Contemporary Moral Issues

Contemporary Moral Issues
Second Edition

edited by

HARRY K. GIRVETZ

University of California, Santa Barbara

Wadsworth Publishing Company, Inc.
Belmont, California

FIFTH PRINTING: *October 1969*

L.C. Cat. Card No.: 68–24201

Printed in the United States of America

Preface

This book deals with some of the major moral issues of our time. To call them issues is to say that they are not yet resolved, at any rate not among thoughtful and responsible men of good will; or, if they are resolved, the manner of resolution is not one that has decisively affected practice. Admittedly the determination of good will, wisdom, and responsibility involves judgments of value and might be said, therefore, to reflect personal bias. But, quite apart from the quality of the readings and the competence and distinction of their authors, I have employed a principle of selection that should commend itself to reasonable readers of every persuasion. I have chosen authors who might be presumed to encounter dissent without branding it as evidence of malice or stupidity—authors who, in short, claim no monopoly of wisdom and virtue. Presumably these are people who could engage in debate without denouncing each other as knaves or fools.

I have employed another related principle of selection, although obviously with no pretense to infallibility in its application. The authors are, it will be evident, committed people. But they have not, in my judgment, subordinated the pursuit of truth to defense of their commitments; their loyalties, however strong and even passionate, have not blinded them to alternatives.

Such, in addition to evidence of scholarship, are the requirements by which great universities recruit their faculties. The upshot of adherence to such principles is the exclusion of bigots and blind partisans. Their utterances too are of interest, for they often have an impact on history and afford interesting evidence of the extremes to which men may be led by their passions and prejudices, but our concern here is a different one—namely, better understanding of some of the still unsettled moral problems of our day. This is not a project to which fanatics can make a significant contribution. However, such a view does not imply endorsement of what has been called the "ultramiddle"; to reject blind partisanship is not to praise moral timidity or apathy.

The selections in this volume are not concerned with the problems that would occupy a theoretical treatise on ethics. Such a study, although it would do well to deal with specific moral problems and issues, would by necessity go beyond them to an analysis of the concepts of right and good and ought, of moral law and conscience, concepts that most moral controversy takes for granted—as it does the relevance and demonstrability of judgments of moral value. How judgments of value are demonstrated (if indeed they can be demonstrated at all), and the sense in which they may therefore be regarded as meaningful, is a cause of much difference of opinion among professional philosophers. But this is not a question that will concern us here beyond one important comment. Behind the assertions of the writers included in these pages is the assumption that there exists a difference between good and evil that is more than a simple affirmation of preference. The point to moral discourse—unless those who partake of it are in quest of emotional catharsis—is to persuade. Quite obviously, if nothing but preferences were involved, all efforts to persuade would founder on the retort that there is no disputing about tastes.

Persuasion is often and most simply accomplished by calling attention to facts concerning the antecedents and consequences of a course of action, or to its consistency or inconsistency with accepted values or standards. One may point out, for example, that the repeal of capital punishment has or has not been followed by an increase of the crimes previously punishable by death, that loyalty oaths have or have not been helpful in exposing Communists or that such oaths are or are not consistent with heretofore accepted standards concerning test oaths. One may cite evidence to indicate the discrepancy between precept and practice in sex conduct, or refer to what psychologists have told us about the causes and consequences of the state of mind that required loincloths to be painted over Michelangelo's nudes in the Sistine Chapel. In all such cases persuasion is accomplished and agreement effected within the framework of a common set of values.

Often, however, the facts do not prevail, and considerations of consistency become hopelessly obscured. When this happens one may conclude that the conflict lies deeper and involves values themselves. It is here, in disputes over standards of value, that our differences are crucial. Can such differences be reconciled?

The question here raised concerns moral suasion in the true sense. When the President of the United States and the president of United States

Steel clashed bitterly, in 1962, over the respective responsibilities of business management and government concerning the price of steel, they were not merely differing over matters of fact—although many facts were, of course, relevant and in need of clarification. One may assume that they had different notions concerning what *ought* to be the prevailing conduct in our society, a basic difference over values that no amount of appeal to verbally identical principles like "the common welfare" or "the public good" can conceal.

The city of Coventry recently completed a cathedral to replace the great Gothic church destroyed by Germany's *Luftwaffe* on the night of November 14, 1940. However, during the years following the war the city council of Coventry refused a building permit for a new cathedral, arguing that there was a prior need for schools, houses, and clinics. The council was overruled, it so happened, by the British Minister of Works, who wrote: "Can we be sure that a cathedral would be so useless? We have never had a greater need for an act of faith." The difference, although perhaps not as acrimonious as the dispute between President Kennedy and the steel industry, surely reflects competing sets of values.

"Hippies," as they have taught us to know them, reject middle-class values. Work, discipline, ambition are scorned, as are their fruits in money, status, and power. Often the offspring of middle-class parents, they think of their parents as chained to a treadmill and of themselves as having repudiated what William James once called the "bitch-goddess, Success." Others think of them as shiftless and slovenly free-loaders seeking escape from responsibility in drugs and antic affectations. The difference between our self-styled "flower-children" and their critics hardly arises from disputes about questions of fact; it is a deep divergence over ideals and standards.

If such differences are to be reconciled and moral suasion is indeed to occur, an *act of will* must take place. This is something more than the act of perception or act of thought required of those who differ because of obscured facts or inconsistent reasoning from accepted moral premises. People must be *willing* (in the double sense of that word) to suspend their prevailing standards of value in order to entertain an alternative—an alternative not envisaged when they first formulated their standards. In the ensuing reevaluation they may reaffirm or revise their heretofore accepted values, but one thing is certain: such values will have new meaning to them by virtue of having been thus tested. Moreover, in this way they may find enhancement that would otherwise have been denied them had they resisted such reappraisal.

What precise circumstances occasion such reevaluations and what occurs as we reappraise our prevailing standards of value are complex questions that must be left to more technical discussions. But this much is clear: bigots and fanatics will not submit their position to reexamination.

Neither, for other reasons, will members of preliterate or authoritarian societies, where the individual is so submerged in the group or so submissive that he would not think of challenging the prevailing mores. Reappraisal is possible only for free men conscious of themselves as agents capable of guiding their own development—capable, that is, of an exercise of free will in what is perhaps the only meaningful sense of that term. Such a capacity is not an original endowment, but an achievement laboriously won over the long centuries during which a relatively few men have emancipated themselves from tyranny, whether of law and custom or of their own unrestrained impulses and appetites.

The issues discussed in this volume are arranged into six groupings, although other ways of relating them might be equally appropriate. With each grouping are brief introductory comments, which suggest the main problems in that area and indicate the rationale for that particular grouping. The groupings are subdivided into topics, and accompanying each topic is a brief formulation of the issue. With each selection are comments concerning the author's background. For the most part I have made an attempt to represent important differences in point of view and to emphasize the contributions of living Americans.

I would like to acknowledge the able assistance of Dr. Vernon Nash whose semi-retirement has brought to our community a rare spirit who combines moral fervor with good humor—thereby enabling us to deplore our follies and at the same time smile at them. In addition, I have been helped by my wife, by Sharon McKenna, secretary to the Department of Philosophy, and by the unfailing cooperation of Dr. Leonard Freedman, University of California Extension, Los Angeles, editor of the series to which this volume is a contribution.

Contents

*PART ONE / SECURITY AND ITS MORAL
IMPLICATIONS*   1

1. National Security in the Nuclear Age: Three Moral
    Appraisals   5

    Karl Barth, *No Angels of Darkness and Light*   6
    George F. Kennan, *Foreign Policy and Christian
       Conscience*   9
    David Sarnoff, *Turn the Cold War Tide in America's
       Favor*   18

2. Internal Security and Civil Disobedience   24

    Harold Laski, *The Case for Disobedience*   28
    John Dickinson, *The Case against Disobedience*   34
    Martin Luther King, Jr., *Where Do We Go from Here?*   43
    Stokely Carmichael, *What We Want*   52
    Will Herberg, *A Religious "Right" To Violate the Law?*   62
    Ronald L. Goldfarb, *Three Conscientious Objectors*   65
    Jeff Greenfield, *The Selective CO*   71

3. Internal Security and the Loyalty Program   76

    Alan Barth, *The Cult of Loyalty*   78
    Sidney Hook, *Heresy, Yes—Conspiracy, No!*   87
    John Steinbeck, *The Trial of Arthur Miller*   97
    Richard H. Rovere, *Arthur Miller's Conscience*   101

4.   Crime and Punishment   106

David L. Bazelon, *The Dilemma of Punishment*   109
Karl Menninger, M.D., *Therapy, Not Punishment*   121
Thomas S. Szasz, M.D., *A Psychiatrist Dissents from
    Durham*   125
Jacques Barzun, *In Favor of Capital Punishment*   132
Caryl Chessman, *A Letter to the Governor*   140

PART TWO / THE VALUES OF A BUSINESS SOCIETY   149

5.   The Acquisitive Ideal   153

John Dewey, *The House Divided against Itself*   154
Max Lerner, *Capitalist Economy and Business Civilization*   161
Peter Viereck, *The Cash-Nexus*   166
Peter Drucker, *The Profit Motive*   171

6.   The Problem of Priorities   177

John Kenneth Galbraith, *The Theory of Social Balance*   179
Henry E. Wallich, *Private vs. Public*   188

7.   Corporate "Citizenship"   197

Richard Eells, *Corporation Giving in a Free Society*   198
Theodore Levitt, *The Dangers of Social Responsibility*   203

8.   Honesty in Business   214

Arthur Selwyn Miller, *Business Morality: Some Unanswered
    (and Perhaps Unanswerable) Questions*   216
Clarence B. Randall, *A New Code of Business Ethics*   221

9.   Television on Trial   226

Newton N. Minow, *The Broadcasters Are Public Trustees*   227
Frank Stanton, *In Defense of Television*   237

10. The Ethics of Persuasion   245

Aldous Huxley, *The Arts of Selling*   246
James Webb Young, *Wanted: Responsible Advertising
    Critics*   253

PART THREE / SEX AND SOCIETY   261

11.   Pornography and Its Control   263

John Fischer, *The Harm Good People Do*   266
John Courtney Murray, S.J., *The Bad Arguments Intelligent
    People Make*   271
United States Circuit Court of Appeals, *Besig v.
    United States*   279
Supreme Judicial Court of Massachusetts, *Attorney General
    v. The Book Named "Tropic of Cancer"*   282
Henry Miller, *The Author's Defense*   283

12.   Extramarital Sexual Experience   290

Bertrand Russell, *Marriage and Morals*   291
Walter Lippmann, *Love in the Great Society*   296
Sarah Gibson Blanding, *The Day I Spoke Off the Cuff to the
    Girls of Vassar*   309
David Boroff, *Sex: The Quiet Revolution*   312
Midge Decter, *Sex, My Daughters, and Me*   319

13.   Homosexuality   328

Edwin M. Schur, *Crimes without Victims*   330
Patrick Devlin, *Morals and the Criminal Law*   336
H. L. A. Hart, *Law, Liberty and Morality*   349

PART FOUR / DISCRIMINATION
AND THE NEGRO   355

14.   The Law and Discrimination   359

Donald R. Richberg, *Freedom of Association*   360
Milton R. Konvitz, *Stand Out of My Sunshine*   364

15.   Persisting Areas of Controversy   372

Daniel P. Moynihan, *The President and the Negro:
    The Moment Lost*   373
James Baldwin, *The American Dream Is at the Expense of
    the American Negro* (debating the affirmative)   396
William F. Buckley, Jr., *The American Dream Is at the
    Expense of the American Negro* (debating the negative)   400

PART FIVE / THE CHURCH AND SOCIETY 405

16. Church and State 407

John Courtney Murray, S.J., *Civil Unity and Religious
  Integrity* 409
Frederick A. Olafson, *Two Views of Pluralism* 425
Supreme Court of the United States, *Everson v. Ewing
  Township Board of Education* 437

17. The Church and Social Reform 444

Walter Rauschenbusch, *Christianity and the Social Crisis* 445
Reinhold Niebuhr, *The Ethic of Jesus and the
  Social Problem* 450
H. Richard Niebuhr, *The Grace of Doing Nothing* 460
Reinhold Niebuhr, *Must We Do Nothing?* 465
H. Richard Niebuhr, *The Only Way into the Kingdom
  of God* 470

PART SIX / ALIENATION IN THE MODERN WORLD 473

18. Modern Society and Its Discontents 475

June Bingham, *The Intelligent Square's Guide to
  Hippieland* 479
Irving Kristol, *What's Bugging the Students* 489
Christopher Jencks, *The New Left* 495
Daniel Bell, *The New Right* 501

19. Drugs: The Magic Carpet 511

President's Advisory Commission on Crime and Law
  Enforcement, *Marihuana* 515
Richard Blum, *LSD—"Utopiate"* 519
Diana Trilling, *Celebrating with Dr. Leary* 532

20. Escape from Alienation 548

Kenneth Keniston, *Toward a More Human Society* 548

Part One

Security and Its Moral Implications

Security of person and property is the first concern of a well-ordered society. Few passages in the literature of political philosophy are more remembered than Thomas Hobbes' observation in the *Leviathan* that in the "war of all against all," there can be "no culture of the earth, no navigation . . . no commodious building . . . no knowledge of the face of the earth . . . no arts; no letters; no society . . ." In Hobbes' famous phrase, life in such circumstances is "solitary, poor, nasty, brutish, and short."

Hobbes lived during a period of prolonged civil strife, and his first concern was with internal order. Today, our first concern is with world order. In such times security takes on new meaning, and nations take special precautions to protect themselves. As a consequence, new moral issues come to the fore—or old issues appear in a new context. In our day the quest for national security is complicated by the threat, posed for the first time, of total destruction from nuclear warfare and by the effect on future generations of the slow contamination of the atmosphere from nuclear testing.

The complications are not only technological; they are also ideological, stemming from the peculiar circumstance that in our present world crisis the division is not primarily between "haves" and "have nots," but between competing ways of ordering the whole scheme of social relationships. The difference could therefore take on a religious character, which is a dangerous possibility because religious wars, as we know from bitter experience, evoke a fanaticism that is heedless of consequences. Fortunately, zealous ideologues rarely achieve high office. Statesmen and politicians are not generally given to religious fervor. They shun holy crusades; and, if the price of the objectives they normally pursue is too high, they content themselves with less—in the present case with coexistence.

The ideological implications of the international crisis, whether these are central or peripheral, bring the problem of defending ourselves from an external threat a great deal closer to the issue of internal security than it would otherwise be. Ideologies are notoriously scornful of national boundaries. Our differences with the Soviet Union have therefore greatly increased concern about Communism at home.

A nation's internal security requires that it protect itself from disloyalty. Such disloyalty may manifest itself in revolutionary activities culminating in efforts to overthrow the government or, where a foreign foe is involved, in sabotage and espionage. Efforts to achieve internal security inevitably come into conflict with individual rights and liberties. The conflict of values thereby generated has sorely tried our national conscience since the loyalty program was first initiated by President Truman in 1947.

Often the conflict appears to be more than a difference over questions of fact. Is there really a danger of revolution in this country requiring that we take special precautions? Is Communism an authentic revolutionary movement or a conspiracy? In either case does the Communist movement undermine and menace our institutions? Is a given device (for example, loyalty oaths) or a given legal measure (say the McCarran Act or the Smith Act) effective in combating Communism? Here, as usual, one may safely assume that where such questions of fact do not get resolved, differences concerning the facts conceal a more basic difference over values. Spokesmen for the radical right find that Communists inside our country pose an imminent threat even more to be feared than the threat of the Soviet Union. Others would say that this is a preposterous exaggeration. Clearly, more than a difference over questions of fact is involved in this disagreement. The so-called naked facts rarely (in fact) present themselves without raiment; we sometimes forget that they come with a thick cloak of interpretation heavily colored by our interests and values.

Readers of the selections that follow should look for unexpressed or tacit disagreements over values as well as for avowed differences. Often the unavowed difference is the more important one. Thus, the question is rarely raised: is revolution *ever* morally justifiable, and, if so, under what conditions? How far does "loyalty" require that we go in obeying the law of the state? Are we, in fact, obligated to obey a law that we are convinced is morally wrong? How shall we view a draftee's refusal to fight in a war that outrages his conscience?

The classical answers to such questions were given by Socrates in the *Apology* and by Sophocles in his *Antigone*—by Socrates, who warned an Athenian jury that he would not stop teaching philosophy and then, as the *Crito* reports, faced the consequences by refusing to escape prison and the death to which the jury condemned him; by Antigone, who refused to obey the law of Creon when it decreed that the body of her brother lie unburied. Refusal to obey the law, it has been said, leads to anarchy. But exclusive stress on obedience enabled the men in charge of the Third Reich's extermination camps to plead that they were conforming to the law which decreed that they obey their superiors: "Ein Befehl ist ein Befehl!" What shall our answer be?

There are other points at which the quest for security raises profound moral issues. We must secure ourselves against thieves, murderers, and the like—against those, that is, who would do violence to us as individuals. Here no political or ideological issues are at stake. Even so, the problems are often similar.

The police are responsible for protecting us from criminals. How far ought they to be allowed to go in ignoring individual rights and invading privacy (for example, with wire-tapping) as they go about the difficult business of detecting crime and catching the culprit? How ought the criminal to be dealt with once he is caught? The crime rate is mounting with alarming rapidity. What can we do to curb crime without flouting accepted moral imperatives? Shall we inflict severer penalties? Many now clamor that we must deal more harshly with the culprit who traffics in narcotics. Shall we say, with the Queen of Hearts, "Off with his head!"? Or is there a more humane and effective way?

Above all, should crime *ever* be punishable by death? Professor Jacques Barzun prefers the term "judicial homicide" to "capital punishment," since the latter designation implies a reason—namely, punishment —to which some who favor the death penalty do not subscribe. In any event, since respect for the sanctity of human life provides the moral basis of our society, the issues raised by the use of the death penalty are fundamental and have therefore occasioned some of our most excruciating moral perplexities.

Such are the diverse and manifold problems raised by the quest for security. Needless to say, they have inspired comparably diverse and manifold solutions.

1

National Security in the
Nuclear Age:
Three Moral Appraisals

The quest for national security in a nuclear age poses some ancient moral problems as well as a number of radically new ones. Is the position of the pacifist morally justifiable? It often manifests itself nowadays in a slogan that seems more like an appeal to expediency than the invocation of a high moral principle: "Better red than dead!" And it calls for unilateral disarmament if necessary. Is this craven capitulation to the forces of evil, or, as some have argued, is the position supported by moral insights that the critics ignore?

The position of the pacifist does not preclude him from making moral comparisons and from allying himself with one or the other of the parties to the conflict; he simply affirms the futility of armed conflict and opposes the use of force under any circumstances. On the other hand, neutralism, at least in one of its major manifestations, is the view that good and evil in what we call the Cold War are too evenly distributed to justify taking sides. Whether Americans like it or not, morally perceptive men defend such a position. Indeed, the sheer massiveness of neutralist sentiment in the world not only puzzles and disturbs Americans, it presents a potential threat to the bonds that tie us to our allies. Unlike doctrinaire pacifism, which finds few converts and will not be debated in these pages, neutralism is a significant force in the world. Hence, no matter how indignant we may feel, we must examine the neutralist's position. Since there are hardly any influential American neutralists, it has been necessary to find a spokesman from abroad.

At the other extreme are those who challenge our present commitment to a policy of coexistence. Is coexistence morally defensible, or shall we, with Senator Goldwater and the far right, answer the title of his book *Why Not Victory?* with a resounding affirmative? Ironically, the Kremlin, also apparently committed to a policy of coexistence, encounters strikingly similar criticism from its far left—in this instance the Chinese Communists. One may well marvel at the curious trick of circumstances (not to mention the hazards of moral discourse) that has made schismatics of Mao Tse-tung and Barry Goldwater and has them raising the same moral questions. In the selections that follow, three distinguished men—a theologian, a diplomat, and a business executive—provide answers to some of these questions.

NO ANGELS OF DARKNESS AND LIGHT

Karl Barth

To many Americans there could be no more disconcerting exponent of the neutralist view than Karl Barth. He is Protestantism's most eminent continental theologian. He has been called "the master theologian of our age" and "the colossus from Basel." President James McCord of Princeton Theological Seminary has said that "he bestrides the theological world like a colossus," and theologian Hans Frei of Yale has called him a "Christ-intoxicated man." Although, as a professor in Germany, he led the fight against Hitlerism, he has refused to take sides against the Russians, even to avoiding open condemnation of the Russian brutalities in Hungary. His advice to us has been to surrender our nuclear weapons—unilaterally if need be. Even so, Time *magazine dedicated its 1962 Easter issue to him, commenting that in this century "no man has been a stronger witness to the continuing significance of Christ's death and Christ's return than the world's ranking Protestant theologian, Swiss-born Karl Barth." Most Americans may not like what Karl Barth says, but they should read him. This need not preclude us from reflecting that if he were to direct similar animadversions at the USSR the Soviets would drown them in vituperation—and from wondering why this has not tempered his impeachment.*

. . . The East-West question has accompanied and shadowed us all since the end of World War II. On this question I cannot agree with the great majority of those around me. Not that I have any inclination toward Eastern communism, in view of the face it presents to the world. I decidedly prefer not to live within its sphere and do not wish anyone else to be forced to do so. But I do not comprehend how either politics or Christianity require or even permit such a disinclination to lead to the conclusions which the West has drawn with increasing sharpness in the past 15 years. I regard anticommunism as a matter of principle an evil even greater than communism itself. Can one overlook the fact that communism is the unwelcomed yet—in all its belligerence—natural result of Western developments? Has not its total, inhuman compulsion which we complain of so much haunted from remotest times in another form our avowedly free Western societies and states? And was it then something suddenly new and worthy of special horror when communism presented itself as a doctrine of salvation blessing all men and nations and therefore one to be spread over the whole world? Are there not other systems of this kind and tendency? Further, could we really intend to help the peoples governed by communism and the world threatened by it, or even one individual among those suffering under its effects, by proclaiming and seeking to practice toward it a relationship exclusively that of enemies? Have we forgotten that what is at stake in this "absolute enemy" relationship, to which every brave man in the West is now obligated and for which he would give his all, is a typical invention of (and a heritage from) our defunct dictators—and that only the "Hitler in us" can be an anticommunist on principle?

Who in the West has even once taken the trouble to think through from the Eastern and particularly from the Russian standpoint the painful situation which has arisen since 1945? Were we not rather happy, and with good reason, over the Soviet contribution to the conquest of the National Socialist danger? Was it not the leaders of the West who toward the end of the war conceded and guaranteed the Soviet Union a determining influence in eastern Europe? Taking into consideration all that had happened since 1914, was the undoubtedly exaggerated need for security by which the Soviet Union tried to fortify itself and to hold the things offered it so completely incomprehensible? With what right did we begin after 1945 to speak forthwith of a necessary "roll back"? When the communists on their part took measures against such a roll back, was it inevitable to view this as an offensive military threat to the rest of the world?

Did we give the Eastern partner any choice? Did we not provoke him by erecting a massive Western defense alliance, by encircling him with artillery, by establishing the German Federal Republic—which seemed to him like a clenched fist pushed under his nose—and by rearming this republic and equipping it with nuclear missiles? Did we not challenge our former partner to corresponding countermeasures of power display and thus in no small measure strengthen him in his peculiar malice? Did the West finally know no better counsel than to put its trust in its infamous A- and H-bombs? And did it not serve the West right to have to realize that the other side had not remained idle in regard to such weapons? Was there no better diplomacy for the West than the one which now maneuvers the world into what seems a blind alley?

Moreover, what kind of Western philosophy and political ethics— and unfortunately even theology—was it whose wisdom consisted of recasting the Eastern collective man into an angel of darkness and the Western "organization man" into an angel of light? And then with the help of such metaphysics and mythology (the fact of an Eastern counterpart is no excuse!) bestowing on the absurd "cold war" struggle its needed higher consecration? Were we so unsure of the goodness of the Western cause and of the power of resistance of Western man that we could bring ourselves to admit only senselessly unequal alternatives—freedom and the dignity of man as against mutual atomic annihilation—then venture to pass off just this latter alternative as a work of true Christian love?

To the madness (I cannot call it anything else) outlined above I have been unable to accommodate myself in any way in all these years. I think that out of fear of fire we are irresponsibly playing with fire. I think that the West, which should know better, must seek and find a better approach to the necessary confrontation with the power and ideology of the communist East. Possibilities of a worthily, circumspectly and firmly guided policy of coexistence and neutrality were more than once offered to the West in past years. More honor would have accrued to the name of the "free world" had it taken up these possibilities; also, more useful and more promising results would have been achieved than those which stand before us today. In particular I think that the Western press and literature instead of meeting the inhuman with inhumanity should have put to the test the vaunted humanity of the West by quietly observing and understanding Eastern individuals and relationships in their dialectical reality. And I think above all that the Christian churches should have considered it their commission to influence by superior witness to the peace and hope of the kingdom of God both public opinion and the leaders who are politically responsible. The churches have injured the cause of the gospel by the manner, to a great extent thoughtless, in which they have identified the gospel (in this Rome is no better than Geneva and Geneva no better than Rome!) with the badly planned and ineptly guided cause of the West. The cause of the gospel cannot from the human perspective be healed for a long time by even the best ecumenical and missionary efforts. The churches have provided Eastern godlessness with new arguments difficult to overcome instead of refuting it by practical action. . . .

FOREIGN POLICY AND CHRISTIAN CONSCIENCE

George F. Kennan

This selection was presented as a lecture at the Princeton Theological Seminary. George F. Kennan spoke from this forum as a Presbyterian addressing himself to fellow Christians, although he would no doubt be the first to say that his remarks were intended for most other communicants.

Ambassador Kennan is perhaps the outstanding authority in the United States on our relations with the Soviet Union as evidenced by a monumental study, Soviet-American Relations, *the second volume of which appeared in 1958, followed in 1961 by* Russia and the West under Lenin and Stalin, *and in 1964 by* On Dealing with the Communist World. *As one who has explored the deeper moral implications of conduct, both individual and collective, he has much to contribute to a volume that deals with the moral dilemmas of our time. Few people are more qualified to discuss the moral implications of the Cold War. Formerly our ambassador to the Soviet Union and to Yugoslavia and chief long-range adviser to the Secretary of State, he is now permanent professor at the Princeton Institute of Advanced Studies. Ambassador Kennan was one of the architects of the policy of containment initiated under the Truman Administration and is today one of the major spokesmen for a policy of coexistence with the USSR. He has condemned what he calls "blind and sterile competition in the ability to wreak indiscriminate destruction." And observing that the Russians breathe the same atmosphere that we breathe, he has said:*

> *Their idea of peace is, of course, not the same as ours. There will be many things we shall have to discuss with them about the meaning of this term before we can agree on very much else. But I see no reason for believing that there are not, even in Moscow's interpretation of this ambiguous word, elements more helpful to us than all the implications of the weapons race in which we are now caught up. And I refuse to believe that there is no way in which we could combine a search for these elements with a pursuit of a reasonable degree of military security in a world*

From *The Atlantic Monthly* (May 1959), pp. 44–49. Copyright © 1959 by The Atlantic Monthly Company, Boston, Mass. Reprinted by permission.

where absolute security has become an outmoded and dangerous dream.[1]

More recently, before the Foreign Relations Committee of the U.S. Senate in 1966, Mr. Kennan characterized the Viet Cong as "ruthless fanatics," but he insisted that "our country should not be asked, and should not ask of itself, to shoulder the main burden of determining the political realities in any other country, and particularly not in one remote from our shores, from our culture, and from the experience of our people." The comments which follow, although they were delivered some years ago and deal with the Cold War in general, are strikingly relevant to our participation in the Vietnam War.

I should like to say at the outset that questions of method in foreign policy seem to me to be generally a much more fitting subject for Christian concern than questions of purpose. It is very difficult for us to know which of the specific undertakings of government in foreign affairs might have Christian significance and which might not. If there is any one thing that is plain about international statesmanship, it is the extreme difficulty of establishing in advance the relationship between cause and effect—of gauging the likely results of one's own acts.

The English historian Herbert Butterfield has shown us with great brilliance, and so has our own Reinhold Niebuhr, the irony that seems to rest on the relationship between the intentions of statesmen and the results they achieve. I can testify from personal experience that not only can one never know, when one takes a far-reaching decision in foreign policy, precisely what the consequences are going to be, but almost never do these consequences fully coincide with what one intended or expected. This does not absolve the statesman of his responsibility for trying to find the measures most suitable to his purpose, but it does mean that he is best off when he is guided by firm and sound principle instead of depending exclusively on his own farsightedness and powers of calculation. And if he himself finds it hard to judge the consequences of his acts, how can the individual Christian onlooker judge them?

All this is quite different when we come to method. Here, in a sense, one can hardly go wrong. The government cannot fully know what it is doing, but it can always know how it is doing it; and it can be as sure that good methods will be in some way useful as that bad ones will be in some way pernicious. A government can pursue its purpose in a patient and conciliatory and understanding way, respecting the interests of others and infusing its behavior with a high standard of decency and honesty and humanity, or it can show itself petty, exacting, devious, and self-righteous.

---

[1] *Russia, The Atom and the West* (New York: Harper & Row, Inc., 1957), pp. 92–93.

If it behaves badly, even the most worthy of purposes will be apt to be polluted; whereas sheer good manners will bring some measure of redemption to even the most disastrous undertaking. The Christian citizen will be on sound ground, therefore, in looking sharply to the methods of his government's diplomacy, even when he is uncertain about its purposes.

In the fabric of international life, there are a great many questions that have no certain Christian significance at all. They represent conflicts between those elements of secular motivation which are themselves without apparent Christian meaning: commercial interests, prestige considerations, fears, and what not. I do not think we can conclude that it matters greatly to God whether the free trade area or the Common Market prevails in Europe, whether the British fish or do not fish in Icelandic territorial waters, or even whether Indians or Pakistani run Kashmir. It might matter, but it is hard for us, with our limited vision, to know.

But these are all questions which reflect the normal frictions between peace-loving nations. How about the issues of the cold war? How about colonialism? How about aid to the underdeveloped areas? How about the United Nations as an institution? How about the atom? Are not Christian values involved in our attitude toward these questions?

Our Competition with Moscow

In its internal policies, the state can create a decent human atmosphere, in which the individual has the maximum possibility for grappling in a hopeful and constructive way with the moral problems of personal life. Or it can, as we have seen in the examples of Hilter and Stalin and the Chinese Communists, strike out on the most appalling lines of viciousness and cruelty, deliberately fostering a real sickness of the human spirit and inculcating in people's minds, for its own purposes, suspicion, terror, callousness, and the habit of brutality—creating conditions dreadfully adverse to the success of the Christian cause. Christianity cannot be indifferent to the existence of such doctrines and methods; and whatever prevents their spread and their triumph on a world scale serves . . . a Christian purpose.

But I do not think this means that every measure that is damaging to international Communism is necessarily good and every measure that is acceptable to a Communist government is necessarily bad. The world is not that simple. Our competition with Moscow is not the only significant reality of international affairs. Our policies, furthermore, must take into account the interests of the peoples under Communist rule as well as those of their governments. Again, we have the question of method and the fact that not even the greatest conviction of righteousness in our purposes absolves us from the obligation of decency in method. If we allow ourselves to copy our adversary's methods as a means of combating him, we may have lost the battle before we start; for this is, after all, what is most essentially at stake.

Furthermore, we must not make the mistake of regarding international Communism as a static, unchanging quantity in the pattern of world realities. While the full-blown totalitarian state in all its unnatural, nightmarish horror is certainly an abomination in the sight of God, one cannot say this of the conservative authoritarian state which has been the norm of Western society in the Christian era. And we must not forget that it is in this direction that the Soviet government, as distinct from the Chinese Communist government, has been rapidly evolving since Stalin's death. Its gravitation in this direction has not been final or decisive, but it has not been negligible. The mere fact that the most characteristic feature of totalitarian horror, the punishment of whole categories of people for abstract or preventive reasons, has been abolished shows how far the Russians have come since Stalin's day.

Now between democracy and traditional authoritarianism there are still differences, but they are relative and do not present clear-cut issues. The authoritarian regime, despite its origins and its sanctions, often rests on a wide area of popular acceptance and reflects popular aspirations in important degree. In democratic countries, on the other hand, such things as the operations of lobbies and political parties and the inevitable control of nominations by small groups of people tend to reduce the ideal representativeness of government and to make it hard to view the political process as much more than a negative expression of the popular will.

And if you consider, as I do, that the value of a democratic society in the Christian sense depends not just on the fact of its enjoying certain rights and liberties but on the nature of the use made of them, then I think you have to raise questions about our American society of this day. These questions do not need to make us lose hope or hang our heads, but they should cause us to be cautious in drawing conclusions about the merit in God's eyes of any particular form of society.

All these considerations lead me to feel that while Christian values often are involved in the issues of Amerian conflict with Soviet power, we cannot conclude that everything we want automatically reflects the purpose of God and everything the Russians want reflects the purpose of the devil. The pattern is complex, fuzzy, and unstable. We must look sharply at each individual issue before we jump to conclusions. We must bear in mind that there are things we do not know and cannot know. We must concede the possibility that there might be some areas of conflict involved in this cold war which a Divine Power could contemplate only with a sense of pity and disgust for both parties, and others in which He might even consider us to be wrong. . . .

The UN as a Symbol of Conscience

The sovereign national state, to which so much reverent devotion is paid in the various gradations of patriotism and chauvinism that make up national feelings, has no foundation in Christian principle, whatever its secular justification. Nowhere in Christ's teachings was it suggested that mankind ought to be divided into political families of this nature, each a law unto itself, each recognizing no higher authority than its own national ego, each assuming its interest to be more worthy of service than any other with which it might come into conflict. Surely this whole theory is an absurdity from the Christian standpoint. Before we could achieve Christian foreign policy we would have to overcome this unlimited egotism of the sovereign national state and find a higher interest which all of us could recognize and serve.

How about the United Nations? it will be asked. Is this not an institution which, insofar as it represents an endeavor to transcend national sovereignty, deserves our support as a vehicle of the Christian purpose?

The UN represents not a supergovernment, not a separate institutional personality, but one of a number of forums on which governments communicate with one another. It does not, in reality, transcend the barrier of sovereignty. Its members are governments, not peoples, and such slender authority as it sometimes possesses is conferred upon it by these governments, each still acting within the sovereign framework.

There is no particular Christian sanctity lent to decisions taken in the United Nations by the fact that they represent the views of a majority of governments. Little countries are not necessarily more virtuous or more enlightened than big ones; and an international majority does not necessarily reflect the Christian answer, or even the most wise and courageous answer, to anything.

On the other hand, the UN does represent the germ of something immensely necessary and immensely hopeful for this endangered world: namely, a sense of conscience higher than the national one, a sense of the fellowship of fate by which we are all increasingly bound together. I cannot conceive of a satisfactory future for humanity that does not embrace, and draw its strength from, the growth of this consciousness. The present UN is the symbol of it. This symbol is still weak and tender, but it is not insignificant. We must therefore cherish it and guard it, not burdening it beyond its strength, not looking to it for the impossible, but strengthening it where and when we can, above all in our own thoughts and attitudes.

This does not mean that all UN decisions are to be taken as automatically right and good. It does not mean that all diplomatic questions should be uncritically consigned to the UN, whether or not this is a suitable place for their discussion. But it does mean that we should be careful and respectful of the organization as such, remembering that if the idea which it symbolizes is ever allowed to depart from international life, nothing else can stand between us and the horrors of a wholly chaotic world in the atomic age.

The Moral Implications of War

This brings me now to the questions on which I think a Christian might, with good conscience, really take a stand. They involve not just the national interests of individual governments but rather the interests of civilization: the question of war, and the atom, and the other weapons of mass destruction.

I am aware that the institution of war has always represented dilemmas for Christian thought to which no fully satisfactory answer has ever been offered. I have, in the past, found myself unable to go along with the Quakers in their insistence on a sweeping renunciation of power as a factor in international affairs. I do not see the reality of so clear a distinction as they draw between domestic affairs and international affairs. The Communists have taught us that these two things are intimately connected, that civil wars have international implications and that international wars have domestic implications everywhere. I am unable therefore to accept the view which condemns coercion on the international sphere but tolerates it within the national borders.

But that we cannot rule out force completely in international affairs does not seem to me to constitute a reason for being indifferent to the ways in which force is applied—to the moral implications of weapons and their uses. It is true that all distinctions among weapons from the moral standpoint are relative and arbitrary. Gunpowder was once viewed with a horror not much less, I suppose, than are atomic explosives today. But who is to say that relative distinctions are not meaningful? I cannot help feeling that the weapon of indiscriminate mass destruction goes farther than anything the Christian era can properly accept. The older weapons, after all, were discriminate in the sense that they had at least a direct coherent relationship to political aims. They were seen as means of coercing people directly into doing things an enemy government wished them to do: evacuating territory, desisting from given objectives, accepting a given political authority. A distinction was still generally drawn, further-more, prior to World War I at least, between the armed forces and the civilian population of a hostile country. Efforts were made to see that military action was directed only against those who themselves had weapons in their hands and offered resistance. The law of war did not yet permit the punishment of whole peoples as a means of blackmail against governments.

In all of these respects, the atom offends. So do all the other weapons of mass destruction. So, for that matter, did the conventional bomber of World War II when it was used for area bombing. In taking responsibility for such things as the bombing of Dresden and Hamburg, to say nothing of Nagasaki and Hiroshima, Americans went beyond what it seems to me the dictates of Christian conscience should have allowed (which is not to say that I think their problem was an easy one).

I regret, as an American and as a Christian, that these things were done. I think it should be our aim to do nothing of the sort in any future military encounter. If we must defend our homes, let us defend them as well as we can in the direct sense, but let us have no part in making millions of women and children and noncombatants hostages for the behavior of their own governments.

It will be said to me: This means defeat. To this I can only reply: I am skeptical of the meaning of "victory" and "defeat" in their relations to modern war between great countries. To my mind the defeat is war itself. In any case it seems to me that there are times when we have no choice but to follow the dictates of our conscience, to throw ourselves on God's mercy, and not to ask too many questions.

Atomic Testing

But this is not the only moral connotation of the atom. There is another in the great controversy that has raged over the question of atomic testing, its effect on the atmosphere, and its consequences for human health. My colleagues in the scientific field advise me to stay away from this subject. They point out that there is a great deal about it which is not yet known; that scientists are themselves in wide disagreement about its seriousness; that I, as a scientific layman, would not even be able to understand the terms in which it is put. All this I readily concede; but even the little that is known to the general public is enough to pose a problem of Christian conscience.

Let us take a random sampling of recent press reports. During the first eight months of 1958, we are told, the fall-out of radioactive strontium on New York City increased by 25 per cent. Readings in Los Angeles are said by the health department of that city to have revealed for limited periods a count of five hundred to one thousand times the normal radioactivity in the atmosphere and double the intensity considered safe for continuous exposure over a lifetime. Only a few weeks ago observations in Sweden showed radioactivity at ten kilometers above sea level to be five times as intense as it was earlier in the year, and individual particles were detected (apparently at ground level), "larger and thought to be more radioactive, than any yet reported except from the immediate area of a test explosion." A similar report has come from Brazil.

All this is only the beginning; a large part of the fall-out from the tests conducted thus far is, we are told, still in the higher atmosphere and will not descend for years. Furthermore, the effect of radioactive substances on human health is cumulative, so that any unnatural exposure presumably reduces the tolerance of exposure from natural causes or for medical purposes.

In the face of these facts, I listen with some amazement to the statements with which some of the scientists endeavor to reassure us about such developments. The damages, they say, have been "negligible" so far. Not *many* deaths, they say, can be expected to ensue from this increase in radioactivity compared with those which occur from natural causes. One scientist, pained and astounded at the concern about the radioactive particles in Sweden, explained that if, for example, 100 people would be killed by the effects of a normal atomic explosion, then only 102 could be expected to die from the effects of the increased radioactivity which Sweden has been experiencing.

But whoever gave us the right, as Christians, to take even one innocent human life, much less 102 or 102,000? I recall no quantitative stipulation in the Sixth Commandment. God did not say through Moses that to take 102,000 lives was wicked but 102 was all right. I fail to see how any of this can be reconciled with the Christian conscience.

I am delighted that our government now shows a serious readiness to work toward the termination of these experiments with atomic explosives. We must go farther and work toward the elimination of the use of atomic weapons in war as well. This cannot be done in a day, and not all that needs to be done can be done by us. But we can at least make a beginning by endeavoring to free ourselves from our unwise dependence on atomic weapons in our own military calculations, from our fateful commitment to the first use of these weapons, whether or not they are used against us.

Our Obligation to the Future

There is a principle involved here which has application beyond just the field of weapons, to a number of other effects in the introduction of modern technology. We of this generation are only the custodians, not the owners, of the earth on which we live. There were others who lived here before, and we hope there will be others who are going to live here afterward. We have an obligation to past generations and to future ones, no less solemn than our obligations to ourselves. I fail to see that we are in any way justified in making, for the safety or convenience of our own generation, alterations in our natural environment which may importantly change the conditions of life for those who come afterward.

The moral laws which we acknowledge predicate the existence of a certain sort of world—a certain sort of natural environment—in which people live. This setting presumably reflects God's purpose. We did not create it; we do not have the right to destroy it. We know the problems which this environment poses for man. We know the nature of the Christian effort to find answers to them. We live by this lore. When we permit this environment to be altered quite basically by things we do today, we are taking upon ourselves a responsibility for which I find no authority in the Christian faith.

Obviously, we do not know what the ultimate effects will be of the atomic weapons tests we have already conducted. I am not sure that we know what will be the ultimate effects of our methods of disposal of radioactive wastes. I doubt that we know what we are doing to the sea through the use of modern detergents and the fouling of its surface with oil. I am not sure that we know what we are doing with modern insecticides, which we employ quite recklessly in agriculture for our immediate purposes, giving little thought to their ultimate effects. We who call ourselves Christians must acknowledge responsibility in these matters, most of which are international in their implications.

We will unavoidably find in the motives and workings of the political process much that is ambiguous in the Christian sense. In approaching the individual conflicts between governments which make up so much of international relations, we must beware of pouring Christian enthusiasm into unsuitable vessels which were at best designed to contain the earthy calculations of the practical politicians. But there are phases of the government's work in which we can look for Christian meaning. We can look for it, first of all, in the methods of our diplomacy, where decency and humanity of spirit can never fail to serve the Christian cause.

Beyond that there loom the truly apocalyptic dangers of our time, the ones that threaten to put an end to the very continuity of history outside which we would have no identity, no face, either in civilization, in culture, or in morals. These dangers represent for us not only political questions but stupendous moral problems, to which we cannot deny the courageous Christian answer. Here our main concern must be to see that man, whose own folly once drove him from the Garden of Eden, does not now commit the blasphemous act of destroying, whether in fear or in anger or in greed, the great and lovely world in which, even in his fallen state, he has been permitted by the grace of God to live.

TURN THE COLD WAR TIDE
IN AMERICA'S FAVOR

David Sarnoff

*Brigadier General David Sarnoff (U.S. Army Hon. Re-
serve) is chairman of the Radio Corporation of America and
one of the nation's most prominent business executives. His
life is a success story in the Horatio Alger tradition; he began
as a messenger boy and wireless operator and rose to the position of general manager and chairman of the board. General
Sarnoff was born in Russia and came to the United States at
the age of nine. The selection below was one of a series published by the editors of* Life *magazine entitled "The National
Purpose."*

. . . Five years ago I submitted a memorandum to the White
House sketching a Program for a Political Offensive against World Communism. "For Moscow," it said, "the real alternative to a nuclear show-
down is not 'peace' but political-psychological warfare of a magnitude to
weaken, demoralize, chip away and ultimately take over what remains of
the free world." The memorandum therefore urged that we renounce all
delusions of easy solutions and compromise; that instead we mount a
political counterstrategy as massive, as intensive and as clear about its
ultimate goals as the strategy of the enemy himself.

Events in the intervening years have, if anything, fortified this
point of view. The essence of my proposed program, for which I claim no
originality, was—and still is—an unequivocal decision to fight the so-called
cold war with a will and on a scale for complete victory.

The decision would have to be communicated to the entire world
as boldly and energetically as the Communists communicate their intentions. Our message to humankind must be that America has decided,
irrevocably, to win the cold war and thereby to cancel out the destructive
power of Soviet-based Communism. A national commitment of this scope,
I submit, would be consistent with American instincts and experience, a
restatement of historic purposes in contemporary terms.

The nature of those purposes . . . is explicit in basic American
documents, beginning with the Declaration of Independence. It is implicit

From *Life* (June 6, 1960), pp. 108 ff. Reprinted by permission.

in the widespread assertion—presented by some as an accusation—that our foreign policies have been "idealistic." Through the generations Americans have always thought of themselves as being in the vanguard of freedom. They cherished the image of their country as the citadel of democracy and morality and a living defiance to despotism anywhere.

The Rockefeller Brothers Fund Report on U.S. Foreign Policy— prepared by a panel of which I was a member and published last year—put it this way: "The United States at its best has always seen its national life as an experiment in liberty . . . [Americans] have known that the hopes of the world were, in some measure, bound up with their success. . . . Whenever [the United States] has wielded effective power in the world, its ideals and its moral convictions have played a vital part in its decisions. Whenever, on the contrary, the United States has tried to act without moral conviction, or in ways that went counter to its basic beliefs, it has found itself inhibited and has ultimately had to rechart its course. . . . Ideas and ideals are thus to the United States an essential element of reality."

If this is so, why is there such a pervasive skepticism about our historic national purpose and such a widespread search for substitutes? Why the shrinking from lofty goals for all mankind in favor of the safe, the compromising, or mere survival?

The easy answer—that it is all due to the advent of terrible new weapons—will hardly do. The calendar refutes it: the retreat began before those weapons were forged and grew more panicky during the time when America had a monopoly on the atom bomb. It was precisely in the years before Soviet Russia produced the bomb that Communism scored its greatest gains, and it did so almost always by the default of the free world. The Soviet advantages were not military and technological but political and psychological.

The true answer, as I see it, is related to the ever-rising costs of idealism in terms of the sacrifices and the hazards involved. The trouble is not that the older purposes have become irrelevant but that they have become too relevant. I mean that the time when America could serve passively as an example or inspiration to other nations has run out. Today, professions of principle have serious consequences: they must be implemented in policy and action. To say it in slang, the time has come to put up or shut up.

As far as the contest with Communism is concerned we had "shut up," quite literally. We had curbed our tongues for fear of offending the delicate sensibilities of those who daily offend *us*. Few democratic leaders dare to speak as uninhibitedly about the coming doom of the Communist empire as Khrushchev and Mao Tse-tung regularly speak about our impending doom. Our opponents defy, denounce and challenge, while we plead and propitiate. We have left the vocabulary of confidence and victory to the other side, contenting ourselves with such solacing and temporizing words as accommodation, *modus vivendi,* relaxed tensions and coexistence.

This semantic timidity, of course, is merely a symptom and a minor one. The all-encompassing malady is a loss of nerve, marked by depleted self-esteem and purpose. It has impelled us, whenever we have been faced with a choice of interpretations on some aspect of the Communist affliction, to choose the more agreeable one, the one more conducive to complacency and less likely to tax our courage. With rare exceptions the choice has turned out to be the wrong and often the disastrous one, regardless of the political parties in power in this country and in the free world.

Thus in the 1930s we eagerly found assurance in Stalin's talk about "socialism in one country." Later we relaxed in the cozy conviction that the Chinese Communists were simply "agrarian reformers." We prefer to believe in the "evolution" of Communism, though there has not been the slightest revision of ultimate Communist goals. We seek a comforting answer to our prayers in tensions between Moscow and Peking, though these are strictly within the framework of their unshakable alliance against the West, no more significant than Anglo-American tension within our alliance.

A familiar gambit is to list Communism as just one item in a long inventory of problems. But if the Sino-Soviet bloc[1] wins world dominion, the other problems will cease to matter: they will have been solved for the free world in about the way that death solves all bodily ills.

. . . sheer survival, in the elementary physical sense, is not enough. The world has become too small for physical, economic or political isolationism. The polarization of forces dueling for supremacy has gone too far to permit the survival of an island of humanism in a sea of dehumanized totalitarianism. No single nation can survive unless the civilization of which it is part survives.

Our civilization, too, cannot remain isolated, confined to a delimited segment of the earth and indifferent to the humanity beyond those limits. The world cannot be frozen in its present patterns. In this period of great flux and of intermeshed revolutions, static and passive arrangements are doomed to disruption. If the area of freedom is not expanded, then assuredly it will continue to contract.

Despite this, "survival of the free world"—side by side with an unfree world—has been and remains the maximum goal of Western diplomacy. Not the weakening and eventual defeat of Communism but a lasting accommodation seems to mark the farthest reach of hope. It is

---

[1] Editor's note: General Sarnoff was, of course, writing before the breakup of the Sino-Soviet bloc.

scarcely a vision to inspire confidence or zeal, and in any case it is utterly utopian, because two parties are needed to make an accommodation.

The best analysis of Communist strategy that I know is in a recent book called *Protracted Conflict* by Dr. Robert Strausz-Hupé of the University of Pennsylvania and three associates. The book's title is a phrase used by Mao Tse-tung. The Communist plan, say the authors, is protracted in time and space and in the limitless variety of its techniques and weapons, and the weapons can even include "the final and total knockout punch." Short of surrender, the authors see for our world no alternative but a many-sided, continuous, long-range counteroffensive.

Such a policy would reject all illusions of an enduring truce, let alone a negotiated division of the globe. The historic contest will be with us for a long, long time. We may delay, maneuver, bargain and compromise, but it will be so much flailing of water unless all such moves become for us—as they have always been for the enemy—calculated holding actions geared to long-range objectives, means not ends, tactics not strategy.

Whatever we do or fail to do in the years and decades ahead, we shall be forced to take great risks and make great sacrifices. These cannot be evaded even by piecemeal surrenders. In fact, if Americans and other free people are to understand and accept these costs and exertions, there must be some rational relation between the magnitude of the goal and the magnitude of the burdens it imposes.

This means that in the conflict with Communism we must become the dynamic challenger rather than remain the inert target of challenge. Only then can freedom regain the initiative. Only then will we have a global goal to match that of Communism, and the incentive to apply the full weight of our brains, energies and resources to its achievement. The great decision, once made and communicated to all concerned, will dictate its appropriate program of policy and action. The strategy will shape the necessary tactics.

Even the things we are now doing and must continue to do will become more relevant and more effective when geared to a conscious ultimate goal. Military and economic aid to our allies, to underdeveloped areas and to neutral nations will cease to be hit-or-miss improvisations. They will be integral elements of an affirmative program. Propaganda, cultural exchanges, diplomatic moves, summit meetings will all acquire for us—as they always have for the Communists—dimensions of purpose beyond their limited immediate effects.

Before the Soviet Union attained its present technological stature, America's paramount problem appeared to be the struggle for men's minds. Today it is dangerous to concentrate on any one facet of the conflict. I think of the image in terms of a table with four legs, military, political, economic and psychological. The significance of the last three is self-evident, since they relate to activities short of all-out war. But the "military leg" must not be underrated.

The present approximate balance of terror presents a false appearance of stability. But it may be upset. And if we relax in this area it will be upset. The enemy is constantly probing our vitality and resolution. Any one of these probes may lead to the brink of war and possibly to war itself. No matter how often we repeat that war is "unthinkable" it remains possible. War may be touched off by accident, or it may come because the Communist high command considers itself ready to deliver the "final and total knockout punch." The maintenance of adequate military power, both offensive and defensive, is therefore of paramount importance. Whether it is ever used or not, moreover, it is the indispensable shield for all other types of action in the protracted conflict.

A strategy for victory in the cold war would, however, begin with a complete reappraisal of present efforts. It would aim to seize the initiative in every possible arena of competition. Not merely the expansion of present projects and the addition of new ones would be considered but how to give each of them a clear role within the framework of the over-all objective.

It would not reject courses of action simply because they are unconventional. We would no longer disdain to use against the enemy some of the weapons used against us. Having finally acknowledged that the struggle is decisive and therefore as real as a "real" war, we would not hesitate to fight fire with fire.

American ingenuity would be called upon to evolve devices and techniques to exploit weaknesses and vulnerabilities in the Communist world, to keep the enemy constantly off balance, to impose upon him problems and crises instead of always waiting to counteract crises of his making. By all the instruments of communication and through the loud-speakers of events, we would aim to saturate the Communist world with reminders that we intend to keep alive the memory of human dignity, the hatred of injustice, the hope of liberation and the courage needed for resistance.

Debates in the United Nations and at diplomatic conferences would be made sounding boards for our views as well as for theirs. No allusions to "colonialism" would be permitted to pass without our throwing the limelight on Red imperialism and on the principles of self-determination.

Thus the Communist world, rather than ours, would tend increasingly to become the principal battlefield of ideological and political conflict. The immunity their world has so long enjoyed would be shattered.

A bill to establish a Freedom Academy for training cold war specialists—what a LIFE editorial called a Political West Point—is before Congress. Whatever the merits or demerits of this particular bill, it is in line with a commitment to victory. Various proposals have been made for setting up a Liberation Force, a volunteer formation drawn largely from among refugees from captive nations and ready to serve in emergencies. That, too, is in line with a strategy for victory. And a new department of Cabinet rank could and should be established to plan and coordinate all cold war activities.

Certainly this new approach would call for substantial sacrifices in material terms. But the notion that it would require a deep cut in American living standards underestimates the wealth and productive genius of our country. The more demanding sacrifices, indeed, would be in the psychological and moral domains. Our people, in short, would have to renounce complacency, euphoria and illusion; they would have to embrace the grim but inspiring realities of our epoch.

The ultimate rise of a world order under law is dictated by the logic of devastating weaponry and modern communications. What remains to be settled is whether it will be an order rooted in freedom or in universal tyranny.

I do not doubt that we have what it takes to assure that it will be an order that we may cherish. The Western concepts of open societies, of liberty under law, of government by the consent of the governed, or the supremacy of the individual rather than the state—these are far closer to the natural aspirations of man than the anthill concepts of Communism. In any equal propaganda contest, what these Western concepts have brought in human well-being will become obvious and irresistible to the majority of mankind. . . .

2

Internal Security and Civil Disobedience

When a given law or the whole system of laws outrages his conscience, the individual has two recourses: he may abide by the law until such time as he (and others) can change it; or he may refuse to obey. Such disobedience might take either a peaceful or a violent form. And violent disobedience may be either individual or collective.

In the vocabulary that designates such phenomena, individual violence is called terroristic and is exemplified historically by anarchism of the Bakunin or Kropotkin schools. The Russian Social Revolutionary Party was committed to acts of individual violence—a policy that (contrary to popular assumption) the Russian Communist Party rejected. Disobedience in its terroristic manifestation (it was exemplified by the recent bloodshed in Algeria as well as by that in Czarist Russia) has found hardly any advocates in the United States.

On the other hand, collective disobedience involving the use of force has in the past found us ambivalent: wavering between pride in our revolutionary past and fear of the destructive consequences of revolution. However, there is not now a revolutionary movement in our country nor even a recent revolutionary literature. Although in the 'thirties the American Communist Party reflected and generated some marginal revolutionary sentiments and inspired a considerable literature, it is now virtually moribund as a political movement; and, as Sidney Hook suggests below, its remnants are more aptly described as witting or unwitting agents of a foreign government than as authentic and indigenous revolutionaries. Even so, the moral issues raised by an evaluation of the revolutionary principle are of enduring concern, and some of them are inseparable from a discussion of peaceful resistance, which does have immediate relevance in this country. So much for disobedience committed to the use of force.

Peaceful disobedience, or—as we call it—civil disobedience,[1] like violent disobedience may be individual or collective. And here Americans are less ambivalent. One particular American's individual act of civil disobedience has indeed become so celebrated that it is almost legendary. Henry Thoreau's refusing to pay his taxes was no mean, penurious evasion of his responsibilities; it was an act of individual defiance against a government that was using his taxes to wage an unjust war against Mexico—and was tolerating slavery besides. He was promptly jailed. "Can there not be a government in which majorities do not virtually decide right and wrong, but conscience? . . . Must the citizen ever for a moment, or in the least degree, resign his conscience to the legislator? Why has every man a conscience, then?" asked Thoreau. He added:

> I think we should be men first and subjects afterward. It is not desirable to cultivate a respect for the law, so much as for the right. . . . Unjust laws exist: shall we be content to obey them, or shall we endeavor to amend them, and obey them until we have succeeded, or shall we transgress at once? Men generally under such a government as this, think they ought to wait until they have persuaded the majority to alter them. They think that, if they should resist, the remedy would be worse than the evil. But it is the fault of the government itself that the remedy *is* worse than the evil. *It* makes it worse. . . . As for adopting the ways the state has provided for remedying the evil, I know not of such ways. They take too much time, and a man's life will be gone. I have other affairs to attend to.[2]

Gandhi read these words. There is a direct link between the collective civil disobedience of India's teeming millions and the solitary American who wrote: "I am not born to be forced. I will breathe after my own fashion." The Reverend Martin Luther King, Jr., also read Thoreau's essay—as one of the articles reprinted below suggests.

However, also echoing in our memories are contrary words such as St. Paul's: "Let every person be subject to the

---

[1] Strictly, one should distinguish between nonresistance to evil and passive resistance. The roots of the former are to be found in Buddha and the Gospels ("whoever shall compel thee to go a mile, go with him twain"), and the intent is to shame the perpetrator of evil and violence.

[2] From *On the Duty of Civil Disobedience.*

governing authorities. For there is no authority except from God, and those that exist have been instituted by God."[3] Or Luther's: "Even if those in authority are evil or without faith, nevertheless the authority and its power is good and from God."[4]

While many in an age of stifling conformity will applaud the spirit of spontaneous protest that inspired Thoreau, they will also insist on a sober second thought when it comes to trifling with the law, especially in a democracy where men are free—or said to be free—to persuade others to join with them in making changes. They will agree that the freedom to persuade is often too tenuous; and they will concede that the machinery of democracy often works only for "the long run" when, as Lord Keynes once reminded us, we shall all be dead. They will even agree that inert majorities need an occasional act of defiance to jolt them out of their apathy. Even so, they will draw back at the brink of disobedience. Such a man was John Dickinson, whose views on this problem are included below.

Once the universals about sovereignty and law, obedience and disobedience, have been explored, it becomes necessary to test them against particular cases. One critical case immediately before us is the civil resistance of the Negro. With Thoreau, Negroes are saying that the remedy the state provides for their grievances takes too much time. Competing claims to sovereignty by state and federal government complicate the problem. However, Negro leaders have recently quarreled over the form resistance should take, and their differences have grown increasingly bitter. A new slogan, "Black Power," hints at violence; and a new breed of Negro militant scorns cooperation with white sympathizers, espouses Negro or "black" nationalism, and sneers at moderates like Roy Wilkins and Dr. Martin Luther King as "Uncle Toms." Advocates of both views speak in these pages.

Another critical case involves military service in a war which has provoked the condemnation of large and influential segments of the community. When, on ten California campuses alone, more than 600 faculty members sign a "declaration of

---

[3] St. Paul continues: "Therefore he who resists the authorities resists what God has appointed and those who resist will incur judgment. For rulers are not a terror to good conduct but to bad. Would you have no fear of him who is an authority? Then do what is good and you will receive his approval, for he is God's servant for your good." (Rom. 13:1 ff.)

[4] *Römerbrief*, 13:1. Again: "God would prefer to suffer the government to exist no matter how evil, rather than allow the rabble to riot, no matter how justified they are in doing so. . . . A prince should remain a prince no matter how tyrannical he may be. He beheads necessarily only a few since he must have subjects in order to be a ruler."

conscience" in which they pledge "full and active support" to "all who determine that they will not participate in this [the Vietnam] war," it is clear that we are in the throes of a moral crisis of unprecedented dimensions.[5]

Conscientious objection is not at issue when it is based on religious training and belief and when it takes the form of opposition to all war. The right to such objection (at first limited by the Draft Law of 1917 to the historic peace churches—the Society of Friends, the Mennonites, and the Brethren) was recognized by the 1948 Universal Military Training Act. In 1965 this act was liberalized by judicial interpretation when the Supreme Court held in *United States* v. *Seeger* that Congress did not mean to require belief in God as a condition of exemption. However, the Court's decision left many questions unanswered, questions which have acquired dramatic prominence since the advent of the Vietnam war. The Court was silent concerning the question of conscientious objection on other than religious grounds and sufficiently ambiguous concerning the meaning of "religious" to strain the capabilities of the most earnest draft board. Moreover, the Court sidestepped constitutional issues, such as the ban against establishment of religion, and limited itself to interpreting the meaning of the Congressional statute.

But quite apart from the issues thereby raised, it is clear that the statute applies only to *pacifists,* those who object to all wars. It provides no exemption for those who are not opposed to war in general but plead the right of *selective* conscientious objection. Thus, those who find the Vietnam war unjust and

---

[5] The full text of the declaration published in campus newspapers (May 1967) is as follows:

Many young American men have announced that they will refuse to participate in the barbarism of the Vietnam war. We, too, believe our war in Vietnam is immoral, unjust, unconscionable.

The undersigned, like the majority of our countrymen, are not among those called on to offer their lives in Vietnam. No sacrifice demanded of us can equal the loss of a single life, Vietnamese or American. With all Americans, we share a responsibility for those of our youth who have been ordered off to war.

We believe that every young man has the obligation to choose for himself whether he will train to kill and perhaps be killed in this war. This decision of conscience cannot be made for him by any external authority, including the American government. We therefore urge young men to consider whether they are willing to be executioners and victims.

To all who determine that they will not participate in this war, we pledge our full and active support. We also affirm that we will join with them in a shared effort to assure that their moral rejection of the war results in effective political opposition to it.

irreconcilable with the dictates of conscience, whether these dictates are or are not "religiously" inspired, have no recourse but civil disobedience.

Here, then, are two new issues: selective conscientious objection and the moral status of civil disobedience in this new context. The first case actually to test the right of conscientious objection to a *particular* war was appealed to the Supreme Court (July 1967) following denial to Captain Dale E. Noyd of his request to be released from the Air Force or reassigned to duties not in conflict with his conscientious objection to the Vietnam war. The appeal was turned down without judicial comment. Although the war in Vietnam precipitated this issue, it is a moral predicament that will inevitably recur so long as men wage wars that other men find unjust.

In the discussions that follow, the issue of civil disobedience will be explored first in broad philosophical terms by two eminent political theorists and then in terms of the crises concerning the Negro protest movement and resistance to the Vietnam war and the draft.

THE CASE FOR DISOBEDIENCE

Harold Laski

Harold Laski must be regarded as one of the foremost political philosophers of our time, even by those who do not share his socialist orientation. In the 'thirties his socialism took on a strong Marxian cast. For many years, until his premature death in 1950, he held England's most prestigious chair in political economy at the London School of Economics. He was at the same time chairman of the executive committee, and generally recognized as the chief theoretician, of the British Labour Party. Professor Laski was as much an authority on the American as on the British system of govern-

From *The State in Theory and Practice* by Harold J. Laski (New York: The Viking Press, Inc., 1935), pp. 65–76. Copyright 1935 by Harold J. Laski, © 1963 by Frida Laski. Reprinted by permission of The Viking Press, Inc.

*ment. Of his many books [for example, Authority in the
Modern State (1919), A Grammar of Politics (1925), The
Rise of Liberalism (1936), The American Presidency (1940),
Reflections on the Revolution of Our Time (1943)] the vol-
ume from which the following selection was taken has been
perhaps the most influential.*

. . . Neither formal competence . . . nor political power can
confer a just title to obedience. With what are we left? Only, I think, with
the insistence that law to be ethically valid must conform with the requirements of the system of rights the purposes of which the state exists to
maintain. And since law is a command seeking to control my behaviour in
some particular way, I must judge that conformity for myself as the test of
its ethical adequacy. The roots of valid law, that is, are, and can only be,
within the individual conscience. I make law legal, so to say, by giving to
its operation the consent of my conscience.

If it is said that such a view, by justifying refusal to obey, opens
the door to anarchy, the answer is that the accusation is true. But it is not a
serious accusation. In the life of states the door to anarchy is always open
because men are never willing to admit the unconditional conference of
power. If, further, it be said that the individual conscience is at least as
likely to be wrong as the consciences of those who rule the state, the
answer, again, is that, while this may be true, the citizen who yields his
conviction on the ground that he may be mistaken will soon cease, in any
meaningful sense, to be a citizen at all. There is no way of making a state
active in the fulfilment of its function except the knowledge that men will
refuse to obey its commands where they regard them as a violation of that
function. That was the truth that Pericles saw when he told the citizens of
Athens that the secret of liberty was courage. Unless men are prepared to
act by the insights they have, even when these insights are erroneous, they
are bound to become no more than the passive recipients of orders to
whose moral quality they are indifferent. When they do that, they poison
the foundations of the state. For they then cease to be moral beings in any
sense of the word that has meaning. They associate truth and justice and
right automatically with the possession of physical power. No people
prepared in that fashion to abdicate its humanity is likely to be long
capable of creative achievement. For so to abdicate the duty of moral
judgment is to sell oneself into slavery.

It is said that the individual is powerless, and that he wastes his
energy by acting upon his judgment. But there are at least two answers to
this view. A moral obligation is not less compelling because it may end in
failure. To adopt that canon of effort is to accept the view that justice is the
will of the stronger—a doctrine against which, as I have pointed out, the
whole history of humanity is a protest. And to argue, secondly, that the
individual is powerless is, on the record, quite untrue. He is powerless only

when his perceptions are so completely unshared that he fails to arouse any note of response among his fellow-citizens; and he has always to remember that the shift of events may cause them to be shared at a later stage. The early Christians must have appeared singularly futile to their own generation when they challenged the majesty of Rome; but their steadfastness conquered the Western world. Luther's recalcitrance must have appeared akin to madness to a church which remembered its successful emergence from the stresses of the Conciliar revolt; but he changed the history of the world by his courage. Even so liberal a mind as Emerson could write of the American abolitionists that they were "narrow, self-pleasing, conceited men, and affect us as the insane do"; but it was hardly a generation afterwards that so respectable an observer as Oliver Wendell Holmes, not given to extreme views, could say of his friend's judgment that "it would have taken a long time to get rid of slavery if some of Emerson's teachings in that lecture had been accepted as the whole gospel of liberty."

History, indeed, abounds with such instances. The individual who protests against the law he deems unjust is far less alone than he is likely to imagine. He is acting in a mental climate in which the experience borne in upon him is likely to be shared by others; and the gesture he makes may awaken others to the understanding of their obligations. No one who looks back upon their history can doubt that the suffragettes, who for eight years defied the law, awakened the British government to a sense that their claims were serious in a way that altered the whole perspective of those claims. No one can doubt either that the unbreakable will of Lenin was central to the success of the Bolshevik Revolution in 1917. That we must fight for our philosophy if we believe in it seems to me the inescapable implication of the record.

Against this view two considerations are urged, in both of which there is, unquestionably, considerable force. It is said that to challenge the government is to weaken the authority of all law, and that to do so is to open the floodgates to chaos. It was the sense of this danger which made T. H. Green, who admitted, in the last resort, the right to revolution, insist that we must approach the state in fear and trembling. But it is surely not less important to realize that respect for law must always mean respect for what the law does; and, if the individual, whether alone or in concert with others, judges what the law does to be ethically intolerable, he must act upon the basis of his judgment. To decide otherwise is to argue that the highest duty of the individual is to maintain order, without regard to the quality of the order that is maintained. I do not find this argument compatible with the notion of the individual as a moral being.

It is said, secondly, that this view admits the right of any doctrine to support itself by force, if it can. Men have only to announce that they are moved by some profound conviction to be justified in using violence to attain their ends. Such an attitude, it is argued, is utterly destructive of the foundations of social well-being.

But the answer is surely that no doctrine, however evil, moves to the use of force unless it is rooted in a profound grievance which it sees no other way to remedy. We may believe the Bolshevik Revolution to have been wholly evil; but it is clear that the previous conditions of the Russian state alone account for its origin and methods. We may argue, with the communists, that Hitler has been no more than the agent of finance-capitalism in Germany; but it is also clear that his victory was built upon the profound grievances of millions of Germans who saw no adequate redress for them in the habits of the Weimar republic. The truth is that men in general are so accustomed to obey that their departure from the normal canons of political behaviour is always an index to grave disease in the state. They have, as Burke said, "no interest in disorder; where they do wrong it is their error and not their crime." We need not argue that a doctrine which arms itself is wise or right to do so. But, on the facts, we have to argue that no doctrine ever does successfully arm itself unless the government it attacks has failed to deal with the grievances it expresses in a reasonable way.

That is, I think, apparent in the history of most revolutions. Certainly the student of the English civil wars, of the revolutions of France and of Russia, will note as not the least remarkable of their features the patient efforts of the common people to await reform before they turned to violence. And in any society violence is unlikely if the conviction is widespread that the state is seriously attempting to fulfil its obligations. Violence comes when the facts persuade men to believe that the bona-fides of their rulers are no longer to be trusted. They may be mistaken in that belief. There have certainly been occasions in history when the members of a government which has been overthrown have been well-intentioned men struggling with adverse circumstances it has been impossible to conquer. There have been other occasions, also, when the ends sought by men who resisted the state could not be attained within the framework of existing institutions. The overthrow of Dr. Brüning is, I believe, an instance of the first; the history of the French Revolution is a clear instance of the second.

But, not seldom, the use of violence to defeat the law is the outcome of a clash of values between which compromise is impossible. What is the situation when this arises? No one, at least, can say that the problem is a simple one. It is no answer to it, for example, to argue that the duty of a minority whose values are denied is the simple one of becoming a majority, and so using constitutional processes to obtain power by persuasion. For, in the first place, those constitutional processes may not exist. It is no use telling the citizen of one of the European dictatorships today that he should use the methods of peaceful persuasion to get his views accepted; for, *a priori,* the right, legally, to use those methods has been abrogated. He, at least, has no alternative save revolution if he seeks the realization of his purposes. The German socialist cannot be asked to hope for the peaceful conversion of Hitlerite Germany.

The situation, it is said, is different in a state of which the form is a constitutional democracy. There, at any rate, freedom to criticize exists; and provision is deliberately made for those who differ from the government of the day to take its place if they can persuade a majority of their fellow-citizens to vote with them. There is, I think, a vital truth in this view. In general, it is impossible to condone the use of violence in politics except as a weapon of last resort; it must be shown that all alternative avenues of action have been exhausted before violence is resorted to. But it is, I think, important to realize that even in a constitutional democracy dependence upon reasonable persuasion alone is a function of certain conditions, upon the realization of which the minority concerned must be able to count. First among those conditions is the right to expect the unbiased operation of state-institutions; they must weigh with equal incidence upon all parties to the political equation. In a state even so free as Great Britain that equal incidence does not obtain. For the House of Lords is an instrument in the hands of a single party in the state; and its authority can be deliberately exercised to flout the will of its opponents even when they possess a majority in the electorate. And if it is said that the House of Lords will always give way when the will of the electorate is decisively known (after a general election, for instance, which is fought upon some special issue), the answer surely is that, even if this be the case, it subjects one party in the state to grave disabilities from which its rival is wholly free; and the consequence of those disabilities may render abortive the effort of a party which has won its electoral majority, by reason of the technical conditions under which it may seek to make its purposes effective.

Nor is this all. It is important that the incidence of state-institutions should be unbiased. It is important, also, that those who operate them should be able to assume that the principles of constitutional democracy will be observed by their opponents. It would be facile to argue that this assumption is justified as even approximately an invariable rule. We may say, with some assurance, that in a society long accustomed to those principles departure from them will be less likely than in one where habituation to their exercise is novel. But, even there, it is, I suggest, a reasonable generalization that they will be observed only when the interests which an important minority deems, rightly or wrongly, to be fundamental, are not in jeopardy. . . . Unless, in a constitutional democracy, a government can be certain that its decisions will be respected, one can be certain that the assumptions of such a system will not be long preserved.

It is argued from this that it leads to the obligation, incumbent upon the governments of all such states, not to outrage the fundamental sentiments of an important minority. There are, that is to say, limits to the rights of a majority whose representatives are exercising the sovereign power. That is a platitude which has not even the merit of being profound. Anyone can see that, if the King in Parliament prohibited the exercise of the Roman Catholic religion, those who professed it would break the law rather than obey the law. Anyone can see, also, that, if the King in Parliament were foolish enough to declare trade unions illegal organizations, the trade unions would fight rather than give way. No one ever takes the legal right to exercise the powers of sovereignty as equivalent to the moral right to do anything one pleases.

But to say that there are limits to the rights of a majority is not to define those limits; and that, after all, is the real core of the problem. We cannot seriously argue that no government is entitled to take any decision which may outrage the conscience of a significant minority. A significant minority of American opinion was outraged by the decision to abolish slavery; but that did not render unjustifiable the decision to abolish it. A significant minority thought the Reform Act of 1832 an outrage; but, again, we should not attempt to justify a decision to withdraw it on that ground. A significant minority in Great Britain today thinks the "Means Test" in connexion with unemployment insurance outrageous; that is not held to justify its withdrawal. There is hardly, indeed, a single social expedient of any magnitude, adversely affecting an important interest involved, which has not been deemed, at some time or other, "outrageous" by the minority so affected. . . .

Are we then to say that the point at which the limits of majority rule become apparent are defined when the minority proposes to fight rather than to give way? This raises several issues. Does a proposal to fight mean actual conflict in the streets, or is it sufficient that action like a general strike, in which the use of some violence at least is pretty inevitably inherent, should be attempted? But it is impossible to conduct the process of ordered government upon the terms that a majority must not use its power when a minority threatens resistance. In a situation, for instance, like that of Ireland in 1914, the will of the government would have been completely paralysed. For there the Ulster extremists threatened to fight if the Home Rule Bill went into operation, and the Irish nationalists threatened to turn out the government if the bill was withdrawn; and the Asquith solution, which was to enact the bill, but suspend its operation, effectively resulted in a complete victory for the Ulster extremists.

There are, no doubt, occasions when it is wise for a government so threatened to compromise rather than to seek the maintenance of its prestige without regard to the price that may have to be paid for it. . . . But it is certainly not a method which can be made a general rule, for the simple reason that it would make majority government invariably impossible. Normally, a government that is challenged is obliged, so long as it feels

confident that it has public opinion behind it, to meet the challenge; for it is
the primary thesis of constitutional democracy that it can be overthrown
only in ways specifically provided for by law. The limits of majority rule,
therefore, cannot really be defined with any precision in terms of principle.
They rest upon felt insights rather than exact measurements of what particular situations involve. Certainly a government which estimates their
meaning must always remember that any consistent series of surrenders to
the clamour of interest will rapidly prevent it from being able to embark
upon any measures of serious importance.

What seems to emerge from our historic experience is the lesson
that a government can impose its will upon the citizens of a constitutional
democracy so long, but only so long, as those citizens are in fundamental
agreement about the actual purposes of the state. . . . Valid law, we must
affirm, is law judged adequate by men as it seeks for their consent. It has
no final title to acceptance because it emanates from the sovereign power.
It has no title to acceptance, even, because it presents itself as an effort to
realize the right. Its claim to be obeyed is in the decision men make about
the legitimacy of its pretensions. It becomes valid law by its power to
satisfy the demands they make upon the institutions whose will it represents. . . .

THE CASE AGAINST DISOBEDIENCE

John Dickinson

*John Dickinson taught at Harvard and Princeton and at the
law school of the University of Pennsylvania. He was Assistant U.S. Secretary of Commerce, Assistant U.S. Attorney
General, and chief counsel and vice-president of the Pennsylvania Railroad. He wrote* Administrative Justice and the Supremacy of Law in the United States *(1927).*

. . . a régime of law in the positive sense, in so far as it is realized
at all, prevails only within the limits of each nation-state, and does so only

Reprinted from *Political Science Quarterly,* 43, No. 1 (March 1928), 32–59.
Reprinted by permission.

because, and only in so far as, such a state is organized on the principle of sovereignty.

. . . there can be no doubt that a régime of positive law, where it is strictly realized, has its disadvantages as well as its advantages. It emphasizes order and stability and uniformity, sometimes at the expense of what may be thought to be justice, but almost always at the expense, to some degree, of adaptability and progress. Its mode of operation is to set human conduct into theoretically rigid grooves for the sake of certainty and predictability, and to that extent to put barriers in the way of an experimental quest by private individuals and groups for new and more satisfactory adjustments. Hence arises the familiar and age-old conflict between the claims of order on the one side and of liberty on the other—a conflict which becomes progressively acute when extensive changes in the setting of human life and in the technique of satisfying human wants crowd upon the world and make new adjustments imperative. We are living in the welter of such a period of change today.

At such a time either of two courses seems open to the protagonists of progress. On the one hand they may direct their efforts toward bringing positive law as near as may be into step with the march of the new demands by attempting to so constitute the sovereign organ as to make it more and more delicately responsive to the new impulses within the community. Along this path, and along this path alone, will seriously emerge the challenge to improve the machinery of government, as well as the sole hope and chance of effecting such improvements; for the improvement of government means precisely the difficult task of so altering its machinery as to increase its responsiveness to the needs of the community without impairing its value as an instrument of certainty and order. If we adopt this line of approach, there will be no occasion to question the validity of sovereignty in the sense in which I have sought to describe it. . . .

But of course another method of approach is open. We may take a short cut, and directly challenge sovereignty itself; which, whether we realize it or not, means questioning the value of a régime of positive law as an instrument for the achievement by a community of its internal adjustments. We may be so distrustful lest the sovereign organ fall under the influence of forces which we regard as malign and mischievous that we will refuse to vest any agency with final authority to pronounce what is law, and what is not, as between contending individuals or groups or interests. . . .

The importance of the controversy over sovereignty in its current form hinges precisely on the fact that consciously or unconsciously it is a challenge to choose between these two different attitudes of approach to the disputed issues of political and social reform. Shall we admit that because of the limitations and dangers of positive law, freedom to break through it at the will of the individual who thinks himself right must be erected into a normal working-part of the system of government, available at all times, rather than kept in reserve in the form of an extra-legal power of revolution for use only as an abnormal safety-valve and last resort in exceptional cases of great oppression? This admission is in substance what is demanded by writers who are attacking the concept of sovereignty; they seem to be seeking primarily for a way to regularize and legalize diso-bedience to existing positive law. Of course this is really to make a régime of positive law impossible; for a law which can be legally broken at the will of the lawbreaker can never be positive law in any intelligible sense. The basic question at stake in the controversy over sovereignty is therefore what our attitude shall be toward breaches of positive law, and so how we shall approach the age-old question of obedience—the question of the *Antigone* and the *Crito*. Shall we regard disobedience as properly a normal, i.e., a *legal* thing, or as only the abnormal, and therefore illegal, though perhaps at times morally justifiable, thing? What concessions to sovereignty are inevitable if we would have the advantages of a legally ordered society? . . .

The capital indictments which so-called political pluralists, as represented by Mr. G. D. H. Cole and Mr. Laski in his earlier books, have brought against the concept of sovereignty seem to be all based on this fundamental confusion between legal considerations on the one hand and moral, social, and factual considerations on the other hand. Thus Mr. Laski has pointed out insistently that the "will" of the so-called sovereign can never be an absolute "will"—that it is almost certain to be controlled by some group, some interest, or combination of interests and forces within or without the community; and that the identity, the nature, of this con-trolling influence is of major practical consequence. So indeed it is, in connection with all questions of the goodness and badness of laws and forms of government, and with the reform of constitutional machinery; but hardly in connection with the question of the positive legality of a govern-mental act or pronouncement.

. . . in saying that the sovereign is only sovereign when serving the common good, [Laski] seems to be taking altogether too high and mystical a view of the nature of sovereignty, and of the positive law which proceeds from it. He apparently vests positive law—i.e., a valid pro-nouncement of the sovereign—with a sanctity so elevated that he is un-willing to admit to it anything that is not in accordance with his own conception of the ultimate philosophical purposes of the state. This is a recurrence of the ancient unwillingness among men to admit that there can ever be discrepancy between law and justice; the unwillingness to vest with the character of law any rule which is not thought to be objectively the one and only best rule for application to the particular circumstances of the case in hand. Now of course positive law ought so far as is humanly possible to conform to the highest ideal standards of justice conceivable at the time and place; if it does not so conform, it is doubtless the civic duty of all members of the community to do their best to bring about such conformity; and if the machinery of government does not readily permit progressive improvement in this direction, it should be overhauled in order that it may do so. But even so, we cannot be purists and insist that until the necessary improvements are brought about, the bad old rule with which we are dissatisfied is not entitled to be considered as law in even the positive sense. Positive law is and must always be a thing of rough and ready adjustments; much of convenience, policy, compromise, doubtful experiment, inevitably enter into its make-up. All the members of the community will by no means be able to agree on what justice in the highest sense is, or on what particular demands it makes in any given situation; meanwhile if they are not to fight out their differences, there must be some rule to settle them by. We can never proceed toward getting the best rule until we first consent that there shall at least be a rule, and we will never consent that there shall be a rule if we insist on having what we privately regard as the best rule, or else on having no rule at all. We must therefore be willing to allow the character of positive law to much that we might well wish were otherwise. . . . Unless we are sheer anarchists, a rule sanctioned by the highest authority in the state is ordinarily preferable to no rule at all, until we can get a better one; and if we feel that because of exceptional circumstances this is not so in a particular case, then we must frankly face in that special case the moral or social issue of revolution, and not hide our heads in the sand by pretending that we are only upholding law when we are resisting the ordinances of the authorized law-declaring organ of the community.

In the second place, the language quoted from Mr. Laski seems to show a certain confusion in refusing to regard as law a rule proclaimed by the sovereign organ whenever such a rule can be thought to result from selfish pressure brought to bear upon the sovereign by contending interests. We get off the track if we proceed to say that such a rule is in reality nothing more than an expression of the "private" will of the strongest special interest, on the ground that the interest exerting the decisive force is really the sovereign. Factually, it may indeed be called the cause of the sovereign's action, but still it must act through the sovereign; and if there were no sovereign through which it had to act, its action might well be quite different. The helm controls the ship no less because some one must give direction to the helm; and the sovereign controls the law no less because some one may give direction to the sovereign. The fact that forces will exert pressure is not the important thing; of course they will; the important thing is the way they must go about exerting it. Now in a community politically organized under sovereignty, they must exert it through the sovereign; in the absence of sovereignty there is no legal obstacle to prevent them from exerting it directly against their opponents to the point of actual intimidation and violence. The difference is not un-important; it may be only a difference of degree, but still it produces vital differences in both methods and results. It is never quite enough to see in the politically organized community only a pressure of competing interests, as the pluralists so often do. The competition and the pressure undeniably exist, but there exists also a structure of legal processes which set limits to their action, and often deflect its direction. The kind of competition which goes on between opposing interests within a nation-state is certainly a different kind of competition in enough important particulars from that which goes on between "independent" nation-states to warrant recognizing the differences. . . .

Government, if it performs its function, is simply a great central coordinating agency from which these adjustments ultimately emerge . . . But even if government is not well organized, and performs its functions ill, still it sometimes accomplishes one important purpose; even if it habitually favors one group in the community at the expense of others, and advances the interests of the former to the utter disregard of the latter, it may yet afford the advantages, whatever we hold them worth, of peace and order. It at least enables men to know the rules they must live under and the authority to which they must submit if they would be law-abiding. Now there are times, no doubt, when this is not a good thing; there is a peace which is the "bitterest bitterness" and worse than any war; and at such times the anarchy of resistance and civil war may be the only thinkable portal to a fairer and better world. But admitting all this, there is still a truth in the old commonplace that one tyrant is preferable to many; and the age of Augustus, the age of the Medici and of the Tudors, bear witness that as a general rule men appear to find the peace and order even of a despotism a more satisfactory environment wherein to work out their purposes than a continual conflict of authorities, though the latter be shot through with the purest passion for civil or religious liberty of a Brutus or a Becket. . . .

Suppose . . . that we do not accept the doctrine of sovereignty. We will then insist that laws do not derive their validity from the stamp of the sovereign, but that a rule may be validly a law which is directly con-trary to the rule which the sovereign is seeking to enforce. But if this is the case, and if we must look not to the sovereign but to some other source to assure us what is the law, where else are we to look? Mr. Laski has suggested the only possible answer—we must look within, each man to his own individual conscience. If we use this method of approach we have no choice but to say that the validity of all law is derived from the conscience of the individual. The question of obedience or resistance then becomes a simple one. All that is involved is for each individual to set side by side and compare the law as promulgated by the sovereign with what his own con-science tells him is the law, and if there is a discrepancy between the two precepts, then he is not merely morally justified, he is legally authorized, to disobey. There are but two factors to be taken into account in solving the problem—the sovereign's pronouncement on the one hand and the individual's own conception of the law—i.e., of what is right—on the other. His career as a member of civil society becomes a continuous process of such comparisons, and he stands at every moment on the brink of disobedience and resistance. "The only ground upon which the individual can give or be asked his support for the state is from the conviction that what it is aiming at is, in each particular action, good. . . . It deserves his allegiance, it should receive it, only where it commands his conscience. . . . Its purpose is at each stage subject to examination." The individual is thus invited to assume habitually what Mr. Laski has elsewhere called the "Athanasius attitude."

The doubt which suggests itself in connection with this attitude is that possibly it may be too naïve—that possibly it may not be sophisticated enough to comprehend the full challenge of civil society. It is the primitive attitude of Antigone, rather than the mature comprehension of Socrates. Its capital defect is that it leaves fundamentally out of account the chief and most difficult factor in the whole problem—the question, namely, of the advantage, not merely to all individuals but to each individual, of having a legally ordered society to live in, and of the price which he must perforce pay for it. This factor is the thing which really causes all the difficulty; and it is the major factor. If there were no question but of a conflict between two opposing wills, the will of the citizen as one individual and the will of the sovereign as another, the problem would be quite easy; the individual could not fairly be expected to surrender his will until convinced intellectually and morally that he was wrong. But so to state the problem is to simplify it out of all recognition. It is not a question of a bare conflict between the individual and the sovereign; the conflict must be regarded as rather between the individual and all that the sovereign stands for. The individual may be convinced and reasonably convinced that the sovereign is wrong, unfairly, brutally wrong; but the deeper question must at once arise of what is involved in disobeying the sovereign.

For sovereignty, as we have seen, is a prerequisite of legal order; a prerequisite, that is, of a condition of affairs where the disputes which will honestly and inevitably arise between man and man, and which will as often be due to a real and involuntary difference in intellectual outlook as to a clash between purely selfish purposes, are settled peaceably by a publicly authorized arbiter, and, so far as possible, by impartial rules, rather than by the rough arbitrament of force and chance. The very essence and meaning of civil society is precisely the fact that the former method rather than the latter is the one which habitually prevails; and this essential method of civil society is just the thing which we strike at whenever we disobey or resist the sovereign. The question of obedience thus raises far more than the mere question of the agreement or disagreement in a particular case between the sovereign's law applying to the case in hand, and what the individual's private conscience tells him the law ought to be; properly approached, it brings dominantly into the foreground the large issue of the desirability of preserving public authority and civil society itself. This is the great truth so clearly put by Socrates, when in answer to Crito's plea for disobedience he represents the City as standing before him and saying, "Tell us, Socrates, what is it you mean to do? Nothing more nor less than to overthrow us by this attempt of yours—to overthrow the laws and the whole commonwealth so far as in you lies. For do you imagine that a city can stand and not be overthrown, when the decisions of the judges have no power, when they are made of no effect and destroyed by private persons?" In other words, something of vastly superior consequence is involved than the essential rightness or wrongness in the given case of any particular exercise of sovereign power; what is involved, fundamentally, is the value and validity of civil society in contrast with the freedom, the flexibility, the experimentalism, of anarchy, whether the latter take the form of benevolent cooperation or of forceful competition. Civil society cannot stand when the decisions of the judges are made of no effect by private persons; and the Athanasius attitude, to be defensible, must balance not particular differences of opinion between the individual conscience and the sovereign will, but the value of the end which conscience has at stake as against the value of civil society.

For there are of course ends which from time to time do validly outweigh the maintenance for the time being of the orderly processes of civil society. Revolution, like war, is no doubt entitled to a place as one of the indispensable ingredients of progress in the existing, and perhaps in any, state of human nature. The only point I am insisting on is that revolution should always be recognized for what it is—a lapse into anarchy. Only so, in any specific case, can the wisdom of taking the plunge be fairly assessed; only so can the full meaning of the alternative between obedience and resistance be grasped in all its awful implications. The chief defect in the doctrine of the denial of sovereignty is that it glosses over with thin sugarcoating this fundamental alternative. The doctrine that there exists somewhere a law above, and independent of, the law of the sovereign, and capable of being discovered for himself by each private individual so as to justify disobedience to the positive law, carries with it the implication that civil society itself exists, and can exist, apart from and independently of obedience to the sovereign; and that therefore resistance by the individual to the sovereign is not necessarily anything like so serious and ultimate a thing as an assault on civil society is readily seen to be. The essential meaning of resistance is obscured, the price which it entails belittled. And at the same time the price that we must pay for civil society itself is belittled. For the demand which civil society makes that private individual will and purpose be always subordinated to the will of the authorized public representative of the society, on no other and no better ground than merely that the one is private and the other public, is by implication denied, if we accept the doctrine that civil society does not depend for its existence and functioning on obedience to its constituted representative. A view of civil society is thus produced which evades the necessity for political organization—which tolerates the claim of separate and discrete groups within the state to be independent of the jurisdiction of, and immune from interference by, the state, and which in pursuance of the same conviction is capable of seeing in an unorganized "society of nations" a substantial substitute for an organized League. The theory seeks to have its cake of order without having to pay the price of organization.

This was the theory that dominated the thought of the Western world throughout the medieval centuries. It is a theory the defectiveness of which is in large cured if we are able to accept a presupposition which to the mind of the Middle Ages was a commonplace—the presupposition, namely, that there not merely exists a body of law above and independent of human choice, but that the precepts of that law are fixed, definite and capable of being as clearly perceived in identical form by every human intelligence as are the elementary truths of mathematics. Men obviously need no sovereign to exercise a prerogative of choice in order to tell them whether twice two is five or four. If the laws which distinguish right from wrong are equally well defined by "nature," we need no sovereign to tell us whether the issue of watered stock by a corporation is illegal, or whether or not relief by injunction is a lawful remedy to apply in a labor dispute. Men thought, not so long ago, that the one right answer to every such question could be reached by mathematical demonstration. If this were so, there would be no need for a sovereign law-declaring agency. But during the past few centuries there has been growing doubt as to whether it is really so; and the conflict between the faith and the doubt is quaintly reflected in the inconsistency of a central passage of Locke's *Second Treatise of Civil Government:* "In the state of Nature there are many things wanting. Firstly, there wants an established, settled, known law. . . . For though the law of Nature be plain and intelligible to all rational creatures, yet men, being biased by their interest, as well as ignorant for want of study of it, are not apt to allow of it as a law binding to them in the application of it to their particular cases." In other words, the law of nature is there, but we need an authoritative human organ to tell us what it is. "Those who are united into one body and have a common established law and judicature to appeal to . . . are in civil society with one another, but those who have no such common appeal are in the state of nature."

Even, then, if we grant the existence of a "law" that is not of men's making, but recognize that room remains for possible differences of opinion as to its specific precepts, we shall still have to admit the need for political organization, the need for a sovereign to "declare" that law authoritatively; and we shall then be driven forward to face the important practical problems incidental to devising a mechanism of organization best adapted to cause the precepts of the sovereign to conform to the precepts of the "higher" law. But this is a task which the doctrine of resistance minimizes and discourages. If each individual is entitled to search in his own conscience for the precept of the higher law applicable to the case in hand, and then to disobey the sovereign should his inquiry lead to a different conclusion from that which that sovereign has reached, the importance of having a sovereign who will reach the right conclusion in the first place is vastly decreased; for if no law made by the sovereign need be obeyed unless it is a good law, the question of whether the sovereign makes bad laws becomes of relatively secondary consequence. From this point of view, therefore, the real guaranty of good government is the "right" of resistance, not the perfecting of the government machinery adapted to produce the best results under given circumstances. In answer to this theory it should be sufficient to point out that the whole history of progress in the art of government has consisted in the gradual substitution of the latter for the former of these guaranties. Revolution was during long ages the only effective way by which the ordinary acts of government could be corrected; the efforts of many centuries have been spent on devising less wasteful and more orderly methods of control. These efforts have proceeded on the assumption that it is not compatible with the existence of civil society to leave to each individual the protection of his own rights; that so long as the normal conditions of civil order prevail, the sovereign, as the organ of the community, must be entitled to the obedience of the individual precisely because, and for no other reason than because, the sovereign *is* the organ of the community; and that therefore the protection of the individual under normal circumstances must be found not in the "right" of resistance, but in the manner and plan whereby sovereign power is organized and constituted.

The fact that in civil society the individual is thus not entitled to set his own idea of the "higher" precepts which the government should follow against the sovereign's version of them, does not mean that there are no such precepts. Whether they constitute a body of "higher law" or not, is of course a wholly different question; but nothing that has been said implies that there are no canons of morality and justice which the sovereign ought to embody in his positive laws. On the contrary, the institution of sovereignty exists primarily because of the need of an organ to focus and formulate these fundamental, but more or less vague and disputed, canons into precise and uniform rules which on the one hand have the fixity and generality necessary for a rule of law, and which on the other hand represent the moral conceptions that command acceptance among the most influential members of the community rather than views which are held merely by isolated private thinkers. In a realm of ideas where there is so much room for differences of opinion as in connection with the precepts of morality, it is absolutely necessary to have such an authoritative declaration of the rule before there can properly be any thought of enforcing it as a rule of community action. It may, and doubtless often will, result that the rule selected by the sovereign for enforcement, precisely because it will be a rule reflecting the morality of the crowd or the morality of the wealthy or military class, will offend the consciences of the individuals who constitute the most enlightened and morally advanced element of the community. Under such circumstances is not the right of this class to resist essential in order to secure moral progress? As a last resort and in extraordinary situations where the stake is sufficiently high, the answer must certainly be, yes; but always with full recognition of the fact that such resistance constitutes rebellion, and entails for the time being a dissolution of the conditions of civil order. Under a properly adjusted constitution, the necessity should seldom occur, because such a constitution would, on the one hand, provide adequate channels for the views of this class to exert an influence upon the sovereign as far as is compatible with the obvious fact that laws must be made to fit the average rather than the exceptional man; and because, on the other hand, under such a constitution the sovereign would doubtless be wise enough to limit to the narrowest point his interference with those kinds of individual action from which moral improvement can properly be expected to occur. . . .

· WHERE DO WE GO FROM HERE?

Martin Luther King, Jr.

Of all those who have fought racial injustice Dr. Martin Luther King, Jr. is easily the best known. Born in the South and educated in the North, he first came to national prominence as leader of the boycott of segregated buses in Montgomery, Alabama. His work was recognized by the award in 1964 of the Nobel Peace Prize. An eloquent and tireless cru-

sader for equality for his people, he became embroiled not only in a struggle against racist whites, but in controversies with Negro leaders who preach a different gospel of resistance.

The following selection was written before protesting marchers began chanting "black power" as they trudged across the state of Mississippi. Of this slogan Dr. King had later observed, even before the Newark and Detroit riots, that it "was an unwise choice at the outset. With the violent connotations that now attach to the words it has become dangerous and injurious. . . . Black supremacy or aggressive black violence is as invested with evil as white supremacy or white violence."[1] More recently, however, in an effort to contain the "black power" movement, the Southern Christian Leadership Conference (SCLC), which he headed, adopted new phrases such as "sense of negritude" and "Afro-American unity" to reckon with the Negro identity crisis.

The selection should be read primarily for its bearing on the issue of civil disobedience. However, it will be clear that Dr. King was concerning himself with more than a defense of the duty to disobey an unjust law and with more than a commentary on the technique of nonviolent resistance; included is an examination of such more general moral phenomena as the spiritual invigoration that comes from selfless dedication to a common purpose.

. . . Violence as a way of achieving racial justice is both impractical and immoral. It is impractical because it is a descending spiral ending in destruction for all. The old law of an eye for an eye leaves everybody blind. It is immoral because it seeks to humiliate the opponent rather than win his understanding; it seeks to annihilate rather than to convert. Violence is immoral because it thrives on hatred rather than love. It destroys community and makes brotherhood impossible. It leaves society in monologue rather than dialogue. Violence ends by defeating itself. It creates bitterness in the survivors and brutality in the destroyers. A voice echoes through time saying to every potential Peter, "Put up your sword." History is cluttered with the wreckage of nations that failed to follow this command.

If the American Negro and other victims of oppression succumb to the temptation of using violence in the struggle for freedom, future generations will be the recipients of a desolate night of bitterness, and our chief legacy to them will be an endless reign of meaningless chaos. Violence is not the way.

[Another] way open to oppressed people in their quest for freedom is the way of nonviolent resistance. Like the synthesis in Hegelian

---

[1] "Black Power," *The Progressive*, XXX (November 1966), 15–16.

philosophy, the principle of nonviolent resistance seeks to reconcile the truths of two opposites—acquiescence and violence—while avoiding the extremes and immoralities of both. The nonviolent resister agrees with the person who acquiesces that one should not be physically aggressive toward his opponent; but he balances the equation by agreeing with the person of violence that evil must be resisted. He avoids the nonresistance of the former and the violent resistance of the latter. With nonviolent resistance, no individual or group need submit to any wrong, nor need anyone resort to violence in order to right a wrong.

It seems to me that this is the method that must guide the actions of the Negro in the present crisis in race relations. Through nonviolent resistance the Negro will be able to rise to the noble height of opposing the unjust system while loving the perpetrators of the system. The Negro must work passionately and unrelentingly for full stature as a citizen, but he must not use inferior methods to gain it. He must never come to terms with falsehood, malice, hate, or destruction.

Nonviolent resistance makes it possible for the Negro to remain in the South and struggle for his rights. The Negro's problem will not be solved by running away. He cannot listen to the glib suggestion of those who would urge him to migrate en masse to other sections of the country. By grasping his great opportunity in the South he can make a lasting contribution to the moral strength of the nation and set a sublime example of courage for generations yet unborn.

By nonviolent resistance, the Negro can also enlist all men of good will in his struggle for equality. The problem is not a purely racial one, with Negroes set against whites. In the end, it is not a struggle between people at all, but a tension between justice and injustice. Nonviolent resistance is not aimed against oppressors but against oppression. Under its banner consciences, not racial groups, are enlisted.

If the Negro is to achieve the goal of integration, he must organize himself into a militant and nonviolent mass movement. All three elements are indispensable. The movement for equality and justice can only be a success if it has both a mass and militant character; the barriers to be overcome require both. Nonviolence is an imperative in order to bring about ultimate community.

A mass movement of a militant quality that is not at the same time committed to nonviolence tends to generate conflict, which in turn breeds anarchy. The support of the participants and the sympathy of the uncommitted are both inhibited by the threat that bloodshed will engulf the community. This reaction in turn encourages the opposition to threaten and resort to force. When, however, the mass movement repudiates violence while moving resolutely toward its goal, its opponents are revealed as the instigators and practitioners of violence if it occurs. Then public support is magnetically attracted to the advocates of nonviolence, while those who employ violence are literally disarmed by overwhelming sentiment against their stand.

Only through a nonviolent approach can the fears of the white community be mitigated. A guilt-ridden white minority lives in fear that if the Negro should ever attain power, he would act without restraint or pity to revenge the injustice and brutality of the years. It is something like a parent who continually mistreats a son. One day that parent raises his hand to strike the son, only to discover that the son is now as tall as he is. The parent is suddenly afraid—fearful that the son will use his new physical power to repay his parent for all the blows of the past.

The Negro, once a helpless child, has now grown up politically, culturally, and economically. Many white men fear retaliation. The job of the Negro is to show them that they have nothing to fear, that the Negro understands and forgives and is ready to forget the past. He must convince the white man that all he seeks is justice, *for both himself and the white man*. A mass movement exercising nonviolence is an object lesson in power under discipline, a demonstration to the white community that if such a movement attained a degree of strength, it would use its power creatively and not vengefully.

Nonviolence can touch men where the law cannot reach them. When the law regulates behavior it plays an indirect part in molding public sentiment. The enforcement of the law is itself a form of peaceful persuasion. But the law needs help. The courts can order desegregation of the public schools. But what can be done to mitigate the fears, to disperse the hatred, violence, and irrationality gathered around school integration, to take the initiative out of the hands of racial demagogues, to release respect for the law? In the end, for laws to be obeyed, men must believe they are right.

Here nonviolence comes in as the ultimate form of persuasion. It is the method which seeks to implement the just law by appealing to the conscience of the great decent majority who through blindness, fear, pride, or irrationality have allowed their consciences to sleep.

The nonviolent resisters can summarize their message in the following simple terms: We will take direct action against injustice without waiting for other agencies to act. We will not obey unjust laws or submit to unjust practices. We will do this peacefully, openly, cheerfully because our aim is to persuade. We adopt the means of nonviolence because our end is a community at peace with itself. We will try to persuade with our words, but if our words fail, we will try to persuade with our acts. We will always be willing to talk and seek fair compromise, but we are ready to suffer when necessary and even risk our lives to become witnesses to the truth as we see it.

The way of nonviolence means a willingness to suffer and sacrifice.

It may mean going to jail. If such is the case the resister must be willing to fill the jail houses of the South. It may even mean physical death. But if physical death is the price that a man must pay to free his children and his white brethren from a permanent death of the spirit, then nothing could be more redemptive.

What is the Negro's best defense against acts of violence inflicted upon him? As Dr. Kenneth Clark has said so eloquently, "His only defense is to meet every act of barbarity, illegality, cruelty and injustice toward an individual Negro with the fact that 100 more Negroes will present themselves in his place as potential victims." Every time one Negro school teacher is fired for believing in integration, a thousand others should be ready to take the same stand. If the oppressors bomb the home of one Negro for his protest, they must be made to realize that to press back the rising tide of the Negro's courage they will have to bomb hundreds more, and even then they will fail.

Faced with this dynamic unity, this amazing self-respect, this willingness to suffer, and this refusal to hit back, the oppressor will find, as oppressors have always found, that he is glutted with his own barbarity. Forced to stand before the world and his God splattered with the blood of his brother, he will call an end to his self-defeating massacre.

American Negroes must come to the point where they can say to their white brothers, paraphrasing the words of Gandhi: "We will match your capacity to inflict suffering with our capacity to endure suffering. We will meet your physical force with soul force. We will not hate you, but we cannot in all good conscience obey your unjust laws. Do to us what you will and we will still love you. Bomb our homes and threaten our children; send your hooded perpetrators of violence into our communities and drag us out on some wayside road, beating us and leaving us half dead, and we will still love you. But we will soon wear you down by our capacity to suffer. And in winning our freedom we will so appeal to your heart and conscience that we will win you in the process."

Realism impels me to admit that many Negroes will find it difficult to follow the path of nonviolence. Some will consider it senseless; some will argue that they have neither the strength nor the courage to join in such a mass demonstration of nonviolent action. As E. Franklin Frazier points out in *Black Bourgeoisie,* many Negroes are occupied in a middle-class struggle for status and prestige. They are more concerned about "conspicuous consumption" than about the cause of justice, and are probably not prepared for the ordeals and sacrifices involved in nonviolent action. Fortunately, however, the success of this method is not dependent on its unanimous acceptance. A few Negroes in every community, unswervingly committed to the nonviolent way, can persuade hundreds of others at least to use nonviolence as a technique and serve as the moral force to awaken the slumbering national conscience. Thoreau was thinking of such a creative minority when he said: "I know this well, that if one thousand, if one hundred, if ten men whom I could name—if ten honest men only— aye, if one honest man, in the state of Massachusetts, ceasing to hold slaves, were actually to withdraw from the copartnership, and be locked up in the county jail therefore, it would be the abolition of slavery in America. For it matters not how small the beginning may seem to be, what is once well done is done forever."

Mahatma Gandhi never had more than one hundred persons absolutely committed to his philosophy. But with this small group of devoted followers, he galvanized the whole of India, and through a magnificent feat of nonviolence challenged the might of the British Empire and won freedom for his people.

This method of nonviolence will not work miracles overnight. Men are not easily moved from their mental ruts, their prejudiced and irrational feelings. When the underprivileged demand freedom, the privileged first react with bitterness and resistance. Even when the demands are couched in nonviolent terms, the initial response is the same. Nehru once remarked that the British were never so angry as when the Indians resisted them with nonviolence, that he never saw eyes so full of hate as those of the British troops to whom he turned the other cheek when they beat him with lathis. But nonviolent resistance at least changed the minds and hearts of the Indians, however impervious the British may have appeared. "We cast away our fear," says Nehru. And in the end the British not only granted freedom to India but came to have a new respect for the Indians. Today a mutual friendship based on complete equality exists between these two peoples within the Commonwealth.

In the South too, the initial white reaction to Negro resistance has been bitter. I do not predict that a similar happy ending will come to Montgomery in a few months, because integration is more complicated than independence. But I know that the Negroes of Montgomery are already walking straighter because of the protest. And I expect that this generation of Negro children throughout the United States will grow up stronger and better because of the courage, the dignity, and the suffering of the nine children of Little Rock, and their counterparts in Nashville, Clinton, and Sturges. And I believe that the white people of this country are being affected too, that beneath the surface this nation's conscience is being stirred.

The nonviolent approach does not immediately change the heart of the oppressor. It first does something to the hearts and souls of those committed to it. It gives them new self-respect; it calls up resources of strength and courage that they did not know they had. Finally it reaches the opponent and so stirs his conscience that reconciliation becomes a reality.

I suggest this approach because I think it is the only way to reëstablish the broken community. Court orders and federal enforcement agencies will be of inestimable value in achieving desegregation. But desegregation is only a partial, though necessary, step toward the ultimate goal which we seek to realize. Desegregation will break down the legal barriers, and bring men together physically. But something must happen so to touch the hearts and souls of men that they will come together, not because the law says it, but because it is natural and right. In other words, our ultimate goal is integration which is genuine intergroup and inter-personal living. Only through nonviolence can this goal be attained, for the aftermath of nonviolence is reconciliation and the creation of the beloved community.

It is becoming clear that the Negro is in for a season of suffering. As victories for civil rights mount in the federal courts, angry passions and deep prejudices are further aroused. The mountain of state and local segregation laws still stands. Negro leaders continue to be arrested and harassed under city ordinances, and their homes continue to be bombed. State laws continue to be enacted to circumvent integration. I pray that, recognizing the necessity of suffering, the Negro will make it a virtue. To suffer in a righteous cause is to grow to our humanity's full stature. If only to save himself from bitterness, the Negro needs the vision to see the ordeals of this generation as the opportunity to transfigure himself and American society. If he has to go to jail for the cause of freedom, let him enter it in the fashion Gandhi urged his countrymen, "as the bridegroom enters the bride's chamber"—that is, with a little trepidation but with a great expectation.

Nonviolence is a way of humility and self-restraint. We Negroes talk a great deal about our rights, and rightly so. We proudly proclaim that three-fourths of the people of the world are colored. We have the privilege of watching in our generation the great drama of freedom and independence as it unfolds in Asia and Africa. All of these things are in line with the work of providence. We must be sure, however, that we accept them in the right spirit. In an effort to achieve freedom in America, Asia, and Africa we must not try to leap from a position of disadvantage to one of advantage, thus subverting justice. We must seek democracy and not the substitution of one tyranny for another. Our aim must never be to defeat or humiliate the white man. We must not become victimized with a philosophy of black supremacy. God is not interested merely in the freedom of black men, and brown men, and yellow men; God is interested in the freedom of the whole human race.

The nonviolent approach provides an answer to the long debated question of gradualism *versus* immediacy. On the one hand it prevents one from falling into the sort of patience which is an excuse for do-nothingism and escapism, ending up in standstillism. On the other hand it saves one from the irresponsible words which estrange without reconciling and the hasty judgment which is blind to the necessities of social process. It recognizes the need for moving toward the goal of justice with wise restraint and calm reasonableness. But it also recognizes the immorality of slowing up in the move toward justice and capitulating to the guardians of an unjust status quo. It recognizes that social change cannot come overnight. But it causes one to work as if it were a possibility the next morning.

Through nonviolence we avoid the temptation of taking on the psychology of victors. Thanks largely to the noble and invaluable work of the NAACP, we have won great victories in the federal courts. But we must not be self-satisfied. We must respond to every decision with an understanding of those who have opposed us, and with acceptance of the new adjustments that the court orders pose for them. We must act in such a way that our victories will be triumphs for good will in all men, white and Negro.

Nonviolence is essentially a positive concept. Its corollary must always be growth. On the one hand nonviolence requires noncoöperation with evil; on the other hand it requires coöperation with the constructive forces of good. Without this constructive aspect noncoöperation ends where it begins. Therefore, the Negro must get to work on a program with a broad range of positive goals.

One point in the Negro's program should be a plan to improve his own economic lot. Through the establishment of credit unions, savings and loan associations, and coöperative enterprises the Negro can greatly improve his economic status. He must develop habits of thrift and techniques of wise investment. He must not wait for the end of segregation that lies at the basis of his economic deprivation; he must act now to lift himself up by his own bootstraps.

The constructive program ahead must include a campaign to get Negroes to register and vote. Certainly they face many external barriers. All types of underhand methods are still being used in the South to prevent the Negroes from voting, and the success of these efforts is not only unjust, it is a real embarrassment to the nation we love and must protect. The advocacy of free elections in Europe by American officials is hypocrisy when free elections are not held in great sections of America.

But external resistance is not the only present barrier to Negro voting. Apathy among the Negroes themselves is also a factor. Even where the polls are open to all, Negroes have shown themselves too slow to exercise their voting privileges. There must be a concerted effort on the part of Negro leaders to arouse their people from their apathetic indifference to this obligation of citizenship. In the past, apathy was a moral failure. Today, it is a form of moral and political suicide.

The constructive program ahead must include a vigorous attempt to improve the Negro's personal standards. It must be reiterated that the standards of the Negro as a group lag behind not because of an inherent inferiority, but because of the fact that segregation does exist. The "behavior deviants" within the Negro community stem from the economic deprivation, emotional frustration, and social isolation which are the inevitable concomitants of segregation. When the white man argues that segregation should continue because of the Negro's lagging standards, he fails to see that the standards lag because of segregation.

Yet Negroes must be honest enough to admit that our standards do often fall short. One of the sure signs of maturity is the ability to rise to the point of self-criticism. Whenever we are objects of criticism from white men, even though the criticisms are maliciously directed and mixed with half-truths, we must pick out the elements of truth and make them the basis of creative reconstruction. We must not let the fact that we are the victims of injustice lull us into abrogating responsibility for our own lives.

Our crime rate is far too high. Our level of cleanliness is frequently far too low. Too often those of us who are in the middle class live above our means, spend money on nonessentials and frivolities, and fail to give to serious causes, organizations, and educational institutions that so desperately need funds. We are too often loud and boisterous, and spend far too much on drink. Even the most poverty-stricken among us can purchase a ten-cent bar of soap; even the most uneducated among us can have high morals. Through community agencies and religious institutions Negro leaders must develop a positive program through which Negro youth can become adjusted to urban living and improve their general level of behavior. Since crime often grows out of a sense of futility and despair, Negro parents must be urged to give their children the love, attention, and sense of belonging that a segregated society deprives them of. By improving our standards here and now we will go a long way toward breaking down the arguments of the segregationist.

This then must be our present program: Nonviolent resistance to all forms of racial injustice, including state and local laws and practices, even when this means going to jail; and imaginative, bold, constructive action to end the demoralization caused by the legacy of slavery and segregation, inferior schools, slums, and second-class citizenship. The nonviolent struggle, if conducted with the dignity and courage already shown by the people of Montgomery and the children of Little Rock, will in itself help end the demoralization; but a new frontal assault on the poverty, disease, and ignorance of a people too long ignored by America's conscience will make victory more certain.

In short, we must work on two fronts. On the one hand, we must continue to resist the system of segregation which is the basic cause of our lagging standards; on the other hand we must work constructively to improve the standards themselves. There must be a rhythmic alternation between attacking the causes and healing the effects.

This is a great hour for the Negro. The challenge is here. To become the instruments of a great idea is a privilege that history gives only occasionally. Arnold Toynbee says in *A Study of History* that it may be the Negro who will give the new spiritual dynamic to Western civilization that it so desperately needs to survive. I hope this is possible. The spiritual power that the Negro can radiate to the world comes from love, under-standing, good will, and nonviolence. It may even be possible for the Negro, through adherence to nonviolence, so to challenge the nations of the world that they will seriously seek an alternative to war and destruction. In a day when Sputniks and Explorers dash through outer space and guided ballistic missiles are carving highways of death through the stratosphere, nobody can win a war. Today the choice is no longer between violence and nonviolence. It is either nonviolence or nonexistence. The Negro may be God's appeal to this age—an age drifting rapidly to its doom. The eternal appeal takes the form of a warning: "All who take the sword will perish by the sword."

WHAT WE WANT

Stokely Carmichael

Stokely Carmichael was born in Trinidad in 1941 and came from Port-of-Spain to live in New York in 1952. He was one of the first "freedom riders" to be arrested and has been jailed many times since. The treatment he encountered in Southern jails apparently embittered him against all whites. He was elected chairman of the Student Nonviolent Coordinating Committee (SNCC) in 1966. By 1967 he had become the most vocal exponent of black power among Negro militants. In acerbic language he expresses the frustration of young Negroes embittered by the humiliations of life in Northern ghettoes and the meager results in the South of the Civil Rights Act of 1965. His first book, Black Power, the Politics of Liberation in America, *was published in 1967.*

Carmichael is no longer head of SNCC; after a year he an-nounced "I'm going back to the fields where I came from." The "fields" included Havana where, joining with Castro, he seemed quite willing to rekindle the flames that have already

From *The New York Review of Books* (September 22, 1966), pp. 5–7. Reprinted by permission of SNCC International Affairs Commission.

devastated a number of American cities by calling upon American Negroes to take up arms for "total revolution." But surprisingly, in light of Carmichael's other utterances, he refrains from advocating violence in his new book. William Styron must surely have had Carmichael and his kind in mind when he wrote his brilliantly fictionalized account of a 19th-century Negro rebellion, The Confessions of Nat Turner *(1967).*

The slogan "black power" is notorious for its ambiguity. Some who shout it approve the use of violence to bring about reform. Others advocate the use of force only in self-protection against violence. Still others see it as a call for bloc voting to increase the Negro political strength. For many, black power is a frank avowal of Negro separatism mingled, as separatism generally is, with black chauvinism. Carmichael sees in the slogan a reflection of "the necessity to reclaim our history and our identity from . . . cultural terrorism . . ."[1]

One of the tragedies of the struggle against racism is that up to now there has been no national organization which could speak to the growing militancy of young black people in the urban ghetto. There has been only a civil rights movement whose tone of voice was adapted to an audience of liberal whites. It served as a sort of buffer zone between them and angry young blacks. None of its so-called leaders could go into a rioting community and be listened to. In a sense, I blame ourselves— together with the mass media—for what has happened in Watts, Harlem, Chicago, Cleveland, Omaha. Each time the people in those cities saw Martin Luther King get slapped, they became angry; when they saw four little black girls bombed to death, they were angrier; and when nothing happened, they were steaming. We had nothing to offer that they could see, except to go out and be beaten again. We helped to build their frustration.

For too many years, black Americans marched and had their heads broken and got shot. They were saying to the country, "Look, you guys are supposed to be nice guys and we are only going to do what we are supposed to do—why do you beat us up, why don't you give us what we ask, why don't you straighten yourselves out?" After years of this, we are at almost the same point—because we demonstrated from a position of weakness. We cannot be expected any longer to march and have our heads broken in order to say to whites: come on, you're nice guys. For you are not nice guys. We have found you out.

An organization which claims to speak for the needs of a community—as does the Student Nonviolent Coordinating Committee—must speak in the tone of that community, not as somebody else's buffer zone.

---

[1] *The Massachusetts Review,* Vol. VII, No. 4 (Autumn 1966).

This is the significance of black power as a slogan. For once, black people are going to use the words they want to use—not just the words whites want to hear. And they will do this no matter how often the press tries to stop the use of the slogan by equating it with racism or separatism.

An organization which claims to be working for the needs of a community—as SNCC does—must work to provide that community with a position of strength from which to make its voice heard. This is the significance of black power beyond the slogan.

Black power can be clearly defined for those who do not attach the fears of white America to their questions about it. We should begin with the basic fact that black Americans have two problems: they are poor and they are black. All other problems arise from this two-sided reality: lack of education, the so-called apathy of black men. Any program to end racism must address itself to that double reality.

Almost from its beginning, SNCC sought to address itself to both conditions with a program aimed at winning political power for impoverished Southern blacks. We had to begin with politics because black Americans are a propertyless people in a country where property is valued above all. We had to work for power, because this country does not function by morality, love, and nonviolence, but by power. Thus we determined to win political power, with the idea of moving on from there into activity that would have economic effects. With power, the masses could *make or participate in making* the decisions which govern their destinies, and thus create basic change in their day-to-day lives.

But if political power seemed to be the key to self-determination, it was also obvious that the key had been thrown down a deep well many years earlier. Disenfranchisement maintained by racist terror makes it impossible to talk about organizing for political power in 1960. The right to vote had to be won and SNCC workers devoted their energies to this from 1961 to 1965. They set up voter registration drives in the Deep South. They created pressure for the vote by holding mock elections in Mississippi in 1963 and by helping to establish the Mississippi Freedom Democratic Party (MFDP) in 1964. That struggle was eased, though not won, with the passage of the 1965 Voting Rights Act. SNCC workers could then address themselves to the question: "Who can we vote for, to have our needs met—how do we make our vote meaningful?"

SNCC had already gone to Atlantic City for recognition of the Mississippi Freedom Democratic Party by the Democratic convention and been rejected; it had gone with the MFDP to Washington for recognition by Congress and been rejected. In Arkansas, SNCC helped thirty Negroes to run for School Board elections; all but one were defeated, and there was evidence of fraud and intimidation sufficient to cause their defeat. In Atlanta, Julian Bond ran for the state legislature and was elected—twice—and unseated—twice. In several states black farmers ran in elections for agricultural committees which make crucial decisions concerning land use, loans, etc. Although they won places on a number of committees, they never gained the majorities needed to control them.

All of the efforts were attempts to win black power. Then, in Alabama, the opportunity came to see how blacks could be organized on an independent party basis. An unusual Alabama law provides that any group of citizens can nominate candidates for county office and, if they win 20 per cent of the vote, may be recognized as a county political party. The same then applies on a state level. SNCC went to organize in several counties such as Lowndes, where black people—who form 80 per cent of the population and have an average annual income of $943—felt they could accomplish nothing within the framework of the Alabama Democratic Party because of its racism and because the qualifying fee for this year's elections was raised from $50 to $500 in order to prevent most Negroes from becoming candidates. On May 3, five new county "freedom organizations" convened and nominated candidates for the offices of sheriff, tax assessor, members of the school boards. These men and women are up for election in November—if they live until then. Their ballot symbol is the black panther; a bold, beautiful animal, representing the strength and dignity of black demands today. A man needs a black panther on his side when he and his family must endure—as hundreds of Alabamians have endured—loss of job, eviction, starvation, and sometimes death, for political activity. He may also need a gun and SNCC reaffirms the right of black men everywhere to defend themselves when threatened or attacked. As for initiating the use of violence, we hope that such programs as ours will make that unnecessary; but it is not for us to tell black communities whether they can or cannot use any particular form of action to resolve their problems. Responsibility for the use of violence by black men, whether in self-defense or initiated by them, lies with the white community.

This is the specific historical experience from which SNCC's call for "black power" emerged on the Mississippi march last July. But the concept of "black power" is not a recent or isolated phenomenon: It has grown out of the ferment of agitation and activity by different people and organizations in many black communities over the years. Our last year of work in Alabama added a new concrete possibility. In Lowndes county, for example, black power will mean that if a Negro is elected sheriff, he can end police brutality. If a black man is elected tax assessor, he can collect and channel funds for the building of better roads and schools serving black people—thus advancing the move from political power into the economic arena. In such areas as Lowndes, where black men have a majority, they will attempt to use it to exercise control. This is what they seek: control. Where Negroes lack a majority, black power means proper representation and sharing of control. It means the creation of power bases from which black people can work to change statewide or nationwide patterns of oppression through pressure from strength—instead of weakness. Politically, black power means what it has always meant to SNCC: the coming-together of black people to elect representatives and *to force those representatives to speak to their needs*. It does not mean merely putting black faces into office. A man or woman who is black and from the slums cannot be automatically expected to speak to the needs of black people. Most of the black politicians we see around the country today are not what SNCC means by black power. The power must be that of a community, and emanate from there.

SNCC today is working in both North and South on programs of voter registration and independent political organizing. In some places, such as Alabama, Los Angeles, New York, Philadelphia, and New Jersey, independent organizing under the black panther symbol is in progress. The creation of a national "black panther party" must come about; it will take time to build, and it is much too early to predict its success. We have no infallible master plan and we make no claim to exclusive knowledge of how to end racism; different groups will work in their own different ways. SNCC cannot spell out the full logistics of self-determination but it can address itself to the problem by helping black communities define their needs, realize their strength, and go into action along a variety of lines which they must choose for themselves. Without knowing all the answers it can address itself to the basic problem of poverty; to the fact that in Lowndes County, 86 white families own 90 per cent of the land. What are black people in that county going to do for jobs, where are they going to get money? There must be reallocation of land, of money.

Ultimately, the economic foundations of this country must be shaken if black people are to control their lives.

The colonies of the United States—and this includes the black ghettoes within its borders, north and south—must be liberated. For a century, this nation has been like an octopus of exploitation, its tentacles stretching from Mississippi and Harlem to South America, the Middle East, southern Africa, and Vietnam; the form of exploitation varies from area to area but the essential result has been the same—a powerful few have been maintained and enriched at the expense of the poor and voiceless colored masses. This pattern must be broken. As its grip loosens here and there around the world, the hopes of black Americans become more realistic. For racism to die, a totally different America must be born.

This is what the white society does not wish to face; this is why that society prefers to talk about integration. But integration speaks not at all to the problem of poverty, only to the problem of blackness. Integration today means the man who "makes it," leaving his black brothers behind in the ghetto as fast as his new sports car will take him. It has no relevance to the Harlem wino or to the cotton-picker making three dollars a day. As a lady I know in Alabama once said, "the food that Ralph Bunche eats doesn't fill my stomach."

Integration, moreover, speaks to the problem of blackness in a despicable way. As a goal, it has been based on complete acceptance of the fact that *in order to have* a decent house or education, blacks must move into a white neighborhood or send their children to a white school. This reinforces, among both black and white, the idea that "white" is automatically better and "black" is by definition inferior. This is why integration is a subterfuge for the maintenance of white supremacy. It allows the nation to focus on a handful of Southern children who get into white schools, at great price, and to ignore the 94 per cent who are left behind in unimproved all-black schools. Such situations will not change until black people have power—to control their own school boards, in this case. Then Negroes become equal in a way that means something, and integration ceases to be a one-way street. Then integration doesn't mean draining skills and energies from the ghetto into white neighborhoods; then it can mean white people moving from Beverly Hills into Watts, white people joining the Lowndes County Freedom Organization. Then integration becomes relevant.

Last April, before the furor over black power, Christopher Jencks wrote in a *New Republic* article on white Mississippi's manipulation of the anti-poverty program:

> The war on poverty has been predicated on the notion that there is such a thing as *a community* which can be defined geographically and mobilized for a collective effort to help the poor. This theory has no relationship to reality in the Deep South. In every Mississippi county there are *two* communities. Despite all the pious platitudes of the moderates on both sides, these two communities habitually see their interests in terms of conflict rather than cooperation. Only when the Negro community can muster enough political, economic and professional strength to compete on somewhat equal terms, will Negroes believe in the possibility of true cooperation and whites accept its necessity. En route to integration, the Negro community needs to develop greater independence —a chance to run its own affairs and not cave in whenever "the man" barks . . . Or so it seems to me, and to most of the knowledgeable people with whom I talked in Mississippi. To OEO, this judgment may sound like black nationalism . . .

Mr. Jencks, a white reporter, perceived the reason why America's anti-poverty program has been a sick farce in both North and South. In the South, it is clearly racism which prevents the poor from running their own programs; in the North, it more often seems to be politicking and bureaucracy. But the results are not so different: In the North, non-whites make up 42 per cent of all families in metropolitan "poverty areas" and only 6 per cent of families in areas classified as not poor. SNCC has been working with local residents in Arkansas, Alabama, and Mississippi to achieve control by the poor of the program and its funds; it has also been working with groups in the North, and the struggle is no less difficult. Behind it all is a federal government which cares far more about winning the war on the Vietnamese than the war on poverty; which has put the poverty program in the hands of self-serving politicians and bureaucrats rather than the poor themselves; which is unwilling to curb the misuse of white power but quick to condemn black power.

To most whites, black power seems to mean that the Mau Mau are coming to the suburbs at night. The Mau Mau are coming, and whites must stop them. Articles appear about plots to "get Whitey," creating an atmosphere in which "law and order must be maintained." Once again, responsibility is shifted from the oppressor to the oppressed. Other whites chide, "Don't forget—you're only 10 per cent of the population; if you get too smart, we'll wipe you out." If they are liberals, they complain, "what about me?—don't you want my help any more?" These are people supposedly concerned about black Americans, but today they think first of themselves, of their feelings of rejection. Or they admonish, "you can't get anywhere without coalitions," when there is in fact no group at present with whom to form a coalition in which blacks will not be absorbed and betrayed. Or they accuse us of "polarizing the races" by our calls for black unity, when the true responsibility for polarization lies with whites who will not accept their responsibility as the majority power for making the democratic process work.

White America will not face the problem of color, the reality of it. The well-intended say: "We're all human, everybody is really decent, we must forget color." But color cannot be "forgotten" until its weight is recognized and dealt with. White America will not acknowledge that the ways in which this country sees itself are contradicted by being black—and always have been. Whereas most of the people who settled this country came here for freedom or for economic opportunity, blacks were brought here to be slaves. When the Lowndes County Freedom Organization chose the black panther as its symbol, it was christened by the press "the Black Panther Party"—but the Alabama Democratic Party, whose symbol is a rooster has never been called the White Cock Party. No one ever talked about "white power" because power in this country is white. All this adds up to more than merely identifying a group phenomenon by some catchy name or adjective. The furor over that black panther reveals the problems that white America has with color and sex; the furor over "black power" reveals how deep racism runs and the great fear which is attached to it.

Whites will not see that I, for example, as a person oppressed because of my blackness, have common cause with other blacks who are oppressed because of blackness. This is not to say that there are no white people who see things as I do, but that it is black people I must speak to first. It must be the oppressed to whom SNCC addresses itself primarily, not to friends from the oppressing group.

From birth, black people are told a set of lies about themselves. We are told that we are lazy—yet I drive through the Delta area of Mississippi and watch black people picking cotton in the hot sun for fourteen hours. We are told, "If you work hard, you'll succeed"—but if that were true, black people would own this country. We are oppressed because we are black—not because we are ignorant, not because we are lazy, not because we're stupid (and got good rhythm), but because we're black.

I remember that when I was a boy, I used to go to see Tarzan movies on Saturday. White Tarzan used to beat up the black natives. I would sit there yelling, "Kill the beasts, kill the savages, kill 'em!" I was saying: Kill *me*. It was as if a Jewish boy watched Nazis taking Jews off to concentration camps and cheered them on. Today, I want the chief to beat hell out of Tarzan and send him back to Europe. But it takes time to become free of the lies and their shaming effect on black minds. It takes time to reject the most important lie; that black people inherently can't do the same things white people can do, unless white people help them.

The need for psychological equality is the reason why SNCC today believes that blacks must organize in the black community. Only black people can convey the revolutionary idea that black people are able to do things themselves. Only they can help create in the community an aroused and continuing black consciousness that will provide the basis for political strength. In the past, white allies have furthered white supremacy without the whites involved realizing it—or wanting it, I think. Black people must do things for themselves; they must get poverty money they will control and spend themselves, they must conduct tutorial programs themselves so that black children can identify with black people. This is one reason Africa has such importance: The reality of black men ruling their own natives gives blacks elsewhere a sense of possibility, of power, which they do not now have.

This does not mean we don't welcome help, or friends. But we want the right to decide whether anyone is, in fact, our friend. In the past, black Americans have been almost the only people whom everybody and his momma could jump up and call their friends. We have been tokens, symbols, objects—as I was in high school to many young whites, who liked having "a Negro friend." We want to decide who is our friend, and we will not accept someone who comes to us and says: "If you do X, Y, and Z, then I'll help you." We will not be told whom we should choose as allies. We will not be isolated from any group or nation except by our own choice. We cannot have the oppressors telling the oppressed how to rid themselves of the oppressor.

I have said that most liberal whites react to "black power" with the question, What about me? rather than saying: Tell me what you want me to do and I'll see if I can do it. There are answers to the right question. One of the most disturbing things about almost all white supporters of the movement has been that they are afraid to go into their own communities—which is where the racism exists—and work to get rid of it. They want to run from Berkeley to tell us what to do in Mississippi; let them look instead at Berkeley. They admonish blacks to be nonviolent; let them preach nonviolence in the white community. They come to teach me Negro history; let them go to the suburbs and open up freedom schools for whites. Let them work to stop America's racist foreign policy; let them press this government to cease supporting the economy of South Africa.

There is a vital job to be done among poor whites. We hope to see, eventually, a coalition between poor blacks and poor whites. That is the only coalition which seems acceptable to us, and we see such a coalition as the major internal instrument of change in American society. SNCC has tried several times to organize poor whites; we are trying again now, with an initial training program in Tennessee. It is purely academic today to talk about bringing poor blacks and whites together, but the job of creating a poor-white power bloc must be attempted. The main responsibility for it falls upon whites. Black and white can work together in the white community where possible; it is not possible, however, to go into a poor Southern town and talk about integration. Poor whites everywhere are becoming more hostile—not less—partly because they see the nation's attention focused on black poverty and nobody coming to them. Too many young middle-class Americans, like some sort of Pepsi generation, have wanted to come alive through the black community; they've wanted to be where the action is—and the action has been in the black community.

Black people do not want to "take over" this country. They don't want to "get whitey"; they just want to get him off their backs, as the saying goes. It was for example the exploitation by Jewish landlords and merchants which first created black resentment toward Jews—not Judaism. The white man is irrelevant to blacks, except as an oppressive force. Blacks want to be in his place, yes, but not in order to terrorize and lynch and starve him. They want to be in his place because that is where a decent life can be had.

But our vision is not merely of a society in which all black men have enough to buy the good things of life. When we urge that black money go into black pockets, we mean the communal pocket. We want to see money go back into the community and used to benefit it. We want to see the cooperative concept applied in business and banking. We want to see black ghetto residents demand that an exploiting store keeper sell them, at minimal cost, a building or a shop that they will own and improve cooperatively; they can back their demand with a rent strike, or a boycott, and a community so unified behind them that no one else will move into the building or buy at the store. The society we seek to build among black people, then, is not a capitalist one. It is a society in which the spirit of community and humanistic love prevail. The word love is suspect; black expectations of what it might produce have been betrayed too often. But those were expectations of a response from the white community, which failed us. The love we seek to encourage is within the black community, the only American community where men call each other "brother" when they meet. We can build a community of love only where we have the ability and power to do so: among blacks.

As for white America, perhaps it can stop crying out against "black supremacy," "black nationalism," "racism in reverse," and begin facing reality. The reality is that this nation, from top to bottom, is racist; that racism is not primarily a problem of "human relations" but of an exploitation maintained—either actively or through silence—by the society as a whole. Camus and Sartre have asked, can a man condemn himself? Can whites, particularly liberal whites, condemn themselves? Can they stop blaming us, and blame their own system? Are they capable of the shame which might become a revolutionary emotion?

We have found that they usually cannot condemn themselves, and so we have done it. But the rebuilding of this society, if at all possible, is basically the responsibility of whites—not blacks. We won't fight to save the present society, in Vietnam or anywhere else. We are just going to work, in the way *we* see fit, and on goals *we* define, not for civil rights but for all our human rights.

A RELIGIOUS "RIGHT"
TO VIOLATE THE LAW?

Will Herberg

Dr. Herberg is professor at Drew University, where he has specialized in Judaic studies and social philosophy. He has written Judaism and Modern Man; An Interpretation of Jewish Religion *(1951) and is editor of* The Writings of Martin Buber *(1956). He is an associate editor of the conservative* National Review.

Early last month, Yale University conferred the degree LL.D. upon Martin Luther King, who had already been celebrated on the cover of *Time* Magazine. True enough, nowadays the LL.D., *legum doctor,* doctor of laws (both canon and civil), no longer implies any special distinction in jurisprudence or legal learning; but it does imply a moral and social distinction which sets off its recipient as a man of intelligence, eminence, and respectability, a force in society and a leader of men—and this Dr. Martin Luther King certainly is (Dr. King is also a Christian, and sees the movement he leads as a Christian movement grounded in Christian teachings.)

It is therefore of considerable interest to inquire a little more closely into Dr. King's notions of political responsibility and social order, particularly into his central contention that Christian principles permit, perhaps even require, the violation of laws the individual conscience may hold to be "unjust." In this contention Dr. King is supported by that other influential Negro Christian leader, the Rev. Adam Clayton Powell, who is also a member of the House of Representatives. Here are their words:

> *Dr. Martin Luther King:* One may well ask, "How can you advocate breaking some laws and obeying others?" The answer lies in the fact that there are two types of laws: There are just laws and there are unjust laws. . . . I submit that an individual who breaks a law that conscience tells him is unjust, and willingly accepts the penalty . . . is in reality expressing the highest respect·for law . . . ("A Letter From the Birmingham City Jail").
> *Rev. Adam Clayton Powell:* People say it's against the law. What law? And who made them? There is only one great and un-

From *National Review* (July 14, 1964), pp. 579–580. Reprinted by permission of National Review, 150 East 35th Street, New York, N.Y. 10016.

breakable law, and that's the law of God (recorded Feb. 4, 1964, by NBC-WRC News).

The two are in substantial agreement (Dr. King too derives "just" laws from "the moral law or the law of God"); and, in more or less cautious form, their position is shared by thousands of churchmen, Negro and white, throughout the country. But how does this position square with well-established Christian teaching on government, law, and civil obedience?

The essential Christian teaching on government, law, and civil obedience is grounded on that celebrated Chapter XIII of Paul's Epistle to the Romans, which itself reflects earlier Jewish teaching. "Let every one be subject to the governing authorities," the Apostle enjoins. "For there is no authority except from God, and the existing authorities have been ordained by God. Therefore, he who resists the authorities resists what God has appointed, and those who resist will incur judgment. . . ." This is balanced in the New Testament by the conviction of Peter and the Apostles, "We must obey God rather than Man" (Acts 5:29).

When does loyalty to God come into conflict with obedience to earthly rulers? When earthly rulers are insensate enough (as totalitarian states invariably are) to demand for themselves what is owing only to God—worship and ultimate allegiance. The classical Christian teaching emerges most profoundly perhaps in the writings of St. Augustine, whose position Professor Deane thus summarizes:

> All the laws promulgated by the ruler must be obeyed by all citizens, with the sole exception of laws or commands that run contrary to God's ordinances . . . When Augustine says that God's command overrules [human] laws and customs, it seems clear that he is referring to those commands of God that have been directly revealed to men in the Scriptures, such as the prohibition against idol worship . . . He does not say that if the ruler is unwise or evil, and fails to take the eternal law into account when he frames temporal laws, these laws have no validity, and the subjects have no obligation to obey them; nor does he say that the subjects have a right to determine for themselves, by reference to the natural or eternal law, whether or not such a temporal law is valid and is to be obeyed (Herbert A. Deane, *The Political and Social Ideas of St. Augustine,* Columbia U-P 1963, pp. 147, 89, 90; Dr. Deane is professor of government at Columbia).

This, in substance, early became the normative Christian doctrine, stated and restated by Thomas Aquinas, Martin Luther, John Calvin, and every other great moralist and theologian of the Church. It is the standard by which the position advanced by Dr. King and Rep. Powell *as Christian* must be judged; and, judged by that standard, their position permitting the violation of any law disapproved of by the individual conscience as "unjust," must be judged as not Christian at all, but seriously deviant and heretical.

The early Christians, under the teaching of the apostles, were enjoined to obey the laws of the state, a pagan state, mind you, whether they held these laws to be just or unjust—just so long as the state (the Emperor) did not claim for itself the worship and allegiance owing only to God. At that point, they knew how to draw the line. But even at that point, where they were compelled to disobey, their disobedience was limited to *refusal to participate* in the pagan abominations. The Christian refused, at the risk of life, to take part in the pagan cult, or to sacrifice to the Emperor; he did not set up mass picketing of the temples, or organize sit-ins in the public buildings in which the "blasphemies" (Tertullian) were being performed. Dr. King will get as little support for his position from authoritative Christian practice as from authoritative Christian teaching.

Would it not be well for Dr. King, as a responsible community leader honored with a Doctor of Laws by Yale University, to consider the consequences of his strange doctrine? Every man has his conscience; and if the individual conscience is absolutized (that is, divinized), and made the final judge of laws to be obeyed or disobeyed, nothing but anarchy and the dissolution of the very fabric of government would result. Thousands and thousands of Americans, eminent, respectable, and responsible, are convinced in their conscience that the new Civil Rights Act is utterly wrong, unjust, and unconstitutional; are they therefore entitled to disobey it, and to organize civil disobedience campaigns to impede its effectuation? Grant this "right" and there would be no law at all, nothing but a clash of "consciences" that could not hope to escape becoming a clash of raw power.[1] Strange as it may seem to Dr. King, the very purpose of government is to make us obey laws of which we do not approve, which indeed we may even regard as "unjust." Laws that we approve of, and regard as just, we hardly need much coercion to get us to obey.

In its essential aims, the civil rights movement led by Dr. King is not at all revolutionary: it strives not to subvert and new-model the American system, but to win for the Negro a fair and equal place within it. Its methods, however, and the political philosophy that informs these methods —the deliberate creation of "crisis-packed situations" through systematic civil disobedience—are consistent neither with Christian teaching nor with

---

[1] One important exception must be noted. Under the American system of judicial review, the constitutionality, and therefore the legality of a law, when challenged cannot be finally determined until it comes to court; and very frequently, it cannot come to court until it is somehow violated. Such technical violation for the sake of a *test case* is to be fundamentally distinguished from the mass civil disobedience advocated by Dr. King.

ordinary political responsibility.[2] Dr. King, the Christian leader, now a Yale Doctor of Laws, might do well to rethink the theological foundations of a doctrine so dubious in its social and political consequences.

---

[2] The pitch of irresponsibility this kind of thing can lead to is painfully illustrated by the words addressed by the eminently respectable citizen, Adlai E. Stevenson to the graduating class at Colby College in Maine: "I think especially of the participation of American students in the great struggle to advance civil and human rights in America. Indeed, even a jail sentence is no longer a dishonor, but a proud achievement. Perhaps we are destined to see in this lawloving land people running for office not on their stainless record, but on their prison records."

THREE CONSCIENTIOUS OBJECTORS

Ronald L. Goldfarb

Ronald L. Goldfarb was educated at Syracuse University (A.B. 1954, LL.B. 1956) and has LL.M. and J.S.D. degrees from Yale University. He is the author of The Contempt Power *(1963) and* Ransom: A Critique of the American Bail System *(1965), and he is now working on a book on free press and fair trial with Alfred Friendly.*

Lewis B. Hershey, Director of the Selective Service System, has spoken out against draft shirkers and "political pacifists" who burn their draft cards as an expression of disapproval of American policy in Vietnam. "They shouldn't be prosecuted . . . they should be inducted. They might learn what it's all about," he was quoted as saying. This same attitude was voiced by a number of our troops in Vietnam on a special television program. It is a feeling that has common currency. Yet there is an organized student movement to protest the war in Vietnam by claiming conscientious objector status in *this* war on essentially political grounds. This situation, likely to come to the courts, raises anew the seemingly endless debate over when it may be proper to object on grounds of conscience to the draft.

From *American Bar Association Journal* (June 1966), pp. 564–567. Reprinted by permission of the publisher.

The United States Constitution and one of our draft laws crashed head-on recently in the cases of three unorthodox conscientious objectors, but the Supreme Court saved them all by what might facetiously be called artificial legislation.

Section 6(j) of the Universal Military Training and Service Act provides that selective service (our military draft) should not be construed to ". . . require any person to be subject to combatant training and service in the armed forces of the United States who, *by reason of religious training and belief, is conscientiously opposed to participation in war in any form* [emphasis added]." The statute then goes on to make the qualification that the reference to "religious training and belief" means "an individual's belief in a relation to a Supreme Being involving duties superior to those arising from any human relation" and that those words were *not* intended to include "essentially political, sociological, or philosophical views or a merely personal moral code."

Three young men recently refused to be drafted into the Armed Forces and in doing so sought shelter under the protective provisions of Section 6(j). All three were convicted of refusing to submit to induction. Two convictions were reversed, and the Government appealed; one conviction was upheld, and the defendant appealed.

Two constitutional issues were raised when the cases came to the Supreme Court: (1) that the law in exempting only religious conscientious objectors violated the establishment of religion and the free exercise clauses of the First Amendment by preferring certain religious groups and (2) that Section 6(j) discriminated between different forms of religious expression in violation of the guarantee of equal protection of the law implicit within the due process clause of the Fifth Amendment.

The Cases of the Three Objectors

Forest Britt Peter was a student at Reed College when he was first called upon to register with selective service. He filed the standard forms but added a poem expressing his views against war. A few years later, he formally requested to be classified as a conscientious objector. He said in response to a question about his belief in a "Supreme Being" that "it depends on the definition." He referred to the writings of Blake, Emerson and Reverend John Haynes Holmes; he expressed his conviction, based on his readings, that human life is a final value and the taking of it a violation of moral law; he expressed his approval of Gandhian nonviolence; he admitted that he was not a member of any religious organization.

During later proceedings others testified that Peter was sincere and unshakeable in his conscientious objections to war and "military service as an implement of present day policy." Some described his views as Buddhist; others said he was under the influence of the theologian, Martin Buber.

A series of proceedings ensued between Peter and the Government. No one questioned anything except the religiosity of his feelings. He said finally, "I do not know what you mean. . . . I have tried . . . to give you a picture of my own 'religiousness' and show how it motivates my objection." When pressed for further substantiation of his attitude, Peter referred to Schweitzer's "reverence for life," to the examples and inspirations of Gautama's fourfold truth, to *Tao Te Ching* by Lao-tse and its discussion of the natural world, to the teachings of nonviolence by Jesus and St. Francis, to the teachings of love by Bal Shem Tov of the European Hassidic movement. He said his conclusions were not intellectual alone but were based also on "the promptings of my heart and the sense of relationship with all living elements in nature."

He was convicted in California and sentenced to six months' imprisonment.

Arno Sascha Jakobson first registered with his draft board in New York in 1953. After some years in student status and some discussion about a possible physical disability, he claimed he was a conscientious objector. Reason, faith and contemplation led him, he said, to the conclusions that "the method of war itself . . . must be fought if we are to have a lasting peace," that war reduces enemy people to mere abstractions and killing humans cannot be a statistical necessity, that war breeds war, that the ends don't justify the means, and that peaceful coexistence is the better way. He said that he had reached his personal conclusions with the aid of readings from Remarque, Sorokin, Koestler, Fromm and Dostoevski.

He asked for complete exemption because *any* military service would involve him with situations that would strain his conscience. He said his relationship to Godness was not direct but horizontal through mankind. Though he argued that his conclusions came from "my inner light," the authorities decided his views were essentially sociological, philosophical or a matter of personal morality and not properly religious.

He was convicted and sentenced to imprisonment for a year and a day. The Court of Appeals for the Second Circuit reversed on the ground that the draft board's rejection of his claim might have rested on an erroneous finding that he did not believe in a Supreme Being. The Government appealed.

Daniel Andrew Seeger registered at eighteen in 1953. Four years later he wrote his draft board requesting classification as a conscientious objector. He claimed that he was conscientiously opposed to participation in war in any form based on his developed beliefs about the welfare and the preservation of democratic values. He refused to tie his convictions to a "belief in a Supreme Being" because he felt that the existence of God cannot be proved or the essence of his nature determined. His beliefs were for their own sake. But, he argued, his beliefs were superior to any arising from any mere human relation. He discussed Tolstoy's views about evil and violence, the failure of previous world wars and the need to resort to better principles lest we pass away "like the dinosaurs before us." He pointed to the writings of Gandhi, Bertrand Russell, Aldous Huxley, Erich Fromm and Herbert J. Muller as the sources for his pacifistic ideas. A Federal Bureau of Investigation report revealed that he had a common reputation for sincerity in his views. Seeger himself testified that though he had sympathies for the views of certain religious sects, he was not affiliated with any.

The hearing officer concluded that Seeger's views were sincere and were based on his training and beliefs, which included research into religious fields. Nevertheless, the Justice Department concluded that the exemption could not apply because Seeger's objections were not based on religious training and belief in relation to a Supreme Being.

He was tried and convicted. The Court of Appeals for the Second Circuit reversed his conviction on the ground that the Supreme Being requirement of the law created a classification that the due process clause of the Fifth Amendment makes impermissible "in that it distinguished between internally derived and externally compelled beliefs." The Government appealed.

The Cases Arrive in the Supreme Court

The three cases were consolidated, and Justice Tom C. Clark wrote the opinion for a unanimous Supreme Court affirming the reversal of the convictions of Seeger and Jakobson and reversing Peter's conviction. But critics who might have said that God was repulsed again by the Court, since it gave recognition to people who do not believe in God through some organized religious commitment, would have been quite wrong; He really was given a much broader recognition.

Both Justice Clark and Justice Douglas, who wrote an opinion concurring with the majority but ruminating about the case, agreed that the issue presented was not one between theistic and atheistic beliefs. Rather, it merely involved the question whether Section 6(j) meant, in referring to belief in a Supreme Being, only an "orthodox God" or whether it included some "broader concept."

The majority opinion suggested that the long Congressional history of conscientious objector legislation has recognized consistently that one might be religious without belonging to an organized church. Applying this rationale to the present cases, Justice Clark held that it is one's individual belief rather than membership in a particular recognized church or sect that determines the duties God imposes upon man and the religiosity of one's compulsions. The test is, he held, whether one's belief is "sincere and meaningful" and "occupies a place in the life of its possessor parallel to that filled by the orthodox belief in God of one who clearly qualifies for the exemption." And so the Court held, in the summing-up words of Justice Douglas, that "any person opposed to war on the basis of a sincere belief, which in his life fills the same place as a belief in God fills in the life of an orthodox religionist, is entitled to exemption under the statute."

Thus, the statute was upheld, although its literal interpretation would not seem to have protected these defendants; the relevant constitutional guarantees were not dissipated, if only because the issues were avoided by the Court's strained interpretations of the statute; and the defendants were exonerated, although they provide only the most questionable precedent for draft boards or others with similar problems about the meaning of the statute or their protection under the Constitution. This leaves draft boards with the duty to determine if the beliefs of registrants are sincerely held and "religious" in the individual's own scheme of things. It is an inappropriate if not impossible chore for such agencies to decide this metaphysical issue, which Justice Clark referred to as "the threshold question of sincerity."

Justice Clark recognized the quandary of matching factual disputes with general principles in an intellectually satisfying way when subjective philosophical claims conflict with positivistic law: "Few would quarrel with the proposition that in no field of human endeavor has the tool of language proved so inadequate in the communication of ideas as it has in dealing with the fundamental questions of man's predicament in life, in death, or in final judgment and retribution." He went on to cite Paul Tillich's *Systematic Theology,* the Bishop of Woolwich, John A. T. Robinson's *Honest to God,* David Saville Muzzey's *Ethics as a Religion* and the schema of the recent Ecumenical Council in articulating the Court's appreciation of the religiosity of these defendants' stated beliefs.

In his statement of appropriate legal principles, he was able to quote Chief Justice Hughes's remark in a 1931 case that "in the forum of conscience, duty to a moral power higher than the state has always been maintained" and Chief Justice Stone's statement in an article that "both morals and sound policy require that the state should not violate the conscience of the individual . . . and it may well be questioned whether the state which preserves its life by a settled policy of violation of the conscience of the individual will not in fact ultimately lose it by the process."

The Court Avoids the Difficult Question

Thus armed with theory and principle, the Court ducked the difficult question whether one could legally be a conscientious objector to military service on grounds of conscience based on some epistemological exercise and not conscience elevated through interpretation to the level of some draft board's or court's concept of "religion." Perhaps these cases did not on their facts reach this question. Arguably, at least, they did. But the Court did not think so, and held only that these defendants' beliefs were religious and, therefore, within the protection of the statute—a law that tried with the inadequate tools of language to make the distinction suggested if not clearly raised by these cases.

The key question was not whether these defendants' feelings about war were religious, but whether people ought to be released from military service because their personal philosophical outlooks prohibit such service. It is not difficult to ascribe religiosity to one's views about such matters; it is quite difficult to define a sensitive and wise state policy about draft exemption. Should exemption be confined to objections based on traditional, nonpersonal, organized religious scruples only? Or should it apply when objections are based on personal codes, notwithstanding the religiosity that may inhere in these codes? The latter case is not covered by the statute in question, and was not dealt with clearly by this decision.

And no wonder. As a matter of national policy and morality, it might be well to encourage antiwar attitudes even amongst antireligionists.[1] As a matter of national defense, such a policy could be problematical.[2] Everyone is against war in principle, but relatively few carry the principle to acts of conscientious objection. To avoid this issue, the Court equated these defendants' "personal moral codes" with religion and, it could be argued, thus read the essential distinction out of the statute.

The most difficult policy decision—one which was not clearly made in these opinions—is whether to confine special treatment for conscientious objectors to those whose antiwar compulsions arise from orthodox theological beliefs grounded in church membership and belief in a traditional deity. This judgment must include a determination whether, when and by what standard "religion," insofar as it receives special legal treatment, may include a personal decision compelled by one's conscience or individual inner spirit.[3]

Perhaps this decision was prompted by a desire on the part of the Court to do the just and equitable thing in a technically difficult situation

---

[1] At the time of the debates over the Constitution, Mr. Tredell of North Carolina said: "True religion is derived from a much higher source than human laws. When any attempt is made by any government to restrain men's consciences, no good consequence could possibly follow." ELLIOTT, DEBATES 138 (1830).

[2] For a critical view of the United States policy, see Heisler, *The Law Versus the Conscientious Objector,* 20 U. CHI. L. REV. 441 (1953).

[3] Two interesting articles dealing with this subject generally and with this issue specifically are: Cornell, *Exemption from the Draft,* 56 YALE L. J. 258 (1947), and Russell, *Development of Conscientious Objector Recognition in the United States,* 20 GEO. WASH. L. REV. 409 (1952).

and to avoid further public confrontations on religious issues. It is easier to live with Congress's laws by making them livable than to throw them out. As Justice Douglas wrote: ". . . It is, in my opinion, not a *tour de force* if we construe the words Supreme Being to include the cosmos, as well as an anthropomorphic entity . . . it is no more so than other instances where we have gone to extremes to construe an Act of Congress to save it from demise on constitutional grounds."

But where this case leaves General Hershey and our young protestors is not certain. If provoked, the Court may be moved to invigorate the classic distinction made by the statute but relaxed in the cases of the three conscientious objectors.

THE SELECTIVE CO

Jeff Greenfield

Jeff Greenfield was Note and Comment editor of the Yale Law Journal and got his LLB degree from the Yale University Law School in 1967. He has written articles for Harper's *and* The New York Times Book Review. *He was a legislative aide to the late Senator Robert F. Kennedy of New York.*

For thousands of young Americans, the government's call to arms—an inherent power of the state—cannot be obeyed. Some draw the line at service in Vietnam; others will not be a part of the armed forces while the United States prosecutes that war. Their refusal is more than the basis for a nice debate on ethics and conscience; it has stark legal implications. As objectors to *this* war, and not to "war in any form," they do not meet the statutory definition of a conscientious objector. They have no legal right to refuse either induction or combat status in the military.

To some, the plight of the selective objector causes little concern. We cannot allow everyone to pick and choose the wars in which he will serve, it is argued. If the government were to grant exemption to selective military objectors, why not to those who have scruples about paying taxes

From *The New Republic* (July 1, 1967), pp. 15–16. Reprinted by permission from *The New Republic,* © 1967, Harrison-Blaine of New Jersey, Inc.

for public housing, or who "conscientiously" oppose civil rights legislation?

As it now stands, Section 6(j) of the 1948 Universal Military Training Act exempts from military service anyone who, "by religious training and belief, is conscientiously opposed to participation in war in any form." Most controversy over CO status, as the conviction of Cassius Clay illustrates, has centered around the "religious training and belief" requirement.

Many civil libertarians argued that the requirement was an invalid establishment of religion, since Congress had defined it to mean belief "in relation to a Supreme Being involving duties superior to those arising from any human relation, but [not including] essentially political, sociological or philosophical views or a merely personal moral code." The Supreme Court ducked a constitutional challenge in 1965, holding in *United States* v *Seeger* that Congress didn't mean to require belief in God as a condition of being a conscientious objector. Congress, said the Court, meant to determine "whether a given belief that is sincere and meaningful occupies a place in the life of its possessor parallel to that filled by the orthodox belief in God." Even as thus stretched by the Court, however, the law does not embrace avowed atheists or rationalists who are still pacifists.

The significance of the religious test is the light it throws on why *selective* objection is so resisted. A person religiously opposed to *all* wars is in no sense a political threat to the state. He is somehow "above" politics, answering what he believes is the command of God or an equivalent mystical force. In accommodating him (and both Congress and the courts have stressed that exemption is purely a matter of legislative grace), the state recognizes this "other worldly" quality. To be accepted as a CO, Congress has made clear, you must not base your plea on mundane considerations of this world.

But the selective objector is more often than not inherently *political*. He may be a Marxist who will fight only in wars of national liberation, or an economist whose cost-benefit approach convinces him that a certain war is inefficient, or a democratic absolutist who will not fight for unrepresentative regimes. Or he may object to *this* war but not *that* war because he accepts the "just war" theory identified with St. Augustine, under which a war can be supported by Christians only if it meets certain standards: It must be declared by legitimate authority, waged to avenge injustice, fought with maximum effort to distinguish fighters from civilians, and must be a last resort after peaceful means have failed. Obviously, any application of the "just war" theory requires political and social judgments. Is the war in Vietnam to avenge injustice? Are we making the effort required to distinguish between civilians and soldiers? Do you believe the Congress is constitutionally obligated to declare war in a case like Vietnam?

Generally speaking, this is the key distinction between the total and selective objector. The former rests his case on no political objection to an act of the state; a kind of resistance is carved out which the government can afford to honor with no embarrassment; indeed the government may feel ennobled by the concession it makes to the conscience of a relatively few. The selective objector, on the contrary, is making a statement of political opposition, even when he bases his dissent on something like Augustinian theory. The roots may be buried in religious tradition, but the application depends on whether you accept Alsop or Lippmann, Douglas Pike or Donald Duncan, Dean Rusk or William Fulbright. The selective objector is arguing that it is wrong to kill men in battle for *this* cause at *this* time under *this* condition. In sum, he is one of us: a participant in political debate who now raises the claim of conscience to avoid honoring the will of the majority.

This is not the end of the inquiry, for it avoids the ultimately persuasive, practical arguments for accommodating the selective objector. First, we should understand what conscientious objection means. It does *not* mean evading an obligation to one's country. Even total pacifists do not gain CO status if they are "noncooperators." They must register with their draft boards and serve for the requisite two years, either as noncombatants (most typically in the Medical Corps), or in alternative civilian service. Usually this is discharged by hospital work, or by menial service for charitable organizations. Wage rates, according to Selective Service, are lower than that of a private. To grant CO status does not give the objector freedom from obligation; it changes the service he renders.

Second, the question the state should concern itself with is the *sincerity* of the objection from conscience, not the wisdom of it. The law today does not accommodate the pacifist because he is objectively right, or because his religious teachings are universally accepted. Rather, it recognizes the powerful claim of "sincere and meaningful" belief, the claim of objectors that their consciences—shaped by *their* interpretation of religious teaching—will not let them participate in war.

Now, whether they are right or wrong, the vast majority of Vietnam objectors are impelled by conscience, not by personal convenience. (Those who worked in civil rights drives in Mississippi or the Peace Corps cannot be accused of cowardice or sloth.) These dissenters, Steve Rockefeller recently said at a commencement address at Marymount College, "are not afraid to fight, but they are afraid to betray their consciences and unwilling to abandon their intelligence." Or, as John Swomley Jr. of the St. Paul School of Theology puts it, "the concept of a just war is a theological formulation based on moral judgments about war which can be as readily acceptable to nonbelievers in God as to believers." Indeed, much of the "new politics," in which churches are taking an increasingly active role, stems from exactly this concept that morals and politics *do* mix. (At Cassius Clay's trial, the prosecutor said the Muslim religion was "as much political as it is religious.")

A man may believe in using force to defend himself or his nation if it is attacked. Yet he may not accept the domino rhetoric by which each ideological clash in Asia or Latin America or Africa is said to represent a threat to US security. In the judgment of many men, religious and atheist alike, the war in Vietnam in no way justifies the massive destructive power we have committed there. That judgment is political, but does that make it any the less "sincere and meaningful"? There is, moreover, something special about the call of conscience when the demand of the state is to help kill other men. I may object to tax money being spent on supersonic airplanes or moonshots or poverty programs. In such cases, however, democratic theory demands that, having lost the fight in the decision-making forum, the majority must prevail and I must go along. The selective objector, though, is on very different footing. Here the majority calls on him to help kill for a cause he believes to be wrong or worthless. If the choice before society is to put the objector in jail or put him to work elsewhere in the national interest, why should the objector not prevail? The stakes of conscience are the highest imaginable; the demand of the state as grim as a command to join a firing squad. Recognizing selective objection in this limited field helps avoid the "slippery slope" of exempting everybody from laws they don't like. By requiring objectors to serve in other, vitally needed, equally burdensome service when the question is literally one of life and death, we impose substantial barriers to those who claim freedom from other laws.

But what of national survival? What if half of all draft-eligible men refused to fight? First, if full mobilization were needed, accommodation could cease—by dropping conscientious objection, Congress would presumably propel many objectors into the military. Second, if a nation's survival were at stake, the number of CO's would almost certainly be small. Britain retained a generous CO policy during World War II, and in the United States there were about 65,000 claims for CO status out of 2.8 million registrants.

Finally, if massive numbers of draftees filed selective objector claims in a war like the one in Vietnam, it might well provide a healthy check. Perhaps there is no anomaly in Congress, whose average member is well over 60, voting and speaking for a war whose average soldier is under 21. But if a war were so unpopular that a huge number of soldiers demanded alternative service, might that suggest that we should not be fighting it?

I want to make it clear that conscientious selective objection would of necessity include those who are ideological sympathizers with our foe; it would include those who strongly disagree for reasons rooted in tactics, economics, politics, philosophy or religion; it would in sum include all who claim a refusal to fight on grounds other than personal inconvenience (by virtually accepting such claims at face value, the administrative burden on the Selective Service department would not be great). The demanding character of alternative service (which could be rendered longer, or more burdensome), the social pressure to conform, and the history of citizen support for all our wars, no matter how dubious, make a rush for CO status unlikely.

3

Internal Security and
the Loyalty Program

In no area has the quest for security inspired more bitter controversy than with the loyalty program, in part because those same world tensions that call for reasonable precautions also generate unreasoned fears; in part also because of a tendency in many quarters to identify disagreement with disloyalty. Many of the measures adopted as part of the so-called security program have been nullified by the courts. On March 3, 1967, for example, the U.S. Court of Appeals set aside the conviction of the Communist Party for failing to register with the government, finding the 1950 Subversive Activities Control Act "hopelessly at odds" with the Fifth Amendment's protection against self-incrimination. The Supreme Court had already struck down (November, 15, 1965) registration requirements for individual party members. A new bill intended to avoid the Supreme Court's objections will almost certainly be passed by the Senate; but, as a result of a compromise, the Subversive Activities Control Board which the bill set up will automatically die by June 30, 1969, unless it hears two cases on internal communism before the end of 1968. It is considered unlikely that Attorney General Ramsey Clark will give the board a lease on life by referring two such cases to it.

A 1962 law requiring the Post Office to hold all incoming "Communist political propaganda" for 20 days and then destroy it unless the addressee requests delivery was voided by the Supreme Court in 1965 by an 8–0 vote. In 1967, in the *Keyisbian* case, the Court threw out the Feinberg laws, New York State's contribution to the "security" program.

In general, then, there has been a mitigation of the excesses of the McCarthy period. However, much of the legislation intended or purporting to protect internal security remains on the books. New laws, especially at the state level, are constantly proposed. Loyalty oaths still abound. Attorney General Katzenbach announced in 1966 that the Justice Department had found evidence in the peace movement of Communist infiltration, and he was echoed by the chairman of the House Committee on Un-American Activities who said that "the Communist Party, U.S.A., and other Communist organizations and their adherents have been importantly involved in the great majority of them [peace demonstrations] and have been the originating and guiding force in the major demonstrations" (July 3, 1967). Although many will charge that such statements are intended to discourage honest criticism of our Vietnam policy, fear of subversion is hardly quieted in these circumstances, nor are attempts to control it likely to abate. The issue is very much alive.

Among the many anti-Communists who are deeply disturbed by our internal security program is Alan Barth who while affirming that Communists are enemies of America and American values and that the American Communist Party is an instrument of Russian foreign policy nevertheless condemns the internal security program somewhat more categorically than does Professor Sidney Hook. Hook characterizes Barth as a "ritualistic liberal."[1] The difference between the two as reflected in the pages that follow is all the more significant in that both men are liberals and would probably agree on most questions of public policy.

Barth and Hook deal eloquently with the universals involved in our quest for internal security. But universals require more than excellent prose to make them truly evocative and moving. This is accomplished only in rare instances—sometimes by nature, as when a shattered tree testifies mutely to the force of lightning; or by history, as when the corpses of a tyrant and his mistress dangle grotesquely from meat hooks in a petrol station on Milan's Piazzale Loreta; or, most often, by art, as when the impersonal brutality of war is dramatized by a soldier's destruction as he reaches from his trench for a butterfly, and when man's inhumanity to man is epitomized in a doomed Jewish child's diary. So, too, the 1957 contempt-of-Congress trial of Arthur Miller, one of America's best playwrights, dramatized the moral contradictions and ambivalences in which the American people have become involved as, seeking internal security, we grope for the meaning of loyalty.

Arthur Miller testified freely before the House Un-Amer-

---

[1] See his "Security and Freedom" in the *New Leader* (June 21, 1954), pp. 8–10.

ican Activities Committee that he had once been a member of the Communist Party. In all respects he was what the Committee calls a "cooperative witness"—in all respects, that is, except one. Miller was asked to identify other writers whom he had known to be Communists. He refused. "I will protect my sense of myself," he said. "I could not use the name of another person and bring trouble on him."

The refusal resulted in his being cited for contempt of Congress and his conviction by a judge who found his motives "commendable," but his action legally indefensible. The problem raised by his refusal to answer must be viewed, of course, as involving much more than possible abuses of Congressional prerogative, or the issue of informing. It raises the supreme question mentioned earlier concerning the relation of law and conscience. The selections below were written before the contempt conviction was reversed.[2]

---

[2] By 1963, the United States Supreme Court had upset ten such convictions for contempt of Congress.

THE CULT OF LOYALTY

Alan Barth

Alan Barth is an editorial writer for the Washington Post, *a former Nieman Fellow at Harvard, and holder of distinguished awards in the field of journalism; he wrote* The Loyalty of Free Men *in 1950 before the eclipse of Senator McCarthy. Perhaps he would write less pessimistically now, although a new wave of radical rightism might temper his optimism.*

The relation of the individual to the State—or of individual liberty to national security—is the crucial issue of our time. The emphasis in this relation marks the essential distinction between a totalitarian society and a free society. A totalitarian society emphasizes the supremacy of the State, seeking national security through rigid governmental control of individual activity and expression. A free society emphasizes the supremacy of the individual, relying for its national security upon a democratic adjustment of diverse views and interests and upon the freely accorded devotion of its constituents.

The function of national security in a totalitarian society is to preserve the State, while the function of national security in a free society is to preserve freedom. Those who established the American Republic counted freedom among man's "unalienable" or "natural" rights and believed that it was in order to secure these rights that governments are instituted among men. But there is a looseness about freedom that makes it seem hazardous to security. It involves an inescapable element of risk. There have always been men everywhere who viewed it skeptically as a luxury to be enjoyed only within prescribed limits and when the nation is not subject to any external threat. It is commonly in the name of national security that individual liberty is lost.

The purpose here is to show: (1) that we have accepted, without full awareness of their meaning, piecemeal encroachments on personal freedom that threaten to corrupt our richest inheritance; (2) that these encroachments have been accepted as the result of what are in large part groundless and neurotic fears; (3) that, although accepted in the name of national security, they operate, in fact, to impair the security they are intended to protect; and (4) that whether or not individual liberty is, as the founders of the United States believed it to be, an "unalienable" or "natural" right, it serves vital practical purposes and is an affirmative source of national strength.

This is by no means to suggest that national security can be neglected. The institutions of liberty are under attack. They are threatened by an aggressive totalitarianism abroad, and they need the protection of a strong and resolute government. If that government should fall, the institutions of liberty would fall with it. In some measure, too, the institutions are threatened in novel ways by agents of that totalitarianism at home. They are threatened most of all, however, by well-meaning and patriotic but frightened Americans, who have come to think of liberty as a liability rather than an asset.

The error of these men is that they confuse loyalty with orthodoxy. Acting upon this confusion, they tend to suppress diversity and to insist upon a rigid conformity. But loyalty may take as many forms as religious worship. This much about it seems indisputable: like love, it must be freely given. It can be evoked but it cannot be commanded or coerced. Members of a family are loyal to one another, not through any oath or compulsion, but as a result of shared experiences, community of interest, and long mutual dependence. A great aggregation of individuals and families becomes and remains a nation, not through geographical propinquity alone, but rather through much this same process of shared experiences—which is to say, a common history—and, above all, through common acceptance of certain fundamental values. The national loyalty of free men is not so much to their government as to the purposes for which their government was created. . . .

The tolerance on which freedom and opportunity must rest was a necessity of early life in America. Conquest of a continental wilderness fostered a tradition of individualism. The opening of successive frontiers widely different in physical conditions and in the problems of settlement encouraged a variety of political forms. Differences of religion, of social background, of economic interest among the settlers required tolerance of diversity. Out of this necessity the early Americans made a virtue. The idea that they had raised a standard to which the lovers of liberty could repair became a source of tremendous pride to them. "This new world," Thomas Paine boasted in *Common Sense,* "hath been the asylum for the persecuted lovers of civil and religious liberty from *every part* of Europe." . . .

Whatever may have been the vices and weaknesses of this country in the past, want of confidence in itself was not one of them. The nation knew that the American dream would inspire all who had a chance to dream it.

But that sublime self-confidence has now disappeared. Aliens are suspect; there is no longer the old certainty that they will be swept into the mainstream of American life. Prospective immigrants must prove that they are not the bearers of contagious opinions, and even transient visitors are feared. In 1950 the State Department denied visas to the Dean of Canterbury and later to twelve members of the Communist-sponsored World Congress of Partisans for Peace, Pablo Picasso among them, because of their political and economic views. The faith of Americans in their own institutions is apparently no longer considered strong enough to withstand Communist propaganda. Eminent artists have been barred merely because their political sympathies were suspect. The German conductor Wilhelm Furtwängler was kept out because he had collaborated with the Nazis. Later Joseph Krips, the conductor of the Vienna State Opera, was forbidden to fill a summer engagement with the Chicago Symphony Orchestra because he had previously conducted performances at Moscow and Leningrad. Tolerance of diversity and faith in the democratic process are giving way to reliance on the quarantine of hostile doctrines.

Indeed, even those born into the American heritage are now only tentatively trusted; they are obliged to affirm and reaffirm their allegiance. And beyond this ritual of affirmation, in the potency of which there is no longer any confidence, they are commonly required before entering upon any post affecting the national interest to deny disloyalty. Anyone who goes to work for the government of the United States today must swear that he does not advocate its overthrow. In point of fact, Congress thought it necessary in 1940 to make it a penal offense for any citizen to teach or advocate the duty or necessity of overthrowing "any government in the United States by force or violence."

A terrible distrust lies behind this shift to negativism. The country's doubts about the loyalty of its citizens are not unlike the doubts of a husband about the fidelity of his wife. The protestations that answer his doubts are never convincing and are likely to dissipate the mutual confidence that is the essence of a marriage. When men lose faith in one another, they lose the substance of what constitutes a community among them. Thus, to a national community, there is nothing that so dangerously corrupts its integrity as such a loss of faith. As in the case of the suspicious husband, this distrust is the expression of a neurotic insecurity.

Such insecurity is perhaps the most pervasive characteristic of our time. The fear of freedom and the difficulties of realizing its potentialities have been illuminatingly treated by the psychiatrists and the socal psychologists. They have contributed invaluable insights of which political theorists have as yet made too little use. The forces that have led great numbers of Europeans and Asiatics to seek the fellowship of disciplined submission to authority as an escape from the responsibilities and isolation of freedom are at work here too. They exhibit themselves in the exertion of powerful pressures, cultural as well as political, toward conformity and in an attitude novel among Americans that they can neither comprehend nor change the awful tides in which they feel themselves engulfed. The consequence is a stultifying tendency to seek unity through uniformity.

"Loyalty" has become a cult, an obsession, in the United States. But even loyalty itself is now defined negatively. It is thought of not so much in terms of an affirmative faith in the great purposes for which the American nation was created as in terms of stereotypes the mere questioning of which is deemed "disloyal." The whole postwar accent is on something called "un-Americanism"—a hyphenated synonym for unorthodoxy. Deviations to the Left are regarded as more suspicious or criminal than deviations to the Right; but the tendency is to question all deviations. "Loyalty" consists today in not being un-American, which is to say, in not being different or individualistic. The very diversity which was the wellspring of loyalty in the past is now distrusted.

The term "disloyalty" as it is commonly used today is nothing more or less than a circumlocution for treason. The authors of the Constitution went to a great deal of trouble in dealing with the subject of treason because they knew from experience how readily the term can be twisted to make discontent or dissent, or mere criticism of the government, a major crime. They took care, therefore, to define treason in the narrowest terms. "Treason against the United States," they declared in Article III, Section 3, of the Constitution, "shall consist only in levying war against them or in adhering to their enemies, giving them aid and comfort." No acts other than those specified in the Constitution can be made treasonable by legislation. Congress can neither extend, nor restrict, nor define the crime. Its power over the subject is limited to prescribing the punishment.

The Constitution is no less exacting as to the means by which conviction of treason may be obtained. "No person shall be convicted of treason," Section 3 continues, "unless on the testimony of two witnesses to the same overt act, or on confession in open court."

James Madison explained in Number 43 of *The Federalist*—that brilliant exegesis of the Constitution characterized by Thomas Jefferson as "the best commentary on the principles of government which ever was written"—the reasons that prompted the Constitutional Convention to define treason so narrowly and to make conviction of it so difficult:

> As treason may be committed against the United States, the authority of the United States ought to be enabled to punish it. But as newfangled and artificial treasons have been the great engines by which violent factions, the natural offspring of free government, have usually wreaked their alternate malignity on each other, the convention have, with great judgment, opposed a barrier to this peculiar danger, by inserting a constitutional definition of the crime, fixing the proof necessary for conviction of it, and restraining the Congress, even in punishing it, from extending the consequences of guilt beyond the person of its author.

There is a whole lesson in political science in this paragraph—a lesson peculiarly applicable today. The use of "disloyalty" as a "newfangled and artificial" form of treason has indeed promoted the rise of violent factions and led to a wreaking of "their alternate malignity on each other." There is no way to measure the impairment of national security that has resulted from this disruption of the sense of national community.

Disloyalty, to be sure, has not officially been held to constitute treason. But when a congressional committee or a quasi-judicial government board says that an individual is disloyal—or that he is un-American, or subversive, or a security risk, or ineligible for employment by the United States, or any of the other circumlocutions of the circumlocution—it is saying in not very euphemistic terms, or at least is encouraging the public to believe, that he is a traitor. The difference is that disloyalty is nowhere to be found detailed as a crime upon the statute books, that nowhere has it been defined, that nowhere has a punishment been prescribed for it by law. This ambiguity merely makes the charge more difficult to avoid and a condemnation less difficult to obtain.

Real disloyalty presents a threat to national security. It might find expression in betrayal of the nation—even in espionage or sabotage. Of course these are statutory crimes, clearly defined and punishable through the normal processes of indictment and trial by jury. The law can easily be used to punish any actual spy or saboteur. But the law can no more be used to punish a potential spy or a potential saboteur than it can be used to punish a potential pickpocket or a potential embezzler. The law punishes specifically prohibited antisocial acts. It does not prohibit and cannot punish antisocial ideas or intentions. The distinction has always been considered basic to a free society.

In a period of international tension, however, a potential spy or saboteur is likely to seem very dangerous—so dangerous that there is enormous temptation to deal with him outside the law. The United States, engaged in a world-wide struggle that has led to armed conflict in Asia, has yielded to this temptation to an alarming degree. It has devised an elaborate system and ritual for punishing men—and punishing them most cruelly—for crimes they have not committed but are suspected of desiring to commit. It punishes them by stigmatizing them as disloyal.

Anyone so stigmatized becomes to some degree an outcast. If he retains any friends, he knows himself to be a menace to them. Any association with them may result in their stigmatization too. Wherever he goes he is marked as a man who would be willing to betray his country. He remains at large but is regarded as a menace to society. He is expatriated without being exiled and denied the opportunity to gain a livelihood without the compensation of being maintained in prison at the community's expense. He and his fellows might come, in time, to constitute something new in American life—a caste of untouchables.

The punishment in such cases is something like that in the old story about the Quaker and his dog Tray. " 'Go to,' said the Quaker to poor Tray, 'I will not kill thee, but I will give thee a bad name,' as he turned him into the streets with the cry of 'mad dog,' and somebody else did kill Tray."

Perhaps the punishments meted out on the ground of disloyalty are not too severe for anyone who clearly and demonstrably intends to serve the interest of a foreign government to the detriment of his own countrymen. The fact is, however, that these penalties are meted out without any of the safeguards embodied in the Anglo-American system of justice for the protection of innocent persons against unjust conviction. They are inflicted on the loyal and the disloyal almost without discrimination.

By the simple stratagem of charging a man with disloyalty, instead of with treason or espionage or sabotage, it is possible to evade the constitutional requirements that he be indicted by a grand jury, that he enjoy a speedy and public trial by an impartial petit jury, that he be informed of the nature and cause of the accusation and confronted with the witnesses against him, that he be accorded the benefit of compulsory process to obtain witnesses in his favor. He is indicted and tried and sentenced by congressional committee or administrative tribunal, with the same men acting as prosecutors, judges, and jury. The presumption of innocence supposed to surround him is ignored. The mere charge of disloyalty is treated as evidence of guilt.

. . . it is the press which executes, so to speak, the sentences passed by congressional committees or by mere individuals speaking under the immunity from suits for slander or libel afforded by Congress. Newspapers especially tend to make headlines out of accusations and to treat denials less prominently. This stems in large measure from the concept of news as sensation and is scarcely less true of those newspapers that strive for objectivity than of those that deliberately use their news pages to serve editorial biases.

The tradition of objectivity, which is the great virtue of the American press, has operated in this context to make the press an instrument of those seeking to inflict punishment by publicity. Allegations which would otherwise be ignored because they would be recognized as groundless and libelous are blown up on front pages and given a significance out of all relation to their intrinsic merit after they have been made before a committee of Congress. Thus, what is one day properly regarded as unpublishable gossip is treated the next day as news of great moment because it has been uttered under official auspices. Refutation, no matter how compelling, never catches up with charges of disloyalty and never erases their imprint. In addition, of course, many newspapers welcome such charges and inflate them for political reasons or for their commercial value in stimulating street sales. . . .

The short-cut to punishment has an effect on society in other ways as well. The knowledge that men may be accused and found guilty of disloyalty in so summary a manner becomes a restraint on the exercise of constitutional rights. It is no longer safe to talk recklessly or foolishly. If the effect of this were no more than to silence recklessness and folly, perhaps the loss would not be great. But the discouragement of reckless and foolish talk tends inescapably to suppress sound and sensible dissent which may seem unpatriotic because it happens to be unpopular.

The trouble with putting any halter upon individual freedom to talk nonsense—even subversive or seditious nonsense—is that it tends to frustrate the democratic process. That process is one in which nonsense cannot be silenced by authority; it can be silenced, or overcome, only by sense. Since it is often not altogether easy to distinguish between the two, silencing of the one cannot help but result in silencing of the other. What happens, of course, is that unorthodox ideas, whether sensible or not, are suppressed in favor of orthodoxy. And consequently the attention of the society is diverted from its real problems, which call for adaptation and change, and focused instead upon a preservation of things as they are.

The situation should not be overstated. There has been, as yet, no formal or statutory suppression of speech in the United States beyond the prohibition of advocacy of violent overthrow of the government and the punitive restrictions of the McCarran Act. Men may, and fortunately a number of them still do, express nonconformist views liable to be termed treasonable. But, as Senator Margaret Chase Smith observed in a speech expressing her revulsion against the name-calling tactics of Senator Joseph McCarthy, "Freedom of speech is not what it used to be in America. It has been so abused by some that it is not exercised by others." Freedom of speech does not mean, to be sure, that a man who says what is unpopular should be protected from the penalties of unpopularity. Heretics and reformers must expect denunciation. The alarming characteristic about what is happening today lies partly in the official source of the denunciation, partly in the easy identification of dissent with disloyalty, partly in the punishment of it by the government itself through extralegal mechanisms.

The cult of loyalty, and its attendant hunt for heresy as a symptom of disloyalty, has generated an intellectually shackled feeling for which terror is too strong a term, but which is marked nevertheless by widespread anxiety. The feeling is most acute, naturally, in Washington, and among government employees. . . . But outside the capital, the pressures for conformity are mounting to a degree never before experienced by the American people. The Committee on Un-American Activities in the national House of Representatives has spawned imitators in state legislatures; some of them, such as the Tenney Committee in California,[1] the Canwell Committee in Washington, the Broyles Commission in Illinois, have rivaled the tactics of the congressional body. In their role of investigators and with the stated object of protecting national security, they have had the effect of penalizing Americans for exercising the fundamental rights of advocacy and association.

Similarly, the Federal Employee-Loyalty Program has been aped and embellished in states and municipalities—where there is far less warrant for such restrictions.[2] Protective measures designed to keep disloyal persons out of jobs that directly affect the national security become merely punitive when applied indiscriminately to all forms of public employment. In many states extremely repressive legislation, of doubtful constitutionality, has been adopted. These laws are aimed at Communists, but their result is to penalize all forms of heterodoxy. Some of the laws deny a place on the ballot to Communists, thereby revealing a distrust of

---

[1] Editor's note: Senator Tenney has been long retired from the California State Senate, but his committee carries on, claiming, in its last report, that the administration of the University of California "welcomes Communist organizations, throws the portals open to Communist speakers, and exhibits an easy tolerance of Communist activities." Other committees, for example the Broyles Commission, have been dissolved.

[2] The Maryland version was nullified on November 7, 1967 by the U.S. Supreme Court.

the democratic process. Some, like the Ober Law in Maryland, drastically restrict the right of citizens to join in voluntary associations if the purpose of these associations is officially regarded as subversive. A number of municipalities, especially in the South, have adopted ordinances banning Communists and Communist *sympathizers* from the city limits. Birmingham, Alabama, for instance, announced that it would jail anyone found guilty of "voluntary association" with a Communist. Other cities have undertaken to require the registration of all Communists. The patent invalidity of such edicts from a constitutional point of view has given no apparent pause to local legislative and law-enforcement bodies. In a number of places, police chiefs have intimated that they mean to apply virtual lynch law to political undesirables. Behind all these measures is a fear of freedom and a panicky willingness to disregard the great procedural safeguards that distinguish a free from a totalitarian society.

The hounding of heterodoxy in the name of loyalty takes an especially ugly and mischievous form in connection with schools and universities. The proliferation of loyalty tests and oaths required of teachers inhibits discussion precisely where it should be most free. But perhaps the gravest consequence of the official cult of loyalty is the inflammation of public opinion to a sometimes hysterical pitch. When political disagreement is branded as disloyalty, when neighbor is invited to look with suspicion on neighbor, the bonds of national unity are strained in a way that is directly injurious to national security. . . .

Censorship in the name of patriotism occurs on an unorganized basis too. Perhaps the most sensitive example of it was provided by a Hollywood motion-picture studio which, after six months of work, shelved plans to produce a film dealing with the life and exploits of Hiawatha, the Onondaga Indian chief immortalized by Longfellow. Hiawatha had succeeded in establishing peace among the warring Five Nations; and it was felt, according to a studio spokesman, that this might cause the film to be regarded as a message for peace and thus as Communist propaganda.

Political discussion has been debased to a species of fishwifery by shrill and redundant accusations of disloyalty. The immunity from suit for slander afforded by the floor of Congress has been abused over and over again to launch extravagant attacks on the good faith of opponents in every issue of policy. . . .

The point is patently illustrated in connection with events in the Far East. The readiness of the China Lobby to impute disloyalty to every realistic appraisal of the collapse of the Chinese Nationalist government has made a rational China policy impossible. The State Department has been forced to cling to a transparent fiction. In other areas as well, mere anti-communism has taken the place of a reasoned evaluation of American interests, allying this country with discredited regimes abroad. Those who dared to protest or dissent were liable to vilification as Communist sympathizers. . . .

The disloyalty of the Americanists [super-patriots] impairs national security more seriously than the comparable disloyalty of the Communists. . . . It is more deeply subversive, strikes more injuriously at the real roots of loyalty and of American strength. It would, in fact, meet the threat of communism by the substitution of Communist techniques for the techniques of freedom. If the relatively impotent Communists aim at overthrowing the government of the United States, the Americanists, whether they are aware of it or not, aim at overthrowing the essential values which that government was instituted to secure.

HERESY, YES—CONSPIRACY, NO!

Sidney Hook

Sidney Hook, one of America's foremost philosophers, was fighting Stalinism in the thirties, long before anti-Stalinism became intellectually fashionable. As a spokesman for the Left, his opposition was especially effective, although he may no longer be described as a Marxist. He is the author of From Hegel to Marx *(1936),* John Dewey: An Intellectual Portrait *(1950),* The Hero in History *(1943),* Toward the Understanding of Karl Marx *(1933) and* The Paradoxes of Freedom *(1962). His now well-known discussion of the difference between heresy and conspiracy is reprinted here.*

The most comprehensive and adequate definition in positive terms of the meaning of liberalism, from Socrates to John Dewey, is suggested by the memorable words of Justice Holmes. It is the belief "in the free trade of ideas—that the test of truth is the power of thought to get itself accepted in the competition of the market." This is not a program of action nor a philosophical theory of truth, but an attitude or temper of mind towards all programs. Liberals may disagree among themselves about everything else; but all of them have this faith in common. It is a faith which marks off

From *Heresy, Yes—Conspiracy, No!* (New York: John Day Co., Inc., 1953), pp. 19–36. Reprinted by permission of the author.

liberal from totalitarian culture. Any action which restricts the freedom of ideas to develop or circulate is illiberal.

There are at least two presuppositions of this belief in the free market of ideas. One of them is explicitly drawn by Justice Holmes and already recognized by Jefferson; the other is implicit and perhaps more important, for around it center most of our present difficulties.

The first is that the free expression and circulation of ideas may be checked wherever their likely effects constitute a clear and present danger to public peace or the security of the country. This is a specific application of the principle that no right is absolute when it endangers rights of equal or greater validity. In ordinary affairs, this is a commonplace. The right to inquire is innocent, but not when it leads someone to experiment on a human being to determine how long he can survive torture. The right to free speech is precious, but not when it blasts a reputation by libelous accusation. Truth is sacred, but a person who revealed it knowing that it would be used to destroy his country is a traitor. Freedom to worship God according to one's conscience is one of the historical cornerstones of the structure of American liberties, but it cannot be invoked to protect rituals which require human sacrifice or practices like plural marriages or refusal to submit to vaccination against plagues.

In the context of public affairs, however, there is a certain ambiguity involved in the conception of clear and present danger. Clear to whom? To the public enforcement agencies, to Congress, to the Justices of the Supreme Court (who are notoriously at odds with each other and who, on matters of fact, are less well informed than many laymen)? And how present must a "present danger" be? Must a riot be in progress before an anti-Semitic orator ranting about the forged *Protocols of Zion* is stopped from speaking? Must we await the actual delivery of an atomic bomb by a foreign power, or a formal declaration of war, before the incitements to treason by its fifth columnists in this country are curbed? These are some of the difficulties that attend the clear and present danger formula. They cannot be solved by fiat. In all such questions of "proximity and degree," good judgment is required. The most we can expect is that those who make the judgment will be competently informed and ultimately responsible to the community at large. According to our practice, a clear and present danger exists in the United States when a majority of the Supreme Court says it does; in England, when Parliament says it does.

The second presupposition of the liberal's faith in the free market of ideas is that the competition will be honestly and openly conducted. For unless there are certain rules, so to speak, of honest competition, analogous to those which hold in other domains of testing and inquiry, freedom of choice is an illusion. If the market is rigged by money, power or fraud, what gets accepted is anything but the truth. If ability to withstand honest competition is not a sufficient condition of truth it is at least a necessary one. From the point of view of the liberal, it is not doctrines "fraught with death" which he fears, for his faith in intelligence is such that he is confident that in the open and honest exchange of opinion the majority of men will choose life, not death, and that if they choose death they deserve their fate. Men cannot be compelled to remain free, any more than they can be compelled to love one another. What the liberal fears is the systematic corruption of the free market of ideas by activities which make intelligent choice impossible. In short, what he fears is not heresy but conspiracy.

The failure to recognize the distinction between heresy and conspiracy is fatal to a liberal civilization, for the inescapable consequence of their identification is either self-destruction, when heresies are punished as conspiracies, or destruction at the hands of [our] enemies, when conspiracies are tolerated as heresies.

A heresy is a set of unpopular ideas or opinions on matters of grave concern to the community. The right to profess publicly a heresy of any character, on any theme, is an essential element of a liberal society. The liberal stands ready to defend the honest heretic no matter what his views against any attempt to curb him. It is enough that the heretic pays the price of unpopularity which he cannot avoid. In some respects each of us is a heretic, but a liberal society can impose no official orthodoxies of *belief,* disagreement with which entails loss of liberty or life.

A conspiracy, as distinct from a heresy, is a secret or underground movement which seeks to attain its ends not by normal political or educational processes but by playing outside the rules of the game. Because it undermines the conditions which are required in order that doctrines may freely compete for acceptance, because where successful it ruthlessly destroys all heretics and dissenters, a conspiracy cannot be tolerated without self-stultification in a liberal society.

A heresy does not shrink from publicity. It welcomes it. Not so a conspiracy. The signs of a conspiracy are secrecy, anonymity, the use of false names and labels, and the calculated lie. It does not offer its wares openly but, by systematic infiltration into all organizations of cultural life, it seeks to capture strategic posts to carry out a policy alien to the purposes of the organization. There is political conspiracy, which is the concern of the state; but there may also be a conspiracy against a labor union, a cultural or professional association, or an educational institution which is not primarily the concern of the state but of its own members. In general, whoever subverts the rules of a democratic organization and seeks to win by chicanery what cannot be fairly won in the process of free discussion is a conspirator.

Communist *ideas* are heresies, and liberals need have no fear of them where they are freely and openly expressed. They should be studied and evaluated in the light of all the relevant evidence. No one should be punished because he holds them. The Communist *movement,* however, is something quite different from a mere heresy, for wherever it exists it operates along the lines laid down by Lenin as guides to Communists of all countries, and perfected in great detail since then. . . .

Under present conditions of political and military warfare, it is not hard to see what immense dangers to the security of liberal institutions is implicit in this strategy of infiltration and deceit. Even a few men in sensitive posts can do incalculable harm. These instructions—and there are many more detailed ones, combined with explicit directives to Communists to transform any war in which their country is involved, except one approved by the Soviet Union, into a civil war against their own government—indicate that members of the Communist party are not so much heretics as conspirators and in actual practice regard themselves as such.

There may be some justification for conspiratorial activity in undemocratic countries where heresies are proscribed, but Lenin . . . makes no exceptions. Since 1917, he maintains, in no country of the world can the revolution be peacefully achieved. . . .

How faithfully the Communist movement pursues the pattern laid down by its authoritative leaders in the political sphere is a matter of historical record. But unfortunately for the peace of mind of liberals, the same tactics are followed in other areas of social and cultural life. The history of American labor is replete with illustrations.

Every large labor organization in the United States has been compelled to take administrative action against Communist party elements not because of their beliefs—their heresies—but because their pattern of conduct made the Communist party, and ultimately the Kremlin, the decisive power in the life of the union, and not the needs and wishes of the membership. President Philip Murray of the CIO exposed the technique in detail when his organization ousted the Mine, Mill and Smelter Workers Union. In all these situations, it is not fear of Communist ideas which has led to disciplinary action. The charge against the Communists is that it is *they* who fear the open and honest confrontation of ideas. They operate through "fronts," the charge continues, because they fear that, given a free choice of honestly labeled alternatives, they will be rejected; once they slip into power, they consolidate their position by terror.

Under existing law punishment is provided for criminal conspiracy, whether this be conspiracy in restraint of trade or conspiracy to overthrow the government by insurrection or to advocate such overthrow in time of clear and present danger. But there are noncriminal conspiracies in sectors of life which are not affected by legislative power. These sectors of life are social and cultural and are regulated by tradition, common standards of propriety or decency in personal relations, and sometimes by explicit rules. The transfer of some of the techniques by which conspirators in the past have seized the state to capturing control of benevolent associations, social, chess, and athletic clubs, literary societies, research groups, professional and trade unions, even philanthropic agencies is unique to modern totalitarian movements. In the past, it was here if anywhere that honest opposition openly declared itself. The elaborate devices adopted by Communists to disguise the nature of their opposition and to prevent others from functioning in opposition to them when they seize control may have been anticipated in earlier times by other groups but they never were previously employed with such fanaticism, rationalized by such body of doctrine, and executed with such lack of scruple.

By now it should be apparent that liberals in the twentieth century are confronted by a situation quite unfamiliar to their forbears. For they must contend not with fearless heretics, indigenous elements of the community who, like the abolitionists and revolutionists of old, scorn concealment, and who make no bones about their hospitality to the principles of liberalism. They find themselves in the unique historical predicament of having to deal with native elements who, by secrecy and stratagem, serve the interests of a foreign power which believes itself entitled to speak for all mankind, and whose victory spells the end of all liberal civilization and with it the right to heresy. It is now plain that the Communist regimes of the world have turned out to be the greatest and cruelest heresy-hunters in history, not merely in politics but in every branch of theory and practice. They have even abolished the right to be silent, for on any matter on which the Central Committee of any Communist party has laid down the law, silence is construed as treason.

It is a great pity and a source of much confusion that present-day Communists are often referred to as Marxists, without further qualification. For this overlooks the radical departure from Marx's own position initiated by Lenin and Stalin on the question of conspiracy. Marx was an unconcealed heretic. Even when writing in nondemocratic countries, subject to repression and imprisonment, he scorned the use of conspiratorial techniques and excoriated Bakunin and others for adopting them. The concluding sentence of the *Communist Manifesto* frankly tells the rulers of the nondemocratic countries of Europe: "The Communists disdain to conceal their views and aims. They openly declare that their ends can be attained only by the forcible overthrow of all existing social conditions."

Contrast with this the instructions given to Communists by the Kremlin in democratic countries, to adopt para-military organizational forms, to work underground even when legal work is permitted, and to develop systematic techniques of deception, and we can see the difference between honest and open revolutionists and underground conspirators.

The problems which underground conspiracy creates for a liberal society are of tremendous magnitude. They cannot be dismissed by a quotation from Jefferson. Nor can they be solved by indiscriminately placing the Communist movement and its entire periphery outside the law by special legislation. They require constructive intelligence, the discovery and application of techniques in each field which will meet conspiratorial threats to the proper functioning of liberal institutions without creating still greater ones. Legal outlawry of the Communist Party will not prevent it from reappearing under different names.

Failure to take this approach is characteristic of some current wholesale responses to the problem. The first is that of frightened reactionaries who cannot distinguish between heresy and conspiracy, and identify communism with any decent thing they wish to destroy. By making reckless charges of conspiracy where there is only honest heresy, they prevent intelligent choice. And by labeling all progressive ideas as Communist heresies, they help Communist strategy. For the Communist strategy is to make it appear that Communists are an integral part of the indigenous progressive movement, instead of a cancerous growth upon it, and that any legitimate measure directed against them is actually an attack upon all progressives, and indeed upon the philosophy of liberalism itself. There is nothing new about this unreasoning reaction. It emanates from the same quarters which called the Taft-Ellender Housing Bill "Communist," and plans for national health insurance "un-American."

A second response is made by a small but influential group of men who believe that they can check Communist conspiracy merely by passing laws against it, and that they can protect institutions from subversives by requiring all individuals, particularly teachers, to take loyalty oaths. As if any member of the Communist Party regarded any oaths except one to the Communist Party and the Soviet Union as binding! This results in foolish legislation like the Feinberg Law in New York and the Ober Law in Maryland, which are potentially dangerous in that they fail to make proper distinctions between conspirators and heretics.

A third group consists of those whom we may call ritualistic, as distinct from realistic, liberals. They ignore or blithely dismiss as comparatively insignificant the mass of evidence concerning the conspiratorial character of the Communist movement in all institutions in which it is active. They regard communism merely as an unpleasant heresy just a little worse than a crotchety theory of disease or finance. They sometimes characterize prosecution of a conspirator for espionage or perjury as persecution of a heretic. Or they condemn as "witch hunting," measures taken to deny access to sensitive posts in government or social institutions to members of the Communist Party, who are under explicit instructions to sabotage the purposes of these organizations. The ritualistic liberals would wait until the sabotage has been carried out before proceeding against Communists. This gives a new lease of life to the reactionaries, who now tend to regard the ritualistic liberals as the dupes or accomplices of the Communists, thus confirming the illusions of the ritualistic liberals that there really is no problem of Communist conspiracy.

One of the most ambiguous phrases in current use among ritualistic liberals is "guilt by association." . . . It is or should be now clear that "association" by way of membership in the Communist Party is not innocent or coincidental but is *a form of active co-operation and collaboration* in carrying out the purposes of a conspiratorial organization. The Communist Party sees to it that all members are instructed about the purposes as soon as they join. Continued membership is possible only in virtue of a series of continued *acts* of obedience to instructions. Those who dub the active co-operation required of all members of the Communist Party "guilt by association" coyly suggest by that phrase the innocuous association of chance or occasional encounters with Communists in social gatherings. They simply ignore the fact that all members of the Communist Party must "associate" by active co-operation with its purposes or be expelled.

Ritualistic liberals legitimately criticize the dangerous nonsense of those who proscribe heresy. But they carry their criticism to a point where they give the impression that the country is in the grip of a deadly reign of terror or hysteria much more dangerous than Communist expansion from without and infiltration from within. Because someone has given a silly characterization of a subversive organization, they imply that there are no subversive organizations. The sad history of recent American liberal movements, however, shows that the instructions given to American Communists by Otto Kuusinen, as Secretary of the Communist International, bore bitter fruit for liberals. Kuusinen advised: "We must create a whole solar system of organizations and smaller committees around the Communist Party, so to speak, smaller organizations working under the influence of the Party." (*American Communist,* May 1931.)

The problem of membership in Communist front organizations which often conceal their purposes is much more difficult. Many innocent people have been ensnared by these organizations. No hard and fast rule can be laid down as a guide. The number of such organizations an individual has joined, the time he joined, his function and activities upon joining—all these, as we shall see, are highly relevant in determining the degree to which an individual is untrustworthy from the point of view of security. Only those exceptional souls who have never made a mistake or have never been fooled can shut the gates of understanding and charity against all members of such groups and pronounce a blanket judgment against them. This troublesome question should not be made a matter of legislation but of judicious administration.

Because some security regulations in government are questionable, and because some blunders have been made, ritualistic liberals intimate that no security regulations are necessary and that the existing laws against treason and criminal conspiracy are sufficient for all purposes. They do not understand that the purpose of the security program is not punishment for acts committed but prevention of acts threatened by those who are under instructions to commit them or whose behavior or habits make them dangerous risks. By artfully collecting instances of foolishness from the press and blowing up their significance, they convey a very misleading picture comparable to what an account of American business would be like if only bankruptcies were reported, or an account of public order that featured only crime stories.

David Lilienthal, a realistic not a ritualistic liberal, has warned us against the "Scare-the-dopes!" method of discussing nuclear energy. There is also a "Scare-the-dopes!" method of discussion of the problem of Communistic conspiracy. It is used by those who employ the term Communist with scandalous looseness as a synonym for any economic or political heresy, and who shout conspiracy where there is only heresy. It is also used by those who do not tell us how to meet the real dangers of Communist conspiracy but shout "Hysteria!" "Fascism!" or "Police State!" when the first faltering efforts are made to cope with dangers hitherto unprecedented in the history of American democracy.

The position of realistic liberalism in three trouble centers of American life in which overt conspiratorial activity of a criminal nature is not involved may be briefly indicated as illustrative of its attitude.

Where government service is concerned, the operating maxim for every sensitive and policy-making post should be a principle enunciated by Roger Baldwin, former head of the American Civil Liberties Union: "A superior loyalty to a foreign government disqualifies a citizen for service to our own." This is not a matter of civil rights but of common sense. Once a policy is adopted by the governing agencies of a liberal society empowered by a democratic consensus to safeguard the public welfare, it is not only its right but its duty to insure its loyal execution. It cannot wait for a major piece of sabotage or leak of information in order to act. Yet this is precisely the procedure advocated by those who urge that once an individual has been appointed and served a probationary period, he should be dismissed only if he is caught engaging in espionage or sabotage. Presumably, even if it had been known that Hiss, Fuchs, Boyer, et al. were members of the Communist Party, once employed they should not have been dismissed until they had carried out their objectives or were on the verge of doing so.

The difficulty lies in determining what constitutes sufficient evidence to warrant the inference that a particular individual is unsafe, for in some cases even past membership in subversive organizations is not conclusive. On the other hand, notoriously bad judgment might bar someone from an important post whose loyalty is not impugned. A fool may sometimes be as dangerous as a rogue. Nor can the principles that apply in a courtroom in determination of *criminal* guilt be applied in these situations.

The criteria for establishing "unreliability" must obviously be less stringent than those which lead us to deprive an individual of his life or freedom.

It is not impossible to find knowledgeable individuals who can supervise such a program. Where certain procedural safeguards are adopted and individuals allowed in doubtful cases to resign quietly without prejudice when they do not wish to accept posts in nonsensitive sectors, the likelihood of injustice diminishes. The more fanfare and publicity, however, the greater are the chances of error and injury to reputation. Ritualistic liberals who insist that everything be decided in the public eye, and that a case be made out that can stick in a court of law before an individual is dropped as a security risk, are inviting political circuses and a reaction that will sweep away all administrative safeguards against arbitrary dismissal. It cannot be emphasized too often that there is a difference between legal rules of evidence absolutely essential to our tradition where a man's life or liberty is at stake and rules of evidence that bear only on an individual's qualifications for a position of trust. There is certainly room for criticism of present procedures, but whoever speaks up will be more persuasive if he presents alternative positive proposals which show that he at least recognizes the problem.

In labor organizations, the existence of Communist leaders is extremely dangerous because of their unfailing use of the strike as a political instrument at the behest of the Kremlin. The history of Communist-led trade unions here and abroad is instructive enough. The most effective way of meeting this situation, however, is not by requiring non-Communist oaths on the part of union officers; for this can be circumvented by delegating office to individuals who are faithful but non-card-holding Communists. The most intelligent procedure for labor here is to let labor clean its own house. Free and independent trade unions, which are essential to a democracy, cannot be liberated from the organizational stranglehold of the Communist Party by government intervention. Only an aroused membership together with other labor organizations can do the job.[1]

. . . the question [of freedom and responsibility in the schools] is not primarily political. It does not involve civil rights so much as the ethics of professional conduct. Heresy in the schools—whether in science, economics, or politics—must be protected against any agency which seeks to impose orthodoxy. For the scholar there is no subversive doctrine, but only that which is valid or invalid or not proven in the light of evidence. The primary commitment of the teacher is to the ethics and logic of inquiry. It is not his beliefs, right or wrong—it is not his heresies—which disqualify

---

[1] Editor's note: Professor Hook would undoubtedly agree that since these words were written the trade union movement has done the job.

the Communist Party teacher, but his declaration of intention, as evidenced by official statements, to practice educational fraud. Must one catch him in the act before dismissing him? Not necessarily; any more than we must catch a judge who is a *present* and *active* member of the Ku Klux Klan in the act of discriminating against Negroes or Jews before concluding he is unfit for judicial office. It is amazing to hear from ritualistic liberals that it is a violation of academic freedom to prevent a man from carrying out the professional misconduct which he has pledged himself to engage in by virtue of his membership in an organization whose publicly professed aim is to indoctrinate for the Communist Party in classrooms, enroll students in Communist Youth organizations, rewrite textbooks from the Communist point of view, build cells on campuses, capture departments, and inculcate the Communist Party line that in case of war students should turn their arms against their own government.

This is a matter of ethical hygiene, not of political heresy or of persecution. And because it is, the enforcement of the proper professional standards should rest with the teachers themselves, and not with the state or regents or even boards of trustees. The actual techniques of handling such issues must be worked out, but the problem cannot be confused with the issue of heresy. If the conspiratorial purposes of Communist Party teachers is glossed over by ritualistic liberals as merely a manifestation of heresy, then all heresy comes under fire. This does not mean that faculties must engage in a hue and cry to rout out the few unfaithful members of the profession who are betraying their trust. But they must not refuse to act whenever evidence of such unfitness is established thus making clear that "not everything gives." . . .

Liberalism in the twentieth century must toughen its fibre, for it is engaged in a fight on many different fronts. It must defend the free market in ideas against the racists, the professional patrioteers, and those spokesmen of the status quo who would freeze the existing inequalities of opportunity and economic power by choking off criticism. It must also be defended against those agents and apologists of Communist totalitarianism who, instead of honestly defending their heresies, resort to conspiratorial methods of anonymity and other techniques of fifth columnists. I will not be taken in by labels like "left" and "right." These terms came into use after the French Revolution, but the legacy of the men who then called themselves "left"—the strategic freedoms of the Bill of Rights—is today everywhere repudiated by those who are euphemistically referred to as "leftists" but who are actually Communists more reactionary than many of those who are conventionally called "rightists."

There is always a danger of excesses being committed when exposure of Communist conspiracy is left to the leadership of reactionaries. When this happens, it testifies to the fact that the liberals have failed to do the necessary job of moral education which is implicit in their dedication to the "free market in ideas." Similarly, they lose by default when, instead of taking the leadership in the struggle against "Know-Nothingism," racial persecution, and cultural repression, they permit Communists to exploit for their own political purposes the idealism of youth and the just resentments of the underprivileged.

Realistic liberalism recognizes that to survive we must solve many hard problems, and that they can be solved only by intelligence, and not by pious rhetoric. Our greatest danger is not fear of ideas but *absence* of ideas—specific ideas, addressed to concrete problems, here and now, problems of such complexity that only the ignorant can claim to know all the answers to them.

Finally, liberalism today conceives life not in terms of bare survival or of peace at any price, but in the light of ideas and ideals without which a life worthy of man cannot be attained. Among them are the strategic freedoms of those American traditions which make the continuous use of intelligence possible. . . .

THE TRIAL OF ARTHUR MILLER

John Steinbeck

The author of novels like The Grapes of Wrath, In Dubious Battle, *and* Of Mice and Men *would have needed no introduction even before the award of a Nobel prize brought him greater prominence and world-wide recognition. That same conscience which led him, in* Grapes of Wrath, *to protest against social injustice brings him here to the defense of a fellow writer.*

The trial of Arthur Miller for contempt of Congress brings close to all of us one of the strangest and most frightening dilemmas that a people and a government have ever faced. It is not the first trial of its kind, nor will it in all probability be the last. But Arthur Miller is a writer—one of our very best. What has happened to him could happen to any writer; could happen to me. We are face to face with a problem by no means easy of solution. . . .

No man knows what he might do in a given situation, and surely many men must wonder how they would act if they were in Arthur Miller's shoes. I wonder what I would do.

Let me suppose that I were going to trial for contempt of Congress as he is. I might be thinking somewhat as follows:

There is no doubt that Congress has the right, under the law, to ask me any question it wishes and to punish my refusal to answer with a contempt charge. The Congress has the right to do nearly anything conceivable. It has only to define a situation or an action as a "clear and present danger" to public safety, public morals, or public health. The selling or eating of mince pie could be made a crime if Congress determined that mince pie was a danger to public health—which it probably is. Since many parents raise their children badly, mother love could be defined as a danger to the general welfare.

Surely, Congress has the right to ask me anything on any subject. The question is: Should the Congress take advantage of that right?

Let us say that the Congressional Committee feels that the Communist Party and many groups which have been linked with it—sometimes arbitrarily—constitute a clear and present danger to the nation. Now actually it is neither virtue nor good judgment on my part that has kept me from joining things. I am simply not a joiner by nature. Outside of the Boy Scouts and the Episcopal choir, I have never had an impulse to belong to things. But suppose I had. And suppose I have admitted my association with one or more of these groups posted as dangerous. As a writer, I must have been interested in everything, have felt it part of my profession to know and understand all kinds of people and groups. Having admitted these associations, I am now asked by the Committee to name individuals I have seen at meetings of such groups. I hope my reasoning then would go as follows:

The people I knew were not and are not, in my estimation, traitors to the nation. If they were, I would turn them in instantly. If I give names, it is reasonably certain that the persons named will be called up and questioned. In some cases they will lose their jobs, and in any case their reputations and standing in the community will suffer. And remember that these are persons who I honestly believe are innocent of any wrongdoing. Perhaps I do not feel that I have that right; that to name them would not only be disloyal but actually immoral. The Committee then is asking me to commit an immorality in the name of public virtue.

If I agree, I have outraged one of our basic codes of conduct, and if I refuse I am guilty of contempt of Congress, sentenced to prison and fined. One way outrages my sense of decency and the other brands me as a felon. And this brand does not fade out.

Now suppose I have children, a little property, a stake in the community. The threat of the contempt charge jeopardizes everything I love. Suppose, from worry or cowardice, I agree to what is asked. My deep and wounding shame will be with me always.

I cannot be reassured by the past performance of the Committee. I have read daily for a number of years the testimony of admitted liars and perjurers whose charges have been used to destroy the peace and happiness of people I do not know, and many of whom were destroyed without being tried.

Which path am I to choose? Either way I am caught. It may occur to me that a man who is disloyal to his friends could not be expected to be loyal to his country. You can't slice up morals. Our virtues begin at home. They do not change in a courtroom unless the pressure of fear is put upon us.

But if I am caught between two horrors, so is the Congress caught. Law, to survive, must be moral. To force personal immorality on a man, to wound his private virtue, undermines his public virtue. If the Committee frightens me enough, it is even possible that I may make up things to satisfy the questioners. This has been known to happen. A law which is immoral does not survive and a government which condones or fosters immorality is truly in clear and present danger.

The Congress had a perfect right to pass the Alien and Sedition Act. This law was repealed because of public revulsion. The Escaped Slave laws had to be removed because the people of free states found them immoral. The Prohibition laws were so generally flouted that all law suffered as a consequence.

We have seen and been revolted by the Soviet Union's encouragement of spying and telling, children reporting their parents, wives informing on their husbands. In Hitler's Germany, it was considered patriotic to report your friends and relations to the authorities. And we in America have felt safe from and superior to these things. But are we so safe or superior?

The men in Congress must be conscious of their terrible choice. Their legal right is clearly established, but should they not think of their moral responsibility also? In their attempts to save the nation from attack, they could well undermine the deep personal morality which is the nation's final defense. The Congress is truly on trial along with Arthur Miller.

Again let me change places with Arthur Miller. I have refused to name people. I am indicted, convicted, sent to prison. If the charge were murder or theft or extortion I would be subject to punishment, because I and all men know that these things are wrong. But if I am imprisoned for something I have been taught from birth is a good thing, then I go to jail with a deep sense of injustice and the rings of that injustice are bound to spread out like an infection. If I am brave enough to suffer for my principle, rather than to save myself by hurting other people I believe to be innocent, it seems to me that the law suffers more than I, and that contempt of the law and of the Congress is a real contempt rather than a legalistic one.

Under the law, Arthur Miller is guilty. But he seems also to be brave. Congress feels that it must press the charge against him, to keep its prerogative alive. But can we not hope that our representatives will inspect their dilemma? Respect for law can be kept high only if the law is respectable. There is a clear and present danger here, not to Arthur Miller, but to our changing and evolving way of life.

If I were in Arthur Miller's shoes, I do not know what I would do, but I could wish, for myself and for my children, that I would be brave enough to fortify and defend my private morality as he has. I feel profoundly that our country is better served by individual courage and morals than by the safe and public patriotism which Dr. Johnson called "the last refuge of scoundrels."

My father was a great man, as any lucky man's father must be. He taught me rules I do not think are abrogated by our nervous and hysterical times. These laws have not been annulled; these rules of attitudes. He taught me—glory to God, honor to my family, loyalty to my friends, respect for the law, love of country and instant and open revolt against tyranny, whether it come from the bully in the schoolyard, the foreign dictator, or the local demagogue.

And if this be treason, gentlemen, make the most of it.

ARTHUR MILLER'S CONSCIENCE

Richard H. Rovere

Richard Rovere writes the New Yorker's *"Letter from Washington," is American correspondent for* The Spectator, *and co-author with Arthur Schlesinger, Jr., of* The General and the President. *His most recent work is a collection of essays,* The American Establishment and Other Reports, Opinions, and Speculations (*1962*).

"I will protect my sense of myself," Arthur Miller told the House Committee on Un-American Activities when he refused to identify some writers who had once been Communists. "I could not use the name of another person and bring trouble on him." The refusal brought Miller a conviction for contempt of Congress from a judge who found his motives "commendable" but his action legally indefensible.

A writer's sense of himself is to be projected as well as protected. It becomes, through publication and production, a rather public affair. For this and other reasons, it is fitting that what Miller saw as the testing of his integrity—the challenge to his sense of himself—was a question involving not himself but others. Of himself, he had talked freely, not to say garrulously. He chatted, almost gaily, about his views in the Thirties, his views in the Forties, his views in the Fifties, about Ezra Pound and Elia Kazan and other notables, about the Smith Act and Congressional investigations and all manner of things. . . . His self-esteem was offended only when he was asked to identify others.

Thus, one might say, it was really a social or political ethic that he was defending, while of his sense of himself he gave freely. . . . (It was, of course, a symbolic act, a gesture, for Miller knew very well that the committee knew all about the men he was asked to identify. He could not really shield: he could only assert the shielding principle.) What he was protecting was, in any case, a self-esteem that rested upon a social rule or principle or ethic.

One could almost say that Miller's sense of himself *is* the principle that holds "informing" to be the ultimate in human wickedness. It is certainly a recurrent theme in his writing. In *The Crucible,* his play about the

---

From *The New Republic* (June 17, 1957), pp. 13–15. Reprinted by permission of the author.

Salem witchcraft trials, his own case is so strikingly paralleled as to lend color—though doubtless not truth—to the view that his performance in Washington was a case of life paying art the sincere flattery of imitation. To save his life, John Proctor, the hero, makes a compromise with the truth. He confesses, falsely, to having trafficked with Satan. "Did you see the Devil?" the prosecutor asks him. "I did," Proctor says. He recognizes the character of his act, but this affects him little. "Good, then—it is evil, and I do it," he says to his wife, who is shocked. He has reasoned that a few more years on earth are worth his betrayal of his sense of himself. (It is not to be concluded that Proctor's concession to the mad conformity of the time parallels Miller's testimony, for Proctor had never in fact seen the devil, whereas Miller had in fact seen Communists.) The prosecutor will not let him off with mere self-incrimination. He wants names; the names of those Proctor has seen with the Devil. Proctor refuses; does not balk at a self-serving lie, but a self-serving lie that involves others will not cross his lips. "I speak my own sins," he says, either metaphorically or hypo-critically, since the sins in question are a fiction. "I cannot judge another. I have no tongue for it." He is hanged, a martyr. . . .

Today, in most Western countries, ethics derive mainly from so-ciety and almost all values are social. What we do to and with ourselves is thought to be our own affair and thus not, in most circumstances, a matter that involves morality at all. People will be found to say that suicide, for a man or woman with few obligations to others, should not be judged harshly, while the old sanctions on murder remain. Masochism is in one moral category, sadism in another. Masturbation receives a tolerance that fornication does not quite receive. A man's person and his "sense of himself" are disposable assets, provided he choose to see them that way; sin is only possible when we involve others. Thus, Arthur Miller's John Proctor was a modern man when, after lying about his relations with the Devil, he said, "God in heaven, what is John Proctor, what is John Proctor? I think it is honest, I think so. I am no saint." . . . He was speaking for the social ethic which is Arthur Miller's—and he resisted just where Miller did, at "informing."

It is, I think, useful to look rather closely at Miller's social ethic and at what he has been saying about the problems of conscience, for circumstances have conspired to make him the leading symbol of the militant, risk-taking conscience in this period. I do not wish to quarrel with the whole of his morality, for much of it I share—as do, I suppose, most people who have not found it possible to accept any of the revealed religions. Moreover, I believe, as Judge McLaughlin did, that the action Miller took before the committee was a courageous one. Nevertheless, I think that behind the action and behind Miller's defense of it there is a certain amount of moral and political confusion. If I am right, then we ought to set about examining it, lest conscience and political morality come to be seen entirely in terms of "naming names"—a simplification which the House Un-American Activities Committee seems eager to foist upon us and which Miller, too, evidently accepts.

A healthy conscience, Miller seems to be saying, can stand anything but "informing." On the one hand, this seems a meager view of conscience. On the other, it makes little political sense and not a great deal of moral sense. Not all "informing" is bad, and not all of it is despised by the people who invariably speak of it as despicable. The question of guilt is relevant. My wife and I, for example, instruct our children not to tattle on one another. I am fairly certain, though, that if either of us saw a hit-and-run driver knock over a child or even a dog, we would, if we could, take down the man's license number and turn him in to the police. Even in the case of children, we have found it necessary to modify the rule so that we may be quickly advised if anyone is in serious danger of hurting himself or another. (The *social* principle again.) Proctor, I think, was not stating a fact when he said, "I cannot judge another"—nor was Miller when he said substantially the same thing. For the decision *not* to inform involves judging others. "They think to go like saints," Proctor said of those he claimed he could not judge, and Miller must have had something of the sort in mind about the writers he refused to discuss. He reasoned, no doubt, that their impulses were noble and that they had sought to do good in the world. We refuse to inform, I believe, either when we decide that those whose names we are asked to reveal are guilty of no wrong or when we perceive that what they have done is no worse than what we ourselves have often done. Wherever their offenses are clearly worse—as in the case of a hit-and-run driver or a spy or a thief—we drop the ban.

If the position taken by Miller were in all cases right, then it would seem wise to supplement the Fifth Amendment with one holding that no man could be required to incriminate another. If this were done, the whole machinery of law enforcement would collapse; it would be simply impossible to determine the facts about a crime. Of course, Congressional committees are not courts, and it might be held that such a rule would be useful in their proceedings. It would be useful only if we wished to destroy the investigative power. For we live, after all, in a community, in the midst of other people, and all of our problems—certainly all of those with which Congress has a legitimate concern—involve others. It is rarely possible to conduct a serious inquiry of any sort without talking about other people and without running the risk of saying something that would hurt them. We can honor the conscience that says "I speak my own sins. I cannot judge another," but those of us who accept any principle of social organization and certainly those of us who believe that our present social order, whatever changes it may stand in need of, is worth preserving cannot make a universal principle of refusing to inform. If any agency of the community is authorized to undertake a serious investigation of any of our common problems, then the identities of others—*names*—are of great importance. What would be the point of investigating, say, industrial espionage if the labor spies subpoenaed refused to identify their employers? What would be the point of investigating the Dixon-Yates contract if it were impossible to learn the identity of the businessmen and government officials involved?

The joker, the source of much present confusion, lies in the matter of *seriousness*. Miller and his attorneys have argued that the names of the writers Miller had known were not relevant to the legislation on passports the Committee was supposed to be studying. This would certainly seem to be the case, and one may regret that Judge McLaughlin did not accept this argument and acquit Miller on the strength of it. Nevertheless, the argument really fudges the central issue, which is that the Committee wasn't really investigating passport abuses at all when it called Miller before it. It was only pretending to do so. The rambling talk of its members with Miller was basically frivolous, and the Un-American Activities Committee has almost always lacked seriousness. In this case, as Mary McCarthy has pointed out, the most that it wanted from Miller was to have him agree to its procedure of testing the good faith of witnesses by their willingness to produce names. It was on this that Miller was morally justified in his refusal.

Still, Miller's principle, the social ethic he was defending, cannot be made a universal rule or a political right. For it is one thing to say in *The New Republic* that a committee is frivolous or mischievous and another to assert before the law that such a judgment gives a witness the right to stand mute without being held in contempt. As matters stand today, Miller was plainly in contempt. At one point in *The Crucible,* John Proctor is called to justify his failure to attend the church of the Reverend Mr. Parris and to have his children baptized by that divine. He replies that he disapproves of the clergyman. "I see no light of God in that man," he says. "That is not for you to decide," he is told. "The man is ordained, therefore the light of God is in him." And this, of course, is the way the world is. In a free society, any one of us may arrive at and freely express a judgment about the competence of duly constituted authority. But in an orderly society, no one of us can expect the protection of the law whenever we decide that a particular authority is unworthy of our cooperation. We may stand by the decision, and we may seek the law's protection, but we cannot expect it as a matter of right. There are many courses of action that may have a sanction in morality and none whatever in law.

Yet the law is intended to be, among other things, a codification of morality, and we cannot be pleased with the thought that a man should be penalized for an act of conscience—even when his conscience may seem not as fully informed by reason as it ought to be. In a much more serious matter, war, we excuse from participation those who say their consciences will permit them no part in it. One of the reasons the order of American society seems worth preserving is that it allows, on the whole, a free play to the individual's moral judgment. In recent years, Congressional committees have posed the largest single threat to this freedom. The issues have often been confused by the bad faith of witnesses on the one hand and committee members on the other. Still and all, the problem is a real one, as the Miller case shows. If there is not sufficient latitude for conscience in the law, then there ought to be. It would be unrealistic, I think, simply to permit anyone who chooses to withhold whatever information he chooses. The Fifth Amendment seems to go as far as is generally justified in this direction. Changes in committee procedures have often been urged, but it is doubtful if much clarification of a problem such as this can be written into rules and by-laws. The problem is essentially one of discretion and measurement; it is, in other words, the most difficult sort of problem and one of the kind that has, customarily, been dealt with by the establishment of broad and morally informed judicial doctrines. It is surely to be hoped that in the several cases, including Arthur Miller's, now in one stage or another of review, the courts will find a way of setting forth a realistic and workable charter for the modern conscience.[1]

---

[1] Editor's note: Miller's conviction was reversed by the U.S. Supreme Court.

4

Crime and Punishment

At the point where other restraints fail to provide security for persons and property from criminal acts, society provides for a penal system. Such a system is intended (a) to deter would-be criminals, (b) to isolate those who have not been deterred, (c) to reform those who are not incorrigible, and (d) to deter them from repeating criminal acts after their release. The purposes of a penal system are thus to deter, to protect where deterrence has failed, to reform or correct. It also serves another purpose, which responsible penologists acknowledge but do not condone: it punishes and thereby vents the wrath of society on those who flout its rules. Although many will argue that an intellectually respectable or morally responsible case for retributive justice can no longer be formulated, in a state like California, where penological practice is quite advanced, responsible officeholders have nevertheless been forced to make concessions to the demand for harsher sentences on dope peddlers.[1] Clearly, the quest for security is inextricably involved with other motives and purposes.

It is almost universally acknowledged that prevailing penal practices are failing to serve as a deterrent. Some 67 percent of federal prisoners have been incarcerated previously. Few—no more than 15 percent—are reformed. The proportions are no doubt similar in state prisons. Most prisoners, when their terms are

---

[1] No less an authority than J. Edgar Hoover has testified before the House Appropriations Committee (May 1959) that "reports on youth crimes have indicated a mounting savagery, a senseless brutality, which leaves little doubt that in the interest of self-preservation, it is now time for sterner measures to be taken by the communities and by the courts."

over, are eventually released into society more hardened and brutalized and potentially more dangerous than they were before. One of our most distinguished jurists, Judge David Bazelon, has said of prisons: "They breed crime. They breed homosexuality. Society is not getting the protection it requires by our present system of punishment, and neither is the prisoner getting the help he needs." Nearly all competent authorities would agree. Why then do we persist in practices that defeat their own purpose? Judge Bazelon's answer is that the community is concerned with *whether* a crime is committed and generally fails to ask *why*.

The community does of course take into account such circumstances as extreme youth, the presence of duress, entrapment, and the like in determining guilt; and long ago England reckoned in a formal way with the question of sanity in the now generally accepted M'Naghten rule, by which most American jurisdictions are also bound.

In brief, the M'Naghten rule declares that the perpetrator of an illegal act may not be found guilty if he was unable at the time of the crime to distinguish between right and wrong. In general, it represents—usually supplemented by the "irresistible impulse" test—the limit to which adherents of the retributive justice school are willing to go in reckoning with mental disease or defect.

It is the gravamen of the now famous Durham rule laid down by Judge Bazelon in *Durham* v. *United States* (1954) that the M'Naghten rule is not only unjust but, as he said in his Brandeis Lecture reproduced below, symptomatic of limitations in our approach to criminal conduct that account for the glaring failures of our whole penal system.

Dr. Karl Menninger, whose comments also appear below, has described the Durham opinion as "more revolutionary in its total effect than the Supreme Court decision regarding segregation." If the Durham rule were to win general acceptance it would greatly restrict the area of responsibility on the basis of which we now dispense "justice." The overwhelming weight of scientific opinion is on its side. Why, if nearly all psychologists and penologists favor Durham, does M'Naghten still prevail? In part, of course, because of fear. In part because society is still more interested in punishment than in correction and cure. But most of all because society is still groping for the point at which to draw a line between the area where an individual must be regarded as responsible for his conduct and the area where he is the victim (or beneficiary) of circumstances over which he had no control. It is to this most difficult of all problems in ethics—defining the line between blame and exculpation, a problem involving ultimately the basic issue of freedom and determinism—that M'Naghten and Durham direct attention.

Objections to Judge Bazelon's opinion in the Durham case have been largely limited to frustrated police and prosecuting attorneys, to incensed citizens whose lazy way of achieving a sense of civic responsibility and moral righteousness consists of denouncing crime and demanding severer penalties, and to moralists genuinely concerned about whether the Durham rule hopelessly confounds the meaning of responsibility as a moral category.

In general, psychiatrists have joined with Dr. Menninger and hailed the Bazelon opinion as marking a breakthrough in the treatment of criminals and a new rapprochement between psychiatry and criminology. For this reason a dissent voiced by an able psychiatrist is noteworthy. Dr. Thomas S. Szasz is no apologist for the M'Naghten rule, which he describes elsewhere as based on myths and as "utterly nonsensical." However, he has questioned whether "modern diagnostic notions will serve any better,"[2] and he has argued at length that "the *application* of scientific knowledge about human feelings, motivation, and behavior is not *necessarily* 'beneficial' for the individual or for mankind."[3]

The foregoing considerations come to a dramatic focus on the issue of capital punishment. Two voices separated by an astronomic social distance provide an unusual contrast in the selections appearing below. The first is that of a distinguished scholar and teacher, Jacques Barzun, who defends capital punishment as a means of ridding society of undesirable elements, and the other is that of Caryl Chessman, who was executed on May 9, 1960, twelve years after he was installed in Death Row and shortly after his last reprieve. In retrospect it is difficult to believe that the fate of one individual with a long record of criminal misbehavior could have occasioned the vast uproar that preceded his execution. In the end, the governor would have commuted Chessman's sentence, but under the laws of California he was powerless to do so.[4] In a last-minute effort to alter the outcome, the governor called the state legislature into special session to

---

[2] "Psychiatric Expert Testimony—Its Covert Meaning and Social Function," *Psychiatry: Journal for the Study of Interpersonal Processes* (August 1957), p. 314.

[3] "Some Observations on the Relationship Between Psychiatry and the Law," *AMA Archives of Neurology and Psychiatry* (March 1956), p. 16.

[4] Chessman was convicted of assault and kidnapping. Assault alone is not a capital crime in California. The kidnapping charge was a strictly "technical" one. The governor may not under California law commute the sentence of a twice-convicted felon without a recommendation from the state supreme court.

consider repeal of capital punishment, at least for a trial period. In doing so he jeopardized his political career. Clearly, the execution of Chessman was no routine act of retribution. The great causes célèbres—Dreyfus, Sacco and Vanzetti, Tom Mooney—had ideological involvements that were completely lacking in the Chessman case. No issue of anti-semitism, radicalism, or the like, was involved in the spontaneous protest against Caryl Chessman's execution. His case was unique because it evoked such worldwide concern over the life of a single person and the moral right of the state to take such a life.

THE DILEMMA OF PUNISHMENT

David L. Bazelon

Judge David L. Bazelon, member of the U.S. Court of Appeals, Washington, D.C., has written more than twenty-five opinions on the insanity defense in criminal cases, of which the Durham opinion is the most famous. The American Psychiatric Association has recognized his work by awarding him a certificate of commendation, declaring that "he has removed massive barriers between the psychiatric and legal professions and opened pathways wherein together they may search for better ways of reconciling human values with social safety." The following are selections from his Brandeis Lecture delivered at Brandeis University in 1960.

. . . In the criminal law, where one might expect the assistance of the behavioral sciences and especially psychiatry to be most eagerly solicited—because most obviously relevant—the fact of the matter is that they are not. . . . I will not burden your patience by recounting again the century-old struggle against the exclusionary M'Naghten Rules. These Rules have dominated the administration of the insanity defense in England and most American jurisdictions. It should suffice to remind you of their continued vitality. The M'Naghten formula emphasizes the rational

From the Louis D. Brandeis Memorial Lecture, Brandeis University, March 14, 1960. Reprinted by permission of Brandeis University.

capacity of the mind, and excuses from criminal responsibility only the individual who at the time of the crime "was laboring under such a defect of reason, from disease of the mind, as not to know" what he was doing or that it was wrong. However this test *might* have been interpreted—volumes have been written on the possible meanings of the words—it has in fact worked to exclude medical evidence. I am almost tempted to say that under M'Naghten practice the psychiatrist appears in the proceeding at all only to testify to the irrelevance of psychiatry—that is, to confirm the irrelevance that "the law" has already decided upon. It assigns to the psychiatric expert in court a sacrificial role in a ritual of condemnation. The expert is asked a question which—most leaders of the profession inform us—cannot be answered within the terms of their discipline. And unless the Rules are breached—as they frequently are on the trial level— the psychiatrist is not encouraged or permitted to address himself to the clinical questions which are the only ones he is truly expert in answering.

That is the scientific expert testifying at the trial level. But on appeal, you may ask, have there been no "Brandeis briefs" setting forth the relevant facts and insights of modern scientific psychiatry? Yes, for example many psychiatric works were referred to in the appellant's brief in the *Durham* case, which, as many of you know, resulted in the adoption in the District of Columbia of a broadened insanity test—a rule designed to relax the rigors of M'Naghten and to welcome genuine psychiatric testimony presented in its own terms. The Durham test simply asks whether the accused was suffering from a mental disease or defect, and inquires as to the relation between any such condition and the criminal act. . . .

In the administration of the criminal law today, we desperately need all the help we can get from modern behavioral scientists—before trial, during trial, and after trial. The law by itself, without these workers, is cast in the hopeless role of a socially isolated, traditional bulwark against the welter of personal, social and economic forces which create today's problem of crime and the so-called criminal population. And in this losing struggle, the law—by which I mean police, judges, lawyers, and prison guards—would have at its disposal a limited set of concepts honored largely by time alone. In brief, the law would have the *lex talionis*—the idea of retributive punishment based on absolute moral principles of purportedly universal application. *By itself,* the law would dispose of both the problem of crime and the criminal himself with the one idea of punishment. The "program" would be: Repress crime and all antisocial behavior by punishment alone; rehabilitate the offender by punishment alone; achieve social understanding of wrongdoing and the wrongdoer by the sole mechanical response—"Punish them—they deserve it!"

If the foregoing remarks seem intemperate, that is of course because they do *not* describe our actual system of criminal law administration. For one thing, stern retributive justice has always been tempered by mercy and forgiveness—by the ubiquitous impulse to afford the transgressor a "second chance." This happens in practice even when it is not allowed by theory. We simply find it too difficult, too non-human to punish, punish, punish—even though we may hold most seriously the moral imperative to punish, and even though our feeling is that we are wrong when we do not. And for another thing, the behavioral scientists—along with their facts, ideas, and methodology—have as a matter of fact intervened increasingly at many stages of the administrative process. Social workers, clinicians, welfare agencies, even the police, as well as many others, attempt to deal constructively with the juvenile delinquent before he is sent to a reformatory to begin his professional training as the criminal of the future. The psychiatrist comes to court and sometimes his presence there *does* have something other than a ritualistic effect on the outcome of the proceeding. . . .

So clearly our criminal system is a very mixed affair—some would say a very *mixed-up* affair. But things are happening, there is agitation and movement, much heat and a certain amount of light. To put it simply, it is a system in transition. We are, painfully and slowly, coming to a clearer understanding of alternatives and necessities. . . .

If our system is in transition, then the question properly arises—Transition from what to what? From M'Naghten to Durham? Hardly. Certainly *from* M'Naghten—but not *just* from that ritualistic phrase, except perhaps symbolically. And Durham—even viewed as a concept, as an approach, which is the way I prefer to view it, rather than nineteen words of a jury instruction—is merely one way of welcoming the psychiatrist into the courtroom. It is a beginning, not an ending—and it relates to the insanity defense, which is only [the] visible one-ninth of the iceberg.

I believe that the deeper part of the iceberg consists of the retributive urge to punish irrespective of effect, and the accompanying intellectual justification of this primitive urge, the so-called theory of deterrence. A deep emotion and a complicated rationalization. . . .

Wherever one turns in an effort at reform in the treatment of offenders, one comes up against this need to punish and its defense by the theory of deterrence. Of course there are many other arguments put forward at various times in justification of the present system, with its great emphasis on punishment for its own sake or punishment as the answer to all problems. For example, both Judge Learned Hand in this country and Lord Justice Denning in England—the first sadly and the latter more firmly—have referred to the *public's* demand that the sinner shall suffer. Judge Hand stated that he did "not share that feeling, which is a vestige . . . of very ancient primitive and irrational beliefs and emotions." Lord Justice Denning spoke more strongly by saying:

> It is a mistake to consider the objects of punishment as being deterrent or reformative or preventive, and nothing else. . . . The truth is that some crimes are so outrageous that society insists on adequate punishment, because the wrongdoer deserves it, irrespective of whether it is a deterrent or not.

I can assure you that similar views are frequently expressed from the bench in courts throughout our land—and often enough when the crime is no more "outrageous" than juvenile car-theft. Sometimes the court in relieving itself of these sentiments will refer to society's demand for retribution—communicated to the court by some unknown intermediary, or perhaps so obvious as not to require communication. On other occasions a court will abandon that rhetorical flourish and speak directly, saying—"You are going to be punished good and proper because you deserve it, and because too many of you hoodlums have been getting away with it."

So it is still the need to punish that confronts us—although at times not *my* need, but somebody else's. All this, as Judge Hand suggests, is highly irrational. I am sure that we must recognize this irrational need as a social fact, but I cannot see that we must abandon attempts at reform because of it. After all, that public out there that needs to punish also needs to forgive—and it especially needs to be given, for its own protection and well-being, the most rationally effective administration we can devise for it. It is not getting it now. The excessive emphasis on punishment, with the consequent neglect of genuine rehabilitation, is accompanied by a disastrously high level of recidivism. In the relatively progressive Federal Prison System, for example, the rate increased between 1949 and 1958 from 61 percent to 67 percent. In this same period, the number of serious offenders who have had two or more previous commitments has grown from 39 percent to 46 percent. Please realize what these figures mean: In two-thirds of the cases, punishment neither reforms nor deters the individual who has served one sentence. And with those who have served a second sentence, it fails again in nearly half of the cases. . . .

This being the case, why such persistent, irrational emphasis on punishment? I think one thing is the deep childish fear that with any reduction of punishment, multitudes would run amok. It seems to me this fear must be based on exaggerated notions of the role of punishment when we were children. The reasoning is: We are good adults because we were punished when we were bad children; any adult who is bad should get some more of what we got when we were children. *"They"* must be punished to reconfirm our adulthood and our goodness—to distinguish us from them. But most of us who have been good for many years—or at least haven't been caught—have not maintained our high estate because of witnessing frequent public hangings and whippings or stopping to observe a malefactor being drawn-and-quartered on the corner of a busy intersection. Quite the opposite. According to the famous Warden Lawes of Sing Sing

Prison, this is especially true of the prosecutors and judges who so zealously take upon themselves the rhetorical burden of carrying out society's need to punish. He sent invitations to the appropriate officers of the law to attend each of the 114 executions carried out at Sing Sing while he was warden. Not one ever found time to attend.

Perhaps one should be encouraged by the fact that the modern urge to punish is no longer so immediately personal. I suppose we should all be pleased by the recent report from Saudi Arabia announcing an important reform in criminal law administration—that hereafter a thief's hand will be cut off by an "expert surgeon" using anesthetics rather than by an amateur with a hatchet. An accompanying reform is that adulteresses will no longer be stoned to death, as in biblical times. As Saudi Arabia enters the modern world, they will now be shot.

So there is something like progress in these matters. I would remind you that not half a century before the M'Naghten Rules were enunciated, more than 200 crimes were punishable by death in England. It is interesting to speculate as to whether England could possibly have become the civilized place it is today if the number of capital crimes had not been reduced. But Lord Justice Denning still believes in punishment for its own sake—or still believes that society believes in it. . . .

. . . what has to be explained—and finally understood—is the really frightening scope of the irrationality of our notions and practices regarding punishment. It seems that we just do not know how to be practical about the matter. For example, most of us, I imagine, have achieved major control over our own aggressive and vindictive impulses. We would be revolted to watch a hanging or a beating, and even more to participate in one. When we are personally called upon to administer punishment or any form of serious deprivation, we take the task as a heavy duty and think very hard to make certain that we do no more and no less than we feel to be necessary and effective in the circumstances. This would be so in the disciplining of our own children or any subordinates. But when it comes to the administration of crime, we hand the whole matter over to a distant bureaucratic machine, and we want to hear no more about it. Our attitude is—"Let the State take care of them."

In other words, our personal resolution of the issue of vindictiveness seems to be achieved at the cost of our human capacity to identify with the offender. Isn't it strange that the criminal law tradition which not so long ago was based on the supposedly deterrent spectacle of public punishment has come full circle and now can be said to be based in effect on the distance and even the secrecy of actual punishment? I wonder how many in this audience have ever seen the inside of a prison? What you would see there can be justified only on the assumption that the prisoners are less than human, and that therefore the obviously de-humanizing process they are undergoing is appropriate for them. Because they have stolen property or committed acts of violence, they are outside the pale of human society, and that is the end of the matter. But of course after having further brutalized them, after having failed to deal with the causes of their behavior, and having failed to effect any serious rehabilitation, we then release them into society where they can experience their second or third or fourth opportunity to fail. As Karl Menninger has said, these people are failures first and "criminals" later. To be a criminal is not strictly speaking merely to have committed a crime—it is a social branding plus penitentiary training, all of which serves only to confirm the initial personal failure which led to the first antisocial act. (As I speak of crime and the criminal tonight, I should emphasize that I am thinking of the delinquent car-thief, the mugger, the amateur burglar and the armed robber, the sex offender, and the man who commits assault and other crimes of violence—my attention is not directed toward the special problems represented by the criminal elite consisting of competent professionals, the organization men of the syndicates, or the whole separate area of white-collar crime.)

It is as if society cooperates with certain human beings who are social failures to create this object called the criminal. Our present system of punishment is an essential part of *this* process, not of any process that can be called reforming or rehabilitative. Why does society go to all the trouble and expense of creating this special class of human beings? I think chiefly because we really do not comprehend what we are doing, because we do not want to deal with the facts of social failure to begin with, and because we are not prepared to follow out the logic of our attitude and "dispose" of these failures outright. There results a sort of half-way house, neither disposal nor rehabilitation, but a new class of human beings to mirror society's confusion on the profound issue of failure in the educative process—and reliance on punishment to cure or cover over all such failure.

What I am suggesting is that the criminal serves as a "scapegoat." And this as much as anything is impeding obvious and sorely needed reform in the treatment of offenders. I use the word "scapegoat" in the specific sense in which it has become a key term in the psycho-sociological analysis of prejudice. That is, a deeply held, unrealistic, projective image of a minority group indulged by members of a dominant group. The essential fact in this form of prejudiced perception is that the member of the dominant group refuses ordinary, human one-to-one identification with representatives of the minority group, sometimes for lack of opportunity, sometimes because of a deeper unwillingness. . . .

Another point to be understood about punishment is that it is not a universal solvent. Different people react differently to it. This is perfectly obvious with regard to children, and needs no elaboration. Our response to punishment is like anything else we learn; some learn better than others, and some learn the same lesson differently than others. In this broad sense, the criminal is the person who has been miseducated with respect to punishment and the threat of punishment. His re-education must consist of something in addition to just more of the same, more punishment. To conceive otherwise would be like giving harder and harder lessons in algebra to a student who has already evidenced his inability to absorb the basic lessons. Only an incompetent teacher, a man of ill-will or one with very limited resources, would go about destroying a student in such a fashion. But that is just what we do with so many people who, if they had had the proper capacity to respond to punishment, would not have gotten into trouble in the first place. We do just the wrong thing by confirming all of their wrong feelings about punishment. And so we create a class of hopelessly recidivistic criminals. . . .

I would not want to leave you with the impression that I am opposed to all measures of punishment, or deprivation. It seems super-fluous to state that I recognize their necessity, but perhaps I had better do so because thinking in this field tends to be characterized by an either-or, all-or-nothing attitude. It is just this attitude which I object to and from which I wish to dissociate myself. Let me illustrate its unfortunate effects. When the *Durham* case was decided in the District of Columbia, a great hue and cry was raised that great numbers of vicious criminals would soon be roaming the streets of the city. Nothing could have been more off the mark, as subsequent events have shown. But at the time many people felt that *either* offenders are punished by execution or a penitentiary term, *or* they in effect get off scotfree—that *all* of them must be punished and just punished, or *nothing* would be done to protect society against them. . . . The Court now requires a positive instruction to the effect that the defendant acquitted by reason of insanity will be put in a mental institution until cured and judicially determined to be no longer a danger to himself or others. Such commitments, incidentally, may continue for a longer term than would have been served in a penitentiary for the offense charged. They are clearly a deprivation, a negative sanction—and in this sense a "punishment"—but with the very important difference that it is not retributive, it is no more than may be necessary, and it is punishment subordinate to the purpose of rehabilitation.

. . . Some people seem to feel that whenever trained workers including psychiatric therapists supplement the work of police and prison guards, or play any independent role at all, the offender will be molly-coddled and consequently society's bulwark against crime will crumble. This is nonsense, but the attitude persists. Dr. Melitta Schmideberg of the Association for the Psychiatric Treatment of Offenders is one of the most devoted and distinguished workers in her field. I am not competent to underwrite the validity of her views, but she is a richly experienced ther-apist in this special and rather neglected area of treatment. She believes in a strongly directive therapy, and in the course thereof gives practical recognition to the fact that the threat of loss of liberty—of going to jail or going back to jail—plays an important part in her work with probationed offenders or repeaters. This threat is an ever-present backdrop to her efforts to help the patient get along with his probation officer, to stop breaking the law, to get a job and hold it, and so on. She feels that—"Fear of punishment and guilt keep normal people in check, but an overdose of anxiety can react in the opposite direction on criminals." She states the problem as follows: "If the therapist condemns the offender out and out, he cannot treat him; if he condones his offense, he cannot change him." This is certainly not a mollycoddling approach. On the other hand, she objects eloquently to the psychological effect on offenders of a period in the usual penitentiary. She feels one of the most imperative uses of therapy is to help the ex-convict overcome the effects of prison! Now does it strike anyone here as sensible to deny early treatment of first offenders, send them to a penitentiary where their dangerous problems will be dangerously augmented, and then end up with an infinitely more difficult problem-personality to deal with later on?

Why do we do it? Why do we treat offenders this way? . . . any satisfactory answer will be found to lie very deep indeed—probably at the core of man's inhumanity to man, in each of us and in the history of all of us. . . .

But when we transcend our emotional urge to punish, and begin to think seriously about crime and the criminal without such undue reliance on the one idea of punishment, we very shortly come right up against an intellectually much more formidable barrier. And that is the ubiquitous theory of deterrence. On the intellectual level, it turns out to be the greatest barrier to progress in the criminal law.

This theory proposes that actual malefactors be punished in order to deter potential malefactors. In its pure form, it is willing to assume arguendo that punishment may not reform and may even damage the particular individual being punished. But this unfortunate person must be sacrificed to the common good—he must be punished as an example to all, to keep all the rest of us from committing his crime. Of course the theory is not always stated in this pure form. Indeed, there is a common confusion which you may notice in arguments based on the premise of deterrence—a confusion between deterrence of the person being punished and deterrence of all others. Now clearly the convicted prisoner was not deterred by the prior punishment of others from committing the crime which placed him in prison. And to speak of deterring him from committing another offense later takes us back to the previous discussion of the effectiveness of punishment, and concerns rehabilitation not deterrence. So the theory, properly considered, involves only the justification of punishment because of its show-effect, its supposed effect on others. I need not labor the point that the individual so used is a scapegoat, a sacrificial victim. This is an admitted feature of the theory.

Logically, of course, the more we witness the pains of punishment, the more apt they would be actually to deter us from crime. (That is, if active fear deters.) Originally, this logic was a part of the deterrence theory. But in our day it is not. To illustrate this I would like to quote from the 1953 Report of the Royal Commission on Capital Punishment:

> In the first half of the nineteenth century executions still took place in public. This indeed was thought to be an essential part of the deterrent value of the death penalty. But public executions, "though the publicity was deterrent in intention . . . became in practice a degrading form of popular entertainment, which could serve only to deprave the minds of the spectators."

Parliament ended the practice in 1868. The Report also suggests that the method of hanging was invented and found favor because of its "advertisement value." But at the hearings before the Commission, "witness after witness" defended hanging because it was the most humane method of execution! The Report notes this "surprising inversion" succinctly as follows:

> Thus a method of execution whose special merit was formerly thought to be that it was peculiarly degrading is now defended on the ground that it is uniquely humane.

So clearly the deterrence theory is not quite so logical as it used to be. (And just as well!) . . .

A common argument offered in support of deterrence is this: The ordinary citizen would not obey traffic signals if sanctions were not imposed on all drivers for breach of the rules. This argument, please notice, depends for its persuasiveness on a supposed identity between a traffic violation, on the one hand, and murder, assault, and grand theft, on the other—all these being "breach of the rules." Although I suppose they all do come under this category, the empirical differences are more impressive to me than the abstract similarity. But more important, because of the preconditioning of licensing, the persons to whom traffic rules are addressed are a select group to begin with: Those who are incompetent to conform to the rules, for whatever reasons, are weeded out before the sanction system is applied. And that is an important point. Although traffic rules have very little moral force behind them, the system works tolerably well just because reliance is not placed solely on sanctions, but also on the judgment of competence.

I think we all understand that the maintenance of public order must be backed up by a system of sanctions . . . deprivations . . . *punishments,* if you please. Neither law nor morality can sustain itself, from generation to generation, without the threat of some form of punishment. But the difficult point to be comprehended here is that the system requires the *threat* of punishment, not punishment itself. An internal control system generated by our mores and received beliefs keeps most of us from stealing. For those who require external controls, it is the threat of going to jail, not actual time spent there, that keeps them from stealing. Actual sanctions are needed—as far as the system is concerned—only to give substance to the threat, to keep it from being reduced to impotence. The problem really posed by the question of deterrence is, how much actual punishment—and what kind of actual punishment—is required in order to sustain the threat of punishment at an effective level? Or, stated inversely—now looking at the problem from the point of view of the individual rather than the system—how much non-punishment, how much besides punishment, can be allowed in treatment of the individual without inviting a breakdown of the system of sanctions?

I do not propose to solve this problem [now], even stated in such fashion. . . . But I do want to conclude with a few observations about this critical and perplexing question. First of all, I believe that in the absence of decisive empirical data, we should take a developmental approach. That is, we should view the issue historically and not assume that any particular status quo is ultimate and unalterable. I will confess that I am subjectively distrustful of many ponderous proponents of deterrence who answer the question, how much punishment is necessary, with the quick reply, exactly as much as we now have. And those who use the necessity of deterrence to justify the scandal of our prison system, also earn my suspicion.

Some people have argued in favor of the M'Naghten ritual on the grounds of a deterrent effect—that the mentally ill offender should not be recognized as such and treated as such because to do so would encourage crime and perhaps even mental illness. This argument I consider beneath contempt. The M'Naghten Rules were adopted twenty-five years before the English saw fit to do away with public hangings. . . . Why I wonder, are these Rules considered still necessary to deter crime, when public hangings and capital punishment for petty offenses are not? And if M'Naghten is so necessary for this purpose, why do the same people justify it by reminding us that trial courts frequently ignore it?

To sum up briefly: Punishment has a role to play in the education and re-education of the individual. The threat of some form of deprivation is of course essential in the functioning of any moral or legal system—and the threat must have substance. But these basic requirements of the criminal law have been used—I will say misused—to justify the present system which contains a preposterous predominance of senseless punitive elements. The theory of deterence, as too frequently applied, results in degrading the individual for a purported social purpose—contrary to the democratic ethos and with no convincing evidence that the purpose is promoted. In doing so, in casting the individual offender in the role of a scapegoat, it begs the entire question of justice. And while no socio-legal system can reach a perfect incarnation of justice, none can survive in the hearts of the people which by-passes or does not engage the issue seriously.

If we were not so set on punishing the offender for the sake of punishment, if we did not justify this practice by reference to its deterrent effect, we could understand that rehabilitation lies at the spiritual heart of any vital moral system. The alternative can only be destructiveness. Even the violent corporal punishments of the past were designed to rehabilitate the wrongdoer's soul, which was held to be of much greater concern than his body. In our secular age, we have lost sight of this spiritual truth. But we still punish—without hope of reformation, without belief in saving the soul by damning the earthly body. And our entire moral system necessarily suffers thereby.

Would it really be the end of the world if all jails were turned into hospitals, or "Rehabilitation Centers"? The offender would then—just as the committed mental patient is today—be deprived of his dearest possession, his personal liberty. "Punishment" enough, I should think—to satisfy our punitive urge and to induce a deterrent fear. The offender's purpose in such a Rehabilitation Center would be to change his personality, his very style of responding to life. I would like to suggest, quite seriously, that the effort toward such a personal alteration is the greatest sanction of them all. To make this is indeed the true command of all religion and all morality. And it is the normal law-abiding person's most profound and continuous "punishment." The difference between the offender or the mental patient and the rest of us happily normal citizens, is that "they" have a special problem and need special help in living up to society's expectations. A few of us have had "special problems" in the course of our lives but were lucky enough to get the help we needed, or strong enough to get by on our own. We are entitled to congratulate ourselves on the superiority of our endowment or good fortune—but not, I think, to celebrate our triumphs by degrading our less fortunate neighbors. Is it in any way necessary for our own benefit to perpetuate the shame of our penitentiaries—where a youthful offender, having been processed through the homosexual auction block, will be taught the ways of crime and perversity by a hardened expert? . . .

Among the many serious issues I have not discussed, . . . prominent mention should be made of the current and future limits of that omnibus grouping called the behavioral sciences. How much of their promise is valid hope, how much wishful thinking? We can only find out by trying—by experimenting. Take the question of psychiatric "treatment," for example. It seems clear that new, more sophisticated techniques will have to be developed with more pointed relevance to the problems of offenders. But where are the experimental clinics, where are the budgets to attract competent staff, where is the administrative approach that would welcome and facilitate this urgent work? Blocked, I have suggested, by the belief in punishment. Many critics of the reforming attitude in criminal law adminstration fear the unknown contours of a future dominated by the experimental ideas of rehabilitation. Reformers may share some of these fears, but they are motivated even more by fear of the consequences of continuing our present practices. For example, I am deeply disturbed by the whole question of the indeterminacy of the period of incarceration, which is a very serious problem today and will undoubtedly grow in importance as reforms favoring rehabilitation are instituted. The image of one class of experts administering the lives of another class of "unfortunates" has some very disquieting aspects. I comfort myself with the thought that images of the future are frequently discomforting, and that early surgery, for example, was probably greeted with the same disquiet. . . .

Perhaps we can take comfort that new problems have a way of begetting new solutions and that, in this instance, solutions may be found which are consonant with our traditional concern for civil liberties. I, for one, have no intention of ushering in permanent incarceration for behavior not seriously dangerous to society. . . .

Crime and criminals belong very much to their particular time and place. They grow out of very specific social settings. Moreover, any system of sanctions and any system of rehabilitation applies to and within a society, it does not substitute for one. And these systems cannot be much better than the society in which they exist. On the other hand, they should not be worse.

THERAPY, NOT PUNISHMENT

Karl Menninger, M.D.

Dr. Karl Menninger is one of America's most distinguished psychiatrists, with headquarters at the famous Menninger Clinic in Topeka, Kansas. His is the psychiatrist's verdict on the principles enunciated by Judge Bazelon in the Durham case. Dr. Menninger has written The Human Mind (*1930*), Man against Himself (*1938*), *and* Love against Hate (*1942*).

. . . On the other hand most lawyers have no really clear idea of the way in which a psychiatrist functions or of the basic concepts to which he adheres. They cannot understand, for example, why there is no such thing (for psychiatrists) as "insanity." Most lawyers have no conception of the meaning or methods of psychiatric case study and diagnosis. They seem to think that psychiatrists can take a quiet look at a suspect, listen to a few anecdotes about him, and thereupon be able to say, definitely, that the awful "it"—the dreadful miasma of madness, the loathsome affliction of "insanity"—is present or absent. Because we all like to please, some timid psychiatrists fall in with this fallacy of the lawyers and go through these preposterous antics.

It is true that almost any offender—like anyone else—when questioned for a short time, even by the most skillful psychiatrist, can make responses and display behavior patterns which will indicate that he is enough like the rest of us to.be called "sane." But a barrage of questions is not a psychiatric examination. Modern scientific personality study depends upon various specialists—physical, clinical, and sociological as well as psychological. It takes into consideration not only static and presently observable factors, but dynamic and historical factors, and factors of environmental interaction and change. It also looks into the future for correction, re-education, and prevention.

Hence, the same individuals who appear so normal to superficial observation are frequently discovered in the course of prolonged, intensive scientific study to have tendencies regarded as "deviant," "peculiar," "unhealthy," "sick," "crazy," "senseless," "irrational," "insane."

But now you may ask, "Is it not possible to find such tendencies in

---

From "Verdict Guilty—Now What?" in *Harper's Magazine* (August 1959), pp. 63–64. Reprinted by permission of the author.

any individual if one looks hard enough? And if this is so, if we are all a little crazy or potentially so, what is the essence of your psychiatric distinctions? Who is it that you want excused?"

And here is the crux of it all. We psychiatrists don't want *anyone* excused. In fact, psychiatrists are much more concerned about the protection of the public than are the lawyers. I repeat; psychiatrists don't want anyone excused, certainly not anyone who shows antisocial tendencies. We consider them all responsible, which lawyers do not. And we want the prisoner to take on that responsibility, or else deliver it to someone who will be concerned about the protection of society and about the prisoner, too. We don't want anyone excused, but neither do we want anyone stupidly disposed of, futilely detained, or prematurely released. We don't want them tortured, either sensationally with hot irons or quietly by long-continued and forced idleness. In the psychiatrist's mind nothing should be done in the name of punishment, though he is well aware that the offender may regard either the diagnostic procedure or the treatment or the detention incident to the treatment as punitive. But this is in *his* mind, not in the psychiatrist's mind. And in our opinion it should not be in the public's mind, because it is an illusion.

It is true that we psychiatrists consider that all people have potentialities for antisocial behavior. The law assumes this, too. Most of the time most people control their criminal impulses. But for various reasons and under all kinds of circumstances some individuals become increasingly disorganized or demoralized, and then they begin to be socially offensive. The man who does criminal things is less convincingly disorganized than the patient who "looks" sick, because the former more nearly resembles the rest of us, and seems to be indulging in acts that we have struggled with and controlled. So we get hot under the collar about the one and we call him "criminal" whereas we pityingly forgive the other and call him "lunatic." But a surgeon uses the same principles of surgery whether he is dealing with a "clean" case, say some cosmetic surgery on a face, or a "dirty" case which is foul-smelling and offensive. What we are after is results and the emotions of the operator must be under control. Words like "criminal" and "insane" have no place in the scientific vocabulary any more than pejorative adjectives like "vicious," "psychopathic," "bloodthirsty," etc. The need is to find all the *descriptive* adjectives that apply to the case, and this is a scientific job—not a popular exercise in name-calling. Nobody's insides are very beautiful; and in the cases that require social control there has been a great wound and some of the insides are showing.

Intelligent judges all over the country are increasingly surrendering the onerous responsibility of deciding in advance what a man's conduct will be in a prison and how rapidly his wicked impulses will evaporate there.

With more use of the indeterminate sentence and the establishment of scientific diagnostic centers, we shall be in a position to make progress in the science of *treating* antisocial trends. Furthermore, we shall get away from the present legal smog that hangs over the prisons, which lets us detain with heartbreaking futility some prisoners fully rehabilitated while others, whom the prison officials know full well to be dangerous and unemployable, must be released, *against our judgment,* because a judge far away (who has by this time forgotten all about it) said that five years was enough. In my frequent visits to prisons I am always astonished at how rarely the judges who have prescribed the "treatment" come to see whether or not it is effective. What if doctors who sent their seriously ill patients to hospitals never called to see them!

As more states adopt diagnostic centers directed toward getting the prisoners *out* of jail and back to work, under modern, well-structured parole systems, the taboo on jail and prison, like that on state hospitals, will begin to diminish. Once it was a lifelong disgrace to have been in either. Lunatics, as they were cruelly called, were feared and avoided. Today only the ignorant retain this phobia. Cancer was then considered a *shameful* thing to have, and victims of it were afraid to mention it, or have it correctly treated, because they did not want to be disgraced. The time will come when offenders, much as we disapprove of their offenses, will no longer be unemployable untouchables.

To a physician discussing the wiser treatment of our fellow men it seems hardly necessary to add that under no circumstances should we kill them. It was never considered right for doctors to kill their patients, no matter how hopeless their condition. True, some patients in state institutions have undoubtedly been executed without benefit of sentence. They were a nuisance, expensive to keep and dangerous to release. Various people took it upon themselves to put an end to the matter, and I have even heard them boast of it. The Hitler regime had the same philosophy.

But in most civilized countries today we have a higher opinion of the rights of the individual and the limits to the state's power. We know, too, that for the most part the death penalty is inflicted upon obscure, impoverished, defective, and friendless individuals. We know that it intimidates juries in their efforts to determine guilt without prejudice. We know that it is being eliminated in one state after another, most recently Delaware.[1] We know that in practice it has almost disappeared—for over seven thousand capital crimes last year there were less than one hundred executions. But vast sums of money are still being spent—let us say wasted—in legal contests to determine whether or not an individual, even

---

[1] Editor's note: Although Delaware abolished the death penalty for all crimes in 1958, it reintroduced the death penalty for murder in 1961.

one known to have been mentally ill, is now healthy enough for the state to hang him. (I am informed that such a case has recently cost the State of California $400,000!)

Most of all, we know that no state employees—except perhaps some that ought to be patients themselves—want a job on the killing squad, and few wardens can stomach this piece of medievalism in their own prisons. For example, two officials I know recently quarreled because each wished to have the hanging of a prisoner carried out on the other's premises.

Capital punishment is, in my opinion, morally wrong. It has a bad effect on everyone, especially those involved in it. It gives a false sense of security to the public. It is vastly expensive. Worst of all it beclouds the entire issue of motivation in crime, which is so importantly relevant to the question of what to do for and with the criminal that will be most constructive to society as a whole. Punishing—and even killing—criminals may yield a kind of grim gratification; let us all admit that there are times when we are so shocked at the depredations of an offender that we persuade ourselves that this is a man the Creator didn't intend to create, and that we had better help correct the mistake. But playing God in this way has no conceivable moral or scientific justification. . . .

We, the agents of society, must move to end the game of tit-for-tat and blow-for-blow in which the offender has foolishly and futilely engaged himself and us. We are not driven, as he is, to wild and impulsive actions. With knowledge comes power, and with power there is no need for the frightened vengeance of the old penology. In its place should go a quiet, dignified, therapeutic program for the rehabilitation of the disorganized one, if possible, the protection of society during his treatment period, and his guided return to useful citizenship, as soon as this can be effected.

A PSYCHIATRIST DISSENTS FROM DURHAM

Thomas S. Szasz, M.D.

Dr. Szasz was a staff member of the Institute for Psycho-analysis, Chicago, and when the following article was written, a member of the Department of Psychiatry, State University of New York. His Ethics of Psychoanalysis *and* Psychiatric Justice *both appeared in 1965.*

The following brief comments are intended to call attention to what I believe are inroads of serious import which organized psychiatry is making into the area of civil liberties. The significance of this encroachment transcends the specialized interests of psychiatry and jurisprudence, for it involves the most basic value of Anglo-American democracy, namely, the worth of the individual's autonomy and dignity. Cast in the context of current political and social events, it would seem that what the Western democracies can put against the claims of opposing ideologies is not a high standard of living; nor is it the abstract notions of free enterprise, capitalism, or even the Christian ethic. What democracies, and *only* democracies, possess, and what can not be imitated by other ideologies—without themselves becoming democracies—is respect for the dignity and autonomy of the individual. Stripped of proud adjectives, this simply means that people must be taken seriously for what they do; and this implies holding them accountable for their actions.

Having argued elsewhere that psychiatric testimony concerning mental illness (as presently conceived) is distracting to judicial proceedings, and that acquittal from a criminal charge by reason of insanity followed by commitment to a mental hospital constitutes a serious infringement of a person's civil liberties, I shall turn, without further comment, to a recent case to illustrate and add to the points made previously.

The case is that of Miss Edith L. Hough. The following are the salient facts, as abstracted from the records of her appeal to the U.S. Court of Appeals for the District of Columbia Circuit. On May 30, 1957, Miss Hough shot and killed a male friend who came to call on her to express his sympathy over the recent death of her father. The next day she was ordered to St. Elizabeths Hospital for determination of her competency to stand

From *The Journal of Nervous and Mental Disease* (July 1960), pp. 58–63. Copyright © 1960, The Williams & Wilkins Co., Baltimore, Md. 21202, U.S.A. Reprinted by permission.

trial. She was subsequently found incompetent to stand trial and was committed to the hospital until restoration of her competency. In May, 1958, she was declared competent. She was tried for her offense—first degree murder—on July 10, 1958, and was acquitted by reason of insanity. She was then committed to St. Elizabeths Hospital.

On October 20, 1958, the Superintendent of St. Elizabeths Hospital filed in the District Court a certificate stating in part:

> Miss Hough has now recovered sufficiently to be granted her conditional release from Saint Elizabeths Hospital pursuant to section 927 (e) of Public Law 313.

The District Court denied conditional release, whereupon the "patient" appealed to a higher court seeking reversal of this decision. The U.S. Court of Appeals for the District of Columbia Circuit heard the case and, on September 14, 1959, affirmed the decision of the lower court. In hearing the appeal, psychiatric testimony was obtained from Doctors Benjamin Karpman and Winfred Overholser, and judicial opinions were rendered by Judges David Bazelon and Wilbur K. Miller. In the context of decision-making in an actual, real-life situation, the opinions and actions of the various participants become clearer than any statement, concerning psychiatry and law, that could be made in the abstract. My comments will be based on testimony and opinion recorded in the transcript of the decision rendered by the Appellate Court.

The first point on which I shall comment is the problem of acquitting a person of a crime and then committing him. Once he is acquitted, he must be considered (legally) innocent. If he is not so considered, the word "acquittal" and the deed it designates will lose their customary meanings.

Commitment of the insane—a complex, and in my opinion, highly questionable procedure as presently practiced—must now be scrutinized. Courts are legally empowered to commit people to mental hospitals, provided that certain conditions obtain. Illustrative is the case of a person who manifests such behavior as is considered patently deranged in our culture. A young man, for example, may become increasingly withdrawn and uncommunicative; he may stop eating and start masturbating in the presence of others. Sooner or later in the course of these events, the patient's family would very likely seek the aid of a physician (who may or may not be a psychiatrist). The latter would then make out the necessary papers *certifying* that the patient is in need of involuntary hospitalization. Finally, the judge under whose jurisdiction this matter falls would, in the ordinary course of events, order the patient *committed*.

Another type of situation in which people might be committed as mentally ill has traditionally been associated with the general area of criminal behavior. Without entering into the complexities of this matter, I wish to note only that according to the Durham Rule and its implementations, persons charged with offenses but acquitted by reason of insanity are committed to St. Elizabeths Hospital. If this practice were to be carried out *seriously* such persons would have to be treated as if they were *bona fide innocent.* This is required by the fact that they have been tried and have been pronounced *"not guilty* (by reason of insanity)." While the court has the right to order commitment, once a patient has been committed he comes under the jurisdiction of the hospital authorities. Hospital psychiatrists should be able to release the patient should they wish to do so. In cases of ordinary civil commitment, the court has no jurisdiction over the actions of the hospital staff vis-à-vis patients. To be more exact, the courts do have a say concerning hospital-patient relationships even in such cases, but this is essentially limited to giving the patient freedom. In other words, if the patient wishes to be released from the hospital over the opposition of the psychiatrists, he can, by availing himself of the appropriate legal safeguards, *e.g., habeas corpus,* enlist the aid of the court to gain his freedom. The reverse of this does not obtain! Should the hospital wish to release the patient, the court cannot interfere and keep the patient confined. It can not do this simply because commitment is legally justified—and this shows how poor this justification really is—by the psychiatric testimony of the physicians involved. Hence, if they (*i.e.,* the state hospital physicians) testify that the patient is sane, how can the court commit?

In the present case, it is to be noted that the court had the power not only to commit but also to regulate the patient's movements in and out of the hospital. This was in accord with a statute of the District of Columbia (D.C. Code #24.301 (e) Supp. VII, 1959). This meant, in effect, that the hospital functioned as an arm of the court. It had no real autonomy, but was merely a subordinate body to the superordinate power of the courts. If a hospital superintendent and his staff can not discharge a patient from their "hospital" when they wish, then, I submit, they are but the functionaries of those who do have the power to make this decision.

All this points to the fact that hospitals functioning in such a fashion are, in fact, jails. But we can go further than this, for jails have a high degree of regulatory autonomy over their inmates. Parole boards, for example, can decide—within certain legally set limits—when prisoners may be released. The courts, once having passed sentence, can not interfere in this process. The regulations governing the release of mental patients from St. Elizabeths Hospital thus give the staff of this institution *less* jurisdiction over (some of) its "patients" than have jails over their prisoners.

We must infer from this that the courts, after having relinquished their responsibility to the psychiatrists for judging and sentencing criminals, have turned around and have arrogated to themselves the responsibilities of physicians and psychiatrists. This conclusion must be drawn from the fact that the courts take it upon themselves to decide when a person—

officially designated a "patient," and one who has been acquitted of a criminal charge in a duly conducted trial, and is therefore "innocent"—may or may not be released from a place called "hospital." As matters now stand, psychiatric testimony in criminal trials—to the effect that the accused is mentally ill—makes it virtually unnecessary to have juries and judges, for acquittal follows almost automatically. Similarly, judicial authority of the type considered makes it virtually unnecessary, for patients of *this type* at least, to have psychiatrists and psychotherapists in mental hospitals—for it is the court, in the last analysis, that will decide when the "patient" is well enough to be released. The tragi-comedy that has been called "psychiatric testimony" has traversed a full circle: The psychiatrists who displaced the legal authorities (the latter having abdicated their responsibilities for decision-making of this type) have, in their turn, been displaced by the legal authorities, who now function in the guise of psychiatrists and social therapists.

All this leads finally and inevitably to the psychiatrist's surrender of his professional responsibility. For, if a psychiatrist in charge of a patient—who is *not* a convicted criminal!—regards him, in his own best judgment, as ready to leave a hospital and assume the duties of a job, how can he, in his professional conscience, let a court tell him that this he can not do? What is the psychiatrist "treating" the patient for, anyway? To make him a good "prisoner"? The farcical, were it not tragic, character of the notion of mental illness is well illustrated by these impossible dilemmas into which psychiatrists and lawyers place themselves, each other, their patients, and their clients.

The peculiar legal condition of a person such as Miss Hough has not escaped the participants in this difficult affair. Judge Bazelon expressly affirmed that such a person is a "patient," not a "prisoner." The facts of the matter, however, vitiate the practical meaning of these terms. Judge Bazelon's words illustrate the crux of the problem:

> Nothing in the history of the statute—and nothing in its language—indicates that an individual committed to a mental hospital after acquittal of a crime by reason of insanity is other than a patient. The individual is confined in the hospital for the purpose of treatment, not punishment; and the length of confinement is governed solely by considerations of his condition *and* the public safety. Any preoccupation by the District Court with the need of punishment for crime is out of place in dealing with an individual who has been acquitted of the crime charged.
>
> It does not follow, however, that the hospital authorities are free to allow such a patient to leave the hospital without supervision. We readily grant that periodic freedom may be valuable therapy. So, we suppose, may outright release sometimes be. But the statute makes one in appellant's situation a member of "an

exceptional class of people." It provides generally, that the District Court have a voice in any termination of her confinement, whether unconditional or conditional.

There is an attempt here to circumvent the problem by creating the somewhat mystical entity of "an exceptional class of people." What is meant by this? Are these people who are "legally innocent but really guilty"? Or are these people who, by virtue of their actions, shall henceforth and forever after be considered second-class citizens? Does this mean that we shall have two sets of laws, one for ordinary citizens and ordinary criminals, and another for the "mentally ill"? If these questions are answered in the affirmative—as they seem to be in this case—then surely we ought to ask: Is this in accord with the spirit and the letter of our Constitution, our Bill of Rights, and with the ethics of democracy?

Before bringing this discussion to an end, I wish to comment briefly on two other items found in this record. One is an opinion by Judge Wilbur K. Miller, stating:

> It is, of course, much easier to believe that a sane person will not in the reasonable future be dangerous to himself or others than to believe that an insane person will not be.

Here is an ancient view, equating violence and insanity, dressed in slightly more modern garb. What is being asserted here, if anything? Both "insanity" and "dangerousness" are such vague terms that it is impossible to know what is being asserted by such a statement. But not only is this statement vague, worse, it is tautologous, for we habitually infer a condition of "insanity" from acts of violence. This was precisely the case in the present instance, for Miss Hough was considered legally sane until after she committed a murder. But if we infer insanity from violence, naturally we shall always expect violence when we speak of insanity, even though, in everyday life, the latter term is often used quite independently of whether or not a person is considered "dangerous."

In this connection, we must also note that the common-sense formulation of "insanity" propounded by Judge Miller seems to serve the function of enabling the observer—and this means all of us, and especially juries and judges—to wrestle with the problem of a person's so-called possible future dangerousness. At the very least, by codifying acts of violence as expressions of "mental illness" and some sort of irrationality (which, according to *certain* criteria, they might well be), we neatly rid ourselves of the task of dealing with criminal offenses as rational, goal-directed acts in principle no different from other forms of conduct.

Finally, I wish to call attention to a portion of Doctor Overholser's testimony. Being challenged by the attorney for the appellee to show reason why the patient should be released from the hospital, he was asked this question:

> Now, if this woman, who has this major mental disease, were released conditionally into the community and met a great number of frustrations in adjusting herself in getting along, isn't there a probability or possibility that she might explode, so to speak, and even do harm to herself or to others?

His answer was:

> Well, there is that possibility with a great many people, some of whom have never been in mental hospitals. I can't make any guarantee about permanence, or even about the conduct.

Here, it seems to me, Doctor Overholser spoke as a psychiatric scientist. As such, he could not predict with certainty, and surely could not guarantee, that this woman would not kill again. But if this is true, how can psychiatrists justify hospitalizing and "psychiatrically treating" someone whose "illness" appears to be mainly that she killed someone. Is being a murderer an illness? And if psychiatric treatment still leaves open the possibility of future crime, as obviously it must, then why use it as a *substitute* for legally codified imprisonment?

Does all this not mean that a logically simpler, and legally and psychiatrically clearer approach to a problem such as this might lie in treating persons in Miss Hough's predicament with the same dignity and firmness as we treat others confronted by serious problems? Why could she not be found guilty of a crime she obviously committed? Why could she not be imprisoned for a given term and, if necessary, given psychiatric help in jail? Is it not a truism that in a democracy, imprisonment (or loss of liberty) is justified only by conviction for a crime? But Miss Hough, and others in similar positions, were never convicted of a crime, but are, nevertheless, deprived of their liberty. This is clearly done as a *preventive measure!* Herein lies, I think, the worst and most dangerous feature of this procedure: it establishes legal precedent, and hence a measure of sanction, for prophylactic imprisonment! Let us not forget that this social act has, and with good reason, been regarded as the hallmark of the totalitarian state. The legal restraint of a person justified by *what he might do* (in the future) is there used with the explicit aim of social reform. Although not explicitly formulated, and perhaps only as an unwitting and undesired side-effect, this tactic of preventive restraint seems to be implicit in the operations of the Durham Rule and its subsequent modifications and applications.

The merits and risks of preventive imprisonment—even if some choose to call it "hospitalization"—are well worth the attention of every informed and intelligent person. This was my reason for stating at the outset that many problems of psychiatry and law transcend the boundaries of these disciplines and rightly concern all the people of the land. Let us at least entertain the possibility that by engaging in certain modifications of social living—for this is what we are doing—we run the risk of squandering the greatest asset of our Nation and its distinctive form of government, namely, the autonomy, integrity, responsibility, and freedom of the individual.

A recent decision rendered by the United States Court of Appeals for the District of Columbia Circuit was examined for the light it threw on some problems concerning crimes, psychiatry, and civil liberties. It was shown that acquittal by reason of insanity, followed by automatic commitment, seems to lead by easy steps to preventive jailing (hospitalization) of persons because of their alleged future dangerousness.

Increased psychiatric participation in the disposition of criminals seems to invite its corollary, namely, increased legal participation in psychiatric operations. We might raise the question: Do the questionable benefits of the Durham Rule (and its implementation) justify the risks of this "social therapy"? Could it be, perchance, that the cure, in this case, is worse than the disease? In other words, are the political and ethical risks of preventive jailing (preventive mental hospitalization) worth running, even if the psychiatric value of this measure were firmly established? (The psychiatric-scientific rationale of this procedure is hardly clear-cut or well established.) Personally, I hold that the value of formal psychiatric therapy for "criminals"—under present medico-legal conditions—is, at best, highly questionable. But beyond this, I believe that even if this psychiatric-legal procedure could be shown to be highly efficacious in restoring offenders of a certain type to useful social existence (which is the most that even its proponents claim for it), I would doubt that, *in a hierarchy of values,* such therapy of a small group could be justified *if* its results could be achieved *only* at the cost of a significant reduction in the autonomy and dignity of the majority of the people. In any case, the problem of crime and "mental illness" should be cast in a much broader context, and should be scrutinized by many more people, than it is at present.

IN FAVOR OF CAPITAL PUNISHMENT

Jacques Barzun

Jacques Barzun is a well-known historian and critic and Dean of Faculties and provost of Columbia University. His works include The House of Intellect (*1959*) *and* Science, the Glorious Entertainment (*1964*). *Professor Barzun's defense of capital punishment is all the more interesting in that it comes from an unexpected quarter.*

. . . I readily concede at the outset that present ways of dealing out capital punishment are as revolting as Mr. Koestler says in his harrowing volume, *Hanged by the Neck*. Like many of our prisons, our modes of execution should change. But this objection to barbarity does not mean that capital punishment—or rather, judicial homicide—should not go on. The illicit jump we find here, on the threshold of the inquiry, is characteristic of the abolitionist and must be disallowed at every point. Let us bear in mind the possibility of devising a painless, sudden and dignified death, and see whether its administration is justifiable.

The four main arguments advanced against the death penalty are: (1) punishment for crime is a primitive idea rooted in revenge; (2) capital punishment does not deter; (3) judicial error being possible, taking life is an appalling risk; (4) a civilized state, to deserve its name, must uphold, not violate, the sanctity of human life.

I entirely agree with the first pair of propositions, which is why . . . I replace the term capital punishment with "judicial homicide." The uncontrollable brute whom I want put out of the way is not to be punished for his misdeeds, nor used as an example or a warning; he is to be killed for the protection of others, like the wolf that escaped not long ago in a Connecticut suburb. No anger, vindictiveness or moral conceit need preside over the removal of such dangers. But a man's inability to control his violent impulses or to imagine the fatal consequences of his acts should be a presumptive reason for his elimination from society. This generality covers drunken driving and teen-age racing on public highways, as well as incurable obsessive violence; it might be extended (as I shall suggest later) to other acts that destroy, precisely, the moral basis of civilization.

But why kill? I am ready to believe the statistics tending to show

Reprinted from *The American Scholar*, 31, No. 2 (Spring 1962), 182–191. Copyright © 1962 by the United Chapters of Phi Beta Kappa. By permission of the publishers.

that the prospect of his own death does not stop the murderer. For one thing he is often a blind egotist, who cannot conceive the possibility of his own death. For another, detection would have to be infallible to deter the more imaginative who, although afraid, think they can escape discovery. Lastly, as Shaw long ago pointed out, hanging the wrong man will deter as effectively as hanging the right one. So, once again, why kill? If I agree that moral progress means an increasing respect for human life, how can I oppose abolition?

I do so because on this subject of human life, which is to me the heart of the controversy, I find the abolitionist inconsistent, narrow or blind. The propaganda for abolition speaks in hushed tones of the sanctity of human life, as if the mere statement of it as an absolute should silence all opponents who have any moral sense. But most of the abolitionists belong to nations that spend half their annual income on weapons of war and that honor research to perfect means of killing. These good people vote without a qualm for the political parties that quite sensibly arm their country to the teeth. The West today does not seem to be the time or place to invoke the absolute sanctity of human life. As for the clergymen in the movement, we may be sure from the experience of two previous world wars that they will bless our arms and pray for victory when called upon, the sixth commandment notwithstanding.

"Oh, but we mean the sanctity of life *within* the nation!" Very well: is the movement then campaigning also against the principle of self-defense? Absolute sanctity means letting the cutthroat have his sweet will of you, even if you have a poker handy to bash him with, for you might kill. And again, do we hear any protest against the police firing at criminals on the street—mere bank robbers usually—and doing this, often enough, with an excited marksmanship that misses the artist and hits the bystander? The absolute sanctity of human life is, for the abolitionist, a slogan rather than a considered proposition.

Yet it deserves examination, for upon our acceptance or rejection of it depend such other highly civilized possibilities as euthanasia and seemly suicide. The inquiring mind also wants to know, why the sanctity of *human* life alone? My tastes do not run to household pets, but I find something less than admirable in the uses to which we put animals—in zoos, laboratories and space machines—without the excuse of the ancient law, "Eat or be eaten."

It should moreover be borne in mind that this argument about sanctity applies—or would apply—to about ten persons a year in Great Britain and to between fifty and seventy-five in the United States. These are the average numbers of those executed in recent years. The count by itself should not, of course, affect our judgment of the principle: one life spared or forfeited is as important, morally, as a hundred thousand. But it should inspire a comparative judgment: there are hundreds and indeed thousands whom, in our concern with the horrors of execution, we forget: on the one hand, the victims of violence; on the other, the prisoners in our jails.

The victims are easy to forget. Social science tends steadily to mark a preference for the troubled, the abnormal, the problem case. Whether it is poverty, mental disorder, delinquency or crime, the "patient material" monopolizes the interest of increasing groups of people among the most generous and learned. Psychiatry and moral liberalism go together; the application of law as we have known it is thus coming to be regarded as an historic prelude to social work, which may replace it entirely. Modern literature makes the most of this same outlook, caring only for the disturbed spirit, scorning as bourgeois those who pay their way and do *not* stab their friends. All the while the determinism of natural science reinforces the assumption that society causes its own evils. A French jurist, for example, says that in order to understand crime we must first brush aside all ideas of Responsibility. He means the criminal's and takes for granted that of society. The murderer kills because reared in a broken home or, conversely, because at an early age he witnessed his parents making love. Out of such cases, which make pathetic reading in the literature of modern criminology, is born the abolitionist's state of mind: we dare not kill those we are beginning to understand so well.

If, moreover, we turn to the accounts of the crimes committed by these unfortunates, who are the victims? Only dull ordinary people going about their business. We are sorry, of course, but they do not interest science on its march. Balancing, for example, the sixty to seventy criminals executed annually in the United States, there were the seventy to eighty housewives whom George Cvek robbed, raped and usually killed during the months of a career devoted to proving his virility. "It is too bad." Cvek alone seems instructive, even though one of the law officers who helped track him down quietly remarks: "As to the extent that his villainies disturbed family relationships, or how many women are still haunted by the specter of an experience they have never disclosed to another living soul, these questions can only lend themselves to sterile conjecture."

The remote results are beyond our ken, but it is not idle to speculate about those whose death by violence fills the daily two inches at the back of respectable newspapers—the old man sunning himself on a park bench and beaten to death by four hoodlums, the small children abused and strangled, the middle-aged ladies on a hike assaulted and killed, the family terrorized by a released or escaped lunatic, the half-dozen working people massacred by the sudden maniac, the boatload of persons dispatched by the skipper, the mindless assaults upon schoolteachers and shopkeepers by the increasing hordes of dedicated killers in our great cities. Where does the sanctity of life begin?

It is all very well to say that many of these killers are themselves "children," that is, minors. Doubtless a nine-year-old mind is housed in that 150 pounds of unguided muscle. Grant, for argument's sake, that the misdeed is "the fault of society," trot out the broken home and the slum environment. The question then is, What shall we do, not in the Utopian city of tomorrow, but here and now? The "scientific" means of cure are more than uncertain. The apparatus of detention only increases the killer's antisocial animus. Reformatories and mental hospitals are full and have an understandable bias toward discharging their inmates. Some of these are indeed "cured"—so long as they stay under a rule. The stress of the social free-for-all throws them back on their violent modes of self-expression. At that point I agree that society has failed—twice: it has twice failed the victims, whatever may be its guilt toward the killer.

As in all great questions, the moralist must choose, and choosing has a price. I happen to think that if a person of adult body has not been endowed with adequate controls against irrationally taking the life of another, that person must be judicially, painlessly, regretfully killed before that mindless body's horrible automation repeats.

I say "irrationally" taking life, because it is often possible to feel great sympathy with a murderer. Certain *crimes passionnels* can be forgiven without being condoned. Blackmailers invite direct retribution. Long provocation can be an excuse, as in that engaging case of some years ago, in which a respectable carpenter of seventy found he could no longer stand the incessant nagging of his wife. While she excoriated him from her throne in the kitchen—a daily exercise for fifty years—the husband went to his bench and came back with a hammer in each hand to settle the score. The testimony to his character, coupled with the sincerity implied by the two hammers, was enough to have him sent into quiet and brief seclusion.

But what are we to say of the type of motive disclosed in a journal published by the inmates of one of our Federal penitentiaries? The author is a bank robber who confesses that money is not his object:

> My mania for power, socially, sexually, and otherwise can feel no degree of satisfaction until I feel sure I have struck the ultimate of submission and terror in the minds and bodies of my victims. . . . It's very difficult to explain all the queer fascinating sensations pounding and surging through me while I'm holding a gun on a victim, watching his body tremble and sweat. . . . This is the moment when all the rationalized hypocrisies of civilization are suddenly swept away and two men stand there facing each other morally and ethically naked, and right and wrong are the absolute commands of the man behind the gun.

This confused echo of modern literature and modern science defines the choice before us. Anything deserving the name of cure for such a man presupposes not only a laborious individual psychoanalysis, with the means to conduct and to sustain it, socially and economically, but also a re-education of the mind, so as to throw into correct perspective the garbled ideas of Freud and Nietzsche, Gide and Dostoevski, which this power-seeker and his fellows have derived from the culture and temper of our times. Ideas are tenacious and give continuity to emotion. Failing a second birth of heart and mind, we must ask: How soon will this sufferer sacrifice a bank clerk in the interests of making civilization less hypocritical? And we must certainly question the wisdom of affording him more than one chance. The abolitionists' advocacy of an unconditional "let live" is in truth part of the same cultural tendency that animates the killer. The Western peoples' revulsion from power in domestic and foreign policy has made of the state a sort of counterpart of the bank robber: both having power and neither knowing how to use it. Both waste lives because hypnotized by irrelevant ideas and crippled by contradictory emotions. If psychiatry were sure of its ground in diagnosing the individual case, a philosopher might consider whether such dangerous obsessions should not be guarded against by judicial homicide *before* the shooting starts.

I raise the question not indeed to recommend the prophylactic execution of potential murderers, but to introduce the last two perplexities that the abolitionists dwarf or obscure by their concentration on changing an isolated penalty. One of these is the scale by which to judge the offenses society wants to repress. I can for example imagine a truly democratic state in which it would be deemed a form of treason punishable by death to create a disturbance in any court or deliberative assembly. The aim would be to recognize the sanctity of orderly discourse in arriving at justice, assessing criticism and defining policy. Under such a law, a natural selection would operate to remove permanently from the scene persons who, let us say, neglect argument in favor of banging on the desk with their shoe. Similarly, a bullying minority in a diet, Parliament or skupshtina would be prosecuted for treason to the most sacred institutions when fists or flying inkwells replace rhetoric. That the mere suggestion of such a law sounds ludicrous shows how remote we are from civilized institutions, and hence how gradual should be our departure from the severity of judicial homicide.

I say gradual and I do not mean standing still. For there is one form of barbarity in our law that I want to see mitigated before any other. I mean imprisonment. The enemies of capital punishment—and liberals generally—seem to be satisfied with any legal outcome so long as they themselves avoid the vicarious guilt of shedding blood. They speak of the sanctity of life, but have no concern with its quality. They give no impression of ever having read what it is certain they have read, from Wilde's *De Profundis* to the latest account of prison life by a convicted homosexual. Despite the infamy of concentration camps, despite Mr. Charles Burney's remarkable work, *Solitary Confinement,* despite riots in prisons, despite the round of escape, recapture and return in chains, the abolitionists' imagination tells them nothing about the reality of being caged. They read without a qualm, indeed they read with rejoicing, the hideous irony of "Killer Gets Life"; they sigh with relief instead of horror. They do not see and suffer the cell, the drill, the clothes, the stench, the food; they do not feel the sexual racking of young and old bodies, the hateful promiscuity, the insane monotony, the mass degradation, the impotent hatred. They do not remember from Silvio Pellico that only a strong political faith, with a hope of final victory, can steel a man to endure long detention. They forget that Joan of Arc, when offered "life," preferred burning at the stake. Quite of another mind, the abolitionists point with pride to the "model prisoners" that murderers often turn out to be. As if a model prisoner were not, first, a contradiction in terms, and second an exemplar of what a free society should not want.

I said a moment ago that the happy advocates of the life sentence appear not to have understood what we know they have read. No more do they appear to read what they themselves write. In the preface to his useful volume of cases, *Hanged in Error,* Mr. Leslie Hale, M.P., refers to the tardy recognition of a minor miscarriage of justice—one year in jail: "The prisoner emerged to find that his wife had died and that his children and his aged parents had been removed to the workhouse. By the time a small payment had been assessed as 'compensation' the victim was incurably insane." So far we are as indignant with the law as Mr. Hale. But what comes next? He cites the famous Evans case, in which it is very probable that the wrong man was hanged, and he exclaims: "While such mistakes are possible, should society impose an irrevocable sentence?" Does Mr. Hale really ask us to believe that the sentence passed on the first man, whose wife died and who went insane, was in any sense *revocable?* Would not any man rather be Evans dead than that other wretch "emerging" with his small compensation and his reasons for living gone?

Nothing is revocable here below, imprisonment least of all. The agony of a trial itself is punishment, and acquittal wipes out nothing. Read the heart-rending diary of William Wallace, accused quite implausibly of having murdered his wife and "saved" by the Court of Criminal Appeals— but saved for what? Brutish ostracism by everyone and a few years of solitary despair. The cases of Adolf Beck, of Oscar Slater, of the unhappy Brooklyn bank teller who vaguely resembled a forger and spent eight years in Sing Sing only to "emerge" a broken, friendless, useless, "compensated" man—all these, if the dignity of the individual has any meaning, had better have been dead before the prison door ever opened for them. This is what counsel always says to the jury in the course of a murder trial and counsel is right: far better hang this man than "give him life." For my part, I would choose death without hesitation. If that option is abolished, a demand will one day be heard to claim it as a privilege in the name of human dignity. I shall believe in the abolitionist's present views only after he has emerged from twelve months in a convict cell.

The detached observer may want to interrupt here and say that the argument has now passed from reasoning to emotional preference. Whereas the objector to capital punishment *feels* that death is the greatest of evils, I *feel* that imprisonment is worse than death. A moment's thought will show that feeling is the appropriate arbiter. All reasoning about what is right, civilized and moral rests upon sentiment, like mathematics. Only, in trying to persuade others, it is important to single out the fundamental feeling, the prime intuition, and from it to reason justly. In my view, to profess respect for human life and be willing to see it spent in a penitentiary is to entertain liberal feelings frivolously. To oppose the death penalty because, unlike a prison term, it is irrevocable is to argue fallaciously.

In the propaganda for abolishing the death sentence the recital of numerous miscarriages of justice commits the same error and implies the same callousness: what is at fault in our present system is not the sentence but the fallible procedure. Capital cases being one in a thousand or more, who can be cheerful at the thought of all the "revocable" errors? What the miscarriages point to is the need for reforming the jury system, the rules of evidence, the customs of prosecution, the machinery of appeal. The failure to see that this is the great task reflects the sentimentality I spoke of earlier, that which responds chiefly to the excitement of the unusual. A writer on Death and the Supreme Court is at pains to point out that when that tribunal reviews a capital case, the judges are particularly anxious and careful. What a left-handed compliment to the highest judicial conscience of the country! Fortunately, some of the champions of the misjudged see the issue more clearly. Many of those who are thought wrongly convicted now languish in jail because the jury was uncertain or because a doubting governor commuted the death sentence. Thus Dr. Samuel H. Sheppard, Jr., convicted of his wife's murder in the second degree is serving a sentence that is supposed to run for the term of his natural life. The story of his numerous trials, as told by Mr. Paul Holmes, suggests that police incompetence, newspaper demagogy, public envy of affluence and the mischances of legal procedure fashioned the result. But Dr. Sheppard's vindicator is under no illusion as to the conditions that this "lucky" evader of the electric chair will face if he is granted parole after ten years: "It will carry with it no right to resume his life as a physician. His privilege to practice medicine was blotted out with his conviction. He must all his life bear the stigma of a parolee, subject to unceremonious return to confinement for life for the slightest misstep. More than this, he must live out his life as a convicted murderer."[1]

What does the moral conscience of today think it is doing? If such a man is a dangerous repeater of violent acts, what right has the state to let

---

[1] Editor's note: Dr. Sheppard has since been freed.

him loose after ten years? What is, in fact, the meaning of a "life sentence" that peters out long before life? Paroling looks suspiciously like an expression of social remorse for the pain of incarceration, coupled with a wish to avoid "unfavorable publicity" by freeing a suspect. The man is let out when the fuss has died down; which would mean that he was not under lock and key for our protection at all. He *was* being punished, just a little—for so prison seems in the abolitionist's distorted view, and in the jury's and the prosecutor's, whose "second-degree" murder suggests killing someone "just a little."[2]

If, on the other hand, execution and life imprisonment are judged too severe and the accused is expected to be harmless hereafter—punishment being ruled out as illiberal—what has society gained by wrecking his life and damaging that of his family?

What we accept, and what the abolitionist will clamp upon us all the more firmly if he succeeds, is an incoherence which is not remedied by the belief that second-degree murder merits a kind of second-degree death; that a doubt as to the identity of a killer is resolved by commuting real death into intolerable life; and that our ignorance whether a maniac will strike again can be hedged against by measuring "good behavior" within the gates and then releasing the subject upon the public in the true spirit of experimentation.

These are some of the thoughts I find I cannot escape when I read and reflect upon this grave subject. If, as I think, they are relevant to any discussion of change and reform, resting as they do on the direct and concrete perception of what happens, then the simple meliorists who expect to breathe a purer air by abolishing the death penalty are deceiving themselves and us. The issue is for the public to judge; but I for one shall not sleep easier for knowing that in England and America and the West generally a hundred more human beings are kept alive in degrading conditions to face a hopeless future; while others—possibly less conscious, certainly less controlled—benefit from a premature freedom dangerous alike to themselves and society. In short, I derive no comfort from the illusion that in giving up one manifest protection of the law-abiding, we who might well be in any of these three roles—victim, prisoner, licensed killer—have struck a blow for the sanctity of human life.

---

[2] The British Homicide Act of 1957, Section 2, implies the same reasoning in its definition of "diminished responsibility" for certain forms of mental abnormality. The whole question of irrationality and crime is in utter confusion, on both sides of the Atlantic.

A LETTER TO THE GOVERNOR

Caryl Chessman

The voice of Caryl Chessman is stilled; he was executed at San Quentin on May 20, 1960. His words, in a letter written to the Governor after a temporary reprieve, survive as a remarkable commentary on the moral implications of capital punishment.

Name: Caryl Chessman
Box 66565, San Quentin, Calif.
Date: February 26, 1960

The Hon. Edmund G. Brown
Governor of the State of California
State Capitol
Sacramento, California

Dear Governor Brown:

As you know, at approximately 4:45 P.M. on Thursday, February 18, 1960, I was removed from the Death Row Unit located on the fifth floor of the North Block here at San Quentin and locked in the small holding cell, just a few feet from the State's lethal gas chamber, where California's condemned spend their last night on earth. The death watch began. So far as I knew, I would be put to death at ten o'clock in the morning.

I was permitted to see an early edition of a Friday newspaper. Its headlines were large and black: CHESSMAN MUST DIE, BROWN SAYS. Again, only an hour earlier, the members of the California Supreme Court had voted 4 to 3 against a recommendation to you for clemency. Thus, by a simple vote, you were foreclosed from exercising your commutation powers. The court had made its order "final forthwith." I had been notified of that action a few hours before being taken downstairs to the holding cell. In anticipation of it, had put my affairs in order and executed a new will. . . .

And death appeared inevitable. I held out no feverish, desperate

---

Unpublished correspondence.

hope for a life-sparing miracle. On the contrary, what sustained me, what made it possible for me to await the morning and oblivion with a detached, almost clinical calm was hope of an entirely different sort: the burning hope that my execution would lead to an objective reappraisal of the social validity or invalidity of capital punishment, and that such a reexamination would lead, in turn, to an awareness on the part of all Californians that Death Rows, and death chambers and executioners were unworthy of our society, that the former, in fact, were gross obscenities, solving nothing but rather confounding solution.

The minutes passed, the hours. The prison's Catholic Chaplain, Father Edward Dingberg, visited me. Associate Wardens Walter D. Achuff and Louis S. Nelson saw me for a few minutes. Dr. David G. Schmidt, San Quentin's chief psychiatrist, came in. Attorney George Davis conferred with me hurriedly, intending to return later. Warden Fred R. Dickson dropped by for a talk.

Contrary to published accounts that I consumed the condemned man's traditional hearty meal of "fried chicken, French fried potatoes, vegetable salad, coffee and two kinds of pie—apple and chocolate cream," I am compelled to confess these reports, seemingly attesting to my capacity as a trencherman, are somewhat exaggerated. Actually, my wants were more modest. I had a hamburger and a coke about 7:30, and during the course of the evening I drank three cups of coffee. I also puffed on a cigar, although I normally do not smoke.

I waited. Midnight came. All my visitors had left but Warden Dickson. Then the telephone rang mutedly, and one of the death watch officers said, "It's for you, Warden." I watched Mr. Dickson disappear around a bend in the hallway. I paced the floor, my steps reduced to almost soundlessness by the cloth slippers. The radio outside the cell played quietly. Over it I had listened to a succession of newscasts. The news was all negative. One commentator reported Miss Asher[1] had been unable to see you but, in vain, had talked with two members of your staff. A second commentator solemnly quoted you as having said, "Only an act of God can save Caryl Chessman now."

My eyes fell on the newspaper I had been allowed whose stark headline I quoted above. One of its front-page lead paragraphs reads: "The world was disturbed last night as the hour for Caryl Chessman's execution drew near. Protests echoed from continent to continent." This San Francisco daily also reported: "There was little question that the Governor . . . was undergoing great emotional stress as Chessman's last hours ticked away," and: "The mail—most of it running about three to one for clemency—continued to pour in. So did the telegrams and the zero-hour telephone calls. . . ."

---

[1] Editor's note: Chessman's attorney.

On page two were pictures of the gas chamber and this account of how I would die in less than ten hours:

> . . . He'll get a physical examination from the prison's chief physician, Dr. Herman H. Gross, at 9 A.M. and undoubtedly will once again be found to be in perfect condition.
>
> At 9:45 A.M. come the last, formal visits from Warden Dickson and his aide to hear any last requests. Once again the chaplains will wait silently.
>
> Over a carpeted floor, his stockinged feet should take the last walk at 10 A.M. on the dot.
>
> There have been 164 people in the gas chamber before him, and experience gives the prison staff an almost split-second foretelling of the rest.
>
> By 10:01 A.M. he should be in one of the two death chairs—chair B. in his case.
>
> Two straps for each arm and leg, one across the chest and another for the waist. That, and the final slamming of the great iron door—less than three minutes.
>
> At 10:03½, by schedule, Warden Dickson would nod at a guard and a lever will send the cyanide pellets into the sulphuric acid basins.

I smiled, grimly, I'm sure. I knew how it felt to be a dead man. Only the ritualized formalities of physically extinguishing my life with hydrocyanic acid gas remained.

"Has the Warden gone?" I asked one of the death watch. "No," I was told, "he's still on the phone."

I gave no thought to the significance of the call. Then, audibly, I heard Warden Dickson say, "All right, Governor." A few seconds later the Warden reappeared. I'd glanced up from the paper I was reading. As he approached the cell, the Warden's face was a thoughtful mask.

"I have some news for you, Caryl." Mr. Dickson paused. "Oh?" I responded. He nodded, smiled. "The Governor has just granted you a 60-day reprieve."

The words had been spoken softly—but they crashed and reverberated in my mind like thunder in an echo chamber. Except possibly in a mocking, sadistic nightmare, they were words I truly never had expected to hear up to the instant of their utterance. I had been prepared to die; now I must be ready to go on living, I realized, for at least another 60 days.

I drew a deep breath as my thoughts raced. My words have been reported in the press: "Thank you. This is a great surprise. I really didn't expect it. Tell the Governor I thank him. I am surprised and grateful."

The Warden said he would see me again later in the morning. We said goodnight. Swiftly I was taken back upstairs in the elevator to Death Row. Swiftly, in the office, I changed into my regular clothing. Accompanied by the officers, I was passed through the "Bird Cage"—with its double doors and multiplicity of bolts and bars and locks—into the Row proper. From most of the occupied cells, yellow light spilled out into the corridor. The condemned were awake, listening to their earphones, silent, waiting—for what? Somehow, even better than I, they had sensed their fate was tied to mine, and mine to a pressing social issue of far greater significance than what might, individually or collectively, happen to any or all of us. They had heard me say repeatedly that obviously the greatest hope for abolition of the death penalty lay with my death. They—even the tortured and troubled ones—knew this to be true. Their obvious course was to accept this fact and hope it might lead them out from the cold shadow of the gas chamber. But, as I later learned, they had sent you a telegram, urging your intercession in my behalf. They had refused to believe that death—even another's—was a solution. I don't know whether that telegram ever came to your attention in the flood of messages you were receiving. I do know it had a profound effect on me. . . .

I continued along the corridor, stopping for a moment or two to speak to the occupant of each cell. The reaction was the same. Here was a genuine and spontaneous expression of brotherhood, commingled for them with a miracle. And make no mistake, Governor, I was for my doomed fellows no arrogant, swaggering hero returned after breathing defiance into the teeth of the cosmos. On the contrary, since they had come to know the man rather than the counterfeit black criminal legend, I was a flesh and blood human being whose appointment with man-imposed death had come to symbolize the critical and yet unresolved basic struggle of social man to rise above wrath and vengeance, to trust not the executioner, but their— mankind's—own reason and humanity in building a saner world for their children and their children's children. These men had been accused and convicted of homicidal violence, and so, better than any, they knew the futility of such violence. Now, after a bitter contest, life in my case had claimed at least a temporary victory. . . .

We got the word [that] you had granted the reprieve because, since the people of California were sharply divided on the issue, you wanted "to give the people . . . an opportunity, through the Legislature, to express themselves once more on capital punishment." . . .

And then, as well as in the hectic days to come, before there were calmer reflections and clearer analysis, the paradoxical evidence mounted: While the Chessman case had made evident the urgent need for a calm, careful and objective reexamination of the question whether capital punishment should not be discarded as a barbarous anachronism, productive finally of nothing but division and uneasy doubt among us, my continued existence, if only for another few weeks, and the fearful Chessman legend, which portrayed me as a cunning, fiendish, Cataline-like mocker of justice, threatened to throttle such a reexamination and reevaluation at the outset.

I remain haunted by that paradox. Beyond the descriptive power of words, these have been troubled and difficult days for me. I do not resort to hyperbole when I say they have been hell, even more than the past 11½ years have been hell. I cannot escape the fact I owe you my life for whatever days remain to me. I cannot forget that literally millions of people from nations around the world spoke out for me. In terms of the larger social good that is your goal, my obligation is a heavy one, and I refuse to try to rationalize it away. Over and over I have asked myself the questions. What possibly can I do, if anything, to divorce the ugly, emotion-inflaming image of Caryl Chessman from the grave social issue of capital punishment? What can I say—and mean, and demonstrate?

. . . I decided I can and I do, without theatrics, offer them my life. If the hysteria and the mob wrath that surrounds the problem only can be propitiated by my death and if otherwise they agree that the death penalty should be abolished, then I earnestly urge the members of our Legislature to frame their bill in such a way as to exclude me. This can be done readily—for example, by a declaration in the law that anyone convicted of a capital offense during or subsequent to the year 1950, whose sentence of death remains in force and unexecuted, shall be treated as though serving a sentence of life imprisonment. I give my solemn word before the world that I will never challenge such a law in the courts and I will disavow any attempt by any attorney purporting to act in my behalf.

. . . If the legislators do not necessarily demand my death but do believe the final question of my fate, under the California Constitution, should be resolved by yourself and the majority opinion of the State Supreme Court, then I urge them so to indicate. This way, by the passage of the type of bill mentioned above, they can sever the two problems. . . .

Except for the days I was out to court, I have occupied a death cell continuously since Saturday morning, July 3, 1948. I have had eight dates for execution in California's lethal gas chamber fixed and then canceled, some in the very last hours. A ninth date soon will be set. Ninety-odd men have taken that last, grim walk by my cell to their deaths since I came to Death Row. If it gives them any satisfaction, Californians may be assured my prolonged half-life in the shadow of the gas chamber has been an indescribably punishing ordeal. The shock of it, I think, has brought me to maturity; it has forced upon me keen social awareness of the problem that, in exaggerated form, I am said to typify.

I am now 38 years of age. I was 26 when arrested. Behind me is a long record of arrest. I am a graduate of California reform schools and prisons. I have been called a "criminal psychopath." Certainly, as a young man, I was a violent, rebellious, monumental damn fool. I was at odds with my society; I resisted authority. I am ashamed of that past but I cannot change it. However, with my writings, I have tried to salvage something of larger social significance from it. Without shifting responsibility for my conduct, I endeavored in my first book to tell the story of my life and hence to explain how young men like myself got that way. I realized that Death Rows made sense only because people like Caryl Chessman didn't.

After being brought to the death house, the change in me and my outlook came slowly and painfully. Defiantly, I stood and fought in the courts for survival, asking no quarter and expecting none. But, ironically, to have any chance for survival, I had to turn to the law; I had to invoke the protections of the Constitution; I had to study, often as much as 18 to 20 hours a day; I had to learn to impose upon myself a harsh self-discipline; I had to think and to be ruthlessly honest with myself; in time, I forced myself to admit, "Chessman, you have been, and to some degree still are, an irrational, impossible fool. What are you going to do about it?"

At that juncture, the traditional thing, the conventional response almost certainly would have been for me to confess my past folly and to beg for mercy. But I hesitated, not out of pride or false pride. I couldn't escape the fact that such a response on my part would, in practical effect, amount to affirmation that gas chambers and a system of justice ultimately based upon retribution possessed a genuine—rather than a mistakenly conceived and defended—social validity. I knew they did not possess such a validity. Without mock heroics, I became aware then that the greatest contribution I could make was to cause people, all people, to become angrily aware of places like Death Row and the administration of criminal justice in general. This, in my own way, I did: by continued total resistance. I was told I could not write another line for publication and I wrote anyway. When concerted efforts were made to suppress my manuscripts, I found a way to smuggle them from the prison. I intensified my court fight, winning some battles, losing others. Vituperation was heaped upon me. I became known as a mocker of justice. Editorial writers and public officials roundly denounced me. The public clamored for "this cunning fiend's" execution. Often I was half-mad with doubt; often I was ready to collapse with a brutal fatigue; often I sardonically sneered at myself and my goal. But I kept on somehow. A remorseless voice within told me, "This is your penance, fool—to be reviled and hated. This, if you call yourself a man, is the price you must pay."

I had certain advantages, and almost impossible handicaps. Among others, I had been convicted of unsavory sex offenses, sordid acts that, when recounted, inflamed the mind of the listener. They had inflamed the judge, the prosecutor, the jury. A Red Light Bandit—so-called because the bandit had operated, according to trial testimony, with a car equipped with a red spotlight such as those on police cars. He had accosted couples in lonely lovers' lanes. Armed with a gun, he would sometimes rob the couples, if they had any money. On two occasions testified to at my trial, he took the woman to his car. In one of these instances, under threat of death, he compelled her, the victim, to commit an unnatural sex act before letting her out and driving off. On a second occasion, he drove off with a 17-year-old girl to another secluded area, compelled her, too, to commit a perverted sexual act and attempted to rape her. Then he let her off near her home. (This tragic young woman, who had a history of serious mental disturbance, was committed to a mental hospital some 19 months after her traumatic experience. "Today," the wire services have quoted her mother as saying, "she just sits and stares"—lost in the withdrawn unreal world of the schizophrenic.)

It is no wonder, then, that the Red Light Bandit crimes so aroused judge, jury and prosecutor and antagonized them against the man accused of their commission. They angered and outraged me to an equal or greater degree, to an extent where in a red haze of emotion, I was unable to defend myself as effectively as otherwise I might. Stupidly and stubbornly, as well, I had withheld certain vital facts about my involvement in a violent internecine struggle for control of an illegal but police protected book-making syndicate. The convict's code said I shouldn't talk, or name names. I didn't. Then, not by myself, other critical evidence got suppressed. Witnesses disappeared. And a damning net was drawn around me. The jury returned verdicts of guilty, doomed me. I was brought to Death Row, twice sentenced to death and to 15 consecutive prison terms. The question of guilt or innocence was closed unless I could convince an appellate court I had been convicted illegally. Otherwise, branded a loathsome sex predator, I would die. I would have no chance to establish California had convicted the wrong man. It would make no difference that the description furnished the police of the bandit didn't remotely fit me; that the 17-year-old girl said her attacker had been "shorter than the usual man" and had weighed nearly 50 pounds less than the evidence showed I did, while I was six feet tall; or that she said the bandit had spoken with a slight accent, had appeared to be Italian and had a linear cut scar extending back from his right ear; or that this bandit usually gave his victims a look at his face before pulling up a handkerchief mask, while I just had been released from prison on parole and knew that my photographs almost certainly would be the first shown robbery victims; or that I had absolutely no history as a sex offender; or that I had been refused the right to produce witnesses at the trial who would testify to my reputation for sexual normality as well as to produce expert psychiatric evidence that I did not possess the psychological disposition to commit sexual crimes, particularly those involving force or violence, and that I was not a sexual psychopath.

All this made no difference. In the eyes of the law, I was guilty and would remain guilty unless I could win a new trial and acquittal. This galled but it also drove and sustained me. . . .

I wait to die. I remain locked in a death cell. More than 12 years have passed since my arrest. The State has spent nearly a million dollars in trying to kill me.

Now, in a few days, the California Legislature will be called into special session to consider abolition of capital punishment. Disturbed that a vote against the death penalty will be a vote for me, the man they believe has embarrassed their State and made a mockery of their laws, many legislators have vowed publicly to see that capital punishment is retained. I do not presume to tell them what to do; I do pray they will reconsider and reevaluate. . . . I am more than willing that they separate me decisively from the greater issue. I am quite willing to die if that will bring about this desperately needed social reform. I do suggest that if our positions were reversed and they had found themselves occupying a death cell under the conditions I have they too, and honorably, would have done as I have done, even though it meant bringing the wrath of the State down upon them. Happily, they will never know what it means to be doomed, to be within hours and minutes of execution, to feel the full, terrible impact of mob wrath, to have a claim of innocence brushed impatiently aside, to be called a "monster" and vilified, to seek redemption, not through hypocritical groveling, but by a harder, perhaps impossible road, to win friends and want desperately to justify their friendship and their faith, to want to live and to believe, humbly, that within them is a gift for words that can enrich our literature and, their own case aside, contribute significantly to the pressing social problems of our day.

I do not overstate when I say I gladly would die ten thousand gas chamber deaths if that would bring these truths into the hearts and minds of those who make our laws: A vote for either abolition or a moratorium is not an indication of approval of murder or other capital crimes, for the death penalty does not deter; it does not protect society. On the contrary, it leaves it defenseless, since as long as we have an executioner and a gas chamber, we will be content to believe that we can bury the problem with the offender. We will think that revenge is enough. It isn't. We must find why men kill and we must learn to prevent killing. We must become as intensely concerned with tomorrow's prospective victims as yesterday's actual ones. We must learn how to save lives and to salvage lives.

As long as the death penalty is on our statute books, there will be too much emotionality and circus atmosphere tainting our administration of justice. And for those who doubt this, there is a ready and rational test at hand: Let a moratorium be ordered on the supreme penalty for a period of, say, five years. I am certain during that period there will be no rise in the per capita crimes. Rather, I am convinced the crime rate will drop appreciably, and that justice will function in a far more even-handed and fair way. The sensationalism inevitably attending capital cases will vanish. The citizen will be reassured. He will know that the man who has killed has been isolated. The accused is more likely, if he is guilty, to plead guilty. Our courts thus will be able to perform their duties more efficiently. And if an innocent man is later found to have been mistakenly convicted, it will not be too late to correct the error.

Unfortunately, as investigation will confirm, too often it is the friendless and the fundless upon whom the death penalty is imposed. The man with means or who knows the angles does not come to Death Row. As well, under our outmoded tests for legal sanity or insanity, too often the man who is executed is one who, while not legally insane, suffers from some serious mental disability. It needlessly demeans our society to engage in killing the mentally ill. Still further, among this group, as psychiatrists and penologists will attest, is the type of personality who is inflamed by the thought and threat of the gas chamber. His response to it, his overt expression of defiance, is to strike out homicidally. In effect, he gets his revenge in advance, and we in turn get ours after the tragedy.

That is why so many thoughtful citizens advocate abolition or a moratorium. They feel, as I do, a sense of guilty responsibility at a lethal act that is both more than futile and less than futile when the State takes a life. They want their laws to express humanity's ideal of nobility, compassion, understanding and social awareness. They know that our laws can do so without endangering the citizens of California. The basis for their opposition to man's government killing man is thus, in the highest sense, ethical, social, practical and religious. They do not want to see their society needlessly degraded, their system of justice compromised.

I must close, and in closing I again earnestly urge you to ask the Legislature to consider the question of capital punishment apart from Caryl Chessman and the Chessman case. I urge you to request that they consider framing their bill as suggested above, to exclude me. You can do this honorably by taking my life back into your hands alone. You can let me die. Indeed, as the matter now stands, you are powerless to do otherwise because of the present 4–3 vote against me in the California Supreme Court. But, at the same time, you can give your proposal to the Legislature a chance.

It deserves that chance. It deserves your forceful leadership. You are right in the position you have taken. It is time to speak out, for too seldom does unlightened humanity in this age of fear and awesome nuclear devices have a spokesman with the courage to advocate that death and hate are not and never can be an answer to the problems that beset our civilization. Mankind and future generations ever will remain in your debt and ever will honor your name.

Yours respectfully,
/s/ Caryl Chessman

Part Two

The Values of a Business Society

"The business of America is business." Thus did Calvin Coolidge, a man not given to prolixity, sum up America's ideals and aspirations. In this he seemed to confirm Dickens' harsh impeachment of Americans in *Martin Chuzzlewit:* "All their cares, hopes, joys, affections, virtues, and associations, seemed to be melted down into dollars. . . . Men were weighed by their dollars; life was auctioneered, appraised, put up and knocked down for its dollars."

The image of Americans and America that such statements perpetuate is of a materialist civilization exclusively preoccupied with the accumulation of wealth and physical goods,[1] an image inspired these days, one suspects, as much by secret envy of our wealth as by an accurate estimate of the difference in taste and refinement between Europeans and Americans. Our European cousins are prone to such an appraisal of us, and they have succeeded in converting some American intellectuals to the same view. In truth, now that prosperity has come to the West Europeans, they generally display that same regard for mechanical gadgets that overwhelmed many of us;[2] they pursue wealth just as

---

[1] For some, Coca-Cola has unaccountably become the symbol of our degradation. Thus, in a letter to the editor of *The New York Times* (June 14, 1962) a prominent British historian, A. R. Burns, refers to the "Coca-Cola-vization of the American way of life" and adds that "if the only way to keep Europe from Communism were to have it completely Americanized, I should have my doubts about the merits of the bargain." It is reassuring to learn in the same letter that some of historian Burns' best friends are Americans.

[2] Peter Viereck's comment is surely apt: "Old world disdainers of us soulless American vulgarians still engage in heated debates about the rival aesthetics of the 'Cinquecents' and 'Seicents.' These two Italian labels, however, no longer refer to Renaissance art but to Fiat automobiles. Soon it may be necessary for left-bank sensitive plants to flee from modern, rootless, gadget-giddy Europe to ancient, medieval, traditionalist America." (*The Unadjusted Man,* p. 69.)

avidly, and, if public benefactions and tax avoidance are measures, their capitalists are far more grasping.

We often find in others the faults that are most conspicuous in ourselves—the psychological mechanism involved may aptly be called a disowning projection—and the European in stigmatizing Americans as materialistic may well be guilty of this rationalization. The libel is compounded when critics ignore the growing concern in America for scholarship and the fine arts. However, once all this is said and we have expressed our righteous indignation over what is an unfair caricature of American culture, the question may well be raised: ought not our concern for the arts and letters and sciences to be greater? Is it not true that, however overstated by unfair critics, profoundly important values are overshadowed and obscured by the emphasis in our society on the pursuit of wealth? Is it not the case that the motives of the marketplace invade the church, the school, government, the professions, the arts, deflecting them from their proper mission? In particular, how has the profit motive affected the quality of the so-called mass media to which we give so many of our leisure hours? May it not be said that business monopolizes too much of our lives? Many years ago De Tocqueville, most perceptive of foreign observers of American life, spoke of "the business-like qualities" of the Americans and of their "trading passions." The question is, have we carried these passions too far?

There is another aspect to the problem. A society that emphasizes pecuniary motives is organized about the satisfaction of *individual* needs and interests. Must this result in a neglect of national or community goals and purposes? Our cities, for example, have been called by Lewis Mumford a "crystallization of chaos." The rich and moderately well-to-do of the most affluent country in all history are engaged in an ignominious evacuation of their cities, leaving them—except for well-guarded islands of high commerce and plush living—to ethnic minorities, to marginal members of the majority group, and to the superannuated. In the past this occurred because there was an invader at the gates; today it occurs because our cities are less and less viable as communities. Does this suggest, as many have charged, that in our quest for consumer goods we have starved our social services, neglected public amenities, ignored national goals?

A major reason for our preoccupation with consumer goods is that the talents and energies of a great many able people are concentrated on promotion and salesmanship, which in effect bias the outlay we make as a people in favor of consumption to the neglect of such social needs as urban redevelopment, education, recreation, and conservation. Quite apart from the fact that supersalesmanship may—by persuading people to buy what they would not in ordinary circumstances want—lead to such neglect and to a misdirection of resources, how are we morally to evaluate the main manifestation of such promotion in the form of advertising? Is the effect desirable? Without reference to the tastelessness of the average commercial message on television or radio, or the influence of advertisers on newspaper or program content, how shall we morally assess the deception that characterizes most advertising? Is it discounted by the listener or viewer and therefore innocuous and morally irrelevant, or are we so institutionalizing mendacity that we dull our capacity to be morally discriminating?

Such a line of inquiry leads to two issues of increasing concern to responsible business leaders and to the community at large. Both issues concern the ethics of the business community. Industry in this country, according to a number of its most distinguished leaders, is facing a moral crisis. The issue quite simply is honesty—honesty as commonly defined and understood. To what extent are businessmen honest with each other, honest with their government, honest with the public? The same question may of course be put to labor leaders. But businessmen are leaders of the larger community as well as of their own enterprises in a sense in which labor leaders are not. The answer of businessmen to this question is therefore crucially important. Quite probably if they are dishonest—the reference here is not to marginal businessmen or even to an occasional Billie Sol Estes but to the respected and established businessman—we as a people will be dishonest, with ourselves and with others.

The second question is more difficult and the answer more controversial. It involves much more than considerations of simple honesty. What are the responsibilities of the business community to the larger community of which it is a part? In recent years we have heard much of "corporate citizenship." It is said by many that the robber-baron days are over and that business executives have a new sense of the larger social responsibilities of the corporations over which they preside. Large-scale financial aid to colleges and universities is often cited as an example. Others will argue that the stewardship of private ownership and management has degraded our mass media, that the action of the management of basic industries in initiating price increases has indicated an obliviousness to the impact such action would have on the nation's economy, that industry (as in the case of automobile manufacture) is more concerned with a saleable appearance than with basic quality (and safety), that—in sum—the ideal of corporate citizenship is a veneer and a pretense. Clearly, such questions are of profound interest to every American.

It is all too easy to come up with simple answers and sweeping generalizations. All of them, including many of the adverse judgments implied above, must be weighed against the achievements of an open society in which, uniquely in man's history, vast strides towards banishing want and suffering have been made and in which—to borrow from Pericles—"Although only a few may originate a policy, we are all able to judge it." Such a judgment is made in the challenging comments that follow.

5

The Acquisitive Ideal

The acquisitive impulse is as old as man and has manifested itself wherever men have lived, but what R. H. Tawney has called the Acquisitive Society hardly antedates the third quarter of the eighteenth century. For a large part of this period its ambit was limited to England, the United States, and a small part of the continent of Europe. Max Weber was referring to a period not too long before the eighteenth century, when he wrote: "That anyone should be able to make it the sole purpose of his life-work, to sink into the grave weighed down with a great material load of money and goods, seems to him [pre-capitalist man] explicable only as the product of a perverse instinct, the *aura sacra fames*."[1]

The acquisitive society institutionalized the profit motive, gave it a central role, made it the driving force that transformed the static and stable economies of an earlier era. This was, as Tawney has said, its "whole tendency and interest and preoccupation."[2] An acquisitive society is one in which the means of production are privately owned and in which the motives of the market, that is to say, the calculated interests of buyers and sellers, determine the allocation of productive resources and the distribution of incomes. Such a society, as Joseph Schumpeter has written, "has been cast in a purely economic mold: its foundations, beams and beacons are all made of economic material. The

---

[1] *The Protestant Ethic and the Spirit of Capitalism,* translated by Talcott Parsons (London: George Allen & Unwin, Ltd., 1930), pp. 71–72.

[2] *The Acquisitive Society* (New York: Harcourt, Brace and World, Inc.), p. 29.

building faces toward the economic side of life. Prizes and penalties are measured in pecuniary terms. Going up and down means making and losing money."[3]

For a long time such a society felt no need to examine its basic premises, including its economic bias and the central place it accorded economic man—viewed always, in Veblen's famous phrase, as a "lightning calculator." In recent years, however, such a review has been going on. Not only did the acquisitive society develop unexpected weaknesses; it had to meet the challenge of competing systems and ideologies. The resulting reexamination has gone far beyond economic analysis to a reappraisal of the basic values of a good society. If the society emerging from appraisals such as those that follow would be unrecognizable to Mr. Gladstone or Mr. Coolidge, there is good reason to believe that it will prove more durable in the end.

---

[3] *Capitalism, Socialism, and Democracy* (New York: Harper & Row, Inc., 1942), p. 73.

THE HOUSE DIVIDED AGAINST ITSELF

John Dewey

Although it is fashionable in some quarters to denigrate him, John Dewey remains the towering eminence among American philosophers. In 1952, when he died at the age of 93, he left behind him a prodigious legacy of provocative and important books and articles such as few other men have encompassed in a lifetime. It is safe to say that he influenced our thinking more than any other American. His greatest works in the field of general philosophy are Experience and Nature *(1925) and* The Quest for Certainty *(1929). In ethical theory he waged a long war not only against absolutism, but against the kind of relativism which asserts that judgments of value are not, like judgments of fact, demonstrable and are therefore merely "emotive." Dewey believed that judgments of value are susceptible of validation and hence meaningful,*

Reprinted by permission of G. P. Putnam's Sons from *Individualism, Old and New*, pp. 9–56, by John Dewey. Copyright 1929, 1930 by John Dewey.

even though this is not accomplished by referring them to or deriving them from moral absolutes. Much of what he said on this subject is intended for the professional philosopher, but his Ethics *(1938) (especially Part II, which he wrote without his collaborator, James Tufts) will reward the general reader, as will* Human Nature and Conduct *(1922) and* Reconstruction in Philosophy *(1920).*

Dewey was an ardent social reformer. In this sense he was a philosophe *as well as a philosopher, if we agree with Carl Becker's view of the former as interested not only in ideas but in the impact of ideas on events. Dewey's interest was a logical outcome of his "instrumentalism," to use the term he preferred for his version of the pragmatic philosophy of which he was the leading exponent. But it was also an outcome of his recoil as an individual from what he regarded as the less wholesome features of a pecuniary culture.*

Although Individualism, Old and New *appeared in 1930, much recent social criticism bears a striking resemblance to it. When the book was first published, relatively few students were moved by Dewey's criticism of business. Today student attitudes have changed drastically enough to affect recruitment and concern business leaders. The* Los Angeles Times, *in an article about a weekend seminar of businessmen and students at Pomona College with the headline "Students Tell Why They Shun Business," reported that the two groups are "not on the same beam." Typical student comment, according to the* Times, *stressed that money is not the prime objective of today's students and that students want to do something that is "socially useful."*

Dewey's work is a severe impeachment of patterns of conduct prevalent during the first quarter of this century. We need now to ask ourselves to what extent these patterns still prevail.

. . . Anthropologically speaking, we are living in a money culture. Its cult and rites dominate. "The money medium of exchange and the cluster of activities associated with its acquisition drastically condition the other activities of the people." This, of course, is as it should be; people have to make a living, do they not? And for what should they work if not for money, and how should they get goods and enjoyments if not by buying them with money—thus enabling someone else to make more money, and in the end to start shops and factories to give employment to still others, so that they can make more money to enable other people to make more money by selling goods—and so on indefinitely. So far, all is for the best in the best of all possible cultures: our rugged—or is it ragged?—individualism.

And if the culture pattern works out so that society is divided into two classes, the working group and the business (including professional) group, with two and a half times as many in the former as in the latter, and with the chief ambition of parents in the former class that their children should climb into the latter, that is doubtless because American life offers such unparalleled opportunities for each individual to prosper according to his virtues. If few workers know what they are making or the meaning of what they do, and still fewer know what becomes of the work of their hands . . . this is doubtless because we have so perfected our system of distribution that the whole country is one. And if the mass of workers live in constant fear of loss of their jobs, this is doubtless because our spirit of progress, manifest in change of fashions, invention of new machines and power of overproduction, keeps everything on the move. Our reward of industry and thrift is so accurately adjusted to individual ability that it is natural and proper that the workers should look forward with dread to the age of fifty or fifty-five, when they will be laid on the shelf.

All this we take for granted; it is treated as an inevitable part of our social system. To dwell on the dark side of it is to blaspheme against our religion of prosperity. But it is a system that calls for a hard and strenuous philosophy. If one looks at what we do and what happens, and then expects to find a theory of life that harmonizes with the actual situation, he will be shocked by the contradiction he comes upon. For the situation calls for assertion of complete economic determinism. We live as if economic forces determined the growth and decay of institutions and settled the fate of individuals. Liberty becomes a well-nigh obsolete term; we start, go, and stop at the signal of a vast industrial machine. Again, the actual system would seem to imply a pretty definitely materialistic scheme of value. Worth is measured by ability to hold one's own or to get ahead in a competitive pecuniary race. . . . The philosophy appropriate to such a situation is that of struggle for existence and survival of the economically fit. One would expect the current theory of life, if it reflects the actual situation, to be the most drastic Darwinism. And, finally, one would antici- pate that the personal traits most prized would be clear-sighted vision of personal advantage and resolute ambition to secure it at any human cost. Sentiment and sympathy would be at the lowest discount.

It is unnecessary to say that the current view of life in Middletown, in Anytown, is nothing of this sort. Nothing gives us Americans the horrors more than to hear that some misguided creature in some low part of the earth preaches what we practice—and practice much more efficiently than anyone else—namely, economic determinism. Our whole theory is that man plans and uses machines for his own humane and moral purposes, instead of being borne wherever the machine carries him. Instead of materialism, our idealism is probably the loudest and most frequently professed philosophy the world has ever heard. We praise even our most successful men, not for their ruthless and self-centered energy in getting ahead, but because of their love of flowers, children, and dogs, or their kindness to aged relatives. Anyone who frankly urges a selfish creed of life is everywhere frowned upon. Along with the disappearance of the home, and the multiplication of divorce in one generation by six hundred per cent, there is the most abundant and most sentimental glorification of the sacredness of home and the beauties of constant love that history can record. We are surcharged with altruism and bursting with the desire to "serve" others.

These are only a few of the obvious contradictions between our institutions and practice on one hand, and our creeds and theories on the other, contradictions which a survey of any of our Middletowns reveals. It is not surprising that the inhabitants of these towns are bewildered, uneasy, restless, always seeking something new and different, only to find, as a rule, the same old thing in a new dress. It may all be summed up, perhaps, by saying that nowhere in the world at any time has religion been so thoroughly respectable as with us, and so nearly totally disconnected from life. . . .

. . . the whole story is told in brief when one contrasts what is actually happening to family life and the complete secularization of daily activities with a statement from the pulpit that "the three notable words in the English language are mother, home and heaven," a remark that would certainly pass unquestioned in any representative American audience.

It makes little difference whether one selects important or trivial aspects of the contradiction between our life as we outwardly live it and our thoughts and feelings—or what we at least say are our beliefs and sentiments. The significant question is: What is the cause of this split and contradiction? . . . It is evident enough that the rapid industrialization of our civilization took us unawares. Being mentally and morally unprepared, our older creeds have become ingrowing; the more we depart from them in fact, the more loudly we proclaim them. In effect we treat them as magic formulae. By repeating them often enough we hope to ward off the evils of the new situation, or at least to prevent ourselves from seeing them—and this latter function is ably performed by our nominal beliefs.

With an enormous command of instrumentalities, with possession of a secure technology, we glorify the past, and legalize and idealize the *status quo,* instead of seriously asking how we are to employ the means at our disposal so as to form an equitable and stable society. This is our great abdication. It explains how and why we are a house divided against itself. Our tradition, our heritage, is itself double. It contains in itself the ideal of equality of opportunity and of freedom for all, without regard to birth and status, as a condition for the effective realization of that equality. This ideal and endeavor in its behalf once constituted our essential Americanism; that which was prized as the note of a new world. It is the genuinely spiritual element of our tradition. No one can truthfully say that it has entirely disappeared. But its promise of a new moral and religious outlook has not been attained. It has not become the well-spring of a new intellectual consensus; it is not (even unconsciously) the vital source of any distinctive and shared philosophy. It directs our politics only spasmodically, and while it has generously provided schools it does not control their aims or their methods.

Meanwhile our institutions embody another and older tradition. Industry and business conducted for money profit are nothing new; they are not the product of our own age and culture; they come to us from a long past. But the invention of the machine has given them a power and scope they never had in the past from which they derive. Our law and politics and the incidents of human association depend upon a novel combination of the machine and money, and the result is the pecuniary culture characteristic of our civilization. The spiritual factor of our tradition, equal opportunity and free association and intercommunication, is obscured and crowded out. Instead of the development of individualities which is prophetically set forth, there is a perversion of the whole idea of individualism to conform to the practices of a pecuniary culture. It has become the source and justification of inequalities and oppressions. Hence our compromises, and the conflicts in which aims and standards are confused beyond recognition. . . .

The marks and signs of [the] "impersonalization" of the human soul are quantification of life, with its attendant disregard of quality; its mechanization and the almost universal habit of esteeming technique as an end, not as a means, so that organic and intellectual life is also "rationalized"; and, finally, standardization. Differences and distinctions are ignored and overridden; agreement, similarity, is the ideal. There is not only absence of social discrimination but of intellectual; critical thinking is conspicuous by its absence. Our pronounced trait is mass suggestibility. The adaptability and flexibility that we display in our practical intelligence when dealing with external conditions have found their way into our souls. Homogeneity of thought and emotion has become an ideal.

Quantification, mechanization and standardization: these are then the marks of the Americanization that is conquering the world. They have their good side; external conditions and the standard of living are undoubtedly improved. But their effects are not limited to these matters; they have invaded mind and character, and subdued the soul to their own dye. The criticism is familiar; it is so much the burden of our own critics that one is never quite sure how much of the picture of foreign critics is drawn from direct observation and how much from native novels and essays that are not complacent with the American scene. This fact does not detract from the force of the indictment; it rather adds to it, and raises the more insistently the question of what our life means.

. . . the impoverishment of the individual is accompanied, even now, by an enrichment of community resources. Collectively, present society . . . is marked by a power over nature and by intellectual resource and power exceeding that of the classic Athenian and the man of the Renaissance. Why is it that this collective enrichment does not operate to elevate correspondingly the life of the individual? . . . Failure to consider [this question] constitutes to my mind the chief failure of critics whether foreign or native. Our materialism, our devotion to money making and to having a good time, are not things by themselves. They are the product of the fact that we live in a money culture; of the fact that our technique and technology are controlled by interest in private profit. There lies the serious and fundamental defect of our civilization, the source of the secondary and induced evils to which so much attention is given. Critics are dealing with symptoms and effects. The evasion of fundamental economic causes by critics both foreign and native seems to me to be an indication of the prevalence of the old European tradition, with its disregard for the body, material things, and practical concerns. The development of the American type, in the sense of the critics, is an expression of the fact that we have retained this tradition and the economic system of private gain on which it is based, while at the same time we have made an independent development of industry and technology that is nothing short of revolutionary. When our critics deal with this issue instead of avoiding it there will be something really doing.

Until the issue is met, the confusion of a civilization divided against itself will persist. The mass development, which our European critics tell us has submerged individuality, *is* the product of a machine age; in some form it will follow in all countries from the extension of a machine technology. Its immediate effect has been, without doubt, a subjection of certain types of individuality. As far as individuality is associated with aristocracy of the historic type, the extension of the machine age will presumably be hostile to individuality in its traditional sense all over the world. . . . The problem of constructing a new individuality consonant with the objective conditions under which we live is the deepest problem of our times. . . .

Assured and integrated individuality is the product of definite social relationships and publicly acknowledged functions. Judged by this standard, even those who seem to be in control and to carry the expression of their special individual abilities to a high pitch, are submerged. They may be captains of finance and industry, but until there is some consensus of belief as to the meaning of finance and industry in civilization as a whole, they cannot be captains of their own souls—their beliefs and aims. They exercise leadership surreptitiously and, as it were, absentmindedly. They lead, but it is under cover of impersonal and socially undirected economic forces. Their reward is found not in what they do, in their social office and function, but in a deflection of social consequences to private gain. They receive the acclaim and command the envy and admiration of the crowd, but the crowd is also composed of private individuals who are equally lost to a sense of social bearings and uses.

The explanation is found in the fact that while the actions promote corporate and collective results, these results are outside their intent and irrelevant to that reward of satisfaction which comes from a sense of social fulfillment. To themselves and to others, their business is private and its outcome is private profit. No complete satisfaction is possible where such a split exists. Hence the absence of a sense of social value is made up for by an exacerbated acceleration of the activities that increase private advantage and power. One cannot look into the inner consciousness of his fellows; but if there is any general degree of inner contentment on the part of those who form our pecuniary oligarchy, the evidence is sadly lacking. As for the many, they are impelled hither and yon by forces beyond their control. . . .

The unrest, impatience, irritation and hurry that are so marked in American life are inevitable accompaniments of a situation in which individuals do not find support and contentment in the fact that they are sustaining and sustained members of a social whole. They are evidence, psychologically, of abnormality, and it is as idle to seek for their explanation within the deliberate intent of individuals as it is futile to think that they can be got rid of by hortatory moral appeal. Only an acute maladjustment between individuals and the social conditions under which they live can account for such widespread pathological phenomena. Feverish love of anything as long as it is a change which is distracting, impatience, unsettlement, nervous discontentment, and desire for excitement, are not native to human nature. They are so abnormal as to demand explanation in some deep-seated cause.

I should explain a seeming hypocrisy on the same ground. We are not consciously insincere in our professions of devotion to ideals of "service"; they mean something. Neither the Rotarian nor the big business enterprise uses the term merely as a cloak for "putting something over" which makes for pecuniary gain. But the lady doth protest too much. The wide currency of such professions testifies to a sense of a social function of business which is expressed in words because it is so lacking in fact, and yet which is felt to be rightfully there. If our external combinations in industrial activity were reflected in organic integrations of the desires, purposes and satisfactions of individuals, the verbal protestations would disappear, because social utility would be a matter of course.

CAPITALIST ECONOMY AND BUSINESS CIVILIZATION

Max Lerner

Max Lerner is one of the most discerning observers of the American scene. He makes his views known in the college classroom, through a daily column in the New York Post, *and in books and essays that invariably provide new insights into the American character. Among these are his* It's Later Than You Think (*1943*), Ideas Are Weapons (*1939*), The Mind and Faith of Justice Holmes (*1943*) *and, the two-volume work from which the following selection is taken. Although no apologist for things as they are, Lerner is much less severe with the culture of a business society than was Dewey.*

. . . The reach of the commercial spirit penetrates into every area of American culture. The business principle has sometimes been confused with the machine principle. The latter is used to dispense with human labor and make possible standardized and large-scale production, while the business principle focuses on market sale for profit. It puts the making of money ahead of other craft and civilization values, gives primacy to the cultural and personal traits which lead to that end, and tends to apply money values even to the human personality.

America has often been called a business civilization, but the term is too sweeping. One cannot say that the business principle is the only one operating in American culture. In some areas—religion, education, the arts, the family—it exerts only an incipient influence. But even where it has not become decisive, there has been a creeping imperialism of business over the other domains of life.

The business principle has given a synthetic cohesion to the far-flung diversity of American life. Before the Civil War it could genuinely be said that American culture was a loose collection of principalities—those of politics, of farming and industry, of religion, of literature and art and the press—tied together mainly by a pride of pioneering and a sense of the emerging national strength, and some belief in the democratic idea. The advance of business power and values weakened the hold of the democratic idea, while translating both the pioneering sense and the nationalist pride into the boom terms of growing industrial power and profit. . . .

In America, as everywhere, politics has been vulnerable to bribery. Yet it is a paradox of a business civilization that there has been notably less political corruption in America than in many precapitalist societies such as in Asia, the Middle East, and South America, or even some of the Latin societies of Europe. Perhaps this is exactly because of the importance of business: for those to whom money is all-important there are in America (as in no other culture) more direct channels open to the money-making energies than through the circuitous routes of the political career and political power. Political corruption is most rampant in the cultures where for many men it is the only road to wealth and status; in America it is only one of many.

Yet the business spirit, which directly carries along in its torrential course so many of the talents and energies of men into money-making, also breaks down some of the moral barriers that had been built into the conscience for generations. The big temptation in the era of the expanding frontier was land speculation. In the era of an expanding capitalism the temptations lie less in speculation than in the sale of political influence to businessmen intent on getting some of the Big Money, by crucially placed governmental subalterns who don't see why they too should not get their cut. As in the post-Civil War days of Grant and Conkling, or the post-World War days of Harding and Daugherty, the torrents of fresh business energy which open new opportunities for big profits also carry away with them much of the terrain of social conscience. In this sense it is not the periods of business decay but the periods of business expansion and vitality which play havoc with moral principles, because they fix men's aims at the attainable goals of the Big Money. . . .

Until recently, at least, the appeal of business has been as a way of making money, not as a way of life. Sensitive people have rejected the way of life but then been lured by the money; hence the split in the American attitude toward business, which has been most marked where the tradition of an educated elite has been strongest. The Adams family, for example, showed both a cultivated understanding and a cultivated fear of the new and pushing type of business activity. Writing in *The Education,* Henry Adams expressed the melancholy sense that for all the processes of civilization that had gone to make him, he was unfit to survive in the world that business values were fashioning. Brooks Adams, living as a *rentier* from corporate securities, was able to dissect pitilessly the social sources of his income, all the time ransacking history to explain the emergence of this new form of centralized power to which he owed the leisure he had for ransacking history. The third brother, Charles Francis Adams, was a railroad president who wrote with shriveling contempt for the narrowness of outlook and the niggardliness of spirit of business as a way of life. Henry James, for all his preoccupation with money and what it could buy, always pushed the question of its sources into the background and felt slightly soiled by them. He was most at home with a businessman like the hero of *The Golden Bowl,* spending in Europe the fortune he had made in America, a Maecenas who knew what he wanted and went after it with the practiced assurance that betokened the habitual conqueror. The secret that Sir Joseph Duveen discovered about American businessmen, which made his fortune as an art salesman, was that they gloried in their power over the things that money commanded but hungered for the symbols of the life values that went beyond money. Throughout the history of the business spirit, the monied men have used business first as a way of making the Big Kill, then turned to philanthropy or the life of the patron, travel, or hobbies as a way of making a life.

The business spirit, then, has not in itself been regarded as a nourishing one but as a means to bring a good life within reach. For that reason perhaps it has exerted an attraction for the young men of talent who in other civilizations might have gone into government, the Army, or the priesthood, into literature or the arts or the study of philosophy, into science or the professions. Even those in government service have, when successful, been tempted to turn their knowledge to the service of the corporation: if they have worked in the Treasury Department on taxes, or as economists in government bureaus, they can command good salaries as consultants or executives in business. If they have been good newspapermen they are eagerly recruited for public-relations jobs in the corporate world. And the corporations have learned to go directly to the colleges in recruiting young men of talent who are rarely able to resist the offer of an immediate job as against the uncertainties of a career in the arts or professions.[1]

Even for those who stay outside business, there is a strong drive to conduct themselves in a "businesslike" way. The trade-union movement in America has been largely, as Hoxie first described it, "business unionism," expressing the competing claims to income of the corporate employees as part of the larger structure of the business economy itself. In education the school administrator and the university president have tended to act as corporate executives. Even in the churches the temptation is to be "practical" in administering vast properties rather than unworldly in pursuing the values of the spirit. In the newspaper and magazine fields the pressure is toward building big power aggregates that can command writing talent and the reader market and get a big share of national advertising: the magazine or big newspaper is likely to make its more blatant public boasts not so much about its newsgathering or its crusading spirit as about its circulation

---

[1] Editor's note: Max Lerner might well qualify that statement if he were writing today.

and advertising gains. In radio and television the art forms are subsidiary to the selling of time to the business sponsors. In moviemaking, the final art product has to run the gauntlet of box-office appeal, and the Hollywood values of inflated salaries and skyrocketing careers are a kind of caricature of the corporate executives. In literature the emphasis has shifted to the products that can be marketed to a mass audience, notably crime and detection thrillers.

In fact, it may turn out that the business spirit will leave its most enduring imprint on the adjoining provinces of literature and entertainment, government and opinion: for these are the areas in which capital investment counts least and personality and talent still can carve out empires. They are the last Klondikes of venture skills, which are even more important in the history of business than venture capital. The lure of the acquisitive impulse, wedded to talent and ideas, produces a powerful amalgam.

It is customary to speak of this as the "commercializing" of art and opinion. But the process is more complex. The crux of it is that the dominant activity of any civilization colors the prevailing notions of what is effective or futile in the exercise of men's talents. In a business civilization the stamp of effectiveness is placed on whatever can be exchanged in the personality market for money and success; the stamp of ineffectuality is placed on whatever talent is not vendible, whatever cannot move to a maximum degree into the channels where it is capitalized and reaches a mass market with all the accruing rewards. Thus the business spirit, itself incapable of yielding nourishing life values, has become for Americans the prime gateway to a way of life, with few questions asked about what you find when you have gone through the gates.

When one inquires what may account for the "domination effect" of the business spirit, the answer lies partly in the attractiveness of the big rewards and the big market, partly in the admiration felt for the men who have shown that they can run things best, partly in the pragmatic strain of a culture which accepts whatever is practical and successful as the valid and pays it the flattery of mimicry.

The final tribute to the domination effect of the business spirit is the extent to which the phases of the human personality are measured in its terms. In a seminal analysis of types of character structure that bear aptly on American life, Fromm has spoken of the "marketing orientation" as one that is crowding out much else in the business society. There is little question that the marketable personality is becoming the dominant one, even in areas outside business. Courtesy and charm come to be valued not for themselves but because they pay off in salesmanship; clothes must be worn well to make an impression on a prospective customer or employer; the "dreamer type" of person is dangerous because he will estrange those who seek alertness. America itself, in the impact it makes on other peoples in the struggle for world leadership, must "sell" itself and its ideas; and the clinching argument used even by liberal intellectuals against the denial of civil rights of Negroes and other minority groups is that it will interfere with such international "selling" and acceptance.

This then is what seems to have happened in the American business economy. The more strictly technical problems of production and scarcity, of income distribution, of bigness in the sense distinct from monopoly, even of the business cycle, are fairly on the way to being resolved. But the bureaucratization of life through the new managerial structures in business, the trade-union, the government, and the corrupting reach of marketing values and the money spirit are being extended through the whole culture. The real problems of the business culture are thus less the technical and strictly economic problems than the moral and psychological ones.

Yet, to say, as some foreign observers and American critics have said, that only money talks in America is to vulgarize the impact of the business spirit. Other values than the acquisitive find a place in American life, and often they triumph; and other qualities than the money-making qualities blossom. But even when they do triumph, it is only after they have been measured and defended against the money values and the vendible qualities. That they survive is the final tribute to their hardihood, and when they do survive—in literature and the arts, in human relations, in religion and education and government, in the armed services, in the professions, perhaps even in business itself—they have a greater strength than in those cultures where they do not have to measure themselves so searchingly against the domination effect of the business spirit.

THE CASH-NEXUS

Peter Viereck

*The selection that follows is an evaluation of the business
spirit from the point of view of a conservative who is not himself a member of the business community.*

*Peter Viereck teaches history at Mount Holyoke College
and was an eloquent spokesman for the conservative point of
view even during the 'thirties, when conservatism found few
intellectual adherents. However, many of those who call
themselves conservatives today will derive meager comfort
from his views. Viereck regards the current crop of right-wing
nationalists as spurious conservatives devoid of generous social
impulses and disposes of them in a* New Republic *article
(September 24, 1962) as "rootless, counter-revolutionary doc-
trinaires."*

*Besides the volume from which the present selection is
taken, he has written* Metapolitics: From the Romantics to
Hitler *(1941),* Conservatism Re-Visited *(1949 and 1962),
and* Shame and Glory of the Intellectuals *(1953).*

The conservative philosophy developed partly as an ethical reaction against the value-dissolving huckster-materialism accompanying the
industrial revolution in the early 1800's. Though founded earlier by Burke
as an answer to the French Revolution, the conservative philosophy gained
its depth-psychology only under the agony of industrialism. The main
impact of industrialism on western man was not economic but psychological: the trauma it inflicted on the traditional value-heritage. The post-
Burkean depth-psychology of conservatism derived not from politicians but
from sensitive creative artists like Coleridge, Matthew Arnold, Cardinal
Newman in England; Baudelaire, Dostoyevsky, Nietzsche, Burckhardt on
the continent; Melville, Hawthorne, Poe, Henry Adams, Faulkner in
America. Melville was the one to state the most succinctly the attitude they
all shared:

> The spider in the laurel spins,
> The weed exiles the flower;
> And, flung to kiln, Apollo's bust
> Makes lime for Mammon's tower.

Such literary or religious value-conservers could not endure the dissolving of society's aesthetic, ethical, and religious ties by the arid cash-nexus. Its dissolution of these traditional ties was opposed, long before Marx, by Tory spirits like Donoso Cortés, Metternich, Disraeli. Therefore, most (not all) new conservatives have actively opposed that last Indian summer of hucksterdom which flowered in America after the Republican victory of 1952.

But unlike socialists, with their class-determinism, new conservatives do not indiscriminately equate most businessmen with a huckster-mentality. It is a kind of Aryan racism of economics to brand classes instead of individuals. A mentality characterizing more individual business-men in the McKinley context of yesteryear may, under a new context, characterize more individual trade-unionists, rustics, grand dukes, or pro-fessors. Such a mentality should no more be attributed permanently to a party than to a class. The cash-nexus Old Guard is not the whole Republi-can party, did not represent it in Lincoln's day, need not represent it tomorrow.

It is mere romanticism to ignore the reality of industrialism and flee into some never-existent idealization of the Middle Ages. What is deadly is not the industrial gadgetry itself nor the material prosperity itself but the overadjusted smugness, self-sufficiency, and betrayal of spiritual traditions that accompany this gadgetry, this prosperity unless these be-come servants, not tyrants of man. In their different ways, the starting point 150 years ago of both aristocratic conservatism and democratic socialism was their shared fear that the middleclass *laissez faire* liberalism was allowing industrial mechanization to become not the servant but the tyrant of man. In their historical and European origins, conservatism and socialism are both psychological reactions against the intolerable cash-nexus mentality of the nineteenth-century burgher.

In twentieth-century America, that same capitalism has achieved (in contrast with the high-priced, low-production capitalism of Europe) miraculous economic benefits for all, benefits which its socialist-proletarian and conservative-aristocratic opponents never dreamed of in Europe and in the nineteenth century. The diffusion of these benefits among workers has rendered out of date most of the socialist attacks on capitalism, insofar as these attacks were mainly economic and material. But these admittedly attractive benefits have not rendered out of date the traditional conserva-tive attacks on middleclass capitalism, attacks which were not economic but spiritual (Coleridge, Carlyle, Newman, Ruskin, Arnold, Melville). Nor have these material benefits of modern American capitalism rendered out of date that minority within socialist thinkers who represent not material-ism but Christian ethics.

The benefits of American capitalism, its admirable flexibility, its ability to reform its own weaknesses via free parliamentary channels, its wide diffusion of private property (which Henry Maine in *Popular Government,* 1885, showed to be indispensable to full personal liberty), and the greatest material well-being in history—all these benefits, while refuting and outdating the Marxist predictions of ever greater poverty and inequality under capitalism, have neither outdated nor solved the problem of the Over-adjusted Man. That is, the problem of mass-mechanization leading to an economically delicious but stereotyping prosperity. There is, therefore, no need to abandon smugly those attacks on the cash-nexus which characterized almost all the greatest religious, philosophical, and literary figures of America's past. Today and tomorrow those attacks must continue on cultural, ethical, or religious levels—the three proper levels of conservatism in contemporary America—even though those attacks on capitalism have been outdated on the economic level, the proper level of socialist materialists.

In Europe socialism and conservatism both had a social base, a party, a class: proletariat or landed aristocracy. In America, where the whole country is diffused with middleclass psychology, the two anti-middleclass movements cannot play a role in terms of political parties or economic classes. This obvious lack of a class base for either socialism or conservatism in America has led to their being scorned as having no role to play in America. What their scorners forget is that attitudes can work through diffusion as well as through a movement. Both conservatism and socialism work in America as a whole, equally in all parties and classes, as an unlabeled and unconscious diffusion, not as a movement. When they become a movement, they become small, comical splinter-groups. They become cranks who imagine nostalgically a non-existent class of feudal southern landowners or class-conscious proletarians, as the case may be. To make this statement is not to minimize the important role of conservative and socialist thought. Diffusion can be more influential than any localized movement or party. But that important intellectual influence will be jeopardized if New Conservatives should make the mistake of trying to localize their essentially cultural and ethical thought into one particular party or into apologetics for one particular American class, whether that class be the no-longer-existent agrarian nobles of the Middle Ages and the feudal south or the all-too-existent urban hucksters.

In the case of Europe, conservatism and socialism differ in their class base, their economic base, and their general historical base. In the case of America, neither has inherited any class base from history, and neither is identified with any political party (except for irrelevant splinter-groups, our parties are neither aristocratic nor proletarian but middleclass). Therefore, in the case of America, conservatism and socialism are not only weaker than in Europe (except for diffusion under other labels) but differ far less from each other than they do in Europe. What unites them in America is their distrust of the commercialism prevailing ever since the defeat of the Civil War of the agrarian south as well as the subsequent defeat of the Lincolnian non-commercial idealists inside the north.

In America, ever since the death of the truly conservative Federalist party, we must speak (except for rootless, doctrinaire fringes) not of socialist or conservative ideologies, parties, movements but of diffused and unlabeled conservative or socialist attitudes, at their most effective when least labeled and at their least effective when articulate and conscious. Despite their close kinship in America as fellow anti-commercialists, there is one important area where conservative and socialist attitudes do differ from each other, even in America, with an unbridgeable gap. That area is their view of human nature. Socialism shares with Jeffersonian liberals a faith in human nature, the masses, the natural goodness of man; sometimes it also shares with Progressives and Populists of the Paine heritage a faith in direct democracy. In contrast, the conservative view of human nature takes into account its complexity, its tragic tensions between incompatible impulses, and therefore its inability to plan the long-range rational blueprints desired by socialists. Historically the conservative view of human nature is a secularization of the Christian doctrine of original sin. At the same time the conservative view of human nature is close to the discoveries of the Freudians about the subconscious and about stifled impulses, discoveries that Coleridge and Nietzsche so uncannily anticipated.

The usual capitalist defense of private property against socialists sounds appalling, especially in the ears of idealistic artists and scholars, because of its grubby materialist basis. If the issue is debated on that basis alone, then trade-unions of Europe and the majority of the intellectuals of Asia and Europe are justified in strongly sympathizing with the socialists, who at least have a generous breadth of vision. Yet it is the socialists who are wrong, the American kind of capitalists who are right about the need for a widely-diffused possession of unmolested private property. The capitalists are right, not in sloganizing about a maximum *laissez faire* (which they themselves fail to practice whenever they can get tariffs and state subsidies) but in insisting upon some minimum level of property beyond which not even the kindliest state may intervene. However, the proper argument for their excellent case is not their profit-motive but the fact that capitalist private property has also a non-material, moral function. It educates its possessor in the moral qualities of sturdy independence, sense of responsibility, and the training of judgment and character brought whenever free choice is exercised in any field, including the economic field. It is these moral qualities, not the gluttonous material ones that have historically associated the rise of personal liberty with the rise of personal property. To recognize this concrete historical fact about property and liberty is not, be it added, the same as abstracting that fact into a vast, rigid ideology of Manchester liberalism or into an imagination-stifling cash-nexus.

Most socialists are anti-communists. The horrible example of Soviet terrorist dictatorship, which socialists like George Orwell and Norman Thomas opposed more effectively than most capitalists, has forced most socialists to reconsider their frequent earlier minimizing of the danger of statism to their own lofty ideals. The best socialist thought today, independent and non-sectarian, is ably engaged in trying to work out a formula preserving personal choice in all non-economic spheres at the same time as having centralized economic planning. To a distruster of the abstract, the flaw in even the best of these socialist theories lies not in their sincerity, intellect, and good will (often superior in those three qualities to their detractors). Their flaw lies in their assumption that society can be understood or perfected by over-all formulas in the first place. Thomas I. Cook has defined the new conservatism as the rediscovery that liberty depends on concrete traditions and is menaced by "excessive reliance on human reason, functioning deductively and *a priori* on a foundation of abstract principle.

The proper corollary to the able socialist indictments of Soviet Russia is not to contrive some new and shinier formula to replace the discredited old one but to stop seeing salvation in any brand of over-all formula. The proper corollary is to begin seeing history as the darkly growing relationship of concrete to concrete. No kind of socialist over-all explanation and chart, no pedantic, top-of-the-brain ideology (whether it calls itself socialist, liberal, or conservative), can ever systematize or control the rich, helter-skelter plenitude of man.

The latest thought of certain socialists and of certain *laissez faire* capitalists is producing insights no conservative can neglect without being the loser. A number of those writers are far removed from being the usual grubby caricatures of materialism. And yet, even when one leans over backward to consider their writings without prejudice, how many others turn out to be just that. And how much such big-business materialists and socialist materialists resemble each other! They differ on the non-essentials: on economic theory, on the boring wrangle about whether the fat swine or the lean swine of materialism should hog a bit more of the economic trough. But they agree on certain essentials: a mechanistic view of life, utilitarianism, the unpleasant duty of dutiful pleasure-seeking, faith in bigger and better progress, in sterile efficiency, in doctrinaire apriorism. To these goals both sacrifice what the conservative cherishes: all that is warm, concrete, human in human nature, everything precarious, diversified, unpredictable, unorganized, unadjusted. . . .

Industrialism is still a young force, a post-1789 force, a force still unpatterned and experimental. If its strutting, success-intoxicated children will subordinate the raw material energies of that new force to the old, legitimizing pattern of the Christian-Judaic ethic, then American democratic capitalism will increasingly evolve a non-huckster, non-philistine businessman, just as America has already amazed continental Europe by evolving a non-Marxist workingman. Then the new legitimism of a more deeply-rooted, ethic-centered west can transcend the false choice between plutocratic and Marxist materialism. Such transcendence can still save America from a warning of Emerson that ought especially to haunt an atomic age. "Things are in the saddle and ride mankind."

THE PROFIT MOTIVE

Peter Drucker

Peter Drucker is a well-known authority on the corporation as a social institution. He is both a teacher and management consultant and the author of a number of widely read books, including The End of Economic Man (*1939*), The Future of Industrial Man (*1941*), The New Society (*1950*), *and* Landmarks of Tomorrow (*1959*). *For eighteen months he served as outside consultant to General Motors Corporation, which asked him to study and report on its managerial policies and organization. The volume from which the following selection is taken is a result of this study. While rejecting the hedonistic preconceptions of orthodox economics as a basis on which to plead that the profit motive is inherent in human nature, he argues that the profit motive is nevertheless indispensable to a viable economy and a free society.*

Profit and profitability are objective criteria of economic action. They have nothing to do with the beliefs of a given society or with particular institutions but apply to any society however organized. Essentially profit and profitability are nothing but reformulations of the law of the conservation of energy in economic terms.

The "profit motive" on the other hand pertains to man's actions and reactions. In capitalist society, moreover, it is institutionalized in special institutions, and behavior according to the "profit motive" receives

---

From *The Concept of the Corporation* by Peter F. Drucker (New York: John Day Company, Inc., 1946), pp. 236–245. Copyright © 1946 by Peter F. Ducker. By permission of The John Day Company, Inc., publisher.

social sanctions and rewards. It is this "profit motive," the socially sanctioned behavior of the individual to obtain the maximum material gain, which is under attack as "unnatural" and "antisocial." And since the corporation in a free-enterprise economy is directed by, and dedicated to, the satisfaction of this "profit motive," the question arises whether the "profit motive" is indeed incompatible with a stable, functioning and good society.

The attack on the profit motive as "unnatural" and conflicting with socially and individually more beneficial and more fundamental human motives is, like the attack on profitability, partly the result of an excessive reaction against the wrong psychology of the utilitarian economists. They had proclaimed that man has a natural instinct to "truck and bargain," and they deduced from this instinct the laws of classical economics. We know today that there is no such thing as a natural instinct to "truck and bargain." If we ever needed proof of the fallacy of the utilitarian concept, it has been abundantly supplied by modern cultural anthropology and modern psychology. We also know that in most human activities, motives are thoroughly mixed, and that we will never find anybody acting on the basis of that "simple and clear calculation" of possible gain against possible effort on which the classical economists based their theories of economic behavior. Finally, we know that the orthodox economists were completely mistaken when they used the utilitarian "pleasure-pain calculus" to equate "work" with "pain." The psychological and social ravages of unemployment have certainly shown that idleness, far from being pleasing, is destructive, and that work, far from being disagreeable, is a necessity of human existence and self-respect and in itself a source of pride and satisfaction. There is little left today of that psychology from which the profit motive emerged as the controller of human destinies and as the natural law of human behavior.

To say that the profit motive is not inborn in man and the expression of his true nature is, however, something very different from asserting that it is vicious, unnatural and socially undesirable. This assertion rests on two beliefs which are both as untenable and as fallacious psychologically as the dogma of the preordained profit motive which they tried to replace. The first of these is the belief that man's "creative instinct" is not only good in itself but alone sufficient to make man socially constructive—the belief which is expressed in Veblen's famous juxtaposition of "industry" and "business." The second of these beliefs asserts that, but for the profit motive, human society would be one of equality and peace, and that all drive for power and privilege, all conflict and all inequality are the result of the lust for gain. In other words, both beliefs see in the profit motive the one, or at least the main, obstacle to the millennium.

It cannot be said too emphatically that no society can be based on man's "creative instincts." In order to make social life possible there must always be a principle of organization which reduces individual fulfillment and individual drive to a social purpose. Otherwise that co-ordinated human effort on which social life rests becomes impossible. If we do not use profit and profitability as the reduction gear, we would have to work out some other social mechanism to convert the subjective drive of the individual into the objective performance of society.

If we take, for instance, the people employed in the production of an automobile, we shall find that the "instinct of workmanship" leads in totally different directions, depending upon whether we look at the engineer, the production man or the sales manager. For the engineer the highest standard of achievement and craftsmanship lies in the most functional and most up-to-date car embodying the best and newest in engineering research, in materials and in design. He may be inclined to regard as alien and as in conflict with his ideas of workmanship such considerations as cheapness and ease of production, habits of automobile users, their comfort, etc.; and he would want to change his design all the time in order to· incorporate the latest engineering improvements. The standards by which the production man will measure his workmanship and achievement would be above all cheapness, speed and ease of production. His ideal is an engineering design that will never change. His attitude towards the consumer's preference and desires was summed up perfectly in the epigram attributed to that prince of production men, Henry Ford, when he said that "the customer can have any color as long as it's black." The sales manager finally—or anybody whose business it is to distribute cars—sees maximum achievement in the most salable car, a cheap car that "looks like a million dollars" and satisfies the consumer's desire to keep up with the Joneses—however unreasonable this may appear to the engineer or to the production man. Each has "instincts of workmanship" which are creative. But the instinct of the one can find free rein only at the expense of the instinct of another. If society wants automobiles, it must be able to subordinate the instincts of each man to an objective principle of social satisfaction. However much such an objective principle "violates" individual integrity—a point mooted since the dawn of history—society must have it.

The profit motive may not be the best reduction gear. It certainly is not the only possible one. But to denounce it because it is a reduction gear—Veblen's procedure—begs the question. What we have to answer is not whether the profit motive is good or bad, but whether it is efficient or inefficient as a principle of social integration of individual motives and desires.

In a society which accepts economic advancement and economic goals as socially efficient and as socially desirable the profit motive is socially the most efficient device. In any other society, it is not an efficient mechanism. In the Middle Ages, for instance, the profit motive was clearly socially inefficient from the point of view of an order which regarded economic goals—beyond mere physical survival—as socially irrelevant and as morally suspect. In a society which believes in the desirability of economic progress, as has ours for the last two hundred years, the profit motive is an efficient mechanism of integration, because it relates individual motives and drives directly to accepted social purposes. Obviously, this creates problems in those spheres of social life to which economic rationality is not applicable, such as the arts. But these problems are no greater than those faced by the Middle Ages in applying their noneconomic objective principle of social integration to the economic sphere with its necessarily economic rationality. In other words, while no society and no principle of social integration can be perfect or automatic, the profit motive is the most efficient and the simplest mechanism for the conversion of individual drives into social purpose and action under the given conditions and beliefs of *our* society. It is, perhaps, the best commentary on this conclusion that the Soviet Union has gone as far as any capitalist country —and further—in using economic rewards and incentives in industry. For however different its social tenets and institutions, Russia shares with the West the belief in economic goals.

What about the second count in the popular indictment of the profit motive: that it is the cause of the lust for power and dominance and the sole or main obstacle to peace and equality? Certainly the "profit motive" is not necessarily inherent in human nature. But inherent in human nature there is a drive for power and distinction of which the profit motive is only one possible form. If we eliminate the profit motive, the result will not be the equal and peaceful society of the millennium but the emergence of some other outlet for men's basic lust for power.

The weakness of the traditional argument is beautifully illustrated by the first great sermon on the profit motive as the original sin, and on its abolition as the key to the earthly paradise—Thomas More's *Utopia*. More's ideal society is perfect, peaceful, free of strife and ambition simply because property and gain have been eliminated. At the same time—almost on the same page—More proposes an elaborate system of honors and preferments as the basis for social power and political rulership. And he never sees the obvious: that the competition for these honors and preferments would at once bring back the ambition, the strife, the factionalism and the lust for power and prestige which he had just driven out by banishing the profit motive. Plato—and More was a Platonist—knew better. But his proposal in the *Republic* not to admit anyone to rulership until he be old enough to be past ambition is hardly more realistic; is there an age limit on ambition and pride? Wherever in history a man was kept out of power until very late, his lust for power, his ambition, his dominance and factiousness increased, often to the point of pathological exaggeration.

If I may again point to the findings of modern anthropology: the sentimental concept of "primitive equality" popularized by Rousseau and Marx has been exploded completely. There are many primitive tribes which do not know individual property in the sense in which we use the term. There are however no examples of real communism among primitive tribes; communism is far too complicated a social arrangement to be attainable for a primitive society. And in every single culture we know of, there is a socially accepted motive of advancement to power and prestige around which the social organization is built.

Actually, we should not have needed anthropology to teach us that society is based on man's innate drive for power and social recognition. We have known for thousands of years that Pride is an essentially human quality. We may, with the ancient Greeks and the Renaissance, accept Pride as a virtue. Or we may with the Christian doctrine regard Pride as both cause and result of man's fall from grace and as the center of his corruption. But we can never hope to have a society without it. The statesman may, as a Christian, deplore the weakness of man and strive to overcome it in himself. As a statesman, however, he has to accept the fact that Pride and its manifestations are both the reason for the existence of society, and a constant in any social organization. The problem of the statesman is not to suppress or to overcome the drive for power; that is the concern of philosopher and saint. The political problem is how to direct the drive for power into the socially most constructive or least destructive channels.

To say, as is customary, that the profit motive is bad because all drive for power is bad, evades the issue; it may be good theology but it certainly is not relevant to politics. To say that the profit motive is bad because without it there would be no drive for power, is not even bad theology; it is nonsense. The only relevant and meaningful question is whether the profit motive is the socially most efficient one of the available directions in which the drive for power can be channeled.

I do not think that anyone can give a dogmatic answer; the absolutely best lies in the field of religion or philosophy, not in that of politics or social organization. But we can say that of the channels available and known to us, the profit motive has a very high, if not the highest, social efficiency. All the other known forms in which the lust for power can be expressed, offer satisfaction by giving the ambitious man direct power and domination over his fellow man. The profit motive alone gives fulfillment through power over things. It is an old truth that the richest and most overbearing millionaire in a capitalist society has less power over the individual worker than the worst paid official in a collectivist state, who can grant or withhold a license to do business or a work card. Certainly there is the danger that the power over things may develop into a power over men. But it is not an inevitable danger, and it can be checked by social action. . . .

The profit motive is the one way known to us to divert ambition from the socially destructive goal of power over men, into a socially constructive channel, that of economic production. This, though not by itself sufficient, is a protection against the danger that the lives and the livelihood of the individual citizen will become pawns in the game of human ambition and fair prey for the drive for power. It is no accident that the great villains of history are not found among the "economic royalists" but among the "incorruptibles," whose aim was power and power alone. Neither Robespierre nor Hitler could have been bought off by money; they lacked economic acquisitiveness entirely. But this hardly made them any more beneficial for mankind; their indifference to anything but naked power over men only heightened their inhumanity. . . .

To have a free society we must make it possible for man to act and to live in society without destroying himself or enslaving his fellow men. We must harness the lust for power to a social purpose. This, in a society accepting economic goals, the profit motive can do.

We do not have to regard the drive for gain as noble or as the best man is capable of. But noble or base, it directs the drive for power into the least dangerous channel. Of course the profit motive does not bring about a free society; the identification of capitalism with democracy, so current today, is utterly superficial and is the result of a truly shocking confusion. But while the profit motive by itself leads to a free society as little as any other human drive, it is more compatible with it than the other forms in which the lust for power may manifest itself socially. A free society is not based on man's drive but on his reason; it always has to guard against the danger of its perversion by the drive for power or by any other drive. The profit motive contains potential threats like all other manifestations of human pride. But unlike the other forms in which the drive for power may become socially effective, the profit motive of a free-enterprise society also contains powerful safeguards against the politically most dangerous consequence of human pride, the tyranny of the power-drunk.

6

The Problem of Priorities

The foregoing discussions have dealt in general terms with the way in which the profit motive has shaped our culture and influenced our ideals and aspirations as a people. Traditionally in our country the profit motive operates through the market and ours is known as a "market economy." The alternative to a market economy is some form of planning, either private or public, partial or total. In truth, ours is a "mixed economy" in which private planning and public planning combine with the conventional forces of the market to determine the way in which we allocate our human and physical resources. Even so, the movements of the market are influenced primarily by the decisions of those who own or manage the private sector of the economy. In recent times the beneficence of this influence on our scale of preferences as these are reflected in public and private expenditures has become a subject of much controversy. It will become evident that the problem of priorities, as we have come to know it, is a special one, touched upon, to be sure, in the preceding selections but not in its own terms.

Thus, if an individual were to spend a disproportionate amount of his income on luxuries—flashy automobiles, sports, liquor, etc.—at the same time that his family was badly housed and without adequate medical care, and his children inadequately educated, our moral appraisal of him would be a severe one. The contention is that collectively as a people we dispose of our resources in some analogous fashion.

The disposition of our resources, to repeat, is determined either by the market or by government. In our folklore, if not in fact, the market is thought to reflect the multitudinous decisions of individuals, each one the best judge of his own interest and each choosing freely and rationally[1] within the limitations of his income and thereby guiding the flow of resources into one use or other. Government is generally thought of as consisting of potentially tyrannous individuals arbitrarily imposing their judgment on others. Is this an accurate description of the alternatives? And does the kind of market economy that prevails in the United States bias the allocation of resources in favor of frivolous expenditures to the neglect of fundamental needs? The question has come increasingly into the forefront of our thinking. Although it is generally discussed in economic and political terms, moral issues are clearly involved.

Many would say that, except at the margins, we need not stumble over distinguishing between what is extravagant and frivolous and what is basic and fundamental. Oversized cars, rapid changes of fashion in attire, and built-in obsolescence would appear to fall into the first category; water purification, housing, medical care, and education, into the latter. Even so, some will ask who is to determine what is good or bad in the way we spend our money? Others will answer that the consumer should, but under conditions that enable him to exercise his best judgment. This, then, is the problem of priorities: Do our economic institutions as they now operate make for a wise or foolish allocation of our resources? Two contrasting views are presented in the selections that appear below.

---

[1] To be rational in this sense is to know what one wants and to choose the means most likely to get it and least likely to interfere with the satisfaction of stronger wants.

THE THEORY OF SOCIAL BALANCE

John Kenneth Galbraith

John Kenneth Galbraith, appointed by President Kennedy as ambassador to India, has returned to his professorship at Harvard. As an economist he has generally preferred novel and arresting insights and generalizations to detailed statistical analyses, a preference no doubt abetted by a biting epigrammatic style that has been lacking in the literature of political economy since the days of England's R. H. Tawney and America's Thorstein Veblen. More than any recent book, Galbraith's volume from which the following selection is taken focused attention on the contrast between what he has called "private opulence and public squalor." He has also written Modern Competition and Business Policy (*1938*), American Capitalism: The Concept of Countervailing Power (*1952*), The Liberal Hour (*1960*), *and* The New Industrial State (*1967*). *He was elected national chairman of Americans for Democratic Action at its 1967 convention.*

The final problem of the productive society is what it produces. This manifests itself in an implacable tendency to provide an opulent supply of some things and a niggardly yield of others. This disparity carries to the point where it is a cause of social discomfort and social unhealth. The line which divides our area of wealth from our area of poverty is roughly that which divides privately produced and marketed goods and services from publicly rendered services. Our wealth in the first is not only in startling contrast with the meagerness of the latter, but our wealth in privately produced goods is, to a marked degree, the cause of crisis in the supply of public services. For we have failed to see the importance, indeed the urgent need, of maintaining a balance between the two.

This disparity between our flow of private and public goods and services is no matter of subjective judgment. On the contrary, it is the source of the most extensive comment which only stops short of the direct contrast being made here. In the years following World War II, the papers of any major city—those of New York were an excellent example—told daily of the shortages and shortcomings in the elementary municipal and metropolitan services. The schools were old and overcrowded. The police

From *The Affluent Society* (Boston: Houghton Mifflin Company, 1958), pp. 251–269. Reprinted by permission.

force was under strength and underpaid. The parks and playgrounds were insufficient. Streets and empty lots were filthy, and the sanitation staff was underequipped and in need of men. Access to the city by those who work there was uncertain and painful and becoming more so. Internal transportation was overcrowded, unhealthful, and dirty. So was the air. Parking on the streets had to be prohibited, and there was no place elsewhere. The deficiencies were not in new and novel services but in old and established ones. Cities have long swept their streets, helped their people move around, educated them, kept order, and provided horse rails for vehicles which sought to pause. That their residents should have a nontoxic supply of air suggests no revolutionary dalliance with socialism.

The discussion of this public poverty competed, on the whole successfully, with the stories of ever-increasing opulence in privately produced goods. The Gross National Product was rising. So were retail sales. So was personal income. Labor productivity had also advanced. The automobiles that could not be parked were being produced at an expanded rate. The children, though without schools, subject in the playgrounds to the affectionate interest of adults with odd tastes, and disposed to increasingly imaginative forms of delinquency, were admirably equipped with television sets. We had difficulty finding storage space for the great surpluses of food despite a national disposition to obesity. Food was grown and packaged under private auspices. The care and refreshment of the mind, in contrast with the stomach, was principally in the public domain. Our colleges and universities were severely overcrowded and underprovided, and the same was true of the mental hospitals.

The contrast was and remains evident not alone to those who read. The family which takes its mauve and cerise, air-conditioned, power-steered, and power-braked automobile out for a tour passes through cities that are badly paved, made hideous by litter, blighted buildings, billboards, and posts for wires that should long since have been put underground. They pass on into a countryside that has been rendered largely invisible by commercial art. (The goods which the latter advertise have an absolute priority in our value system. Such aesthetic considerations as a view of the countryside accordingly come second. On such matters we are consistent.) They picnic on exquisitely packaged food from a portable icebox by a polluted stream and go on to spend the night at a park which is a menace to public health and morals. Just before dozing off on an air mattress, beneath a nylon tent, amid the stench of decaying refuse, they may reflect vaguely on the curious unevenness of their blessings. Is this, indeed, the American genius?

In the production of goods within the private economy it has long been recognized that a tolerably close relationship must be maintained between the production of various kinds of products. The output of steel and oil and machine tools is related to the production of automobiles. Investment in transportation must keep abreast of the output of goods to be transported. The supply of power must be abreast of the growth of industries requiring it. The existence of these relationships—coefficients to the economist—has made possible the construction of the input-output table which shows how changes in the production in one industry will increase or diminish the demands on other industries. To this table, and more especially to its ingenious author, Professor Wassily Leontief, the world is indebted for one of its most important of modern insights into economic relationships. If expansion in one part of the economy were not matched by the requisite expansion in other parts—were the need for balance not respected—then bottlenecks and shortages, speculative hoarding of scarce supplies, and sharply increasing costs would ensue. Fortunately in peacetime the market system operates easily and effectively to maintain this balance, and this, together with the existence of stocks and some flexibility in the coefficients as a result of substitution, insures that no serious difficulties will arise. We are reminded of the existence of the problem only by noticing how serious it is for those countries—Poland or, in a somewhat different form, India—which seek to solve the problem by planned measures and with a much smaller supply of resources.

Just as there must be balance in what a community produces, so there must also be balance in what the community consumes. An increase in the use of one product creates, ineluctably, a requirement for others. If we are to consume more automobiles, we must have more gasoline. There must be more insurance as well as more space on which to operate them. Beyond a certain point more and better food appears to mean increased need for medical services. This is the certain result of the increased consumption of tobacco and alcohol. More vacations require more hotels and more fishing rods. And so forth. With rare exceptions—shortages of doctors are an exception which suggests the rule—this balance is also maintained quite effortlessly so far as goods for private sale and consumption are concerned. The price system plus a rounded condition of opulence is again the agency.

However, the relationships we are here discussing are not confined to the private economy. They operate comprehensively over the whole span of private and public services. As surely as an increase in the output of automobiles puts new demands on the steel industry so, also, it places new demands on public services. Similarly, every increase in the consumption of private goods will normally mean some facilitating or protective step by the state. In all cases if these services are not forthcoming, the consequences will be in some degree ill. It will be convenient to have a term which suggests a satisfactory relationship between the supply of privately produced goods and services and those of the state, and we may call it social balance.

The problem of social balance is ubiquitous, and frequently it is obtrusive. As noted, an increase in the consumption of automobiles requires a facilitating supply of streets, highways, traffic control, and parking space. The protective services of the police and the highway patrols must also be available, as must those of the hospitals. Although the need for balance here is extraordinarily clear, our use of privately produced vehicles has, on occasion, got far out of line with the supply of the related public services. The result has been hideous road congestion, an annual massacre of impressive proportions, and chronic colitis in the cities. As on the ground, so also in the air. Planes collide with disquieting consequences for those within when the public provision for air traffic control fails to keep pace with private use of the airways.

But the auto and the airplane, versus the space to use them, are merely an exceptionally visible example of a requirement that is pervasive. The more goods people procure, the more packages they discard and the more trash that must be carried away. If the appropriate sanitation services are not provided, the counterpart of increasing opulence will be deepening filth. The greater the wealth the thicker will be the dirt. This indubitably describes a tendency of our time. As more goods are produced and owned, the greater are the opportunities for fraud and the more property that must be protected. If the provision of public law enforcement services do not keep pace, the counterpart of increased well-being will, we may be certain, be increased crime.

The city of Los Angeles, in modern times, is a near-classic study in the problem of social balance. Magnificently efficient factories and oil refineries, a lavish supply of automobiles, a vast consumption of handsomely packaged products, coupled with the absence of a municipal trash collection service which forced the use of home incinerators, made the air nearly unbreathable for an appreciable part of each year. Air pollution could be controlled only by a complex and highly developed set of public services—by better knowledge stemming from more research, better policing, a municipal trash collection service, and possibly the assertion of the priority of clean air over the production of goods. These were long in coming. The agony of a city without usable air was the result.

The issue of social balance can be identified in many other current problems. Thus an aspect of increasing private production is the appearance of an extraordinary number of things which lay claim to the interest of the young. Motion pictures, television, automobiles, and the vast opportunities which go with the mobility, together with such less enchanting merchandise as narcotics, comic books, and pornographia, are all included in an advancing gross national product. The child of a less opulent as well as a technologically more primitive age had far fewer such diversions. The red schoolhouse is remembered mainly because it had a paramount position in the lives of those who attended it that no modern school can hope to attain.

In a well-run and well-regulated community, with a sound school system, good recreational opportunities, and a good police force—in short a community where public services have kept pace with private production —the diversionary forces operating on the modern juvenile may do no great damage. Television and the violent mores of Hollywood and Madison Avenue must contend with the intellectual discipline of the school. The social, athletic, dramatic, and like attractions of the school also claim the attention of the child. These, together with the other recreational opportunities of the community, minimize the tendency to delinquency. Experiments with violence and immorality are checked by an effective law enforcement system before they become epidemic.

In a community where public services have failed to keep abreast of private consumption things are very different. Here, in an atmosphere of private opulence and public squalor, the private goods have full sway. Schools do not compete with television and the movies. The dubious heroes of the latter, not Miss Jones, become the idols of the young. The hot rod and the wild ride take the place of more sedentary sports for which there are inadequate facilities or provision. Comic books, alcohol, narcotics, and switchblade knives are, as noted, part of the increased flow of goods, and there is nothing to dispute their enjoyment. There is an ample supply of private wealth to be appropriated and not much to be feared from the police. An austere community is free from temptation. It can be austere in its public services. Not so a rich one.

Moreover, in a society which sets large store by production, and which has highly effective machinery for synthesizing private wants, there are strong pressures to have as many wage earners in the family as possible. As always all social behavior is part of a piece. If both parents are engaged in private production, the burden on the public services is further increased. Children, in effect, become the charge of the community for an appreciable part of the time. If the services of the community do not keep pace, this will be another source of disorder.

Residential housing also illustrates the problem of the social balance, although in a somewhat complex form. Few would wish to contend that, in the lower or even the middle income brackets, Americans are munificently supplied with housing. A great many families would like better located or merely more houseroom, and no advertising is necessary to persuade them of their wish. And the provision of housing is in the private domain. At first glance at least, the line we draw between private and public seems not to be preventing a satisfactory allocation of resources to housing.

On closer examination, however, the problem turns out to be not greatly different from that of education. It is improbable that the housing industry is greatly more incompetent or inefficient in the United States than in those countries—Scandinavia, Holland, or (for the most part) England—where slums have been largely eliminated and where *minimum* standards of cleanliness and comfort are well above our own. As the experience of these countries shows, and as we have also been learning, the housing industry functions well only in combination with a large, complex, and costly array of public services. These include land purchase and clearance for redevelopment; good neighborhood and city planning, and effective and well-enforced zoning; a variety of financing and other aids to the housebuilder and owner; publicly supported research and architectural services for an industry which, by its nature, is equipped to do little on its own; and a considerable amount of direct or assisted public construction for families in the lowest income brackets. The quality of the housing depends not on the industry, which is given, but on what is invested in these supplements and supports.

The case for social balance has, so far, been put negatively. Failure to keep public services in minimal relation to private production and use of goods is a cause of social disorder or impairs economic performance. The matter may now be put affirmatively. By failing to exploit the opportunity to expand public production we are missing opportunities for enjoyment which otherwise we might have had. Presumably a community can be as well rewarded by buying better schools or better parks as by buying bigger automobiles. By concentrating on the latter rather than the former it is failing to maximize its satisfactions. As with schools in the community, so with public services over the country at large. It is scarcely sensible that we should satisfy our wants in private goods with reckless abundance, while in the case of public goods, on the evidence of the eye, we practice extreme self-denial. So, far from systematically exploiting the opportunities to derive use and pleasure from these services, we do not supply what would keep us out of trouble.

The conventional wisdom holds that the community, large or small, makes a decision as to how much it will devote to its public services. This decision is arrived at by democratic process. Subject to the imperfections and uncertainties of democracy, people decide how much of their private income and goods they will surrender in order to have public services of which they are in greater need. Thus there is a balance, however rough, in the enjoyments to be had from private goods and services and those rendered by public authority.

It will be obvious, however, that this view depends on the notion of independently determined consumer wants. In such a world one could with some reason defend the doctrine that the consumer, as a voter, makes an independent choice between public and private goods. But given the dependence effect—given that consumer wants are created by the process by which they are satisfied—the consumer makes no such choice. He is subject to the forces of advertising and emulation by which production creates its own demand. Advertising operates exclusively, and emulation mainly, on behalf of privately produced goods and services. Since management and emulative effects operate on behalf of private production, public services will have an inherent tendency to lag behind. Automobile demand which is expensively synthesized will inevitably have a much larger claim on income than parks or public health or even roads where no such influence operates. The engines of mass communication, in their highest state of development, assail the eyes and ears of the community on behalf of more beer but not of more schools. Even in the conventional wisdom it will scarcely be contended that this leads to an equal choice between the two.

The competition is especially unequal for new products and services. Every corner of the public psyche is canvassed by some of the nation's most talented citizens to see if the desire for some merchantable product can be cultivated. No similar process operates on behalf of the non-merchantable services of the state. Indeed, while we take the cultivation of new private wants for granted we would be measurably shocked to see it applied to public services. The scientist or engineer or advertising man who devotes himself to developing a new carburetor, cleanser, or depilatory for which the public recognizes no need and will feel none until an advertising campaign arouses it, is one of the valued members of our society. A politician or a public servant who dreams up a new public service is a wastrel. Few public offenses are more reprehensible.

So much for the influences which operate on the decision between public and private production. The calm decision between public and private consumption pictured by the conventional wisdom is, in fact, a remarkable example of the error which arises from viewing social behavior out of context. The inherent tendency will always be for public services to fall behind private production. . . .

Social balance is also the victim of . . . the truce on inequality . . . With rare exceptions such as the post office, public services do not carry a price ticket to be paid for by the individual user. By their nature they must, ordinarily, be available to all. As a result, when they are improved or new services are initiated, there is the ancient and troublesome question of who is to pay. This, in turn, provokes to life the collateral but irrelevant debate over inequality. As with the use of taxation as an instrument of fiscal policy, the truce on inequality is broken. Liberals are obliged to argue that the services be paid for by progressive taxation which will reduce inequality. Committed as they are to the urgency of goods . . . they must oppose sales and excise taxes. Conservatives rally to the defense of inequality—although without ever quite committing themselves in such uncouth terms—and oppose the use of income taxes. They, in effect, oppose the expenditure not on the merits of the service but on the demerits of the tax system. Since the debate over inequality cannot be resolved, the money is frequently not appropriated and the services not performed. . . .

In practice matters are better as well as worse than this statement of the basic forces suggests. Given the tax structure, the revenues of all levels of government grow with the growth of the economy. Services can be maintained and sometimes even improved out of this automatic accretion.

However, this effect is highly unequal. The revenues of the federal government, because of its heavy reliance on income taxes, increase more than proportionately with private economic growth. In addition, although the conventional wisdom greatly deplores the fact, federal appropriations have only an indirect bearing on taxation. Public services are considered and voted on in accordance with their seeming urgency. Initiation or improvement of a particular service is rarely, except for purposes of oratory, set against the specific effect on taxes. Tax policy, in turn, is decided on the basis of the level of economic activity, the resulting revenues, expediency, and other considerations. Among these the total of the thousands of individually considered appropriations is but one factor. In this process the ultimate tax consequence of any individual appropriation is *de minimus,* and the tendency to ignore it reflects the simple mathematics of the situation. Thus it is possible for the Congress to make decisions affecting the social balance without invoking the question of inequality.

Things are made worse, however, by the fact that a large proportion of the federal revenues are pre-empted by defense. The increase in defense costs has also tended to absorb a large share of the normal increase in tax revenues. The position of the federal government for improving the social balance has also been weakened since World War II by the strong, although receding, conviction that its taxes were at artificial wartime levels and that a tacit commitment exists to reduce taxes at the earliest opportunity.

In the states and localities the problem of social balance is much more severe. Here tax revenues—this is especially true of the General Property Tax—increase less than proportionately with increased private production. Budgeting too is far more closely circumscribed than in the case of the federal government—only the monetary authority enjoys the pleasant privilege of underwriting its own loans. Because of this, increased services for states and localities regularly pose the question of more revenues and more taxes. And here, with great regularity, the question of social balance is lost in the debate over equality and social equity.

Thus we currently find by far the most serious social imbalance in the services performed by local governments. The F.B.I. comes much more easily by funds than the city police force. The Department of Agriculture can more easily keep its pest control abreast of expanding agricultural output than the average city health service can keep up with the needs of an expanding industrial population. One consequence is that the federal government remains under constant pressure to use its superior revenue position to help redress the balance at the lower levels of government. . . .

A feature of the years immediately following World War II was a remarkable attack on the notion of expanding and improving public services. During the depression years such services had been elaborated and improved partly in order to fill some small part of the vacuum left by the shrinkage of private production. During the war years the role of government was vastly expanded. After that came the reaction. Much of it, unquestionably, was motivated by a desire to rehabilitate the prestige of private production and therewith of producers. No doubt some who joined the attack hoped, at least tacitly, that it might be possible to sidestep the truce on taxation vis-à-vis equality by having less taxation of all kinds. For a time the notion that our public services had somehow become inflated and excessive was all but axiomatic. Even liberal politicians did not seriously protest. They found it necessary to aver that they were in favor of public economy too.

In this discussion a certain mystique was attributed to the satisfaction of privately supplied wants. A community decision to have a new school means that the individual surrenders the necessary amount, willy-nilly, in his taxes. But if he is left with that income, he is a free man. He can decide between a better car or a television set. This was advanced with some solemnity as an argument for the TV set. The difficulty is that this argument leaves the community with no way of preferring the school. All private wants, where the individual can choose, are inherently superior to all public desires which must be paid for by taxation and with an inevitable component of compulsion.

The cost of public services was also held to be a desolating burden on private production, although this was at a time when the private production was burgeoning. Urgent warnings were issued of the unfavorable effects of taxation on investment—"I don't know of a surer way of killing off the incentive to investment than by imposing taxes which are regarded by people as punitive." This was at a time when the inflationary effect of a very high level of investment was causing concern. The same individuals who were warning about the inimical effects of taxes were strongly advocating a monetary policy designed to reduce investment. However, an understanding of our economic discourse requires an appreciation of one of its basic rules: men of high position are allowed, by a special act of grace, to accommodate their reasoning to the answer they need. Logic is only required in those of lesser rank.

Finally it was argued, with no little vigor, that expanding government posed a grave threat to individual liberties. "Where distinction and rank are achieved almost exclusively by becoming a civil servant of the state . . . it is too much to expect that many will long prefer freedom to security."

With time this attack on public services has somewhat subsided. The disorder associated with social imbalance has become visible even if the need for balance between private and public services is still imperfectly appreciated.

Freedom also seemed to be surviving. Perhaps it was realized that all organized activity requires concessions by the individual to the group. This is true of the policeman who joins the police force, the teacher who gets a job at the high school, and the executive who makes his way up the hierarchy of Du Pont. If there are differences between public and private organizations, they are of kind rather than of degree. As this is written the pendulum has in fact swung back. Our liberties are now menaced by the conformity exacted by the large corporation and its impulse to create, for its own purposes, the organization man. This danger we may also survive.

Nonetheless, the postwar onslaught on the public services left a lasting imprint. To suggest that we canvass our public wants to see where happiness can be improved by more and better services has a sharply radical tone. Even public services to avoid disorder must be defended. By contrast the man who devises a nostrum for a nonexistent need and then successfully promotes both remains one of nature's noblemen.

PRIVATE VS. PUBLIC

Henry E. Wallich

Among academic economists, Henry E. Wallich might be described as belonging to the "conservative" school. He is Professor of Economics at Yale and author of Mainsprings of the German Revival *(1955) and* The Cost of Freedom: A New Look at Capitalism *(1960). He was a member of President Eisenhower's Council of Economic Advisers between 1959 and 1961.*

From *Harper's Magazine* (October 1961), pp. 12–25. Copyright © 1961 by Harper's Magazine, Inc. Reprinted by permission of the author.

. . . It is one thing to be irritated by certain manifestations of our contemporary civilization—the gadgets, the chrome, the tailfins, and the activities that go with them. It is quite another—and something of a *non sequitur*—to conclude from this that the only alternative to foolish private spending is public spending. Better private spending is just as much of a possibility. My contention here will be that to talk in terms of "public vs. private" is to confuse the issue. More than that, it is to confuse means and ends. The choice between public and private money is primarily a choice of means. The sensible approach for those who are dissatisfied with some of the ends to which private money is being spent, is to specify first what other ends are important and why. Having determined the ends, the next step is to look to the means. That is the order in which I propose to proceed here.

One may share the irritation of the new social critics as they look upon some of the fluff and the floss on our standard of living. My personal feelings can be characterized by noting that I have a 1951 car and no TV. The critics may want to bear in mind, however, that not all the money in this country is spent by people for whom life begins at $25,000. The median family income is $5,600. Would these critics of the affluent society want to try living on much less than that? When Galbraith inveighs eloquently against switchblades, narcotics, and other phases of juvenile delinquency, he deserves the support of all right-thinking representatives of what he calls the "conventional wisdom." But are the sources of these aberrations more intimately tied to affluence or to poverty? The exponents of the new social criticism may also want to remember the outcome of that "noble experiment," Prohibition. It should have taught us that it is futile to become our brother's dietitian. I hope that it has also imbued us with wholesome doubt about the moral right of some members of the community to regulate the lives of the rest.

Irritation with the poor judgment of other people who fail to appreciate one's own more advanced tastes is not new. It was a familiar situation during the 1920s. The critics then quoted T. S. Eliot's *The Waste Land,* and some went off to Paris in search of greener cultural pastures. The feeling behind the new social criticism is not dissimilar. Hence one might suppose that the reaction would likewise turn in a cultural direction. One might expect the critics of contemporary materialism to plead for more intensive preoccupation with things of the mind. Some fits and starts in that direction there have been, to be sure. But they have not been in the main stream of the movement. The principal alternative to private materialism that has been offered to us has been public materialism.

Obviously, the quality of our culture could be greatly improved by public expenditures for education and support of the arts. The sales of good paperbacks and LPs are encouraging signs. But if contemporary materialism is to be leavened by such pursuits, it will be principally because large numbers of individuals make private decisions to that end. Social criticism is constructive if it helps precipitate these decisions. It obstructs a desirable evolution if it suggests that public creature comforts are the only alternative to private.

But while emphasis on nonmaterial ends seems sadly lacking in the new social criticism, the critics are right in pointing out that new material needs also have been carried to the fore by social and economic evolution—even though they mislabel them as public needs. In the good old days, when this was still a nation of farmers, most people had no serious retirement worries, there was no industrial unemployment problem, good jobs could be had without a college degree, most diseases were still incurable—in short, social security, education, and health care found primitive and natural solutions within the family and among the resources of the neighborhood. Today, these solutions are neither adequate nor usually even possible.

Meanwhile mounting wealth and advancing technology have brought within reach the means of meeting these needs. We can afford to live better in every way—more creature comforts, more leisure, more attention to matters of the mind and the spirit. At the same time we can take better care of retirement, of unemployment, of illness, of education, of the possibilities opened by research, than ever before.

There are indeed new needs. The citizen-taxpayer has his choice of meeting them, as well as all his other needs, in one of two ways. He can buy the goods or services he wants privately, for cash or credit. Or he can buy them from the government, for taxes.

The nation as a whole pays taxes to buy public services as it pays grocery bills to buy groceries. The tax burden may be heavier for some individuals than for others. But the nation as a whole has no more reason to complain about the "burden" of taxes than about the "burden" of grocery bills—and no more reason to hope for relief.

Of the two stores, the private store today still is much the bigger. The public store is smaller, but it is growing faster.

Each store has some exclusive items. The private store sells most of the necessities and all of the luxuries of life, and in most of these has no competition from the government side. The public store has some specialties of its own: defense, public order and justice, and numerous local services that the private organization has not found profitable. But there is a wide range of items featured by both stores: provision for old age, health services, education, housing, development of natural resources.

The bulk of the new needs are in this competitive area. The fashionable notion is to claim them all for the public store and to label them public needs. The statistics say otherwise. They say in fact two things: First, the supply of this group of goods and services has expanded very rapidly in recent years; and second, they are being offered, in varying degrees, both by the private and the public suppliers. Let us run down the list.

Provision for old age is predominantly private. The average American family, realizing that while old age may be a burden, it is the only known way to achieve a long life, takes care of the matter in three ways: (1) by private individual savings—home ownership, savings deposits, securities; (2) by private collective savings—life insurance, corporate pension funds; and (3) by public collective savings through social security. Statisticians report that the two collective forms are advancing faster than the individual. The increases far exceed the rise in the Gross National Product of almost 80 per cent (in current prices) over the past ten years; they do not indicate either that these needs are neglected or that they are necessarily public in character.

Education: the bulk of it is public; but a good part, particularly of higher education, is private. Total expenditures for all education have advanced in the last ten years from $9.3 billion to $24.6 billion ($19.3 billion of it public). Education's share in the national income has advanced from 3.8 per cent to 5.8 per cent. The silly story that we spend more on advertising than on education is a canard, though with its gross of over $10 billion, advertising does take a lot of money.

Health expenditures are still mainly private. At considerable expense, it is now possible to live longer and be sick less frequently or at least less dangerously. In the past, most people paid their own doctors' bills, although health care for the indigent has always been provided by public action or private philanthropy. Since the war, the proliferation of health insurance has given some form of collective but private insurance to three-quarters of our 182 million people. This has greatly reduced pressure for a national health service along British lines. For the aging, whose health-care needs stand in inverse proportion to their capacity to pay or insure, public insurance has finally been initiated and needs to be expanded. The total annual expenditure on health is estimated at over $25 billion, a little more than on education. Of this, about $6 billion is public.

So much for the allegation that the "new needs" are all public needs. Now for some further statistics on the public store, which is said to have been neglected. Some of them could make an investor in private growth stocks envious. Research expenditures (mainly for defense and atomic energy) have gone from about $1 billion to over $8 billion in the last ten years. Federal grants to the states have advanced from $2.2 billion to $7 billion during the same period. Social-security benefits rose from $1 billion to over $10 billion. All in all, public cash outlays (federal and state) advanced from $61 billion to $134 billion over ten years, 57 per cent faster than the GNP.

For those who feel about public spending the way Mark Twain felt about whiskey, these figures may still look slim. (Mark Twain thought that while too much of anything was bad, too much whiskey was barely enough.) To others, the data may suggest that the advocates of more public spending have already had their way. Could their present discontent be the result of not keeping their statistics up-to-date? In one of his recent pamphlets, Arthur M. Schlesinger, Jr. claims that the sum of the many neglects he observes (including defense) could be mended by raising public expenditures by $10 to $12 billion. That is well below the increase in public cash outlays that actually did take place in one single fiscal year, from $118.2 billion in 1958 to $132.7 billion in 1959. In the three fiscal years 1957–59, these outlays went up more than $31 billion, though the advance slowed down in 1960. More facts and less indignation might help to attain better perspective.

Some parts of federal, state, and local budgets have expanded less rapidly than those cited—in many cases fortunately. The massive buildup in defense expenditures from the late 'forties to the 'fifties has squeezed other programs. Unfortunately, on the other hand, some programs that both political parties have favored—including aid to education, to depressed areas, for urban renewal—have been delayed unduly by the vicissitudes of politics. But the figures as a whole lend little support to the thesis that politicians don't spend enough, and that the government store is not expanding fast enough.

The two stores—private and public—work very hard these days to capture the business of the citizen-taxpayer. Here is what he hears as he walks into the private store.

"The principal advantage of this store," the private businessman says, "is that you can shop around and buy exactly what you want. If I don't have it I'll order it. You, the consumer, are the boss here. To be sure, I'm not in business for charity but for profit. But my profit comes from giving you what you want. And with competition as fierce as it is, you can be sure the profit won't be excessive."

If the proprietor has been to Harvard Business School, he will perhaps remember to add something about the invisible hand which in a free economy causes the self-seeking of competitors to work for the common good. He will also, even without benefit of business school, remember to drop a word about the danger of letting the public store across the street get too big. It might endanger freedom.

As the citizen turns this sales talk over in his mind, several points occur to him. Without denying the broad validity of the argument, he will note that quite often he has been induced to buy things he did not really need, and possibly to neglect other, more serious needs. Snob appeal and built-in obsolescence promoted by expensive advertising don't seem to him to fit in with the notion that the consumer is king. Looking at the brand names and patents and trademarks, he wonders whether most products are produced and priced competitively instead of under monopoly conditions. The invisible hand at times seems to be invisible mainly because it is so deep in his pocket.

Bothered by these doubts, the citizen walks across the street and enters the public store.

"Let me explain to you," says the politician who runs it—with the aid of a horde of hard-working bureaucrats doing the chores. "The principles on which the store is run are known as the political process, and if you happen to be familiar with private merchandising they may seem unusual, but I assure you they work. First of all, almost everything in this store is free. We simply assess our customers a lump sum in the form of taxes. These, however, are based largely on each customer's ability to pay, rather than on what he gets from the store. We have a show of hands from the customers once a year, and the majority decides what merchandise the store is to have in stock. The majority, incidentally, also decides how much everybody, including particularly the minority, is to be assessed in taxes.

"You will observe," the politician continues, "that this store is not run for profit. It is like a co-operative, run for the welfare of the members. I myself, to be sure, am not in politics for charity, but for re-election. But that means that I must be interested in your needs, or you would not vote for me. Moreover, there are some useful things that only I can do, with the help of the political process, and in which you and every citizen have an interest. For instance, everybody ought to go to school. I can make them go. Everybody ought to have old-age insurance. I can make that compulsory too. And because I don't charge the full cost of the service, I can help even up a little the inequalities of life.

"By the way," the politician concludes, "if there is any special little thing you want, I may be able to get it for you, and of course it won't cost you a nickel."

The citizen has some fault to find with the political process too. He notes that there is not even a theoretical claim to the benefits of an invisible hand. Majority rule may produce benefits for the majority, but how about the other 49 per cent? Nor is there the discipline of competition, or the need for profits, to test economy of operation. There is no way, in the public store, of adjusting individual costs and benefits. And the promise to get him some small favor, while tempting, worries him, because he wonders what the politician may have promised to others. The political process, he is led to suspect, may be a little haphazard.

He asks himself how political decisions get to be made. Sometimes, obviously, it is not the majority that really makes a decision, but a small pressure group that is getting away with something. He will remember that—after payments for major national security and public debt interest— the largest single expenditure in the federal budget is for agriculture, and the next for veterans. He may also recall that one of the first budgetary actions of the new Administration was to increase funds for agriculture by $3 billion.

Next, the citizen might consider the paralyzing "balance-of-forces" effect that often blocks a desirable reshuffling of expenditures. The allocation of public funds reflects the bargaining power of their sponsors, inside or outside the government. A classical example was the division of funds that prevailed in the Defense Department during the late 'forties. Army, Navy, and Air Force were to share in total resources in a way that would maximize military potential. By some strange coincidence, maximum potential was always achieved by giving each service the same amount of money. It took the Korean War to break this stalemate.

What is the consequence of the balance-of-forces effect? If the proponents of one kind of expenditure want to get more money for their projects, they must concede an increase also to the advocates of others. More education means more highways, instead of less; more air power means more ground forces. To increase a budget in one direction only is as difficult as letting out one's belt only on one side. The expansion tends to go all around. What this comes down to is that politicians are not very good at setting priorities. Increases in good expenditures are burdened with a political surcharge of less good ones.

The last-ditch survival power of federal programs is a specially illuminating instance of the balance of forces. If a monument were built in Washington in memory of each major federal program that has been discontinued, the appearance of the city would not be greatly altered. In contrast, when the Edsel doesn't sell, production stops. But the government is still reclaiming land to raise more farm surpluses and training fishermen to enter an occupation that needs subsidies to keep alive. Old federal programs never die, they don't even fade away—they just go on.

The citizen will remember also the ancient and honorable practice of logrolling. The unhappy fate of the Area Development bill illustrates it admirably. As originally proposed, the bill sought to aid a limited number of industrial areas where new jobs were badly needed. It got nowhere in the Congress. Only when it was extended to a large number of areas with less urgent or quite different problems were enough legislators brought aboard to pass it. Because of the heavy political surcharge with which it had become loaded, President Eisenhower vetoed the bill. A bill was finally enacted early this year, long after aid should have been brought to the areas that needed it.

Finally, the citizen might discover in some dark corner of his mind a nagging thought: Any particular government program may be a blessing, but could their cumulative effect be a threat to freedom? He has heard businessmen say this so often that he has almost ceased to pay attention to it. He rather resents businessmen acting the dog in the manger, trying to stop useful things from being done unless they can do them. He is irritated when he hears a man talk about freedom who obviously is thinking about profit. And yet—is there any conclusive rebuttal?

The citizen would be quite wrong, however, if he blamed the politician for the defects of the political process. The fault lies with the process, or better with the way in which the process, the politician, and the citizen interact. The citizen therefore would do well to examine some of his own reactions and attitudes.

First, when he thinks about taxes, he tends to think of them as a burden instead of as a price he pays for a service. As a body, the nation's taxpayers are like a group of neighbors who decide to establish a fire department. Because none is quite sure how much good it will do him, and because each hopes to benefit from the contribution of the rest, all are prudent in their contributions. In the end they are likely to wind up with a bucket brigade.

But when it comes to accepting benefits, the citizen-taxpayers act like a group of men who sit down at a restaurant table knowing that they will split the check evenly. In this situation everybody orders generously; it adds little to one's own share of the bill, and for the extravagance of his friends he will have to pay anyhow. What happens at the restaurant table explains—though it does not excuse—what happens at the public trough.

Finally, in his reaction to public or free services, the citizen takes a great deal for granted, and seldom thinks of the cost. Public beaches mistreated, unmetered parking space permanently occupied, veterans' adjustment benefits continued without need—as well as abuses of unemployment compensation and public assistance—are some examples. This applies also, of course, to privately offered benefits, under health insurance, for instance. The kindly nurse in the hospital—"Why don't you stay another day, dearie, it won't cost you anything, it's all paid for by Blue Cross"— makes the point.

By removing the link between costs and benefits, the political process also reduces the citizen's interest in earning money. The citizen works to live. If some of his living comes to him without working, he would be less than rational if he did not respond with a demand for shorter hours. If these public benefits increase his tax burden so that his over-all standard of living remains unchanged, the higher taxes will reduce his work incentive. Why work hard, if much of it is for the government?

These various defects of the political process add up to an obvious conclusion: the dollar spent by even the most honest and scrupulous of politicians is not always a full-bodied dollar. It often is subject to a discount. It buys less than it should because of the attrition it suffers as it goes through the process, and so may be worth only 90 cents or 80 cents and sometimes perhaps less. The private dollar, in too many cases, may also be worth less than 100 per cent. But here each man can form his own judgment, can pick and choose or refuse altogether. In the political process, all he can do is say Yes or No once a year in November.

The discount on the public dollar may be compensated by the other advantages of government—its ability to compel, to subsidize, to do things on a big scale and at a low interest cost. Whether that is the case needs to be studied in each instance. Where these advantages do not apply, the private market will give better service than the political process. For many services, there is at least some leeway for choice between the private and public store—health and retirement, housing, research, higher education, natural-resource development. Defense, on the other hand, as well as public administration, public works of all kinds, and the great bulk of education—while perhaps made rather expensive by the political process—leave no realistic alternative to public action.

The argument I have offered is no plea to spend more or less on any particular function. It is a plea for doing whatever we do in the most effective way.

7

Corporate "Citizenship"

Private ownership of the means of production in a highly industrialized economy has produced the modern corporation, through which the financial resources of large numbers of people are pooled, ownership and management are separated, and vast enterprises launched and operated. Given the central place of the private corporation in our institutional life, the ideals and standards of management, in particular management's conception of the social obligations of the corporation, will have a great deal to do with the kind of society in which we live. In recent times, the strategic place of the corporation has presented management with a new problem: whether to construe the role of the corporation narrowly as a strictly amoral business enterprise organized to maximize profits, or to accept a broader, socially oriented interpretation of the responsibilities of the corporation that would include the welfare of the community. A measure of the influence of the latter view is suggested by the prediction of Dr. Wilson Compton, president of the Council for Financial Aid to Education, that by 1970 corporate aid to higher education will amount to one-half billion dollars annually. Inseparably related to the solution of the moral problem are complex economic and political issues only briefly explored here, especially the question of managerial power and its control. (For further examination of this question, see Girvetz, *The Evolution of Liberalism* (1963), Chapter XII.)

CORPORATION GIVING IN A FREE SOCIETY

Richard Eells

Richard Eells is Public Policy Research Consultant for the
General Electric Company and Adjunct Professor in Business
of the Graduate School of Business, Columbia University. He
is the author of The Meaning of Modern Business (*1960*) *and*
The Government of Corporations (*1962*) *and co-author of*
Conceptual Foundations of Business (*1961*).

A searching question facing the corporations of today is: Should business corporations make gifts for scientific, educational, and charitable purposes; and if they do, what principles and policies should they adopt as a guide to their philanthropic programs? . . .

We have reached a stage in the evolution of corporate enterprise and the development of philanthropy where the two are meeting. The corporation has become a philanthropic force in the sheer bulk of its contributions.

Most Americans have an awareness of the constructive contributions to society of such private philanthropic work as that done by Carnegie, Rockefeller, Ford, Guggenheim, Harkness, and others, and of the magnitude and significance of their support. But the American corporation is in a position to reduce previous philanthropy to pioneering efforts. . . .

The basic justification for corporate giving is a philosophy of enlightened self-interest. For if a company merely engages in "charity *qua* charity," it reflects an altruism more laudable than defensible as an exercise of corporate authority. Yet, if its gifts fail to serve the broader interests of mankind, they cease to qualify as philanthropy, with implications that will concern the tax collector. Corporation philanthropy, in short, must get in between the horns of a rather difficult dilemma.

It is hardly surprising that public policy deliberately encourages corporate boards to develop aggressive solutions for this dilemma. Public law invites the business corporation to benefit mankind through tax-deductible gifts. The trend of judicial decision is to widen corporate authority to engage in philanthropic pursuits, even though the benefits accruing to the corporate donor and its share owners may appear to be incommensurable when noted on a company's financial balance sheet. . . . A significant result is a strengthening of the American faith in the autonomy of private sectors.

The concept of private sectors is of key importance to a philosophy of corporation philanthropy in a country engaged in an epochal struggle to defend free institutions. The higher duty of corporate giving is to defend and preserve these sectors. It is the private sectors that constitute the foundations of a society of free men. The private sectors constitute all the areas of meaningful human activity apart from public government: the multifold activities of the family; the local community; the indigenous welfare groups of the local community; the private schools, the colleges, and the universities; the churches; the healers of body and soul; the associations of scholars, scientists, writers, and artists; the labor unions; the business enterprises—indeed, the whole spectrum of voluntary associations through which men hope in their own ways to achieve their goals, mundane and divine.

The constitution of a society of free men must preserve the vital private sectors as a counterpoise to tyranny. If they were to be progressively absorbed into the State, the corporate environment of free enterprise for industry would rapidly disappear.

No denial of the legitimate regulative powers of national, state, and local governments is necessarily implicit in the vigorous defense of private sectors. Corporate philanthropy will not patronize any pluralistic renunciation of state sovereignty. The controlling consideration . . . is not the negative one of forestalling government intervention into these private sectors. Stated affirmatively, the objective must always be to strengthen a balanced multigroup social structure that makes intervention unnecessary. More, the social structure to be preserved must be one that lends vitality to American values of individual freedom and human dignity.

What specific objectives should a donor company set for itself in the light of the philosophy of corporation philanthropy which has as its goal the strengthening of the private sectors in society? The bases for a policy of giving in a given company will depend upon a considered view of its enlightened self-interest. How should the donor proceed in the task of appraising the wider social responsibilities as they relate to the more immediate economic interests a corporate board is obligated to preserve and protect?

One function of corporate management, in the years ahead, will be to open up new avenues of social and economic research with support comparable to the financial resources thrown hitherto into technological research.

It is a truism that our social sciences have lagged dangerously behind our physical sciences and engineering skills. A major responsibility of corporation philanthropy today is to throw its weight on the side of developing the social sciences, with courage to withstand the assaults that are being made, and will be made, upon studies of the structure and dynamics of a free society. Business has such a large stake in the outcome of such research that it must stand resolutely against the anti-intellectualism and obscurantism now rising in powerful quarters aimed at thwarting scientific analysis of human relations. It would seem that economists, political scientists, jurists, anthropologists, and social psychologists still require a common language and terminology through which a frontal attack can be made upon the broad problem of maintaining a free society in which private enterprise can prosper. Corporation philanthropy will advance both corporate interests and the interests of the nation as a whole if it supports such collaborative research.

Despite the deep concern of businessmen with the constant encroachment of government into business, there is a growing fear that corporations dare not give any money for "scientific, educational, and charitable" purposes that have anything to do with politics, or even with studies of the governmental process. There are even those who would shy away from any projects in the "dubious" area of the social sciences.

One reason for this reluctance to give corporate support to the necessary study—and action—in the whole field of social and governmental forces that play upon business enterprise is the fear of political retaliation. The path of caution is to steer clear of such corporation giving as may rouse the least suspicion that tax-exempt funds are being used for any "political" purpose, however remote the political implication may be. Yet, what will the result be if this rule of caution is adhered to? It will mean that no funds will be allocated even for membership in an organization that undertakes in any way to influence the direction of public policy, unless such payments come from other than tax-exempt funds.

Business might elect to withdraw completely from any support—whether by tax-exempt funds or otherwise—of efforts to influence legislation directly or indirectly. To do so, of course, would be to abdicate an elementary right of corporate citizenship and to avoid clear responsibilities to the stockholders of the corporation. The corporation is, and must be, concerned with the governmental process at all levels. This does not imply that corporation foundations will have to engage in "politics," in the popular sense of that term; it does mean that business leaders must accept the responsibilities of corporate citizenship by concerning themselves in an enlightened way with the health of the body politic.

Corporate management faces the general problem of effective restraints upon the power of both public and private government. Through the selective disbursal of gifts and grants, it should attempt to implant throughout the private sectors of American organized life a lively appreciation of our constitutional tradition, with its emphasis on the limitation of both public and private governmental powers. . . .

This goal is not a doctrinaire stand against public education, public health measures, or social legislation in general. One always assumes that public efforts may be required where private efforts fail. But in a constitutional system such as ours there is a presumption against restraint when freedom of action can produce the desired results. . . .

Requirements for philanthropic support of education, and especially of private educational institutions, [have] been mentioned. A recent survey of educational philanthropy published by the Council for Financial Aid to Education indicated the nation's colleges and universities will need new funds for buildings, facilities and operations, in addition to present support, averaging at least $500 million a year for the next ten years. Corporation philanthropy should aim toward continuous support in one form or another for a much longer time, in fact indefinitely, not as charity but as a sound and indispensable investment in the future of our human resources. Further, we must provide a more solid educational base at the primary and secondary school level. The "fourth level" of adult education requires increasing attention. And finally at the highest level of education—the production of scientists and scholars—we face, as a nation, grave shortages.

Corporate support of education should not necessarily be confined to private institutions. The design of a company's plan of educational support may cut across both public and private schools and colleges. Corporation philanthropy has to set for itself, and for others, high standards of nonencroachment upon the "academic republic." The principle involved here is not academic freedom in any narrow sense. In mankind's pursuit and cultivation of knowledge, it is the business, not of outsiders, but of scholars, academic and nonacademic, to find the best organizational and procedural means.

Other major categories of private sectors deserve corporate support. Among the more important of these are the religious sectors. Corporate donors have too often shied away from contributions for any religious purposes whatever. Such gifts are frequently regarded as being "dangerous" or "dubious." Since the "danger" does not lie in religiousness as such this trepidation is comparable to the self-defeating fears about philanthropic work in the social sciences.

But is not the pursuit of the religious way of life at least as important as the pursuit of knowledge in the physical sciences, engineering, and the social sciences? Is it not as important to survival of the free society in which corporate enterprise hopes to live? Is there valid justification for the neglect of churches as objects of corporation philanthropy?

It is a strange argument to say that corporations ought to support the *welfare* and *educational* work of religious groups but avoid like a plague any support of the centers of religion—the churches themselves.

There is no sound ground for excluding gifts for the construction and maintenance of places of worship themselves, if it be conceded that a pervasive and pluralistic religious life is basic to American constitutionalism.

Corporation philanthropy can with good reason also lend support to the creative arts, libraries, museums, recreation, and to fraternal groups. Activities that now seem remote from managerial interests in the immediate business operation will assume more important proportions as our understanding of social, cultural, and political processes widens and deepens.

It may well turn out to be far more fruitful, for example, in combating subversive trends in our political system, to strengthen the "primary groups" in society—groups that provide cohesion in close and personal grounds—than to engage in the more dramatic political struggle on the domestic national level. The cohesive force of nonpolitical groupings, where people are intent upon creative endeavor, provides a community with resistive powers against disintegration more effectively than outright propagandistic indoctrination.

Corporate giving represents one of the great fruits of the free enterprise system. It provides new and unusual opportunities for business leadership. Imaginatively conceived, wisely planned, and well administered, it can become one of the formative factors of our time. For corporate giving is essentially an allocation of certain corporate assets to uses regarded as best in the long run for both the corporation and the society on which it depends. Society is now willing to leave far more discretion in the hands of corporate boards and trustees than formerly in such distribution of corporate assets.

Today, corporate managers find themselves at the core of a "twentieth-century capitalist revolution"—a humane movement that stands in contrast to inhumane collectivist drives in some other parts of the world. Many business leaders will take in their stride the responsibilities inherent in this position at the heart of our "capitalist revolution." The rise of philanthropy as a facet of corporate action relates directly to the central position of business leadership. In the years just ahead many executives will strive to do a bigger job at the higher levels of human aspiration as well as at the economic level. Many will succeed; and one of their instruments is certain to be corporation philanthropy.

The defense of our way of life is predicated upon the preservation of individual dignity and freedom. If we are able to link the future affairs of the corporation to these human values we will succeed in laying a secure foundation both for the corporation and our Western culture.

THE DANGERS OF SOCIAL RESPONSIBILITY

Theodore Levitt

Theodore Levitt is a consultant to big business. He has been adviser to the top management of Standard Oil Company (Indiana) on long-range marketing policy, strategy, and organization and has served as consultant to the Ohio Industrial Council.

Concern with management's social responsibility has become more than a Philistinic form of self-flattery practiced at an occasional community chest banquet or at a news conference celebrating a "selfless example of corporate giving" to some undeserving little college in Podunk. It has become more than merely intoning the pious declarations of Christian brotherhood which some hotshot public relations man has pressed into the outstretched hands of the company president who is rushing from an executive committee meeting to a League of Women Voters luncheon. It has become a deadly serious occupation—the self-conscious, soul-searching preoccupation with the social responsibilities of business, with business statesmanship, employee welfare, public trust, and with all the other lofty causes that get such prominent play in the public press.

Contrary to what some uncharitable critics may say, this preoccupation is not an attitudinizing pose. Self-conscious dedication to social responsibility may have started as a purely defensive maneuver against strident attacks on big corporations and on the moral efficacy of the profit system. But defense alone no longer explains the motive.

The Nonprofit Motive

When outnumbered by its critics at the polls, business launched a counterattack via the communications front. Without really listening to what the critics alleged, business simply denied all that they were saying. But a few executives did listen and began to take a second look at themselves. Perhaps this criticism was not all captious. And so they began to preach to their brethren.

From *Harvard Business Review* (September–October, 1958), pp. 41–50. © 1958 by the President and Fellows of Harvard College; all rights reserved.

Before long something new was added to the ideological stockpile of capitalism. "Social responsibility" was what business needed, its own leaders announced. It needed to take society more seriously. It needed to participate in community affairs—and not just to take from the community but to give to it. Gradually business became more concerned about the needs of its employees, about schools, hospitals, welfare agencies, and even aesthetics. Moreover, it became increasingly clear that if business and the local governments failed to provide some of the routine social-economic amenities which people seemed clearly intent on getting, then that Brobdingnagian freewheeling monster in far-off Washington would.

So what started out as the sincere personal viewpoints of a few selfless businessmen became the prevailing vogue for them all. Today pronouncements about social responsibility issue forth so abundantly from the corporations that it is hard for one to get a decent play in the press. Everybody is in on the act, and nearly all of them actually mean what they say! Dedication reverberates throughout the upper reaches of corporate officialdom.

This, it is widely felt, is good. Business will raise itself in the public's esteem and thereby scuttle the political attacks against it. If the public likes big business, nobody can make capital by attacking it. Thus social responsibility will prolong the lifetime of free enterprise. Meanwhile, the profit motive is compromised in both word and deed. It now shares its royal throne with a multitude of noncommercial motives that aspire to loftier and more satisfying values. Today's profits must be merely adequate, not maximum. If they are big, it is cause for apologetic rationalization (for example, that they are needed to expand the company's ability to "serve" the public even better) rather than for boastful celebration. It is not fashionable for the corporation to take gleeful pride in making money. What *is* fashionable is for the corporation to show that it is a great innovator; more specifically, a great public benefactor; and, very particularly, that it exists "to serve the public."

The mythical visitor from Mars would be astonished that such a happy tableau of cooperative enterprise can create such vast material abundance. "People's Capitalism" is a resounding success. The primitive principle of aggrandizing selfishness which the Marxists mistakenly contend activates capitalism does not count at all. What we have instead is a voluntary association of selfless entrepreneurs singularly dedicated to creating munificence for one and all—an almost spiritually blissful state of cooperative and responsible enterprise. We are approaching a jet-propelled utopia. And, unlike some other periods in the short and turbulent history of capitalism, today has its practicing philosophers. These are the men busily engaged in the canonistic exposition of a new orthodoxy—the era of "socially responsible enterprise."

Occasionally some big business representative does speak less sanctimoniously and more forthrightly about what capitalism is really all about. Occasionally somebody exhumes the apparently antique notion that the business of business is profits; that virtue lies in the vigorous, undiluted assertion of the corporation's profit-making function. But these people get no embossed invitations to speak at the big, prestigeful, and splashy business conferences—where social responsibility echoes as a new tyranny of fad and fancy.

About a year ago, Frank O. Prior, then president and now board chairman of Standard Oil Company (Indiana), made a speech that was in part reminiscent of the late but apparently unlamented tycoon. Without terminological pretensions, pseudodialectical profundity, or rhetorical subtlety, he called on his big business colleagues to run their businesses as they are intended to be run—for profit. Regarding people who publicly consider profit making a doubtful morality, he called on his colleagues to "move over to the offensive," "to stand up and fight," to talk about profits in terms of their central function, and to throw all sentiment to the wolves.

His remarks must have sounded strange and harsh to people accustomed to a decade of viewing the corporation as a sort of miniature welfare state. Good human relations, he said, makes sense only when it "rests on a foundation of economic good sense and not just on sentiment. Sentiment has a tendency to evaporate whenever the heat is on. Economic good sense is durable."

Then he said: "You aren't supposed to use language like that these times. You're supposed to talk about high ideals using high-flown words. You're expected to be mainly aware of what they call social responsibility. . . . This is fine, but I still say management's No. 1 problem is profits."

And where was this vigorous affirmation of no-nonsense capitalism made? Was it Chicago, the seat of Standard's home office and one of the few places where some think the old orthodoxy retains some semblance of primeval integrity? No. This was too unreconstructed a view even for Chicago, the city of broad shoulders. So the Chamber of Commerce of distant and isolated Casper, Wyoming, provided the platform. And even there Prior could not afford to let his forthright remarks stand as boldly as he started out. The corporation, he allowed, must develop "a fuller sense of responsibility and a much broader outlook on the facts of life"—and prices should be "fair."

The fact is, the profit motive is simply not fashionable today among emancipated conferees of the Committee for Economic Development or even in the National Association of Manufacturers. It has been dying a lingering, unmourned death for ten years. Rarely can a big business leader eulogize it today without being snubbed by his self-consciously frowning peers.

Things have come to a remarkable pass. And if anyone doubts it, let him contemplate the spectacle of a recent NAM convention interrupting its urgent deliberations to hear Siobhan McKenna reading Yeats's poetry, presumably to set an appropriate tone of cultural emancipation and dedication. Can anybody picture this happening 25 years ago? Or the board chairman of Sears, Roebuck & Co., stating, as he did last year, that not only is business's first responsibility social but business executives, like Secretary Benson's farmers, should look less to their pocketbooks and more to their spirits? Not even his suggestion that the top brass are overpaid ruffled any managerial feathers.

There is nothing mysterious about the social responsibility syndrome. It does not reflect a change in businessmen's nature or the decay of self-interest. Quite to the contrary, often it is viewed as a way of maximizing the lifetime of capitalism by taking the wind out of its critics' sails. Under direct questioning it will be confessed that activities such as supporting company intramural athletic programs, hiring a paid director for a company choral society, or underwriting employee dramatic performances (even on company time) are not charity. They are hardheaded tactics of survival against the onslaught of politicians and professional detractors. Moreoever, they build morale, improve efficiency, and yield returns in hard cash.

In other words, it pays to play. If it does not pay, there is no game. For instance, when it comes to choosing between the small Arkansas supplier whose town would be ruined if orders stopped and the Minneapolis supplier who can make it cheaper, there is no doubt that even the most socially responsible corporation will take the latter. It can always fall back on responsibility to its employees, stockholders, or customers, and still pretend it is being fashionable.

In some respects, therefore, all this talk *is* merely talk. It stops at the pocketbook. How, then, can it be dangerous? I think the answer is very simple: what people say, they ultimately come to believe if they say it enough, and what they believe affects what they do. . . .

The talk about social responsibility is already more than talk. It is leading into the believing stage; it has become a design for change. I hope to show why this change is likely to be for the worse, and why no man or institution can escape its debilitating consequences. . . .

A New Feudalism

The function of business is to produce sustained high-level profits. The essence of free enterprise is to go after profit in any way that is consistent with its own survival as an economic system. The catch, someone will quickly say, is "consistent with." This is true. In addition, lack of profits is not the only thing that can destroy business. Bureaucratic ossification, hostile legislation, and revolution can do it much better. Let me examine the matter further. Capitalism as we like it can thrive only in an environment of political democracy and personal freedom. These require a pluralistic society—where there is division, not centralization, of power; variety, not unanimity, of opinion; and separation, not unification, of workaday economic, political, social, and spiritual functions.

We all fear an omnipotent state because it creates a dull and frightening conformity—a monolithic society. We do not want a society with one locus of power, one authority, one arbiter of propriety. We want and need variety, diversity, spontaneity, competition—in short, pluralism. We do not want our lives shaped by a single viewpoint or by a single way of doing things, even if the material consequences are bountiful and the intentions are honorable. Mussolini, Stalin, Hitler, Franco, Trujillo, Peron, all show what happens when power is consolidated into a single, unopposed, and unopposable force.

We are against the all-embracing welfare state not because we are against welfare but because we are against centralized power and the harsh social discipline it so ineluctably produces. We do not want a pervasive welfare state in government, and we do not want it in unions. And for the same reasons we should not want it in corporations.

But at the rate we are going there is more than a contingent probability that, with all its resounding good intentions, business statesmanship may create the corporate equivalent of the unitary state. Its proliferating employee welfare programs, its serpentine involvement in community, government, charitable, and educational affairs, its prodigious currying of political and public favor through hundreds of peripheral preoccupations, all these well-intended but insidious contrivances are greasing the rails for our collective descent into a social order that would be as repugnant to the corporations themselves as to their critics. The danger is that all these things will turn the corporation into a twentieth-century equivalent of the medieval Church. The corporation would eventually invest itself with all-embracing duties, obligations, and finally powers—ministering to the whole man and molding him and society in the image of the corporation's narrow ambitions and its essentially unsocial needs.

Now there is nothing wrong as such with the corporation's narrow ambitions or needs. Indeed, if there is anything wrong today, it is that the corporation conceives its ambitions and needs much too broadly. The trouble is not that it is too narrowly profit-oriented, but that it is not narrowly profit-oriented *enough*. In its guilt-driven urge to transcend the narrow limits of derived standards, the modern corporation is reshaping not simply the economic but also the institutional, social, cultural, and political topography of society.

And there's the rub. For while the corporation also transforms itself in the process, at bottom its outlook will always remain narrowly materialistic. What we have, then, is the frightening spectacle of a powerful economic functional group whose future and perception are shaped in a tight materialistic context of money and things but which imposes its narrow ideas about a broad spectrum of unrelated noneconomic subjects on the mass of man and society.

Even if its outlook were the purest kind of good will, that would not recommend the corporation as an arbiter of our lives. What is bad for this or any other country is for society to be consciously and aggressively shaped by a single functional group or a single ideology, whatever it may be.

If the corporation believes its long-run profitability to be strengthened by these peripheral involvements—if it believes that they are not charity but self-interest—then that much the worse. For, if this is so, it puts much more apparent justification and impulse behind activities which are essentially bad for man, bad for society, and ultimately bad for the corporation itself.

The belief that one institution should encompass the complete lives of its members is by no means new to American society. One example can be taken from the history of unionism:

In the latter part of the nineteenth century America's budding labor unions were shaken by a monumental internal struggle for power. On the one side were the unctuous advocates of the "whole man" idea of the union's function. For them the union was to be an encompassing social institution, operating on all conceivable fronts as the protector and spokesman of the workingman at large. In the process they acknowledged that the union would have to help shape and direct the aspirations, ideas, recreations, and even tastes—in short, the lives—of the members and the society in which they functioned.

Opposing this view were the more pragmatic "horny-handed sons of toil," the "bread and butter" unionists. All they wanted, in the words of Samuel Gompers, was "more, more, more." At the time it was widely believed that this made Gompers a dangerous man. Lots of pious heads shook on the sidelines as they viewed the stark contrast between the dedicated "uplifters" and Gompers' materialistic opportunism. Who would not side with the "uplifters"? Yet Gompers won, and happily so, for he put American unionism on the path of pure-and-simple on-the-job demands, free of the fanciful ideological projects and petty intellectualism that drain the vitality of European unions.

As late as the early 1930's the American Federation of Labor remained true to Gompers' narrow rules by opposing proposed Social Security legislation. And when, in the 1930's, the communists and the pseudo humanitarians pushed the "whole man" concept of unionism, they also lost. Today, however, without ideologically sustained or conscious direction, the more "progressive" unions have won the battle for what the nineteenth century ideologists lost. With all their vast might and organizational skill, these unions are now indeed ministering to the whole man:

> Walter Reuther's United Auto Workers runs night schools, "drop-in" centers for retired members, recreation halls; supports grocery cooperatives; publishes and broadcasts household hints, recipes, and fashion news; and runs dozens of social, recreational, political, and action programs that provide something for every member of the family every hour of the day.
> David Dubinsky's International Ladies' Garment Workers' Union has health centers, citizenship and hobby classes, low-cost apartment buildings, and a palatial summer resort in the Poconos.
> A Toledo union promotes "respectability" in clothes and hair styles among teenagers as a way of counteracting leather-jacketed, duck-tail, rock-'n-roll delinquency.

Thus, the union is transformed in such cases from an important and desirable economic functional group into an all-knowing, all-doing, all-wise father on whom millions become directly dependent for womb-to-tomb ministration.

This is the kind of monolithic influence the corporation will eventually have if it becomes so preoccupied with its social burden, with employee welfare, and with the body politic. Only, when the corporation does this, it will do a much more thorough job than the union. For it is more protean and potentially more powerful than any democratic union ever dreamed of being. It is a self-made incubator and instrument of strength, more stable and better able to draw and hold a following than is the union. It creates its own capital and its own power by the sheer accident of doing what it is expected to do. . . .

If the corporate ministry of man turns out to be only half as pervasive as it seems destined to be, it will turn into a simonist enterprise of Byzantine proportions. There is a name for this kind of encircling business ministry, and it pains me to use it. The name is fascism. It may not be the insidious, amoral, surrealistic fascism over which we fought World War II, or the corrupt and aggrandizing Latin American version, but the consequence will be a monolithic society in which the essentially narrow ethos of the business corporation is malignantly extended over everyone and everything.

This feudalistic phantasmagoria may sound alarmist, farfetched, or even patently ridiculous. For one thing, it will be said, not all corporations see alike on all things. At the very least there will be the pluralism of differences arising out of corporate differences in productive functions and their differences as competitors. But look at it this way: When it comes to present-day corporate educational, recreational, welfare, political, social, and public relations programs, attitudes, ideas, promotions, and preferences, how much difference is there? Are they more alike or more unlike? Are they growing more similar or more dissimilar?

It may also be protested, "What is wrong with the corporate ideology, anyway? Who will deny the material abundance, the leisure, and even the aesthetic values it has created and fostered in the United States? Nobody!" But that is irrelevant. The point is: we do not want a monolithic society, even if its intentions are the best. Moreoever, a group's behavior in the pluralistic, competitive past is no guarantee of its behavior once it reaches complete ascendance. . . .

There is nothing more dangerous than the sincere, self-righteous, dedicated proselyte sustained by the mighty machinery of a powerful institution—particularly an economic institution. The reformer whose only aim is personal aggrandizement and whose tactics are a vulgar combination of compulsive demagoguery and opportunistic cynicism is much less dangerous than the social evangelist who, to borrow from Nietzsche, thinks of himself as "God's ventriloquist." As Greek tragedies show, there is nothing more corrupting than self-righteousness and nothing more intolerant than an ardent man who is convinced he is on the side of the angels.

When the spokesmen for such causes begin to make speeches and write books about their holy mission, to canonize their beliefs into faith, conviction, and doctrine, and to develop ways of thinking by which their particular institutional ambitions are ideologically sustained—that is the time for us to begin trembling. They will then have baptized their mission with a book—still the most powerful instrument of change devised by man. . . .

So far the movement is a young and rather unassuming one. But when it really gathers momentum, when its forms become crystallized and its primal innocence becomes more professionalized, its success should amaze us. The corporation is not handicapped by the cumbersome authority that has always characterized the church and the state. It can make its authority sweet as honey by making itself the embodiment of material welfare, of unbounded security, of decorous comfort, amusing diversion, healthful recreation, and palatable ideology. It can far surpass even the medieval Church in efficiency and power.

It may have no intention of doing this (and I firmly believe that this is the last thing that the apostles of corporate humanity want), but what we get is seldom what we want. History is fortuitous. It does not move on tracks made by rational social engineers.

Business wants to survive. It wants security from attack and restriction; it wants to minimize what it believes is its greatest potential enemy—the state. So it takes the steam out of the state's lumbering engines by employing numerous schemes to win its employees and the general public to its side. It is felt that these are the best possible investments it can make for its own survival. And that is precisely where the reasoning has gone wrong. These investments are only superficially *easy* solutions, not the best.

Welfare and society are not the corporation's business. Its business is making money, not sweet music. The same goes for unions. Their business is "bread and butter" and job rights. In a free enterprise system, welfare is supposed to be automatic; and where it is not, it becomes government's job. This is the concept of pluralism. Government's job is not business, and business's job is not government. And unless these functions are resolutely separated in all respects, they are eventually combined in every respect. In the end the danger is not that government will run business, or that business will run government, but rather that the two of them will coalesce, as we saw, into a single power, unopposed and unopposable.

The only political function of business, labor, and agriculture is to fight each other so that none becomes or remains dominant for long. When one does reach overwhelming power and control, at the very best the state will eventually take over on the pretense of protecting everybody else. At that point the big business executives, claiming possession of the tools of large-scale management, will come in, as they do in war, to become the bureaucrats who run the state.

The final victor then is neither government, as the representative of the people, nor the people, as represented by government. The new leviathan will be the professional corporate bureaucrat operating at a more engrossing and exalted level than the architects of capitalism ever dreamed possible.

The functions of the four main groups in our economy—government, business, labor, agriculture—must be kept separate and separable. As soon as they become amalgamated and indistinguishable, they likewise become monstrous and restrictive.

Tending to Business

If businessmen do not preach and practice social responsibility, welfare, and self-restraint, how can management effectively deal with its critics, the political attacks, the confining legislation—that is, the things which have induced it to create its own private welfare state? The answer is fairly simple: to perform its main task so well that critics cannot make their charges stick, and then to assert forthrightly its function and accomplishments with the same aroused spirit that made nineteenth-century capitalism as great as it was extreme.

It seems clear that today's practices fall far short of this prescription. When it comes to material things, the accomplishments of American capitalism are spectacular. But the slate is not clean. American capitalism also creates, fosters, and acquiesces in enormous social and economic cancers. Indeed, it fights against the achievement of certain forms of economic and social progress, pouring millions into campaigns against things which people have a right to expect from their government and which they seem to want their government to provide. For example:

> Business motives helped to create slums, and now business seems all too frequently to fight their abolition. The free operation of the profit motive has not abolished them. Indeed, it sustains them. But if abolishing slums is not a sound business proposition, business should cease its campaign against government doing a job which nobody in his right mind can deny should be done. If supporting state and federal efforts at urban renewal does not raise the public's esteem of business's good intentions, few things will. Certainly self-righteous claims of good intentions are not enough.
>
> The same is true of health insurance, pensions, school construction, and other proposals for activities which are best handled by government (for reasons of administration as well as of ability to meet the commitments) and are therefore logical government functions. Businessmen will simply have to accept the fact that the state can be a powerful auxiliary to the attainment of the good life. This is particularly so in a free enterprise economy where there is a natural division of social and economic functions, and where this division is fortified by countervailing institutional checks and balances.

Yet in both word and deed business constantly denies the potentially beneficial role of the state. Where it does not fight the public interest, it often adopts a placid air of indifference or a vapid neutrality. . . .

I am not arguing that management should ignore its critics. Some of them have made a good case from time to time against business's social delinquencies and against its shortsightedness in fighting practically all of Washington's efforts to provide security. (Indeed, if business had not always fought federal welfare measures, perhaps the unions would not have demanded them from business itself.)

Nor am I arguing that management has no welfare obligations at all to society. Quite to the contrary. Corporate welfare makes good sense *if* it makes good economic sense—and not infrequently it does. But if something does not make economic sense, sentiment or idealism ought not let it in the door. Sentiment is a corrupting and debilitating influence in business. It fosters leniency, inefficiency, sluggishness, extravagance, and hardens the innovationary arteries. It can confuse the role of the businessman just as much as the profit motive could confuse the role of the government official. The governing rule in industry should be that *something is good only if it pays*. Otherwise it is alien and impermissible. This is the rule of capitalism. . . .

In the end business has only two responsibilities—to obey the elementary canons of everyday face-to-face civility (honesty, good faith, and so on) and to seek material gain. The fact that it is the butt of demagogical critics is no reason for management to lose its nerve—to buckle under to reformers—lest more severe restrictions emerge to throttle business completely. Few people will man the barricades against capitalism if it is a good provider, minds its own business, and supports government in the things which are properly government's.

8

Honesty in Business

The issue of honesty is related to, yet nevertheless distinct from, a discussion of the social obligations of the business community. The area of social responsibility embraces much terra incognita: should business acknowledge responsibility (as few businesses have) for the employment of workers during slack periods and off-seasons; should a large corporation shut down a marginal plant in a community completely dependent on its operation; should a plant foul a nearby stream or incur added costs in disposing of pollutants; should corporations (as distinguished from individuals) give aid to churches and institutions of higher learning; should the steel industry reckon with the impact of its pricing policies on the economy as a whole? The nature of obligation is not clearly defined in these areas, and standards are in flux.

On the other hand, the question of honesty involves no comparable perplexities, not even in certain practices not banned by law. Normal people generally know when they are dishonest. At issue here is adherence to precepts that the business community itself accepts. Quite simply, honesty is opposed to lying, cheating, or stealing. Also, it involves practicing what we preach, especially when we preach with moral fervor.

Are incidents of illegal or unethical business conduct isolated and unrepresentative, or do they indicate the presence of widespread dishonesty and moral obtuseness in the business community?[1] In the case of the General Electric and Westinghouse

---

[1] For example, in 1961 a federal judge upheld the conviction of eleven major oil firms on gasoline price-fixing charges. In 1962, five steel corporations were

executives who were jailed a few years ago for illegal conduct, the defense pleaded in extenuation that the violations were part of a "prevailing business morality." Was counsel exaggerating to save his client or was he describing a true state of affairs?

Again, the business community affirms its dedication to the ideal of consumer "sovereignty" with moral fervor and great vigor.[2] Yet the "Truth in Lending" bill, authored by former Senator Paul H. Douglas, which required disclosure of simple annual interest rates and the actual cost in dollars of buying on the installment plan has been bitterly opposed by retailers and lenders and required seven years for a compromise version to pass the Senate before going to the House in July 1967. One revealing compromise was the exclusion of first mortgages on houses because (according to the AP report) the "industry" said disclosure of full dollar cost of the financing might discourage home buyers! (The exemption was removed from a somewhat stricter House bill reported out of committee on December 13, 1967.) Quite apart from the ethics of calling, say, a 14-percent interest rate 7 percent, is it honest to call the consumer sovereign while energetically opposing a measure intended to let him know what he is doing? Only a few such questions can be answered here. But they will be raised more and more persistently until the business community comes up with satisfactory answers.

As we appraise the answers we must, in all fairness, reckon with notable improvements in the last several decades, as with the difference between American businessmen and their counterparts in other countries. Moreover, we must be on guard against

---

fined a total of $44,000 on their plea of no contest to charges of conspiracy to fix prices and rig bids in steel sales. In 1964 six of the nation's largest aluminum firms were accused by the Justice Department of submitting rigged bids and overcharging government agencies for aluminum conductor cable. They settled out of court, paying the U.S. Government $563,000. In 1967, it was the turn of the drug industry. For another kind of example, shipments of General Foods' Maxwell House instant coffee were seized recently by the Food and Drug Administration because the giant "economy" size was costing the consumer more per ounce than the small jar. Instances can be multiplied.

[2] "Within the market society the working of the price mechanism makes the consumer supreme. . . . In that endless rotating mechanism the entrepreneurs and capitalists are servants of the consumer. The consumers are the masters. . . . The market is a democracy in which every penny gives a right to vote . . ." Ludwig Von Mises, *Omnipotent Government* (New Haven: Yale University Press, 1944), pp. 49–50. So, too, John Chamberlain, whose book *The Roots of Capitalism* is one of a series designed to promote understanding of prevailing business practices, writes: "The test of an economic system lies in the choices it offers. . . ." In a free system such as ours "the consumer directs production, forcing or luring energy, brains, and capital to obey his will" (New York: D. Van Nostrand Co., 1959), p. 165. If there is need for reform here, Mr. Chamberlain is powerless since, in the title of an earlier book, he bade *Farewell to Reform*.

regarding dishonesty as an exclusive monopoly of the business
community. We are helped in this by the Teamsters Union and
similarly managed labor organizations, by the refusal of congress
to pass a "conflict of interest" law applicable to its own members,
and by the precautions that must be taken even in the rarefied
atmosphere of a college campus against book thefts and cheating
on examinations. In a more inclusive survey these would deserve
close attention. Even so, one may still ask whether such evidences
of widespread dishonesty suggest an inherent depravity in human
nature or reflect the influence of the acquisitive ideal in our
society.

It is unlikely that business management, whatever the
prevailing practice, would dissent from the criticism contained in
the two following articles. Disagreement occurs between those who
believe that dishonesty is built into the "business system," as
Professor Miller seems to imply when he says that "the law of the
jungle prevails," and those who, like Clarence Randall, believe
that business leaders "can and must set off a moral and spiritual
reawakening."

BUSINESS MORALITY: SOME UNANSWERED
(AND PERHAPS UNANSWERABLE)
QUESTIONS

Arthur Selwyn Miller

*Arthur Selwyn Miller is Professor of Law in the Law School
and in the Graduate School of Public Law at The George
Washington University. While Professor of Law at Emory
University from 1953 to 1961, he was Editor of the* Journal
of Public Law. *He is the author of* Racial Discrimination and
Private Education: A Legal Analysis (*1957*), Private Governments and the Constitution (*1959*), *and other works, including
numerous articles in legal and other periodicals. He was Spe-*

From *The Annals* of the American Academy of Political and Social Science
(Jan. 1966), Vol. 363, 95–101. Reprinted by permission of the author.

cial Editor of the September 1962 issue of The Annals *on* The Ethics of Business Enterprise. *Since 1962 he has been a Lecturer in the Advanced Study Program of the Brookings Institution.*

That there is more to corporate decision-making than profit-making, although it is the irreducible minimum and doubtless the principal desideratum, is the teaching of the many assertions of social responsibility by corporate executives. If the published statements of businessmen are to be believed—and one must, of course, be wary of the public-relations man busily engaged in building a favorable "image" for his client—then there can be little doubt that something more than profit-maximization motivates the businessman. (Whether they can or should be believed is another question which itself poses interesting moral questions.) In this connection, one may compare the observation of Rabbi Louis Finkelstein with a finding of The Reverend Raymond C. Baumhart, s.j. Said the former: "The American business executive tends to ignore the great ethical laws as they apply immediately to his work. He is preoccupied chiefly with gain."[1] Father Baumhart found that in a survey of American businessmen, 73 per cent of the respondents agreed that "for corporation executives to act in the interest of shareholders alone, and not also in the interest of employees and consumers, is unethical."[2]

How much, and to what extent, businessmen are, in fact, ethical cannot, of course, be so effortlessly answered. . . . it may be valid to suggest that, as with nation-states in the conduct of what are considered to be their vital interests, so it is with the corporation: the law of the jungle prevails. Very possibly, it is externally imposed *power,* not morality and not law, that is the determinant of corporate behavior. True it is that there is adherence to the standards of conduct *precisely* demanded by the legal system. But, as lawyers know, the law is not very certain; it leaves a great deal of flexibility and freedom to maneuver. And it is also true that the business enterprise has been insulated from the direct interdictory command of law in most of its important activities. That is to say, the law protects and aids, rather than substantially circumscribes, the businessman;

---

[1] Editor's note: It is a tribute to the business community's capacity for self-criticism that Rabbi Finkelstein's comments were published in the pages of *Fortune* (September, 1958, p. 116). Rabbi Finkelstein also found "distressing validity" in the remark of an executive that "It is impossible to conduct business in the U.S. today without breaking the law."

[2] Editor's note: He also found that almost half of the businessmen surveyed agreed with Rabbi Finkelstein's statement, pointing out that, although most of his respondents "profess a lofty level of ethical aspiration for themselves," they have a strikingly lower opinion of the practices of other businessmen. See *Harvard Business Review* (July–August 1961), pp. 7 ff.

it provides a favorable arena in which he can operate and only asks that the more grotesque of his preferences be blunted.

Who Sets the Standards?

Under the "classical" theory of economics, often identified with Adam Smith, the businessman does not have to worry about ethical behavior. Acting as the personification of "economic man" bent ceaselessly upon maximizing his profit, he is considered to be controlled by the market. The intervention of government or the moral leaders of the community is not necessary, simply because the "invisible hand" magically translates the pursuit of selfish gain into the over-all public good. The market, in other words, is said to operate as an external standard. By merely being, it performs its vital societal function.

That this simplistic model of politico-economic behavior no longer is adequate is evident. (Likely it never was, except in the published lucubrations of economists who sat secure in their ivory aeries taking an Olympian and magisterial view of human affairs.) Social Darwinism as a prevailing philosophy does not and cannot work to the benefit of many, perhaps most, people. Something else is needed in an economy dominated by corporate giants—those latter-day disembodied economic men. That "something" is provided in part by government through the use of officially imposed norms of conduct. The antitrust and labor laws are the obvious examples. How much these, in fact, circumscribe corporate behavior is difficult to ascertain. No doubt both do to some degree; the "robber baron" has become anachronistic, as have the "dark, satanic mills" of the early Industrial Revolution. The "public be damned" attitude has become "the public be cajoled or enticed (or perhaps cozened)," the "exploitive capitalism" of the nineteenth century having become the "service" capitalism of the twentieth. Why this change has taken place is the critical, unanswered question. Perhaps it is more traceable to technological advance than to anything else. The antitrust laws burst into recent prominence in the convictions in the "electrical conspiracy" cases of a number of high executives of such corporate giants as General Electric and Westinghouse.[3] Whether these convictions mark a change in corporate behavior (or reflect the corporate norm) is difficult to determine, although in the summer of 1965 another price-fixing conspiracy was found in the steel industry. The very light sentences given the corporate delinquents and the subsequent tax write-off of fines and judgments mysteriously granted by a complaisant Internal Revenue Service would lead one to believe that the cases are a

---

[3] Editor's note: The convictions, occurring at a time when "Big Business" was enjoying a revival of prestige, rocked the business world and led to an orgy of self-examination probably without precedent in economic history.

light slap on the wrist, rather than a sharp rein on corporate activity. What the cases further indicate is that the corporation—for example, General Electric—has become so large that top management does not know what is going on within the entity itself. President Ralph Cordiner of General Electric was absolved of blame in those cases, on his assertion that he was unaware of what his colleagues were doing. This might mean one of two things, assuming, as one must, that Mr. Cordiner is telling the truth: either the corporation has gotten out of hand, so that nobody is really running it (it runs itself) or that the top management of some of our corporations are chosen for reasons other than supervising their subordinates. In either event, it is not a particularly savory picture.

Outside of the law—and, to repeat, no one should be sanguine about law being a prime method of social control of corporations—the acceptance of externally imposed norms by corporate managers seems to be more the resultant of power positions by other segments of the entity (for example, labor) than the acceptance by those managers of commands or suggestions to "be good." For the over-all well-being of the corporation, the manager thus takes into consideration the demands and interests of labor and the consumer, as well as of the other elements. This may well be not because he wants to, but because of an "I have to live with him, don't I?" attitude. It may also reflect economic reality, which means that good morals become good economics—not an uncomfortable position.

Who, then, sets the standards? The short answer is that the corporate manager does for himself. Ethical leaders, save for a few industries, are irrelevant. The business executive, like Mr. Ralph Cordiner, talks of "self-discipline." Some effort has been made to draft a code of ethics for business enterprise, but as with most of such codes they would have no effective technique for enforcement and are written in such nebulous language as to leave large areas for interpretation. In practical effect, accordingly, the injunction to the businessman to "be good" requires him to "be God." . . .

What Standards?

If the businessman . . . is enjoined to be good and thus has to be God, a final question is what standards are to guide those Olympians? What should their celestial majesties decide when particular problems face them? The law gives little or no guidance; the ethical leaders of the community are mute; ethical codes are more hortatory than interdictory. A few representative examples of corporate decisions pose some of the problems in better focus:

Item: According to the *Wall Street Journal,* an executive of the Bethlehem Steel Company "was fired in March 1964 after local newspaper articles identified him as a member of the Community Civic League, a voluntary race relations group." *Query:* What is the morality of this corporate action? The answer is dependent upon the ethical obligations owed internally to a member of the managerial hierarchy.

Item: Not long ago the United States Steel Company maintained that it had no responsibility at its Birmingham, Alabama plant to do anything about the state of race relations in Alabama or Birmingham. *Query:* Is this ethical? The answer involves consideration of the external obligations of a corporation.

Item: In 1960, at a time when the United States was experiencing severe "balance of payments" difficulties, the Ford Motor Company transferred $300 million to England for the purpose of acquiring full ownership of Ford-England. At about the same time, in an effort to help the balance of payments, the Pentagon announced that servicemen could no longer take dependents abroad with them. The Secretary of Defense said that servicemen are used to hardship. *Query:* What are the relative equities of these situations? The answer seems to depend upon the obligations owed by a corporation (an artificial person) to the nation at large as compared with those owed by natural persons. (In this instance, the artificial person came off better, in itself an illustration of the lack of real power government presently has over giant enterprise. Government dominance of business is a myth.)

Item: In 1962, the Council of Economic Advisers announced so-called "guideposts" for wage negotiations in collective bargaining, in an effort to stave off further inflation. In 1964, Mr. George Meany, a leading labor official, said that he did not think that labor should be bound by such guideposts. *Query:* What should be the response of corporate management?

In these examples, as well as many others, the broad question is whether moral or ethical considerations should be brought within the crucible of decision-making. The suggestion here is that neither political nor economic theory offers anything viable by way of analysis and explication, and that, accordingly, the question of morality cannot be meaningfully answered. The corporate manager really has little or no external guide to decisions. It is high time that this parlous condition be rectified. When it is—as it must be—then the question of the legitimacy of the power of the large corporation will reach some sort of reasonable resolution. Until it is, the corporate manager must mill around in the dark, without effective guidance from the law or from the ethical leaders of the community and without really knowing to what signals he should listen when it comes to morals.

A NEW CODE OF BUSINESS ETHICS

Clarence B. Randall

Clarence B. Randall had occupied a rare vantage point from which to view business morality. He had been president and chairman of the board of Inland Steel Company, which he joined in 1925, and had served three administrations as an expert on foreign economic policy. He was the author of The Folklore of Management (*1959*). *It is unlikely that management, whatever its prevailing practice, would dissent from his criticism. Disagreement is likely to come from those who believe that the kinds of practices he castigated are built into the "business system."*

. . . Industry in this country is facing a moral crisis. The American people are taking a new, hard look at us and are asking themselves whether by any chance the whole lot of us are dishonest.

They demand urgently to know whether we operate behind a pious façade, whether our public posture is a fraud, whether deep down inside we are completely antisocial in our purposes. We are not yet convicted in the public mind, but a heavy cloud of suspicion surrounds us.

We must face this issue squarely . . . In my opinion, we must at once do one of two things. If our ethical practices are in fact shameful, we must change them forthwith, and make it clear that we have done so. If conscience tells us that they are completely above reproach, we must offer a new declaration of faith to the American people, and then by our conduct demonstrate the complete integrity of our purposes.

No man of senior years, like myself, can fail to sense that the moral climate in industry today is greatly improved over what we knew in earlier years, but this is partly because it was so bad in the period when we first went to work. We remember all too vividly practices which prevailed then, and which we would now like to forget.

For example, in the steel industry, I knew a time when it was common for one company to endeavor continuously by subversive means to steal the research secrets of its competitors. This was done in many ways, with all the stealth of a Communist agent. Technicians in other laboratories would be suborned and for a fixed payment per month,

From *The New York Times Magazine* (April 8, 1962), pp. 24 ff. © 1962 by The New York Times Company. Reprinted by permission.

delivered in rolls of bills at secret rendezvous, would turn over copies of blueprints or duplicates of new formulae. A second and even more effective way was simply to hire away the chief chemist or other research officer by doubling his pay, on condition that he would bring his secrets with him.

During the Great Depression, these methods were applied to sales. The vice-president of a company whose pay had been severely cut was an easy mark for the competitor who offered a big increase. When he changed jobs, he brought his little black book with him, and revealed the secret rebates which he had been giving customers. The trouble was that his aroused former employer often hired him back at the end of the first year, and when he returned he crossed up his new employer and took his new little black book with him.

There was another kind of venality—a betrayal of trust within a company for a cold cash payment. I was once trapped in the midst of one such nasty situation where, for every carload of steel scrap shipped to the steel plant, the inspector was paid handsomely for not looking beneath the top layer. Nor was that enough. A further shocker was in store for me, because I found that the shipper who had bought the inspector had also bought the court.

Bribery of public officials, the crude buying of legislators, was also widely practiced in earlier days. The notorious black bag was not a fiction in my day but reality, and devious indeed were the mental processes by which otherwise high-minded men justified the practice. For example, I knew a company which for years secretly put a particular member of the legislature on its payroll for $400 a month (that was real money then) with the justification that he was making a great personal sacrifice in accepting the office. I do not recall, however, that he ever voted for a measure of which the company disapproved.

And I knew another corporation in which the officer who handled the taxes was directed by the president to get the assessment reduced, and not to report back. He did in fact get the assessment down. He did it by meeting the assessor in a hotel room. And he did not tell the boss what he had done—but he did tell me.

Now most of those crude and crass practices have disappeared from American business practices—most, but not all. For example, the large-scale pirating of trade secrets in big industry is no longer resorted to. In steel, at least, technical information is now openly and freely exchanged. Advances based upon research by one company become available to all. Competitors have learned that they gain more that way than they lose. Nevertheless, in new industries which depend heavily on design factors and advanced technology, or in fields where only a few large companies carry on research programs, I suspect that the stealing still goes on.

Graft, unhappily, is still practiced by many at the municipal level, in such cases as buying off an alderman for an alley permit and this is very wrong. Though undoubtedly rare, money may still sometimes actually pass to a member of a state legislature, or of Congress, to influence his attitude.

I regret, too, that in all candor I must record the unsavory fact that there is a related area of business endeavor where the state of morality is very low indeed, and where there is a stain on the conscience of industry which needs to be removed soon. I mean the bribery of officials in the governments of new countries in the underdeveloped parts of the world.

In the course of my government service, I visited many of these areas. I know whereof I speak, and I say that there are many otherwise respectable companies which still buy their way in when it comes to securing a mineral concession or establishing an operation in a remote part of the world.

This must stop, and it can only be accomplished by self-discipline. Surprisingly enough, I happen to have grave doubt whether it is a violation of any present Federal law for an American citizen to corrupt an officer of a foreign government, but that fact merely highlights the challenge to our business leadership. I reject the argument that other nations are doing it, and therefore we must if we are to compete. Better to lose the business than to deny our heritage. The entire prestige of our country, and its ability to preserve our way of life in the world, is at stake. Those precious values must not be jeopardized by individual dishonor.

In the host countries, someone always knows the facts. What could be more tragic than for us to lose an air base that is vital to our national security because of moral turpitude on the part of American business? What will be our position when some demagogue from the desert calls his people to arms with the cry "Drive the filthy Americans into the sea. We have been robbed of our ancient heritage"?

Either we have a code of morals, or we do not. If we do, it is for universal application, and must be adhered to in all circumstances, regardless of the impact on earnings. This is the acid test of our integrity.

That was the moral point at issue in the investigations of the electrical industry—setting artificially high prices to keep profits up. It is perhaps unfair to pass judgment upon those cases without personal knowledge of the facts, but who among us can avoid it, when so much is at stake?

For myself, there is no doubt whatever that serious mistakes were made. Things were done which have prejudiced the continuing development of the private-enterprise system, and this is bad for all of us. How could this have come to pass? How may one explain these incredible circumstances? All that an outsider may do is to speculate.

Conceivably, for example, these were mistakes of the head, and not of the heart, committed by overzealous executives. It might be argued that here were men who in their daily lives were decent, law-abiding citizens, and who responded to the highest loyalty they knew, the desire to advance the interests of their companies. In other words, it is possible that they put corporate welfare above that of their country merely because they knew no better. It is possible that they simply did not understand the vital function of a free market in a democratic society.

If this were the answer, it would still be bad. To hold the confidence of our public, we in industry must not only have the moral courage to do the right, but sufficient insight to know the right. Our minds must be clear, as well as our consciences.

This hypothesis does not ring true, however. These executives were men of long years of service and broad experience, and it is hard to believe that they did not know that they were violating the law. Our moral crisis is there, either way.

But beyond these proved and punished aberrations there are large, new, somewhat peripheral areas of moral problems, of such comparatively recent origin that the issues have not yet been sharply defined, nor full corrective measures taken. Here the impeccable conduct of the many is being placed in jeopardy by the rascality of the few.

This is a partial list:

(1) *Lack of truth in advertising.* There is still an occasional business buccaneer who misrepresents the quality of the product, or who understates the price by concealing the fact that there are indispensable accessories which will also be required.

(2) *The credit racket.* There are still unscrupulous vendors who overpersuade the unwary buyer of modest means by the no-payment-down, take-all-the-time-you-need pitch. The true interest charge on the deferred balance is not revealed, and the seller makes his money out of the financing of the debt rather than as legitimate profit on the merchandise.[1]

(3) *The union agent racket.* There are still evil-minded employers who cross the palm of the organizer, and buy exemption from legitimate worker grievances, thus cheating the employes, and rejecting the responsibilities of orderly collective bargaining.

(4) *Denial of promotion on merit to minority groups.* There are still those who give lip service in public to the doctrine of fair opportunity for all workers, regardless of creed or color, but who deny it in actual practice.

(5) *Expense account cheating.* No well-informed observer can doubt for a moment that the Federal Government is still being deprived of large sums of revenue by the unscrupulous padding of income-tax deductions claimed as business expenses. The honest citizen pays more than his share of the tax load when the man who cheats pays less.

---

[1] Editor's note: A truth-in-lending bill has since been passed.

In listing this catalogue of corporate sins one must, in fairness, point out that industry is not alone in having its moral lapses. The commercial world has no monopoly on character weakness. There are newspaper reporters who state as fact that for which they have no documentation; there are clergymen whose conduct is such that they have to be unfrocked; there are scholars who must be dismissed from faculties; there are surgeons who split fees, and lawyers who are disbarred.

But the human frailty of others can never justify moral turpitude in business. The American people are entitled to expect the very best from us at all times. We have no present alternative other than to submit forthwith all our practices to the most intensive re-examination, done in an atmosphere of heart-searching humility, and thereafter we must have the fortitude to do the right, wherever that may take us. We can and must set off a moral and spiritual reawakening which will touch every segment of American life.

Here is a unique challenge for our trade associations. Let our two great groups, the National Association of Manufacturers and the United States Chamber of Commerce, seize the initiative in denouncing obvious misconduct and in proclaiming new codes of ethical conduct. Then let the trade groups, industry by industry, promote the doing of the right as zealously as they now promote the sale of the product.

Above all, let each corporate officer determine in his own heart that never again will he put expediency above principle, never again let a chance for a quick profit stifle the dictates of his conscience.

Only thus can the survival of private enterprise in this troubled world be assured.

9

Television on Trial

The effects of the free enterprise system or, as Max Lerner calls it, the "business spirit" or, to use Viereck's term, the "cash-nexus" are on full display in television broadcasting, which— whether we like it or not—provides a kind of showcase for our society. Most television stations depend on advertising revenue and are run as a private enterprise for a profit. How does this affect the quality or value of their contribution to the community? Here the business spirit has operated with nearly unrestrained exuberance; have its effects on the culture been good or bad? Here great corporations have an opportunity to display citizenship in a highly sensitive area; do they? Here a bewildering variety of skills is enlisted to influence our scale of preferences; quite apart from the question whether we have been bored or entertained, is the outcome a people whose tastes and values have been vulgarized or elevated? The statements which follow represent opposing answers to these questions by two highly qualified spokesmen.

THE BROADCASTERS ARE PUBLIC TRUSTEES

Newton N. Minow

Newton N. Minow was a law partner of Adlai Stevenson and the chairman of the Federal Communications Commission, a post to which he was appointed by President Kennedy. It would not be an overstatement to say that this, his maiden address, had a traumatic effect on the television industry. In commenting that Minow "has exercised greater influence over broadcasting than the FCC has ever shown before" and that he "could justifiably take credit that his campaign . . . had forced the TV industry to think a little more about its responsibility to its audience," Time magazine probably reflects the verdict of many students of the television industry. Others will have recourse to an old French proverb: "Plus cela change, plus c'est la même chose."[1]

It may . . . come as a surprise to some of you, but I want you to know that you have my admiration and respect. Yours is a most honorable profession. Anyone who is in the broadcasting business has a tough row to hoe. You earn your bread by using public property. When you work in broadcasting you volunteer for public service, public pressure, and public regulation. You must compete with other attractions and other investments, and the only way you can do it is to prove to us every three years that you should have been in business in the first place.

I can think of easier ways to make a living.

But I cannot think of more satisfying ways.

I admire your courage—but that doesn't mean I would make life any easier for you. Your license lets you use the public's airwaves as Trustees for 180,000,000 Americans. The public is your beneficiary. If you want to stay on as Trustees, you must deliver a decent return to the

---

From an address delivered to the 39th Annual Convention of the National Association of Broadcasters in Washington, D.C., May 9, 1961, and reprinted in *Vital Speeches of the Day* (June 15, 1961), pp. 533 ff. Reprinted by permission.

[1] These will include Mr. Fred Friendly, whose book *Due to Circumstances Beyond Our Control* (1967), written after his resignation as head of the CBS news division, is a damaging criticism of the television industry. Mr. Friendly suggests that "one reason why Americans know more about detergents and bleaches than they do about Viet Nam or Watts" is that the networks devote 17 percent of their time to commercials.

public—not only to your stockholders. So, as a representative of the public, your health and your product are among my chief concerns.

As to your health: let's talk only of television today. 1960 gross broadcast revenues of the television industry were over $1,268,000,000; profit before taxes was $243,900,000, an average return on revenue of 19.2%. Compared with 1959, gross broadcast revenues were $1,163,900,-000, and profit before taxes was $222,300,000, an average return on revenue of 19.1%. So, the percentage increase of total revenues from 1959 to 1960 was 9%, and the percentage increase of profit was 9.7%. This, despite a recession. For your investors, the price has indeed been right.

I have confidence in your health.

But not in your product.

It is with this and much more in mind that I come before you today.

One editorialist in the trade press wrote that "the FCC of the New Frontier is going to be one of the toughest FCC's in the history of broadcast regulation." If he meant that we intend to enforce the law in the public interest, let me make it perfectly clear that he is right—we do.

If he meant that we intend to muzzle or censor broadcasting, he is dead wrong.

It would not surprise me if some of you had expected me to come here today and say in effect, "Clean up your own house or the government will do it for you."

Well, in a limited sense, you would be right—I've just said it.

But I want to say to you earnestly that it is not in that spirit that I come before you today, nor is it in that spirit that I intend to serve the FCC.

I am in Washington to help broadcasting, not to harm it; to strengthen it, not weaken it; to reward it, not punish it; to encourage it, not threaten it; to stimulate it, not censor it.

Above all, I am here to uphold and protect the public interest.

What do we mean by "the public interest"? Some say the public interest is merely what interests the public.

I disagree.

So does your distinguished president, Governor Collins. In a recent speech he said, "Broadcasting to serve the public interest must have a soul and a conscience, a burning desire to excel, as well as to sell; the urge to build the character, citizenship and intellectual stature of people, as well as to expand the gross national product. . . . By no means do I imply that broadcasters disregard the public interest . . . But a much better job can be done, and should be done."

I could not agree more.

And I would add that in today's world, with chaos in Laos and the Congo aflame, with Communist tyranny on our Caribbean doorstep and relentless pressure on our Atlantic alliance, with social and economic problems at home of the gravest nature, yes, and with technological knowledge that makes it possible, as our President has said, not only to destroy our world but to destroy poverty around the world—in a time of peril and opportunity, the old complacent, unbalanced fare of Action-Adventure and Situation Comedies is simply not good enough.

Your industry possesses the most powerful voice in America. It has an inescapable duty to make that voice ring with intelligence and with leadership. In a few years, this exciting industry has grown from a novelty to an instrument of overwhelming impact on the American people. It should be making ready for the kind of leadership that newspapers and magazines assumed years ago, to make our people aware of their world.

Ours has been called the jet age, the atomic age, the space age. It is also, I submit, the television age. And just as history will decide whether the leaders of today's world employed the atom to destroy the world or rebuild it for mankind's benefit, so will history decide whether today's broadcasters employed their powerful voice to enrich the people or debase them.

If I seem to address myself chiefly to the problems of television, I don't want any of you radio broadcasters to think we've gone to sleep at your switch—we haven't. We still listen. But in recent years most of the controversies and cross-currents in broadcast programming have swirled around television. And so my subject today is the television industry and the public interest.[2]

Like everybody, I wear more than one hat. I am the Chairman of the FCC. I am also a television viewer and the husband and father of other television viewers. I have seen a great many television programs that seemed to me eminently worthwhile, and I am not talking about the much bemoaned good old days of Playhouse 90 and Studio One.

I am talking about this past season. Some were wonderfully entertaining, such as The Fabulous Fifties, the Fred Astaire Show, and the Bing Crosby Special; some were dramatic and moving, such as Conrad's Victory and Twilight Zone; some were marvelously informative, such as The Nation's Future, CBS Reports, and The Valiant Years. I could list many more—programs that I am sure everyone here felt enriched his own life and that of his family. When television is good, nothing—not the theatre, not the magazines or newspapers—nothing is better.

---

[2] Editor's note: A year later, addressing the same audience, Minow turned his attention to radio. Noting that there are three times as many radio stations now as there were at the end of World War II, he added with some astringency: "In too many communities to twist the radio dial today is to be shoved through a bazaar, a clamorous casbah of pitchmen and commercials which plead, bleat, pressure, whistle, groan and shout. Too many stations have turned themselves into publicly franchised jukeboxes." He added: "Moreover, radio stations do not fade away, they just multiply."

But when television is bad, nothing is worse. I invite you to sit down in front of your television set when your station goes on the air and stay there without a book, magazine, newspaper, profit and loss sheet or rating book to distract you—and keep your eyes glued to that set until the station signs off. I can assure you that you will observe a vast wasteland.

You will see a procession of game shows, violence, audience participation shows, formula comedies about totally unbelievable families, blood and thunder, mayhem, violence, sadism, murder, western badmen, western good men, private eyes, gangsters, more violence, and cartoons. And, endlessly, commercials—many screaming, cajoling, and offending. And most of all, boredom. True, you will see a few things you will enjoy. But they will be very, very few. And if you think I exaggerate, try it.

Is there one person in this room [who] claims that broadcasting can't do better?

Well, a glance at next season's proposed programming can give us little heart. Of 73½ hours of prime evening time, the networks have tentatively scheduled 59 hours to categories of "action-adventure," situation comedy, variety, quiz, and movies.

Is there one network president in this room who claims he can't do better?

Gentlemen, your trust accounting with your beneficiaries is overdue.

Never have so few owed so much to so many.

Why is so much of television so bad? I have read many answers: demands of your advertisers; competition for ever higher ratings; the need always to attract a mass audience; the high cost of television programs; the insatiable appetite for programming material—these are some of them. Unquestionably, these are tough problems not susceptible to easy answers.

But I am not convinced that you have tried hard enough to solve them.

I do not accept the idea that the present over-all programming is aimed accurately at the public taste. The ratings tell us only that some people have their television sets turned on and of that number, so many are tuned to one channel and so many to another. They don't tell us what the public might watch if they were offered half a dozen additional choices. A rating, at best, is an indication of how many people saw what you gave them. Unfortunately, it does not reveal the depth of the penetration, or the intensity of reaction, and it never reveals what the acceptance would have been if what you gave them had been better—if all the forces of art and creativity and daring and imagination had been unleashed. I believe in the people's good sense and good taste, and I am not convinced that the people's taste is as low as you assume.

My concern with the rating services is not with their accuracy.

Perhaps they are accurate. I really don't know. What, then, is wrong with the ratings? It's not been their accuracy—it's been their use.

Certainly, I hope you will agree that ratings should have little influence where children are concerned. The best estimates indicate that during the hours of 5 to 6 P.M. 60% of your audience is composed of children under 12. And most young children today, believe it or not, spend as much time watching television as they do in the schoolroom. I repeat— let that sink in—most young children today spend as much time watching television as they do in the schoolroom. It used to be said that there were three great influences on a child: home, school, and church. Today, there is a fourth great influence, and you ladies and gentlemen control it.

If parents, teachers, and ministers conducted their responsibilities by following the ratings, children would have a steady diet of ice cream, school holidays, and no Sunday School. What about your responsibilities? Is there no room on television to teach, to inform, to uplift, to stretch, to enlarge the capacities of our children? Is there no room for programs deepening their understanding of children in other lands? Is there no room for a children's news show explaining something about the world to them at their level of understanding? Is there no room for reading the great literature of the past, teaching them the great traditions of freedom? There are some fine children's shows, but they are drowned out in the massive doses of cartoons, violence, and more violence. Must these be your trademarks? Search your consciences and see if you cannot offer more to your beneficiaries whose future you guide so many hours each and every day.

What about adult programming and ratings? You know, newspaper publishers take popularity ratings too. The answers are pretty clear: it is almost always the comics, followed by the advice to the lovelorn columns. But, ladies and gentlemen, the news is still on the front page of all newspapers, the editorials are not replaced by more comics, the newspapers have not become one long collection of advice to the lovelorn. Yet newspapers do not need a license from the government to be in business— they do not use public property. But in television—where your responsibilities as public trustees are so plain, the moment that the ratings indicate that westerns are popular there are new imitations of westerns on the air faster than the old coaxial cable could take us from Hollywood to New York. Broadcasting cannot continue to live by the numbers. Ratings ought to be the slave of the broadcaster, not his master. And you and I both know that the rating services themselves would agree.

Let me make clear that what I am talking about is balance. I believe that the public interest is made up of many interests. There are many people in this great country and you must serve all of us. You will get no argument from me if you say that, given a choice between a western and a symphony, more people will watch the western. I like westerns and private eyes too—but a steady diet for the whole country is obviously not in the public interest. We all know that people would more often prefer to be entertained than stimulated or informed. But your obligations are not satisfied if you look only to popularity as a test of what to broadcast. You are not only in show business; you are free to communicate ideas as well as relaxation. You must provide a wider range of choices, more diversity, more alternatives. It is not enough to cater to the nation's whims—you must also serve the nation's needs.

And I would add this—that if some of you persist in a relentless search for the highest rating and the lowest common denominator, you may very well lose your audience. Because, to paraphrase a great American who was recently my law partner, the people are wise, wiser than some of the broadcasters—and politicians—think.

As you may have gathered, I would like to see television improved. But how is this to be brought about? By voluntary action by the broadcasters themselves? By direct government intervention? Or how?

Let me address myself now to my role not as a viewer but as Chairman of the FCC. I could not, if I would, chart for you this afternoon in detail all of the actions I contemplate. Instead, I want to make clear some of the fundamental principles which guide me.

First: the people own the air. They own it as much in prime evening time as they do at 6 o'clock Sunday morning. For every hour that the people give you—you owe them something. I intend to see that your debt is paid with service.

Second: I think it would be foolish and wasteful for us to continue any worn-out wrangle over the problems of payola, rigged quiz shows, and other mistakes of the past. There are laws on the books which we will enforce. But there is no chip on my shoulder. We live together in perilous, uncertain times; we face together staggering problems; and we must not waste much time now by re-hashing the clichés of past controversy. To quarrel over the past is to lose the future.

Third: I believe in the free enterprise system. I want to see broadcasting improved and I want you to do the job. I am proud to champion your cause. It is not rare for American businessmen to serve a public trust. Yours is a special trust because it is imposed by law.

Fourth: I will do all I can to help educational television. There are still not enough educational stations, and major centers of the country still lack usable educational channels. If there were a limited number of printing presses in this country, you may be sure that a fair proportion of them would be put to educational use. Educational television has an enormous contribution to make to the future, and I intend to give it a hand along the way. If there is not a nation-wide educational television system in this country, it will not be the fault of the FCC.

Fifth: I am unalterably opposed to governmental censorship. There will be no suppression of programming which does not meet with bureaucratic tastes. Censorship strikes at the tap root of our free society.

Sixth: I did not come to Washington to idly observe the squandering of the public's airwaves. The squandering of our airwaves is no less important than the lavish waste of any precious natural resource. I intend to take the job of Chairman of the FCC very seriously. I believe in the gravity of my own particular sector of the New Frontier. There will be times perhaps when you will consider that I take myself or my job *too* seriously. Frankly, I don't care if you do. For I am convinced that either one takes this job seriously—or one can be seriously taken.

Now, how will these principles be applied? Clearly, at the heart of the FCC's authority lies its power to license, to renew or fail to renew, or to revoke a license. As you know, when your license comes up for renewal, your performance is compared with your promises. I understand that many people feel that in the past licenses were often renewed *pro forma*. I say to you now: renewal will not be *pro forma* in the future. There is nothing permanent or sacred about a broadcast license.

But simply matching promises and performance is not enough. I intend to do more. I intend to find out whether the people care. I intend to find out whether the community which each broadcaster serves believes he has been serving the public interest. When a renewal is set down for hearing, I intend—wherever possible—to hold a well-advertised public hearing, right in the community you have promised to serve. I want the people who own the air and the homes that television enters to tell you and the FCC what's been going on. I want the people—if they are truly interested in the service you give them—to make notes, document cases, tell us the facts. For those few of you who really believe that the public interest is merely what interests the public—I hope that these hearings will arouse no little interest.

The FCC has a fine reserve of monitors—almost 180 million Americans gathered around 56 million sets. If you want those monitors to be your friends at court—it's up to you.

Some of you may say—"Yes, but I still do not know where the line is between a grant of a renewal and the hearing you just spoke of." My answer is: Why should you want to know how close you can come to the edge of the cliff? What the Commission asks of you is to make a conscientious, good faith effort to serve the public interest. Every one of you serves a community in which the people would benefit by educational, religious, instructive or other public service programming. Every one of you serves an area which has local needs—as to local elections, controversial issues, local news, local talent. Make a serious, genuine effort to put on that programming. When you do, you will not be playing brinkmanship with the public interest.

What I've been saying applies to broadcast stations. Now a station break for the networks:

You know your importance in this great industry. Today, more than one-half of all hours of television station programming comes from the networks; in prime time, this rises to more than three-fourths of the available hours.

You know that the FCC has been studying network operations for some time. I intend to press this to a speedy conclusion with useful results. I can tell you right now, however, that I am deeply concerned with concentration of power in the hands of the networks. As a result, too many local stations have foregone any efforts at local programming, with little use of live talent and local service. Too many local stations operate with one hand on the network switch and the other on a projector loaded with old movies. We want the individual stations to be free to meet their legal responsibilities to serve their communities.

I join Governor Collins in his views so well expressed to the advertisers who use the public air. I urge the networks to join him and undertake a very special mission on behalf of this industry: you can tell your advertisers, "This is the high quality we are going to serve—take it or other people will. If you think you can find a better place to move automobiles, cigarettes and soap—go ahead and try."

Tell your sponsors to be less concerned with costs per thousand and more concerned with understanding per millions. And remind your stockholders that an investment in broadcasting is buying a share in public responsibility.

The networks can start this industry on the road to freedom from the dictatorship of numbers.

But there is more to the problem than network influences on stations or advertiser influences on networks. I know the problems networks face in trying to clear some of their best programs—the informational programs that exemplify public service. They are your finest hours—whether sustaining or commercial, whether regularly scheduled or special—these are the signs that broadcasting knows the way to leadership. They make the public's trust in you a wise choice.

They should be seen. As you know, we are readying for use new forms by which broadcast stations will report their programming to the Commission. You probably also know that special attention will be paid in these reports to public service programming. I believe that stations taking network service should also be required to report the extent of the local clearance of network public service programming, and when they fail to clear them, they should explain why. If it is to put on some outstanding local program, this is one reason. But, if it is simply to carry some old movie, that is an entirely different matter. The Commission should consider such clearance reports carefully when making up its mind about the licensee's over-all programming.

We intend to move—and as you know, indeed the FCC was rapidly moving in other new areas before the new administration arrived in Washington. And I want to pay my public respects to my very able predecessor, Fred Ford, and my colleagues on the Commission who have welcomed me to the FCC with warmth and cooperation.

We have approved an experiment with pay TV, and in New York we are testing the potential of UHF broadcasting. Either or both of these may revolutionize television. Only a foolish prophet would venture to guess the direction they will take, and their effect. But we intend that they shall be explored fully—for they are part of broadcasting's New Frontier.

The questions surrounding pay TV are largely economic. The questions surrounding UHF are largely technological. We are going to give the infant pay TV a chance to prove whether it can offer a useful service; we are going to protect it from those who would strangle it in its crib.

As for UHF, I'm sure you know about our test in the canyons of New York City. We will take every possible positive step to break through the allocations barrier into UHF. We will put this sleeping giant to use and in the years ahead we may have twice as many channels operating in cities where now there are only two or three. We may have a half dozen networks instead of three.

I have told you that I believe in the free enterprise system. I believe that most of television's problems stem from lack of competition. This is the importance of UHF to me: with more channels on the air, we will be able to provide every community with enough stations to offer service to all parts of the public. Programs with a mass market appeal required by mass product advertisers certainly will still be available. But other stations will recognize the need to appeal to more limited markets and to special tastes. In this way, we can all have a much wider range of programs.

Television should thrive on this competition—and the country should benefit from alternative sources of service to the public. And . . . I hope the NAB will benefit from many new members.

Another and perhaps the most important frontier: television will rapidly join the parade into space. International television will be with us soon. No one knows how long it will be until a broadcast from a studio in New York will be viewed in India as well as in Indiana, will be seen in the Congo as it is seen in Chicago. But as surely as we are meeting here today, that day will come—and once again our world will shrink.

What will the people of other countries think of us when they see our western badmen and good men punching each other in the jaw in between the shooting? What will the Latin American or African child learn of America from our great communications industry? We cannot permit television in its present form to be our voice overseas.

There is your challenge to leadership. You must reexamine some fundamentals of your industry. You must open your minds and open your hearts to the limitless horizons of tomorrow.

I can suggest some words that should serve to guide you:

"Television and all who participate in it are jointly accountable to the American public for respect for the special needs of children, for community responsibility, for the advancement of education and culture, for the acceptability of the program materials chosen, for decency and decorum in production, and for propriety in advertising. This responsibility cannot be discharged by any given group of programs, but can be discharged only through the highest standards of respect for the American home, applied to every moment of every program presented by television.

"Program materials should enlarge the horizons of the viewer, provide him with wholesome entertainment, afford helpful stimulation, and remind him of the responsibilities which the citizen has towards his society."

These words are not mine. They are yours. They are taken literally from your own Television Code. They reflect the leadership and aspirations of your own great industry. I urge you to respect them as I do. And I urge you to respect the intelligent and farsighted leadership of Governor LeRoy Collins, and to make this meeting a creative act. I urge you at this meeting and, after you leave, back home, at your stations and your networks, to strive ceaselessly to improve your product and to better serve your viewers, the American people.

I hope that we at the FCC will not allow ourselves to become so bogged down in the mountain of papers, hearings, memoranda, orders, and the daily routine that we close our eyes to the wider view of the public interest. And I hope that you broadcasters will not permit yourselves to become so absorbed in the chase for ratings, sales, and profits that you lose this wider view. Now more than ever before in broadcasting's history the times demand the best of all of us.

We need imagination in programming, not sterility; creativity, not imitation; experimentation, not conformity; excellence, not mediocrity. Television is filled with creative, imaginative people. You must strive to set them free.

Television in its young life has had many hours of greatness—its Victory at Sea, its Army-McCarthy hearings, its Peter Pan, its Kraft Theaters, its See It Now, its Project 20, the World Series, its political conventions and campaigns, The Great Debates—and it has had its endless hours of mediocrity and its moments of public disgrace. There are estimates that today the average viewer spends about 200 minutes daily with television, while the average reader spends 38 minutes with magazines and

40 minutes with newspapers. Television has grown faster than a teen-ager, and now it is time to grow up.

What you gentlemen broadcast through the people's air affects the people's taste, their knowledge, their opinions, their understanding of themselves and of their world, and their future.

The power of instantaneous sight and sound is without precedent in mankind's history. This is an awesome power. It has limitless capabilities for good—and for evil. And it carries with it awesome responsibilities, responsibilities which you and I cannot escape.

IN DEFENSE OF TELEVISION

Frank Stanton

Frank Stanton is president of Columbia Broadcasting Company. He and General Sarnoff may be regarded as the two chief spokesmen for the television industry. In effect, his is the television industry's response to Mr. Minow's "wasteland" speech and the criticism of program content that Mr. Minow was voicing.

Television . . . is a medium bringing the sights and sounds of every area of life into ninety per cent of America's 52 million homes. Here is a medium obliged, by its nature, to provide something for everybody in a heterogeneous nation of 185 million people. Here is a medium calling for resources of untold millions of dollars, unprecedented in communications, to support it. Here is a medium as fraught with the public interest as printing was in Franklin's day, and to which freedom is as vital. Here is a medium on the verge of directly linking together all the continents of a troubled and divided world. . . .

Today television is very nearly at the beginning of its international era. It has, I think, an enormous potential contribution to make towards world order. But American television faces that era with many unresolved problems. It is, of course, inevitable that a medium that has grown so fast

---

From the Benjamin Franklin Lecture, University of Pennsylvania, December 7, 1961. Reprinted by permission.

should create unique problems just as it has presented unique opportunities.

Some of them are transitory in nature. Some are fundamental. In an impatient society, hard pressed with the ugly potentials of a cold war, these fundamental problems can invite dangerously precipitous solutions, superficially attractive perhaps but full of land mines.

Chief among these fundamental problems is the arrival at standards for programming. Whose standards should they be? How should they be determined? Can you trust the people to know what is good for them? Or must they be told by some authority? I want to discuss this problem against the total context—social, cultural, economic and political—in which television must function, and against the background of a free society that has been particularly alert to abridgments of the freedom of communications—whether of the press, of speech, of assembly, or of any extension of these that technical developments since the Bill of Rights have made possible.

The volume and variety of programming produced by the three television networks are, I think, wholly without precedent in the history of communications. In the month of November, for example, the three networks provided their affiliates with over a thousand hours of programming. This consisted chiefly of 99½ hours of actual news events and straight news broadcasts, 22¾ hours of documentary news, 19 hours of discussion, 45 hours of education and religion, 77 hours of sports, 63¼ hours of general drama, 8 hours of panel shows, 84 hours of situation comedy, 42½ hours of variety, 84¾ hours of serial drama, and 74¾ hours of children's programs. Of the total, 56 hours were mysteries and 60½ hours were Westerns—a combined total of 11 per cent of all the programming.

The range of subjects and material that appeared on the three networks in November was extremely wide. There were biographical studies of such diverse men as U. S. Grant and Vincent Van Gogh, Al Smith and Sinclair Lewis. There were several special half-hour biographies of speaker Sam Rayburn. There were long reports on such countries as Germany, Spain, Yugoslavia, and France. There were interviews with men representing a provocative cross section of the world today: Prime Minister Nehru, Igor Stravinsky, Hugh Gaitskell, John Kenneth Galbraith, Bertrand Russell. Full-length dramatic productions included Hans Conried and Jane Wyatt in *Little Lost Sheep,* Julie Harris in *Victoria Regina,* and Fred Astaire in *Moment of Decision.*

It is true, of course, that much of the television fare of the month was light. But most fiction published every month is light reading. It is relevant to remember, too, that of the hundreds of popular magazines published in this country, only four are news magazines and only four more are of generally serious editorial content. And many Sunday newspapers, with from sixteen to eighteen pages devoted to sports and amusements, have a single page devoted to editorials and a single column to education.

The press in this country, nevertheless, is carrying out its responsibilities far better than that of any other country and better than it ever has before, given the economic and social context in which it must function. Newspapers and magazines must attract and hold their readers. They must attract and hold their advertisers. They have arrived at patterns of content after a good deal of tough trial and error. They are not, of course, an exact parallel to television, for they are not subject to licensing; most publications, however, are objects of partial government subsidy through advantageous postal rates.

Like the magazines and newspapers, television fills a dual role of entertaining and informing, diverting and instructing, relaxing and stimulating. There are those, I am sure, who would have television exclusively informative and instructive. There are those, too, who would have it exclusively entertaining and diverting. But the economic demands of the medium and the capacities and interests of human beings require it to be both. Despite this diversity of taste, somebody has to set standards. Broadcasters have turned to the general public. In the absence of the kind of physical circulation that publications have to measure their public acceptance, there is a nationwide rating service to provide the networks with means of determining public acceptance of programs. This does not mean that no network would broadcast a program that does not attract a high rating. This is obviously not so, since year after year many important broadcasts, particularly of an informational character, do go on the air in spite of consistently low ratings.

In October, for example, the CBS Television Network broadcast the first of a series of three hour-long interviews with General Eisenhower on the problems of the Presidency. The first was universally acclaimed by the critics. It was on the air in prime evening time. Its rating indicated that some six million people saw the broadcast as compared to 21 million who tuned to the suspense drama and 26 million to the popular song program that were on the air at the same time on the other two networks.

Now there are several ways that you can look at that figure, six million. Compared to the audience of a popular entertainment television show, it is small. Compared to the audience of a best selling book, whether informative or escape fiction, it is gigantic. Compared to the largest metropolitan newspapers, it ranges from three to ten times their daily circulation. Now consider what an hour-long discussion is equal to in terms of the written word. It is about nine thousand words—twenty-seven typed pages. So the real gauge of public interest in what General Eisenhower had to say on the problems he faced as President can be judged by the fact that more people, by many times over, were exposed to twenty-seven pages of comment on serious matters than read any newspapers, or any best seller. We broadcast a second conversation with General Eisenhower on Thanksgiving night, and we are scheduled to broadcast another early in 1962.

On December first, the CBS Television Network broadcast a Young People's Concert of the New York Philharmonic in prime evening time. Although we knew that this concert would interest fewer viewers than RAWHIDE, which it displaced that evening, we believed that there was enough following of good serious music in America to justify the experiment of making such a distinguished orchestra available to the family in prime time. As it turned out, 40 times as many people heard the Philharmonic that night as heard it during the entire season at Carnegie Hall last year. But we were certainly not under any illusion that there would be more than sing along with Mitch every week.

This illustrates, I think, the kind of perplexing questions that are evoked by the phrase "meeting the standards set by the people." Should we meet the standards set by *most* of the people *all* of the time? I think that the answer to that is clearly No. We must be constantly aware that ours is a most varied population, with a wide range of degrees of sophistication, of education, of interest, of tastes. We must make an effort to accommodate that endless variety. But we must do it with some sort of scale and balance in mind. For the second perplexing question is: At what point should a mass medium stop moving towards the interests of a relative few? How few is the "relative few"?

I think that it would be a misuse of the air waves, for example, to carry very esoteric, avant-garde material that experienced observers know would be meaningless to all but a handful of the initiated. On the other hand, there is a great and restless potential in the American people to broaden their cultural horizons. Television can, and does, play an enormous role in stimulating that potential. I don't think, however, that these stirrings are visited upon all of the people, or even most of them, at the same time. And so we have to experiment. We know pretty clearly, after a reasonable trial, when a program of popular entertainment registers with the people. We assume that if it does, they are entitled to see it and we ought to continue it. We assume that if a vast majority of the people vote against it, we ought to discontinue it and try something else. . . .

I don't know any satisfactory or democratic alternative to letting the people set the standards of programming by the simple act of accepting or rejecting what is offered. It has been said that the public is getting no choice of kinds of television fare, but with rare exceptions in the schedules this is simply not the case. It has also been said—contradictory as it may sound—that television is ruled by two tyrannies: the tyranny of the majority, and the tyranny of the mercantilists; that, on the one hand, its sole purpose is to drug the great mass of citizens and, on the other hand, it is the tool exclusively of greedy men who will foist anything on the public if it will serve their purpose in selling things that nobody wants. . . .

The tyranny of the majority is, of course, a classical dilemma of the democratic state. It has been asserted from ancient times that it leads to a rule of mediocrity, or even of the lowest common denominator. It seems to me that the American political experience—and I believe also the American social and cultural experiences—have minimized this danger by a widely respected recognition of the right and interests of minorities. . . .

The unique problem in this respect with regard to television is that, both because of the technical limitations on the number of channels and because of the economic demands of the medium, it is impossible to have separate channels to serve every worthwhile minority whatever its size.[1] . . .

Television is concerned with the relative size of cultural minorities, because television has a primary responsibility to serve more than quantitatively minute minorities. It is unlikely that we will do anything to stimulate discussion of the use of classical images in early eighteenth century poetry—although I am quite sure that somewhere there are several passionately dedicated students of the subject. But we would do something about the general subject of art in American life, even though an overwhelming share of the audience is not interested. . . .

We all know that many . . . programs will not attract a large share of the viewers watching television at the time that they are on the air. They . . . are broadcast because the interest of significant minorities are recognized by broadcasters. But the broadcasters are thoroughly justified, under any principles of cultural democracy, in basing such recognition to some extent on reasonable assurance that the program is not so specialized as virtually to black out the station. In fact, responsible programming should have the opposite effect and invite the many to come in with the interested few—and get something out of it.

The blanket charge that the trouble with television is that it permits the tyrannizing of the public by the manufacturers of consumer goods and their advertising agencies—in league with the broadcasters and in contempt of any except mercantile values—seems to me to impede any useful discussion. We live in a mercantile society, and our material life is

---

[1] Editor's note: The addition of ultra-high-frequency (UHF) bands has already greatly increased the number of available channels in many areas of the country. It may be noted also that all major cities in the United States have educational TV stations. Furthermore, in November, 1967, Congress passed and the President signed a bill appropriating $9 million for "public" broadcasting. This is in addition to $38 million authorized over a three-year period in grants for the construction of facilities for educational television and radio. Commercial sponsorship is to be eliminated from the educational and cultural broadcasts contemplated under this program. A nonprofit corporation governed by a 15-member board will be in charge.

based on the sale and purchase of goods and services. This is not unique to our century or to our land. The development of mercantilism has coincided in modern history with the development of democracy—not because it was a philosophic ideal but because it worked best, even if imperfectly, with democratic institutions. The reason, of course, is that, for all its faults, mercantilism is not categorical, not authoritative. It is open-ended and gives room to move around economically; and, without that, political democracy would be meaningless in practical life.

. . . the advertiser has no immunity from the verdict of the public. Every time his program is on the air, it is submitted to the viewer's vote. If it lost or never attained that vote, it would go off the air with absolute inevitability. And so again we get back to the fundamental question: Should it be the public or should it be some authority—whether in the government or a czar in the industry or some independent commission—that makes the verdict?

The public verdict is, I have no doubt, the safest and surest, the most valid and most enduring, one. But it has its price. It is less swift and less efficient, but it shares such limitations with all other procedural aspects of the democratic life. We in America have over and over again faced that particular dilemma, and we have refused to put a premium on speed and efficiency at any cost. . . .

A decade from now, if the public verdict prevails, television will be unrecognizable from what we have today. The medium will change because there is a constant, slow but inevitable upward movement in the standards and interests and capacities of a free people. If this were not so, the American experience would be meaningless, for life consists in growth. If we say that it is not so, if we start making exceptions, we are losing faith in the democratic dynamic. If we liken the mass of people and their ability to make their own decisions to unsupervised children and their desire for a constant diet of sweets, we are striking at the heart of what a democracy is all about—that the people, whatever their temporary errors or inadequacies, are, in the long run, the best judges of their own interests, and that they will make themselves heard.

In a pluralistic society like ours there are a great many additional built-in safeguards against persistent excesses. These are far more effective over the long haul than paternal authority. The variety of pressures that make themselves felt in such a society—civic organizations, academic groups, churches, the newspapers, articulate and forceful individuals—are the indirect influences that set the pace for the evolution of culture in a democracy. The important thing is that essential freedom remains—there is freedom to yield to pressures or to resist them, to respect those that seem enlightened and to ignore those that seem self-serving, to make mistakes, to take risks. All this takes time, and all this involves the chance of error. But there is no finality about it. And *that* is the rub with any pressure stemming from authority. The pressures normal in a democracy say, "You should." The pressure of authority says, "You shall."

We have also on the side of the public verdict the continued rise in the educational level of the people: they are better qualified each year to make the verdict. Isn't this—and not salvation by authority—our real, in fact our only, hope?

The material available on the television networks pretty much parallels, in kind, the material that characterizes such other mass media as the paperback book—the rise of which chronologically has matched that of television and which now sells 294 million copies annually. Reassuring as it is to know that you can get Plato's dialogues or Trevelyan's histories in inexpensive editions at Liggett's, it is still not surprising that Mickey Spillane remains the all-time best seller. Or that, of the 248 new titles in paperback fiction in the present fall season, 92, or 37 per cent, are Westerns, adventures and mysteries. Or even that the majority of the other titles are obviously light romances and other escape fiction.

But I would think that a literary critic would be something less than perceptive if he picked up the first fifty titles and used them as a base for a report on the achievement of the American novel. I would question also the judgment of an historian who concluded that a sound basis for appraising the role of the magazine in American life was to read indiscriminately every magazine that he found on the first shelf of his neighborhood newsstand. Such a method would be considered an aberration in critical methodology and its results could not be taken seriously.

But isn't this exactly what has happened in the case of television? The process by which it was concluded that television programming was "a vast wasteland" was described in these words: ". . . sit down in front of your television set when your station goes on the air . . . and keep your eyes glued to that set until the station signs off." A writer in a series for a magazine with a long history of Westerns and mysteries, began with the same specious approach: ". . . arose at five-thirty . . . turned the family television set to Channel 5, sat down in front of it and stayed there until Channel 5 went off the air twenty hours later."

The danger of this kind of sensationalized and oversimplified approach, with its broad brush conclusions, is not only that it grotesquely distorts the situation as it is, a clear perception of which is necessary to improvement, but also that it invites impulsive measures directed at making fundamental changes on the ground that any change is a change for the better. Actually, the only change that I have seen suggested is that the government supervise programming by use of its licensing power and by regulating a major program source, the networks.

How much improvement can either of these really bring about? If government authority sets standards, qualitative or quantitative, for television programming, whose standards are they going to be? The chairman of a commission? A majority of a commission? A Congressional committee?

You would have authoritative standards that would stifle creativity. You would have a rigidity that would discourage experimentation. You would have the subjective judgment of a small group imposed on the many. And you would have the constant danger of the misuse of the medium for political purposes.

Television does need improving. So do private colleges and charitable organizations. So do motion pictures and magazines. So do typewriters and cameras. All these have improved immeasurably over the years, and they will improve further. But they did not improve because some central authority said they must. They improved because they had elbow room to move forward in response to the demands put upon them and the new opportunities that new conditions brought them. Are we so bereft of that trust in the people . . . that we must now turn over the substance of the most promising medium we have to the control of the government because the people do not know what is good for them? I think not.

10

The Ethics of Persuasion

The question of business and morality and corporate citizenship is hardly separable from the more specific issue of how private enterprise conducts one of its two most important activities. As every commercial on television reminds us, it is engaged in *selling* as well as producing—and this involves making representations to the buying public. Are these representations, whether through advertisements, labels, or simple statements concerning the rate of interest charged for a loan, honest or dishonest? This question should focus not on marginal practices that are illegal, or universally characterized as shady even by those who engage in them, but on the more or less general conduct of selling as it prevails in our economy.

THE ARTS OF SELLING

Aldous Huxley

*Aldous Huxley was one of the noted writers of our time.
Novelist, essayist, poet, dramatist, he was also justly called a
humanist because he was interested in people and what happens to them. This interest extended from (quite literally) improving their sight* (The Art of Seeing) *to improving their
vision* (The Perennial Philosophy). *Of his many works the
best known are no doubt* Point Counter Point *and* Brave New
World. *In* Brave New World, *written in 1931, he prophesied
for the sixth or seventh century* "A.F. *(After Ford)" the coming of a completely organized society with, in his summary
words, a "scientific caste system, the abolition of free will by
methodical conditioning, servitude made acceptable by regular
doses of chemically induced happiness, . . . orthodoxies
drummed in by nightly courses of sleep-teaching. . . ." The
depression-ridden world of the 1930's was, he said, "a nightmare of too little order," the world of the seventh century,
A.F., of too much. He had hoped that during the long interval
in between the more fortunate third of the human race would
make the best of both worlds. Later he was no longer so sure,
and in* Brave New World Revisited, *from which the selection
below is taken, he tells us why. Among the uncontrolled impersonal forces that he finds accelerating the speed with which
his depressing prophecies are being brought to pass is modern
advertising.*

The survival of democracy depends on the ability of large numbers
of people to make realistic choices in the light of adequate information. A
dictatorship, on the other hand, maintains itself by censoring or distorting
the facts, and by appealing, not to reason, not to enlightened self-interest,
but to passion and prejudice, to the powerful "hidden forces," as Hitler
called them, present in the unconscious depths of every human mind.

In the West, democratic principles are proclaimed and many able
and conscientious publicists do their best to supply electors with adequate
information and to persuade them, by rational argument, to make realistic
choices in the light of that information. All this is greatly to the good. But
unfortunately propaganda in the Western democracies, above all in Amer-

ica, has two faces and a divided personality. In charge of the editorial department there is often a democratic Dr. Jekyll—a propagandist who would be very happy to prove that John Dewey had been right about the ability of human nature to respond to truth and reason. But this worthy man controls only a part of the machinery of mass communication. In charge of advertising we find an anti-democratic, because anti-rational, Mr. Hyde—or rather a Dr. Hyde, for Hyde is now a Ph.D. in psychology and has a master's degree as well in the social sciences. This Dr. Hyde would be very unhappy indeed if everybody always lived up to John Dewey's faith in human nature. Truth and reason are Jekyll's affair, not his. Hyde is a motivation analyst, and his business is to study human weaknesses and failings, to investigate those unconscious desires and fears by which so much of men's conscious thinking and overt doing is determined. And he does this, not in the spirit of the moralist who would like to make people better, or of the physician who would like to improve their health, but simply in order to find out the best way to take advantage of their ignorance and to exploit their irrationality for the pecuniary benefit of his employers. But after all, it may be argued, "capitalism is dead, consumerism is king"—and consumerism requires the services of expert salesmen versed in all the arts (including the more insidious arts) of persuasion. Under a free enterprise system commercial propaganda by any and every means is absolutely indispensable. But the indispensable is not necessarily the desirable. What is demonstrably good in the sphere of economics may be far from good for men and women as voters or even as human beings. An earlier, more moralistic generation would have been profoundly shocked by the bland cynicism of the motivation analysts. Today we read a book like Mr. Vance Packard's *The Hidden Persuaders,* and are more amazed than horrified, more resigned than indignant. Given Freud, given Behaviorism, given the mass producer's chronically desperate need for mass consumption, this is the sort of thing that is only to be expected. But what, we may ask, is the sort of thing that is to be expected in the future? Are Hyde's activities compatible in the long run with Jekyll's? Can a campaign in favor of rationality be successful in the teeth of another and even more vigorous campaign in favor of irrationality? These are questions which, for the moment, I shall not attempt to answer, but shall leave hanging, so to speak, as a backdrop to our discussion of the methods of mass persuasion in a technologically advanced democratic society.

The task of the commercial propagandist in a democracy is in some ways easier and in some ways more difficult than that of a political propagandist employed by an established dictator or a dictator in the making. It is easier inasmuch as almost everyone starts out with a prejudice in favor of beer, cigarettes and iceboxes, whereas almost nobody starts out with a prejudice in favor of tyrants. It is more difficult inasmuch as the commercial propagandist is not permitted, by the rules of his particular game, to appeal to the more savage instincts of his public. The advertiser of dairy products would dearly love to tell his readers and listeners that all their troubles are caused by the machinations of a gang of godless international margarine manufacturers, and that it is their patriotic duty to march out and burn the oppressors' factories. This sort of thing, however, is ruled out, and he must be content with a milder approach. But the mild approach is less exciting than the approach through verbal or physical violence. In the long run, anger and hatred are self-defeating emotions. But in the short run they pay high dividends in the form of psychological and even (since they release large quantities of adrenalin and noradrenalin) physiological satisfaction. People may start out with an initial prejudice against tyrants; but when tyrants or would-be tyrants treat them to adrenalin-releasing propaganda about the wickedness of their enemies— particularly of enemies weak enough to be persecuted—they are ready to follow him with enthusiasm. In his speeches Hitler kept repeating such words as "hatred," "force," "ruthless," "crush," "smash"; and he would accompany these violent words with even more violent gestures. He would yell, he would scream, his veins would swell, his face would turn purple. Strong emotion (as every actor and dramatist knows) is in the highest degree contagious. Infected by the malignant frenzy of the orator, the audience would groan and sob and scream in an orgy of uninhibited passion. And these orgies were so enjoyable that most of those who had experienced them eagerly came back for more. Almost all of us long for peace and freedom; but very few of us have much enthusiasm for the thoughts, feelings and actions that make for peace and freedom. Conversely almost nobody wants war or tyranny; but a great many people find an intense pleasure in the thoughts, feelings and actions that make for war and tyranny. These thoughts, feelings and actions are too dangerous to be exploited for commercial purposes. Accepting this handicap, the advertising man must do the best he can with the less intoxicating emotions, the quieter forms of irrationality.

Effective rational propaganda becomes possible only when there is a clear understanding, on the part of all concerned, of the nature of symbols and of their relations to the things and events symbolized. Irrational propaganda depends for its effectiveness on a general failure to understand the nature of symbols. Simple-minded people tend to equate the symbol with what it stands for, to attribute to things and events some of the qualities expressed by the words in terms of which the propagandist has chosen, for his own purposes, to talk about them. Consider a simple example. Most cosmetics are made of lanolin, which is a mixture of purified wool fat and water beaten up into an emulsion. This emulsion has many valuable properties: it penetrates the skin, it does not become rancid, it is mildly antiseptic and so forth. But the commercial propagandists do not speak about the genuine virtues of the emulsion. They give it some picturesquely voluptuous name, talk ecstatically and misleadingly about feminine beauty and show pictures of gorgeous blondes nourishing their tissues with skin food. "The cosmetic manufacturers," one of their number has written, "are not selling lanolin, they are selling hope." For this hope, this fraudulent implication of a promise that they will be transfigured, women will pay ten or twenty times the value of the emulsion which the propagandists have so skilfully related, by means of misleading symbols, to a deep-seated and almost universal feminine wish—the wish to be more attractive to members of the opposite sex. The principles underlying this kind of propaganda are extremely simple. Find some common desire, some widespread unconscious fear or anxiety; think out some way to relate this wish or fear to the product you have to sell; then build a bridge of verbal or pictorial symbols over which your customer can pass from fact to compensatory dream, and from the dream to the illusion that your product, when purchased, will make the dream come true. "We no longer buy oranges, we buy vitality. We do not buy just an auto, we buy prestige." And so with all the rest. In toothpaste, for example, we buy, not a mere cleanser and antiseptic, but release from the fear of being sexually repulsive. In vodka and whisky we are not buying a protoplasmic poison which, in small doses, may depress the nervous system in a psychologically valuable way; we are buying friendliness and good fellowship, the warmth of Dingley Dell and the brilliance of the Mermaid Tavern. With our laxatives we buy the health of a Greek god, the radiance of one of Diana's nymphs. With the monthly best seller we acquire culture, the envy of our less literate neighbors and the respect of the sophisticated. In every case the motivation analyst has found some deep-seated wish or fear, whose energy can be used to move the consumer to part with cash and so, indirectly, to turn the wheels of industry. Stored in the minds and bodies of countless individuals, this potential energy is released by, and transmitted along, a line of symbols carefully laid out so as to bypass rationality and obscure the real issue.

Sometimes the symbols take effect by being disproportionately impressive, haunting and fascinating in their own right. Of this kind are the rites and pomps of religion. These "beauties of holiness" strengthen faith where it already exists and, where there is no faith, contribute to conversion. Appealing, as they do, only to the aesthetic sense, they guarantee neither the truth nor the ethical value of the doctrines with which they have been, quite arbitrarily, associated. As a matter of plain historical fact, the beauties of holiness have often been matched and indeed surpassed by the beauties of unholiness. Under Hitler, for example, the yearly Nuremberg rallies were masterpieces of ritual and theatrical art. "I had spent six years in St. Petersburg before the war in the best days of the old Russian ballet," writes Sir Nevile Henderson, the British ambassador to Hitler's Germany, "but for grandiose beauty I have never seen any ballet to compare with the

Nuremberg rally." One thinks of Keats—"Beauty is truth, truth beauty." Alas, the identity exists only on some ultimate, supramundane level. On the levels of politics and theology, beauty is perfectly compatible with nonsense and tyranny. Which is very fortunate; for if beauty were incompatible with nonsense and tyranny, there would be precious little art in the world. The masterpieces of painting, sculpture and architecture were produced as religious or political propaganda, for the greater glory of a god, a government or a priesthood. But most kings and priests have been despotic and all religions have been riddled with superstition. Genius has been the servant of tyranny and art has advertised the merits of the local cult. Time, as it passes, separates the good art from the bad metaphysics. Can we learn to make this separation, not after the event, but while it is actually taking place? That is the question.

In commercial propaganda the principle of the disproportionately fascinating symbol is clearly understood. Every propagandist has his Art Department, and attempts are constantly being made to beautify the billboards with striking posters, the advertising pages of magazines with lively drawings and photographs. There are no masterpieces; for masterpieces appeal only to a limited audience, and the commercial propagandist is out to captivate the majority. For him, the ideal is a moderate excellence. Those who like this not too good, but sufficiently striking, art may be expected to like the products with which it has been associated and for which it symbolically stands.

Another disproportionately fascinating symbol is the Singing Commercial. Singing Commercials are a recent invention; but the Singing Theological and the Singing Devotional—the hymn and the psalm—are as old as religion itself. Singing Militaries, or marching songs, are coeval with war, and Singing Patriotics, the precursors of our national anthems, were doubtless used to promote group solidarity, to emphasize the distinction between "us" and "them," by the wandering bands of paleolithic hunters and food gatherers. To most people music is intrinsically attractive. Moreover, melodies tend to ingrain themselves in the listener's mind. A tune will haunt the memory during the whole of a lifetime. Here, for example, is a quite uninteresting statement or value judgment. As it stands nobody will pay attention to it. But now set the words to a catchy and easily remembered tune. Immediately they become words of power. Moreover, the words will tend automatically to repeat themselves every time the melody is heard or spontaneously remembered. Orpheus has entered into an alliance with Pavlov—the power of sound with the conditioned reflex. For the commercial propagandist, as for his colleagues in the fields of politics and religion, music possesses yet another advantage. Nonsense which it would be shameful for a reasonable being to write, speak or hear spoken can be sung or listened to by that same rational being with pleasure and even with a kind of intellectual conviction. Can we learn to separate the pleasure of singing or of listening to song from the all too human tendency to believe in the propaganda which the song is putting over? That again is the question.

Thanks to compulsory education and the rotary press, the propagandist has been able, for many years past, to convey his messages to virtually every adult in every civilized country. Today, thanks to radio and television, he is in the happy position of being able to communicate even with unschooled adults and not yet literate children.

Children, as might be expected, are highly susceptible to propaganda. They are ignorant of the world and its ways, and therefore completely unsuspecting. Their critical faculties are undeveloped. The youngest of them have not yet reached the age of reason and the older ones lack the experience on which their new-found rationality can effectively work. In Europe, conscripts used to be playfully referred to as "cannon fodder." Their little brothers and sisters have now become radio fodder and television fodder. In my childhood we were taught to sing nursery rhymes and, in pious households, hymns. Today the little ones warble the Singing Commercials. Which is better—"Rheingold is my beer, the dry beer," or "Hey diddle-diddle, the cat and the fiddle"? "Abide with me" or "You'll wonder where the yellow went, when you brush your teeth with Pepsodent"? Who knows?

"I don't say that children should be forced to harass their parents into buying products they've seen advertised on television, but at the same time I cannot close my eyes to the fact that it's being done every day." So writes the star of one of the many programs beamed to a juvenile audience. "Children," he adds, "are living, talking records of what we tell them every day." And in due course these living, talking records of television commercials will grow up, earn money and buy the products of industry. "Think," writes Mr. Clyde Miller ecstatically, "think of what it can mean to your firm in profits if you can condition a million or ten million children, who will grow up into adults trained to buy your product, as soldiers are trained in advance when they hear the trigger words, Forward March!" Yes, just think of it! And at the same time remember that the dictators and the would-be dictators have been thinking about this sort of thing for years, and that millions, tens of millions, hundreds of millions of children are in process of growing up to buy the local despot's ideological product and, like well-trained soldiers, to respond with appropriate behavior to the trigger words implanted in those young minds by the despot's propagandists.

Self-government is in inverse ratio to numbers. The larger the constituency, the less the value of any particular vote. When he is merely one of millions, the individual elector feels himself to be impotent, a negligible quantity. The candidates he has voted into office are far away, at the top of the pyramid of power. Theoretically they are the servants of the people; but in fact it is the servants who give orders and the people, far off at the base of the great pyramid, who must obey. Increasing population and advancing technology have resulted in an increase in the number and complexity of organizations, an increase in the amount of power concentrated in the hands of officials and a corresponding decrease in the amount of control exercised by electors, coupled with a decrease in the public's regard for democratic procedures. Already weakened by the vast impersonal forces at work in the modern world, democratic institutions are now being undermined from within by the politicians and their propagandists.

Human beings act in a great variety of irrational ways, but all of them seem to be capable, if given a fair chance, of making a reasonable choice in the light of available evidence. Democratic institutions can be made to work only if all concerned do their best to impart knowledge and to encourage rationality. But today, in the world's most powerful democracy, the politicians and their propagandists prefer to make nonsense of democratic procedures by appealing almost exclusively to the ignorance and irrationality of the electors. "Both parties," we were told in 1956 by the editor of a leading business journal, "will merchandise their candidates and issues by the same methods that business has developed to sell goods. These include scientific selection of appeals and planned repetition. . . . Radio spot announcements and ads will repeat phrases with a planned intensity. Billboards will push slogans of proven power. . . . Candidates need, in addition to rich voices and good diction, to be able to look 'sincerely' at the TV camera."

The political merchandisers appeal only to the weaknesses of voters, never to their potential strength. They make no attempt to educate the masses into becoming fit for self-government; they are content merely to manipulate and exploit them. For this purpose all the resources of psychology and the social sciences are mobilized and set to work. Carefully selected samples of the electorate are given "interviews in depth." These interviews in depth reveal the unconscious fears and wishes most prevalent in a given society at the time of an election. Phrases and images aimed at allaying or, if necessary, enhancing these fears, at satisfying these wishes, at least symbolically, are then chosen by the experts, tried out on readers and audiences, changed or improved in the light of the information thus obtained. After which the political campaign is ready for the mass communicators. All that is now needed is money and a candidate who can be coached to look "sincere." Under the new dispensation, political principles and plans for specific action have come to lose most of their importance. The personality of the candidate and the way he is projected by the advertising experts are the things that really matter.

In one way or another, as vigorous he-man or kindly father, the candidate must be glamorous. He must also be an entertainer who never bores his audience. Inured to television and radio, that audience is accustomed to being distracted and does not like to be asked to concentrate or make a prolonged intellectual effort. All speeches by the entertainer-candidate must therefore be short and snappy. The great issues of the day must be dealt with in five minutes at the most—and preferably (since the audience will be eager to pass on to something a little livelier than inflation or the H-bomb) in sixty seconds flat. The nature of oratory is such that there has always been a tendency among politicians and clergymen to over-simplify complex issues. From a pulpit or a platform even the most con-scientious of speakers finds it very difficult to tell the whole truth. The methods now being used to merchandise the political candidate as though he were a deodorant positively guarantee the electorate against ever hearing the truth about anything.

WANTED: RESPONSIBLE ADVERTISING CRITICS

James Webb Young

James Webb Young is regarded as one of the elder statesmen of the advertising industry. He helped build the world's largest advertising agency and now serves as an advertising consultant. He has taught business history and advertising at the University of Chicago.

I learned my trade as a writer of advertisements in a religious publishing house, selling books by mail to Methodist ministers. My first big success was with a book called "Personal Evangelism," which had the worthy purpose of telling these ministers how to increase the membership of their church and, as the saying had it, to "bring more souls to Christ."

In such an activity I had no suspicion that I was entering upon what—much later—President Angell of Yale told me was a *"déclassé* profession." And I dare say the present writer of an effective series of advertisements, now being published by the Knights of Columbus for the Catholic faith, would have been as astonished as I was when I heard this.

From *Saturday Review* (April 23, 1960), pp. 35 ff. Reprinted by permission.

My first warning on the status of the advertising man came on another campus. Early in the 1920s, in the midst of a busy advertising life, I had undertaken to get a solid physiological base for the study of psychology. And the famous Anton J. Carlson at the University of Chicago had agreed personally to give it to me in his laboratory.

One day Dr. Carlson introduced me to the late C. Judson Herrick, notable for his researches on the brain and nervous system, whose latest book I had been given to study. I said: "Dr. Herrick, it may surprise you to know that an advertising man is finding your new book on the brain of the greatest interest." Said Dr. Herrick, looking at me sourly over his glasses: "I am not only surprised; I am chagrined. As far as I can see there is no connection between brains and advertising."

Since then, through the years, in my notes on many kinds of human behavior, I have recorded other equally sweeping generalizations about advertising, made by faculty members of Harvard, Columbia, Princeton, Cornell, Wisconsin, Johns Hopkins, and McGill.

But sweeping generalizations about advertising are not confined to the academic groves, nor to recent times. A notable piece on the subject came from the pen of Dr. Samuel Johnson, in the mid-eighteenth century. And currently, triggered by the revelation of rigged TV quiz shows, any number of people have gotten into the act.

Thus, for example, in a recent column Walter Lippmann seems to transfer the responsibility for this rigging wholly to the shoulders of "advertisers"—not to particular advertisers, and not in any degree to those of the educator-idol whose feet of clay furnished all the drama.

Note, too, the adverbs used by Father P. P. Harbrecht, S.J., in a recent booklet issued by the Twentieth Century Fund on his excellent study, "Toward the Paraproprietal Society." Speaking of such big corporations as General Motors, du Pont, U.S. Steel, Alcoa, and General Electric, he says (italics mine): "Their research and innovations transform our lives, *quietly* with home appliances or *dramatically* with atomics and space flight; *brashly* with TV advertising or *culturally* with subsidies to education." Is all the TV advertising of all these firms done "brashly"?

Now, let me say clearly that advertising needs, is entitled to, and can profit from criticism of the most public kind. It needs it more than ever today because advertising has become one of the most potent forces in our culture—ranking as an "institution" with the church and education, according to Professor Potter of Yale, in his book "People of Plenty."

But it needs that criticism in the form that the dictionary defines as "the act of passing judgment on the merits of anything"; that is, discriminating criticism, which applauds the good and damns the bad.

No one is more concerned about the misuses of advertising than the responsible people in advertising. And, in fact, they have been trying for a very long time to do something about these misuses. If any of the shoot-from-the-hip critics of this activity would take the same trouble to understand my specialty as I was taking to understand that of Dr. Herrick, these are some of the things they would find:

First, that the technical literature of advertising is currently filled with the kind of "good-and-bad" criticism advertising needs.

Second, that advertising people have promoted and secured the adoption of "Truth in Advertising" laws in over half our states, and have supported the work of Better Business Bureaus in policing these laws.

Third, that they have supported the purposes, if not always the methods, of the Federal Trade Commission, to prevent the use of advertising in ways unfair to competition.

Fourth, that in their various trade and professional organizations advertising men have drafted any number of codes of "ethical" practices—and have been busy reactivating these lately!

Fifth, that many important advertising media refuse to accept advertising for certain classifications of products; and that the largest advertising agency in the world has never undertaken advertising for "hard" liquors—all at a considerable cost to their revenues.

All these things have, in fact, brought improvements in the use of advertising, as a recent writer noted. "In front of us," he says, "is a 1913 advertisement pointing out the advantages of Postum over Brazilian coffee. Among the ills attributed to coffee: 'Sallow Complexions; Stomach Trouble; Bad Liver; Heart Palpitations; Shattered Nerves; Caffeine, a Drug; Weakness from Drugging.' We doubt if the present owners of Postum would O.K. copy like this today. Even if they didn't own Maxwell House."

But all this is not enough, and nobody knows it better than those hard-working creators of much of our advertising, inaccurately stereotyped as "Madison Avenue."

The reason why it is not enough is that, as developed in America, the set of facilities and techniques called advertising has become the most powerful single means that the world has ever seen for informing, persuading, and inspiring a people to action. As such, it becomes vital that its potentialities for good or ill become fully recognized; that the responsibilities for its use be squarely shouldered; and that the magnificent opportunities for its use in the public service, as now amply demonstrated in the work of the Advertising Council, be fully exploited.

It is therefore my thesis that what advertising now needs is to be given, in public print, the same kind of continuing, knowing, responsible criticism as that given to the theatre, music, the arts, books, and other major aspects of our culture. It needs a "career critic," keeping a steady spotlight on both the good and the bad in the uses of advertising, and on its unexploited social potentialities.

What would be the qualifications for such a public critic of advertising—assuming the judicial temperament of the responsible man?

First, he should know that "advertising" is a set of facilities and techniques as impersonal as electricity or atomic energy, and thus equally usable for noble ends or shabby ones. Hence he will avoid the "pathetic fallacy" of animating the inanimate, into which so many critics of advertising fall. It is *advertisers* who need criticism—not advertising.

Second, he will understand clearly the economic necessities which brought advertising into existence, and still control its use. These were well stated in 1870 by Walter Bagehot in his classic work "Lombard Street." Said Bagehot:

> Our current political economy does not sufficiently take account of *time* as an element in trade operations. But as soon as the division of labour has once established itself in a community, two principles at once begin to be important, of which time is the very essence. These are—
> *First,* that as goods are produced to be exchanged, it is good that they should be exchanged as quickly as possible.
> *Secondly,* that as every producer is mainly occupied in producing what others want, and not what he wants himself, it is desirable that he should always be able to find, without effort, without delay, and without uncertainty, others who want what he can produce.

These words are even truer today than when Bagehot wrote them. To understand the workhorse job of advertising in a high production-consumption economy such as ours is primary for any intelligent criticism of its uses.

Third, he must understand that the methods by which advertising gets the workhorse job done in today's economy have been greatly developed since Bagehot's day; and why in these methods are to be found some of the roots of the criticisms of advertising.

. . . early in the expansion of the use of advertising it was discovered that the mere repetition of a name or trademark could produce a preference for one product over another. Remember "Gold Medal flour—Eventually, Why Not Now?" This sort of advertising worked because mere familiarity is a *value* to the human being. It satisfies one of his deepest needs: for a sense of "at-homeness" in this world. You can check this, perhaps, by recalling when, in a crowd of strangers, you have found yourself gravitating toward one familiar face—possibly even that of a person not well liked. Familiarity is a value, and no advertising works which does not, in some form, deliver a value to somebody.

Then it was discovered that there is a function for advertising merely as a "re-minder" of something we are already "minded" to do. For example, to "Say it with flowers!" when you have a wedding anniversary coming up. A service, surely, in the cause of domestic tranquillity!

After this, as railroads made a national market possible, came a development in the *news* use of advertising. Just as the Associated Press came into being to gather and transmit general news, so the advertising agency came into being to gather and transmit commercial news, thus making possible the announcement, say, of a new model automobile on the same day everywhere.

But there is also another kind of "news," in the advertising sense. It is the kind of news you pay no attention to until you need to know it. In our long march from the cradle to the grave we pass into, and out of, many areas of experience. And as we do, our receptivity to all sorts of news changes. Thus the young woman who ignores the infant-feeding advertisement of today may become its most eager reader next year.

Then, along the way, came the discovery that advertising could be used to overcome human inertia. Hell is indeed paved with many good intentions, toward such things as making a will, taking out adequate life insurance, seeing the dentist regularly, and so on. In all such things the reward for action taken, or the punishment for action postponed, is remote and delayed. Advertising, by making more vivid such rewards or punishments, can often overcome the inertia—to the profit of the reader or listener as well as the advertiser.

Religions have always had to deal with this problem in the training of ministers, and here it seems always to have been a moot question whether portrayal of the rewards of heaven or of the punishments of hell converted more sinners.

Then, finally, came the discovery that advertising could *add a value not in the product.* And because these values were subjective ones (such as status symbols; or, say, the luxury of bathing with the same soap the movie stars use; or what Edith Wharton once called "the utility of the useless"), here advertising really got into trouble. For in this area of subjective values, one man's meat is definitely another man's poison.

In this area, too, our critic will come face to face with one of his most difficult problems. Advertising, like editing, politics, and even to some extent education, always operates within the context of the culture of its day. One irony of its present situation is that some of the people who are most vocal in their negative attitudes toward advertising may themselves have contributed to some aspects of it which they most deplore. By supporting liberal policies for the wider distribution of wealth in this country, they have helped bring into existence a mammoth class of *nouveau riche,* whose incomes have improved faster than their tastes and subjective values.

In addition to such an understanding of the ways in which advertising works, our critic must grasp some of the trends in our economy which have major impacts on the creation of advertising.

The most important of these lie in our technology. Innovation has become an industry, as Dr. Sumner Slichter pointed out. Theoretically, our accelerated rate of innovation should produce more and more advertising news about distinction in products. But counter forces produce in some considerable degree an opposite effect.

One of these counter forces is governmental pressure for the preservation of competition. This tends to force a cross-licensing of patents which rapidly spreads any given innovation throughout an industry. Thus, for instance, when one manufacturer of television sets produces a more compact tube, soon many of his major competitors have the benefit of it.

Then, too, innovation often comes, not from the end-producer of the product or service, but from the supplier of an ingredient or part, whose interest is to gain its adoption by as many end-producers as possible. See, for example, the current jet plane advertising of our airlines.

Added to these we have, in this country, a widespread "free trade" in technological ideas, through such channels as the Society of Automotive Engineers and numerous trade and technical journals. The result is that innovating ideas get "in the air," and soon all our automobiles, for example, become more and more alike.

All these forces result in the reverse of a distinction between competitive products and services. But the advertising man is expected to present each of them as one with important differences, leading to the manufacture of mountains out of molehills in the advertising. Our critic must be knowledgeable about this problem, and about the constructive ways to deal with it.

Finally, and most importantly, our critic should be conscious of the still underdeveloped use of advertising as a social force outside the exchange of goods and services.

He must know of the remarkable results that the Advertising Council has produced over the last fifteen years for some fifty "good causes"—through the voluntary services of advertising men, and with contributions of some $180 million annually, in time and space, from advertisers and media.

And he should know, too, of the following-up of this lead in such fine corporation advertising campaigns as:

a. The striking campaign of the Standard Oil Company (N.J.) in the interest of international friendship.

b. The Weyerhaeuser Company's campaign for the preservation of our forests and for conservation through tree-farming.

c. The campaign for better schools, safer highways, forest fire prevention, and other useful purposes of the Caterpillar Tractor Co.

d. The campaign of the New York Life Insurance Company to help parents guide their children in career choices, or the notable campaign of the Metropolitan Life Insurance Company on behalf of better health.

e. The campaign for citizen responsibility of Nationwide Insurance.

An alert critic might see, too, in such uses of advertising, potentialities for our great foundations; for the use of some of their funds in the *distribution* of knowledge, through this most modern high-speed means of communication.

In all this let our critic be not only objective but specific. Let him deal, not with "advertising," but with its uses, good and bad. Let him examine:

> Whether there is too much crowding of advertising in time and space—such as commercials per TV program, and billboards per scenic mile?
>
> Whether there is too much stridency and bad manners in some advertising, now that it can project personal salesmanship into the living room?
>
> Whether the paucity of real buying information, and the superfluity of adjectives in some advertising is, not a crime, but worse —a mistake?

Would such a critic have any real effect on the advertising scene? All I know is that the genius of advertising is reiteration, and that its prophet, Isaiah, said: "Whom shall he teach knowledge? and whom shall he make to understand doctrines? . . . For precept must be upon precept; precept upon precept; line upon line; line upon line; here a little, and there a little."

What I am looking for is a publisher or editor with the insight and courage to enter this new field of criticism—and for the competent critic to aid him. Such a publisher or editor will have to take some risks with his advertisers, yes. But he will, I believe, make a major contribution to the better and wiser use of advertising in our day; he will find himself attracting a surprising volume of mail from his readers; and, in the longer haul, profiting from the sharp attention given his publication by advertisers and advertising men.

Are there any takers in the house?

Part Three

Sex and Society

A large number of our moral problems revolve about sex. Here more than anywhere else is the area in which institutional restraints are pitted against persistent drives, where there are radical discrepancies between what we preach and what we practice,[1] and where, therefore, values are in a state of tension and flux.

In many instances, to be sure, we know where we stand: there is no difference among us and no question concerning the immorality of obscenity, promiscuity, prostitution. Differences arise, however, concerning whether a particular book or moving picture is obscene. Prudery can be as objectionable as prurience, and in our time prudery—which is not to be confused with modesty—is regarded with as much misgiving as promiscuity. Other differences arise concerning the kind of precaution to take: shall pornography and prostitution be outlawed; or shall we avoid legal curbs and rely on the power of education and public opinion? The evil of both pornography and prostitution is acknowledged; the problem here is the recurrent one of not courting a greater evil as we endeavor to combat a lesser one.

In other instances, however, the moral problems are more acute and they grow even more so. These concern such issues as premarital and extramarital sexual experience, divorce, and birth control. Here standards have undergone drastic change as reflected in new attitudes towards the use of contraceptives, greater ease in obtaining divorce and an enormous increase in the divorce rate, and surveys in-

---

[1] It is reliably estimated, for example, that in the United States, where abortion is illegal unless the life of the mother is at stake, 5,000 women die each year at the hands of illegal, unqualified abortionists, and from 1 to 3 million abortions are performed each year. Since it is illegal to abort a woman who contracts an illness (e.g., German measles) that may result in the birth of a blind or mentally retarded child, or even to abort a victim of rape, flouting of the law is almost certain. Recently California and Colorado liberalized their abortion laws.

dicating a significantly large proportion of women reporting extramarital sexual experience. Everywhere one encounters perplexity and a need for moral guidance. But authorities are themselves in doubt and disagreement, and the counsel we get is conflicting.

Conflicts, deep or otherwise, are best dramatized by particular events. It was not many years ago that Bertrand Russell, by common consent the world's greatest living philosopher and one of the greatest men of our age, was dismissed by the City College of New York, where he was visiting lecturer, because, in a book written many years before, he had advocated experimental marriage. That one of the most cosmopolitan and reputedly tolerant cities in the world suffered an agony of shame over this episode suggests the dimensions of the conflict, as does the invitation to teach at Harvard that its faculty promptly extended Lord Russell.

Topics dealing with sexual conduct fall logically into two parts. One part embraces deviant or aberrational sexuality, specifically perversion, obscenity, prudery, and prostitution. Here concern is with the psychopathic or sociopathic and with how to deal with it. The second part embraces "normal" sexuality, that is, questions concerning guidance of the sexual development of adolescents, the role of love, extramarital relationships, marriage and divorce, birth control. Here sex deviancy is irrelevant and psycho- or sociopathic behavior are only indirectly if at all involved.

Considerations of space limit the number of selected topics to three: pornography and how to control it, homosexuality, and extramarital sexual experience.

11

Pornography and Its Control

What is pornography? We have traveled a long distance since Walter Hines Page, then with Doubleday, Page and Co., refused to publish a book which contained the word "chaste" because it was too "suggestive." The Massachusetts Supreme Court would not now sustain the conviction of a publisher for selling Theodore Dreiser's *An American Tragedy* as it did in 1930. Even so, it was only yesterday that *Lady Chatterley's Lover* became available to American readers (pirated editions were sold, of course, from the beginning); and it was only a day before yesterday that producers of the motion picture version of *A Streetcar Named Desire* were persuaded to delete the last three words from a line in the Tennessee Williams play that reads, "I would like to kiss you softly and sweetly on the mouth."

In a book he wrote in 1927 about Anthony Comstock, Heywood Broun reminded his readers that sex is not an invention of the novelists, not even the modern ones. "Both the fundamentalists and the evolutionists agree," Broun wrote, "that the scheme has at least the merit of antiquity. Anthony Comstock may have been entirely correct in his assumption that the division of living creatures into male and female was a vulgar mistake, but a conspiracy of silence about the matter will hardly alter the facts."[1]

---

[1] *Anthony Comstock* (New York: A. & C. Boni, Inc., 1927), p. 274. Written with Margaret Leech. This, with *The Censor Marches On* by Morris L. Ernst and Alexander Lindey, is a good account of early difficulties with the censors. Comstock, a professional anti-vice crusader who devoted himself chiefly to the suppression of what he regarded as salacious literature, was primarily responsible for the notorious Comstock Laws of 1873.

Today, nearly all responsible people will applaud Broun's verdict, and, with motion pictures dealing in such taboo themes as Lesbianism, incest, and even child molestation, and mass-circulation periodicals using words heretofore banned in all except the most vulgar company, the day of permissiveness has dawned. Even so, the nature of obscenity and its control remains controversial.

If the canon ecclesiastical lawyers did not spell out the meaning of the word "obscene," says Father Gardiner, this was because they did not conceive that the word was complicated or obscure. They took it for granted, as it were, that the word was rather self-evident." But Father Gardiner concedes that "in a pluralistic society such as ours" the problem *has* arisen, and he therefore defines obscenity in a book or painting as "the intrinsic tendency or bent of the work to arouse sexual passion, or, to put it more concretely, the motions of the genital apparatus which are preparatory to the complete action of sexual union." Father Gardiner adds that "a particular work . . . may not always and in all circumstances so arouse this or that individual. It is not so much a matter of the individual's own reaction here and now as the nature of the work under consideration . . . it must, of its nature, be such as actually to arouse in the viewer or reader such venereal pleasure."[2]

Psychologists Eberhard Kronhausen and Phyllis Kronhausen disagree. They distinguish between erotic realism and pornography: "In pornography . . . the main purpose is to stimulate erotic response in the reader. And that is all. In erotic realism, truthful description of the basic realities of life is of the essence. . . ." And, ". . . if while writing realistically on the subject of sex the author succeeds in moving his reader, this too is erotic realism, *and it is axiomatic that the reader should respond erotically to such writing,* just as the sensitive reader will respond, perhaps by actually crying, to a sad scene . . ."[3]

Pondering such differing views of obscenity and recalling that reproductions of Goya's famous Nude (or Naked) Maja decorate an official postage stamp in Catholic Spain whereas in "pluralistic" America reproductions were banned in the mails, we have turned for enlightenment to an exchange between a distinguished Catholic prelate and the editor of one of our best monthly periodicals.

---

[2] Harold C. Gardiner, S.J., *Catholic Viewpoint on Censorship,* Image Books Edition (Garden City, N.Y.: Doubleday & Company, Inc., 1961), pp. 64–65.

[3] *Pornography and the Law* (New York: Ballantine Books, Inc., 1959), p. 18. With an introduction by Dr. Theodore Reik.

But here, as in other cases, moral perplexities are best exhibited by viewing them in a particular context. The experience of a noted writer provides such a context. Henry Miller has engaged over a long period of years in a series of self-revelations that his severer critics have denounced as exercises in scatology. Among the most notable of these disclosures are *Tropic of Cancer* and *Tropic of Capricorn,* both banned from this country until 1961, when federal restraints were removed. Their fate in local jurisdictions, as the selections below will indicate, has been an uneven one, although some would say they are more likely—if Judge Woolsey's language in the *Ulysses* case may be borrowed— to act as an emetic than as an aphrodisiac. The two court decisions below illustrate the problems involved in first defining and then controlling pornography. The first is an opinion of Judge Stephens for the majority of the U.S. Court of Appeals (Ninth Circuit). The second is an opinion of Justice Cutter for the majority of the Supreme Judicial Court of Massachusetts.[4] A third selection gives the author an opportunity to speak for himself.

---

[4] Until recently the U.S. Supreme Court guided itself by the so-called Hicklin test of obscenity, which was first affirmed in 1868 in England by Lord Chief Justice John Campbell: "Whether the tendency of the matter charged . . . is to deprave and corrupt those whose minds are open to such immoral influences, and into whose hands . . . [it] may fall." Typical of works suppressed by this test were Hemingway's *For Whom the Bell Tolls,* Lillian Smith's *Strange Fruit* and Tolstoy's *Kreutzer Sonata.* In its famous *Roth-Alberts* decision (June 24, 1957) the Court, while affirming the constitutionality of obscenity laws, rejected the Hicklin test declaring that the test of obscenity is "Whether to the average person, applying contemporary community standards, the dominant theme of the material taken as a whole appeals to prurient interest." Hailed by the censors, the Court had in fact liberalized the test of obscenity as became clear in a series of decisions in which movies like *The Moon Is Blue* and books like Miller's *Tropics* and Lawrence's *Lady Chatterley* were given constitutional protection. However, on March 21, 1966, in three historic decisions, the Court upheld obscenity convictions in the cases of Ralph Ginzburg, publisher of *Eros,* and Edward Mushkin, a Times Square bookseller, while reversing a lower-court ruling that *Fanny Hill,* the eighteenth-century minor classic, is obscene. The significance of the Ginzburg-Mushkin decisions is the Court's finding that the context of a work's production and sales promotion is relevant. That is to say, the manner in which a purveyor promotes a work may now bring it under a ban as when the redoubtable Mr. Ginzburg sought out the town of Intercourse (Pa.) for a franking permit and, denied one there, settled for Middlesex (N.J.).

THE HARM GOOD PEOPLE DO

John Fischer

> *John Fischer, editor in chief of* Harper's Magazine *for fourteen years, succeeded Bernard De Voto as the occupant of its "Easy Chair." However upholstered the chair may be, its occupants have rarely given comfort to the smug and sanctimonious. Fischer's articles have enjoyed a wide circle of thoughtful and appreciative readers and many of these articles are collected in his book,* The Stupidity Problem, and Other Harassments *(1964). He has announced his resignation as editor in chief of* Harper's *in order to concentrate on writing.*

A little band of Catholics is now conducting a shocking attack on the rights of their fellow citizens. They are engaged in an un-American activity which is as flagrant as anything the Communist party ever attempted—and which is, in fact, very similar to Communist tactics. They are harming their country, their Church, and the cause of freedom.

Their campaign is particularly dangerous because few people realize what they are up to. It can hurt you—indeed, it already has—without your knowing it. It is spreading rapidly but quietly; and so far no effective steps have been taken to halt it.

Even the members of this organization probably do not recognize the damage they are doing. They are well-meaning people, acting from deeply moral impulses. They are trying, in a misguided way, to cope with a real national problem, and presumably they think of themselves as patriots and servants of the Lord. Perhaps a majority of Americans, of all faiths, would sympathize with their motives—though not with their methods.

They do not, of course, speak for all Catholics. On the contrary, they are defying the warnings of some of their Church's most respected teachers and theologians. The Catholic Church as a whole certainly cannot be blamed for their actions, any more than it could be held responsible a generation ago for the political operations of Father Coughlin.

This group calls itself the National Organization for Decent Literature. Its headquarters are in Chicago; its director is the Very Reverend Monsignor Thomas Fitzgerald. Its main purpose is to make it impossible

---

for anybody to buy books and other publications which it does not like. Among them are the works of some of the most distinguished authors now alive—for example, winners of the Nobel Prize, the Pulitzer Prize, and the National Book Award.

It chief method is to put pressure on news dealers, drug stores, and booksellers, to force them to remove from their stocks every item on the NODL blacklist. Included on this list are reprint editions of books by Ernest Hemingway, William Faulkner, John Dos Passos, George Orwell, John O'Hara, Paul Hyde Bonner, Emile Zola, Arthur Koestler, and Joyce Cary. In some places—notably Detroit, Peoria, and the suburbs of Boston —the organization has enlisted the local police to threaten booksellers who are slow to "co-operate."

This campaign of intimidation has no legal basis. The books so listed have not been banned from the mails, and in the overwhelming majority of cases no legal charges have ever been brought against them. Indeed, it seems that the National Organization for Decent Literature deliberately prefers to ignore the established legal channels for proceedings against books which it thinks improper. Its chosen weapons are boycott and literary lynching.

For example, early last year committees of laymen from Catholic churches in the four northern counties of New Jersey—Union, Hudson, Essex, and Bergen—began to call on local merchants. These teams were armed with the NODL lists. They offered "certificates," to be renewed each month, to those storekeepers who would agree to remove from sale all of the listed publications. To enforce their demands, they warned the merchants that their parishioners would be advised to patronize only those stores displaying a certificate.

Contact, a bulletin published by the Sacred Heart Parish Societies of Orange, New Jersey, listed fourteen merchants in its March 1955 issue. "The following stores," it said, "have agreed to co-operate with the Parish Decency Committee in not displaying or selling literature disapproved by the National Organization for Decent Literature. . . . Please patronize these stores only. They may be identified by the certificate which is for one month only."

Similar tactics have been followed in scores of other communities. Even in Nevada—a state not noted for Puritanical temper—the Council of Catholic Men has asked booksellers to purge from their shelves a list of books which included such widely read novels as *Mr. Roberts* and *From Here to Eternity.* When an Associated Press reporter pointed out that millions of people already were familiar with these works, in print and on film, the state chairman of the campaign, Paul Laxalt of Carson City, replied:

"We've got to stand by the list. If we make one exception the list would be chopped up."

Such tactics are highly effective. Most news dealers, druggists, and similar merchants carry paper-bound books only as a minor side line. Moreover, they receive from the wholesalers more books than they have space for; if they remove one title from their racks, there are plenty of others to take its place. They don't want trouble. It is never good business to argue with a customer—so most of them readily comply with this form of private censorship. After all, their other customers, who might want to read a book by Faulkner or Hemingway or Zola, will never know that it has been suppressed, and when they don't find it on the shelves they probably will buy something else.

For these reasons it was possible for the Archdiocesan Council of Catholic Men in St. Louis to report recently that it had "obtained the consent of about one-third of the store owners approached in a campaign to ask merchants to submit to voluntary screening. . . ."

Something—but not much—can be said in defense of the National Organization for Decent Literature and its local campaigners. A good many tawdry and disreputable magazines, paper-bound reprints, and comic books have been offered for sale on a lot of newsstands. A few publishers unquestionably have tried to base their sales appeal on sex and violence; the pictures and text on the covers of their publications often hint that the contents are far more salacious than they are in fact. (Such misrepresentation, however, is less common now than it was a few years ago, and both the contents and the covers of most pocket-size books seem to be growing less lurid.)

It can be argued, too, that law enforcement agencies in some cities have not been vigorous in enforcing the statutes against obscene publications. Finally, the "decent literature" campaigners apparently feel that their main mission is to protect young people, whose judgment is unformed and who might be attracted to sleazy reading matter by a provocative newsstand display; they seem to take far less interest in the hard-bound editions of the same books available in libraries or regular book stores. The Detroit NODL, for example, states that its list is "not intended as a restrictive list for adults"—though it does not explain how adults could purchase the books if merchants have been persuaded not to stock them.

But the motives of these zealous people are not the issue. The real issue is whether any private group—however well-meaning—has a right to dictate what other people may read.

Clearly any church, or any sub-group within a church, has a right to advise its own members about their reading matter.

Clearly, too, anybody has a right to try to *persuade* other people to read or refrain from reading anything he sees fit.

The National Organization for Decent Literature, however, goes much further. Its campaign is not aimed at Catholics alone, and it is not attempting to *persuade* readers to follow its views. It is *compelling* readers, of all faiths, to bow to its dislikes, by denying them a free choice in what they buy.

This principle is of course unacceptable to Catholics—as it is to all Americans—if they take the trouble to think about it for a moment. How would Catholics react if, say, a group of Jewish laymen were to threaten merchants with boycott unless they banned from their shops all publications which referred to the divinity of Christ? Some religious denominations believe that gambling is immoral; most Catholics do not, and many of their parishes raise considerable sums by means of bingo games and raffles. What if some Protestant sect were to try to clean out of the stores all publications which spoke tolerantly of gambling, and to boycott every merchant who bought a raffle ticket?

The principle at stake was set forth with admirable clarity by Father John Courtney Murray, S.J., professor of moral theology at Woodstock College, Maryland, in a recent address on "Literature and Censorship." He listed four rules, which ought to command the enthusiastic support of all Americans regardless of religious belief:

(1) "Each minority group has the right to censor for its own members, if it so chooses, the contents of the various media of communication, and to protect them, by means of its own choosing, from materials considered harmful according to its standards." (He also pointed out that in the United States "all religious groups . . . are minority groups.")

(2) "No minority group has the right to demand that government should impose a general censorship" on material "judged to be harmful according to the special standards held within one group."

(3) "Any minority group has the right to work toward the elevation of standards of public morality . . . through the use of the methods of persuasion and pacific argument."

(4) "No minority group has the right to impose its own religious or moral views on other groups, through the use of methods of force, coercion, or violence."

And Father Murray went on to warn that methods of coercion are especially imprudent for Catholic associations.

"The chief danger," he said, "is lest the Church itself be identified in the public mind as a power-association. The identification is injurious; it turns into hatred of the faith. And it has the disastrous effect of obscuring from the public view the true visage of the Church as God's kingdom of truth and freedom, justice and love."

He quoted from Jacques Leclercq "of the Catholic University of Louvain, who is no slight authority" the dictum that "no government has ever succeeded in finding a balanced policy of combating unhealthy sexual propaganda without injuring legitimate freedom or provoking other equally grave or worse disorders."

Finally, Father Murray emphasized that "censorship in the civil order must be a judicial process," carried out under the statutes and according to the due processes of law.

The conclusions which flow from Father Murray's teachings seem plain enough:

(1) *For the National Organization for Decent Literature.* It should stop immediately its campaign of threats, blacklisting, and boycott. It should then pursue its aims by the legitimate methods of persuasion, propaganda, and action through the courts. Most states have adequate laws against the publication and sale of indecent literature. In cases where the law seems inadequate, the legislature can be persuaded to amend it, by the normal means of lobbying and petition. In cases where the law is not enforced, public officials should certainly be reminded of their duty—and opposed at the polls, in the democratic way, if they fall down on their jobs.

Above all, the NODL ought to consider the possibility of guiding young readers by positive rather than negative techniques. Youngsters are not likely to read trash whenever they have good books readily available. If they are brought up in homes where good literature is a constant part of their environment—where parents read to them from infancy, and encourage them to build up their own libraries—then there is scant chance that they will be attracted by comics or two-bit horrors.

What has the NODL done to urge parents to give their children such basic moral training? Has it done all it can to foster topnotch libraries—public, school, church, and family? In how many communities has it sponsored campaigns to stimulate good reading?

(2) *For news dealers, booksellers, and other merchants.* They should muster the courage to defy any group of private citizens which tries to impose its own brand of censorship on the publications they offer for sale. And, with equal courage, they should set their own house in order; they should refuse to sell any publication which—in their own untrammeled judgment—falls below their own standards as responsible business men.

(3) *For the patriotic citizen.* He should protest against the lynching of books just as vigorously as against the lynching of people. He should go out of his way to support the merchants who resist such coercion. He should point out to the members of the National Organization for Decent Literature (and to any other self-appointed censors in his community) the immeasurable damage they are doing to the American way of life, to the very foundation of democratic government.

For the gravest harm done here is not to the Catholic Church—

though, as Father Murray noted, that is dangerous enough—or to the individual who is denied the right to choose his own books. The great peril is to the fabric of orderly government. It is always injured when any group takes the law into its own hands. And whenever such a band of vigilantes succeeds in imposing its will by force, some other—and perhaps more sinister—group is encouraged to try the same thing.

Dean Joseph O'Meara of the Notre Dame Law School recently put it like this:

> Unfortunately many sincere people do not comprehend the genius of our democracy . . . such people would deny free speech to those with whom they are in fundamental disagreement. . . . They would establish a party line in America—*their* party line, of course. This is an alien concept, a totalitarian concept; it is not consonant with the American tradition; it is anti-democratic; it is, in short, subversive and it should be recognized for what it is.

Still another eminent Catholic—Senator John Kennedy of Massachusetts—summed up the case in even more prophetic terms.

> The lock on the door of the legislature, the parliament, or the assembly hall by order of the King, the Commissar, or the Führer —has historically been followed or preceded by a lock on the door of the printer's, the publisher's, or the bookseller's.

THE BAD ARGUMENTS
INTELLIGENT PEOPLE MAKE

John Courtney Murray, S.J.

Since he was one of American Catholicism's most brilliant and fluent spokesmen, this volume relies on Father Murray for comments on two topics instead of one. His views concerning the relation of church and state will be found on pages 409–425. Although another competent spokesman for the Catholic view on the present topic might have been found,

From *America, The National Catholic Weekly Review*, 106 W. 56 Street, New York, N.Y. 10019 (November 3, 1956), pp. 120–123. © 1956 America Press, Inc. Reprinted by permission.

Father Murray has been enlisted because his remarks are directly responsive to John Fischer and hence provide a clear joining of some of the basic issues involved in current debates about pornography. John Courtney Murray was, until his recent death, Professor of Theology at Woodstock College, Maryland. He is the author of We Hold These Truths *(1961),* The Problem of God: Yesterday and Today *(1963),* The Problem of Religious Freedom *(1965).*

From his "Editor's Easy Chair" John Fischer looks out and sees "immeasurable damage" being done "to the American way of life and to the very foundations of democratic government." This has become a familiar vision; many of us share it. But we frequently differ on the question, who or what is doing the damage?

In Mr. Fischer's view the damage is being done by "a little band of Catholics" who are "conducting a shocking attack on the rights of their fellow citizens" through the medium of an organization called the National Organization for Decent Literature, which undertakes to "censor" certain publications.

I take a rather broader view. I see a large band of people, of all faiths, who are conducting a shocking attack on the reason of their fellow citizens through the medium of passionately irrational argument about important public issues. I believe that nothing is more damaging to democracy than lack of rationality in public argument. The foundations of our society are indeed laid in an identifiable consensus. But they are more importantly laid in a reasonable disposition to argue our many disagreements in intelligent and temperate fashion, using restrained language, avoiding misstatements, overstatements or simplifications, and endeavoring to define issues with precision in the light of all the relevant principles and facts. I believe that whatever corrupts rational public argument corrupts democracy.

It has seemed to me that censorship is one of the public issues that are being deformed by bad argument, emanating from all sides. Hence on May 4, 1956, in a talk given before the Thomas More Association in Chicago and printed in the organ of the Thomas More Book Shop, *Books on Trial,* I made an attempt at a contribution to good public argument on this difficult subject. Part of my argument consisted in stating four practical rules that should govern the action of minority groups in a pluralist society, in their legitimate efforts to improve public morality. These rules were not original. I had seen them stated in substance in a news release of a paper given at Marquette University on March 23, 1956, by Prof. Vernon J. Bourke of St. Louis University.

Mr. Fischer quotes my statement of these four procedural rules in support of certain conclusions of his own with regard to the activities of the

National Organization for Decent Literature. Perhaps Mr. Bourke will undertake to say whether, and how far, Mr. Fischer's conclusions follow from the four norms of action for whose formulation, in language somewhat different from my own, he should be given the credit. . . . My own major concern is with a broader question—the quality of public argument. My question is whether Mr. Fischer has made a contribution to rational public argument on the issue of censorship. I am afraid my answer must be No.

Consider the preliminary question of language. In his opening paragraph Mr. Fischer asserts that a "little band of Catholics" is "engaged in an un-American activity which is as flagrant as anything the Communist party ever attempted—and which is in fact very similar to Communist tactics." Does one open a rational public argument by two such attacks on the reason of the reader? That tired old cuss-word, "un-American activity" —has it not gone the way of all cuss-words, into meaninglessness? And the tactic of slapping the label "Communist" on your adversary's position— have we not agreed that this is a tactic of unreason? As for the later argument by epithet (the NODL is "lynching" books), one hardly expects to find it in *Harper's,* however much it may be used on the hustings.

The more substantive question is this: has Mr. Fischer done justice to the NODL's own understanding of its purposes and methods, as these are stated in its explanatory literature?

The literature is easily obtainable from the central office. . . . On reading it, one would come, I think, to the following conclusions. The NODL is simply a "service organization," not an "action group." Its major service consists in offering to "responsible individuals and organizations an evaluation of current comic books, magazines and pocket-size books." This is the famous "NODL list." The evaluation of these types of publications (only these) is done singly from the standpoint of what is objectionable as juvenile reading. The standards of evaluation are nine in number. All of them are common-sense norms; none of them are special tenets of any type of "group morality." Methods of review vary for each type of publication. Five reviewers vote on each item. The purpose is to "encourage the publishing and distribution of good literature," as well as to discover what is unfit for adolescents.

NODL also distributes information about ways of organizing decent-literature campaigns on the community or parish levels. It is clearly stated that the list is merely an expression of a publication's nonconformity with the NODL code and that "the list is not to be used for purposes of boycott or coercion." The recommended procedures seem to rest on the suppositions that the ordinary merchant is a responsible man; that he would welcome some assistance in ridding his shop of stuff that responsible parents fairly judge to be unfit for their children; that if he accepts the assistance, he is to be commended; that if he rejects it, he is to be left alone. (NODL says: "Instruct your committee workers to leave silently if the owner, manager or clerk refuses cooperation.")

The general conclusion, on the basis of its own statements about itself, would be that the NODL looks to voluntary reform, through co-operation between parent-citizens and merchants, in an area where a special problem of public morality exists. That problem arises out of the ready accessibility to boys and girls of a rather immense amount of cheap literature that is objectionable on common-sense grounds of morality and taste.

Consider now Mr. Fischer's description of the NODL. "Its main purpose is to make it impossible for anybody to buy books and other publications which it does not like." "Its chief method is to put pressure on newsdealers, drugstores and booksellers to force them to remove from their stocks every item on the NODL blacklist." It "deliberately prefers to ignore the established legal channels for proceedings against books which it thinks improper. Its chosen weapons are boycott and literary lynching." It is embarked upon a "campaign of intimidation."

Something is wrong here. When Mr. Fischer describes the NODL he is obviously not describing the same thing that NODL describes when it describes itself. Thus you have reproduced the perfect pattern—the perfectly wretched pattern—of so much American public argument at the moment. There is really no argument at all—at least not yet. The two sides are not talking about the same thing. Hence the exchange proceeds to the customarily futile end. On the basis of his own description Mr. Fischer asserts that NODL "is *compelling* [emphasis his] readers, of all faiths, to bow to its dislikes, by denying them a free choice in what they buy." Hence he defines the issue thus: "The real issue is whether any private group—however well-meaning—has a right to dictate what other people may read."

To Mr. Fischer's charges the NODL would, I expect, reply to this effect: "But we are not compelling anybody to do or not to do anything. We are not doing any such arbitrary thing as making our own 'dislikes' the coercive standard for the reading of the general public. We are not trying to do any 'dictating.' And as for denying to readers of all faiths a free choice in what they buy—that is not the real issue at all."

Thus the argument fulfils the customary American pattern. The next step is for the contestants to retire from the field, either in sorrow or in anger or in both. Thereafter their partisans move in. Epithets are bandied; labels are exchanged; *non sequiturs* proliferate. Until finally, both sides mutter disgustedly, "So's your old man." And there is, for a time, a sullen silence.

Maybe the argument could be rescued from this dismal end, to which most arguments in America seem to be condemned. Mr. Fischer could have rescued it, but he didn't. The *NODL* could have obviated the need for rescue, but it hasn't. The point where rescue begins is, of course, a fact. Mr. Fischer notes the fact, but he abuses it to advance his own purposes. The NODL must surely recognize the fact, but it has not acted on the recognition, to the detriment of its own purposes. The fact is that in half-a-dozen or more cities and towns the police have made use of the NODL list in order to threaten, coerce or punish dealers in reading matter.

Unquestionably, officers of the law have full right to use the weapons of law, which are coercive. The point in question, however, is their use of the NODL list. This puts NODL in an ambiguous position. It cannot expect to have the thing both ways. It cannot, on the one hand, protest that "the list is not to be used for purpose of boycott or coercion," and, on the other hand, fail to protest against the use of the list by the police. It has to choose its cooperators—either the merchant or the police. It cannot choose both; for the choice is really between opposed methods of cooperation—the method of voluntary cooperation as between equal citizens, or the method of coercion as used by the police.

If NODL consents to the use of its list by the police, it creates an ambiguity that its critics may rightly seize upon, as Mr. Fischer did; what is worse, it obscures from public view its own "idea," the altogether valid idea of voluntary reform. On the other hand, if NODL does not consent to the use of its list by the police, it should say so—publicly, and on every necessary occasion. Surely part of its service must be the supervision, conducted on its own principles, of the uses to which its list is put.

There is another inappropriateness here. Officers of the law must operate under statutes which in this matter are, or ought to be, narrowly drawn. On the other hand, voluntary reform, precisely because it is voluntary, may be based on the somewhat broader categories of common-sense judgment. The latter are employed by the NODL, rightly enough. But for this very reason it is not right for the police to use NODL's judgments in enforcing the law. The law must have its own standards, minimal enough to sustain the challenge of due process.

In this connection another fact must be noted. The fact is that on NODL lists there appear some twenty-odd works that either have received literary honors or at least have been acclaimed by serious critics. Doubtless high-school teachers could not, without absurdity, make them required reading for their students. But the police cannot, without equal absurdity, make them prohibited reading. Such stultification of the law is itself immoral.

There is a third fact of some consequence. The history of censorship has been a history of excess. The NODL has the problem of the local zealot, operating far from the central office in Chicago, and way outside the four pages of sensible procedures sent out from it. He or she "has the zeal of God indeed, but not according to understanding" (Romans 10:2). Such zealots are righteous, usually indignant, people. They have a good cause.

They want results. What they lack is St. Paul's "understanding," which bears, he said, on "the *way* of justification."

I shall not labor the analogy. The point of it, in our case, is that the zealot at times fails to see how his zeal for results may betray him into the use of methods that will in turn betray his cause. Mr. Fischer, for example, in his zeal for his own cause, which is a good one, fell into a bad method of argument. Among other faults, he fails to distinguish between the "idea" of the NODL, which is the substantive issue, and the applications of the idea, which raise issues of procedure. In good "liberal" fashion he assigns the primacy to the procedural over the substantive. Contrariwise, in good "Catholic" fashion, the local zealot for the NODL cause assigns the primacy to the substantive over the procedural. He, or she, wants the newsstands "cleaned up"; and he, or she, in some instances doesn't greatly care how.

At that, Mr. Fischer is more nearly right. In this sensitive area the question of procedure is all-important. Part of the service of NODL to its own cause should be what I can only call a service of fraternal correction. It should somehow find a way of rebuking, or at least disavowing, the local zealot who violates, or goes beyond, the cooperative procedures, none of them coercive, which it officially stands for. (As for Mr. Fischer, maybe I have myself done him some service of intellectual charity?)

At this point, with all the ambiguities at least sorted out, if not cleared up, we could begin the rational public argument. The starting-point would be a fact—the existence of a "real national problem" (Mr. Fischer's words). Then the questions arise. For instance, does Mr. Fischer adequately measure the dimensions of the problem? He says:

"A good many tawdry and disreputable magazines, paperbound reprints and comic books have been offered for sale on a lot of newsstands. A few publishers unquestionably have tried to base their sales appeal on sex and violence; the pictures and text on the covers of their publications often hint that the contents are far more salacious than they are in fact."

He adds that "law-enforcement agencies in some cities have not been vigorous in enforcing the statutes against obscene publications." And that's it.

Or is it? Others would maintain that this is an astonishing understatement of the real national problem. They see the problem much more ominously large. A major issue in public morality has arisen; the morals of youth are particularly involved in it; the problem is growing. They further see a causal line between bad magazines, etc., and immorality. And they feel it imperative to "do something" about the bad literature.

When these last statements are made, they start up the current argument between sociology and common sense. The sociologist expresses professional doubt about the causal line between bad reading and immorality; he finds insufficient evidence for it. The common-sense view asserts that the causal line is sufficiently established by the nature, content, tendency, etc., of the literature itself. At least a strong presumption is thus created; and it furnishes reason for action, until—and maybe after—all the Ph.D. theses, pro and con, have been written.

The word "action" disturbs the jealous advocate of civil rights. He therefore comes up with his own causal line—between any attempt at suppressing any kind of literature and the subversion of the foundations of the Republic. The common-sense view expresses doubt about this causal line. There is, it says, insufficient evidence that any such alarming consequences will follow, if the action taken is rational and prudent.

Here the real issue begins to appear: what kinds of action, as taken by whom, are rational and prudent in the circumstances? And what promise of effectiveness do they offer?

Mr. Fischer has his own program of action, which deserves consideration. He recommends two positive courses. The first is self-regulation by newsdealers, booksellers and other merchants. They should, he says, "set their own house in order; they should refuse to sell any publication which—in their own untrammeled judgment—falls below their own standards as responsible businessmen."

A question of fact occurs here: how effective so far has the principle of self-regulation been in the solution of our real national problem? The evidence suggests a discouraging answer. Some efforts in this direction have been made, always under the pressure of public opinion; but their slim success bases little hope for the future. Second, the principle itself may be, and has been, called in question. For instance, in a report entitled *The Freedom to Read,* written for the National Book Committee, Richard McKeon, Walter Gellhorn and Robert K. Merton say this:

> The dangers of police censorship are obvious; but we are convinced that the dangers of a code of self-censorship are even greater. It provides the means by which all kinds of restrictions can be put on freedom of expression, and it places the freedom to read in the hands of a group which does not even have the accountability to the public which a chief of police has.

I don't necessarily endorse this judgment; but it may suggest that Mr. Fischer is on shaky ground.

There are other questions too. What, I might ask, is the right of a newsdealer to "untrammeled judgment"? Is his judgment, as a matter of fact, untrammeled? And whether it is or not, why should one trust it as a means of solution for our real national problem? Is he a better critic of literature, a better judge of morality, than the average parent? How is one even to know what his "standards as a responsible businessman" are? And if they could be known, is there to be no possibility of public judgment on them? On what title is this Olympian immunity claimed? One would like to know.

The second positive course is the action of law—legislative and court action. I am inclined to think that Mr. Fischer's confidence in the efficacy of legal action as a corrective in this difficult field of printed media will be astonishing to students of the law. If I mistake not, it is pretty generally admitted that the present legal picture is a muddle. It is further admitted that the difficulties encountered in trying to straighten it out are immense. There are the two sacred legal doctrines that must be protected—prior restraint and due process. Furthermore, there are certain adverse high-court decisions that seem to have reduced the law to a state of practical impotence, not least in the two crucial areas of obscenity and violence.

What is even more decisive, even if the law could be lifted to the full height of its legitimate potency, it would still be largely impotent to cope with the new problem of mass media, whose crude subtleties seem to defeat the subtle crudities of the law. The grounds for accepting the relative ineffectiveness of law in this special field, where the moral issue is not justice, are both theoretical and practical—to be found both in the art of jurisprudence and in the lessons of history.

Mr. Fischer suggests two manners of action—one private, the other public—whose possibilities ought by all means be explored and exploited. But in the course of rational public argument it would, I think, appear that his program of positive action is inadequate to the real national problem that confronts us. His negative demand is more acceptable. He wants organizations of private right to stop campaigns of coercion. So do I. Mr. Fischer's reasons are, I think, doctrinaire; further argument would have to illuminate the fact, if it is a fact. Whereas, I, a Catholic, am not a doctrinaire.

In my Chicago lecture I said that ". . . it is not possible to prove the position, taken by some, that an action like the boycott of a moving picture is somehow 'unrightful,' or 'undemocratic' or 'unconstitutional.' No one can show that such an action lies beyond the limits of a primeval American right to protest and object. The action may indeed be strenuous; but the American right to protest and object is permitted to run to some pretty strenuous extremes. This said against the doctrinaire, it remains true that methods of action which verge upon the coercive exhibit some incongruity when used by citizen-groups in the interests of morality in literature or on the screen. Even if they raise no issue of abstract right, they do raise the concrete issue of prudence, which, equally with justice, is one of the cardinal virtues."

I hold to this position now, against Mr. Fischer (I think), and also (I think) against the NODL in its present ambiguous situation—certainly in its representation by local zealots and by the secular arm of the police.

I further hold to my previous position that private agencies such as the NODL can perform an indispensable public function in the promotion of public morality—provided they understand what their function is. It is not to supplant the coercive function of the agencies of public law. It is to represent, soberly and honestly, the principle of voluntary reform, to be accomplished on the basis of social cooperation—that sincere cooperation which in America is always ready to be stimulated but often needs stimulation.

This principle of reform is altogether valid in itself. Its applications call for prudence—concretely, as I have previously said, for "men and women of prudence, who understand the art of procedure, and understand too that we are morally bound, by the virtue of prudence, to a concrete rightness of method in the pursuit of moral aims." For the rest, the rationality of this method of social reform will be understood, and its pitfalls will be avoided, if we can all somehow hold to high standards of public discussion. In this respect the editor of *Harper's* has failed. But his failure is less reprehensible than that of Catholics who miss their present opportunity—and duty—to perform the instant task, which is to inject the Catholic tradition of rationality into a mass democracy that is rapidly slipping its moorings in reason.

BESIG v. UNITED STATES

United States Circuit Court of Appeals

Two books entitled respectively "Tropic of Cancer" and "Tropic of Capricorn," which were written by Henry Miller and were printed in Paris, were intercepted at an American port of entry and labeled . . . as obscene. The district court found them to be obscene and ordered them destroyed. Besig, the owner of the books, is here appealing upon the ground that neither of the two books, which are commonly referred to together as "The Tropics," is obscene.

The word "obscene" is not uncommon and is used in English and

---

From the decision of the Ninth Circuit, before Stephens, Orr, and Pope, San Francisco, California, October 23, 1953 (208 F.2d 142).

American speech and writings as the word symbol for indecent, smutty, lewd or salacious reference to parts of the human or animal body or to their functions or to the excrement therefrom. Each of The Tropics is written in the composite style of a novel-autobiography, and the author as a character in the book carries the reader as though he himself is living in disgrace, degradation, poverty, mean crime, and prostitution of mind and body. The vehicle of description is the unprintable word of the debased and morally bankrupt. Practically everything that the world loosely regards as sin is detailed in the vivid, lurid, salacious language of smut, prostitution, and dirt. And all of it is related without the slighest expressed idea of its abandon. Consistent with the general tenor of the books, even human excrement is dwelt upon in the dirtiest words available. The author conducts the reader through sex orgies and perversions of the sex organs, and always in the debased language of the bawdy house. Nothing has the grace of purity or goodness. These words of the language of smut, and the disgraceful scenes, are so heavily larded throughout the books that those portions which are deemed to be of literary merit do not lift the reader's mind clear of their sticky slime. And it is safe to say that the "literary merit" of the books carries the reader deeper into it. For this reason, The Tropics are far more dangerous than "Confessions of a Prostitute" which was the subject of our opinion in Burstein v. United States. . . . There, the scenes depicted are obscene because of the scene itself which in its stark ugliness might well repel many. The Tropics lure on with the cleverness of scene, skilfulness of recital, and the use of worse than gutter words. All of this is sought to be justified through the sophistry, as the trial judge, Honorable Louis E. Goodman, put it, of "confession and avoidance." It is claimed that they truthfully describe a base status of society in the language of its own iniquities. And that, since we live in an age of realism, obscene language depicting obscenity in action ceases to be obscenity.

Whether the moral conventions should be flouted in the cause of frankness, art, or realism, we have no occasion to decide. That question is for the policy branches of the government. Nor do we understand that we have the legal power to hold that the statute authorizing the seizure of obscene books is inapplicable to books in which obscenity is an integral part of a literary work. So that obscenity, though a part of a composition of high literary merit, is not excepted from operation of the statute, whether written in the style of the realists, surrealists, or plain shock writers. The civilization of our times holds to the premise that dirt in stark nakedness is not generally and at all times acceptable. And the great mass of the people still believe there is such a thing as decency. Indecency is easily recognizable. Such is the premise of the statute. The Congress has chosen to enact a censorship which would not have been possible except for the self-styled prophets of truth who offend so grievously.

It is of course true that the ears of some may be so accustomed to words which are ordinarily regarded as obscene that they take no offense at them, but the law is not tempered to the hardened minority of society. The statute forbidding the importation of obscene books is not designed to fit the normal concept of morality of society's dregs, nor of the different concepts of morality throughout the world, nor for all time past and future, but is designed to fit the normal American concept in the age in which we live. It is no legitimate argument that because there are social groups composed of moral delinquents in this or in other countries, that their language shall be received as legal tender along with the speech of the great masses who trade ideas and information in the honest money of decency.

Adequate provision is made in the statute in the interests of classics and the technical, by the following proviso:

> *Provided further,* That the Secretary of the Treasury may, in his discretion, admit the so-called classics or books of recognized and established literary or scientific merit, but may, in his discretion, admit such classics or books only when imported for non-commercial purposes. . . .

It is claimed that these books (The Tropics) are not for the immature of mind, and that adults read them for their literary and informative merits, but, whether true or untrue, we cannot measure their importability by such a yardstick. The Congress probably saw the impracticability of preventing the use of the books by the young and the pure. And of course they knew that salacious print in the hands of adults, even in the hands of those whose sun is near the western horizon, may well incite to disgusting practices and to hideous crime.

We agree that the book as a book must be obscene to justify its libel and destruction, but neither the number of the "objectionable" passages nor the proportion they bear to the whole book are controlling. If an incident, integrated with the theme or story of a book, is word-painted in such lurid and smutty or pornographic language that dirt appears as the primary purpose rather than the relation of a fact or adequate description of the incident, the book itself is obscene. We are not well acquainted with Aristophanes or his times, but we know they were different from ours. We have chanced upon Chaucer and we know his times were different from ours. Boccaccio is lurid. The Bible is not free from the recounting of immoral practices. But the translators, from the languages in which The Bible was originally written, did not word-paint such practices in the lurid-Miller-morally-corrupt manner. Dirty word description of the sweet and sublime, especially of the mystery of sex and procreation, is the ultimate of obscenity. We have referred to Aristophanes, Chaucer, Boccaccio, and The Bible only because those works were taken as examples by the author of the opinion in the case of United States v. One Book Entitled Ulysses . . . a case cited by appellant to illustrate his point that " 'No work may be judged from a selection of such paragraphs alone . . . ,' " but the point is not relevant because we have adjudged each book as an integrated whole. . . .

Appellant thinks the district court committed error in deciding contrary to the great weight of opinion evidence as to the quality of Mr. Miller's writings. The point has no merit. Opinion evidence is useful, but not controlling. We have carefully read and analyzed the voluminous affidavits and exhibits contained in the record. To a large extent they are opinions of authors who resent any limitation on their writings. Their opinions are relevant and competent evidence, but their views are advisory only as to the norm of the meaning of the word "obscene." We share the general antipathy to censorship and we are aware that individual tastes and special occasions and different times and different peoples differ as to what is offensive language. Yet we risk the assertion that there is an underlying, perhaps universal, accord that there is a phase of respectable delicacy related to sex, and that those compositions which purposefully flout such delicacy in language generally regarded as indecent come under the ban of the statute. . . .

ATTORNEY GENERAL v. THE BOOK NAMED "TROPIC OF CANCER"

Supreme Judicial Court of Massachusetts

We think . . . that the First Amendment protects material which has value because of ideas, news, or artistic, literary, or scientific attributes. If the appeal of material (taken as a whole) to adults is not predominantly prurient, adults cannot be denied the material. When the public risks of suppressing ideas are weighed against the risks of permitting their circulation, the guaranties of the First Amendment must be given controlling effect. The dangers of subjective judgments in the matter of censorship lead to a strong presupposition against suppression. We conclude, therefore, . . . that, with respect to material designed for general circulation, only predominantly "hard core" pornography, without redeeming social significance, is obscene in the constitutional sense.

From the decision of July 17, 1962 (184 N.E.2d 328).

Whether Tropic is "obscene" in the constitutional sense thus depends upon whether the appeal (if any) of Tropic (taken as a whole) to the normal adult is predominantly prurient. It is not relevant that we think that the book at many places is repulsive, vulgar, and grossly offensive in the use of four letter words, and in the detailed and coarse statement of sexual episodes. That a serious work uses four letter words and has a grossly offensive tone does not mean that the work is not entitled to constitutional protection. Much in modern art, literature, and music is likely to seem ugly and thoroughly objectionable to those who have different standards of taste. It is not the function of judges to serve as arbiters of taste or to say that an author must regard vulgarity as unnecessary to his portrayal of particular scenes or characters or to establish particular ideas. Within broad limits each writer, attempting to be a literary artist, is entitled to determine such matters for himself, even if the result is as dull, dreary, and offensive as the writer of this opinion finds almost all of Tropic.

Competent critics assert, and we conclude, that Tropic has serious purpose, even if many will find that purpose obscure. There can be no doubt that a significant segment of the literary world has long regarded the book as of literary importance. A majority of the court are of opinion that the predominant effect and purpose of the book as a whole is not prurient. . . . a majority of the court are of opinion that Tropic is more likely to discourage than "to excite lustful thoughts." We think that the book must be accepted as a conscious effort to create a work of literary art and as having significance, which prevents treating it as hard core pornography.

THE AUTHOR'S DEFENSE

Henry Miller

Henry Miller is described by his admirers as a "free spirit"
in the tradition of Thoreau and Whitman and as having "a deep
and pure sense of morality." He is described by his detractors
as a man wallowing in prurience. His works, notably the
Tropics, *have won him the approval of such established* literati

From *The Henry Miller Reader,* Lawrence Durrell, Ed. (New York: New Directions, 1959), pp. 371–379. © 1959 by Henry Miller. Reprinted by permission of New Directions Publishing Corporation.

as George Orwell, Ezra Pound, and Lawrence Durrell. Miller is a long-time rebel, but of a peculiar kind. As John Ciardi, poet and poetry editor of the Saturday Review, *observes, "Miller's protest includes mockery, a great roaring laughter, and a certain violent joy in flouting all the values socially accepted as sacred. He flatly refuses society the honor of taking it seriously." Some, like Ciardi, will hail such exposures of the meretricious; others will see little more than lingering adolescence.*

Despite his animadversions about America ("Fresh from Europe, the American scene held about as much charm for me as a dead rattlesnake lying in a deep freeze"), Miller has abandoned the Parisian Left Bank, where he was long an expatriate, for the coasts of California—an exile's return that has evoked mixed feelings among his countrymen. Now an aging guru dispensing controversial wisdom to a coterie of admirers, his personal trials are over, thanks to legal trials that have probably brought enough notoriety to his books to assure him a comfortable income.

The letter reprinted below was addressed by Miller to his counsel in Norway to be used before the Supreme Court of that country in defending a Miller book (Sexus) *against the charge of obscenity.*

Big Sur, California
February 27th, 1959

Mr. Trygve Hirsch
Oslo, Norway

Dear Mr. Hirsch:

To answer your letter of January 19th requesting a statement of me which might be used in the Supreme Court trial to be conducted in March or April of this year. . . . It is difficult to be more explicit than I was in my letter of September 19th, 1957, when the case against my book *Sexus* was being tried in the lower courts of Oslo. However, here are some further reflections which I trust will be found *à propos*.

When I read the decision of the Oslo Town Court, which you sent me some months ago, I did so with mingled feelings. If occasionally I was obliged to roll with laughter—partly because of the inept translation, partly because of the nature and the number of infractions listed—I trust no one will take offense. Taking the world for what it is, and the men who make and execute the laws for what they are, I thought the decision as fair and honest as any theorem of Euclid's. Nor was I unaware of, or indifferent to, the efforts made by the Court to render an interpretation beyond the strict letter of the law. (An impossible task, I would say, for if laws are made for

men and not men for laws, it is also true that certain individuals are made
for the law and can only see things through the eyes of the law.)

I failed to be impressed, I must confess, by the weighty, often
pompous or hypocritical, opinions adduced by scholars, literary pundits,
psychologists, medicos and such like. How could I be when it is precisely
such single-minded individuals, so often wholly devoid of humor, at whom
I so frequently aim my shafts?

Rereading this lengthy document today, I am more than ever
aware of the absurdity of the whole procedure. (How lucky I am not to be
indicted as a "pervert" or "degenerate," but simply as one who makes sex
pleasurable and innocent!) Why, it is often asked, when he has so much
else to give, did he have to introduce these disturbing, controversial scenes
dealing with sex? To answer that properly, one would have to go back to
the womb—with or without the analyst's guiding hand. Each one—priest,
analyst, barrister, judge—has his own answer, usually a ready-made one.
But none go far enough, none are deep enough, inclusive enough. The
divine answer, of course, is—first remove the mote from your own eye!

If I were there, in the dock, my answer would probably be—
"Guilty! Guilty on all ninety-seven counts! To the gallows!" For when I
take the short, myopic view, I realize that I was guilty even before I wrote
the book. Guilty, in other words, because I am the way I am. The marvel is
that I am walking about as a free man. I should have been condemned the
moment I stepped out of my mother's womb.

In that heart-rending account of my return to the bosom of the
family which is given in *Reunion in Brooklyn,* I concluded with these
words, and I meant them, each and every one of them: "I regard the entire
world as my home. I inhabit the earth, not a particular portion of it labeled
America, France, Germany, Russia. . . . I owe allegiance to mankind,
not to a particular country, race or people. I answer to God, not to the
Chief Executive, whoever he may happen to be. I am here on earth to work
out my own private destiny. My destiny is linked with that of every other
living creature inhabiting this planet—perhaps with those on other planets
too, who knows? I refuse to jeopardize my destiny by regarding life within
the narrow rules which are laid down to circumscribe it. I dissent from the
current view of things, as regards murder, as regards religion, as regards
society, as regards our well-being. I will try to live my life in accordance
with the vision I have of things eternal. I say 'Peace to you all!' and if you
don't find it, it's because you haven't looked for it."

It is curious, and not irrelevant, I hope, to mention at this point
the reaction I had upon reading Homer recently. At the request of the
publisher, Gallimard, who is bringing out a new edition of *The Odyssey,* I
wrote a short Introduction to this work. I had never read *The Odyssey*
before, only *The Iliad,* and that but a few months ago. What I wish to say
is that, after waiting sixty-seven years to read these universally esteemed

classics, I found much to disparage in them. In *The Iliad,* or "the butcher's manual," as I call it, more than in *The Odyssey.* But it would never occur to me to request that they be banned or burned. Nor did I fear, on finishing them, that I would leap outdoors, axe in hand, and run amok. My boy, who was only nine when he read *The Iliad* (in a child's version), my boy who confesses to "liking murder once in a while," told me he was fed up with Homer, with all the killing and all the nonsense about the gods. But I have never feared that this son of mine, now going on eleven, still an avid reader of our detestable "Comics," a devotee of Walt Disney (who is not to my taste at all), an ardent movie fan, particularly of the "Westerns," I have never feared, I say, that he will grow up to be a killer. (Not even if the Army claims him!) I would rather see his mind absorbed by other interests, and I do my best to provide them, but, like all of us, he is a product of the age. No need, I trust, for me to elaborate on the dangers which confront us all, youth especially, in *this* age. The point is that with each age the menace varies. Whether it be witchcraft, idolatry, leprosy, cancer, schizophrenia, communism, fascism, or what, we have ever to do battle. Seldom do we really vanquish the enemy, in whatever guise he presents himself. At best we become immunized. But we never know, nor are we able to prevent in advance, the dangers which lurk around the corner. No matter how knowledgeable, no matter how wise, no matter how prudent and cautious, we all have an Achilles' heel. Security is not the lot of man. Readiness, alertness, responsiveness—these are the sole defenses against the blows of fate.

I smile to myself in putting the following to the honorable members of the Court, prompted as I am to take the bull by the horns. Would it please the Court to know that by common opinion I pass for a sane, healthy, normal individual? That I am not regarded as a "sex addict," a pervert, or even a neurotic? Nor as a writer who is ready to sell his soul for money? That, as a husband, a father, a neighbor, I am looked upon as "an asset" to the community? Sounds a trifle ludicrous, does it not? Is this the same *enfant terrible,* it might be asked, who wrote the unmentionable *Tropics, The Rosy Crucifixion, The World of Sex, Quiet Days in Clichy?* Has he reformed? Or is he simply in his dotage now?

To be precise the question is—are the author of these questionable works and the man who goes by the name of Henry Miller one and the same person? My answer is yes. And I am also one with the protagonist of these "autobiographical romances." That is perhaps harder to swallow. But why? Because I have been "utterly shameless" in revealing every aspect of my life? I am not the first author to have adopted the confessional approach, to have revealed life nakedly, or to have used language supposedly unfit for the ears of school girls. Were I a saint recounting his life of sin, perhaps these bald statements relating to my sex habits would be found enlightening, particularly by priests and medicos. They might even be found instructive.

But I am not a saint, and probably never will be one. Though it occurs to me, as I make this assertion, that I have been called that more than once, and by individuals whom the Court would never suspect capable of holding such an opinion. No, I am not a saint, thank heavens! nor even a propagandist of a new order. I am simply a man, a man born to write, who has taken as his theme the story of his life. A man who has made it clear, in the telling, that it was a good life, a rich life, a merry life, despite the ups and downs, despite the barriers and obstacles (many of his own making), despite the handicaps imposed by stupid codes and conventions. Indeed, I hope that I have made more than that clear, because whatever I may say about my own life which is only *a* life, is merely a means of talking about life itself, and what I have tried, desperately sometimes, to make clear is this, that I look upon life itself as good, good no matter on what terms, that I believe it is *we* who make it unlivable, *we,* not the gods, not fate, not circumstance.

Speaking thus, I am reminded of certain passages in the Court's decision which reflect on my sincerity as well as on my ability to think straight. These passages contain the implication that I am often deliberately obscure as well as pretentious in my "metaphysical and surrealistic" flights. I am only too well aware of the diversity of opinion which these "excursi" elicit in the minds of my readers. But how am I to answer such accusations, touching as they do the very marrow of my literary being? Am I to say, "You don't know what you are talking about"? Ought I to muster impressive names—"authorities"—to counterbalance these judgments? Or would it not be simpler to say, as I have before—"Guilty! Guilty on all counts, your Honor!"

Believe me, it is not impish, roguish perversity which leads me to pronounce, even quasi-humorously, this word "guilty." As one who thoroughly and sincerely believes in what he says and does, even when wrong, is it not more becoming on my part to admit "guilt" than attempt to defend myself against those who use this word so glibly? Let us be honest. Do those who judge and condemn me—not in Oslo necessarily, but the world over—do these individuals truly believe me to be a culprit, to be "the enemy of society," as they often blandly assert? What is it that disturbs them so? Is it the existence, the prevalence, of immoral, amoral, or unsocial behavior, such as is described in my works, or is it the exposure of such behavior in print? Do people of our day and age really behave in this "vile" manner or are these actions merely the product of a "diseased" mind? (Does one refer to such authors as Petronius, Rabelais, Rousseau, Sade, to mention but a few, as "diseased minds"? Surely some of you must have friends or neighbors, in good standing too, who have indulged in this questionable behavior, or worse. As a man of the world, I know only too well that the appanage of a priest's frock, a judicial robe, a teacher's uniform provides no guarantee of immunity to the temptations of the flesh. We are all in the same pot, we are all guilty, or innocent, depending on whether we take the frog's view or the Olympian view. For the nonce I shall refrain from pretending to measure or apportion guilt, to say, for example, that a criminal is more guilty, or less, than a hypocrite. We do not have crime, we do not have war, revolution, crusades, inquisitions, persecution and intolerance because some among us are wicked, mean-spirited, or murderers at heart; we have this malignant condition of human affairs because all of us, the righteous as well as the ignorant and the malicious, lack true forebearance, true compassion, true knowledge and understanding of human nature.

To put it as succinctly and simply as possible, here is my basic attitude toward life, my prayer, in other words: "Let us stop thwarting one another, stop judging and condemning, stop slaughtering one another." I do not implore you to suspend or withhold judgment of me or my work. Neither I nor my work is that important. (One cometh, another goeth.) What concerns me is the harm you are doing to yourselves. I mean by perpetuating this talk of guilt and punishment, of banning and proscribing, of whitewashing and blackballing, of closing your eyes when convenient, of making scapegoats when there is no other way out. I ask you pointblank—does the pursuance of your limited role enable you to get the most out of life? When you write me off the books, so to speak, will you find your food and wine more palatable, will you sleep better, will you be a better man, a better husband, a better father than before? These are the things that matter—what happens to *you,* not what you do to *me.*

I know that the man in the dock is not supposed to ask questions, he is there to answer. But I am unable to regard myself as a culprit. I am simply "out of line." Yet I am in the tradition, so to say. A list of my precursors would make an impressive roster. This trial has been going on since the days of Prometheus. Since before that. Since the days of the Archangel Michael. In the not too distant past there was one who was given the cup of hemlock for being "the corrupter of youth." Today he is regarded as one of the sanest, most lucid minds that ever was. We who are always being arraigned before the bar can do no better than to resort to the celebrated Socratic method. Our only answer is to return the question.

There are so many questions one could put to the Court, to any Court. But would one get a response? Can the Court of the Land ever be put in question? I am afraid not. The judicial body is a sacrosanct body. This is unfortunate, as I see it, for when issues of grave import arise the last court of reference, in my opinion, should be the public. When justice is at stake responsibility cannot be shifted to an elect few without injustice resulting. No Court could function if it did not follow the steel rails of precedent, taboo and prejudice.

I come back to the lengthy document representing the decision of the Oslo Town Court, to the tabulation of all the infractions of the moral code therein listed. There is something frightening as well as disheartening about such an indictment. It has a medieval aspect. And it has nothing to do with justice. Law itself is made to look ridiculous. Once again let me say that it is not the courts of Oslo or the laws and codes of Norway which I inveigh against; everywhere in the civilized world there is this mummery and flummery manifesting as the Voice of Inertia. The offender who stands before the Court is not being tried by his peers but by his dead ancestors. The moral codes, operative only if they are in conformance with natural or divine laws, are not safeguarded by these flimsy dikes; on the contrary, they are exposed as weak and ineffectual barriers.

Finally, here is the crux of the matter. Will an adverse decision by this court or any other court effectively hinder the further circulation of this book? The history of similar cases does not substantiate such an eventuality. If anything, an unfavorable verdict will only add more fuel to the flames. Proscription only leads to resistance; the fight goes on underground, becomes more insidious therefore, more difficult to cope with. If only one man in Norway reads the book and believes with the author that one has the right to express himself freely, the battle is won. You cannot eliminate an idea by suppressing it, and the idea which is linked with this issue is one of freedom to read what one chooses. Freedom, in other words, to read what is bad for one as well as what is good for one—or, what is simply innocuous. How can one guard against evil, in short, if one does not know what evil is?

But it is not something evil, not something poisonous, which this book *Sexus* offers the Norwegian reader. It is a dose of life which I administered to myself first, and which I not only survived but thrived on. Certainly I would not recommend it to infants, but then neither would I offer a child a bottle of *aqua vite*. I can say one thing for it unblushingly— compared to the atom bomb, it is full of life-giving qualities.

Henry Miller

12

Extramarital Sexual Experience[1]

The mores are flexible with reference to male chastity and comparatively rigid as regards female chastity. Such a double standard in a society that frowns upon prostitution and does not, like ancient Corinth, accept hetairas (or what the French call "women of the demimonde") is, of course, contradictory. If, besides this, one reckons with the emancipation or semi-emancipation of women, the great disparity between what we preach about chastity and what we practice should come as no surprise. In the samples studied by three authoritative surveys of premarital sexual behavior (Terman, Burgess and Wallen, Kinsey) approximately 50 percent of the women among those born after 1900 had entered marriage "nonvirginal." It is reliably estimated that over 30 percent of all unmarried women between the ages of twenty-one and twenty-five have some premarital experience.

In a country such as Sweden the mores are permissive and in our country, as might be expected, very much in transition. Meanwhile we vary in our responses to these awkward revelations between titillating ourselves with the risqué and wrestling with feelings of guilt. Few rise above the level of oblique reference to examine a subject of surpassing importance in a frank and honest way. Outside of a limited circle, the causes and consequences of the disparity between precept and practice are rarely explored, even in an age which has known Havelock Ellis and Sigmund Freud, and, in its literature, no longer bans James Joyce, D. H. Lawrence,

---

[1] "Extramarital" is used here to designate all relationships outside of marriage and hence to include premarital sexual experience.

Henry Miller, and Jean Genet. It will surprise many to find this whole dimly lit world of embarrassment and evasion explored in the 1920's with engaging frankness by two renowned men who would be the first to disqualify themselves as sexologists. Nevertheless, it seems worthwhile to avail ourselves of their wisdom. It seems appropriate also to hear from lesser mortals writing in the new era of permissiveness. One of these is the retired head of our best known women's college; the other a professor of English whose interest in campus life clearly embraces more than its classroom manifestations.

MARRIAGE AND MORALS

Bertrand Russell

Many who read the following selection from Bertrand Russell's Marriage and Morals *will wish that this ruthlessly frank philosopher had limited himself to such harmless pursuits as logic, epistemology, and metaphysics. Russell is no sexologist, of course, and not an authority on marriage and the family. The volume from which the following selection is taken may well be regarded as among the less important of his works. The selection is simply offered as a sample of what one of the most profound thinkers of our time had to say about a delicate and still much neglected subject.* Marriage and Morals *was published in 1929, but there is no reason to believe that Russell would change it materially if he were writing in 1972, when at the age of 100, he will no doubt be embarking with youthful vigor on some new mission—provided he succeeds in his present one, which is to alert the world to the imminence and finality of an atomic war. Those who would savor the details of this great man's personal life are advised to read his autobiography, the first volume of which appeared in 1967. It begins with these memorable words: "Three passions, simple but overwhelmingly strong, have governed my life: the longing for love, the search for knowledge, and unbearable pity for the suffering of mankind . . . Love and knowledge, as far as they were possible, led upward toward the heavens. But always pity brought me back to earth."*

From *Marriage and Morals* by Bertrand Russell (New York: H. Liveright, 1929), pp. 125–133. Reprinted by permission of Liveright, Publishers, New York. Copyright CR 1957 by Bertrand Russell; Copyright 1929 by Horace Liveright, Inc.

In a rational ethic, marriage would not count as such in the absence of children. A sterile marriage should be easily dissoluble, for it is through children alone that sexual relations become of importance to society, and worthy to be taken cognisance of by a legal institution. This, of course, is not the view of the Church, which, under the influence of St. Paul, still views marriage rather as the alternative to fornication than as the means to the procreation of children. In recent years, however, even clergymen have become aware that neither men nor women invariably wait for marriage before experiencing sexual intercourse. In the case of men, provided their lapses were with prostitutes and decently concealed, they were comparatively easy to condone, but in the case of women other than professional prostitutes, the conventional moralists find what they call immorality much harder to put up with. Nevertheless, in America, in England, in Germany, in Scandinavia, a great change has taken place since [World War I] . . . many girls of respectable families have ceased to think it worth while to preserve their "virtue," and young men, instead of finding an outlet with prostitutes, have had affairs with girls of the kind whom, if they were richer, they would wish to marry. It seems that this process has gone farther in the United States than it has in England, owing, I think, to Prohibition and automobiles. Owing to Prohibition, it has become *de rigueur* at any cheerful party for everybody to get more or less drunk. Owing to the fact that a very large percentage of girls possess cars of their own, it has become easy for them to escape with a lover from the eyes of parents and neighbours. The resulting state of affairs is described in Judge Lindsey's books.[1] The old accuse him of exaggeration, but the young do not. As far as a casual traveller can, I took pains to test his assertions by questioning young men. I did not find them inclined to deny anything that he said as to the facts. It seems to be the case through America that a very large percentage of girls who subsequently marry and become of the highest respectability have sex experience, often with several lovers. And even when complete relations do not occur, there is so much "petting" and "necking" that the absence of complete intercourse can only be viewed as a perversion.

I cannot say myself that I view the present state of affairs as satisfactory. It has certain undesirable features imposed upon it by conventional moralists, and until conventional morality is changed, I do not see how these undesirable features are to disappear. Bootlegged sex is in fact as inferior to what it might be as bootlegged alcohol. I do not think anybody can deny that there is enormously more drunkenness among young men, and still more among young women, in well-to-do America than there was before the introduction of Prohibition. In circumventing the

---

[1] *The Revolt of Modern Youth,* 1925. *Companionate Marriage,* 1927.

law there is, of course, a certain spice and a certain pride of cleverness, and while the law about drink is being circumvented it is natural to circumvent the conventions about sex. Here, also, the sense of daring acts as an aphrodisiac. The consequence is that sex relations between young people tend to take the silliest possible form, being entered into not from affection but from bravado, and at times of intoxication. Sex, like liquor, has to be taken in forms which are concentrated and rather unpalatable, since these forms alone can escape the vigilance of the authorities. Sex relations as a dignified, rational, wholehearted activity in which the complete personality co-operates, do not often, I think, occur in America outside marriage. To this extent the moralists have been successful. They have not prevented fornication; on the contrary, if anything, their opposition, by making it spicy, has made it more common. But they have succeeded in making it almost as undesirable as they say it is; just as they have succeeded in making much of the alcohol consumed as poisonous as they assert all alcohol to be. They have compelled young people to take sex neat, divorced from daily companionship, from a common work, and from all psychological intimacy. The more timid of the young do not go so far as complete sexual relations, but content themselves with producing pro-longed states of sexual excitement without satisfaction, which are ner-vously debilitating, and calculated to make the full enjoyment of sex at a later date difficult or impossible. Another drawback to the type of sexual excitement which prevails among the young in America is that it involves either failure to work or loss of sleep, since it is necessarily connected with parties which continue into the small hours.

A graver matter, while official morality remains what it is, is the risk of occasional disaster. By ill luck it may happen that some one young person's doings come to the ears of some guardian of morality, who will proceed with a good conscience to a sadistic orgy of scandal. And since it is almost impossible for young people in America to acquire a sound knowledge of birth-control methods, unintended pregnancies are not in-frequent. These are generally dealt with by procuring abortion, which is dangerous, painful, illegal, and by no means easy to keep secret. The complete gulf between the morals of the young and the morals of the old, which exists very commonly in present-day America, has another unfortu-nate result, namely that often there can be no real intimacy or friendship between parents and children, and that the parents are incapable of helping their children with advice or sympathy. When young people get into a difficulty, they cannot speak of it to their parents without producing an explosion—possibly scandal, certainly a hysterical upheaval. The relation of parent and child has thus ceased to be one performing any useful function after the child has reached adolescence. How much more civilized are the Trobriand Islanders, where a father will say to his daughter's lover: "You sleep with my child: very well, marry her."[2]

In spite of the drawbacks we have been considering, there are great advantages in the emancipation, however partial, of young people in America, as compared with their elders. They are freer from priggery, less inhibited, less enslaved to authority devoid of rational foundation. I think also that they are likely to prove less cruel, less brutal, and less violent than their seniors. For it has been characteristic of American life to take out in violence the anarchic impulses which could not find an outlet in sex. It may also be hoped that when the generation now young reaches middle age, it will not wholly forget its behaviour in youth, and will be tolerant of sexual experiments which at present are scarcely possible because of the need of secrecy.

The state of affairs in England is more or less similar to that in America, though not so developed owing to the absence of Prohibition and the paucity of motor-cars. There is also, I think, in England and certainly on the Continent, very much less of the practice of sexual excitement without ultimate satisfaction. And respectable people in England, with some honourable exceptions, are on the whole less filled with persecuting zeal than corresponding people in America. Nevertheless, the difference between the two countries is only one of degree.

Judge Ben B. Lindsey, who was for many years in charge of the juvenile court at Denver, and in that position had unrivalled opportunities for ascertaining the facts, proposed a new institution which he calls "companionate marriage." Unfortunately he has lost his official position, for when it became known that he used it rather to promote the happiness of the young than to give them a consciousness of sin, the Ku Klux Klan and the Catholics combined to oust him. Companionate marriage is the proposal of a wise conservative. It is an attempt to introduce some stability into the sexual relations of the young, in place of the present promiscuity. He points out the obvious fact that what prevents the young from marrying is lack of money, and that money is required in marriage partly on account of children, but partly also because it is not the thing for the wife to earn her own living. His view is that young people should be able to enter upon a new kind of marriage, distinguished from ordinary marriage by three characteristics. First, that there should be for the time being no intention of having children, and that accordingly the best available birth-control information should be given to the young couple. Second, that so long as there are no children and the wife is not pregnant, divorce should be possible by mutual consent. And third, that in the event of divorce, the wife should not be entitled to alimony. He holds, and I think rightly, that if such an institution were established by law, a very

---

[2] Malinowski, *The Sexual Life of Savages,* p. 73.

great many young people, for example students at universities, would enter upon comparatively permanent partnerships, involving a common life, and free from the Dionysiac characteristics of their present sex relations. He brings evidence to bear that young students who are married do better work than such as are unmarried. It is indeed obvious that work and sex are more easily combined in a quasi-permanent relation than in the scramble and excitement of parties and alcoholic stimulation. There is no reason under the sun why it should be more expensive for two young people to live together than to live separately, and therefore the economic reasons which at present lead to postponement of marriage would no longer operate. I have not the faintest doubt that Judge Lindsey's plan, if embodied in the law, would have a very beneficent influence, and that this influence would be such as all might agree to be a gain from a moral point of view.

Nevertheless, Judge Lindsey's proposals were received with a howl of horror by all middle-aged persons and all newspapers throughout the length and breadth of America. It was said that he was attacking the sanctity of the home; it was said that in tolerating marriages not intended to lead at once to children he was opening the floodgates to legalized lust; it was said that he enormously exaggerated the prevalence of extramarital sexual relations, that he was slandering pure American womanhood, and that most businessmen remained cheerfully continent up to the age of thirty or thirty-five. All these things were said, and I try to think that among those who said them were some who believed them. I listened to many invectives against Judge Lindsey, but I came away with the impression that the arguments which were regarded as decisive were two. First, that Judge Lindsey's proposals would not have been approved by Christ; and second, that they were not approved by even the more liberal of American divines. The second of these arguments appeared to be considered the more weighty, and indeed rightly, since the other is purely hypothetical, and incapable of being substantiated. I never heard any person advance any argument even pretending to show that Judge Lindsey's proposal would diminish human happiness. This consideration, indeed, I was forced to conclude, is thought wholly unimportant by those who uphold traditional morality.

For my part, while I am quite convinced that companionate marriage would be a step in the right direction, and would do a great deal of good, I do not think that it goes far enough. I think that all sex relations which do not involve children should be regarded as a purely private affair, and that if a man and a woman choose to live together without having children, that should be no one's business but their own. I should not hold it desirable that either a man or a woman should enter upon the serious business of a marriage intended to lead to children without having had previous sexual experience. There is a great mass of evidence to show that the first experience of sex should be with a person who has previous knowledge. The sexual act in human beings is not instinctive, and apparently never has been since it ceased to be performed *a tergo*. And apart from this argument, it seems absurd to ask people to enter upon a relation intended to be lifelong, without any previous knowledge as to their sexual compatibility. It is just as absurd as it would be if a man intending to buy a house were not allowed to view it until he had completed the purchase. The proper course, if the biological function of marriage were adequately recognized, would be to say that no marriage should be legally binding until the wife's first pregnancy. At present a marriage is null if sexual intercourse is impossible, but children, rather than sexual intercourse, are the true purpose of marriage, which should therefore be not regarded as consummated until such time as there is a prospect of children. This view depends, at least in part, upon that separation between procreation and mere sex which has been brought about by contraceptives. Contraceptives have altered the whole aspect of sex and marriage, and have made distinctions necessary which could formerly have been ignored. People may come together for sex alone, as occurs in prostitution, or for companionship involving a sexual element, as in Judge Lindsey's companionate marriage, or, finally, for the purpose of rearing a family. These are all different, and no morality can be adequate to modern circumstances which confounds them in one indiscriminate total.

LOVE IN THE GREAT SOCIETY

Walter Lippmann

Over a long period Walter Lippmann has been a brilliant political analyst and commentator. Through his syndicated column and numerous books and articles he has influenced public policy in America at least as much as any living writer. The Good Society (*1937*), The Public Philosophy (*1955*), The Communist World and Ours (*1959*), The Coming Test with Russia (*1961*), *and* Western Unity and the Common

Reprinted by permission of The Macmillan Company from *A Preface to Morals* by Walter Lippmann, pp. 285–313. Copyright 1929 by The Macmillan Company; renewed 1957 by Walter Lippmann.

Market (*1962*) *are among his many works. Because in late years he has limited himself to questions of public policy— if, indeed, such an interest can be viewed as restricted—it is not always remembered that in an older work,* A Preface to Morals, *he wrote about the foundations of belief and conduct. Unlike behavior, which is the province of the psychologist, conduct is the concern of the humanist and moralist; and it is as such that Lippmann writes about sexual conduct. Although these comments were published in the same year as Russell's (*1929*), it is doubtful that Lippmann any more than Russell would find a need to change the text (except perhaps the frequency of his reference to Havelock Ellis) if he were writing it today.*

. . . In the popular mind it is immediately assumed that when morals are discussed it is sexual morals that are meant. The morals of the politician and the voter, of the shareholder and executive and employee, are only moderately interesting to the general public: thus they almost never supply the main theme of popular fiction. But the relations between boy and girl, man and woman, husband and wife, mistress and lover, parents and children, are themes which no amount of repetition makes stale. The explanation is obvious. The modern audience is composed of persons among whom only a comparatively negligible few are serenely happy in their personal lives. Popular fiction responds to their longings: to the unappeased it offers some measure of vicarious satisfaction, to the prurient an indulgence, to the worried, if not a way out, then at least the comfort of knowing that their secret despair is a common, and not a unique, experience.

Yet in spite of this immense preoccupation with sex it is extraordinarily difficult to arrive at any reliable knowledge of what actual change in human behavior it reflects. This is not surprising. In fact this is the very essence of the matter. The reason it is difficult to know the actual facts about sexual behavior in modern society is that sexual behavior eludes observation and control. We know that the old conventions have lost most of their authority because we cannot know about, and therefore can no longer regulate, the sexual behavior of others. It may be that there is, as some optimists believe, a fine but candid restraint practiced among modern men and women. It may be that incredible licentiousness exists all about us, as the gloomier prophets insist. It may be that there is just about as much unconventional conduct and no more than there has always been. Nobody, I think, really knows. Nobody knows whether the conversation about sex reflects more promiscuity or less hypocrisy. But what everybody must know is that sexual conduct, whatever it may be, is regulated personally and not publicly in modern society. If there is restraint it is, in the last analysis, voluntary; if there is promiscuity, it can be quite secret.

The circumstances which have wrought this change are inherent in modern ways of living. Until quite recently the main conventions of sex were enforced first by the parents and then by the husband through their control over the life of the woman. The main conventions were: first, that she must not encourage or display any amorous inclinations except where there was practical certainty that the young man's intentions were serious; second, that when she was married to the young man she submitted to his embraces only because the Lord somehow failed to contrive a less vile method of perpetuating the species. All the minor conventions were subsidiary to these; the whole system was organized on the premise that procreation was the woman's only sanction for sexual intercourse. Such control as was exercised over the conduct of men was subordinate to this control over the conduct of women. The chastity of women before marriage was guarded; that meant that seduction was a crime, but that relations with "lost" or unchaste women was tolerated. The virtuous man, by popular standards, was one who before his marriage did not have sexual relations with a virtuous woman. There is ample testimony in the outcries of moralists that even in the olden days these conventions were not perfectly administered. But they were sufficiently well administered to remain the accepted conventions, honored even in the breach. It was possible, because of the way people lived, to administer them.

The woman lived a sheltered life. That is another way of saying that she lived under the constant inspection of her family. She lived at home. She worked at home. She met young men under the zealous chaperonage of practically the whole community. No doubt, couples slipped away occasionally and more went on than was known or acknowledged. But even then there was a very powerful deterrent against an illicit relationship. This deterrent was the fear of pregnancy. That in the end made it almost certain that if a secret affair were consummated it could not be kept secret and that terrible penalties would be exacted. In the modern world effective chaperonage has become impracticable and the fear of pregnancy has been virtually eliminated by the very general knowledge of contraceptive methods. The whole revolution in the field of sexual morals turns upon the fact that external control of the chastity of women is becoming impossible.

. . . . liberal reformers have . . . been urging for the removal of prohibitory laws [on birth control] and they have built their case on two main theses. They have argued, first, that the limitation of births was sound public policy for economic and eugenic reasons; and second, that it was necessary to the happiness of families, the health of mothers, and the welfare of children. All these reasons may be unimpeachable. I think they are. But it was idle to pretend that the dissemination of this knowledge, even if legally confined to the instruction of married women by licensed physicians, could be kept from the rest of the adult population. Obviously that which all married couples are permitted to know every one is bound to know. Human curiosity will make that certain. Now this is what the Christian churches, especially the Roman Catholic, which oppose contraception on principle, instantly recognized. They were quite right. They were quite right, too, in recognizing that whether or not birth control is eugenic, hygienic, and economic, it is the most revolutionary practice in the history of sexual morals.

For when conception could be prevented, there was an end to the theory that woman submits to the embrace of the male only for the purpose of procreation. She had to be persuaded to cooperate, and no possible reason could be advanced except that the pleasure was reciprocal. She had to understand and inwardly assent to the principle that it is proper to have sexual intercourse with her husband and to prevent conception. She had, therefore, to give up the whole traditional theory which she may have only half-believed anyway, that sexual intercourse was an impure means to a noble end. She could no longer believe that procreation alone mitigated the vileness of cohabiting with a man, and so she had to change her valuation and accept it as inherently delightful. Thus by an inevitable process the practice of contraception led husbands and wives to the conviction that they need not be in the least ashamed of their desires for each other.

But this transvaluation of values within the sanctity of the marital chamber could hardly be kept a secret. What had happened was that married couples were indulging in the pleasures of sex because they had learned how to isolate them from the responsibilities of parenthood. When we talk about the unconventional theories of the younger generation we might in all honesty take this fact into account. They have had it demonstrated to them by their own parents, by those in whom the administering of the conventions is vested, that under certain circumstances it is legitimate and proper to gratify sexual desire apart from any obligation to the family or to the race. They have been taught that it is possible to do this, and that it may be proper. Therefore, the older generation could no longer argue that sexual intercourse as such was evil. It could no longer argue that it was obviously dangerous. It could only maintain that the psychological consequences are serious if sexual gratification is not made incidental to the enduring partnership of marriage and a home. That may be, in fact, I think it can be shown to be, the real wisdom of the matter. Yet if it is the wisdom of the matter, it is a kind of wisdom which men and women can acquire by experience alone. They do not have it instinctively. They cannot be compelled to adopt it. They can only learn to believe it.

That is a very different thing from submitting to a convention upheld by all human and divine authority.

With contraception established as a more or less legitimate idea in modern society, a vast discussion has ensued as to how the practice of it can be rationalized. In this discussion the pace is set by those who accept the apparent logic of contraception and are prepared boldly to revise the sexual conventions accordingly. They take as their major premise the obvious fact that by contraception it is possible to dissociate procreation from gratification, and therefore to pursue independently what Mr. Havelock Ellis calls the primary and secondary objects of the sexual impulse. They propose, therefore, to sanction two distinct sets of conventions: one designed to protect the interests of the offspring by promoting intelligent, secure, and cheerful parenthood; the other designed to permit the freest and fullest expression of the erotic personality. They propose, in other words, to distinguish between parenthood as a vocation involving public responsibility, and love as an art, pursued privately for the sake of happiness.

As a preparation for the vocation of parenthood it is proposed to educate both men and women in the care, both physical and psychological, of children. It is proposed further that mating for parenthood shall become an altogether deliberate and voluntary choice: the argument here is that the duties of parenthood cannot be successfully fulfilled except where both parents cheerfully and knowingly assume them. Therefore, it is proposed, in order to avert the dangers of love at first sight and of mating under the blind compulsion of instinct, that a period of free experimentation be allowed to precede the solemn engagement to produce and rear children. This engagement is regarded as so much a public responsibility that it is even proposed, and to some extent has been embodied in the law of certain jurisdictions, that marriage for parenthood must be sanctioned by medical authority. In order, too, that no compulsive considerations may determine what ought to be a free and intelligent choice, it is argued that women should be economically independent before and during marriage. As this may not be possible for women without property of their own during the years when they are bearing and rearing children, it is proposed in some form or other to endow motherhood. This endowment may take the form of a legal claim upon the earnings of the father, or it may mean a subsidy from the state through mothers' pensions, free medical attention, day nurseries, and kindergartens. The principle that successful parenthood must be voluntary is maintained as consistently as possible. Therefore, among those who follow the logic of their idea, it is proposed that even marriages deliberately entered into for procreation shall be dissoluble at the will of either party, the state intervening only to insure the economic security of the offspring. It is proposed, furthermore, that where women find the vocation of motherhood impracticable for one reason or another, they may be relieved of the duty of rearing their children.

Not all of the advanced reformers adopt the whole of this program, but the whole of this program is logically inherent in the conception of parenthood as a vocation deliberately undertaken, publicly pursued, and motivated solely by the parental instincts.

The separate set of conventions which it is proposed to adopt for the development of love as an art have a logic of their own. Their function is not to protect the welfare of the child but the happiness of lovers. It is very easy to misunderstand this conception. Mr. Havelock Ellis, in fact, describes it as a "divine and elusive mystery," a description which threatens to provide a rather elusive standard by which to fix a new set of sexual conventions. But baffling as this sounds, it is not wholly inscrutable, and a sufficient understanding of what is meant can be attained by clearing up the dangerous ambiguity in the phrase "love as an art."

There are two arts of love and it makes a considerable difference which one is meant. There is the art of love as Casanova, for example, practiced it. It is the art of seduction, courtship, and sexual gratification: it is an art which culminates in the sexual act. It can be repeated with the same lover and with other lovers, but it exhausts itself in the moment of ecstasy. When that moment is reached, the work of art is done, and the lover as artist "after an interval, perhaps of stupor and vital recuperation" must start all over again, until at last the rhythm is so stale it is a weariness to start at all; or the lover must find new lovers and new resistances to conquer. The aftermath of romantic love—that is, of love that is consummated in sexual ecstasy—is either tedium in middle age or the compulsive adventurousness of the libertine.

Now this is not what Mr. Ellis means when he talks about love as an art. "The act of intercourse," he says, "is only an incident, and not an essential in love." Incident to what? His answer is that it is an incident to an "exquisitely and variously and harmoniously blended" activity of "all the finer activities of the organism, physical and psychic." I take this to mean that when a man and woman are successfully in love, their whole activity is energized and victorious. They walk better, their digestion improves, they think more clearly, their secret worries drop away, the world is fresh and interesting and they can do more than they dreamed that they could do. In love of this kind sexual intimacy is not the dead end of desire as it is in romantic or promiscuous love, but periodic affirmation of the inward delight of desire pervading an active life. Love of this sort can grow; it is not, like youth itself, a moment that comes and is gone and remains only a memory of something which cannot be recovered. It can grow because it has something to grow upon and to grow with; it is not contracted and stale because it has for its object, not the mere relief of physical tension, but all the objects with which the two lovers are concerned. They desire their worlds in each other, and therefore their love is as interesting as their worlds and their worlds are as interesting as their love.

It is to promote unions of this sort that the older liberals are proposing a new set of sexual conventions. There are, however, reformers in the field who take a much less exalted view of the sexual act, who regard it, indeed, not only as without biological or social significance, but also as without any very impressive psychological significance. "The practice of birth control," says Mr. C. E. M. Joad, for example, "will profoundly modify our sexual habits. It will enable the pleasures of sex to be tasted without its penalties, and it will remove the most formidable deterrent to irregular intercourse." For birth control "offers to the young . . . the prospect of shameless, harmless, and unlimited pleasure." But whether the reformers agree with Mr. Ellis that sexual intimacy is, as he says, a sacrament signifying some great spiritual reality, or with Mr. Joad that it is a harmless pleasure, they are agreed that the sexual conventions should be revised to permit such unions without penalties and without any sense of shame.

They ask public opinion to sanction what contraception has made feasible. They point out that "a large number of the men and women of to-day form sexual relationships outside marriage—whether or not they ultimately lead to marriage—which they conceal or seek to conceal from the world." These relationships, says Mr. Ellis, differ from the extramarital manifestations of the sexual life of the past in that they do not derive from prostitution or seduction. Both of these ancient practices, he adds, are diminishing, for prostitution is becoming less attractive and, with the education of women, seduction is becoming less possible. The novelty of these new relations, the prevalence of which is conceded though it cannot be measured, lies in the fact that they are entered into voluntarily, have no obvious social consequences, and are altogether beyond the power of law or opinion to control. The argument, therefore, is that they should be approved, the chief point made being that by removing all stigma from such unions, they will become candid, wholesome, and delightful. The objection of the reformers to the existing conventions is that the sense of sin poisons the spontaneous goodness of such relationships.

The actual proposals go by a great variety of fancy names such as free love, trial marriage, companionate marriage. When these proposals are examined it is evident they all take birth control as their major premise, and then deduce from it some part or all of the logical consequences. Companionate marriage, for example, is from the point of view of the law, whatever it may be subjectively, nothing but a somewhat roundabout way of saying that childless couples may be divorced by mutual consent. It is a proposal, if not to control, then at least to register publicly, all sexual unions, the theory being that this public registration will abolish shame and furtiveness and give them a certain permanence. Companionate marriage is frankly an attempt at a compromise between marriages that are difficult to dissolve and clandestine relationships which have no sanction whatever.

The uncompromising logic of birth control has been stated more clearly, I think, by Mr. Bertrand Russell than by anyone else. Writing to Judge Lindsey during the uproar about companionate marriage, Mr. Russell said:

> I go further than you do: the things which your enemies say about you would be largely true of me. My own view is that the state and the law should take no notice of sexual relations apart from children, and that no marriage ceremony should be valid unless accompanied by a medical certificate of the woman's pregnancy. But when once there are children, I think that divorce should be avoided except for very grave cause. I should not regard physical infidelity as a very grave cause and should teach people that it is to be expected and tolerated, but should not involve the begetting of illegitimate children—not because illegitimacy is bad in itself, but because a home with two parents is best for children. I do not feel that the main thing in marriage is the feeling of the parents for each other; the main thing is cooperation in bearing children.

In this admirably clear statement there is set forth a plan for that complete separation between the primary and secondary function of sexual intercourse which contraception makes possible.

It is one thing, however, to recognize the full logic of birth control and quite another thing to say that convention ought to be determined by that logic. One might as well argue that because automobiles can be driven at a hundred miles an hour the laws should sanction driving at the rate of a hundred miles an hour. Birth control is a device like the automobile, and its inherent possibilities do not fix the best uses to be made of it.

What an understanding of the logic of birth control does is to set before us the limits of coercive control of sexual relations. The law can, for example, make divorce very difficult where there are children. It could, as Mr. Bertrand Russell suggests, refuse divorce on the ground of infidelity. On the other hand the law cannot effectively prohibit infidelity, and as a matter of fact does not do so to-day. It cannot effectively prohibit fornication though there are statutes against it. Therefore, what Mr. Russell has done is to describe accurately enough the actual limits of effective legal control.

But sexual conventions are not statutes, and it is important to define quite clearly just what they are. In the older world they were rules of conduct enforceable by the family and the community through habit, coercion, and authority. In this sense of the word, convention tends to lose force and effect in modern civilization. Yet a convention is essentially a theory of conduct and all human conduct implies some theory of conduct. Therefore, although it may be that no convention is any longer coercive, conventions remain, are adopted, revised, and debated. They embody the considered results of experience: perhaps the experience of a lonely pioneer or perhaps the collective experience of the dominant members of a community. In any event they are as necessary to a society which recognizes no authority as to one which does. For the inexperienced must be offered some kind of hypothesis when they are confronted with the necessity of making choices: they cannot be so utterly open-minded that they stand inert until something collides with them. In the modern world, therefore, the function of conventions is to declare the meaning of experience. A good convention is one which will most probably show the inexperienced the way to happy experience.

Just because the rule of sexual conduct by authority is dissolving, the need of conventions which will guide conduct is increasing. That, in fact, is the reason for the immense and urgent discussion of sex throughout the modern world. It is an attempt to attain an understanding of the bewilderingly new experiences to which few men or women know how to adjust themselves. The true business of the moralist in the midst of all this is not to denounce this and to advocate that, but to see as clearly as he can into the meaning of it, so that out of the chaos of pain and happiness and worry he may help to deliver a usable insight.

It is, I think, to the separation of parenthood as a vocation from love as an end in itself that the moralist must address himself. For this is the heart of the problem: to determine whether this separation, which birth control has made feasible and which law can no longer prevent, is in harmony with the conditions of human happiness.

Among those who hold that the separation of the primary and secondary functions of the sexual impulse is good and should constitute the major premise of modern sexual conventions, there are, as I have already pointed out, two schools of thought. There are the transcendentalists who believe with Mr. Havelock Ellis that "sexual pleasure, wisely used and not abused, may prove the stimulus and liberator of our finest and most exalted activities," and there are the unpretentious hedonists who believe that sexual pleasure is pleasure and not the stimulus or liberator of anything important. Both are, as we say, emancipated: neither recognizes the legitimacy of objective control unless a child is born, and both reject as an evil the traditional subjective control exercised by the sense of sin. Where they differ is in their valuation of love.

Hedonism as an attitude toward life is, of course, not a new thing in the world, but it has never before been tested out under such favorable conditions. . . . There is now a generation in the world which is approaching middle age. They have exercised the privileges which were won by the iconoclasts who attacked what was usually called the Puritan or Victorian tradition. They have exercised the privileges without external restraint and without inhibition. Their conclusions are reported in the latest works of fiction. Do they report that they have found happiness in their freedom? Well, hardly. Instead of the gladness which they were promised, they seem . . . to have found the wasteland. . . .

If you start with the belief that love is the pleasure of a moment, is it really surprising that it yields only a momentary pleasure? For it is the most ironical of all illusions to suppose that one is free of illusions in contracting any human desire to its primary physiological satisfaction. Does a man dine well because he ingests the requisite number of calories? Is he freer from illusions about his appetite than the man who creates an interesting dinner party out of the underlying fact that his guests and he have the need to fill their stomachs? Would it really be a mark of enlightenment if each of them filled his stomach in the solitary and solemn conviction that good conversation and pleasant companionship are one thing and nutrition is another?

This much the transcendentalists understand well enough. They do not wish to isolate the satisfaction of desire from our "finest and most exalted activities." They would make it "the stimulus and the liberator" of these activities. They would use it to arouse to "wholesome activity all the complex and interrelated systems of the organism." But what are these finest and most exalted activities which are to be stimulated and liberated? The discovery of truth, the making of works of art, meditation and insight? Mr. Ellis does not specify. If these are the activities that are meant, then the discussion applies to a very few of the men and women on earth. For the activities of most of them are necessarily concerned with earning a living and managing a household and rearing children and finding recreation. If the art of love is to stimulate and liberate activities, it is these prosaic activities which it must stimulate and liberate. But if you idealize the logic of birth control, make parenthood a separate vocation, isolate love from work and the hard realities of living, and say that it must be spontaneous and carefree, what have you done? You have separated it from all the important activities which it might stimulate and liberate. You have made love spontaneous but empty, and you have made home-building and parenthood efficient, responsible, and dull.

What has happened, I believe, is what so often happens in the first enthusiasm for a revolutionary invention. Its possibilities are so dazzling that men forget that inventions belong to man and not man to his inventions. In the discussion which has ensued since birth control became generally feasible, the central confusion has been that the reformers have tried to fix their sexual ideals in accordance with the logic of birth control instead of the logic of human nature. Birth control does make feasible this dissociation of interests which were once organically united. There are undoubtedly the best of reasons for dissociating them up to a point. But how completely it is wise to dissociate them is a matter to be determined not by saying how completely it is possible to dissociate them, but how much it is desirable to dissociate them.

All the varieties of the modern doctrine that man is a collection of separate impulses, each of which can attain its private satisfaction, are in fundamental contradiction not only with the traditional body of human wisdom but with the modern conception of the human character. Thus in one breath it is said in advanced circles that love is a series of casual episodes, and in the next it transpires that the speaker is in process of having himself elaborately psychoanalyzed in order to disengage his soul from the effects of apparently trivial episodes in his childhood. On the one hand it is asserted that sex pervades everything and on the other that sexual behavior is inconsequential. It is taught that experience is cumulative, that we are what our past has made us and shall be what we are making of ourselves now, and then with bland indifference to the significance of this we are told that all experiences are free, equal, and independent.

It is not hard to see why those who are concerned in revising sexual conventions should have taken the logic of birth control rather than knowledge of human nature as their major premise. Birth control is an immensely beneficent invention which can and does relieve men and women of some of the most tragic sorrows which afflict them: the tragedies of the unwanted child, the tragedies of insupportable economic burdens, the tragedies of excessive child-bearing and the destruction of youth and the necessity of living in an unrelenting series of pregnancies. It offers them freedom from intolerable mismating, from sterile virtue, from withering denials of happiness. These are the facts which the reformers saw, and in birth control they saw the instrument by which such freedom could be obtained.

The sexual conventions which they have proposed are really designed to cure notorious evils. They do not define the good life in sex; they point out ways of escape from the bad life. Thus companionate marriage is proposed by Judge Lindsey not as a type of union which is inherently desirable, but as an avenue of escape from corrupt marriages on the one hand and furtive promiscuity on the other. The movement for free divorce comes down to this: it is necessary because so many marriages are a failure. The whole theory that love is separate from parenthood and home-building is supported by the evidence in those cases where married couples are not lovers. It is the pathology of sexual relations which inspires the reformers of sexual conventions.

There is no need to quarrel with them because they insist upon remedies for manifest evils. Deep confusion results when they forget that these remedies are only remedies, and go on to institute them as ideals. It is better, without any doubt, that incompatible couples should be divorced and that each should then be free to find a mate who is compatible. But the frequency with which men and women have to resort to divorce because they are incompatible will be greatly influenced by the notions they have before and during marriage of what compatibility is, and what it involves. The remedies for failure are important. But what is central is the conception of sexual relations by which they expect to live successfully.

They cannot—I am, of course, speaking broadly—expect to live successfully by the conception that the primary and secondary functions of sex are in separate compartments of the soul. I have indicated why this conception is self-defeating and why, since human nature is organic and experience cumulative, our activities must, so to speak, engage and imply each other. Mates who are not lovers will not really cooperate, as Mr. Bertrand Russell thinks they should, in bearing children; they will be distracted, insufficient, and worst of all they will be merely dutiful. Lovers who have nothing to do but love each other are not really to be envied; love and nothing else very soon is nothing else. The emotion of love, in spite of the romantics, is not self-sustaining; it endures only when the lovers love many things together, and not merely each other. It is this understanding that love cannot successfully be isolated from the business of living which is the enduring wisdom of the institution of marriage. Let the law be what it may be as to what constitutes a marriage contract and how and when it may be dissolved. Let public opinion be as tolerant as it can be toward any and every kind of irregular and experimental relationship. When all the criticisms have been made, when all supernatural sanctions have been discarded, all subjective inhibitions erased, all compulsions abolished, the convention of marriage still remains to be considered as an interpretation of human experience. It is by the test of how genuinely it interprets human experience that the convention of marriage will ultimately be judged.

The wisdom of marriage rests upon an extremely unsentimental view of lovers and their passions. Its assumptions, when they are frankly exposed, are horrifying to those who have been brought up in the popular romantic tradition of the Nineteenth Century. These assumptions are that, given an initial attraction, a common social background, common responsibilities, and the conviction that the relationship is permanent, compatibility in marriage can normally be achieved. It is precisely this that the prevailing sentimentality about love denies. It assumes that marriages are made in heaven, that compatibility is instinctive, a mere coincidence, that happy unions are, in the last analysis, lucky accidents in which two people who happen to suit each other happen to have met. The convention of marriage rests on an interpretation of human nature which does not confuse the subjective feeling of the lovers that their passion is unique, with the brutal but objective fact that, had they never met, each of them would in all probability have found a lover who was just as unique. . . .

This is the reason why the popular conception of romantic love as the meeting of two affinities produces so much unhappiness. The mysterious glow of passion is accepted as a sign that the great coincidence has occurred; there is a wedding and soon, as the glow of passion cools, it is discovered that no instinctive and preordained affinity is present. At this point the wisdom of popular romantic marriage is exhausted. For it proceeds on the assumption that love is a mysterious visitation. There is nothing left, then, but to grin and bear a miserably dull and nagging fate, or to break off and try again. The deep fallacy of the conception is in the failure to realize that compatibility is a process and not an accident, that it depends upon the maturing of instinctive desire by adaptation to the whole nature of the other person and to the common concerns of the pair of lovers.

The romantic theory of affinities rests upon an immature theory of desire. It springs from an infantile belief that the success of love is in the satisfactions which the other person provides. What this really means is that in child-like fashion the lover expects his mistress to supply him with happiness. But in the adult world that expectation is false. Because nine-tenths of the cause, as Mr. Santayana says, are in the lover for one-tenth that may be in the object, it is what the lover does about that nine-tenths which is decisive for his happiness. It is the claim, therefore, of those who uphold the ideal of marriage as a full partnership, and reject the ideal which would separate love as an art from parenthood as a vocation, that in the home made by a couple who propose to see it through, there are provided the essential conditions under which the passions of men and women are most likely to become mature, and therefore harmonious and disinterested.

They need not deny, indeed it would be foolish as well as cruel for them to underestimate, the enormous difficulty of achieving successful marriages under modern conditions. For with the dissolution of authority and compulsion, a successful marriage depends wholly upon the capacity of the man and the woman to make it successful. They have to accomplish wholly by understanding and sympathy and disinterestedness of purpose what was once in a very large measure achieved by habit, necessity, and the absence of any practicable alternative. It takes two persons to make a successful marriage in the modern world, and that fact more than doubles its difficulty. For these reasons alone the modern state ought to do what it would none the less be compelled to do: it ought to provide decent ways of retreat in case of failure.

But if it is the truth that the convention of marriage correctly interprets human experience, whereas the separatist conventions are self-defeating, then the convention of marriage will prove to be the conclusion which emerges out of all this immense experimenting. It will survive not as a rule of law imposed by force, for that is now, I think, become impossible. It will not survive as a moral commandment with which the elderly can threaten the young. They will not listen. It will survive as the dominant insight into the reality of love and happiness, or it will not survive at all. That does not mean that all persons will live under the convention of marriage. As a matter of fact in civilized ages all persons never have. It means that the convention of marriage, when it is clarified by insight into reality, is likely to be the hypothesis upon which men and women will ordinarily proceed. There will be no compulsion behind it except the compulsion in each man and woman to reach a true adjustment of his life.

It is in this necessity of clarifying their love for those who are closest to them that the normal problems of the new age come to a personal issue. It is in the realm of sexual relations that mankind is being schooled amidst pain and worry for the novel conditions which modernity imposes. It is there, rather than in politics, business, or even in religion, that the issues are urgent, vivid, and inescapable. It is there that they touch most poignantly and most radically the organic roots of human personality. And it is there, in the ordering of their personal attachments, that for most men the process of salvation must necessarily begin.

For disinterestedness in all things, as Dean Inge says, is a mountain track which the many are likely in the future as in the past to find cold, bleak, and bare: that is why "the road of ascent is by personal affection for man." By the happy ordering of their personal affections they may establish the type and the quality and the direction of their desires for all things. It is in the hidden issues between lovers, more than anywhere else, that modern men and women are compelled, by personal anguish rather than by laws and preachments or even by the persuasions of abstract philosophy, to transcend naive desire and to reach out towards a mature and disinterested partnership with their world.

THE DAY I SPOKE OFF THE CUFF TO THE GIRLS OF VASSAR

Sarah Gibson Blanding

Miss Blanding headed Vassar, probably the best known of America's colleges for women, for eighteen years, retiring in 1964. In 1962 she spoke to a campus assembly in response to a request from the student government that she clarify a statement in the college catalogue that "The College expects every student to uphold the highest standards." Her answer caused unexpected reverberations on campuses throughout

---

From *McCall's* (November 1962), p. 91 ff. Reprinted by permission of the publisher.

> *the country, including her own, where 52 percent of 1,040*
> *students expressed disagreement with Miss Blanding's state-*
> *ment that premarital sex relations constitute "offensive and*
> *vulgar behavior" and her advice that students who differed*
> *should withdraw. Significantly, 40 percent of those who voted*
> *agreed with Miss Blanding, although 81 percent believed that*
> *sex morals are a personal matter of concern to the college*
> *only if its name were brought into public disrepute.*

Recently, with no advance warning, Vassar College hit the head-lines from coast to coast. In April, at a college assembly, I spoke of the standards of behavior expected of Vassar students. I laid it on the line that the college does not condone and will not tolerate the excessive use of alcohol, premarital sexual indulgence, or offensive, vulgar conduct on the part of students, at Vassar or away from the campus. My remarks were in response to a request from student officers for a definition of the handbook statement that students are expected to maintain the highest standards of behavior. For a century, it had not occurred to a president of a college such as Vassar that there was any need to make explicit what I, too, had thought was implicit. What I said was an off-the-cuff, straightforward expression of my belief that the young woman who drinks to excess or engages in premarital sexual relationships is not living up to the highest standards of behavior. I advised those students who did not wish to comply with decent standards of conduct to withdraw from college.

No news releases were thought of for this entirely intramural assembly, which, to be sure, rocked the campus. However, several weeks later the student newspaper, reporting campus reaction, both positive and negative, fell into the hands of a New York newspaper. The fat was in the fire, and a wild fire it has been. Vassar and I made headlines across the country and abroad. Columns of newsprint in dailies and weeklies brought Vassar to the public eye. Cartoonists, columnists, and editorial writers deplored, satirized, and applauded. Other college presidents were variously put on the spot by their alumni (ae), students, parents of students, and the press. And the mail poured into my office. There were hundreds and hundreds of letters, a few critical of my stand, some deploring the type of publicity, a handful of crackpot epistles, including anti-Communist or pro- or antisegregation literature, and even one that related my stand to the fluoridation of water. But the bulk of the mail went into what my secretary refers to as "The Applaud File."

A touching, misspelled, sincere letter from the wife of a long-haul truck driver told of her fears for her talented daughter, who had just earned a splendid college scholarship. An anonymous unmarried mother, whose state-university career had been interrupted by pregnancy, spoke of her heartache. Young mothers who had precipitously left college for early, forced marriages wrote of their frustration at finding themselves trapped in situations they had not intended to invite. Lawyers, doctors, and clergymen told of the increasing number of tragic and perplexing cases of young people who are caught in the philosophy of freedom of experimentation—a freedom that too often lacks the concomitant of responsibility.

Nineteenth-century morality, much of which may be outdated, is anathema to some leaders of the present college generation. But twentieth-century morality is confused, and the college freshman finds herself without guidelines except those provided by apparently sophisticated, popular, self-assured classmates or upperclassmen. Attractive young men met as blind dates on college weekends are persuasive in confirming any philosophy of "experimentation." The immature and anxious-to-please freshman who dreads nothing so much as "not being invited," "not being popular," not being like some of the self-appointed campus leaders, can easily become involved in a sexual affair. In too many instances, once the barriers of anxiety and reserve have been overcome and an affair has occurred, its repetition becomes easy, even casual. The step from the casual to the promiscuous is a short one. Chastity and virginity are no longer carefully guarded virtues. The pendulum has swung a long way from Hawthorne's *The Scarlet Letter* to Miller's *Tropic of Cancer*.

Our culture is built around the monogamous family unit, sanctified by Hebraic-Christian tradition. I believe that it is the responsibility of parents and educators to prepare young people to live within this cultural framework, not as something that is repressive and imprisoning, but as a background for creative development and responsible freedom. The Kinsey report to the contrary, I believe that premarital sexual relationships, especially if casual or promiscuous, set the stage for later extramarital relationships, which weaken or destroy family life. I believe, further, that premarital chastity on the part of young women is conducive to the stability of marriage.

Conscience and moral attitudes are individual matters. Conduct and behavior—except for someone alone on an island—are not. A college has the responsibility and the right to lay down ground rules for the behavior of the young people who are voluntarily enrolled.

It is easy to forget that late teenagers know considerably less than they think they do. The perspective of youth is necessarily limited, and prestige, popularity, romance, sex, passion, and love are easily and frequently confused.

The decision between right and wrong for the individual is not always black or white. There are many subtle grays. Decisions reached by the liberally educated should be wise in terms of immediate goals and in terms of future consequences, both for the individual and for those affected by his or her actions. A college's first responsibility is to offer an excellent education, so that its graduates will be prepared to reach sensitive, independent decisions, based on considered values. I believe that the undergraduate has the right to access to knowledge in all fields, including that of human relations, marriage, and sex. The mature, independent individual may hold to whatever values seem best to him. He may conduct himself as he sees fit, provided that what he does does not injure or threaten any other individual—adult or child.

But the highest standards of behavior referred to in the handbooks and matriculation pledges of most colleges and universities are not subject to the same subtle individual interpretation as one's personal code of moral values. They are a reflection of the best of our cultural traditions, modified gradually and thoughtfully in terms of changing social needs and conditions. Vassar College intends to uphold these traditions and to play a continuing role in seeking and instituting changes where changes are needed for the benefit of both society and individual students. I, for one, do not accept self-indulgence and moral laxity, however well rationalized, as a desirable direction of change. I know that the overwhelming majority of the undergraduates at Vassar, as well as their parents and the alumnae, support this stand.

I hope that the unsolicited publicity will serve a useful purpose. I hope that young women entering college here and elsewhere will regard matriculation pledges as meaningful. I hope that young people will succeed in escaping the slavery of dependence on the dictates of their contemporaries as a means of achieving popularity and prestige. I hope they will recognize that alcoholic and sexual indulgence are not manifestations of adult independence. Man, unlike any other species, does not need to learn only from personal experience.

SEX: THE QUIET REVOLUTION

David Boroff

Mr. Boroff writes frequently about university life and is the author of Campus, U.S.A. *(1961). He is an associate professor of English at New York University.*

What has happened to sex during the last fifteen years? Among those over thirty-five, there is a feeling, half-envious and half-appalled, that

---

From *Esquire* (July 1961), p. 96 ff. Reprinted by permission of Esquire, Inc.
© 1961 by Esquire, Inc.

the younger generation is calmly but insatiably erotic. What was tense sexual melodrama twenty years ago seems to be little more than reflex action today. If the sophisticated young are no longer agitated about sex, it is because sex is no longer a problem for them. We appear to be living through a sexual revolution. It is a quiet revolution—not a rebellion— without ideological fireworks or flamboyance or protest.

The nature of the change-over was expressed by a man in his thirties who recently spent a year at Harvard. "During the day," he re-called, "you never saw a couple on campus holding hands. Yet you knew damn well that these same kids were quietly having affairs." And there is the editor in his early forties who remarked about one of his charges, a talented novelist of twenty-six: "When . . . and I discuss ideas, I feel I have to pin up his diapers; but when we talk about sex, I feel he has to pin up mine."

If a new sex ethic is beginning to crystallize, it is the culmination of the efforts of a long line of sex libertarians—from Wilhelm Reich through Henry Miller to Norman Mailer and the Beats. Norman Brown, author of *Life Against Death,* is only the last of the champions of a freer sexuality. Dr. Brown, whose revaluation of Freud has been widely dis-cussed in intellectual circles, sees in present society the dominion of death-in-life. He calls for the "resurrection of the body," for "erotic exuberance," and for an end to repression. Significantly, many of the official custodians of our culture are beginning to be influenced by such ideas. Lionel Trilling describes Brown's book as "one of the most interesting and valuable books of our time." And Norman Podhoretz, the editor of *Commentary* who just a few years ago derogated the Beats, is now a fervid proponent of Mailer's talent and hipster ideas.

The New Freedom even gains qualified support from liberal church people. Dr. Roger Shinn, who teaches a course in "The Christian Meaning of Sex" in the Union Theological Seminary, summed up the position of liberal Protestantism: "A good deal of the old repressiveness is gone— what we generally associate with the word puritanism. Arising out of Biblical scholarship of the last twenty years is the recognition that the Bible's attitude toward sex is affirmative and that the repressive attitude is actually a heresy. Sex is God-given, and man realizes himself through it. Simultaneously, we have been influenced by the psychological studies that many clergymen now engage in. There is no longer the feeling that the true meaning of sin is sexual. However, the real meaning of the sexual en-counter is still the commitment expressed through marriage vows."

During the last dozen years, there have been some striking changes in American culture with implications for sexual behavior. There has been a loosening in restraints about language. The vindication of the right to distribute *Lady Chatterley's Lover* through the post office was merely a legal consolidation of a development which has been obvious to many people. World War II opened the floodgates of language. In *The Naked and the Dead* Mailer used the familiar four-letter words, but prissily modified. Then James Jones, in *From Here to Eternity,* employed the idiom of the barracks without disguise and won a National Book Award. When James Gould Cozzens, hardly a literary insurgent, used plain Anglo-Saxon diction in *By Love Possessed,* the forces of conservatism were in full retreat. At the Post Office Department hearings for *Lady Chatterley's Lover,* critic Malcolm Cowley sounded the obsequies for the old restrictions: "There are a certain number of short Anglo-Saxon words for bodily functions that were regarded as a secret language of men. These words were used in the smoking room, in the barroom, in the barbershop, but no woman was supposed to know them unless she was an utterly degraded woman. . . . There is no more secret language of males. That has been abolished."

It is perhaps more accurate to say that women have been admitted to the club. Language that a respectable woman would not permit herself to hear years ago, much less use, is now the lingua franca of the sexes. One can hear the newly liberated idiom at cocktail parties, in plays, and even, occasionally, in that most circumspect of media, television. (*The Iceman Cometh* was *not* bowdlerized for TV presentation.) And plain Anglo-Saxon language has even gained a tenuous handhold in academia. A number of professors all around the country who have invited poets to give readings have listened in stunned silence to naked utterance, while wondering nervously what the Dean would say about all this.

Our culture today is highly sexualized. We see it in changing culture heroes. The late Clark Gable, the archetypal hero of the Thirties and Forties, was unquestionably virile, but an ingenuous boy scout in comparison with the stridently phallic movie heroes of today. Even James Dean, who set the new vogue, for all his dark and moody sensitivity, had a kind of sullen but demanding eroticism. And if Marlon Brando is inarticulate it is because his arrogant sexuality clearly announces his intentions. We have been inundated in movies, each one bolder than the next, so that titillation no longer titillates. And in the publishing world, sleazy paperbacks compete with each other in a gaudy Olympiad of sex and sadism. But, contrary to vulgar opinion, it takes more than sex to make a best seller. This merely proves that the sexual beachheads have been achieved, the campaigns won, and the old battle cries no longer rouse. It is only in an atmosphere of repression that lasciviousness can provide kicks. And there are even those who deplore the passing of the delicious pleasures of the Forbidden.

For many, sex is the last arena of adventure in the quasi-welfare state in which we now live. The old dramas have subsided into silence. Sex, according to David Riesman, is the last frontier of our culture. In an era of affluence and muffled sensibilities, "sex provides a kind of defense against the threat of total apathy. . . . [The other-directed person] looks to it for reassurance that he is alive."

In a very real sense, sex is the politics of the Sixties. There was a vivid demonstration of that last February when Norman Mailer gave a reading at the Poetry Center in New York City. He started out tamely enough reading an excerpt from a magazine piece; then, in an atmosphere of mounting excitement, he began to read short verse selections, some of which could be regarded as obscene. Showing a mock solicitude for the squares in the audience, he said he would "semaphore" if a selection he was about to read would jar their sensibilities. He was wagging his arms before reading his seventh or eighth selection when the curtain came down; the management of the Poetry Center decided they had done enough for one evening to advance the cause of freedom. For a while, it looked as if there might be trouble. Many of the young people in the audience, for whom Mailer oozes *charisma,* were hurling imprecations at the weak-kneed guardians of public morality. It was only after Mailer came out, in duffel coat and mischievous smile, and asked them to leave to show their "discipline" that the crowd grumblingly dispersed. . . .

The ascendancy of psychology in our time has given the new sex ethic a solid intellectual underpinning. According to Philip Rieff, author of *Freud: The Mind of the Moralist,* the New Man is psychological man who substitutes health values for moral values. "Freud," says Rieff, "can conceive of a person's feeling guilty not because he has been bad, but because, as a result of his repressions, he is too moral. This is one source of his influence: his diagnosis that we are sick from our ideals and that the one practical remedy lies in an infusion from below." It is clear that sex and sex pleasure are obligatory today. Dr. Albert Ellis, a psychologist who has written extensively about sex, recently remarked: "Instead of coming with problems of guilt about sex, my patients express concern if they don't enjoy it, or if they're fearful or shy."

How much change in sex behavior has there been? Nobody really knows. But one thing is certain: attitudes towards sex among those who grew up after World War II—those under thirty in other words—are strikingly different from those of earlier generations. It can be summed up in this way: Sex is one of life's principal goods. The degree of pleasure one derives from it is a measure of one's self-realization. And since the old moral sanctions have lost much of their authority, there is far less reluctance about premarital sex. In fact, Dr. Ellis reveals that when he lectures on sex before college students, there is almost invariably a wild cheer when he endorses premarital sex. Before World War II, to be a virgin was good; today, after a certain age, it is bad. The loss of chastity is no longer the fall from innocence; it is the fall upwards, so to speak, to maturity and self-fulfillment. . . .

But this does not mean that carnal anarchy prevails. Young people acknowledge the claims of society. Early marriages constitute one imposing piece of evidence for this. The ethos of the under-thirty generation is that sex is fine—nay, indispensable—but it has to be validated either by love or by a steady relationship. This was borne out by the Kinsey Report which revealed that although about half the women interviewed had premarital coitus, forty-six per cent of this group had relations only with their fiancés. And in a recent study of college youth only two per cent of the girls had intercourse with acquaintances, six per cent with friends (men they knew well, but did not love), and seventeen per cent with lovers.

What we have, in other words, is a shift from the old-fashioned double standard—sex is fine for men, but not for women—to a modified single standard. The old sexual serfdom is dead or dying. Sex is being democratized. Confronting the new sexual freedom for women, a college boy I talked with said: "I'm in favor of it—with reservations. You figure that, one time or another, a girl was in love and had an affair. But I wouldn't want to marry a girl who had too many affairs." Another young man, determinedly egalitarian, said: "I can't condemn a girl for having sex. She has the same feelings I have." He pondered the implications of this for a moment: "You know, I say all this, but I'm not sure I really believe it."

Among girls, there is a range of attitudes from the girl who chanted with horror, "If a girl has sex before she is married, she is ruined!" to the twenty-four-year-old worldling who said haughtily, "In my milieu I don't know any virgins." A mainstream response was that of the girl who said: "I used to think it was terrible if people had intercourse before marriage. Now I think each person should find his own values. And if they won't suffer and feel guilty, why not?" But among sophisticated young women there is a cheerful appropriation of sex which is remarkably masculine in tone. "You feel that you can't really communicate with a virgin," a graduate of a good woman's college remarked. "You want to talk about your current affair—it's not true that girls don't share confidences with each other—and you can't with an inexperienced girl." . . .

Despite their sexual divagations, sophisticated girls are as fierce about marriage as their less-venturesome sisters. It's just that their time-table is arranged differently. Marriage for them comes later, after a few discreet, developmental affairs. "The same girls who may be terribly sophisticated and have one affair after another," a psychoanalyst remarked, "still want to marry and have families." And Professor William Barrett of New York University, author of *Irrational Man,* remarked: "There may be a new freedom, but women are different from men. After a while, the sexual bravado of even the most sophisticated woman disappears. Men are interested in sex, but women are interested in curtains and babies."

But . . . amid evidence of greater permissiveness, there are un-answered questions. What about the quality of sex experience? And where are we headed?

There are the beginnings of a second stage in the new sex ethos. If sex is good, then perhaps it's always good—and the more the better. This may account for the sex predators that some girls complain of—the males who make perfunctory overtures as a kind of reflexive gesture of malehood, Dr. Margaret Mead had some harsh things to say about youthful behavior: "We have jumped from puritanism to lust. The breakdown of the double standard means that all girls—not just bad girls—are fair game today. The average college boy is an unprincipled wolf. The reason they stick so close to their dates at college parties is that they won't trust their girls with their friends, since they don't really trust themselves."

Then, here is another corollary. If sex is good—the basic premise of our culture—then perhaps *all* kinds of sex are good. We encounter this in some of the evangelists of a richer, freer sexuality. For example, Paul Goodman, the brilliant author of *Growing Up Absurd,* was recently asked his view of premarital sex by a college student. "In sex, anything you get pleasure from is good," he said peremptorily. "And that's all there is to it." . . .

But serious students of sex are generally agreed about one thing: the sexual freedom we now have is spurious. Dr. Sandor Lorand, an eminent psychiatrist, said soberly: "The reason youth is on a rampage is that we now have a sexual freedom which does not free." And Dr. Alexander Lowen, a Reichian analyst, said: "Superficially, sexual sophisti-cation is increasing, but on an unconscious level there is almost the same measure of guilt and anxiety as in the past. Sociologist Ernest van den Haag talks of the gap between our verbal culture and our actual sex sophis-tication. Some New York college girls use a blunt acrostic, Nato, which stands for "No action—talk only!"

Dr. Roger Shinn, the Protestant clergyman cited earlier, also took a measured view of the new freedom. "The so-called emancipation," he observed, "has led some people to adopt a hurrah-for-sex attitude. I'm prepared to say hurrah-for-sex too, but it doesn't solve very much. Sex can be an expression of love, or it can be a form of exploitation. We must start with a post-Victorian appreciation of sex, but we must also be aware of its corruptions."

And even among the sophisticates, there is the feeling that surely there must be more to it than this. Pleasure is not enough. Sexual health is not enough. Instead of relieving anxiety, today's sex culture compounds it. For in addition to residual Puritan guilt and anxiety, there is the new pressure that both men and women feel to be sexually omnicompetent.

With the new erotic hedonism, people are constantly appraising their sexual performance.

"Among women," Dr. Douglas Spencer said, "there is a tremendous concern about orgasm. They ask themselves, 'Am I missing something?' And this tension actually blocks orgasm. There used to be a time when women hardly knew about these matters. Now it's become a goal, like a Diners' Club credit card. They lose sight of the real joy—even the humor of sex."

For the man, the sexual virtuosity demanded of him may have something to do with the asserted increase in homosexuality. In other words, some precariously poised males may be scared out of heterosexuality by the very demands made upon them. And today sexual pressure is increased by the fact that men can define their masculinity through their sexual role alone as the occupational, social, and even sartorial space between the sexes narrows.

Turn-of-the-century sports, for example, defined their masculinity through jobs, masculine dress, and all-male recreations. In the brothels which they frequented nobody measured their potency. And their wives had to pretend an indifference to sex—and an ignorance of it—in the same fashion that women today have to simulate ardor and appreciation.

What is the impact of the New Freedom on marriage? Very little thus far. We seem to be moving toward increasing premarital sex freedom, but with the same tight restraints after marriage. This is startlingly similar to the pattern of most primitive cultures. According to Charles Rolo, the author of a forthcoming book about the impact of psychoanalysis on our culture, the psychological revolution is responsible for this.

"Premarital sexual freedom no doubt derives from the influence of psychoanalysis. The psychological revolution placed a premium on sex as hygiene. However, as applied to marriage, psychoanalysis is a conservative influence. In marriage, you don't use adultery as hygiene. We disapprove, on psychological grounds, of the Don Juan and the nymphomaniac. We perceive their pathology all too clearly."

In short, the institution of marriage is well-armored. A Westport, Connecticut, resident pointed out that a single man who turns up for a week end in the company of a girl with whom he is having an affair provokes no comment, "but there would be hell to pay if he went off into the bushes with someone's wife." The only marked development, according to most observers, is that when infidelity occurs it is less likely today to break up a marriage. The couple is more likely to sit down and explore psychologically what is wrong with their relationship.

Sex is still a vast, mysterious country. Freud and Kinsey are perhaps the Livingstone and Stanley of this dark continent. Only one thing is certain: at a time of the swiftest technological change in the history of mankind, it would be naïve to expect sexual mores to stand comfortably

still. That our institutions have shown so much survival power is astonishing. But only a reckless prophet would predict the shape of things to
come.

SEX, MY DAUGHTERS, AND ME

Midge Decter

*Midge Decter's writings have appeared in numerous na-
tional magazines. She is a senior editor at* Harper's *and the
mother of four children. She writes from the angle of a
sophisticated and articulate mother not given to banalities and
stale homilies but obviously beset by indecision.*

My adolescent daughters are, as they have been brought up to be,
my "friends." I have two, and they are very different people indeed; but
what I have to say about them here applies equally to both. We discuss
together the day's events in school and office. We gossip together, within
understood limits, about our respective friends. We share a common pride
in the accomplishments, and a common irritation at the naughtinesses, of
the two youngest children in the family. We tell one another jokes—frequently off-color. We trade cosmetics and minor articles of clothing. I am
as likely to seek out their advice in affairs of shopping and dress as they are
mine.

In our talks, to be sure, we are never exactly equals: I know a
good deal more than they about just those things they are most eager to
know, and have far freer access to that big world they are so eager to enter,
while they on their side hold all the secrets to that which most disquiets
me; still we all manage most of the time not to be too patronizing. I
sometimes think them superior to me, as they sometimes think me to them.
And to some extent I envy them, as they do me.

Of course, friendship does not truly define the relationship between
us. What defines it—for after all we are mother and daughters—is a

---

Reprinted from *Harper's Magazine* (August 1967) by permission of the
author.

struggle for power. When the friendliness cracks, as it does with a fair though not permanently disruptive regularity, it is this struggle which stands nakedly revealed beneath. Now, no one of my age and circumstance—a member of what sociologists would call the professional, or educated, middle class in the second half of the twentieth century—can possibly conceal from himself the Freudian implications of this relationship. In fact, no one of my age and circumstance can even mention the subject without being conscious of the idea that a mother and her daughter constitute a primary sexual rivalry. Such indeed, then, must be the case between my daughters and me; how would I, even if I were inclined to, deny it? Nevertheless, that which two of us *experience* as the issue between us in any given hour of battle has far less to do with why we must, at bottom, be contenders than with a whole lot of questions nearer the surface of things. A dispute may arise over something so trivial as the condition of their room, or something so principled as the allocation of their time between work and play, or even something so stark as their choice of friends. These questions, too, boil down to one: the power we struggle for is power over their respective destinies. At least for now, and presumably for the next few years, what is at stake between us is quite simply the fact that they are dependent on me. And I wish them to be and not to be, and they wish to be and not to be.

The struggle is for them an unequal one. For at the moment, anyway, I have the big guns on my side. I have their past record of helplessness and error to use against them and shake their confidence; I have, at least when pushed to an extreme, the unshakable conviction of my right to exercise power; and above all, I have control over money. Their only weapons are to wound with the spectacle of their unhappiness or to hold themselves resisting and out of earshot. These can be very potent weapons—if they were not, all children would be helpless and all parents serene—but they are defensive ones.

Such disadvantages in a relation of power my daughters have in common with every dependent in every age, clime, and culture. They suffer from certain others, however, peculiar to such young girls as have been brought up in their kind of life. For my daughters are supremely children of their time. Whatever their individualities, they are also very much the products of those spiritual pretensions by which their enlightened parents, like all enlightened parents of this generation, chose to bring up their children. In short, they must suffer the great hindrance to growing up of being their mother's friends.

Apart from the emotional burden our casual intimacy places upon them—a burden about which the psychologists have now, too late, a great deal of wisdom to proffer—this intimacy acts as a practical and political handicap of very real dimensions. For it is not merely trite to say the young are trusting. And above all they trust to the appearances of things. Thus in our condition of friendship, an attack of motherhood upon either of them is apt to come quite suddenly and unprepared for. A casual revelation on one of their parts might become the occasion for a far from casual response on mine. Or I might take them nine-tenths of the way through a discussion or story which is proving to be of the keenest interest and then refuse to go on, overcome by some squeamishness or fastidiousness I had not realized was working inside my nerves; within a single sentence, perhaps, they will have become "too young" to hear what their mother has not heart to utter.

Most of all, they are bereft of the defense of thinking me utterly stupid. They may think so now and then, on this point or that, but they have no really solid base in thought or feeling from which to resist me. Just as they have been brought up from earliest infancy on the assumption that they were being "understood"—this time with sympathy, that time with harshness, but with understanding always—so, too, it has been assumed that they "understand" me. Simple stupidity has never been one of the terms between us. Mothers like me do not believe their children to be incompetent. This may in fact be the prime axiom of our kind of parenthood. We take care to know at every moment of our children's development what the attainments of that moment ought properly to be and make our demands accordingly. (A good deal of fun has been poked at us for this, for we are the comic ladies who sit on park benches poring over our volumes of Spock and Gesell and Bettelheim. But the fun has usually been poked by people who are not entitled to it, by the people who think we ought to respect our children *more;* when what we are really doing is seeking out the widest range of possibilities to offer our children our respect.) And since we do not treat them as incompetents, they have no fund of experience from which in later years to retaliate.

Note, for example, the terms of the current adolescent rebellion against people like us. We are accused of being deficient in love, not simple enough, too adept at making our way, too successful. It is not that we know too little of the world—the major accusation of our own adolescence against our parents—but too much. They do not strive to alter our definition of reality, for no matter what they say, they acknowledge our competence to do the defining; they simply repudiate "reality" altogether, putting the word into inverted commas with, among other things, hallucinogens. As it happens, my own daughters' relation to the current intellectual and social fashions among their rebelling cohorts is—so far—that of only fairly sympathetic onlookers. So far I have succeeded in spoiling the idea of direct participation for them. Which is to say, I have managed to talk them out of it.

And talk is of the essence. We happen to do a great deal of it in our house; for us as a family it is recreation, tool, and means of survival. But not only by the particular accident of birth are my daughters surrounded by talk. For all children like them, words constitute a kind of postnatal amniotic fluid in which they grow and are both sheltered from and introduced to their surroundings. On the most primitive level for such children words have taken the place of physical violence as a means of instruction and discipline. They have also by and large replaced that network of instructions and disciplines called "punishment." To be hampered from pursuing a noxious or harmful activity is to be "told no." Being the denizens of city or suburb, the children discover the world around them primarily by a process of giving names to things. Their hours of solitude are spent alone with the speech of others, in the form of books, television, radio.

The schools in which they spend such a large proportion of the waking hours of their childhood are, of course, veritable waterfalls, floods, volcanos of words, phrases, clauses, sentences, paragraphs. As you might expect, my daughters have gone only to "good" schools—that is to say, the most benign, most attentive, most enriching schools that were available. Thus they have not only been instructed by means of their teachers' use of language, they have also been taught through perfecting their own manipulation of language—in other words, to uncover what might be in their own minds by discussing it aloud. In such schools, the desire to fail can be fulfilled merely by keeping silent. As, indeed, can the desire to fail at home.

The society of the enlightened, then, does not beat or drive its children, does not drill them, but rather nags them, into growing up. And the measure of the children's progress along this path is their capacity to nag in turn.

The point about talk is not whether it is a good way or a bad way to bring up the young. As parents have gone—and as societies have gone—the attempt on the part of my contemporaries to give their children certain physical and social freedoms, to confront and harness for good some of their baser impulses, to help them reason their way toward being civilized, to befriend them, seems not so very malign. We are of course doomed by the absurdity of our pretensions—for naturally we are incapable of permitting our children all those things we pretend to permit them. And we are far from being so pure of motive as we imagined—for motives are never pure between adults and the young. Still, we are, I should think, no more pretentious or self-deceived than our own parents, and very likely a good deal less. In any event, my daughters and their friends seem to me far more attractive, more open, and a good deal nicer than I remember myself and my friends in adolescence.

In some ways, however, they seem to me less fortunate than we were. For the point about talk is that it sets up a competition in which the children, particularly the children of the educated and enlightened, must lose.

Once upon a time, or so I imagine, children could manage their powerlessness by biding their time. They could, if they wanted to be comfortable, obey the rules, and in the face of some unwanted imposition from the authorities or some supposed injustice, take to their closets. Their corporeal selves might be rendered up to Caesar but their thoughts—undoubtedly of future vengeance—they could keep to themselves.

But my daughters have no means of retreat from the barrages of those bigger than they: not into the street and not into the closet. The wider world of school and playmates only confirms *me,* for what I have given them of speech is precisely that which best enables them to get along there. The books they read *I* have placed into their hands (even the dirty books with which they and their friends while away so many exciting, secretive hours they have taken from my shelves, where they stand in full view). Their imaginative life is one that I as a companionable mother once encouraged and helped them to invent. Nor are their hiding places of any use, for I understand and even condone their behavior in taking to them. I am, as it were, huddled inside with them.

And if either of them stands and fights, she naturally loses. I know more words than she, and they are bigger words, more impressive. I can make them do such miraculous and unanswerable things as describe an irony, create an analogy, or cite an apposite witticism. I can dazzle her with words, amuse her against her will with them, distract her, frighten her, expose her motives, analyze her character, justify myself with words, and if need be, simply drown her in them. I can—one of the tricks of friendship—seduce her into answering and use what she says as a new supply of grist for my unending mill. Only pure rage can stop the flow. But my daughters, poor things, are not yet enough in command of themselves to produce that merciful condition in me without being already in the grip of it themselves.

So they have no recourse but to meet me on my own ground. It is a predicament from which only the distance and privacy of adulthood can rescue them.

But I, too, am caught in a predicament. Because when I speak to them, I often contradict myself. To the mothers who were trained as I was—by the Freudian precept that children's personalities are shaped not by what used to be called "upbringing" but by the quality of those family relationships into which they enter at birth—our children represent a total responsibility. We do not believe ourselves charged primarily with keeping them healthy and properly sheltered and teaching them the manners of the society into which we will one day send them. We believe ourselves rather to be the very creators of their psyches, their personalities, and above all, their capacities for success and happiness. What such a responsibility demands of us is something more than undying love, more even than wisdom—it demands that we know what is right and what is needed. This is a responsibility I am hardly able to undertake consistently or gracefully for myself, much less for these nearly-grown female creatures who stand opposite me. They naturally do not ask it of me—at least not any longer. But this is the way of our relationship. Without it, I should have to turn away from them. It is too late to go back now.

Thus I contradict myself. I do not always feel what I think; I do not always think what I feel. Or rather, I belie myself—since it is my usual custom to tell them what I think (the words for thought come easier than those for feelings) and only indicate to them, so desperately unfairly, by my sudden passions what I feel.

Nowhere are my contradictions more evident, nor undoubtedly more painful to them, than in dealing with the problem of sex. This problem is about the last genuine one left to the transaction between us. Not that we do not struggle over other things, but we have nothing new to say to one another about these: they have learned what they have learned from me, I have failed them where I have failed them, the rest is for the most part now up to them and fate.

Sex, however, is another matter. As a real issue it is just now coming up in their lives—that is, becoming something they are required to *do* something about. And they are still young enough to ask me, some-times—usually indirectly—what they should do. And I find myself wishing to the very bottom of my being that they would not.

They ask me, I think, for several reasons. First of all, because they are frightened. Such a to-do is made of sex in these days of the new, supposedly freer attitudes toward it that we are probably succeeding in making it as great a mystery to the young as it was in the era when "leg" was a dirty word: a mystery of a different kind, perhaps, now no longer shrouded in evil but partaking in some of those qualities of quest and conquest of the Holy Grail. In any case, it is partly their timidity that drives my daughters to seek the word of the Authorities, for the comfort, either way, of a denial or of permission.

They also ask me for the simple reason that they believe I know a good deal about the subject. They have not been permitted to assume about me—as the children of my generation, say, permitted ourselves to assume about our parents—that I live in ignorance (in both senses) of sex. I have not permitted it by the conversation, my own and that of my friends, which I have allowed to go on in their presence. I have not permitted it, either, by my style of dress, of behavior, of being. They ask me, too, because to do so is a way, and a very effective way, I might add, of announcing to me that they will one of these days be no longer my satellites but my equals.

But most of all, they ask me because they are too innocent of the danger I represent to them. Like all children raised in the advanced and liberal way, their sophistication and worldliness are streaked with an almost incredible naïveté. This naïveté does not have to do with facts, and certainly not with any of the actual facts of sex, about which they and their friends have a fund of knowledge more complete and accurate than that of many adults I know. Nor have they, since the years of fairly early childhood, acquired any of these facts from me; though once learned, they have often taken pleasure in discussing them with me (out of the desire to show off rather than for information). In fact, had they, as the textbooks recommend, come to me for all this information, they might have found out many of my reluctances in the matter a whole lot sooner. Nor is their naïveté psychological exactly—though its effects on me are clearly psychological—for as I said earlier, they understand me rather well. I suppose their innocence would have to be called spiritual.

Anyway, it has to do with the trust that my seeming openness as a mother has bred in them—so early and so thoroughly that all the disappointments they must have suffered have not served to make them appropriately wary. Our children, so wise to the world in other ways, have very little left of the child's genius for duplicity. They are bad liars and ineffective sneaks. We have deprived them of their natural and indispensable talent for keeping their secrets secret, and with it, of a certain insight into the nature of the dangerous or forbidden.

When I was my daughters' age, I knew exactly how much, for both our sakes, it was necessary for my mother to know about my own personal confrontation with sex: namely, nothing. My daughters have considerably more leeway than that; there, perhaps, is the rub. Sex as a subject is profoundly interesting to people like me. We think about it a great deal, wonder at it a great deal, and discuss it only somewhat less. We are amused by it as a phenomenon, find it comical, take it immensely seriously. We would, if we could, like to know how everyone we see around us conducts himself with respect to sex. And, if it would not entail a psychic monstrosity that no amount of self-deception could keep hidden, we would even like to know precisely how our own daughters and their friends conduct themselves. In short, like the highly emancipated persons we are, our minds are totally the creatures of the most fashionable currents of the culture that surround them.

Yet my daughters, too, are restricted, if not in what they may ask, then in what they may expect to receive an answer to. They are restricted by the intensity with which I wish they wouldn't ask me. All their questions, regardless of how they are put or whether the girls know it or not, can only be directed to one end: ought they, now or in the near future, to engage in sexual relations with one or another young man? And the truth of the matter is, I do not know how to answer.

My uncertainty, to be sure, does not take the form of a simple expression of uncertainty. It takes the form, rather, of a series of confident statements which contradict, supersede, or override one another—or which sometimes simply evade the point. I may, for instance, deride some display of sexual priggishness on the part of a relative, a teacher, or their head-master—on this occasion planting myself foursquare on the side of the legitimate erotic expression of the children. I may at some other time, and not apparently apropos of them at all, find myself delivering a rather brutal lecture on the horrors of premarital pregnancy—attacking first the criminal immorality of the official posture by which proper contraception and legal abortion are kept out of the reach of young girls, and in the next breath, the criminal irresponsibility of the same young girls in surrendering themselves to something they have not first learned to manage. Or I may, in the name of civilization and decency, take up the cudgels for the boys, attempting to make my daughters aware of the acute suffering inflicted on their male contemporaries by the self-involved experimentation with their powers, i.e., the teasing, of the girls. One of the things I say to them—and naturally it is the one I have the strongest sensation of conviction about—is simply mean: that the adolescent love affairs I have seen do not seem to me to be emotional and sexual adventures at all but, on the contrary, a series of enormous cop-outs. That is, I say, they seem to me to entail nearly all the commitments of marriage, dulling in people so young, and far from providing a wider range of experience, they are actually protecting their participants from having to undergo too much experience. How this must translate to my daughters' discerning and simplifying ears, of course, is: Even if you have sex, it won't be any good.

This particular piece of cruelty to them is not mine alone. In somewhat different (and as I fancy, in far less subtle and clever) form, it represents the defense of an entire generation against the implications underlying its own sexual liberation. If you begin as we all did with the proposition that lust is not only natural but life-giving and good, and if you travel the path from there straight and true, you arrive at complete sexual promiscuity. Lust as an independent value divorces itself from institutions, personal relations, and travels with utter unconcern from creature contact to creature contact. This is, as a matter of fact, exactly how the Puritans understood the matter, and they were right. We understand it, too, in the pits of our stomachs if not in our minds, and scurry about to improvise our excuses. We do not want to be promiscuous, for if lust is simple, the other major human passions—vanity, pride, acquisitiveness—are not. Our mar-riages barely survive so much of frankness about our desires as we already allow ourselves; and being unmarried is for us an agony of rushing about to stake our claims. And if we do not want promiscuity for ourselves, we will certainly never be able to bear it in our children.

What we want for ourselves and them is to hold on to our imagin-ings of complete sexual abandon and at the same time maintain the kind of emotional requirements which make such abandon impossible for us. The most notable of our excuses for this is one derived at two removes from a vulgarization of Freud. To wit: a mentally healthy and mature person seeks in sex the deepening and enrichment of an already and otherwise satisfying connection. Sexual conquest as an end in itself is "unhealthy"; in girls it is a mark of self-devaluation, and in boys, of "Don Juanism." On the other hand, an affair with one person undertaken out of curiosity or in a spirit of fun is emotionally irresponsible and therefore "immature." Thus while we promise our children a satisfaction that we had to wrest for ourselves, we nevertheless do our best to block their easy passage to it.

To be sure, we make no point of their having to be married. All of us, I believe, have settled, whether we admit it or not, with the idea that our children will have at least some sex experience before marriage. But we have only retreated to a nearer line of defense. The sex experience they have, in order for them not to earn our opprobrium, must be to some purpose. It must be good in itself, it must improve their lives, it must make them better people. And naturally, it must not end in pregnancy. As for myself, I might wish for the further condition that it take place without either my knowledge or complicity.

I ask too much, I know that. We all do. We always have. But then too much was asked of us, and of our parents, and will be of our grandchildren.

This whole problem is in the end really not my daughters', but mine. They will suffer the cruelties of this alternating titillation and denial that has been their introduction to sex and, like the rest of us, if they are tough enough, or brave enough, or lucky enough, they will prevail. But what will be for them their experience and their life will be for me always the record of my inability as a parent to stand behind that person whose face I had so long ago chosen to show to the world. Not that having such a record is necessarily bad, but the chastening seems to have seeped into every corner of my life. My daughters' education at my hands has turned out to be a far profounder one of me at theirs.

13

Homosexuality

Britain's relaxation of its laws against homosexuality, recent disclosures (some of them at least partly misleading) of an unexpectedly high incidence of homosexuality, and the trend toward permissiveness and frankness in the discussion of once forbidden topics have all combined to increase interest in homosexuality and the problems it poses. For the student of ethics (and legal philosophy) an exploration of the general issues raised by these problems will prove more rewarding than an examination of the phenomenon itself.

The specific problems and the general questions they suggest are exasperatingly perplexing. To what extent is the homosexual a product of nature and therefore incorrigible, or a product of nurture and therefore possibly amenable to correction or "cure"? If homosexuals are such by choice, even though only in the sense that they persist in practices (and a way of life) that could be changed through counsel or treatment, how are they to be judged morally? When we remind ourselves that homosexuals were not subject to ridicule, censure, or legal sanctions in ancient Greece,[1] we may ask to what extent the adverse moral judgment that still generally prevails in our society is culturally conditioned.

---

[1] Aristophanes' *The Frogs* suggests the opposite, as far as ridicule is concerned. The homosexuality popular among Athens' upper classes and reflected in Plato's dialogues (*vide,* the *Charmides* and *Symposium*) was not shared by the poorer classes and was borrowed from Sparta where homosexuality was encouraged as a military virtue.

Our society is not exceptional, it may be noted; nearly all societies have condemned homosexuality.

Homosexuals are referred to as sex deviants in our society. Does this imply a pathological condition, whether physical or psychological, and hence an illness or disease, as Freud suggested in a widely quoted "Letter to an American Mother," or simply a behavioral departure or personality variation from the normal? But what is the "normal"? It is not the opposite of the pathological, since in a society of chain-smokers where nearly everyone was afflicted with lung cancer that would be normal—at least in one sense. Is it simply action in conformity with rules (whether or not embodied in laws) which are supported by a strong consensus and largely obeyed in practice, so that departure from them is deviance? Or is there some standard of health, which, like healthy lungs and unlike rules, is independent of any fiat, from which homosexuality is a deviation?

Finally, to what extent ought society to ban and invoke legal sanctions against practices which, whether moral or immoral, involve only consenting adults and result in no harm to others (except in the tenuous sense that one who "takes offense" is thereby "harmed")?

Many of these issues came to the fore when the British parliament, in December 1966, adopted a controversial recommendation of its now famous Wolfenden Committee and removed the legal ban against homosexual relations in private between consenting adults. Overwhelmingly defeated ten years earlier, the bill encountered only token opposition on its final passage. In the United States only Illinois has legalized private acts. With the exception of West Germany, all major European countries have eased the restrictions on deviates.

An ancillary problem, of special interest to the student of literary criticism, is suggested by the prominence of homosexuals among authors, especially playwrights. To what extent does their deviancy influence what they have to say? If, as might be argued, the intent is to get revenge on the "straight" world from which homosexuals are excluded by denigrating and deriding heterosexual love, should the work be judged by reference to its source and its concealed, possibly subconscious, motive, or strictly on its "merits"?

Of the three readings, the first, by an able scientific observer, is primarily descriptive, although by no means morally aloof. The other two represent brilliantly argued opposing sides of the great debate precipitated by the Wolfenden Report over the role of law in regulating morals, an issue in jurisprudence which far transcends in importance the narrower question of passing judgment on homosexuality as such.

CRIMES WITHOUT VICTIMS

Edwin M. Schur

Edwin M. Schur is a sociologist and teaches at Tufts University. He is a graduate of the London School of Economics, where he received his Ph.D. and also has a law degree from the Yale Law School. Dr. Schur is Associate Editor of the journal Social Problems *and, in addition to the volume from which the following selections have been taken, has written* Narcotic Addiction in Britain and America: The Impact of Public Policy *(1962), and edited* The Family and the Sexual Revolution *(1964).*

Psychiatrist Robert Lindner has succinctly criticized some widely accepted yet inadequate definitions of homosexuality. As Lindner states, a very popular definition is based on overt appearance and mannerisms—that is, the homosexual is conceived of as a person who looks and acts like a member of the opposite sex. Actually, this is an erroneous notion. Although some homosexuals do adopt some mannerisms typical of the opposite sex, there is no simple correlation between effeminacy and homosexuality or between masculinism and lesbianism. Both scientific studies and informal accounts by participants in homosexual life confirm that the most obvious types comprise but a tiny percentage of all sexual deviants. In fact, blatant displays of effeminacy are viewed with scorn by many male homosexuals; similarly, in some cases it may be an exaggerated display of masculinity that makes one man an object of sexual desire for another. Reporting on some observations of homosexuality in New York City, a journalist recently expressed his strong surprise that so few of the men he saw dancing with one another in "gay" (i.e., homosexual) bars "looked" homosexual.

From Edwin M. Schur, *Crimes without Victims: Deviant Behavior and Public Policy, Abortion, Homosexuality, Drug Addiction,* pp. 69 ff. © 1965. Reprinted by permission of Prentice-Hall, Inc., Englewood Cliffs, New Jersey.

A second misleading definition of homosexuality Lindner describes as "pseudoscientific and statistical." According to this approach, one could examine the sort of data presented in the Kinsey report (for example, cumulative incidence figures for various types of sexual activities) and classify as homosexual those individuals reporting a certain frequency of homosexual activities. Lindner asserts that such statistics confuse "outlet with inclination, activity with psychic tendency." They do not, for example, take into account whether other sexual outlets were available, or whether the activities engaged in were really satisfying to the participants. Lindner concludes that the term *homosexual* should be applied only to "those individuals who more or less chronically feel an urgent sexual desire toward, and a sexual responsiveness to, members of their own sex, and who seek gratification of this desire predominantly with members of their own sex." As he goes on to comment, this definition recognizes inversion as "an attitude basic to the personality wherein it resides, as a compulsion with all the urgency and driving energy that account for its persistence despite the obvious disadvantages of homosexuality as a way of life." The Church of England Moral Welfare Council, in its statement to the Wolfenden Committee, similarly sought to distinguish between isolated homosexual acts and homosexuality as a basic sexual condition or inclination:

> Although most males and females exhibit that decided propensity toward members of the complementary sex which is rightly regarded as normal and natural in human beings, it is incontestable that a minority display an equally marked orientation toward members of the same sex.

Homosexuality, then, can—and often does—take the form of a basic personality orientation rather than a particular type of sexual activity. An alternative definition, suggested by Erving Goffman, would limit the term *homosexual* to "individuals who participate in a special community of understanding wherein members of one's own sex are defined as the most desirable sexual objects, and sociability is energetically organized around the pursuit and entertainment of these objects." This definition has the merit of focusing on a collective or socially structured aspect of the problem which . . . is extremely important. However, given the possibility that legal policy may significantly reinforce or even indirectly generate the development of such restricted social organization and collective orientations, it would be a mistake to consider such aspects as being necessary elements in all homosexuality.

Just as there are different definitions of homosexuality, there are also highly conflicting explanations of its causes. There have long been attempts to explain homosexuality in terms of "innate" characteristics, but the results of research along these lines have been very unimpressive. According to one recent and careful report, "there is so much evidence on the side of the nurture hypothesis, and so little on the side of the nature hypothesis, that the reliance upon genetic or constitutional determinants to account for the homosexual adaptation is ill founded." It may be worth noting that such "internal" explanations have often been voiced by homosexuals themselves. This may occasionally represent an effort to find some plausible meaning for an otherwise inexplicable compulsion. On the other hand, the value for the deviant in using such statements as a defense against moral blame is obvious.

Today the view is widely accepted that homosexuality constitutes, or at least reflects, some kind of psychological disturbance. The rather vague phrase *some kind. of* is used intentionally—for there is wide variation in the particular factors emphasized by different experts. Oral fixation, castration anxiety, and numerous other psychoanalytic and psychological rubrics abound in the professional literature on homosexuality. Psychoanalytic theories tend to emphasize that adult homosexuality is rooted in childhood situations. In reporting on a recent comparison of over 100 homosexual patients with a matched group of nonhomosexual patients, a team of psychotherapists stated: "Our findings point to the homosexual adaptation as an outcome of exposure to highly pathologic parent-child relationships and early life situations." Analysts also stress that homosexuality may represent a fear of the opposite sex as much as a desire for persons of the same sex. Another key element in some explanations of male homosexuality has been the concept of a flight from masculinity, an actual or feared inability to live up to male-role expectations. This concept is expanded, by some of the more sociologically oriented interpreters, to relate male homosexuality generally to changing sex roles in modern Western society—that is, to formulate a structural explanation of the condition, rather than merely to uncover predisposing factors in individual cases. . . .

There is definitely no sure and simple cure for homosexuality, and the dominant view is that in most cases therapy at best can only make the patient a better-adjusted homosexual. Not surprisingly, many homosexuals insist that they are in no sense sick, and several disinterested students of the problem also have questioned the alleged invariable pathology of the homosexual. Thus Lindner has viewed homosexuality as a form of rebellion generated by the conflict between an urgent sexual drive and the repressive measures of conventional sex morality. . . .

Although there may well be more homosexuality than the average heterosexual imagines, estimates by individual homosexuals are not likely to be very accurate. Apart from their lack of systematic data, many homosexuals have a psychological stake in exaggerating their number—in order to impress nonhomosexuals that a sizable minority is being mistreated, and in order to bolster their own morale. It is also very difficult to evaluate police figures or other official statistics on homosexuality, fluctuations in which may reflect differentials in law enforcement effort or success every bit as much as they do actual variations in behavior rates.

One point on which all observers are agreed is that official statistics reflect but a fraction of the homosexual behavior that is, in fact, occurring. Most specialists also appear convinced that there has been some increase in homosexuality in recent years—though it is extremely difficult to be sure that such apparent increase is not primarily a reflection of greater research on the problem and more open consideration and discussion of the subject. . . .

Perhaps the conclusion of the Wolfenden Committee would apply equally well to the American situation—that although the amount of homosexuality might well be "large enough to present a serious problem," such behavior is "practiced by a small minority of the population, and should be seen in proper perspective, neither ignored nor given a disproportionate amount of public attention."

In line with the prevailing misconceptions regarding the appearance and overt behavior of the homosexual (and the corresponding mistaken assumption that homosexuals are easily and quickly identified), there is a widespread belief that most homosexuals are members of a particular social stratum and are engaged in a narrow range of occupations. Research has shown—and homosexuals themselves are quick to confirm —that homosexuality cuts across all boundaries of class and occupation, race and religion.

Although the discussion thus far has related largely to male homosexuality, many of the general points would apply equally well to homosexuality among females. . . .

Although it is not a crime merely to be a homosexual, all American jurisdictions (with the recent exception of Illinois) proscribe homosexual acts—among adults as well as between adults and minors, and in private as well as in public. The homosexual, in other words, has no legal outlet for the kind of sex life to which he is drawn; his only alternative to law-breaking is abstinence. Although some statutes provide separate definitions of and penalties for particular homosexual offenses, others set forth a vaguely phrased, catch-all offense. Thus the law books are full of such phrases as *unnatural crimes, the infamous crime against nature, any unnatural copulation, the abominable and detestable crime against nature with mankind or beast, unnatural intercourse,* and *any unnatural and lascivious act.* These terms obviously reflect an attitude of moral condemnation; they do not display the degree of specificity usually required in the statutory definition of crimes. . . .

The typical over-all law enforcement policy on homosexuality . . . appears to be a fairly pragmatic one. Police realize that they must, to a certain extent, adopt a live-and-let-live outlook. They act as vigorously as

possible in cases involving force or minors; furthermore, public outrage
over any type of sex crime may be an occasion for stepped-up activity
against known homosexuals and their gathering places. Although some law
enforcement personnel certainly harbor sadistic attitudes toward homosexuals, today such attitudes may not be widespread. A handbook for
plainclothesmen notes:

> In recent years the terms *fag, fairy,* and *queer* have fallen into the
> discard [*sic*] in law enforcement circles. The general term *de-
> generate* has had the same fate. The homosexual is now called a
> *sex deviate,* and *degenerate* is now used as a term to describe the
> more bestial molester of women or children.

Admittedly, the labels in themselves provide no reliable indication of
attitude, yet this change seems to reflect more than a trend toward
euphemisms. Even if the police do not engage in continual and all-out
persecution of homosexuals, however, it may be questioned (given the
relatively meager results) whether the use of policemen as decoys and for
other surveillance of homosexuals is justified—particularly when there are
more urgent social problems to which such efforts might be directed. . . .

Although legal stigmatization and harassment make the homosexual's life difficult, they rarely push him into a life of sexual abstinence.
Often, however, such pressures do significantly color his sexual and social
relationships. An important aspect of the problem of homosexuality in our
society is the development of a special homosexual subculture—not merely
the gathering together of homosexuals, but a more general culture-within-a-
culture, with its distinctive values and behavior norms, modes of speech
and dress, as well as its special patterns of interaction and social differentiation. To the extent that a homosexual immerses himself in this
subculture, he must undergo a particular socialization process. Homosexual inclination, at least where it is exclusive, may reflect a basic personality
orientation. But living as a homosexual, in the sense of the Goffman definition cited earlier, involves the learning of a special social role. This element
is suggested by the phrase *coming out,* which is used among homosexuals
to refer to "one's recognition of oneself as a homosexual or one's entrance
into the ongoing stream of homosexual life, specifically into the bar system
and the privately organized social affairs." . . .

Whether one says that many homosexuals experience shame or
guilt or both, at least it seems valid to assert that many suffer from some
form of low self-esteem. Such poor self-acceptance relates partly to the
very central matter of sexual identity, as such, and partly to the social
condemnation and humiliation which invariably confronts homosexuals. It
is also reinforced by the very patterns of sexual behavior to which
homosexuals are driven by the need for concealment. One-night stands and

commercial sex transactions have been said both to reflect and to increase the considerable ambivalence of the homosexual about his condition and his behavior. . . .

It is interesting that homosexual life is called "gay," but it would seem a mistake to infer from this that the invert society is a predominantly happy one. Homosexuals may feel genuine relief and some considerable pleasure in being able to drop the mask and meet with fellow inverts. Yet many observers have noted a forced gaiety in such activities, and in any case it is questionable whether the pleasurable aspects of the invert's life can often outweigh the frequent loneliness and insecurity. An informal survey among 100 male homosexuals found that while 75 per cent considered themselves generally well-adjusted, 57 per cent did admit to some adjustment difficulties, and 90 per cent reported some concern about exposure. In another study of 300 male inverts, all but a handful stated they did not want to change their own sexual orientation, but the same respondents overwhelmingly stated that they would not want their sons to be homosexuals. . . .

Conceivably one could argue that no special public policy toward homosexuality is needed at all; an individual's sexual inclinations and behavior are strictly his own business, and inversion is just one of the possible alternatives from which people can choose. This view, according to which any attempt at controlling homosexuality is uncalled for, will be acceptable to few people in our society. There is a strong and sound belief that heterosexuality is the preferable adaptation (both for society and for the individual) and that homosexuality should at least be discouraged—to the extent that discouragement is possible. Furthermore, notwithstanding differences of opinion about the degree of psychopathology involved, there is good reason to think that full inversion is not simply an alternative that some people have freely chosen.

It is not at all clear, however, just what can be done to discourage or to prevent homosexuality. Although the causes are somewhat obscure, it seems likely that major alterations of social structure and culture would be necessary in order to reduce homosexuality to any significant degree. And if it is true that inversion is on the increase, then probably the stemming or even the reversal of broad social trends would also be required. A sharpening of sex-role differentiation, and an accompanying relaxation of the multiple burdens of the male role, might be seen as helping to curb any flight from masculinity. Yet, even assuming that this would be effective and that it could somehow be encouraged by policy, the strong current of social change in the opposite direction (i.e., toward "equalizing" the roles of men and women) would be a major obstacle. Prevention in individual cases may be a more realistic goal. The sympathetic counselling of young persons who seem to be heading in the direction of homosexuality may sometimes inhibit that adaptation. If such persons are reached early enough, the likeli-

hood of success would be increased. . . . Most psychotherapists remain
pessimistic about the likelihood of effecting complete reversals of sex
orientation.

MORALS AND THE CRIMINAL LAW

Patrick Devlin

*Lord Devlin, a Fellow of the British Academy, is one of
Great Britain's most distinguished jurists. He served as Justice
of the High Court, Queen's Bench, Lord Justice of Appeal,
and, until his retirement in 1964, as Lord of Appeal in ordinary. He has written* Trial by Jury *(1956),* The Criminal
Prosecution in England *(1957),* Samples of Lawmaking
*(1962). The following selection is from a collection of lec-
tures entitled* The Enforcement of Morals *(1965), in which
Lord Devlin reverses an earlier position supporting reform of
the criminal law dealing with homosexuality.*

What is the connexion between crime and sin and to what extent,
if at all, should the criminal law of England concern itself with the enforcement of morals and punish sin or immorality as such? The statements
of principle in the Wolfenden Report provide an admirable and modern
starting-point for such an inquiry. . . .

Early in the Report the Commiteee put forward:

> Our own formulation of the function of the criminal law so far
> as it concerns the subjects of this enquiry. In this field, its function,
> as we see it, is to preserve public order and decency, to protect the
> citizen from what is offensive or injurious, and to provide sufficient
> safeguards against exploitation and corruption of others, particu-
> larly those who are specially vulnerable because they are young,
> weak in body or mind, inexperienced, or in a state of special physi-
> cal, official or economic dependence.
>
> It is not, in our view, the function of the law to intervene in

From the Maccabean Lecture in Jurisprudence read at the British Academy
on March 18, 1959; printed in the *Proceedings of the British Academy,* vol. xlv, and
reprinted in *The Enforcement of Morals* by Lord Devlin (London: Oxford University
Press, 1965). Reprinted by permission of Oxford University Press.

the private lives of citizens, or to seek to enforce any particular pattern of behaviour, further than is necessary to carry out the purposes we have outlined.

The Committee preface their most important recommendation

that homosexual behaviour between consenting adults in private should no longer be a criminal offence, [by stating the argument] which we believe to be decisive, namely, the importance which society and the law ought to give to individual freedom of choice and action in matters of private morality. Unless a deliberate attempt is to be made by society, acting through the agency of the law, to equate the sphere of crime with that of sin, there must remain a realm of private morality and immorality which is, in brief and crude terms, not the law's business. To say this is not to condone or encourage private immorality.

Similar statements of principle are set out in the chapters of the Report which deal with prostitution. No case can be sustained, the Report says, for attempting to make prostitution itself illegal. The Committee refer to the general reasons already given and add: 'We are agreed that private immorality should not be the concern of the criminal law except in the special circumstances therein mentioned.' They quote with approval the report of the Street Offences Committee, which says: 'As a general proposition it will be universally accepted that the law is not concerned with private morals or with ethical sanctions.' It will be observed that the emphasis is on *private* immorality. By this is meant immorality which is not offensive or injurious to the public in the ways defined or described in the first passage which I quoted. In other words, no act of immorality should be made a criminal offence unless it is accompanied by some other feature such as indecency, corruption, or exploitation. This is clearly brought out in relation to prostitution: 'It is not the duty of the law to concern itself with immorality as such . . . it should confine itself to those activities which offend against public order and decency or expose the ordinary citizen to what is offensive or injurious'.

I must disclose at the outset that I have as a judge an interest in the result of the inquiry which I am seeking to make as a jurisprudent. As a judge who administers the criminal law and who has often to pass sentence in a criminal court, I should feel handicapped in my task if I thought that I was addressing an audience which had no sense of sin or which thought of crime as something quite different. Ought one, for example, in passing sentence upon a female abortionist to treat her simply as if she were an unlicensed midwife? If not, why not? But if so, is all the panoply of the law erected over a set of social regulations? I must admit that I begin with a feeling that a complete separation of crime from sin (I use the term throughout this lecture in the wider meaning) would not be good for the moral law and might be disastrous for the criminal. But can this sort of feeling be justified as a matter of jurisprudence? And if it be a right feeling, how should the relationship between the criminal and the moral law be stated? Is there a good theoretical basis for it, or is it just a practical working alliance, or is it a bit of both? . . . In jurisprudence . . . everything is thrown open to discussion and, in the belief that they cover the whole field, I have framed three interrogatories addressed to myself to answer:

1. Has society the right to pass judgement at all on matters of morals? Ought there, in other words, to be a public morality, or are morals always a matter for private judgement?
2. If society has the right to pass judgement, has it also the right to use the weapon of the law to enforce it?
3. If so, ought it to use that weapon in all cases or only in some; and if only in some, on what principles should it distinguish?

I shall begin with the first interrogatory and consider what is meant by the right of society to pass a moral judgement, that is, a judgement about what is good and what is evil. The fact that a majority of people may disapprove of a practice does not of itself make it a matter for society as a whole. Nine men out of ten may disapprove of what the tenth man is doing and still say that it is not their business. There is a case for a collective judgement (as distinct from a large number of individual opinions which sensible people may even refrain from pronouncing at all if it is upon somebody else's private affairs) only if society is affected. Without a collective judgement there can be no case at all for intervention. Let me take as an illustration the Englishman's attitude to religion as it is now and as it has been in the past. His attitude now is that a man's religion is his private affair; he may think of another man's religion that it is right or wrong, true or untrue, but not that it is good or bad. In earlier times that was not so; a man was denied the right to practise what was thought of as heresy, and heresy was thought of as destructive of society.

The language used in the passages I have quoted from the Wolfenden Report suggests the view that there ought not to be a collective judgement about immorality *per se*. Is this what is meant by 'private morality' and 'individual freedom of choice and action'? Some people sincerely believe that homosexuality is neither immoral nor unnatural. Is the 'freedom of choice and action' that is offered to the individual, freedom to decide for himself what is moral or immoral, society remaining neutral; or is it freedom to be immoral if he wants to be? The language of the Report may be open to question, but the conclusions at which the Committee arrive answer this question unambiguously. If society is not prepared to say that homosexuality is morally wrong, there would be no basis for a law protecting youth from 'corruption' or punishing a man for living on the 'immoral' earnings of a homosexual prostitute, as the Report recommends. This attitude the Committee make even clearer when they come to deal with prostitution. In truth, the Report takes it for granted that there is in existence a public morality which condemns homosexuality and prostitution. What the Report seems to mean by private morality might perhaps be better described as private behaviour in matters of morals.

This view—that there is such a thing as public morality—can also be justified by *a priori* argument. What makes a society of any sort is community of ideas, not only political ideas but also ideas about the way its members should behave and govern their lives; these latter ideas are its morals. Every society has a moral structure as well as a political one: or rather, since that might suggest two independent systems, I should say that the structure of every society is made up both of politics and morals. Take, for example, the institution of marriage. Whether a man should be allowed to take more than one wife is something about which every society has to make up its mind one way or the other. In England we believe in the Christian idea of marriage and therefore adopt monogamy as a moral principle. Consequently the Christian institution of marriage has become the basis of family life and so part of the structure of our society. It is there not because it is Christian. It has got there because it is Christian, but it remains there because it is built into the house in which we live and could not be removed without bringing it down. The great majority of those who live in this country accept it because it is the Christian idea of marriage and for them the only true one. But a non-Christian is bound by it, not because it is part of Christianity but because, rightly or wrongly, it has been adopted by the society in which he lives. It would be useless for him to stage a debate designed to prove that polygamy was theologically more correct and socially preferable; if he wants to live in the house, he must accept it as built in the way in which it is.

We see this more clearly if we think of ideas or institutions that are purely political. Society cannot tolerate rebellion; it will not allow argument about the rightness of the cause. Historians a century later may say that the rebels were right and the Government was wrong and a percipient and conscientious subject of the State may think so at the time. But it is not a matter which can be left to individual judgement.

The institution of marriage is a good example for my purpose because it bridges the division, if there is one, between politics and morals. Marriage is part of the structure of our society and it is also the basis of a moral code which condemns fornication and adultery. The institution of marriage would be gravely threatened if individual judgements were permitted about the morality of adultery; on these points there must be a public morality. But public morality is not to be confined to those moral principles which support institutions such as marriage. People do not think of monogamy as something which has to be supported because our society has chosen to organize itself upon it; they think of it as something that is good in itself and offering a good way of life and that it is for that reason that our society has adopted it. I return to the statement that I have already made, that society means a community of ideas; without shared ideas on politics, morals, and ethics no society can exist. Each one of us has ideas about what is good and what is evil; they cannot be kept private from the society in which we live. If men and women try to create a society in which there is no fundamental agreement about good and evil they will fail; if, having based it on common agreement, the agreement goes, the society will disintegrate. For society is not something that is kept together physically; it is held by the invisible bonds of common thought. If the bonds were too far relaxed the members would drift apart. A common morality is part of the bondage. The bondage is part of the price of society; and mankind, which needs society, must pay its price. . . .

You may think that I have taken far too long in contending that there is such a thing as public morality, a proposition which most people would readily accept, and may have left myself too little time to discuss the next question which to many minds may cause greater difficulty: to what extent should society use the law to enforce its moral judgements? But I believe that the answer to the first question determines the way in which the second should be approached and may indeed very nearly dictate the answer to the second question. If society has no right to make judgements on morals, the law must find some special justification for entering the field of morality: if homosexuality and prostitution are not in themselves wrong, then the onus is very clearly on the lawgiver who wants to frame a law against certain aspects of them to justify the exceptional treatment. But if society has the right to make a judgement and has it on the basis that a recognized morality is as necessary to society as, say, a recognized government, then society may use the law to preserve morality in the same way as it uses it to safeguard anything else that is essential to its existence. If therefore the first proposition is securely established with all its implications, society has a prima facie right to legislate against immorality as such.

The Wolfenden Report, notwithstanding that it seems to admit the right of society to condemn homosexuality and prostitution as immoral, requires special circumstances to be shown to justify the intervention of the law. I think that this is wrong in principle and that any attempt to approach my second interrogatory on these lines is bound to break down. I think that the attempt by the Committee does break down and that this is shown by the fact that it has to define or describe its special circumstances so widely that they can be supported only if it is accepted that the law *is* concerned with immorality as such.

The widest of the special circumstances are described as the provision of 'sufficient safeguards against exploitation and corruption of others, particularly those who are specially vulnerable because they are young, weak in body or mind, inexperienced, or in a state of special physical, official or economic dependence'. The corruption of youth is a well-recognized ground for intervention by the State and for the purpose of any legislation the young can easily be defined. But if similar protection were to be extended to every other citizen, there would be no limit to the reach of the law. The 'corruption and exploitation of others' is so wide that it could be used to cover any sort of immorality which involves, as most do, the co-operation of another person. Even if the phrase is taken as limited to the categories that are particularized as 'specially vulnerable', it is so elastic as to be practically no restriction. This is not merely a matter of words. For if the words used are stretched almost beyond breaking-point, they still are not wide enough to cover the recommendations which the Committee make about prostitution.

Prostitution is not in itself illegal and the Committee do not think that it ought to be made so. If prostitution is private immorality and not the law's business, what concern has the law with the ponce or the brothel-keeper or the householder who permits habitual prostitution? The Report recommends that the laws which make these activities criminal offences should be maintained or strengthened and brings them (so far as it goes into principle; with regard to brothels it says simply that the law rightly frowns on them) under the head of exploitation. There may be cases of exploitation in this trade, as there are or used to be in many others, but in general a ponce exploits a prostitute no more than an impresario exploits an actress. The Report finds that 'the great majority of prostitutes are women whose psychological makeup is such that they choose this life because they find in it a style of living which is to them easier, freer and more profitable than would be provided by any other occupation. . . . In the main the association between prostitute and ponce is voluntary and operates to mutual advantage.' The Committee would agree that this could not be called exploitation in the ordinary sense. They say: 'It is in our view an over-simplification to think that those who live on the earnings of prostitution are exploiting the prostitute as such. What they are really exploiting is the whole complex of the relationship between prostitute and customer; they are, in effect, exploiting the human weaknesses which cause the customer to seek the prostitute and the prostitute to meet the demand.'

All sexual immorality involves the exploitation of human weaknesses. The prostitute exploits the lust of her customers and the customer the moral weakness of the prostitute. If the exploitation of human weaknesses is considered to create a special circumstance, there is virtually no field of morality which can be defined in such a way as to exclude the law.

I think, therefore, that it is not possible to set theoretical limits to the power of the State to legislate against immorality. It is not possible to settle in advance exceptions to the general rule or to define inflexibly areas of morality into which the law is in no circumstances to be allowed to enter. Society is entitled by means of its laws to protect itself from dangers, whether from within or without. Here again I think that the political parallel is legitimate. The law of treason is directed against aiding the king's enemies and against sedition from within. The justification for this is that established government is necessary for the existence of society and therefore its safety against violent overthrow must be secured. But an established morality is as necessary as good government to the welfare of society. Societies disintegrate from within more frequently than they are broken up by external pressures. There is disintegration when no common morality is observed and history shows that the loosening of moral bonds is often the first stage of disintegration, so that society is justified in taking the same steps to preserve its moral code as it does to preserve its government and other essential institutions. The suppression of vice is as much the law's business as the suppression of subversive activities; it is no more possible to define a sphere of private morality than it is to define one of private subversive activity. It is wrong to talk of private morality or of the law not being concerned with immorality as such or to try to set rigid bounds to the part which the law may play in the suppression of vice. There are no theoretical limits to the power of the State to legislate against treason and sedition, and likewise I think there can be no theoretical limits to legislation against immorality. You may argue that if a man's sins affect only himself it cannot be the concern of society. If he chooses to get drunk every night in the privacy of his own home, is any one except himself the worse for it? But suppose a quarter or a half of the population got drunk every night, what sort of society would it be? You cannot set a theoretical limit to the number of people who can get drunk before society is entitled to legislate against drunkenness. . . .

In what circumstances the State should exercise its power is the third of the interrogatories I have framed. But before I get to it I must raise a point which might have been brought up in any one of the three. How are the moral judgements of society to be ascertained? By leaving it until now, I can ask it in the more limited form that is now sufficient for my purpose. How is the law-maker to ascertain the moral judgements of society? It is surely not enough that they should be reached by the opinion of the majority; it would be too much to require the individual assent of every citizen. English law has evolved and regularly uses a standard which does not depend on the counting of heads. It is that of the reasonable man. He is not to be confused with the rational man. He is not expected to reason about anything and his judgement may be largely a matter of feeling. It is the viewpoint of the man in the street—or to use an archaism familiar to all lawyers—the man in the Clapham omnibus. He might also be called the right-minded man. For my purpose I should like to call him the man in the jury box, for the moral judgement of society must be something about which any twelve men or women drawn at random might after discussion be expected to be unanimous. This was the standard the judges applied in the days before Parliament was as active as it is now and when they laid down rules of public policy. They did not think of themselves as making law but simply as stating principles which every right-minded person would accept as valid. It is what Pollock called 'practical morality', which is based not on theological or philosophical foundations but 'in the mass of continuous experience half-consciously or unconsciously accumulated and embodied in the morality of common sense'. He called it also 'a certain way of thinking on questions of morality which we expect to find in a reasonable civilized man or a reasonable Englishman, taken at random'.

Immorality then, for the purpose of the law, is what every right-minded person is presumed to consider to be immoral. Any immorality is capable of affecting society injuriously and in effect to a greater or lesser extent it usually does; this is what gives the law its *locus standi*. It cannot be shut out. But—and this brings me to the third question—the individual has a *locus standi* too; he cannot be expected to surrender to the judgement of society the whole conduct of his life. It is the old and familiar question of striking a balance between the rights and interests of society and those of the individual. This is something which the law is constantly doing in matters large and small. To take a very down-to-earth example, let me consider the right of the individual whose house adjoins the highway to have access to it; that means in these days the right to have vehicles stationary in the highway, sometimes for a considerable time if there is a lot of loading or unloading. There are many cases in which the courts have had to balance the private right of access against the public right to use the highway without obstruction. It cannot be done by carving up the highway into public and private areas. It is done by recognizing that each have rights over the whole; that if each were to exercise their rights to the full, they would come into conflict; and therefore that the rights of each must be curtailed so as to ensure as far as possible that the essential needs of each are safeguarded.

I do not think that one can talk sensibly of a public and private morality any more than one can of a public or private highway. Morality is a sphere in which there is a public interest and a private interest, often in conflict, and the problem is to reconcile the two. This does not mean that it is impossible to put forward any general statements about how in our society the balance ought to be struck. Such statements cannot of their nature be rigid or precise; they would not be designed to circumscribe the operation of the lawmaking power but to guide those who have to apply it. While every decision which a court of law makes when it balances the public against the private interest is an *ad hoc* decision, the cases contain statements of principle to which the court should have regard when it reaches its decision. In the same way it is possible to make general statements of principle which it may be thought the legislature should bear in mind when it is considering the enactment of laws enforcing morals.

I believe that most people would agree upon the chief of these elastic principles. There must be toleration of the maximum individual freedom that is consistent with the integrity of society. It cannot be said that this is a principle that runs all through the criminal law. Much of the criminal law that is regulatory in character—the part of it that deals with *malum prohibitum* rather than *malum in se*—is based upon the opposite principle, that is, that the choice of the individual must give way to the convenience of the many. But in all matters of conscience the principle I have stated is generally held to prevail. It is not confined to thought and speech; it extends to action, as is shown by the recognition of the right to conscientious objection in war-time; this example shows also that conscience will be respected even in times of national danger. The principle appears to me to be peculiarly appropriate to all questions of morals. Nothing should be punished by the law that does not lie beyond the limits of tolerance. It is not nearly enough to say that a majority dislike a practice; there must be a real feeling of reprobation. Those who are dissatisfied with the present law on homosexuality often say that the opponents of reform are swayed simply by disgust. If that were so it would be wrong, but I do not think one can ignore disgust if it is deeply felt and not manufactured. Its presence is a good indication that the bounds of toleration are being reached. Not everything is to be tolerated. No society can do without intolerance, indignation, and disgust; they are the forces behind the moral law, and indeed it can be argued that if they or something like them are not present, the feelings of society cannot be weighty enough to deprive the individual of freedom of choice. I suppose that there is hardly anyone nowadays who would not be disgusted by the thought of deliberate cruelty to animals. No one proposes to relegate that or any other form of sadism to the realm of private morality or to allow it to be practised in public or in private. It would be possible no doubt to point out that until a comparatively short while ago nobody thought very much of cruelty to animals and also that pity and kindliness and the unwillingness to inflict pain are virtues more generally esteemed now than they have ever been in the past. But matters of this sort are not determined by rational argument. Every moral judgement, unless it claims a divine source, is simply a feeling that no right-minded man could behave in any other way without admitting that he was doing wrong. It is the power of a common sense and not the power of reason that is behind the judgements of society. But before a society can put a practice beyond the limits of tolerance there must be a deliberate judgement that the practice is injurious to society. There is, for example, a general abhorrence of homosexuality. We should ask ourselves in the first instance whether, looking at it calmly and dispassionately, we regard it as a vice so abominable that its mere presence is an offence. If that is the genuine feeling of the society in which we live, I do not see how society can be denied the right to eradicate it. Our feeling may not be so intense as that. We may feel about it that, if confined, it is tolerable, but that if it spread it might be gravely injurious; it is in this way that most societies look upon fornication, seeing it as a natural weakness which must be kept within bounds but which cannot be rooted out. It becomes then a question of balance, the danger to society in one scale and the extent of the restriction in the other. On this sort of point the value of an investigation by such a body as the Wolfenden Committee and of its conclusions is manifest.

The limits of tolerance shift. This is supplementary to what I have been saying but of sufficient importance in itself to deserve statement as a separate principle which law-makers have to bear in mind. I suppose that moral standards do not shift; so far as they come from divine revelation they do not, and I am willing to assume that the moral judgements made by a society always remain good for that society. But the extent to which society will tolerate—I mean tolerate, not approve—departures from moral standards varies from generation to generation. . . . Laws, especially those which are based on morals, are less easily moved. It follows as another good working principle that in any new matter of morals the law should be slow to act. By the next generation the swell of indignation may have abated and the law be left without the strong backing which it needs. But it is then difficult to alter the law without giving the impression that moral judgement is being weakened. This is now one of the factors that is strongly militating against any alteration to the law on homosexuality.

A third elastic principle must be advanced more tentatively. It is that as far as possible privacy should be respected. This is not an idea that has ever been made explicit in the criminal law. Acts or words done or said in public or in private are all brought within its scope without distinction in principle. But there goes with this a strong reluctance on the part of judges and legislators to sanction invasions of privacy in the detection of crime. The police have no more right to trespass than the ordinary citizen has; there is no general right of search; to this extent an Englishman's home is still his castle. The Government is extremely careful in the exercise even of those powers which it claims to be undisputed. Telephone tapping and interference with the mails afford a good illustration of this. . . .

This indicates a general sentiment that the right to privacy is something to be put in the balance against the enforcement of the law. Ought the same sort of consideration to play any part in the formation of the law? Clearly only in a very limited number of cases. When the help of the law is invoked by an injured citizen, privacy must be irrelevant; the individual cannot ask that his right to privacy should be measured against injury criminally done to another. But when all who are involved in the deed are consenting parties and the injury is done to morals, the public interest in the moral order can be balanced against the claims of privacy. The restriction on police powers of investigation goes further than the affording of a parallel; it means that the detection of crime committed in private and when there is no complaint is bound to be rather haphazard and this is an additional reason for moderation. These considerations do not justify the exclusion of all private immorality from the scope of the law. I think that, as I have already suggested, the test of 'private behaviour' should be substituted for 'private morality' and the influence of the factor should be reduced from that of a definite limitation to that of a matter to be taken into account. Since the gravity of the crime is also a proper consideration, a distinction might well be made in the case of homosexuality between the lesser acts of indecency and the full offence, which on the principles of the Wolfenden Report it would be illogical to do.

The last and the biggest thing to be remembered is that the law is concerned with the minimum and not with the maximum; there is much in the Sermon on the Mount that would be out of place in the Ten Commandments. We all recognize the gap between the moral law and the law of the land. No man is worth much who regulates his conduct with the sole object of escaping punishment, and every worthy society sets for its members standards which are above those of the law. We recognize the existence of such higher standards when we use expressions such as 'moral obligation' and 'morally bound'. The distinction was well put in the judgement of African elders in a family dispute: 'We have power to make you divide the crops, for this is our law, and we will see this is done. But we have not power to make you behave like an upright man.'

It can only be because this point is so obvious that it is so frequently ignored. Discussion among law-makers, both professional and amateur, is too often limited to what is right or wrong and good or bad for society. There is a failure to keep separate the two questions I have earlier posed—the question of society's right to pass a moral judgement and the question of whether the arm of the law should be used to enforce the judgement. The criminal law is not a statement of how people ought to behave; it is a statement of what will happen to them if they do not behave; good citizens are not expected to come within reach of it or to set their sights by it, and every enactment should be framed accordingly.

The arm of the law is an instrument to be used by society, and the decision about what particular cases it should be used in is essentially a practical one. Since it is an instrument, it is wise before deciding to use it to have regard to the tools with which it can be fitted and to the machinery which operates it. Its tools are fines, imprisonment, or lesser forms of supervision (such as Borstal and probation) and—not to be ignored—the degradation that often follows upon the publication of the crime. Are any of these suited to the job of dealing with sexual immorality? The fact that there is so much immorality which has never been brought within the law shows that there can be no general rule. It is a matter for decision in each case; but in the case of homosexuality the Wolfenden Report rightly has regard to the views of those who are experienced in dealing with this sort of crime and to those of the clergy who are the natural guardians of public morals.

The machinery which sets the criminal law in motion ends with the verdict and the sentence; and a verdict is given either by magistrates or by a jury. As a general rule, whenever a crime is sufficiently serious to justify a maximum punishment of more than three months, the accused has the right to the verdict of a jury. . . . The juries tend to dilute the decrees of Parliament with their own ideas of what should be punishable. Their province of course is fact and not law, and I do not mean that they often deliberately disregard the law. But if they think it is too stringent, they sometimes take a very merciful view of the facts. . . .

The part that the jury plays in the enforcement of the criminal law, the fact that no grave offence against morals is punishable without their verdict, these are of great importance in relation to the statements of principle that I have been making. They turn what might otherwise be pure exhortation to the legislature into something like rules that the law-makers cannot safely ignore. The man in the jury box is not just an expression; he is an active reality. It will not in the long run work to make laws about morality that are not acceptable to him.

This then is how I believe my third interrogatory should be answered—not by the formulation of hard and fast rules, but by a judgement in each case taking into account the sort of factors I have been mentioning. The line that divides the criminal law from the moral is not determinable by the application of any clear-cut principle. It is like a line that divides land and sea, a coastline of irregularities and indentations. There are gaps and promontories, such as adultery and fornication, which the law has for centuries left substantially untouched. Adultery of the sort that breaks up marriage seems to me to be just as harmful to the social fabric as homosexuality or bigamy. The only ground for putting it outside the criminal law is that a law which made it a crime would be too difficult to enforce; it is too generally regarded as a human weakness not suitably punished by imprisonment. All that the law can do with fornication is to act against its worst manifestations; there is a general abhorrence of the commercialization of vice, and that sentiment gives strength to the law against brothels and immoral earnings. There is no logic to be found in this. The boundary between the criminal law and moral law is fixed by balancing in the case of each particular crime the pros and cons of legal enforcement in accordance with the sort of considerations I have been outlining. The fact that adultery, fornication, and lesbianism are untouched by the criminal law does not prove that homosexuality ought not to be touched. The error of jurisprudence in the Wolfenden Report is caused by the search for some single principle to explain the division between crime and sin. The Report finds it in the principle that the criminal law exists for the protection of individuals; on this principle fornication in private between consenting adults is outside the law and thus it becomes logically indefensible to bring homosexuality between consenting adults in private within it. But the true principle is that the law exists for the protection of society. It does not discharge its function by protecting the individual from injury, annoyance, corruption, and exploitation; the law must protect also the institutions and the community of ideas, political and moral, without which people cannot live together. Society cannot ignore the morality of the individual any more than it can his loyalty; it flourishes on both and without either it dies.

I have said that the morals which underly the law must be derived from the sense of right and wrong which resides in the community as a whole; it does not matter whence the community of thought comes, whether from one body of doctrine or another or from the knowledge of good and evil which no man is without. If the reasonable man believes that a practice is immoral and believes also—no matter whether the belief is right or wrong, so be it that it is honest and dispassionate—that no right-minded member of his society could think otherwise, then for the purpose of the law it is immoral.

This brings me back in the end to a question I posed at the beginning. . . . I have spoken of the criminal law as dealing with the minimum standards of human conduct and the moral law with the maximum. The instrument of the criminal law is punishment; those of the moral law are teaching, training, and exhortation. If the whole dead weight of sin were ever to be allowed to fall upon the law, it could not take the strain. If at any point there is a lack of clear and convincing moral teaching, the administration of the law suffers. . . .

I return now to the main thread of my argument and summarize it. Society cannot live without morals. Its morals are those standards of conduct which the reasonable man approves. A rational man, who is also a good man, may have other standards. If he has no standards at all he is not a good man and need not be further considered. If he has standards, they may be very different; he may, for example, not disapprove of homosexuality or abortion. In that case he will not share in the common morality; but that should not make him deny that it is a social necessity. A rebel may be rational in thinking that he is right but he is irrational if he thinks that society can leave him free to rebel.

A man who concedes that morality is necessary to society must support the use of those instruments without which morality cannot be maintained. The two instruments are those of teaching, which is doctrine, and of enforcement, which is the law.

LAW, LIBERTY AND MORALITY

H. L. A. Hart

*A renowned scholar in the philosophy of law, H. L. A. Hart
is Professor of Jurisprudence in Oxford University and fellow
of University College, Oxford. He has also taught at Harvard,
the University of California at Los Angeles, and Stanford University. He was named a 1966 recipient of the distinguished
Ames Prize for legal scholarship by the Faculty of the Harvard Law School for his* Concept of Law *(1961). Among his
other works are* Law, Liberty and Morality *(1963) and*
Punishment and Responsibility *(1968), a collection of essays
dealing with the theory of punishment and legal criteria of
responsibility.*

Much dissatisfaction has for long been felt in England with the
criminal law relating to both prostitution and homosexuality, and in 1954
the committee well known as the Wolfenden Committee was appointed to
consider the state of the law. This committee reported in September 1957
and recommended certain changes in the law on both topics. As to homosexuality they recommended by a majority of 12 to 1 that homosexual
practices between consenting adults in private should no longer be a
crime . . .

What concerns us here is less the fate of the Wolfenden Committee's recommendations than the principles by which these were supported. These are strikingly similar to those expounded by Mill in his essay
On Liberty. Thus section 13 of the Committee's Report reads:

> [The] function [of the criminal law], as we see it, is to preserve
> public order and decency, to protect the citizen from what is
> offensive or injurious and to provide sufficient safeguards against
> exploitation or corruption of others, particularly those who are
> specially vulnerable because they are young, weak in body or mind
> or inexperienced. . . .

This conception of the positive functions of the criminal law was the
Committee's main ground for its recommendation concerning prostitution

---

that legislation should be passed to suppress the offensive public manifestations of prostitution, but not to make prostitution itself illegal. Its recommendation that the law against homosexual practices between consenting
adults in private should be relaxed was based on the principle stated simply
in section 61 of the Report as follows: "There must remain a realm of
private morality and immorality which is, in brief and crude terms, not the
law's business."

It is of some interest that these developments in England have had
near counterparts in America. In 1955 the American Law Institute published with its draft Model Penal Code a recommendation that all con-
sensual relations between adults in private should be excluded from the
scope of the criminal law. Its grounds were (*inter alia*) that "no harm to
the secular interests of the community is involved in atypical sex practice in
private between consenting adult partners"; and "there is the fundamental
question of the protection to which every individual is entitled against state
interference in his personal affairs when he is not hurting others." This
recommendation had been approved by the Advisory Committee of the
Institute but rejected by a majority vote of its Council. The issue was
therefore referred to the annual meeting of the Institute at Washington in
May 1955, and the recommendation, supported by an eloquent speech of
the late Justice Learned Hand, was, after a hot debate, accepted by a
majority of 35 to 24.

It is perhaps clear from the foregoing that Mill's principles are still
very much alive in the criticism of law, whatever their theoretical deficiencies may be. But twice in one hundred years they have been challenged
by two masters of the Common Law. The first of these was the great
Victorian judge and historian of the Criminal Law, James Fitzjames
Stephen. His criticism of Mill is to be found in the sombre and impressive
book *Liberty, Equality, Fraternity,* which he wrote as a direct reply to
Mill's essay *On Liberty.* It is evident from the tone of this book that
Stephen thought he had found crushing arguments against Mill and had
demonstrated that the law might justifiably enforce morality as such or, as
he said, that the law should be "a persecution of the grosser forms of vice."
Nearly a century later, on the publication of the Wolfenden Committee's
report, Lord Devlin, now a member of the House of Lords and a most
distinguished writer on the criminal law, in his essay on *The Enforcement
of Morals* took as his target the Report's contention "that there must be a
realm of morality and immorality which is not the law's business" and
argued in opposition to it that "the suppression of vice is as much the law's
business as the suppression of subversive activities."

Though a century divides these two legal writers, the similarity in
the general tone and sometimes in the detail of their arguments is very
great. . . . though their arguments are at points confused, they certainly
still deserve the compliment of rational opposition. They are not only

admirably stocked with concrete examples, but they express the considered views of skilled, sophisticated lawyers experienced in the administration of the criminal law. Views such as theirs are still quite widely held especially by lawyers both in England and in this country; it may indeed be that they are more popular, in both countries, than Mill's doctrine of Liberty.

Before we consider the detail of these arguments, it is, I think, necessary to appreciate three different but connected features of the question with which we are concerned.

. . . it is plain that the question is one *about* morality, but it is important to observe that it is also itself a question *of* morality. It is the question whether the enforcement of morality is morally justified; so morality enters into the question in two ways. The importance of this feature of the question is that it would plainly be no sufficient answer to show that in fact in some society—our own or others—it was widely regarded as morally quite right and proper to enforce, by legal punishment, compliance with the accepted morality. No one who seriously debates this question would regard Mill as refuted by the simple demonstration that there are some societies in which the generally shared morality endorses its own enforcement by law, and does so even in those cases where the immorality was thought harmless to others. The existence of societies which condemn association between white and coloured persons as immoral and punish it by law still leaves our question to be argued. It is true that Mill's critics have often made much of the fact that English law does in several instances, apparently with the support of popular morality, punish immorality as such, especially in sexual matters; but they have usually admitted that this is where the argument begins, not where it ends. I shall indeed later claim that the play made by some legal writers with what they treat as examples of the legal enforcement of morality "as such" is sometimes confused. But they do not, at any rate, put forward their case as simply proved by pointing to these social facts. Instead they attempt to base their own conclusion that it is morally justifiable to use the criminal law in this way on principles which they believe to be universally applicable, and which they think are either quite obviously rational or will be seen to be so after discussion.

Thus Lord Devlin bases his affirmative answer to the question on the quite general principle that it is permissible for any society to take the steps needed to preserve its own existence as an organized society, and he thinks that immorality—even private sexual immorality—may, like treason, be something which jeopardizes a society's existence. Of course many of us may doubt this general principle, and not merely the suggested analogy with treason. We might wish to argue that whether or not a society is justified in taking steps to preserve itself must depend both on what sort of society it is and what the steps to be taken are. If a society were mainly devoted to the cruel persecution of a racial or religious minority, or if the steps to be taken included hideous tortures, it is arguable that what Lord Devlin terms the "disintegration" of such a society would be morally better than its continued existence, and steps ought not to be taken to preserve it. Nonetheless Lord Devlin's principle that a society may take the steps required to preserve its organized existence is not itself tendered as an item of English popular morality, deriving its cogency from its status as part of our institutions. He puts it forward as a principle, rationally acceptable, to be used in the evaluation or criticism of social institutions generally. And it is surely clear that anyone who holds the question whether a society has the "right" to enforce morality, or whether it is morally permissible for any society to enforce its morality by law, to be discussable at all, must be prepared to deploy some such general principles of critical morality. In asking the question, we are assuming the legitimacy of a standpoint which permits criticism of the institutions of any society, in the light of general principles and knowledge of the facts.

To make this point clear, I would revive the terminology much favoured by the Utilitarians of the last century, which distinguished "positive morality," the morality actually accepted and shared by a given social group, from the general moral principles used in the criticism of actual social institutions including positive morality. We may call such general principles "critical morality" and say that our question is one of critical morality about the legal enforcement of positive morality.

A second feature of our question worth attention is simply that it is a question of *justification*. In asking it we are committed at least to the general critical principle that the use of legal coercion by any society calls for justification as something *prima facie* objectionable to be tolerated only for the sake of some countervailing good. For where there is no *prima facie* objection, wrong, or evil, men do not ask for or give *justifications* of social practices, though they may ask for and give *explanations* of these practices or may attempt to demonstrate their value.

It is salutary to inquire precisely what it is that is *prima facie* objectionable in the legal enforcement of morality; for the idea of legal enforcement is in fact less simple than is often assumed. It has two different but related aspects. One is the actual punishment of the offender. This characteristically involves depriving him of liberty of movement or of property or of association with family or friends, or the infliction upon him of physical pain or even death. All these are things which are assumed to be wrong to inflict on others without special justification, and in fact they are so regarded by the law and morality of all developed societies. To put it as a lawyer would, these are things which, if they are not justified as sanctions, are delicts or wrongs.

The second aspect of legal enforcement bears on those who may never offend against the law, but are coerced into obedience by the threat of legal punishment. This rather than physical restrictions is what is normally meant in the discussion of political arrangements by restrictions on liberty. Such restrictions, it is to be noted, may be thought of as calling for justification for several quite distinct reasons. The unimpeded exercise by individuals of free choice may be held a value in itself with which it is *prima facie* wrong to interfere; or it may be thought valuable because it enables individuals to experiment—even with living—and to discover things valuable both to themselves and to others. But interference with individual liberty may be thought an evil requiring justification for simpler, utilitarian reasons; for it is itself the infliction of a special form of suffering —often very acute—on those whose desires are frustrated by the fear of punishment. This is of particular importance in the case of laws enforcing a sexual morality. They may create misery of a quite special degree. For both the difficulties involved in the repression of sexual impulses and the consequences of repression are quite different from those involved in the abstention from "ordinary" crime. Unlike sexual impulses, the impulse to steal or to wound or even kill is not, except in a minority of mentally abnormal cases, a recurrent and insistent part of daily life. Resistance to the temptation to commit these crimes is not often, as the suppression of sexual impulses generally is, something which affects the development or balance of the individual's emotional life, happiness, and personality.

Thirdly, the distinction already made, between positive morality and principles of critical morality, may serve to dissipate a certain misunderstanding of the question and to clarify its central point. It is sometimes said that the question is not whether it is morally justifiable to enforce morality as such, but only *which* morality may be enforced. Is it only a utilitarian morality condemning activities which are harmful to others? Or is it a morality which also condemns certain activities whether they are harmful or not? This way of regarding the question misrepresents the character of, at any rate, modern controversy. A utilitarian who insists that the law should only punish activities which are harmful adopts this as a critical principle, and, in so doing, he is quite unconcerned with the question whether a utilitarian morality is or is not already accepted as the positive morality of the society to which he applies his critical principles. If it is so accepted, that is not, in his view, the reason why it should be enforced. It is true that if he is successful in preaching his message to a given society, members of it will then be compelled to behave as utilitarians in certain ways, but these facts do not mean that the vital difference between him and his opponent is only as to the content of the morality to be enforced. For as may be seen from the main criticisms of Mill, the Utilitarian's opponent, who insists that it is morally permissible to enforce morality as such, believes that the mere fact that certain rules or standards of behaviour enjoy the status of a society's positive morality is the reason—or at least part of the reason—which justifies their enforcement by law. No doubt in older controversies the opposed positions were different:

the question may have been whether the state could punish only activities causing secular harm or also acts of disobedience to what were believed to be divine commands or prescriptions of Natural Law. But what is crucial to the dispute in its modern form is the significance to be attached to the historical fact that certain conduct, no matter what, is prohibited by a positive morality. The utilitarian denies that this has any significance sufficient to justify its enforcement; his opponent asserts that it has. These are divergent critical principles which do not differ merely over the content of the morality to be enforced, but over a more fundamental and, surely, more interesting issue.

Part Four

Discrimination
and the Negro

The domination in a society with strong egalitarian traditions of one race over another has produced moral problems which are unique to the American experience. A Martian astronaut, contemplating us for the first time and ignorant of our history, might well conclude that we are a people perversely intent on making unnecessary trouble for ourselves. He would no doubt report back about a so-called "race problem" that was pointless, gratuitous and quite senseless. And so might we consider it. But this would not be to banish it. For there the problem is, looming larger and larger, haunting the national conscience, filling us with anxiety and anguish, almost, it would sometimes seem, devouring us.

On December 5, 1946 events did indeed appear to take a turn for the better. The date is a significant one in the Negroes' struggle for civil rights. On that day President Truman, by executive order, created a Committee on Civil Rights. The now famous report of the Committee, entitled "To Secure These Rights," was issued in 1947.

Since the recommendations of the Committee were often denounced as "Communist inspired" and even the "neutral" *Congressional Digest* refers to the civil-rights program as "weighted down by the unqualified and violent support of extreme left-wing, radical, and Communist organizations," it may be well to list some of the Committee members. The chairman was Charles E. Wilson, then head of General Electric; and it included, among others, Catholic Bishop Frank J. Haas of Michigan; Francis P. Matthews, who was an Omaha, Nebraska, lawyer and utility director, later appointed Secretary of the Navy; Episcopalian Bishop Henry Knox Sherrall of Boston; John S. Dickey, President of Dartmouth College; Charles Luckman, then president of Lever Brothers; Frank P. Graham, then president of the University of North Carolina and later a U.S. Senator; and James B. Carey, who spearheaded the anti-Communist drive in the C.I.O.

The Commitee's report provided the basis for President Truman's "civil-rights" message to Congress in February 1948, in which he urged legislation creating a National Fair Employment Practices Commission and passage of federal laws prohibiting lynching, racial segregation, and the poll tax. Civil-rights legislation was one of the major issues in the presidential election that followed. Both major parties included a "civil-rights" plank in their platform. Despite major defections in the South (not to mention Wallace's abortive third-party movement in the North) Truman scored the now historical upset victory over Dewey. It appeared that a new era might be opening for the victims of race prejudice.

Much has happened since. We have witnessed the Supreme Court's unanimous 1954 decision outlawing segregation in the schools (Brown v. Board of Education of Topeka), the use of federal troops to enforce that decision, and the gradual capitulation of the border states followed by the slower erosion of resistance in the deep South. A new generation of Southern Negroes, committed to nonviolent resistance and helped by the unspeakable brutalities of Selma and Birmingham and Neshoba County, succeeded in enlisting the active sympathy of the North. The great March on Washington not only prodded Congress into action, it also dramatized the essential dignity of the Negro protest. A breakthrough occurred when for the first time the Senate ended a filibuster on a civil rights bill by invoking cloture, thereby making possible the passage of the Civil Rights Act of 1964.

The 1964 law was designed to enforce the constitutional right to vote. It gave U.S. district courts the power to enjoin against discrimination in public accommodations; a Commission on Equal Employment Opportunity to prevent unfair employment practices was established; and the Commission on Civil Rights charged with preventing discrimination in federally assisted programs was given a new lease on life. It was followed shortly by the Economic Opportunity Act of 1964 and, in 1965, by a voting rights law which suspends all literacy, knowledge and character tests for voters in all states and counties where less than 50 percent of the population of voter age was registered or voted in November, 1964. The same law provides for Federal registrars to qualify voters when the Attorney General finds it necessary to enforce the 15th Amendment's guarantee of the right to vote. A new 1967 civil rights bill before the 90th Congress was threatened as usual with a filibuster on the issue of open housing. The Senate invoked cloture in the spring of 1968 to end filibuster and pass a new civil rights bill which, among other things, establishes a precedent for prohibiting discrimination in the sale and rental of housing. It is difficult to say whether the measure as written would have passed the House if Martin Luther King had not been assassinated on April 4, 1968—an event which provoked rioting in more than sixty American cities. The bill was signed by the President on April 11, and by 1970 an estimated 80 percent of the nation's housing will be affected.

Southern Negroes are now voting in growing numbers; they are increasingly enrolled in schools and colleges from which they had been barred; segregation in public places is breaking down. For the first time we witness the appearance of a Negro middle class, and Negroes are being appointed and elected to high public office. But the "American Dilemma," as Myrdal taught us to call it, stubbornly persists and is even exacerbated. The level of living and average income of the Negro remain distressingly low by comparison with the white majority. Meanwhile the Negro's level of expectations, encouraged by legislative reform, has risen. Promising plans to rehabilitate our cities, where most Negroes live, have been shelved because of the Vietnam war.

The Negro concludes that his victory over the more extreme forms of Southern discrimination is hollow; what he has won in the South is no more than he has long had in the North where he is still segregated in blighted ghettoes, still finds himself in disproportionate numbers without employment in a booming economy, and is still viewed by the white majority not as an individual but as a Negro. In any case progress always seems more rapid to those who act to correct an abuse than to those who suffer from it. To the Negro it has seemed painfully slow.

And so we have our long, hot summers. We reap a harvest of individual crime and mass violence. Large areas of our cities, even a city like Detroit where the Negro has made his greatest progress, are devastated. The least grievance is fanned into furious flame, a minor altercation into destructive holocaust. The Negro demagogue is often more heeded than the responsible leader. Whatever else black power may be, Watts, Newark and Detroit know it in an ugly form where arson and looting mingle crazily with valid protest against real grievance.

14

The Law and Discrimination

The emergence of black nationalism, as a response to the identity crisis in which the Negro finds himself, and the challenge of black power have been referred to earlier in the section on civil disobedience. Here the emphasis will be different. In the two articles which follow Donald Richberg attacks and Milton Konvitz defends the idea that law can be used to expand the civil rights of minorities in a democracy, in particular to secure fair employment and ban segregation. Although it might be difficult to find as many individuals of Richberg's stature voicing his views today, his thesis is still widely defended. Involving as it does the extent to which law can be used as an instrument to effect social reform, the issue is broader than civil rights.

FREEDOM OF ASSOCIATION

Donald R. Richberg

*Donald R. Richberg, a constitutional lawyer, was co-author
of the Railway Labor Act of 1926, general counsel and later
chairman of the National Recovery Administration (1933–
35), Executive Director of the National Emergency Council
(1934–35), and Special Assistant to the Attorney General of
the United States.*

People are pleased to be told they have a "right" to do what they
want to do. They applaud the politician who assures them that they have a
"right" to enjoy the things they desire.

It is much more comforting to be assured that you have a right to
obtain a good job from some one, than to be informed that you have a duty
to do a good job for some one. But, let's not forget, that no right can be
enforced for one person without compelling another to fulfill a duty. In the
language of the courts: "When a right is invaded a duty is violated."
"There is no right where there is no remedy."

Even the basic right of my individual liberty cannot be enforced
except by imposing restraints on your individual liberty. The claim of a
right is worthless against more and more domestic conflicts, less and less
internal peace.

Long ago a great philosopher pointed out that "the right of all to
all things" means "the war of all against all." The surest way to destroy the
fundamental freedoms of American life would be to build up a vast legal
structure of social, economic and political rights, all of them creating
corresponding duties, and all of them enforced by governmental restraints
upon individual freedom.

Communists and their dupes complain that a "hysteria" of anti-
communism is causing the suppression of civil rights in the United States.
So now they are diligently fomenting a "counter-hysteria" for expanding
civil rights until the basic rights of life, liberty and property will be completely lost in a maze of petty rights and duties and regulations which only
a communistic dictatorship could possibly enforce.

The horrible and outstanding example of this civil rights hysteria is

From the *Washington Star* (January 4, 1948). Reprinted by permission of
the publisher.

the recent report of the President's Committee on Civil Rights, which is probably the most mischievous document that has been published since Marx and Engels produced the Communist Manifesto 100 years ago.

In the name of "liberty" this report proposes to compel American men, women and children to live and work in a social and economic system created and regulated by Government, a system in which their most profound emotions and ambitions are to be suppressed at the will of political monitors.

Here are the two most fundamental recommendations of the committee, in its own language:

"The elimination of segregation, based on race, color, creed or national origin, from American life."

"The enactment of a Federal Fair Employment Practices Act, prohibiting all forms of discrimination in private employment, based on race, color, creed or national origin."

Please note that segregation is to be eliminated—not only from Government operations, but everywhere "from American life." That is precisely the aim of the committee, which announces, with the voice of omnipotent omniscience: "We can tolerate no restrictions upon the individual which depend upon irrelevant factors such as his race, his color, his religion or the social position to which he was born."

Hundreds of millions of Protestants, Catholics, Jews, Mohammedans, Buddhists and Hindus have believed and taught for centuries the One Way of Living, or the One Road to Salvation, was divinely ordained and revealed in the articles of their particular faith. Any one's religion is necessarily a restriction on him and, if he is to be free in the exercise of his religion (a freedom expressly guaranteed in our Constitution), then he must be free to restrict his associations with others in accordance with his feelings and his convictions as to what is necessary and desirable. Yet the committee would have a man forced by law into associations which may be repulsive to him—not because of any narrow prejudice but because of his profound religious convictions.

Race and color may seem "irrelevant" to the committee. Yet differences of race and color have divided mankind for centuries. They may fade in the coming centuries. But they cannot be wiped out by a state or federal law; and every such foolish effort only intensifies prejudice and intolerance, creates disrespect for law, and is itself an intolerant violation of individual liberty.

Curiously enough the committee observed that an essential part of our freedom is that we "are free to be different." Evidently the committee is willing to have us differ in our taste for cigarettes, but not in our taste for companions. But, in another breath, the committee says: "In a democracy, each individual must have freedom to choose his friends and to control the pattern of his personal and family life." Nevertheless in order to eliminate "segregation" and to prevent "discrimination," the committee insists that this "free" American shall be compelled to spend his working life with undesirable associates, and to send his children to schools, to eat in restaurants, to live in hotels and enjoy all public amusements, in the company of those whose company he would not voluntarily choose.

The logic of the report is very difficult to follow. But, as the King said in Alice in Wonderland, "If there's no meaning in it that saves a world of trouble, you know, as we needn't try to find any."

Let us assume, however, that every like or dislike based on race, color or religion is unreasonable and unfair, and that such prejudices ought to be eliminated from human thinking. Nevertheless, is it proper or even possible for the Government of a free people to attempt to prevent men and women in business or social life from acting in accord with their prejudices? Now this is an entirely different question from asking whether the Government itself should deny equality of opportunity to some of its citizens.

Political equality, in the right to vote, in the administration of justice and in the rendering of public services, is due to all citizens. But unless Government is to destroy an economic system of competitive freedom and a social system of free association, it cannot undertake to level down the inequalities that result from differing abilities and opportunities, or to interfere with the voluntary selection of one's associates in work or play.

No one would dare to propose that an employer be given the right by law to compel a man to work for him. That would be "involuntary servitude"—slavery. Yet it is solemnly proposed that an employer shall be forbidden to refuse to employ a "qualified" man because of his race or religion. This means, in practical effect, that if a Government regulator says that a man is "qualified" and rules that he has been denied employment because of race, color or religion, then he must be employed.

We know from experience under the Wagner Act that the employer would be presumed to be wrong. "Sentence first, verdict afterwards" is the conventional procedure. It seems to be forgotten that an employer works for his employes, just as they do for him. He is obligated by law to do a great many things for his employe. So the proposed law would force an employer into involuntary servitude to men who are under no obligation to work for him.

Superficially, it may seem to be a noble project for government to insure to all citizens an equality of opportunity to earn a livelihood and "to enjoy the benefits of society." But, no government can insure equality of opportunity to human beings who differ so widely in natural capacity and who, because of parental variances in ability and fortune, are so differently nurtured. It should also be pointed out that the benefits of a democratic, free society are not gathered by an omnipotent government into one treasure house for distribution to a dependent population. On the contrary, individuals in a host of big and little enterprises, work and produce things and seek to gain out of their cooperation with others the benefits and satisfactions which they desire and for which they are willing to work and sacrifice.

The concept of a society in which all are working for the common good and obtain only their proportionate share of the total product is the idealism of communism. Now that the world has had a good look at communism in actual operation, it has become quite clear that only a ruthless despotism can compel human beings to live and work in such a regimented society. Furthermore, it has been demonstrated up to date that the productivity of free men and women, working primarily for their own gain and reaping individual rewards, is far, far greater than the productivity of a people working ostensibly for equalitarian progress. Indeed the reward of individual merit has been reluctantly adopted in Russia as a drastic compromise of communistic theory which was necessary to prevent economic disaster.

It is most significant that the shrill slogan of all those fomenting the civil rights hysteria is "equality," although the great declared purpose of the Constitution was, not to achieve an impossible equality among unequal human beings, but to "secure the blessings of liberty" so that men could be free to be different and to realize their differing ambitions with their differing abilities. Every law which seeks to give a man a right to something which as a free man he cannot gain for himself, must impose burdens and restraints on the freedom of other men.

We may, reasonably, tax the fortunate to give aid to the less fortunate. We may, reasonably, prevent the abuse of freedom by those who heedlessly or ruthlessly injure others in the pursuit of selfish gain. We may, reasonably, enact laws to protect the right of every citizen to an equal participation in government and to equal treatment in all government operations. But, let us be watchful against every effort to create by law a "right" in one man to compel others to associate with him or to accept obligations to him in the domain of private enterprise or private life. Let us realize, not only that it is a part of our heritage that "a man's house is his castle," but also that freedom of association in work or play is the most precious of all our liberties.

STAND OUT OF MY SUNSHINE

Milton R. Konvitz

Milton R. Konvitz, author of numerous works on civil rights and civil liberties, is Professor of Industrial and Labor Relations and Professor of Law at Cornell University. He has also been a member of the faculty of the Institute for Advanced Study and the Salzburg Seminar in American Studies. He directed the project that prepared the Code of Laws for the Republic of Liberia and has worked in close association with the National Association for the Advancement of Colored People and the American Civil Liberties Union. His most recent work is Expanding Liberties *(1966).*

In the six years immediately following *Brown* v. *Topeka* [U.S. Supreme Court desegregation decision], President Eisenhower, by his statements and by the things he left unsaid, reflected the views and sentiments of large sections of the American people who were inclined to question the efficacy of law as an instrument of social control and advancement in the field of race relations. Persons with this point of view tended to condemn both those who resorted to legal measures to vindicate and implement the desegregation decision and those who resorted to force, demagoguery, and knavery to defeat that decision. To Eisenhower, both parties were "extremists." He urged "moderation," waiting for an inner change, a change within the heart that would bear fruit in peaceful and constructive actions—on the eve of the centenary of the Civil War.

At a news conference in 1959 Eisenhower declared racial segregation morally wrong when it stands in the way of equality of opportunity in *economic* and *political* fields. By failing to mention, in the context, equality of opportunity in *education,* the statement implied that desegregation of the schools was not a moral imperative. He took this line in his solemn Christmas message of 1960, in which he said:

> Too often we discern an apathy towards violations of laws and standards of public and private integrity. When, through bitter prejudice and because of differences in skin pigmentation, individuals cannot enjoy equality of political and economic opportunity we see another of these imperfections, one that is equally plain to those living beyond our borders.

From *A Century of Civil Rights* by Milton R. Konvitz (New York: Columbia University Press, 1961), pp. 255–272. Reprinted by permission of the publisher.

The omission of any reference to equality of educational opportunity could not but suggest that "he who is silent is understood to consent."

In the same Christmas message Eisenhower again made the point that law will be ineffective if it is more advanced than morals. On this occasion he stated the argument as follows:

> Though we boast that ours is a government of laws, completeness in this work [of living by our national ideals] cannot be achieved by laws alone, necessary though these be. Law, to be truly effective, must command the respect and earnest support of public opinion, both generally and locally. And each of us helps form public opinion.

. . . Eisenhower also expressed a theory of federal-state relations that was reminiscent of the views of Andrew Johnson. His statements suggested that perhaps the "Southern manifesto," issued in 1956 by fifteen United States Senators and eighty-one members of the House of Representatives, was not altogether unwarranted when it called the Supreme Court decision "a clear abuse of judicial power" and an encroachment upon states' rights, and when it blamed the Court for "destroying the amicable relations between the white and Negro races."

Let us examine some of these propositions. . . .

Opposition to *Brown* v. *Topeka* often takes the form of an assertion that racial adjustments must be left to voluntary conduct. They must flow from the heart or conviction. Any attempt to coerce adjustments in the direction of wider equality, it is said, is bound to fail.

Often, however, a distinction is made between equality in some relations and equality in other relations. President Eisenhower, as we have noted, believed that the law may be used to achieve for the Negro political and economic equality, but he refused to assert that the law may also be used to achieve desegregation in the schools—although if the question concerned "separate but equal" schools, it may be assumed that he would have said that the law may be used to compel the states to provide "equal" schools for the Negro race.

In his widely reprinted public letter to the President, Carleton Putnam made the following distinction:

> I would emphatically support improvement of education in Negro schools, if and where it is inferior. Equality of opportunity and equality before the law, when not strained to cover other situations, are acceptable ideals because they provide the chance to earn and to progress—and consequently should be enforced by legal fiat as far as is humanly possible. But equality of association, which desegregation in Southern schools involves, pre-supposes a status which in the South the average Negro has not earned. To force it upon the Southern white will, I think, meet with as much opposition as the prohibition amendment encountered in the wet states.

Most white Southerners would not even concede that equality of economic and political opportunity may be implemented by legal process. The Southern states have not adopted fair employment practices acts, and they have consistently opposed any bill in Congress that would outlaw racial discrimination in employment. The votes in Congress on the Civil Rights Acts of 1957 and 1960—acts that have a bearing on the right of suffrage—clearly showed Southern opposition to legal guarantees of political equality. When it comes to equality of educational opportunity, the record of cases in the courts before 1954 shows that the South had interpreted the "separate but equal" doctrine as permission to deny to the Negro the educational equality that the Constitution commands.

It is difficult to see by virtue of what principle it is possible to distinguish legal coercion in favor of economic and political equality from legal coercion in favor of educational equality, for their interdependence is obvious. In the absence of educational equality, it is hard to see how the Negro can hope to achieve equality in economic and political life. "Today," as Chief Justice Warren said for the unanimous Court,

> education is perhaps the most important function of state and local governments. Compulsory school attendance laws and the great expenditures for education both demonstrate our recognition of the importance of education to our democratic society. It is required in the performance of our most basic responsibilities, even service in the armed forces. It is the very foundation of good citizenship. Today it is a principal instrument in awakening the child to cultural values, in preparing him for later professional training, and in helping him to adjust normally to his environment. In these days, it is doubtful that any child may reasonably be expected to succeed in life if he is denied the opportunity to an education. Such an opportunity, where the state has undertaken to provide it, is a right which must be made avaliable to all on equal terms.

Segregation, said the Court, denotes the inferiority of the Negro race, and a sense of inferiority affects the motivation to learn, retards the development of the Negro children, and deprives them of benefits they would receive in a nonsegregated school.

This deprivation must carry over to later economic and political opportunities. . . .

One may safely say, then, that at the time the Court announced its unanimous decision in *Brown* v. *Topeka,* outside of the states where school segregation was enforced by state laws, the official policies of the federal government, and of the governments of states in which some two-thirds of the American people lived, were against racial segregation or other forms of discrimination.

The letter of Carleton Putnam drew an analogy between opposition to school desegregation and opposition to the Prohibition Amendment, and Senator Fulbright, when he told the Senate that "legislation to regulate men's mores is doomed to failure," also referred to the American experience with prohibition as a precedent. But the analogy disregards crucial differences. At the time when the states were taking action on the Eighteenth Amendment, saloons were illegal in approximately 90 percent of the area of the nation and nearly two-thirds of the population were living in dry territory. When the amendment was ratified, thirty of the forty-eight states had prohibition statutes or constitutional amendments. By 1933, when prohibition was repealed, the overwhelming majority of the people had changed their position. The reasons for this reversal of public opinion are many but not relevant here, except that one point may be made: neither Congress nor the states provided adequate machinery for the enforcement of prohibition, and the local police forces "were either indifferent to the prohibition law or became the allies and protectors of the [racketeering liquor] industry."

With respect to *Brown* v. *Topeka,* on the other hand, the opposition is not national but regional. The American people in general have not found the experiment with equality unsatisfactory. There is no national movement for the repeal of the Fourteenth Amendment. Even in the Deep South—witness Little Rock and St. Louis—school desegregation would have a good chance of success if the demagogic politicians would give the citizens an opportunity to try it. But the rabble-rousing politicians would sooner see their states become a Congolese-like battleground, where law and order were subverted and neighbor lifted sword against neighbor, than let school desegregation be tried even at a snail's pace.

It is odd, to say the least, to hear Southerners argue in favor of "voluntarism." For the record is clear that the people in the South have not practiced voluntarism in race relations. They have always used the full power of the law to compel all persons, without regard to their own thoughts or feelings, to practice racial segregation. They have not left the matter of race relations to education, discussion, and similar methods that are used to reach the mind or heart of a person. They have relied on the power of the law to achieve their ends.

Let us consider an incident that may be taken as typifying the Southern record of action.

In 1855, through the efforts of John G. Fee, a Kentucky abolitionist minister who was disinherited by his slave-holding parents for his anti-slavery views, Berea College was founded as a coeducational, nonsectarian institution of practical and liberal education. Work was suspended in 1859 and resumed in 1865. Berea was located in Kentucky for the benefit mainly of the people of the mountains of the eastern part of the state, and was the only college in Kentucky that admitted both white and Negro students.

In 1904 Berea College had an enrollment of 174 Negro and 753 white students. In that year the Kentucky legislature enacted a statute that made it unlawful to maintain any college or school "where persons of the white and Negro races are both received as pupils for instruction." The penalty for maintaining such a college or school was a fine of $1,000, and an additional fine of $500 for each day the institution was operated after conviction. Any white or Negro student attending such school was subject to a fine of $50 for each day he attended. The law provided that a college could operate a branch for the other race "in a different locality, not less than twenty-five miles distant."

The officers and trustees of Berea College—the only institution affected by the law—protested, but to no avail. When the college opened for the academic year 1904–1905, the Negroes were not admitted but placed by the administration in Negro colleges. . . .

The racism of the South left little to the free will of the citizens. Segregation was required by law at circuses and tent shows; at theaters and public halls; in parks, playgrounds, and at beaches; at race tracks; in billiard and pool rooms. Members of the two races were prohibited from forming fraternal benefit associations together. A Negro minister could not perform the marriage ceremony for a white couple. There were scores of laws that made it *impossible* for persons to use their own judgment as to whether to associate or not associate with members of the other race.

But all this is conveniently forgotten when a court issues a desegregation decree or when Congress considers a civil rights law, for then the cry is heard that Americans are losing their liberty, that the government is invading the private lives of its citizens. Were the Black Codes and the Jim Crow laws attempts at implementing the Declaration of Independence? . . .

Another example of Southern dedication to the philosophy of voluntarism and to freedom of association—which are at the heart of Carleton Putnam's protest against the desegregation decree—may be seen in the all-out attack on the National Association for the Advancement of Colored People (N.A.A.C.P.) in some of the Southern states. In a society in which citizens and public officials are zealously devoted to the maximization of personal freedom, people have the right to join associations for educational, charitable, mutual aid, civil liberties, and other purposes. But Southern practices contradict Southern protestations. Let us examine briefly several Supreme Court decisions in which the Southern practice stands out in total nakedness.

In *N.A.A.C.P.* v. *Alabama,* decided in 1958, the attorney general of Alabama sought an injunction in the state courts to oust the association from the state. He ordered the association to produce records and papers, including names and addresses of all of the association's members and agents in the state. The association produced all the records except the membership lists. As to those lists, the association contended that the state could not compel disclosure without violation of freedom of association.

Unanimously reversing the state courts that had upheld the action of the attorney general of Alabama, the United States Supreme Court, in an opinion by Justice Harlan, said that the association had the right to protect its membership lists on behalf of the right of the members to associate freely with others in the pursuit of their private interests. This right of the members—citizens of the state of Alabama—is protected by the constitutional liberty to engage in association for the advancement of beliefs and ideas pertaining to political, economic, religious, or cultural matters. The attorney general's order to produce the membership lists, supported by the coercive power of the state courts, must be regarded, said Justice Harlan,

> as entailing the likelihood of a substantial restraint upon the exercise by petitioner's members of their right to freedom of association. Petitioner has made an uncontroverted showing that on past occasions revelation of the identity of its rank-and-file members has exposed these members to economic reprisals, loss of employment, threat of physical coercion and other manifestations of public hostility. . . .
> We hold that the immunity from state scrutiny of membership lists which the Association claims on behalf of its members is here so related to the right of the members to pursue their lawful private interests privately and to associate freely with others in so doing as to come within the protection of the Fourteenth Amendment.

In another case, in which two Arkansas cities sought from the N.A.A.C.P. its lists of members and contributors, the Supreme Court said:

> On this record it sufficiently appears that compulsory disclosure of the membership lists of the local branches of the National Association for the Advancement of Colored People would work a significant interference with the freedom of association of their members. There was substantial uncontroverted evidence that public identification of persons in the community as members of the organization had been followed by harassment and threats of bodily harm. There was also evidence that fear of community hostility and economic reprisals that would follow public disclosure of the membership lists had discouraged new members from joining the organizations and induced former members to withdraw. This repressive effect, while in part the result of private attitudes and pressures, was brought to bear only after the exercise of governmental power had threatened to force disclosure of the members' names. . . . Thus, the threat of substantial government encroachment upon important and traditional aspects of individual freedom is neither speculative nor remote.

Before the Civil War the South was willing to repress and stifle the civil rights and liberties of all citizens in order to maintain slavery; today, much of the same antilibertarian atmosphere persists in an effort to maintain "freedom of association," by which is meant, of course, compulsory segregation of the races. The Aesopian language of the South and its protagonists often tends to create the impression that the South is, in fact, fighting for the fundamental liberties of Americans to live as they please, to associate as they please, that the struggle is to give effect to the ideal of "Live and let live!", although the record of the Southern states shows that, when it has been a question of race relations, they have not been willing to let this question be decided by each person for himself. Instead, the force of the states has interposed itself between man and man, just as today some of the Southern states attempt to interpose themselves between the citizen and the Constitution.

A statement against civil rights laws and fair employment practices acts concludes on the following deep and pious note:

> When one's fellow men interpose force and compulsion between him and the Source of his being—whether by the device of government or otherwise—it amounts to interrupting his self-improvement, in conflict with what seems to be the Divine design. Man must be left free to discriminate and to exercise his freedom of choice. This freedom is a virtue and not a vice. And freedom of choice sows the seeds of peace rather than of conflict.

No mention is made of the Jim Crow laws and customs, of the Black Codes, of the private reprisals, of the economic sanctions that the South has used to deny "freedom of choice."

Nor does the South see that by encouraging flouting of the Constitution in the name of voluntarism, freedom of association, and freedom to discriminate, it is sowing the dragon's teeth of criminality and anarchy; for when children see that their parents have no respect for fundamenal law, they cannot help but draw the inference that man lives by might and not by right, that an ounce of force may be worth more than a pound of constitutional law. Enforcement of law in itself is an instrument that aids voluntarism, for when it is certain that "everyone who breaks the law will be dealt with by the law, the less will the power of coercion be felt. The more that resistance is seen to be hopeless, the more can the use of force remain latent."

Often, when these arguments are made against the South, the point is made that there is also racial discrimination in the North, and the inference is drawn that the struggle is not really over civil rights but is rather a sectional feud. Of course there is discrimination in the North, but the orders of magnitude are altogether different. While in the North one needs to look for discrimination—and if one looks for it, he will find it—in the South one needs to look for instances of nondiscrimination—and if one looks for such instances, he will find them. . . .

The American people—through Congress, through the Supreme Court, through states' civil rights and fair employment practices acts, through executive action affecting the military and civilian population, and through a Civil War that was the bloodiest and costliest war in American history—have rejected the slavery arguments for the inherent inferiority of the Negro race. With the ending of slavery, a hundred years ago, there should have come an end to the incidents and badges of slavery, concretized in racial segregation enforced by state law and custom. For these badges and incidents of slavery were based on an immoral opinion of what human nature is. Now Americans must still teach one another what it means to be a human being. The choice is not between law as a means and education as a means; for the law is itself a teaching device and education is itself an enforcing device. The disagreements are only superficially over the means. The real disagreements are over the ends—the inclusion of the Negro race in the community of citizens and in the communion of human beings. But in this instance, end and means are inextricably intertwined; for the Constitution, which is a law, demands that the school shall itself be a means and an end: that it be a demonstration of the ideal of equality, and that it contribute to the establishment of a society in which equality is a working ideal. The question that *Ecclesiasticus* asks about one's self can be asked also of a nation: "Who will justify him that sinneth against his own soul? and who will glorify him that dishonoreth his own life?" As the Negro struggles for freedom from dishonor and freedom from indignity, he struggles, too, to free America from dishonor and from indignity. The demand that the Negro makes today is as reasonable as that which Diogenes made of Alexander: "Stand out of my sunshine!"

15

Persisting Areas
of Controversy

Patrick Moynihan's article has been selected because it deals with a government report which occasioned great controversy and eloquently illustrates the confusions and misunderstandings which beset the Negro's quest for social justice and the efforts of those who would help him. It is more than just another tract on race prejudice or civil rights; it probes problem areas heretofore neglected and provides an insight into how public policy is made and unmade. The somewhat defensive tone of the article will not be understood unless one knows that its thesis as propounded in "The Negro Family" (usually called "The Moynihan Report") was attacked as encouraging "a new form of subtle racism"[1] and as diverting attention from the responsibility of the white majority for the Negro's plight.

Two other selections do not so much add to our knowledge as convey a sense of the wide gap between the Negro's view of his problem and an outspoken conservative's evaluation. The occasion was a debate sponsored by the Cambridge Union Society of Cambridge University which celebrated its 150th anniversary by inviting two well known Americans to argue the motion "The American Dream is at the Expense of the American Negro." In accordance with custom the Cantabrigians voted on the motion after the debate. The result of their balloting is recorded on the last page of this section.

---

[1] "Savage Discovery: The Moynihan Report," William Ryan, *The Nation* (November 22, 1965), pp. 380–384.

THE PRESIDENT AND THE NEGRO: THE MOMENT LOST

Daniel P. Moynihan

Daniel Patrick Moynihan as Assistant Secretary af Labor played an influential role in shaping President Johnson's Great Society programs. Too young to have caught the attention of Horatio Alger, he did indeed begin as one of those legendary bootblacks who survived poverty and the streets of New York to matriculate at Tufts and earn a Ph.D. He was called to Washington at the age of 34 by President Kennedy to work for the New Frontier and continued for a while to work in the Johnson administration. He is now director of the Joint Center for Urban Studies of Harvard University and the Massachusetts Institute of Technology. He is co-author, with Nathan Glazer, of Beyond the Melting Pot *and author of a book on the Negro family which will appear this year.*

Negroes . . . now have enforced legal rights as never in their history, but they remain terribly weak in economic and social terms—a situation that is, if anything, more conspicuous in the face of a booming, full-employment economy now entering its seventh year of unbroken expansion. The basic social legislation and, more importantly, adequate income levels for the Negro poor and the Negro working classes—legislation that would have meant for them what the New Deal measures meant for the population at large—were not enacted. They were, indeed, not even introduced. So long as war persists, economic conditions for Negroes are likely to be tolerable, but peace is more than likely to bring a return to the conditions of, say, the 1950's, conditions which they are no longer willing to accept, but no more than ever, as a group, able to avoid.

The misery is that it did not have to happen. The moment came when, as it were, the nation had the resources, and the leadership, and the will to make a *total* as against a partial commitment to the cause of Negro equality. It did not do so. But it was not Northern conservatives or Southern segregationists who stood in the way. For that one brief moment their opposition would not have prevailed. This time the opposition emanated from the supposed proponents of such a commitment: from Negro leaders

---

Reprinted from *Commentary* (February 1967), pp. 31–45, by permission; copyright © 1967 by the American Jewish Committee.

unable to comprehend their opportunity; from civil-rights militants, Negro and white, caught up in a frenzy of arrogance and nihilism; and from white liberals unwilling to expend a jot of prestige to do a difficult but dangerous job that had to be done, and could have been done. But was not.

One may be confident that Lyndon Johnson will be blamed for this, and with perhaps especial vehemence inasmuch as more than any man in American public life, and any President in American history, he tried to see that the job did get done. Hence the events that led to his effort, and to its subsequent failure, are worth noting: very likely to no greater purpose than the satisfaction of curiosity, but possibly in some small way as a lesson.

In a pattern that has become familiar for major Presidential initiatives, the effort began with an address to a university audience, in this instance the graduating class of Howard University on June 4, 1965. The timing here was perfect. The President had been overwhelmingly elected the preceding fall, and given the largest majorities in the House and Senate since those of the early Congresses that enacted the New Deal. Johnson had sent up a substantial, if not particularly radical, legislative program which was going along nicely. The one measure that promised to reapportion power in a part of American society, the Voting Rights Bill, was also well on its way to enactment. This latter was but one indication of the extraordinarily favored political position which Negro Americans enjoyed at that moment. The nation was proud, in a way, of having so resoundingly turned back the challenge of the Republican right wing, with its penumbra of reaction and racism. The Negro leaders had acted with great wisdom throughout that episode (and by successfully calling off demonstrations had seemed to evince genuine control of the Negro masses). The events in Selma had been almost a caricature of all that is stupid and intolerable in the South, and again the Negro performance was flawless. These events having in effect taken place on television, there was no longer any doubt that the country understood what things could be like in the South, and was determined to place the power of the federal government behind the protection of Negro civil rights in the region.

For just the reason that things were going so well, this was also the moment of maximum danger. To anyone who troubled to look closely at the situation it was clear that the disabilities of Negroes in the North were far wider and of a different order than those involving the deprivation of civil rights in the rural South. Assuring the franchise to Negroes in the South would help them; abolishing the public forms of segregation would also help them. But none of these measures would make any significant difference in the North, and not even that much in the South where Negroes were hopelessly outnumbered and, given the disparities of wealth and position, in important ways outclassed in the competitive struggle for position and wealth. In the meantime, a Negro proletariat was swelling to the bursting point in the cities of the North, its reach so far exceeding its grasp as to force any but the most indomitably complacent to see that trouble was in the offing.

The demands of Negroes in the South had been traditional, orderly, and unassailable in their justice: American citizens were asking that their constitutional rights be observed. Once the facts become clear, middle-class America agreed—instinctively, automatically. This was about the point—granting the looseness of any historical analogy—where things were left after the Civil War: the slaves were emancipated, and that was that. That they might remain penniless and dependent was not an issue touched upon either by John Locke or the American Constitution, and therefore of no concern to government. Just as almost everyone was free in 1863, almost everyone was able to vote a century later. On the other hand, no one had a "right" to own a farm in 1865, and no one had the "right" to hold a job in 1965. Then, as now, going beyond legal entitlements to rights of this kind meant getting involved in large social change—something far more radical than merely eliminating the major inconsistency of the existing system by bringing Negroes into it. Many of the groups now so insistent that the poll tax be abolished and school segregation ended (in the South) would not normally be prepared to support such a change. Moreover, compassion for the suffering, Christlike, non-violent Negro demonstrators of the South was a different thing from loving and understanding the frequently debased and disorderly slum-dwellers of the North. This was a point that anyone who had watched the emergence of "crime-in-the-streets" as a major political issue in New York City would have grasped.

Thus the danger signs were there. Nevertheless, the plain and ascertainable fact was that the nation was going through a moment that had never occurred before—and could not persist indefinitely—in which a willingness to accept a considerable degree of social innovation was combined with genuine feeling for the problems of Negroes. The world was at peace. The President had enormous majorities in Congress. The success of the New Economics was by then manifest: the Bureau of the Budget was already forecasting a $45 billion increase in the level of federal revenues by 1970—an increase, further, which doctrine ordained had to be spent in order to accrue. It was, in addition, a moment of racial calm. No demonstrators were abroad, no confrontation between white power and black protest was building up anywhere. In this atmosphere of maximum reasonableness and calm, an atmosphere in which the President could without great risk do nothing, and which for that very reason provided an opportunity for history to be made, the President, seizing the opportunity, set in motion a major initiative.

He went before an audience of fourteen-thousand persons on hand for the graduating ceremonies at Howard University and made the most advanced commitment to the cause of Negro equality of any President in history. Citing Churchill, he declared that the soon-to-be-enacted Voting Rights Bill, generally deemed at the time the ultimate in civil-rights achievement, was "not the end . . . not even the beginning of the end . . . perhaps the end of the beginning." Once again Negroes were being given their freedom, but, said the President:

". . . freedom is not enough. You do not wipe away the scars of centuries by saying: Now you are free to go where you want, do as you desire; choose the leaders you please.

You do not take a person who for years has been hobbled by chains and liberate him, bring him up to the starting line of a race and then say, You are free to compete with all the others, and still justly believe that you have been completely fair.

Thus it is not enough just to open the gates of opportunity. All our citizens must have the ability to walk through those gates."

For many Negroes there had been great progress, the President continued (speaking in a setting that made that clear enough). "But for the great majority of Negro Americans—the poor, the unemployed, the up-rooted and the dispossessed—there is a much grimmer story. They still are another nation. Despite the court order and the laws, despite the legislative victories and the speeches, for them the walls are rising and the gulf is widening." He went on to recount the facts of this widening gulf, and to insist that "Negro poverty is not white poverty"—the past had been too brutal, the present too distorted, racial prejudice too real for any useful analogy. The disadvantages of the Negro had become "a seamless web. They cause each other, they result from each other. They reinforce each other."

To argue this point, the President then turned to a subject never before mentioned by an American President, never before an acknowledged issue of public concern: the condition of the Negro family, the central fact and symbol of the "one huge wrong of the American nation," a condition that had vastly improved for some, but which remained anguished for many:

> For this, most of all, white America must accept responsibility. It flows from centuries of oppression and persecution of the Negro man. It flows from long years of degradation and discrimination, which have attacked his dignity and assaulted his ability to provide for his family.
>
> This, too, is not pleasant to look upon. But it must be faced by those whose serious intent is to improve the life of all Americans.
>
> Only a minority—less than half—of all Negro children reach the age of eighteen having lived all their lives with both of their parents. At this moment a little less than two-thirds are living with both of their parents. Probably a majority of all Negro children receive federally aided public assistance sometime during their childhood.

The family is the cornerstone of our society. More than any other force it shapes the attitude, the hopes, the ambitions, and the values of the child. When the family collapses it is the children that are usually damaged. When it happens on a massive scale the community itself is crippled.

So, unless we work to strengthen the family, to create conditions under which most parents will stay together—all the rest: schools and playgrounds, public assistance and private concern, will never be enough to cut completely the circle of despair and deprivation.

The President proposed "no single easy answer." Some measures were obvious enough: jobs that enable a man to support his family, decent housing, welfare programs better designed to hold families together, health care, compassion. "But there are other answers still to be found." To seek them out, he announced, he would convene in the fall a White House Conference of scholars and experts, outstanding Negro leaders and government officials. Its theme would be "To Fulfill These Rights," a phrase echoing the great assertion of the Declaration of Independence. And he dedicated his administration to this epic undertaking:

To move beyond opportunity to achievement. To shatter forever not only the barriers of law and public practice, but the walls which bound the condition of man to the color of his skin.

This is the next and more profound stage of the battle for civil rights. We seek not just freedom but opportunity—not just legal equity but human ability—not just equality as a right and a theory, but equality as a fact and as a result.

His audience was not in the least prepared for such a speech, nor was the press. The first accounts were routine enough: the President had promised equality, the ovation was "stunning," he had received an honorary degree. A Gemini flight was the big news of the moment. But over the weekend the reporters thought again and began to assess what they had heard. Douglas Kiker described it in terms of the reaction of an audience "accustomed to hearing national political leaders speak in traditional ways about civil rights":

At first they applauded the traditional lines. Then they sat in stunned silence. And finally they applauded out of shock and self-identification.

Mr. Johnson . . . [spoke] as no President ever has spoken before, but as a result it is doubtful that any future, serious discussion of the problem can be attempted without consideration of what he said.

Tom Wicker described the speech in terms of the Supreme Court decision on school segregation:

At Howard University . . . Mr. Johnson laid down much the
same principle on a much broader scale.

Providing for the Negro an equal "right" to vote, to get a job,
to go to unsegregated schools, to due process of law, Mr. Johnson
was really saying, is providing him with no more than "separate
but equal" citizenship. And just as had been true in education, so
it is true in the broader view that "separate" is inherently "unequal."

Thus did President Johnson face squarely what must be ranked
as the most difficult problem in American life. That problem is not
the enforcing of legal equity for the Negro. It is rather the acceptance of the Negro as an equal human being rather than a "separate
but equal" human being—a man with a darker skin rather than
a "black man."

It was a bold beginning. The speech seemed to attract more attention as time passed, and indeed is almost certain to find a place in the
history of Presidential papers. Yet before half-a-year had passed the initiative was in ruins, and after a year-and-a-half it is settled that nothing
whatever came of it.

Why? The reasons vary. Within weeks of the speech the President
was caught up in the series of decisions that led to the large-scale introduction of ground forces into Vietnam later that summer. The address at
Howard was in a sense his last peacetime speech. Thereafter, one would
assume, his mind was increasingly preoccupied with war in Asia. This did
not entail any backtracking on the commitment "To Fulfill These Rights,"
but it did mean that the White House was not going to think up a program
to do so. The energies of that tiny group at the apex of government were
now directed elsewhere. If a program was to be forthcoming, it would have
to be the work of the civil-rights movement, with whatever assistance it
could muster in government departments and universities. There was no
reason to assume that the movement would fail in this, but in fact it did so:
totally. The civil-rights movement had no program for going beyond the
traditional and relatively easy issues of segregation and discrimination, and
could not organize itself to produce one within the life of the 89th Congress. And in any event it did not do so because it allowed the question of
developing a program to be superseded by a preposterous and fruitless
controversy over a Department of Labor report which had been the
original precipitant of the Howard speech.

The report was entitled *The Negro Family: The Case for National
Action*. It was written by me (I was then Assistant Secretary of Labor for
Policy Planning and Research), with the assistance of Paul Barton and
Ellen Broderick of the Policy Planning Staff. It was an internal document
entirely: intended for the Secretary of Labor, the President, and the
members of their staffs who would accept or reject its proposals and implications. A hundred copies were produced, but with no expectation of using

even that few. The objectives of the report were twofold. First: to argue the need for seizing the opportunity of the moment to make the kind of commitment the President did in fact subsequently make. Second: to urge consideration of a new and different kind of policy, *in addition to* the more familiar ones—namely, a national family policy.

A word about these objectives: traditionally, the American legal and constitutional system has been based on a deliberate blindness to any social reality other than the reality of individuals. Deriving partly from the metaphysics of classical liberalism, and partly from the relative ethnic homogeneity of American society before the Civil War, this emphasis has been a source of much vitality and initiative, but also an obstacle to the entry of a number of groups into a full sharing of the rewards of American life. It was simply not enough, as Anatole France observed, that the law in its majestic equality should forbid the rich equally with the poor to sleep under bridges and to beg bread in the streets. The reality of class had to be acknowledged, for example, in order for the labor movement to make the gains it did under the New Deal. But if this understanding of the Negro in group terms has been widespread enough among scholars, it has not been a consideration in the framing of programs. The report on the Negro family was intended to demonstrate its relevance and thereby to persuade the government that public policy must now concern itself with issues beyond the frame of individualistic political thinking.

The second objective was connected with and flowed from the first. Family is not a subject Americans tend to consider appropriate as an area of public policy. Family affairs are private. For that very reason, to raise the subject in terms of public policy is to arouse immediate interest: edged with apprehension, but interest nonetheless. That was the simple purpose of the report: to win the attention of those in power. The government no less—in fact, more—than the nation at large was caught up in the euphoria and sense of achievement of the moment. This was, after all, an administration of Texans who could hardly help exaggerating the importance of the dismantling of the segregationist social structure that had been the shame and the burden of the South for so long. It was necessary to depict, and in terms that would be felt as well as understood, the internal weakness of the Negro community and the need for immense federal efforts if that community was to go beyond opportunity "to equality as a fact and as a result." Another discourse on unemployment, on housing, on health would not have accomplished this. It would have added little to what persons thought they generally knew. In any event, unemployment was going down, housing was by any criteria improving, health standards were higher than ever. Yet social indicators such as these are relative, while family in a sense remains an absolute: a broken family is broken; a deserted wife is alone; an abandoned child needs help. Describing the plight of so many Negro families appeared the surest way to bring home the reality of their need.

And, should the argument carry within the administration and be extended beyond, it seemed that programs aimed at the family might hope to enlist the support of the more conservative and tradition-oriented centers of power in American life whose enthusiasm for class legislation is limited indeed. To do anything for Negro families would entail assisting the entire population. Certain groups might be hesitant at first, but if the European or Canadian experience was any guide, such programs could quickly become a matter of solid consensus.

However little explored as a subject of public policy, the question of the Negro family has been perhaps the central subject of Negro scholarship in America. The first and in ways the best book, now forgotten, was written by W. E. B. DuBois in 1908, under the title, *The Negro American Family*. A generation later, E. Franklin Frazier published his classic work, *The Negro Family in the United States*. A number of others have contributed important studies since. The destruction of the family under the form of capitalist slavery practiced in the American South was, after all, the unique experience of the Negro American. It was the supreme fact of bondage and, if one likes, the unredeemable sin of the slaveholders. The gradual formation of families by freedmen before emancipation and others thereafter was a central element in the great transformation of the Negro people, but while eminently successful for some, it was slow and painful for many, and from the beginning, Negro families have been exposed to every variety of internal travail and external pounding. Frazier ended his work, which appeared in 1939, on an ominous note. The uprooted, marginal, Southern peasants were then moving To the City of Destruction. "The travail of civilization," he wrote, "is not yet ended."

> First, it appears that the family which evolved within the isolated world of the Negro folk will become increasingly disorganized. Modern means of communication will break down the isolation of the world of black folk, and, as long as the bankrupt system of Southern agriculture exists, Negro families will continue to seek a living in the towns and cities of the country. They will crowd the slum areas of Southern cities or make their way to Northern cities where their family life will become disrupted and their poverty will force them to depend upon charity.

The plan of the Labor Department report was to pick up from Frazier and record what had happened. As the data were assembled—data which had not previously been brought together—a compelling hypothesis began to emerge: *Frazier had been right*. It could not be described as a conclusion, since the information was not that solid, but the impression arose that the Negro community might be dividing. A middle class was clearly consolidating and growing, and yet the overall indicators continued to worsen, not precipitously but steadily. These two things could not be true unless a third fact—that things were falling apart at the bottom—was also true. And that meant trouble in the Northern slums.

The last point is essential to understanding the initial impact of the report and later the reaction to it. The kind of female-headed, female-based family now so common in Negro slums is nothing new. It has been and in places remains a commonplace feature of lower-class life in industrial societies. The Negro experience may be a particularly intensive one, but San Juan and Copenhagen, Glasgow and Dublin have or have had their counterparts. Further, it has its equivalents in primitive societies. In the view of a wide range of anthropologists and sociologists and, of course, of psychiatrists, these families and the communities they make up tend to transmit from one generation to the next, traits and circumstances which help perpetuate their condition. There is nothing absolute about this: as many individuals, no doubt, leave the culture as remain in it, and on one level the proposition amounts to little more than the assertion that the poor rarely inherit large estates. But anyone who has lived in or near the condition knows it to be real. The dissolution, the carelessness, the matriarchy, the violence, the "protest masculinity" are all there. The "massive deterioration of the fabric of society and its institutions," in Kenneth Clark's phrase, sets in and children get caught up in the "tangle of pathology" early. In any event, if, as Kennedy used to say, to govern is to choose, to advise those who govern is to choose positions and press them, and I pressed this one.

The report began: "The United States is approaching a new crisis in race relations." An opening section, "The End of the Beginning," proposed that the Negro demands for liberty in the South would now be met regardless of sporadic opposition, and that the nation must now turn to the issue of equality. On that issue no similar consensus existed. Yet mere equality of opportunity would not be sufficient, for in present terms Negroes were simply not competitive. "The principal challenge of the next phase of the Negro revolution is to make certain that equality of results will now follow. If we do not, there will be no social peace in the United States for generations."

With the warning: "Data are few and uncertain, and conclusions drawn from them, including the conclusions that follow, are subject to the grossest error," the report went on to declare that "At the heart of the deterioration of the fabric of Negro society is the deterioration of the Negro family." A combination of charts and text illustrated the way in which unemployment, in particular, had controlled family stability and welfare dependency, with the latter rising and falling in response to the non-white male unemployment rate, and the prevalence of broken families rising with the long-term rise in unemployment. But then in the 60's employment began to improve, but family conditions did not. *The possibility was real that the situation had begun feeding on itself.* The large number of children born to lower- and working-class Negro parents, combined with the low skills of Negro workers and the sluggishness of the wage structure, argued most powerfully that even full employment would not provide the economic stability that was clearly the basis of family stability for this group. . . . The report concluded that a new and vast national effort was required to enhance "the stability and resources of the Negro American family."

. . . The program response was obvious enough: guaranteed full employment, birth control, adoption services, etc. *But first of all a family allowance.* The United States is the only industrial democracy in the world without a system of automatic income supplements for people living with their children. It is the simplest and possibly the most effective of all social-welfare arrangements, not least because its administration involves no judgments as to whether or not the recipients are worthy and entitled to assistance. If the children are alive, the allowance is paid. The United States has, of course, a family allowance for *broken* families, the AFDC program. It was past time we came to our senses on the subject, and stopped penalizing families with a father in the home. In that far-off spring of 1965 it appeared we might. It was absurd to think that such a precious moment of legislative opportunity would pass without some measure of income redistribution. A family allowance was surely the most promising candidate. It would have cost $5 to $10 billion per year according to the scheme adopted *but we had the money.* To have enacted it would have been a first step in the necessary movement from the "civil-rights" phase— the phase involving legal equality for Negroes—into the phase of "equality as a fact and as a result."

The report was sent to the President by Secretary of Labor Wirtz on May 4th, along with a nine-point program. On May 30th, the White House asked for a draft of a speech at Howard to put forward its thesis. On the night of June 3rd, the draft was rewritten and after being read in the morning to Roy Wilkins, Whitney Young, and Martin Luther King, was delivered without further ado that afternoon.

. . . Predictably, albeit unbeknown to the White House, trouble began within the permanent government, as Arthur Schlesinger Jr. calls the civil-service bureaucracies. The report and the speech were wholly the product of the Presidential government. The welfare bureaucracy knew nothing of either, but as closer inquiry put the two together it was instantly perceived that the adequacy of the welfare bureaucracy's efforts and even the integrity of its view of events had been roundly condemned. The civil service is in an untenable position in this area: they know well enough the inadequacy of the programs they administer, and the ways in which Negroes are discriminated against even within the context of inadequate programs. Rainwater and Yancey write:

Over many years one of the most important ways of coping with this difficult situation has been to try to fuzz it over. Under the guise of civil libertarian reasoning, welfare organizations, both national and local, have tried to "wish away" race as a category, and this has had the latent function of concealing the extent to which discrimination continues. One of the early civil-rights activities of the Kennedy administration was to try to reverse this trend so that at least the government could be informed about the extent to which Negroes were disadvantaged. Having this "color blind" point of view built into their ideology, it was relatively easy for welfare personnel to find Moynihan's intransigent emphasis on color reactionary rather than radical.[1]

Word began to flow forth from the recesses of the Department of Health, Education and Welfare that I was a "subtle racist," that the Negro people had been insulted, and further that the facts were wrong. The Children's Bureau awoke from its torpor to join this effort with singularly feline earnestness.

For the record let it be said that such new information as has come to light since the report was written has substantially confirmed the thesis that the prevalence of family disruption among lower-class Negroes has been on the increase. The weakest statistic in the report had to do with the actual proportion of female-headed non-white families, which had increased only from 18 per cent in 1950 to 21 per cent in 1960. It happens that in March 1965, the month the report was finished, another census was being taken which showed the proportion of female-headed Negro families to have increased to 25 per cent—a sharp acceleration. This is the prevalence at the moment; the incidence over time is, of course, much higher. Probably not much more than a quarter of lower-class Negro children live with both parents during their entire youths. There are more broken families and they are breaking up earlier. Analyzing the non-white data in a paper delivered last summer, Daniel O. Price reported that 1970 will see "significant increases in the percent married with spouse absent. These increases are doubtless related to many factors such as increased urbanization, lack of economic opportunities for non-white males, welfare programs that reduce the financial strains on many female-headed households, differential cultural values, etc."

The white/non-white differential in marriage stability seems to hold at all economic and social levels, but the recent deterioration is clearly concentrated at the lowest ones. In Watts, for example, the proportion of children under 18 living with both parents dropped from 56 per cent in 1960, which was nothing to brag about, to 44 per cent in 1965. Most strikingly, family income levels have also been dropping in these areas.

---

[1] *The Moynihan Report and the Politics of Controversy* (Boston: M.I.T. Press, 1967).

Between 1960 and 1965, family income in America rose 14 per cent. *Non-white* family income rose 24 per cent. But in South Los Angeles, it declined 8 per cent, from $5,122 to $4,736 in constant dollars. The Negro community in that area was going through a serious increase in disorganization; this was not, however, happening to the Mexican American community alongside them in East Los Angeles. In the Hough section of Cleveland, a similar process was underway. In 1959, family income there was $4,732; by 1964, this had dropped to $3,966, a decline almost entirely accounted for by the increase in female-headed households, which rose from 22.5 per cent in 1960 to 32.1 per cent in 1966.

It is plain enough that anyone seeking to discredit a political initiative based on as sensitive a subject as family structure, particularly that of Negroes, will have no difficulty devising arguments. For generations, Negroes have labored under the attribution of genetic inferiority; to raise the question of a "deviant subculture" is to invite the charge of raising the same old canard of innate differences in a more respectable guise. The subject of family introduces the subject of sex, in this instance Negro sex, an issue of intense and not always acknowledged sensitivity for all parties. The subject of broken families raises the specter of welfare cheating charges . . . Further, Negro leaders and activists are apt themselves to come from the most solid, even rigid family backgrounds and probably have real difficulty perceiving or acknowledging the realities of lower-class life. And so on, down a long list of reasons, any one of which is sufficient to explain why, even when the subject is broached, as in the Howard speech, it barely makes its way into the press accounts, being an issue, as the *Economist* noted at the time, that liberals prefer to "skirt."

The attack, as is usual in such cases, came from the outside, in the form of a paper prepared early in the fall by a member of CORE, William Ryan (not the Manhattan congressman) and published in the *Nation*. . . . He charged the report with providing grounds for a massive white "cop out" by means of "a new form of subtle racism that might be termed 'Savage Discovery,' and seduces the reader into believing that it is not racism and discrimination but the weaknesses and defects of the Negro himself that account for the present status of inequality. . . ." One recalls the character in a Disraeli novel said to have been "distinguished for ignorance, in that he had but one idea and that was wrong." Ryan's one idea was that I was obsessed with illegitimacy; I should never have raised the subject, he said, and moreover was inaccurate in my facts. He may have been right about the first allegation, but he was wrong about the statistics. For illegitimacy—which Myrdal judged the best measure of family stability—*is* a serious problem for Negroes (and increasingly for whites as well). A quarter of all non-white births and almost half of first births (and in one large city for which data are available, near to two-thirds of first births) are out of wedlock. The illegitimate first child (the non-white rate rose from 39.5 per cent in 1955 to 47.4 per cent in 1964) seems a particularly poignant problem, as it almost certainly decimates the bargaining power of a young Negro girl with the world around her. Illegitimacy is a painful subject, but one is surprised in this age of the Foul Speech Movement to find that it is also thought to be a dirty word.

Thomas Pettigrew, of Harvard University, author of *Profile of the Negro American,* wrote the editor of the *Nation* describing the Ryan article as "trash . . . replete with errors and written by a man with no past experience in race relations. . . ." But it was widely distributed within the civil-rights movement and seemingly accepted as truth. At the year's end it was reprinted in *Crisis,* the official organ of the NAACP, under the title, "The New Genteel Racism."

The article was a blow to the Howard initiative, but not yet a deadly one. Roy Wilkins wrote to say he had not known the NAACP was reprinting it: "My opinion of the Ryan piece and of similar reasoning is well known to my immediate associate here. . . . It is a silly and sinister distortion to classify as racist this inevitable discussion of a recognized phase of our so-called race problem." Wilkins's attitude was shared by other Negro leaders. During the summer, Whitney Young, Jr. several times noted, properly, that he had for years been writing about just such questions. In October in a speech in Westchester, Martin Luther King, Jr. summed up a general position:

> As public awareness [of the breakdown of the Negro family] increases there will be dangers and opportunities. The opportunity will be to deal fully rather than haphazardly with the problem as a whole—to see it as a social catastrophe and meet it as other disasters are met, with an adequacy of resources. The danger will be that problems will be attributed to innate Negro weaknesses and used to justify neglect and rationalize oppression.

Just so. The Howard speech was playing for high stakes.

The fact was that the civil-rights movement was beginning to think in these terms. The President of a new Asian nation once remarked to an American Assistant Secretary of State that his predecessor, the first President, had had a glorious job. "He had only to go about the country shouting, 'Freedom!' For me it's different. For me it's all arithmetic." Just such a day was approaching for the Negro leaders. On April 3, 1965, in a staff memorandum entitled "Suggested Guidelines for Future Organizational Expansion," James Farmer, then the national head of CORE, had opened the subject: "In the past," he wrote, "any talk of upgrading and improving the Negro community would immediately have been labeled anti-integrationist, separationist, reactionary, and lending grist to the mill of those who cry, 'Not Ready Yet.' But even if such accusations come from thoughtless quarters, we must not delay motion in this direction."

In other circumstances, the Howard speech and even the report might have served to give direction to this developing attitude. Yet just the opposite occurred. The reasons are no doubt many, but an important one seems to have been the war in Vietnam . . .

The real blow was Watts. It threw the civil-rights movement entirely off balance. Until then, theirs had been the aggrieved, the just, the righteous cause. In the South an old game had been going on with a new rule, imperfectly understood by whites, that the first side to resort to violence—lost. Now in the North the Negroes had resorted to violence, in a wild destructive explosion that shattered, probably forever, the image of non-violent suffering. And within hours of the signing of the Voting Rights Act. The same new rule applied. The civil-rights movement could not explain Watts, and could not justify it. Then, of a sudden, the report on the Negro family was being used to do so. Watts made the report a public issue, and gave it a name. Or rather the columnists Rowland Evans and Robert Novak did in their column of August 18, which began:

> Weeks before the Negro ghetto of Los Angeles erupted in violence, intense debate over how to handle such racial powder kegs was under way deep inside the Johnson administration.
> The pivot of this debate: the Moynihan report, a much suppressed, much leaked Labor Department document that strips away usual equivocations and exposes the ugly truth about the big-city Negro's plight.

The report, said they, had raised, as indeed it had, the explosive question of preferential treatment, "a solution far afield from the American dream."

. . . after Watts the report gained notoriety as an explanation of the internal problems revealed by the riots, and in that measure angered and repelled just those Negro leaders who had been on the point of turning to just such problems. Before long I was being denounced, for example, by James Farmer, in terms not at all consistent with his staff memorandum of April 3: "We are sick unto death," he wrote in a syndicated column, "of being analyzed, mesmerized, bought, sold, and slobbered over. . . . Moynihan has provided a massive academic copout for the white conscience and clearly implied that Negroes in this nation will never secure a substantial measure of freedom until we stop sleeping with our wife's sister and buying Cadillacs instead of bread. . . . Nowhere does Moynihan suggest that the proper answer to a shattered family is an open job market where the 'frustrated' Negro male can get an honest day's work." (The gist of the report was, if I may, that full employment, while indispensable, was no longer enough.)

Watts also threw off the White House, which found the moment for the conference "To Fulfill These Rights" almost upon it, but with no adequate preparations for a full-scale meeting. It was decided to hold first a small planning session. This met in November in an atmosphere of near frenzy over the report which was all the militants seemed able to think of. . . . The conference was in truth a shambles; in the aftermath, one Chicago militant declared it had been entirely too much dominated by "whites and Jews," and from within the administration came the verdict: "A disaster."

. . . The essential fact is that neither the government nor the civil-rights movement had the resources to prepare a program in response to the Howard speech. This was the point of unparalleled opportunity for the liberal community and it was exactly the point where that community collapsed.

The collapse had been presaged just before the planning session met in November. A "Pre–White House Conference on Civil Rights" was convened in New York by the Office of Church and Race of the Protestant Council in cooperation with the Commission on Religion and Race of the National Council of Churches. A distinguished group of religious leaders, including Catholics and Jews and a scattering of liberal professors, was in attendance. The key figures were Dr. Robert Spike, Executive Director of the Commission on Religion and Race which had been established in 1963 in the midst of the Birmingham crisis, and Dr. Benjamin F. Payton, a young Negro sociologist and minister, then with the New York Protestant Council, and who a month later succeeded Spike in the national post. The larger purpose of the meeting was to propose that an "Economic Development Budget for Equal Rights in America," to cost $32 billion per year, be placed on the agenda of the White House Conference. But the real heat of the gathering was in the demand "that the question of 'family stability' be stricken entirely from that agenda. . . ."

This demand was supported by a paper written by Dr. Payton analyzing the report. It had already, he said, "had an impact upon the civil-rights movement and upon more general American politics that is quite deadening and utterly misleading." . . .

> Based largely upon Bureau of Census statistics, it summarizes very incomplete data in the form of some highly questionable conclusions, the most important of which are: (1) Since unemployment in general is decreasing in America, the riots breaking out in cities across the land cannot be positively associated with lack of jobs on the part of Negroes; (2) The major causal factor behind the riots, therefore, cannot be associated with *present and continuing* discrimination, or with an inadequate supply of job-training. . . .

Dr. Payton's main assertion was that the report had declared that the employment and income gap between Negroes and whites was closing (where, in fact, the report had said exactly the opposite). . . .

In truth, the Payton paper bordered on the psychopathological. (Although perhaps not: it was broadcast by the hundreds at the time, and achieved its objective brilliantly. . . .) Charles M. Silberman, author of *Crisis in Black and White,* called it "the most blatant distortion that I can remember seeing in a long time." In a letter to a Presbyterian minister he wrote:

> Moynihan's whole emphasis is on the crucial role of unemploy-
> ment in understanding all of the problems of Negro pathology;
> he presents one statistical correlation after another, showing that
> illegitimacy, desertion, and all the other symptoms show an un-
> believably high correlation with changes in Negro unemployment;
> he marshals an enormous amount of evidence demonstrating—
> completely contrary to Payton's allegations throughout his essay—
> that Negro unemployment is very much more serious than the un-
> employment statistics indicate.

And so on. The Presidential assistant most directly responsible for civil-rights matters, a devout Protestant layman, described Payton's paper as "the apotheosis of the big lie." But somehow a nerve had been touched in Liberal Protestantism and there was no undoing the effects. Given the national prominence and the position of the persons who convened the Payton-Spike meeting, and given the absence of any protest or correction from within the church community, it had to be taken as the voice of American Protestantism. The issue of the Negro family was dead. . . .

. . . In February, the President appointed a thirty-member group to organize the White House Conference "To Fulfill These Rights." Reverend Spike was put on this Council and the subject of family—raised by an accused and thereby half-convicted "crypto-racist"—was taken off the agenda. The Department of Labor, the Department of Health, Education and Welfare, and the Office of Economic Opportunity set to work destroying all traces of the original policy, while producing tract on tract to demonstrate that what the President had said at Howard University was not so. The White House dissociated itself from the report and the subject. Order was restored, and soon the old orthodoxies were securely back in place: the problems of Negroes derived from the behavior of whites, and laws would change that behavior. A civil-rights message was sent to Congress proposing a ban on discrimination in housing in about the terms Governor Dewey used to address the New York State legislature in the 1940's.

The Conference, when it met, was a lifeless affair. The Council submitted a long report of unflinching orthodoxy, that missed entirely the import of the Howard speech. It reflected throughout what Rainwater has called "the services strategy," as against an income strategy in dealing with problems of poverty. Thus, the section on public welfare proposed, "There should be a sharp reduction of the number of clients served by each case worker." . . . The Education section proposed that public expenditure per pupil be increased from $532 to $1000. This would reflect an increase of tax outlay per Negro family of $1404, or 37.5 per cent of average Negro family income. But almost every last penny of this increase would go to middle-class persons whose salaries are already well above the poverty level. The thought of giving the money directly to the Negro family in the form of a family allowance is not even suggested in the report, a document in any event destined for instant obscurity. The delegates were bored from the outset, and contented themselves with passing resolutions of no greater political realism than the report itself: "That J. Edgar Hoover be fired," "That the President ask for $2 billion to enforce Civil Rights laws." The President spoke briefly and warned his hearers not to expect miracles.

The question will be asked whether the subject of family was that essential. The answer will depend on a judgment as to the nature of the Negro problem. If one sees it as wholly a white problem, a matter of racial discrimination and oppression which can and should be stamped out, then it will be held that any internal troubles Negroes may have will thereafter take care of themselves. If on the other hand, one sees it as a systemic problem which, *whatever its origins,* is now producing results that no significant portion of the population intends, then family becomes a relevant and politically *useful* issue. I believe it fair to say that family disruption is both a valid measure of the overall impact of external forces on a group such as urban Negroes, and it is also a measure whereby outside groups—white Americans—can be brought to see the realities of life in terms that command attention and demand response. In these terms, the subject of family does not, as has been charged, distract from issues like employment, but rather gives them a reality and urgency which normally they do not command among certain segments of the population. Writing in *Christianity and Crisis* in February 1965, Reverend Spike took particular exception to the fact that *Life* magazine seemed to approve the report. But that was just the point: family is an issue that comes home to responsible and influential, but conservative, persons such as the editors of *Life.* . . .

The administration was and is, as much committed to the goals of the Howard speech as when it was delivered. But it lacked the resources of time and political capital to force the issue. . . . The most that could be hoped for was that the businessmen and liberal leaders on the President's new Council should stick by the Howard thesis and press the matter. They did nothing of the sort. In retrospect it is clear that civil rights had become for them a cause that could no longer stimulate or inspire them to take any grave risks. . . . faced with the prospect that this time there might be some real danger, that a genuinely—horrid word—controversial issue was being raised, the President's Council—persons solidly representative of the civil-rights establishment of that time—did not consider the matter even long enough for it to be said that it collapsed. It did not consider the matter at all. The subject was not dropped, it was never even raised.

The President's Council failed because in the end it had no views: all it sought was agreement. A quest for peace of this kind gives maximum leverage to the group with the most intransigent and assertive opinions, and the greatest ideological discipline. At the moment in question, in matters concerning civil rights, this was a position conspicuously enjoyed by the liberal Left. If that term is vague, anyone with experience in politics will nonetheless recognize the reality behind it. . . .[2]

The nation needs the liberal Left. It has provided a secular conscience in a civilization where the immorality of large organizations has become, as Niebuhr warned us it would, almost the central danger of the age, and where the older voices of conscience have grown confused or silent or worse. Moreover, it has begun to affect and even to "infiltrate" religious institutions in many areas so that, of a sudden, churches stand for something in American public life other than that which is trivial, vulgar, or both. Had it not been for the liberal Left, it is unlikely that the civil-rights movement would have had the extraordinary impact and success of the past decade. But if one accepts the thesis that that was a first phase which now *must* be followed by a second, then the matter becomes more difficult. In the first phase, where issues of principle, of justice, of witness were involved, the liberal Left was an indispensable ally. In the second phase, however, where it becomes necessary to confront the realities of lower-class life, the liberal Left can be a disaster. Consider its reaction to the Watts riot. Anyone with a minimal sense of American social history would have instantly seen this as a calamity. Yet in no time, the liberal Left was depicting the participants not as a mob (and rather a merchandise-minded mob at that) but as an avenging, exultant proletariat. In the March 1966 COMMENTARY, Bayard Rustin explained that it had not been a riot at all, but rather a "Manifesto,"a nicely articulated and discriminating statement of a political viewpoint. For a period after Watts it was not unusual to encounter middle-class civil-rights militants not only repeating the threats and predictions of further violence which had become commonplace on the part of Negroes, but actually enjoying the prospect. . . .

The reaction of the liberal Left to the issue of the Negro family was decisive (the Protestant reaction was clearly triggered by it). They would have none of it. No one was going to talk about their poor people that way. Next ensued a discouragingly familiar form of whipsawing. On

---

[2] Editor's note: Dr. Moynihan's use of the term "liberal left" is misleading and unfortunate. Many mainstream liberals often think of themselves as the "liberal left" and are probably located on the political spectrum in that way by middle-of-the-roaders," conservatives, and the extreme right. Yet such mainstream liberals would agree with Moynihan's indictment of the group to whom he refers, a group which would much more aptly be called the "radical left" or the "New Left."

the one hand, the problems did not exist, the whole affair was a calculated slander; on the other hand, these were not problems at all, but healthful adaptations to intolerable social conditions imposed by an unfeeling racist society. College professors waxed absolutely lyric on the subject of the female-headed household. One of the persisting themes was first sounded by William Ryan who, in his *Nation* article, introduced a novel social indicator, the illegitimacy conception rate. This rate reveals that white bourgeois females fornicate as much as, or even more than (although not of course so well as), Negro girls, and conceive almost as often. But thereafter they resort to (Park Avenue) abortionists. Thus the point becomes to establish *guilt* instead of to deal with a problem.

This is terrifyingly reminiscent of Stanley Elkins's abolitionists who seem never to have seen slavery as a social problem for slaves, but only as an ethical problem for slaveholders. Once legal bondage was at an end, the subject was closed so far as the Northerners were concerned. The fact that the slaves lived on, and the child is born—and needs help—is a matter somehow to be passed over. This is the crux of it. Typically, the refusal of the liberal Left to accept the unpleasant facts of life for the poor—there is delinquency in the slums, but those kids in the suburbs are just as bad and don't get arrested, etc. etc.—leads to the same position as does the insistence of the extreme conservatives on just such facts: namely, to do nothing. The liberal Left will acknowledge the relevance of these facts only to the extent that they serve as an indictment of American society; after that it loses interest. The extreme conservatives harp on these facts in order to indict the poor; after that, *they* lose interest. It does not occur to the liberal Left, for example, that the issue of illegitimacy has nothing to do with whether black women are more or less promiscuous than white women; it has to do with the number of children on the welfare rolls. This is a legitimate concern of public policy. At Howard, however, the President in a radical initiative made the damage to the life-chances of those children a further concern of public policy for the first time in American history. And the liberal Left responded by denying the facts of the damage ("the statistics are wrong") and/or denying that the damage was real ("it is a cultural pattern superior in its vitality to middle-class mores") and/or by arguing about the comparative sexual morals of white and black women.

The insistence, in short, of the liberal Left that the issue of dis-organization in Negro lower-class life not be made a matter of public concern resulted directly in its not being made a matter of public action. . . .

It would be entirely wrong to suggest that resentment over the report was confined to white intellectuals in New York. A great many Negro activists became quite incensed over it, and remained so. A clear concern on the part of many was that the issue would be picked up and used by racists. But there is almost no indication that this occurred, and on the other hand much evidence that Negroes in more ordinary walks of life both recognized what the report was about, and hoped something would come of it. . . .

The urgency of a serious national commitment in the area of income support and guaranteed employment (which would be the central goals of a national family policy) increases as other options close. At the moment, Negroes are placing enormous confidence in the idea that quality education can transform their situation. But it is not at all clear that education has this potential. Last summer, the U.S. Office of Education issued its report on "Equality of Educational Opportunity" based on the study—the second largest in the history of social science—ordered by the Civil Rights Acts of 1964 of the educational facilities available to Negroes and other minority groups as compared with the white majority. The report, of which James S. Coleman of Johns Hopkins was the principal author, radically confounded expectation. Negroes, it turned out, tested badly at the outset of their schooling, and worse at the end of it. But the quality of the schools they attend—shockingly segregated schools—was not in fact significantly different from that of schools attended by whites and others. More important, the regression analyses carried out for the study produced the astounding proposition that the quality of the schools has only a trifling relation to achievement:

> Differences in school facilities and curriculum, which are the major variables by which attempts are made to improve schools, are so little related to differences in achievement levels of students that, with few exceptions, their effects fail to appear even in a survey of this magnitude.

These findings may be modified by further analysis, and it should be noted that for the worst-off groups, better schools do show a distinct if small relation to achievement, and in the right direction. Nonetheless, the two great determinants of outcome turned out to be family background and social peer group. In a later article in *The Public Interest,* Coleman wrote:

> Two points, then, are clear: (1) These minority children have a serious educational deficiency at the start of school, which is obviously not a result of school; and (2) they have an even more serious deficiency at the end of school, which is obviously in part a result of school.
>
> Altogether, the sources of inequality of educational opportunity appear to lie first in the home itself and the cultural influences immediately surrounding the home, then they lie in the schools' ineffectiveness to free achievement from the impact of the home, and in the schools' cultural homogeneity, which perpetuates the social influences of the home and its environs.

Coleman's study is probably the best statistical case for integration ever made: pouring conscience money into slum schools is simply not likely to do the job. He provides strong support for the thesis . . . for despite the many paper gains that Negroes have been making (and some of course more real than that), "There are two areas of bedrock resistance to the progress of the Negro race: residential segregation and the weakness of the Negro family structure." Coleman's data argue that both must be overcome, while the data . . . declare that this is not happening. It now appears it could be a generation before any extensive neighborhood integration is achieved. For the moment the trend is in the opposite direction, owing to changes in the South. Unfortunately, housing integration presents itself as a deceptively simple matter: pass a law. It is likely therefore to preoccupy civil-rights forces, even though it is the area of the most adamant and resourceful opposition. In the meantime, measures to enhance the stability and resources of the family, which might in fact be easier to achieve, will probably continue to be neglected: those who want housing integration most are likely to support these measures least, and very possibly nothing will be achieved on either count.

Given this stalemate, it is altogether possible that the nation will spiral downward into a state of protracted violence and unrest. One infant in six in this country is Negro: the problem will not go away. Yet it may also be that recent events foretell a different outcome. The nation is turning conservative at a time when its serious internal problems may well be more amenable to conservative solutions than to liberal ones—or to solutions carried out by conservatives. It may be that conservatives have more stomach for dealing with the problems of poverty and disorganization in the necessary terms. Republican ranting about welfare contains much meanness and demagoguery, but it is also true that the number of families on welfare in this country *is* a scandal. They ought to be off the dole—not for the sake of the taxpayers, but for *their* sakes. The challenge is to find viable ways of doing this, but that will be impossible unless we first allow that the problem does exist.

The New York experience may be relevant here. Two of the more spectacular political victories of recent times were the election of the Republican John V. Lindsay as Mayor of New York City in 1965 and a year later, the re-election for a third term of Governor Nelson A. Rockefeller. It was not commented upon, but the issue of race was as much present in their campaigns as it was in the more obvious "backlash" affairs elsewhere. In just about every subway car in the New York transit system in 1965 there was a large advertisement that said simply *"Breathe* easier, *Sleep* better, *Feel* safer, with the Lindsay Team." Anyone who does not know what that poster was about is really not eligible to vote. Similarly in 1966 Governor Rockefeller, as the New York *Times* reported, switched his campaign in the last weeks to concentrate almost entirely on crime in the streets.

Lindsay and Rockefeller are humane, progressive men with impec-

cable records of leadership in civil rights. But they perceive the reality of
the internal problems of the slums, and are willing to get elected on that
basis. It remains to be seen whether they and others like them will come
forward with programs that will command conservative support for doing
something about those problems: not necessarily out of compassion for the
oppressed, but out of concern for the stability of society.

But . . . , this is not a likely outcome. There are never enough
Disraelis to go round. The more likely future is one dominated by hyper-
conservatives unwilling to solve problems of the kind Negroes face, hyper-
liberals reluctant to acknowledge the existence of such problems, and
persons of the center increasingly aware that they are probably not competent and certainly not eligible to propose solutions of their own devising.
The era of white initiatives on behalf of Negroes is over. The controversy
over the report on the Negro family had at least this useful outcome: it
raised for Negroes the question of what terms they are willing to accept as
grounds for social action. The continuing controversy among Negroes
themselves over the issue, which for a year now has been dead and forgotten in Washington, suggests that some at least are finding this a timely
and useful development.

Two fairly clear points of view have emerged. On the one hand,
there is that of Martin Luther King Jr., who is willing to describe the
present conditions of life in the lower classes as a "social catastrophe" and
to say in effect to the white world, "Put up or shut up." The basic idea is
that there can and ought to be change. This is a view widely held by
scholars and activists alike. . . . But just as many—more—have taken
quite a different view, namely that the family structure of the lower classes
is a natural and essentially healthful adaptation to special conditions of
life. In an interview in November 1966 the novelist Ralph Ellison, expressing his annoyance with the report, said:

> Moynihan looked at a fatherless family and interpreted it not in
> the context of Negro cultural patterns, but in a white cultural
> pattern. He wasn't looking at the accommodations Negros have
> worked out in dealing with fatherless families. Grandmothers very
> often look after the kids. The mother works or goes on relief. The
> kids identify with stepfathers, uncles, even the mother's boyfriends.
> How children grow up is a cultural, not a statistical pattern.

I would argue that this is a perfectly tenable position. There is no reason
Negroes need conform to anyone's standards but their own, and like no
one else, Ellison has evoked the qualities of endurance and holding-on
which are as much the fact of Negro character in white America as are the
extremes of respectability or disorganization. On the other hand, in order
for this to be a *viable* position as well as a tenable one, it must reject not
only conformity but dependency. It is all very well to point out with whom

it is that impoverished Negro youth identifies: the public issue is who supports them. So long as exceptional numbers of Negro children are dependent on Welfare (recently the U.S. Commissioner of Welfare reported that the majority of families receiving AFDC payments now are nonwhites) and so long as vast numbers of Negro youths have to be helped along with Head Start, Upward Bound, Job Corps, and so on, Negroes will be at the mercy of whites demanding an end to "welfare chiseling" and "immorality" . . . These things ought not to be so, but they are so. As the [Moynihan] report said on its first page: "The racist virus in the American blood stream still afflicts us: Negroes will encounter serious personal prejudice for at least another generation." If at the moment educated, middle-class Negroes are much in demand and doing nicely, this is not so for the lower class and is likely never to be. This country is not fair to Negroes and will exploit any weakness they display. Hence they simply cannot afford the luxury of having a large lower class that is at once deviant *and* dependent. If they do not wish to bring it into line with the working class (*not* middle-class) world around them, they must devise ways to support it from within. It is entirely possible that this could happen, and it might be an eye-opener for all concerned. In all events, one of the most galling forms of dependency is surely behind us. The time when white men, whatever their motives, could tell Negroes what was or was not good for them, is now definitely and decidedly over. An era of bad manners is almost certainly begun. For a moment it had seemed this could be avoided, that the next two decades could be bypassed in a sweep of insight and daring. But the destiny reasserted itself. . . .

"THE AMERICAN DREAM IS AT THE EXPENSE OF THE AMERICAN NEGRO": A DEBATE

Debating the affirmative:

James Baldwin

Novelist and essayist James Baldwin is one of the best known Negro writers in this country. His work has been recognized by numerous fellowships ad awards and he has contributed· many articles to national magazines. He has lectured frequently on civil rights.

I find myself, not for the first time, in the position of a kind of Jeremiah. It would seem to me that the question before the house is a proposition horribly loaded, that one's response to that question depends on where you find yourself in the world, what your sense of reality is. That is, it depends on assumptions we hold so deeply as to be scarcely aware of them.

The white South African or Mississippi sharecropper or Alabama sheriff has at bottom a system of reality which compels them really to believe when they face the Negro that this woman, this man, this child must be insane to attack the system to which he owes his entire identity. For such a person, the proposition which we are trying to discuss here does not exist.

On the other hand, I have to speak as one of the people who have been most attacked by the Western system of reality. It comes from Europe. That is how it got to America. It raises the question of whether or not civilizations can be considered equal, or whether one civilization has a right to subjugate—in fact, to destroy—another.

Now, leaving aside all the physical factors one can quote—leaving aside the rape or murder, leaving aside the bloody catalogue of oppression which we are too familiar with anyway—what the system does to the subjugated is to destroy his sense of reality. It destroys his father's authority over him. His father can no longer tell him anything because his past has disappeared.

In the case of the American Negro, from the moment you are born every stick and stone, every face, is white. Since you have not yet seen a mirror, you suppose you are, too. It comes as a great shock around the age of 5, 6 or 7 to discover that the flag to which you have pledged allegiance, along with everybody else, has not pledged allegiance to you. It comes as a great shock to see Gary Cooper killing off the Indians and, although you are rooting for Gary Cooper, that the Indians are you.

It comes as a great shock to discover that the country which is your birthplace and to which you owe your life and identity has not, in its whole system of reality, evolved any place for you. The disaffection and the gap between people, only on the basis of their skins, begins there and accelerates throughout your whole lifetime. You realize that you are 30 and you are having a terrible time. You have been through a certain kind of mill and the most serious effect is again not the catalogue of disaster— the policeman, the taxi driver, the waiters, the landlady, the banks, the insurance companies, the millions of details 24 hours of every day which spell out to you that you are a worthless human being. It is not that. By that time you have begun to see it happening in your daughter, your son or your niece or your nephew. You are 30 by now and nothing you have done has helped you to escape the trap. But what is worse is that nothing you have done, and as far as you can tell nothing you *can* do, will save your son or your daughter from having the same disaster and from coming to the same end.

We speak about expense. There are several ways of addressing one-self to some attempt to find out what that word means here. From a very literal point of view, the harbors and the ports and the railroads of the country—the economy, especially in the South—could not conceivably be what they are if it had not been (and this is still so) for cheap labor. I am speaking very seriously, and this is not an overstatement: I picked cotton, I carried it to the market, I built the railroads under someone else's whip for nothing. For nothing.

The Southern oligarchy which has still today so very much power in Washington, and therefore some power in the world, was created by my labor and my sweat and the violation of my women and the murder of my children. This in the land of the free, the home of the brave. None can challenge that statement. It is a matter of historical record.

In the Deep South you are dealing with a sheriff or a landlord or a landlady or the girl at the Western Union desk. She doesn't know quite whom she is dealing with—by which I mean, if you are not part of a town and if you are a Northern nigger, it shows in millions of ways. She simply knows that it is an unknown quantity and she wants to have nothing to do with it. You have to wait a while to get your telegram. We have all been through it. By the time you get to be a man it is fairly easy to deal with.

But what happens to the poor white man's, the poor white

woman's, mind? It is this: they have been raised to believe, and by now they helplessly believe, that no matter how terrible some of their lives may be and no matter what disaster overtakes them, there is one consolation like a heavenly revelation—at least they are not black. I suggest that of all the terrible things that could happen to a human being that is one of the worst. I suggest that what has happened to the white Southerner is in some ways much worse than what has happened to the Negroes there.

Sheriff Clark in Selma, Ala., cannot be dismissed as a total monster; I am sure he loves his wife and children and likes to get drunk. One has to assume that he is a man like me. But he does not know what drives him to use the club, to menace with the gun and to use the cattle prod. Something awful must have happened to a human being to be able to put a cattle prod against a woman's breasts. What happens to the woman is ghastly. What happens to the man who does it is in some ways much, much worse. Their moral lives have been destroyed by the plague called color.

This is not being done 100 years ago, but in 1965 and in a country which is pleased with what we call prosperity, with a certain amount of social coherence, which calls itself a civilized nation and which espouses the notion of freedom in the world. If it were white people being murdered, the Government would find some way of doing something about it. We have a civil rights bill now. We had the 15th Amendment nearly 100 years ago. If it was not honored then, I have no reason to believe that the civil rights bill will be honored now.

The American soil is full of the corpses of my ancestors, through 400 years and at least three wars. Why is my freedom, my citizenship, in question now? What one begs the American people to do, for all our sakes, is simply to accept our history.

It seems to me when I watch Americans in Europe that what they don't know about Europeans is what they don't know about me. They were not trying to be nasty to the French girl, rude to the French waiter. They did not know that they hurt their feelings; they didn't have any sense that this particular man and woman were human beings. They walked over them with the same sort of bland ignorance and condescension, the charm and cheerfulness, with which they had patted me on the head and which made them upset when I was upset.

When I was brought up I was taught in American history books that Africa had no history and that neither had I. I was a savage about whom the least said the better, who had been saved by Europe and who had been brought to America. Of course, I believed it. I didn't have much choice. These were the only books there were. Everyone else seemed to agree. If you went out of Harlem the whole world agreed. What you saw was much bigger, whiter, cleaner, safer. The garbage was collected, the children were happy. You would go back home and it would seem, of course, that this was an act of God. You belonged where white people put you.

It is only since World War II that there has been a counterimage in the world. That image has not come about because of any legislation by any American Government, but because Africa was suddenly on the stage of the world and Africans had to be dealt with in a way they had never been dealt with before. This gave the American Negro, for the first time, a sense of himself not as a savage. It has created and will create a great many conundrums.

One of the things the white world does not know, but I think I know, is that black people are just like everybody else. We are also mercenaries, dictators, murderers, liars. We are human, too. Unless we can establish some kind of dialogue between those people who enjoy the American dream and those other people who have not achieved it, we will be in terrible trouble. This is what concerns me most. We are sitting in this room and we are all civilized; we can talk to each other, at least on certain levels, so that we can walk out of here assuming that the measure of our politeness has some effect on the world.

I remember when the ex-Attorney General, Mr. Robert Kennedy, said it was conceivable that in 40 years in America we might have a Negro President. That sounded like a very emancipated statement to white people. They were not in Harlem when this statement was first heard. They did not hear the laughter and bitterness and scorn with which this statement was greeted. From the point of view of the man in the Harlem barber shop, Bobby Kennedy only got here yesterday and now he is already on his way to the Presidency. We were here for 400 years and now he tells us that maybe in 40 years, if you are good, we may let you become President.

Perhaps I can be reasoned with, but I don't know—neither does Martin Luther King—none of us knows how to deal with people whom the white world has so long ignored, who don't believe anything the white world says and don't entirely believe anything I or Martin say. You can't blame them.

It seems to me that the City of New York has had, for example, Negroes in it for a very long time. The City of New York was able in the last 15 years to reconstruct itself, to tear down buildings and raise great new ones and has done nothing whatever except build housing projects, mainly in the ghettoes, for the Negroes. And of course the Negroes hate it. The children can't bear it. They want to move out of the ghettoes. If American pretensions were based on more honest assessments of life, it would not mean for Negroes that when someone says "urban renewal" some Negroes are going to be thrown out into the streets, which is what it means now.

It is a terrible thing for an entire people to surrender to the notion that one-ninth of its population is beneath them. Until the moment comes when we, the Americans, are able to accept the fact that my ancestors are both black and white, that on that continent we are trying to forge a new identity, that we need each other, that I am not a ward of America, I am not an object of missionary charity, I am one of the people who built the country—until this moment comes there is scarcely any hope for the American dream. If the people are denied participation in it, by their very presence they will wreck it. And if that happens it is a very grave moment for the West.

"THE AMERICAN DREAM IS AT THE EXPENSE OF THE AMERICAN NEGRO": A DEBATE

Debating the negative:

William F. Buckley, Jr.

Mr. Buckley first achieved prominence when, upon being graduated from Yale, he castigated the liberalism of the Yale faculty in his God and Man at Yale *(1951). He has been lambasting liberals ever since—including Republican liberals —and has made himself the most vocal exponent of a strict conservatism which, however, contemptuously rejects Mr. Welch and the Birch Society. On the other hand, in* McCarthy and his Enemies *(with C. Bozell, 1954) he ardently defends the late Senator. Mr. Buckley is a tireless polemicist whose vehicles are a national television program, the lecture plat-form, and the arch and archly conservative* National Review *of which he is editor-in-chief.*

It seems to me that of all the indictments Mr. Baldwin has made of America here tonight, and in his copious literature of protest, the one that is most striking involves, in effect, the refusal of the American community to treat him other than as a Negro. The American community has refused

From *The New York Times Magazine* (March 7, 1965), p. 32 ff. © 1965 by The New York Times Company. Reprinted by permission of the author.

to do this. The American community, almost everywhere he goes, treats him with the kind of unction, with the kind of satisfaction that a posturing hero gets for his flagellations of our civilization, so that he quite properly commands the contempt he so eloquently showers upon us.

It is quite impossible in my judgment to deal with the indictments of Mr. Baldwin unless one is prepared to deal with him as a white man, unless one is prepared to say to him that the fact that your skin is black is utterly irrelevant to the arguments you raise. The fact that you sit here, carrying the entire weight of the Negro ordeal on your shoulders, is irrelevant to the argument we are here to discuss.

I am treating you as a fellow American, as a man whose indictments of our civilization are unjustified, as an American who—if his counsels were listened to—would be cursed by all his grandchildren's grandchildren.

About 125 years ago this house was bitterly divided over the question of whether or not some people in England who practiced the faith of Erasmus, your most distinguished lecturer, should be allowed to vote. By a slim margin it was decided that they ought to be allowed to do so. We know that there was more blood shed trying to emancipate the Irish here in the British Isles than has been shed by 10 times the number of people who have been lynched as a result of the delirium of race consciousness, race supremacy, in the United States. Shall we devote the night to these luridities? Shall we devote the evening to examining the sociological facts of human nature? Shall we discuss these class antagonisms in terms of race, in terms of economic standing? Shall we discuss the existential dilemma of humankind?

It is a fact that the position in America is as it is, that the situation in Africa is as it is. The question before the house is not whether we should have purchased slaves generations ago, or ought the blacks to have sold us those slaves. The question, rather, is this: Is there anything in the American dream which intrinsically argues against some kind of deliverance from the system that we all recognize as evil? What shall we do about it? What shall we in America do to eliminate these psychic humiliations which I join Mr. Baldwin in believing are the very worst aspects of this discrimination?

It is the case that seven-tenths of the average white's income in the United States is equal to the entire income of the average Negro. But my great-grandparents worked hard. I do not know of anything which has ever been created without the expense of something. We have a dastardly situation. But I am going to ask you not to make politics as the crow flies.

What is it that we Americans ought to do? I wonder. What is it we should do, for instance, to avoid the humiliations mentioned by Mr. Baldwin as having been part of his own experiences? At the age of 12 he trespassed outside the ghetto of Harlem and was taken by the scruff of his neck by a policeman on 42d Street and Madison Avenue and told, "Here, you nigger, go back to where you belong." Fifteen to 20 years later he asks for a Scotch whisky in Chicago and is told by the white barman that he is obviously under age and under the circumstances cannot be served. I know from your faces that you share with me a feeling of compassion and a feeling of outrage that this kind of thing should have happened. How are we going to avoid the kind of humiliations which are visited perpetually upon members of the minority race?

Obviously, the first element is concern. We have got to care that it happens. We have got to do what we can to change the warp and woof of moral feelings and society to make it happen less and less.

The proposition before us tonight as elaborated by Mr. Baldwin is that we ought precisely to recognize that the American civilization, and indeed the Western civilization, has failed him and his people, that we ought to throw it over. He tells us that our civilization rests on the rantings of the Hebrew, sunbaked fanatic called Jesus—not, says he, truly the founder of the Christian religion. The founder of the Christian religion was actually Paul, whom he describes as a merciless fanatic. And as a result of these teachings of Jesus and Paul, we have Dachau.

If we assume that Dachau was the natural consequence of the teachings of St. Paul and Jesus, what shall we do with the library around here? Shall we descend on it and uproot all the literature that depends in any way on the teachings of Plato and Aristotle because they justified slavery? The primary question before the house is whether or not our civilization has shown itself so flawed as the result of the failure of its response to the Negro problem of the United States that it ought to be jettisoned.

Now I suggest that anyone who argued that English civilization ought to have been jettisoned because Catholics were not allowed to vote in England as late as 1829 and Jews not until 1832 should consider the other possibility. Precisely the reason they *did* get the vote was because English civilization was not jettisoned. The whole point of our philosophical concern ought never to make that terrible fault made so frequently by the positivists, that we should rush forward and overthrow our civilization because we don't live up to our high ideals.

It may be that there has been some sort of sunburst of moral enlightenment that has hit this community so as to make it predictable that if you were the governors of the United States the situation would change overnight. The engines of concern in the United States are working. The presence of Mr. Baldwin here is, in part, a reflection of that concern.

You cannot go to any university in the United States in which practically every other problem of public policy is not pre-empted by the primary concern for the Negro. I challenge you to name me another civilization in the history of the world in which the problems of the minority, which have been showing considerable material and political advancement, are as much a subject of dramatic concern as in the United States.

Americans are not willing, as a result of Mr. Baldwin's aspirations, to say that the whole American proposition was an unfortunate experiment. They are not willing to say that because we have not accelerated Negro progress faster, we are going to desert the constitutional system, the idea of the rule of law, the idea of individual rights of the American citizen, that we are going to burn all the Bibles, burn our books, that we want to reject our entire Judaeo-Christian civilization because of the continued persistence of the kind of evil that has been so eloquently described by Mr. Baldwin.

There is no instant cure for the race problem in America. Anyone who tells you that there is a quick solution is a charlatan and ultimately a boring man—a boring man because he is then speaking in the kind of abstractions which do not relate to human experience. The Negro problem is a very complicated one. I urge those of you who have an actual interest in the problem to read "Beyond the Melting Pot," by Nathan Glazer and Daniel Moynihan. They say that in 1900 there were 3,500 Negro doctors in America. In 1960 there were 3,900, an increase of 400. Is this because there were no opportunities? No, they say. There are a great many medical schools which by no means practice discrimination. It is because the Negro's particular energy is not directed toward that goal.

What should James Baldwin be doing other than telling us to renounce our civilization? He should be addressing his own people and urging them to take advantage of those opportunities which do exist. And urging us to make those opportunities wider.

Where Negroes are concerned, the danger, as far as I can see at this moment, is that they will seek to reach out for some sort of radical solutions, on the basis of which the true problem is obscured. They have done a great deal to focus on the facts of white discrimination against Negroes. They have done a great deal to agitate a moral concern. But where in fact do they go now? They seem to be slipping into some sort of Procrustean formulation which ends up by urging the advancement of the Negro less than the regression of white people.

[Interjection from an American undergraduate: "Mr. Buckley, one thing you can do is to let them vote in Mississippi."

Buckley: "I agree. Except, lest I appear too ingratiating, I think actually what is wrong in Mississippi is not that not enough Negroes have the vote but that too many white people are voting."]

What we need is a considerable amount of frankness that acknowledges there are two sets of difficulties. We must recognize the difficulty that brown people, white people, black people have all over the world to protect their own vested interests. They suffer from a kind of racial narcissism which tends always to convert every contingency in such a way as to maximize their own power. We must acknowledge that problem, but we must also reach through to the Negro people and tell them that their best chances are in a mobile society and the most mobile society in the world today is in the United States.

It is precisely that mobility which can give opportunities to the Negroes, which they must be encouraged to take. But they must not be encouraged to adopt the kind of cynicism, the kind of despair, the kind of iconoclasm that is urged by Mr. Baldwin.

For one thing I believe—that the fundamental trend in the United States is to the good nature, the generosity and good wishes, the decency that do lie in the spirit of the American people. These qualities must not be laughed at, and under no circumstances must America be told that the only alternative is the overthrow of that civilization which we consider to be the faith of our fathers, the faith of your fathers.

If it finally does come to a confrontation between giving up the best features of the American way of life and fighting for them, then we will fight the issue. We will fight the issue not only in the Cambridge Union, but we will fight as you were once asked to fight—on the beaches, in the hills, in the mountains. And just as you waged war to save civilization, you also waged war for the benefit of the Germans, your enemies. We, too, are convinced that if it should ever come to that kind of confrontation, then our determination will be to wage war not only for the whites, but also for the Negroes.

The motion supported by Mr. Baldwin was carried overwhelmingly. The vote: 544 for the motion, 164 against.

Part Five

The Church and Society

16

Church and State

Our churches face many problems with significant moral implications that must go unexplored here. Among such problems are the confusion of superstition, which Thomas Aquinas once called the vice of excess in religion, with religion itself; the polarity between religious fundamentalism and liberalism; the disparity between what one observer has called passion in the pulpit and apathy in the pew, and with this the weakness of the religious commitment in a secular society; the limits and possibilities of the ecumenical movement; the strengths and weaknesses of evangelical Christianity. The selections are limited to two topics, both of great interest to most thoughtful people.

The first of these concerns the relation of church and state. Since America is without an established church, and most American Catholics are reconciled to religious pluralism, the problem is not as acute with us as with some European countries. Nevertheless, persistent controversies remind us that the problem is far from solved. The fate of federal aid to education hinges on the support of Catholics, and the Catholic hierarchy, even in opposition to our first Catholic President, has withheld approval so long as private schools are declared ineligible for public aid. The issues range from this central one to somewhat less urgent matters such as Massachusetts' and Connecticut's use of police power to proscribe the use of contraceptives in order to enforce religious scruples not shared by all their citizens.

Beyond such specific issues and important to their under-standing are certain more general and more fundamental differ-ences. Article I of the Constitution declares that "Congress shall make no law respecting an establishment of religion, or prohibiting the free exercise thereof. . . ." Although the latter provision establishes pluralism as the foundation of our religious life, interpretations of pluralism continue to vary not only in applying it to particular cases but in understanding its essential meaning. Even the first provision of the article suddenly erupts into controversy as when the U.S. Supreme Court ruled (6 to 1) against official prayers in the public schools. The Court, citing the First Amendment, has declared that "it is no part of the business of government to compose official prayers for any group of American people to recite as part of a religious program carried on by the government." The ensuing repercussions[1] suggest that the accommodation of church and state is not yet stable. The first two selections in this part deal with this basic problem. They are supplemented by what might be called a case study.

A second topic is equally important. It concerns the role organized religion and its spokesmen should play and have played in correcting the great social abuses to which most men have been heir. At issue is the very meaning of the religious experience.

Some urge that the church must concern itself with inner rectitude and man's relation to God. If the first is cultivated and the second properly ordered, this is all that matters. Thereupon individuals will pursue the good, and social justice will ensue as a matter of course. It is then with individual vice and virtue that the church must concern itself. There are many variations on this theme—ranging all the way from a naive, simplistic treatment of problems of personal morality by the evangelists to the more worldly dependence of the Buchmanites on suddenly converted moral "heroes."

Others argue that this is sheer religiosity, a desirable escape when men are powerless to remedy the evils of the world in which they live, but irrelevant to our time and place. It is urged that preoccupation with goodness and evil in the abstract is simply an opportunist evasion of responsibility for attacking specific

---

[1] Cardinal Spellman was "shocked and frightened" by the decision, adding that "it strikes at the very heart of the Godly tradition in which America's children have so long been raised." Protestant Dwight Eisenhower said, "I always thought this nation was essentially a religious one" and Herbert Hoover saw in the decision a "disintegration of one of the most sacred of American heritages." None of them remembered that Founding Father James Madison believed even tax exemption for churches to be unconstitutional. Perhaps Father Murray had Madison as well as the Supreme Court in mind when, encountering Justice Douglas at the Center for the Study of Democratic Institutions, he observed that he had been formulating a new school prayer that might be acceptable to the Court. The prayer would start, "To whom it may concern. . . ."

social abuses. When the church shuns the great moral issues—racial segregation, poverty in the midst of opulence, greed and hypocrisy in high places—its role degenerates into an apology for the existing order and a diversionary excoriation of minor, imagined, or harmless vices. The Hebrew prophets and Christian martyrs denounced social abuses. Where are their modern counterparts? Certainly in many places, including Czarist Russia, religion *was* the "opiate of the masses." If too many people have turned to the secular religion of which Karl Marx, who coined that phrase, is the prophet, is this not because the church has abdicated its proper role? This, with variations, has been the argument not only of those who remain outside the church because they find insufficient moral outlet through it, but of the Social Gospel Movement that through the years has imparted significant momentum to the cause of social reform.

A third position is taken by those who argue that, although the Christian ethic provides a basis on which to criticize the social order, attempts to derive a program for the reconstruction of society from the teachings of Jesus are futile. The discussions that follow will reflect some of these standpoints.

CIVIL UNITY AND RELIGIOUS INTEGRITY

John Courtney Murray, S.J.

The late John Courtney Murray's distinction as a theologian has already been noted.[1] Here, in an eloquent and scholarly statement, he explained why he believed that Catholics can in good conscience and without reservation respect the First Amendment.

As it arose in America, the problem of pluralism was unique in the modern world, chiefly because pluralism was the native condition of American society. It was not, as in Europe and in England, the result of a

From *We Hold These Truths: Catholic Reflections on the American Proposition* by Rev. John Courtney Murray, S.J. (New York: Sheed & Ward, Inc., 1960), pp. 45–78 © Sheed & Ward, Inc. 1960. Reprinted by permission.

[1] See above, pp. 271–272.

disruption or decay of a previously existent religious unity. This fact created the possibility of a new solution; indeed, it created a demand for a new solution. The possibility was exploited and the demand was met by the American Constitution.

The question here concerns the position of the Catholic conscience in the face of the new American solution to a problem that for centuries has troubled, and still continues to trouble, various nations and societies. A new problem has been put to the universal Church by the fact of America—by the uniqueness of our social situation, by the genius of our newly conceived constitutional system, by the lessons of our singular national history, which has molded in a special way the consciousness and temper of the American people, within whose midst the Catholic stands, sharing with his fellow citizens the same national heritage. The Catholic community faces the task of making itself intellectually aware of the conditions of its own coexistence within the American pluralistic scene. We have behind us a lengthy historical tradition of acceptance of the special situation of the Church in America, in all its differences from the situations in which the Church elsewhere finds herself. But it is a question here of pursuing the subject, not in the horizontal dimension of history but in the vertical dimension of theory.

The argument readily falls into two parts. The first part is an analysis of the American Proposition with regard to political unity.

The unity asserted in the American device, "E pluribus unum" . . . is a unity of a limited order. It . . . must not hinder the various religious communities in American society in the maintenance of their own distinct identities. Similarly, the public consensus, on which civil unity is ultimately based, must permit to the differing communities the full integrity of their own religious convictions. The one civil society contains within its own unity the communities that are divided among themselves; but it does not seek to reduce to its own unity the differences that divide them. In a word, the pluralism remains as real as the unity. Neither may undertake to destroy the other. Each subsists in its own order. And the two orders, the religious and the civil, remain distinct, however much they are, and need to be, related. All this, I take it, is integral to the meaning attached in America to the doctrine of religious freedom and to its instrumental companion-doctrine called (not felicitously) separation of church and state. I use the word "doctrine" as lawyers or political philosophers, not theologians, use it.

We come therefore to the second question. It concerns the American solution to the problem put by the plurality of conflicting religions within the one body politic. In its legal form (there are other forms, as I shall later say) the solution is deposited in the First Amendment to the Federal Constitution: "Congress shall make no law respecting an establishment of religion or prohibiting the free exercise thereof. . . ." What then is the Catholic view of this constitutional proviso?

The American Catholic is entirely prepared to accept our constitutional concept of freedom of religion and the policy of no establishment as the first of our prejudices. He is also prepared to admit that other prejudices may obtain elsewhere—in England, in Sweden, in Spain. Their validity in their own context and against the background of the history that generated them does not disturb him in his conviction that his own prejudice, within his own context and against the background of his own history, has its own validity.

American Catholics would even go as far as to say of the provisions of the First Amendment what Burke, in his *Reflections,* said of the English Church Establishment, that they consider it as "essential to their state; not as a thing heterogeneous and separable, something added from accommodation, what they may either keep up or lay aside, according to their temporary ideas of convenience. They consider it as the foundation of their whole Constitution, with which, and with every part of which, it holds an indissoluble union." The prejudice formulated in the First Amendment is but the most striking aspect of the more fundamental prejudice that was the living root of our constitutional system—the prejudice in favor of the method of freedom in society and therefore the prejudice in favor of a government of limited powers, whose limitations are determined by the consent of the people. The American people exempted from their grant of power to government any power to establish religion or to prohibit the free exercise thereof. The Catholic community, in common with the rest of the American people, has historically consented to this political and legal solution to the problem created by the plurality of religious beliefs in American society. They agree that the First Amendment is by no means destitute of reason; that it involves profound and extensive wisdom; that its wisdom has been amply substantiated by history. Consequently, they share the general prejudice which it states; often enough both in action and in utterances they have made this fact plain. And that should be the end of the matter.

Theologies of the First Amendment

But, as it happens, one is not permitted thus simply to end the matter. I leave aside the practical issues that have arisen concerning the application of the First Amendment. The question here is one of theory, the theory of the First Amendment in itself and in its relation to Catholic theories of freedom of religion and the church-state relation. It is customary to put to Catholics what is supposed to be an embarrassing question: Do you really believe in the first two provisions of the First Amendment?

The question calls to mind one of the more famous among the multitudinous queries put by Boswell to Dr. Johnson, "whether it is necessary to believe all the Thirty-Nine Articles." And the Doctor's answer has an applicable point: "Why, sir, that is a question which has been much agitated. Some have held it necessary that all be believed. Others have considered them to be only articles of peace, that is to say, you are not to preach against them."

An analogous difference of interpretation seems to exist with regard to the first two articles of the First Amendment.

On the one hand, there are those who read into them certain ultimate beliefs, certain specifically sectarian tenets with regard to the nature of religion, religious truth, the church, faith, conscience, divine revelation, human freedom, etc. In this view these articles are invested with a genuine sanctity that derives from their supposed religious content. They are dogmas, norms of orthodoxy, to which one must conform on pain of some manner of excommunication. They are true articles of faith. Hence it is necessary to believe them, to give them a religiously motivated assent.

On the other hand, there are those who see in these articles only a law, not a dogma. These constitutional clauses have no religious content. They answer none of the eternal human questions with regard to the nature of truth and freedom or the manner in which the spiritual order of man's life is to be organized or not organized. Therefore they are not invested with the sanctity that attaches to dogma, but only with the rationality that attaches to law. Rationality is the highest value of law. In further consequence, it is not necessary to give them a religious assent but only a rational civil obedience. In a word, they are not articles of faith but articles of peace, that is to say, you may not act against them, because they are law and good law. . . .

What is in question is the meaning and the content of the first of our American prejudices, not its genesis. Do these clauses assert or imply that the nature of the church is such that it inherently demands the most absolute separation from the state? Do they assert or imply that the institutional church is simply a voluntary association of like-minded men; that its origins are only in the will of men to associate freely for purposes of religion and worship; that all churches, since their several origins are in equally valid religious inspirations, stand on a footing of equality in the face of the divine and evangelical law; that all ought by the same token to stand on an equal footing in the face of civil law? In a word, does separation of church and state in the American sense assert or imply a particular sectarian concept of the church?

Further, does the free-exercise clause assert or imply that the individual conscience is the ultimate norm of religious belief in such wise that an external religious authority is inimical to Christian freedom? Does it hold that religion is a purely private matter in such wise that an ecclesiastical religion is inherently a corruption of the Christian Gospel? Does it maintain that true religion is religion-in-general, and that the various sects in their dividedness are as repugnant religiously as they are politically dangerous? Does it pronounce religious truth to be simply a matter of personal experience, and religious faith to be simply a matter of subjective impulse, not related to any objective order of truth or to any structural economy of salvation whose consistence is not dependent on the human will?

The questions could be multiplied, but they all reduce themselves to two. Is the no-establishment clause a piece of ecclesiology, and is the free-exercise clause a piece of religious philosophy? The general Protestant tendency, visible at its extreme in the free-church tradition, especially among the Baptists, is to answer affirmatively to these questions. Freedom of religion and separation of church and state are to be, in the customary phrase, "rooted in religion itself." Their substance is to be conceived in terms of sectarian Protestant doctrine. They are therefore articles of faith; not to give them a religious assent is to fall into heterodoxy.

The secularist dissents from the Protestant theological and philosophical exegesis of the first of our prejudices. But it is to him likewise an article of faith (he might prefer to discard the word, "faith," and speak rather of ultimate presuppositions). Within this group also there are differences of opinion. Perhaps the most sharpened view is taken by those who in their pursuit of truth reject not only the traditional methods of Christian illumination, both Protestant and Catholic, but also the reflective methods of metaphysical inquiry.

These men commit themselves singly to the method of scientific empiricism. There is therefore no eternal order of truth and justice; there are no universal verities that require man's assent, no universal moral law that commands his obedience. Such an order of universals is not empirically demonstrable. Truth therefore is to be understood in a positivistic sense; its criteria are either those of science or those of practical life, i.e., the success of an opinion in getting itself accepted in the market place. With this view of truth there goes a corresponding view of freedom. The essence of freedom is "non-committalism." I take the word from Gordon Keith Chalmers. He calls it a "sin," but in the school of thought in question it is the highest virtue. To be uncommitted is to be in the state of grace; for a prohibition of commitment is inherent in the very notion of freedom. The mind or will that is committed, absolutely and finally, is by definition not free. It has fallen from grace by violating its own free nature. In the intellectual enterprise the search for truth, not truth itself or its possession, is the highest value. In the order of morals the norm for man is never reached by knowledge. It is only approximated by inspired guesses or by tentative practical rules that are the precipitate of experience, substantiated only by their unity.

This school of thought, which is of relatively recent growth in America, thrusts into the First Amendment its own ultimate views of truth, freedom, and religion. Religion itself is not a value, except insofar as its ambiguous reassurances may have the emotional effect of conveying reassurance. Roman Catholicism is a disvalue. Nevertheless, religious freedom, as a form of freedom, is a value. It has at least the negative value of an added emancipation, another sheer release. It may also have the positive value of another blow struck at the principle of authority in any of its forms; for in this school authority is regarded as absolutely antinomous to freedom.

Furthermore, this school usually reads into the First Amendment a more or less articulated political theory. Civil society is the highest societal form of human life; even the values that are called spiritual and moral are values by reason of their reference to society. Civil law is the highest form of law and it is not subject to judgment by prior ethical canons. Civil rights are the highest form of rights; for the dignity of the person, which grounds these rights, is only his civil dignity. The state is purely the instrument of the popular will, than which there is no higher sovereignty. Government is to the citizen what the cab-driver is to the passenger (to use Yves Simon's descriptive metaphor). And since the rule of the majority is the method whereby the popular will expresses itself, it is the highest governing principle of statecraft, from which there is no appeal. Finally, the ultimate value within society and state does not consist in any substantive ends that these social forms may pursue; rather it consists in the process of their pursuit. That is to say, the ultimate value resides in the forms of the democratic process itself, because these forms embody the most ultimate of all values, freedom. There are those who pursue this theory to paradoxical lengths—perhaps more exactly, to the lengths of logical absurdity—by maintaining that if the forms of democracy perish through the use of them by men intent on their destruction, well then, so be it.

Given this political theory, the churches are inevitably englobed within the state, as private associations organized for particular purposes. They possess their title to existence from positive law. Their right to freedom is a civil right, and it is respected as long as it is not understood to include any claim to independently sovereign authority. Such a claim must be disallowed on grounds of the final and indivisible sovereignty of the democratic process over all the associational aspects of human life. The notion that any church should acquire status in public life as a society in its own right is per se absurd; for there is only one society, civil society, which may so exist. In this view, separation of church and state, as ultimately implying a subordination of church to state, follows from the very nature of the state and its law; just as religious freedom follows from the very nature of freedom and of truth.

The foregoing is a sort of anatomical description of two interpretations of the religion clauses of the First Amendment. The description is made anatomical in order to point the issue. If these clauses are made articles of faith in either of the described senses, there are immediately in this country some 35,000,000 dissenters, the Catholic community. Not being either a Protestant or a secularist, the Catholic rejects the religious position of Protestants with regard to the nature of the church, the meaning of faith, the absolute primacy of conscience, etc.; just as he rejects secularist views with regard to the nature of truth, freedom, and civil society as man's last end. He rejects these positions as demonstrably erroneous in themselves. What is more to the point here, he rejects the notion that any of these sectarian theses enter into the content or implications of the First Amendment in such wise as to demand the assent of all American citizens. If this were the case the very article that bars any establishment of religion would somehow establish one. . . .

If it be true that the First Amendment is to be given a theological interpretation and that therefore it must be "believed," made an object of religious faith, it would follow that a religious test has been thrust into the Constitution. The Federal Republic has suddenly become a voluntary fellowship of believers either in some sort of free-church Protestantism or in the tenets of a naturalistic humanism. The notion is preposterous. The United States is a good place to live in; many have found it even a sort of secular sanctuary. But it is not a church, whether high, low, or broad. It is simply a civil community, whose unity is purely political, consisting in "agreement on the good of man at the level of performance without the necessity of agreement on ultimates" (to adopt a phrase from the 1945 Harvard Report on General Education in a Free Society). As regards important points of ultimate religious belief, the United States is pluralist. Any attempt at reducing this pluralism by law, through a process of reading certain sectarian tenets into the fundamental law of the land, is prima facie illegitimate and absurd.

The truth of history happens to be more prosaic than the fancies of the secular liberals. In seeking an understanding of the first of our prejudices we have to abandon the poetry of those who would make a religion out of freedom of religion and a dogma out of separation of church and state. We have to talk prose, the prose of the Constitution itself, which is an ordinary legal prose having nothing to do with doctrinaire theories.

Articles of Peace

From the standpoint both of history and of contemporary social reality the only tenable position is that the first two articles of the First Amendment are not articles of faith but articles of peace. Like the rest of the Constitution these provisions are the work of lawyers, not of theologians or even of political theorists. They are not true dogma but only good law. That is praise enough. This, I take it, is the Catholic view. But in thus qualifying it I am not marking it out as just another "sectarian" view. It is in fact the only view that a citizen with both historical sense and common sense can take.

That curiously clairvoyant statesman, John C. Calhoun, once observed that "this admirable federal constitution of ours is superior to the wisdom of any or all the men by whose agency it was made. The force of circumstances and not foresight or wisdom induced them to adopt many of its wisest provisions." The observation is particularly pertinent to the religion clauses of the First Amendment. If history makes one thing clear it is that these clauses were the twin children of social necessity, the necessity of creating a social environment, protected by law, in which men of differing religious faiths might live together in peace. . . . This mark of inevitability is an index of goodness. And it is perhaps nowhere more strikingly manifest than in the institutions which govern the relation of government to religion. These institutions seem to have been preformed in the peculiar conditions of American society. It did indeed take some little time before the special American solution to the problem of religious pluralism worked itself out; but it is almost inconceivable that it should not have worked itself out as it did. One suspects that this would have been true even if there had been no Williamses and Penns, no Calverts and Madisons and Jeffersons. The theories of these men, whatever their merits, would probably have made only literature, not history, had it not been for the special social context into which they were projected. Similarly, the theories of these men, whatever their defects, actually made history because they exerted their pressure, such as it was, in the direction in which historical factors were already moving the new American society.

To say this is not of course to embrace a theory of historical or social determinism. It is only to say that the artisans of the American Republic and its Constitution were not radical theorists intent on constructing a society in accord with the a priori demands of a doctrinaire blueprint, under disregard for what was actually "given" in history. Fortunately they were, as I said, for the most part lawyers. And they had a strong sense of that primary criterion of good law which is its necessity or utility for the preservation of the public peace, under a given set of conditions. All law looks to the common good, which is normative for all law. And social peace, assured by equal justice in dealing with conflicting groups, is the highest integrating element of the common good. This legal criterion is the first and most solid ground on which the validity of the First Amendment rests. . . .

The demands of social necessity were overwhelming. It remains only to insist that in regarding the religion clauses of the First Amendment as articles of peace and in placing the case for them on the primary grounds of their social necessity, one is not taking low ground. Such a case does not appeal to mean-spirited expediency nor does it imply a reluctant concession to *force majeure*. In the science of law and the art of jurisprudence the appeal to social peace is an appeal to a high moral value. Behind the will to social peace there stands a divine and Christian imperative. This is the classic and Christian tradition. . . .

The First Amendment . . . does not say that there is no distinction between true and false religion, good and bad morality. But it does say that in American circumstances the conscience of the community, aware of its moral obligations to the peace of the community, and speaking therefore as the voice of God, does not give government any mandate, does not impose upon it any duty, and does not even communicate to it the right to repress religious opinions or practices, even though they are erroneous and false.

On these grounds it is easy to see why the Catholic conscience has always consented to the religion clauses of the Constitution. They conform to the highest criterion for all legal rulings in this delicate matter. The criterion is moral; therefore the law that meets it is good, because it is for the common good. Therefore the consent given to the law is given on grounds of moral principle. To speak of expediency here is altogether to misunderstand the moral nature of the community and its collective moral obligation toward its own common good. The origins of our fundamental law are in moral principle; the obligations it imposes are moral obligations, binding in conscience. One may not, without moral fault, act against these articles of peace.

The Distinction of Church and State

If the demands of social necessity account for the emergence in America of religious freedom as a fact, they hardly account for certain peculiarities of the first of our prejudices and for the depth of feeling that it evokes. Another powerful historical force must be considered, namely, the dominant impulse toward self-government, government by the people in the most earnest sense of the word. Above all else the early Americans wanted political freedom. And the force of this impulse necessarily acted as a corrosive upon the illegitimate "unions" of church and state which the post-Reformation era had brought forth. The establishments of the time were, by and large, either theocratic, wherein the state was absorbed in the church, or Erastian, wherein the church was absorbed in the state. In both cases the result was some limitation upon freedom, either in the form of civil disabilities imposed in the name of the established religion, or in the form of religious disabilities imposed in the name of the civil law of the covenanted community. The drive toward popular freedom would with a certain inevitability sweep away such establishments. Men might share the fear of Roger Williams, that the state would corrupt the church, or the fear

of Thomas Jefferson, that the church would corrupt the state. In either case
their thought converged to the one important conclusion, that an end had
to be put to the current confusions of the religious and political orders. The
ancient distinction between church and state had to be newly reaffirmed in
a manner adapted to the American scene. Calvinist theocracy, Anglican
Erastianism, Gallican absolutism—all were vitiated by the same taint: they
violated in one way or another this traditional distinction. . . .

    . . . the distinction of church and state, one of the central asser-
tions of this tradition, found its way into the Constitution. There it received
a special embodiment, adapted to the peculiar genius of American government and to the concrete conditions of American society.

    How this happened need not concern us here. Certainly it was in
part because the artisans of the Constitution had a clear grasp of the
distinction between state and society, which had been the historical product
of the distinction between church and state, inasmuch as the latter distinction asserted the existence of a whole wide area of human concerns which
were remote from the competence of government. Calhoun's "force of
circumstances" also had a great deal of influence; here again it was a
matter of the Fathers building better than they knew. Their major concern
was sharply to circumscribe the powers of government. The area of state—
that is, legal—concern was limited to the pursuit of certain enumerated
secular purposes (to say that the purposes are secular is not to deny that
many of them are also moral; so for instance the establishment of justice
and peace, the promotion of the general welfare, etc.). Thus made
autonomous in its own sphere, government was denied all competence in
the field of religion. In this field freedom was to be the rule and method;
government was powerless to legislate respecting an establishment of
religion and likewise powerless to prohibit the free exercise of religion. Its
single office was to take legal or judicial steps necessary on given occasions
to make effective the general guarantee of freedom.

    The concrete applications of this, in itself quite simple, solution
have presented great historical and legal difficulties. This has been inevitable, given the intimacy with which religion is woven into the whole social
fabric, and given, too, the evolution of government from John Adams'
"plain, simple, intelligible thing, quite comprehensible by common sense,"
to the enormously complicated and sprawling thing which now organizes a
great part of our lives, handles almost all education, and much social
welfare. In particular, we have not yet found an answer to the question
whether government can make effective the primary intention of the First
Amendment, the guarantee of freedom of religion, simply by attempting to
make more and more "impregnable" what is called, in Roger Williams'
fateful metaphor, the "wall of separation" between church and state. However, what concerns us here is the root of the matter, the fact that the

American Constitution embodies in a special way the traditional principle of the distinction between church and state.

For Catholics this fact is of great and providential importance for one major reason. It serves sharply to set off our constitutional system from the system against which the Church waged its long-drawn-out fight in the nineteenth century, namely, Jacobinism, or (in Carlton Hayes's term) sectarian Liberalism, or (in the more definitive term used today) totalitarian democracy.

It is now coming to be recognized that the Church opposed the "separation of church and state" of the sectarian Liberals because in theory and in fact it did not mean separation at all but perhaps the most drastic unification of church and state which history had known. The Jacobin "free state" was as regalist as the *ancien régime,* and even more so. Writing as a historian, de Tocqueville long ago made this plain. And the detailed descriptions which Leo XIII, writing as a theologian and political moralist, gave of the Church's "enemy" make the fact even more plain. Within this "free state" the so-called "free church" was subject to a political control more complete than the Tudor or Stuart or Bourbon monarchies dreamed of. The evidence stretches all the way from the Civil Constitution of the Clergy in 1790 to the Law of Separation in 1905.

In the system sponsored by the sectarian Liberals, as has been well said, "The state pretends to ignore the Church; in reality it never took more cognizance of her." In the law of 1905, the climactic development, the Church was arrogantly assigned a juridical statute articulated in forty-four articles, whereby almost every aspect of her organization and action was minutely regulated. Moreover, this was done on principle—the principle of the primacy of the political, the principle of "everything within the state, nothing above the state." This was the cardinal thesis of sectarian Liberalism, whose full historical development is now being witnessed in the totalitarian "people's democracies" behind the Iron Curtain. As the Syllabus and its explicatory documents—as well as the multitudinous writings of Leo XIII—make entirely clear, it was this thesis of the juridical omnipotence and omnicompetence of the state which was the central object of the Church's condemnation of the Jacobin development. It was because freedom of religion and separation of church and state was predicated on this thesis that the Church refused to accept them as a thesis.

This thesis was utterly rejected by the founders of the American Republic. The rejection was as warranted as it was providential, because this thesis is not only theologically heterodox, as denying the reality of the Church; it is also politically revolutionary, as denying the substance of the liberal tradition. The American thesis is that government is not juridically omnipotent. Its powers are limited, and one of the principles of limitation is the distinction between state and church, in their purposes, methods, and manner of organization. The Jacobin thesis was basically philosophical; it derived from a sectarian concept of the autonomy of reason. It was also theological, as implying a sectarian concept of religion and of the church. In contrast, the American thesis is simply political. It asserts the theory of a free people under a limited government, a theory that is recognizably part of the Christian political tradition, and altogether defensible in the manner of its realization under American circumstances.

It may indeed be said that the American constitutional system exaggerates the distinction between church and state by its self-denying ordinances. However, it must also be said that government rarely appears to better advantage than when passing self-denying ordinances. In any event, it is one thing to exaggerate a traditional distinction along the lines of its inherent tendency; it is quite another thing to abolish the distinction. In the latter case the result is a vicious monistic society; in the former, a faultily dualistic one. The vice in the Jacobin system could only be condemned by the Church, not in any way condoned. The fault in the American system can be recognized as such, without condemnation. There are times and circumstances, Chesterton jocosely said, when it is necessary to exaggerate in order to tell the truth. There are also times and circumstances, one may more seriously say, when some exaggeration of the restrictions placed on government is necessary in order to insure freedom. These circumstances of social necessity were and are present in America.

The Freedom of the Church

Here then is the second leading reason why the American solution to the problem of religious pluralism commends itself to the Catholic conscience. . . . In contrast to the Jacobin system in all its forms, the American Constitution does not presume to define the Church or in any way to supervise her exercise of authority in pursuit of her own distinct ends. The Church is entirely free to define herself and to exercise to the full her spiritual jurisdiction. It is legally recognized that there is an area which lies outside the competence of government. This area coincides with the area of the divine mission of the Church, and within this area the Church is fully independent, immune from interference by political authority.

The juridical result of the American limitation of governmental powers is the guarantee to the Church of a stable condition of freedom as a matter of law and right. It should be added that this guarantee is made not only to the individual Catholic but to the Church as an organized society with its own law and jurisdiction. The reason is that the American state is not erected on the principle of the unity and indivisibility of sovereignty which was the post-Renaissance European development. Nowhere in the American structure is there accumulated the plenitude of legal sovereignty possessed in England by the Queen in Parliament. In fact, the term "legal sovereignty" makes no sense in America, where sovereignty (if the alien term must be used) is purely political. The United States has a government, or better a structure of government operating on different levels. The American state has no sovereignty in the classic Continental sense. Within society, as distinct from the state, there is room for the independent exercise of an authority which is not that of the state. This principle has more than once been affirmed by American courts, most recently by the Supreme Court in the *Kedroff* case. The validity of this principle strengthens the stability of the Church's condition at law. . . .

The American Experience

One final ground for affirming the validity of the religion clauses of the First Amendment as good law must be briefly touched on. Holmes's famous dictum, "The life of the law is not logic but experience," has more truth in it than many other Holmesian dicta. When a law ceases to be supported by a continued experience of its goodness, it becomes a dead letter, an empty legal form. Although pure pragmatism cannot be made the philosophy of law, nonetheless the value of any given law is importantly pragmatic. The First Amendment surely passes this test of good law. In support of it one can adduce an American experience. One might well call it *the* American experience in the sense that it has been central in American history and also unique in the history of the world.

This experience has three facets, all interrelated.

First, America has proved by experience that political unity and stability are possible without uniformity of religious belief and practice, without the necessity of any governmental restrictions on any religion. . . .

For a century and a half the United States has displayed to the world the fact that political unity and stability are not necessarily dependent on the common sharing of one religious faith.

The reach of this demonstration is, of course, limited. Granted that the unity of the commonwealth can be achieved in the absence of a consensus with regard to the theological truths that govern the total life and destiny of man, it does not follow that this necessary civic unity can endure in the absence of a consensus more narrow in its scope, operative on the level of political life, with regard to the rational truths and moral precepts that govern the structure of the constitutional state, specify the substance of the common weal, and determine the ends of public policy. Nor has experience yet shown how, if at all, this moral consensus can survive amid all the ruptures of religious division, whose tendency is inherently disintegrative of all consensus and community. But this is a further question, for the future to answer. . . .

The second American experience was that stable political unity, which means perduring agreement on the common good of man at the level

of performance, can be strengthened by the exclusion of religious differences from the area of concern allotted to government. In America we have
been rescued from the disaster of ideological parties. They are a disaster
because, where such parties exist, power becomes a special kind of prize.
The struggle for power is a partisan struggle for the means whereby the
opposing ideology may be destroyed. It has been remarked that only in a
disintegrating society does politics become a controversy over ends; it
should be simply a controversy over means to ends already agreed on with
sufficient unanimity. The Latin countries of Europe have displayed this
spectacle of ideological politics, a struggle between a host of "isms," all of
which pretend to a final view of man and society, with the twin results of
governmental paralysis and seemingly irremediable social division. In
contrast, the American experience of political unity has been striking.
(Even the Civil War does not refute this view; it was not an ideological
conflict but simply, in the more descriptive Southern phrase, a war between
the states, a conflict of interests.) To this experience of political unity the
First Amendment has made a unique contribution; and in doing so it has
qualified as good law.

The third and most striking aspect of the American experience
consists in the fact that religion itself, and not least the Catholic Church,
has benefited by our free institutions, by the maintenance, even in exaggerated form, of the distinction between church and state. Within the same
span of history the experience of the Church elsewhere, especially in the
Latin lands, has been alternately an experience of privilege or persecution.
The reason lay in a particular concept of government. It was alternatively
the determination of government to ally itself either with the purposes of
the Church or with the purposes of some sect or other (sectarian Liberalism, for instance) which made a similar, however erroneous, claim to
possess the full and final truth. The dominant conviction, whose origins are
really in pagan antiquity, was that government should represent tran-
scendent truth and by its legal power make this truth prevail. However, in
the absence of social agreement as to what the truth really was, the result
was to involve the Catholic truth in the vicissitudes of power. It would be
difficult to say which experience, privilege or persecution, proved in the end
to be the more damaging or gainful to the Church.

In contrast, American government has not undertaken to represent
transcendental truth in any of the versions of it current in American
society. It does indeed represent the commonly shared moral values of the
community. It also represents the supreme religious truth expressed in the
motto on American coins: "In God we trust." The motto expresses the two
truths without which, as the Letter to the Hebrews says, "nobody reaches
God's presence," namely, "to believe that God exists and that he rewards
those who try to find him" (Hebrews 11:6). For the rest, government

represents the truth of society as it actually is; and the truth is that American society is religiously pluralist. The truth is lamentable; it is nonetheless true. Many of the beliefs entertained within society ought not to be believed, because they are false; nonetheless men believe them. It is not the function of government to resolve the dispute between conflicting truths, all of which claim the final validity of transcendence. As representative of a pluralist society, wherein religious faith is—as it must be—free, government undertakes to represent the principle of freedom.

In taking this course American government would seem to be on the course set by Pius XII for the religiously pluralist international community, of which America offers, as it were, a pattern in miniature. . . .

In consequence of this American concept of the representative function of government the experience of the Church in America, like the general American experience itself, has proved to be satisfactory when one scans it from the viewpoint of the value upon which the Church sets primary importance, namely, her freedom in the fulfillment of her spiritual mission to communicate divine truth and grace to the souls of men, and her equally spiritual mission of social justice and peace. The Church has not enjoyed a privileged status in public life; at the same time she has not had to pay the price of this privilege. A whole book could be written on the price of such legal privilege. Another book could be written on the value of freedom without privilege. In fact, both books have been written, on the metaphorical pages of history. And looking over his own continually unrolling historical manuscript the American Catholic is inclined to conclude that his is a valid book.

It does not develop a doctrinal thesis, but it does prove a practical point. The point is that the goodness of the First Amendment as constitutional law is manifested not only by political but also by religious experience. By and large (for no historical record is without blots) it has been good for religion, for Catholicism, to have had simply the right of freedom. This right is at the same time the highest of privileges, and it too has its price. But the price has not been envy and enmity, the coinage in which the Church paid for privilege. It has only been the price of sacrifice, labor, added responsibilities; and these things are redemptive.

Conclusion

In the final analysis any validation of the First Amendment as good law—no matter by whom undertaken, be he Protestant, Catholic, Jew, or secularist—must make appeal to the three arguments developed above—the demands of social necessity, the rightfulness within our own circumstances of the American manner of asserting the distinction between church and state, and the lessons of experience. Perhaps the last argument is the most powerful. It is also, I may add, the argument which best harmonizes with the general tone which arguments for our institutions are accustomed to adopt.

In a curiously controlling way the tone was set by the *Federalist* papers. These essays were not political treatises after the manner of Hobbes and Hegel, Rousseau and Comte, or even John Locke. It has been remarked that in America no treatises of this kind have been produced; and it is probably just as well. The authors of the *Federalist* papers were not engaged in broaching a political theory universal in scope and application, a plan for an Ideal Republic of Truth and Virtue. They were arguing for a particular Constitution, a special kind of governmental structure, a limited ensemble of concrete laws, all designed for application within a given society. They were in the tradition of the Revolutionary thinkers who led a colonial rebellion, not in the name of a set of flamboyant abstractions, but in the name of the sober laws of the British Constitution which they felt were being violated in their regard. It has been pointed out that the only real slogan the Revolution produced was: "No taxation without representation." It has not the ring of a trumpet; its sound is more like the dry rustle of a lawyer's sheaf of parchment.

It is in the tone of this tradition of American political writing that one should argue for the First Amendment. The arguments will tend to be convincing in proportion as their key of utterance approaches a dry rustle and not a wild ring. The arguments here presented are surely dry enough. Perhaps they will not satisfy the American doctrinaire, the theologizer. But they do, I think, show that the first of our prejudices is "not a prejudice destitute of reason, but involving in its profound and extensive wisdom." This is all that need be shown; it is likewise all that can be shown.

The Catholic Church in America is committed to this prejudice by the totality of her experience in American history. As far as I know, the only ones who doubt the firmness, the depth, the principled nature of this commitment are not Catholics. They speak without knowledge and without authority; the credence they command has its origins in emotion. If perhaps what troubles them is the fact that the commitment is limited, in the sense that it is not to the truth and sanctity of a dogma but only to the rationality and goodness of a law, they might recall the story of Pompey. After the capture of Jerusalem in 63 B.C. he went to the Temple and forced his way into the Holy of Holies. To his intense astonishment he found it empty. He should not have been astonished; for the emptiness was the symbol of the absence of idolatry. It symbolized the essential truth of Judaism, that One is the Lord. Professor Boorstin, who recounts the tale, adds: "Perhaps the same surprise awaits the student of American culture [or, I add, the American Constitution] if he finally manages to penetrate the arcanum of our belief. And for a similar reason. Far from being disappointed, we should be inspired that in an era of idolatry, when so many nations have filled their sanctuaries with ideological idols, we have had the courage to refuse to do so."

The American Catholic is on good ground when he refuses to make an ideological idol out of religious freedom and separation of church and state, when he refuses to "believe" in them as articles of faith. He takes the highest ground available in this matter of the relations between religion and government when he asserts that his commitment to the religion clauses of the Constitution is a moral commitment to them as articles of peace in a pluralist society.

TWO VIEWS OF PLURALISM

Frederick A. Olafson

Frederick A. Olafson is a member of the Department of Philosophy at Harvard University and editor of Society, Law and Morality *(1961). The following selection is his critical commentary on the views propounded by Father Murray in* We Hold These Truths. *Although his concern is with the American Catholic position on the relation of church and state, Professor Olafson's excellent statement is helpful in understanding the doctrine of natural law that, although primarily associated with the Catholic tradition, has lately attracted many non-Catholics in quest of an escape from moral relativism.*

Since much of Professor Olafson's argument concerning natural law is based on views of Father Murray that are not set forth in the preceding selection, it may be well to summarize these views here. Father Murray's central premise is that the consensus reflected in our constitution whereby we acquire our identity as a people and whereby our society "is endowed with its vital form, its entelechy, its sense of purpose as a collectivity organized for action in history" is no rationalization of an economic interest, no "set of working hypotheses whose value is pragmatic," but an "ensemble of substantive truths . . . an order of elementary affirmations that reflect realities inherent in the order of existence."[1] It is, he says, an "intuitional a priori," and as such it implies not only that there

---

From *The Yale Review* (Summer 1962), pp. 519–531. Copyright 1962 Yale University Press. Reprinted by permission.

[1] *We Hold These Truths* (New York: Sheed & Ward, Inc., 1960), p. 9.

*are certain basic truths we hold in common but also that there
is "a natural law that makes known to all of us the structure
of the moral universe in such wise that all of us are bound by
it in a common obedience."[2] It was this tradition of natural
law, Father Murray urges, that prevailed with the "Fathers of
the Republic" as with the "Fathers of the Church." In its
political implications this tradition means "that government
has a moral basis; that the universal moral law is the foundation of society; that the legal order of society—that is, the
state—is subject to judgment by a law that is not statistical
but inherent in the nature of man; that the eternal reason of
God is the ultimate origin of the law; that this nation in all its
aspects—as a society, a state, an ordered and free relationship
between governors and governed—is under God."[3] It is from
such a concept of natural law and the implications it involves
that Professor Olafson dissents.*

To the many earlier attempts to define the public philosophy of the
American political enterprise, two years ago there was added a closely
argued interpretation of our political tradition by the well-known Jesuit
theologian, Father John Courtney Murray (*We Hold These Truths,* Sheed
and Ward). There can be little doubt that Father Murray's "reflections on
the American proposition" constitute the most considerable effort yet made
by an American Catholic to provide a rationale for the American political
system that remains consistent with the assumptions of the older tradition
of Catholic social thought. To many, the principal interest of these reflections will lie in the support they give to the view that American Catholics
can in good conscience accept American constitutional arrangements and,
in particular, the religious pluralism of American society and the religious
neutrality of our political institutions.

One would be doing less than full justice to Father Murray's
position, however, if on the strength of these conclusions one were simply
to docket him as a "liberal Catholic," without really understanding the
reasoning on which his assessment of our political tradition rests. There is
a real danger that in the easy euphoria of unaccustomed agreement, much
that is important and distinctive in Father Murray's thought will be elided
and its conclusions finally misunderstood because of a failure to set them
firmly in the context of the wider social philosophy by which they are
inspired. This would be all the more unfortunate because one principle
merit of these essays is that they enable us to locate, with considerable
precision, certain radical differences that still separate Catholic and non-
Catholic views of the subjects with which they deal.

---

[2] *We Hold These Truths,* p. 40.
[3] *We Hold These Truths,* p. 42.

In the past these differences have never been more apparent than in just this matter of pluralism that occupies so central a place in Father Murray's thought. While I do not think it was any part of his intention to offer his acceptance of pluralism as an olive branch to liberal opinion in this country, espousals of religious pluralism by Catholic thinkers tend to be wishfully interpreted by American liberals; and there is already some evidence that these essays by Father Murray are, through no lack of clarity on his part, being read in a way that I believe to be quite mistaken. There is, I think, no good reason why liberal opinion should not be as clearly aware of the differences between its conception of pluralism and this Catholic version as Father Murray himself is. This essay is intended to make these differences clear.

Father Murray's statement of what he takes to be the central elements of the American philosphy of government turns on a contrast with what he calls the Jacobin tradition of "totalitarian democracy." This is the view, rather clearly prefigured in Rousseau's political thought, that concentrates the whole moral business of a society in its political institutions and, in its extreme form, refuses to recognize the need for any independent moral appraisal of the political order. By contrast, the Founding Fathers explicitly recognized, so Father Murray tells us, that government is limited and not co-extensive with society; that its acts are not self-validating but must conform to an antecedent moral standard; and that free political institutions that permit the participation of the people in the making of law and the formulation of policy are the indispensable guarantee that government will be responsive to moral opinion. This conception of the role of government is, of course, in sharp contrast both with the ancient Roman unification of *sacerdotium* and *imperium* in the person of the emperor and with the modern totalitarian tendency to attribute an automatic normative significance to the deliverances of the popular will.

The heart of the American political tradition, as Father Murray interprets it, is a rejection of all such forms of social monism and an emphatic assertion that the moral order is independent of and superordinate to political and legal institutions. To use a phrase to which Father Murray later gives a somewhat more controversial sense, one may say that the "American proposition" is that there shall be "not one but two"—not a juridical order but a moral order as well—and that the proper ordering of their relationship to one another is the central problem of good government.

Although this statement of principles is cast in a philosophical vocabulary that is perhaps not widely used by non-Catholic political thinkers in this country, there is probably little in it that would not meet with general acceptance. Broadly speaking, Americans seem to believe that law is an agency designed to serve moral ends and that it is rightly held responsible to moral standards. Indeed, if one may believe certain highly qualified observers of our public life, such as Mr. George Kennan, this conviction has assumed the exaggerated and potentially dangerous form in this country to which the name of "moralism" properly applies.

But when Father Murray goes on to argue that only the doctrine of natural law construes the nature of man and society in a way that does justice to the moral responsibilities of the state, and that it is on the natural-law theory of society that the American polity therefore rests, he is arguing for a position that has been and still is hotly contested. Historically, it is of course true that belief in a "higher law" held an important place in the political philosophy of the Founding Fathers. By the time it reached them, however, the "natural law" of the eighteenth century had been heavily diluted by infusions of a Lockian doctrine of natural rights, which Father Murray declares to be an individualistic corruption of the authentic doctrine of St. Thomas. So his thesis is not likely to be well served by historical arguments. What is much more to the point is Father Murray's contention that the hope of bringing moral considerations to bear upon our thinking about political affairs is dependent on the restoration to a place of honor in our intellectual world of the doctrine of natural law.

What are the merits of natural law theory that justify such an ambitious claim in its behalf? Father Murray's answer is that the morality of natural law alone provides a set of rational procedures by which universally valid and authoritative answers can be given to moral and social questions. The moral imperatives of natural law issue from a rational insight into the nature of man and are therefore entirely free of the taint of voluntarism and subjectivism which Father Murray discovers in a wide range of modern conceptions of morality. The doctrine of natural law, resting as it does on a human nature that is common to all men, is not, according to Father Murray, in any sense distinctively Catholic. It represents, instead, the indispensable minimum of rationally grounded consensus without which even a pluralistic society cannot survive. At this point Father Murray's argument takes on, as he admits, a surprisingly pragmatic cast. He says, in effect, that a return to the abandoned tradition of natural law is a necessary condition of our survival as a civil society.

In the foregoing summary I have been unfaithful to Father Murray's line of thought to the extent that in characterizing the sphere of morality I have spoken of moral "opinion" and not of moral "truth." It is very emphatically the latter that he is interested in and the existence of which he believes to be pre-supposed by the "American proposition." The importance of natural law to his argument can indeed be explained by the fact that it alone is supposed to enable us to make this crucial distinction between opinion and truth in the moral sphere. Now if this were the fundamental option of the moral life it would clearly be perverse to come down on the side of opinion. It is equally apparent, however, that if Father

Murray's somewhat simplistic conception of moral truth is adopted, the case for pluralism, by becoming a case for allowing people to persist in error, would take on a very different aspect. What I wish to suggest here is that the concept of moral truth on which the natural law theory depends is seriously defective and that its repercussions on Father Murray's pluralism are both extensive and disquieting.

It is one thing to adopt an intellectualistic vocabulary for talking about moral deliberation, and quite another to provide solutions to moral problems that command rational assent. Admittedly, many minds find a sort of comfort in the elaborate paraphernalia of rationality with which natural law theory has always surrounded itself, but the real issue has to do with the logical power of that theory as manifested by the justification it is able to provide for the specific directives for conduct which it is supposed to produce. There is unfortunately, in the writings of natural law theorists, and in these essays by Father Murray as well, a kind of abstract and rhetorical intellectualism that runs well ahead of any demonstrated capability to construct justificatory arguments whose validity cannot be challenged.

Consider, for example, those first principles of the practical order from which all moral reasoning is supposed to begin: "the good is to be done and promoted and evil is to be avoided." St. Thomas says that these are necessary truths of reason. From them, by way of a process that Father Murray calls "particularization," moral argument descends to practical conclusions. Unfortunately, these primal truths impose themselves so irresistibly only because they are not the kind of assertion that anyone, no matter what his moral views, would feel obliged to deny. No one except a Satanist goes around preaching that good is to be avoided and evil sought after. Real moral disagreement, on the other hand, cannot be explained by saying that one person apprehends these truths and another does not. Indeed, both parties to a moral conflict could in fact accept these re-sounding truisms in good faith and yet differ in the way they "particularize" the good, i.e. in the criteria by which they identify good things or right actions.

In order to make out a convincing case for the compelling intellectual authority of natural law, it would have to be shown that some ways of particularizing the good are self-contradictory or invalid in some other sense. It is a pity that Father Murray does not cast any new light on this crucially important process. Like many other natural law theorists, he manages to suggest that once the primary truths are accepted, there becomes operative a set of rational controls that guides the well-disposed reasoner to the right answer; but he never gives any indication of what the sequence of the argument is. As a result, the rigorously rational character that he repeatedly attributes to the "moral order" of which he speaks remains unsubstantiated by evidence. It suggests itself that the voluntaristic character of much modern moral philosophy which Father Murray so deplores is due to a recognition that the claims of moral intellectualism cannot in fact be made good and that at crucial points in the process of moral deliberation it is more appropriate to speak of "choice" and "decision" than of "particularizations" and "deductions" that prove on inspection to be disguised choices.

But if "true" answers to substantive moral questions do not follow from first principles without the intervention of more subjective factors, what are we to make of Father Murray's confident assertion that "moral reality" is "permeable to human reason"? Is he just wrong, or is there more to his argument than at first appears? I think the latter is more likely and that at least a partial explanation is to be found in a tacit assumption that Father Murray evidently makes, but the full significance of which for his argument is not developed. This is the assumption that there is an institution that is uniquely qualified to interpret the "moral a priori." That institution is of course the Roman Catholic Church, whose authority in matters of morals can be usefully compared to the authority that in a political society is delegated to judges, whose decisions—or interpretations of statute law—are thereby made the authoritative reading of the law. A judicial decision is binding not because it is possible even in principle to retrace the deductions by which the judge moved from the statute to the decision but because the decision was made by the person or persons whose decision by law counts as the authoritative one. In spite of the great and important differences between straightforward deduction and practical conclusions whose validity rests on a procedural convention of this sort, I would suggest that Father Murray does not clearly distinguish them. Because he fails to do so, he is able to impute a rational necessity to the set of conclusions that the Catholic tradition of social thought has extracted from a "moral a priori" that is in fact logically sterile. The illusion of a seamless logical continuity in moral deliberation that could hardly have been produced by logical operations upon such vacuous "principles" as those noted above is made possible by the covert assumptions of a uniquely empowered interpretative agency. Unfortunately the effect of this added premise is to make it quite impossible for Father Murray to argue, as he does, that there is nothing peculiarly Catholic about the theory of natural law and that it is thus well suited to acceptance as the public philosophy of American society.

The role of the Church as a moral arbiter raises another point that has an important bearing on Father Murray's general thesis. He has argued—rightly, as I believe—that the state must recognize that the moral personality of its citizens is not exhausted by their civic and political functions and that the private associations and the various forms of expression and communication through which moral opinions are formed and revised must not only not be impeded by the state but, wherever possible, encouraged. This view yields the previously noted contrast between the formalized political sphere and the wider and looser sphere of private moral opinion. The traditional American understanding of this contrast, as Father Murray very candidly states, has been that the sphere of moral opinion should never be forced into a single institutional framework. It is par excellence the domain of private associations, no one of which has any privilege or official connection with the political order. The mediating link between "morality," conceived of as sets of opinions held by the members of these groups, and the state is just the individual person who, of course, lives in both spheres and is free to attempt by legal means to translate his moral views into law and public policy. But if Father Murray clearly sees that this moral individualism is basic to the "American proposition," it becomes equally clear to the reader that he does not subscribe to it. The point is a central one and bears close examination.

The traditional Catholic view has been that the individual conscience will inevitably buckle under the weight of the moral responsibility assigned to it by liberalism and that it is foolish to expect a just and stable social order to emerge out of the competition of moral pressure groups, no matter how scrupulously the procedural rules governing this competition are observed. Catholic thought has therefore assumed the necessity of some authoritative direction of moral opinion, and it is clear that the institution that assumes the responsibility becomes, in so doing, more than just a private voluntary association. *Both* the political and the moral sphere must, on this view, have a formalized institutional expression. Furthermore, since the general relationship between the two institutions so created is itself to be determined in accordance with the directives of natural law of which the Church is the final interpreter, it is evident that the Church is the superior member of this "dyarchy." It may of course make certain spheres of action the independent responsibility of the state, just as it may tolerate the existence of other churches. The essential point, however, is that the Church has the right to define its relationship to the state as well as to its direct competitors in the moral-religious sphere.

It is the relation in which Father Murray stands to this tradition of thought that needs clarifying. In the form of rhetorical questions, he seems plainly to indicate his convictions that the liberal faith in the individual conscience is misplaced, but he does not explicitly draw the conclusion—which he as a Catholic can hardly resist—that the mediating function of which he speaks must be performed by the Church and not just by individuals. He does, however, speak of something he calls the "freedom of the Church," which he feels has been sadly neglected in favor of the freedom of individual conscience. He can scarcely mean by the "freedom of the Church" the freedom that the Church enjoys as a private voluntary association, since he recognizes that *that* freedom is complete, at least in this country. One can only suppose, therefore, that in demanding the "freedom of the Church" he is proposing a new and more extensive role for the Church than is permitted by its status as a voluntary association. How such a recognition of the "freedom of the Church" would differ from arrangements in countries where the Church enjoys, by law, a privileged position, Father Murray does not explain.

That Father Murray is dissatisfied with the Church's present status as a voluntary private association is made abundantly clear by his attack on the social "monism" which he believes to be implicit in the doctrine of sovereignty. In this connection, it is to be regretted that Father Murray never gives a neutral statement of what the doctrine of sovereignty really comes to and that, as a result, it functions in these essays as a sort of all-purpose bugaboo. Stripped of its adventitious associations with the various forms of government that have used it for their own purposes, this doctrine emerges as the essentially formal and morally innocuous requirement that the legal order form a self-contained system in the sense that there be a defined procedure available for resolving all questions that come before the body politic. In this sense the United States is as fully sovereign as any European monarchy has ever been. Nothing is implied by this doctrine as to what this juridically complete system will do or what laws it will make. A state that severely limits freedom of expression or the rights of its citizens to participate in the process of government is not a whit more sovereign than the liberal society that recognizes and protects the most extensive political rights for its citizens.

It is surprising and a little disheartening that so judicious a writer as Father Murray should repeat the absurd charge that the Communist state is the logical outcome of the modern doctrine of sovereignty. What is true is that the Communist state does not recognize the desirability of a parallel activity of discussion and deliberation in voluntary associations or otherwise and that it has suppressed the free institutions which, according to the American proposition as stated by Father Murray, are the guarantee of the responsiveness of the state to moral pressures. Through the agency of the one uniquely authorized party, the Communists have regimented opinion and effectively destroyed the fruitful contrast between the political and the moral spheres. In so doing, the Communist state has not made itself more sovereign; it has only made itself illiberal and tyrannical. It is a striking paradox that Father Murray should propose by implication an institutionalization of the moral sphere and thereby place himself in opposition to the liberal tradition and on the side of the totalitarians.

As a result of Father Murray's failure to make these vital distinctions, the morally neutral and the aggressively illiberal forms of "sovereignty" are connected in such a way that, to avoid the latter, one has to reject the former as well. Indeed, it becomes difficult to see how Father Murray could be satisfied with anything short of an explicit recognition by the state that it is not master of its own house. If it claims that it is, it has on his reasoning taken the road that leads to totalitarianism. But if the state is not master of its own house, who is? Not the moral consciousness of its citizens, as expressed through the political process itself, for it is precisely in this role that Father Murray believes that individual conscience has failed; and in any case the supremacy of the moral consciousness is already recognized by the establishment of free institutions that permit the individual citizen to participate in government.

The only sure antidote to the pernicious social disease of "sovereignty," in Father Murray's peculiar use of that term, would inevitably be some form of recognition by the state of an independent institution enjoying at least coordinate status with itself and endowed with special authority in matters of morals, i.e. a church. The precise juridical character of the relationship between these two elements of the "dyarchy" of which Father Murray speaks would no doubt allow for a good deal of slack. The tendency of all such arrangements is, however, as evident as it is, in the light of Father Murray's distaste for "monism," ironical. It would merely transfer sovereignty from the secular state to a new corporate entity—the state-cum-church (or church-cum-state, depending on whether the predominance of power was held by the secular or the spiritual bureaucracy). In either case, society as a whole would be finally contained in a single institutional carapace which would be all the more confining because, unlike the state, a hierarchical church charged with the direction of consciences can hardly allow itself to be judged by an independent moral standard. One could wish that Father Murray, who is markedly sensitive to the temptations of power that are the inseparable accompaniment of political integration, had indicated a corresponding awareness of the even more insidious temptations to which such a church in its "freedom" would be exposed.

These considerations must inevitably qualify any initial enthusiasm that may have been felt over Father Murray's apparent acceptance of religious pluralism. Indeed, the terms in which that acceptance is formulated are in themselves sufficient to inspire some doubts. A great deal of the supporting argument is devoted to the point that American religious pluralism is not a universally valid article of faith, but a sagacious political arrangement that has to be justified by reference to the historical circumstances under which the American polity came into being. To this it might be replied that it matters little what these "articles of peace" are called, so long as the commitment to them of all groups in American society is a firm one and is not based on a tactical situation which is subject to change. Unfortunately when Father Murray carries a qualifying reference to the "given circumstances" over into his assertion that the American government "has neither the mandate nor the duty nor the right to legislate in favor of or against any of the religious confessions existent in American society," one does not have to be a secularist fanatic to be made somewhat uneasy. Elsewhere, Father Murray explicitly declares that it is a "lamentable" truth that American society is religiously pluralistic. It is surely not unreasonable, therefore, to ask what these "given circumstances" are in which the American government does not have this right, and to want to know in what circumstances it would, on the Catholic view, acquire that right. The American proposition, as widely understood, holds that no change in given circumstances would justify the establishment of a confessional state in this country. To speak bluntly, many Americans believe that the leadership of the Roman Catholic Church in this country accepts the religious neutrality of the state only provisionally and lives in expectation of the demographic shifts that will make other more congenial arrangements politically feasible. If this is a false belief, as Father Murray would apparently have us think, then the qualifying phrase, "in the given circumstances," must be elucidated in some other way. It is to be regretted that Father Murray has not performed this much-needed service. Because he has not done so, his acceptance of pluralism retains the very flavor of reluctance and conditionality which he seems to have wished to avoid.

These doubts extend to the very conception of pluralism that Father Murray is at least provisionally defending. At bottom, the question is one that has to do with the various roles or identities that the members of a society sustain by virtue of their membership in various sub-societies, and of the proper relation between these identities. Pluralism in the American tradition is not just a "lamentable" fact that has to be lived with; it is only one aspect of a wider social ideal. This ideal of pluralism is that a society should comprise a variety of institutions that maintain a meaningful degree of independence of one another, and that no individual's identity should be exhausted by his affiliation with any one of them. The one identity that all members of the society share is political: the status of citizens; and the state provides the indispensable legal framework within which limited private associations find their place. When properly understood, this comprehensiveness that is peculiar to the political order has nothing in the least sinister about it; and the liberal pluralist view is that the tendency to elephantiasis, which seems to be latent in every institutional affiliation, must be resisted when it is our identity as citizens that tends to blot out all other identities, as it must in all other cases. Which identity—civic, religious, professional—needs to be strengthened and which needs to be contained within limits is a judgment that will be made differently in the light of tendencies that may be paramount in a given society at a given time.

This at least is the liberal understanding of pluralism as a social philosophy. I do not think that it is Father Murray's. His great fear is that our secular identity as citizens will absorb or distort all our other identities and that it is therefore the most important of these—our religious identity—which requires special attention and solicitude. Here I cannot agree. My own feeling is that our sense of civic identity and of membership and participation in the American political enterprise is not as strong as it might be and that it needs strengthening. I think there is a real danger that our civic identity may be squeezed flat by the expanding demands of other institutional loyalties. But if pluralism is to mean something more than a progressive compartmentalization of our society, steps will have to be taken to give to our public and political life an ideal meaning that it can hardly be said to have for most of us at the present time. Specifically, unless there are occasions on which Americans come together simply as citizens and not as delegates of the religious institutions with which they are affiliated, it is fairly certain that our political institutions will in fact become the "servile and secondary thing" that less careful Catholic apologists have declared them to be.

The case for such a reinforcement of our public identity becomes even stronger when one recalls, as Father Murray does, that in this country a sense of civic participation has never carried with it the kind of aggressively antireligious spirit that has marked the evolution of secular political institutions in Europe. Why then does Father Murray persist in the sterile animosity toward the state that is evident on virtually every page of this book and which seems to have been inspired, in good part, by the experiences of the Church under the Third Republic in France? In the absence of provocation, this competitive and suspicious attitude looks remarkably like a case of projection, in which an unsatisfied aspiration to dominance on the part of the Church is imputed to a secular political institution which does not, at least in this country, make any claim that is really comparable. In particular, the disproportionate emphasis that Father Murray gives to the limited character of government suggests to me not so much any fear that the specific freedoms by which that limitation is realized may be in danger as a generalized suspicion of all forms of secular idealism and particularly of those that find their expression in political activity.

It is this deep hostility to a secular conception of political life that robs Father Murray's acceptance of religious pluralism of any real relevance to the American political situation. One may agree with him that a pluralistic society, like any other, rests on a consensus—a body of shared beliefs—and that these are not just procedural in character (the "democratic method") but in part directly moral as well. Such a society will, however, always come up against the question of the language in which this consensus is to be formulated. Now, if each religious community within the larger society states these principles in a way that makes them dependent on assumptions peculiar to its own religious faith, certain results may be expected. It will almost certainly be more difficult for the members of any given religious community to recognize that they share these principles with other groups, and the distinction between their beliefs as members of a restricted religious community and those they hold as members of a wider political society will be blurred. But just this public awareness that there *is* a body of shared religiously neutral beliefs, whether moral or "procedural," is of vital importance to a pluralistic society which must, after all, recognize itself for what it is. In the absence of such an awareness, the social strategy of religious communities that lack a sense of being part of a larger society with principles of its own will inevitably be absorptive and eventually totalitarian.

Father Murray makes the claim that the theory of natural law can provide the common vocabulary that our pluralistic society needs. I have tried to show why I think he is mistaken. I would argue, against his claim, that if competing religous groups are not going to destroy such social unity as we actually enjoy by futile attempts to pull the "American proposition" into their own orbits of belief, there must be an explicit recognition that our "consensus" is secular in character. By "secular" I do not mean to imply that individuals or groups may not continue to find additional reasons for preferring free institutions in their religious beliefs. What is meant is simply that the public or shared formulation of the principles of a free society must not be one that stands and falls with the special assumptions of particular religious groups about the metaphysical status of moral truth or the nature of human reason. At bottom, these "principles" are very general ways of acting and of comporting oneself in relation to other human beings; and the working out of their precise nature is the task of secular political and social philosophy. There is, I think, every reason to suppose that this enterprise is of central importance to our society and that our public life will in the end be better served by a clear delineation of the "logic" of a free society than by the search for metaphysical underpinnings.

If there is one thing that disfigures these essays by Father Murray, it is the extraordinary and ill-informed animus that he displays toward the whole tradition of secular political philosophy. It is next to impossible to discover in the caricatured versions of Hobbes and Locke and Bentham that he offers us the thinkers who, whatever their failures, really tried to devise a rationale of human society that would be genuinely independent, as Father Murray's is not, of special assumptions of a religious nature. To me there is a strangeness bordering on outright paradox in a procedure that violently rejects virtually the whole intellectual heritage of liberalism but accepts the open and pluralistic society that it has produced. No doubt it is possible to provide a new set of foundations for an older set of political institutions; but in this case I can only think that a pluralistic society that tries to make its unifying political and moral principles religious in any nontrivial sense is in for trouble; and that Father Murray's attempt to organize the public consciousness and the public area of concern around the idea of natural law is most unlikely to allow them the degree of separate identity that will insure effective social unity. By recognizing that public consciousness only when it is willing to express itself in the special moral-political vocabulary of his faith, he has really avoided the problem that he ostensibly set himself: how does one live together in a civil society with those whose religious beliefs one does not share?

EVERSON v. EWING TOWNSHIP BOARD OF EDUCATION

Supreme Court of the United States

As always, a particular case, even a minor one, helps to throw the large conflict of principles into dramatic highlight, especially if it occasions vigorous differences among justices of the U.S. Supreme Court. The fact that Justice Hugo Black, speaking for the majority, and Justice Robert Jackson, dissenting, are usually on the same side of most of the issues dividing the Supreme Court makes their difference in the present instance all the more interesting. The case concerns a township's provision of bus fares for parochial-school pupils. The decision is significant in that, while assenting, the Court for the first time explicitly elaborated the doctrine of separation of church and state as embodied in the First Amendment and invoked the Jeffersonian dictum that the amendment (along with the Fourteenth Amendment, which made it applicable to the states) erected "a wall of separation between Church and State."

Mr. Justice Black delivered the opinion of the Court: A New Jersey statute authorizes its local school districts to make rules and contracts for the transportation of children to and from schools. The appellee, a township board of education, acting pursuant to this statute, authorized reimbursement to parents of money expended by them for the bus transportation of their children on regular busses operated by the public transportation system. Part of this money was for the payment of transportation of some children in the community to Catholic parochial schools. These church schools give their students, in addition to secular education, regular religious instruction conforming to the religious tenets and modes

---

330 USI, 1947.

of worship of the Catholic faith. The superintendent of these schools is a Catholic priest.

The appellant, in his capacity as a district taxpayer, filed suit in a State court challenging the right of the Board of Education to reimburse parents of parochial school students. . . .

The only contention here is that the State statute and the resolution, insofar as they authorized reimbursement to parents of children attending parochial schools, violates the Federal Constitution. . . .

The New Jersey statute is challenged as a "law respecting the establishment of religion." . . .

The meaning and scope of the First Amendment, preventing establishment of religion or prohibiting the free exercise thereof, in the light of its history and the evils it was designed forever to suppress, have been several times elaborated by the decisions of this Court prior to the application of the First Amendment to the states by the Fourteenth. The broad meaning given the Amendment by these earlier cases has been accepted by this Court in its decisions concerning an individual's religious freedom rendered since the Fourteenth Amendment was interpreted to make the prohibitions of the First applicable to state action abridging religious freedom. There is every reason to give the same application and broad interpretation to the "establishment of religion" clause. . . .

The "establishment of religion" clause of the First Amendment means at least this: Neither a state nor the Federal Government can set up a church. Neither can pass laws which aid one religion, aid all religions, or prefer one religion over another. Neither can force nor influence a person to go to or to remain away from church against his will or force him to profess a belief or disbelief in any religion. No person can be punished for entertaining or professing religious beliefs or disbeliefs, for church attendance or non-attendance. No tax in any amount, large or small, can be levied to support any religious activities or institutions, whatever they may be called, or whatever form they may adopt to teach or practice religion. Neither a state nor the Federal Government can, openly or secretly, participate in the affairs of any religious organizations or groups and vice versa. In the words of Jefferson, the clause against establishment of religion by law was intended to erect "a wall of separation between Church and State." . . .

We must consider the New Jersey statute in accordance with the foregoing limitations imposed by the First Amendment. But we must not strike that state statute down if it is within the State's constitutional power even though it approaches the verge of that power. . . . New Jersey cannot consistently with the "establishment of religion" clause of the First Amendment contribute tax-raised funds to the support of an institution which teaches the tenets and faith of any church. On the other hand, other language of the amendment commands that New Jersey cannot hamper its citizens in the free exercise of their own religion. Consequently, it cannot exclude individual Catholics, Lutherans, Mohammedans, Baptists, Jews, Methodists, Non-believers, Presbyterians, or the members of any other faith, *because of their faith, or lack of it,* from receiving the benefits of public welfare legislation. While we do not mean to intimate that a state could not provide transportation only to children attending public schools, we must be careful, in protecting the citizens of New Jersey against state-established churches, to be sure that we do not inadvertently prohibit New Jersey from extending its general state law benefits to all its citizens without regard to their religious belief.

Measured by these standards, we cannot say that the First Amendment prohibits New Jersey from spending tax-raised funds to pay the bus fares of parochial school pupils as a part of a general program under which it pays the fares of pupils attending public and other schools. It is undoubtedly true that children are helped to get to church schools. There is even a possibility that some of the children might not be sent to the church schools if the parents were compelled to pay [for] their children going to and from church [schools out of their own] pockets when transportation to a public school would have been paid for by the State. The same possibility exists where the state requires a local transit company to provide reduced fares to school children including those attending parochial schools, or where a municipally owned transportation system undertakes to carry all school children free of charge. Moreover, state-paid policemen, detailed to protect children going to and from church schools from the very real hazards of traffic, would serve much the same purpose and accomplish much the same result as state provisions intended to guarantee free transportation of a kind which the state deems to be best for the school children's welfare. And parents might refuse to risk their children to the serious danger of traffic accidents going to and from parochial schools, the approaches to which were not protected by policemen. Similarly, parents might be reluctant to permit their children to attend schools which the state had cut off from such general government services as ordinary police and fire protection, connections for sewage disposal, public highways and sidewalks. Of course, cutting off church schools from these services, so separate and so indisputably marked off from the religious function, would make it far more difficult for the schools to operate. But such is obviously not the purpose of the First Amendment. That Amendment requires the state to be a neutral in its relations with groups of religious believers and non-believers; it does not require the state to be their adversary. State power is no more to be used so as to handicap religions than it is to favor them.

This Court has said that parents may, in the discharge of their duty under state compulsory education laws, send their children to a religious rather than a public school if the school meets the secular educational requirements which the state has power to impose. . . . It appears that these parochial schools meet New Jersey's requirements. The State contributes no money to the schools. It does not support them. Its legislation, as applied, does no more than provide a general program to help parents get their children, regardless of their religion, safely and expeditiously to and from accredited schools.

The First Amendment has erected a wall between church and state. That wall must be kept high and impregnable. We could not approve the slightest breach. New Jersey has not breached it here.

Affirmed.

Mr. Justice Jackson, dissenting. I find myself, contrary to first impressions, unable to join in this decision. I have a sympathy, though it is not ideological, with Catholic citizens who are compelled by law to pay taxes for public schools, and also feel constrained by conscience and discipline to support other schools for their own children. Such relief to them as this case involves is not in itself a serious burden to taxpayers and I have assumed it to be as little serious in principle. Study of this case convinces me otherwise. The Court's opinion marshals every argument in favor of state aid and puts the case in its most favorable light, but much of its reasoning confirms my conclusions that there are no good grounds upon which to support the present legislation. In fact, the undertones of the opinion, advocating complete and uncompromising separation of Church from State, seem utterly discordant with its conclusion yielding support to their commingling in educational matters. The case which irresistibly comes to mind as the most fitting precedent is that of Julia who, according to Byron's reports, "whispering 'I will ne'er consent,'—consented."

The Township of Ewing is not furnishing transportation to the children in any form; it is not operating school busses itself or contracting for their operation; and it is not performing any public service of any kind with this taxpayer's money. All school children are left to ride as ordinary paying passengers on the regular busses operated by the public transportation system. What the Township does, and what the taxpayer complains of, is at stated intervals to reimburse parents for the fares paid, provided the children attend either public schools or Catholic Church schools. This expenditure of tax funds has no possible effect on the child's safety or expedition in transit. As passengers on the public busses they travel as fast and no faster, and are as safe and no safer, since their parents are reimbursed as before. . . .

Whether the taxpayer constitutionally can be made to contribute aid to parents of students because of their attendance at parochial schools depends upon the nature of those schools and their relation to the Church. The Constitution says nothing of education. It lays no obligation on the states to provide schools and does not undertake to regulate state systems of education if they see fit to maintain them. But they cannot, through school policy any more than through other means, invade rights secured to citizens by the Constitution of the United States. . . . One of our basic rights is to be free of taxation to support a transgression of the constitutional command that the authorities "shall make no law respecting an establishment of religion, or prohibiting the free exercise thereof." . . .

The function of the Church school is a subject on which this record is meager. It shows only that the schools are under superintendence of a priest and that "religion is taught as part of the curriculum." But we know that such schools are parochial only in name—they, in fact, represent a world-wide and age-old policy of the Roman Catholic Church. Under the rubric "Catholic Schools," the Canon Law of the Church, by which all Catholics are bound, provides:

> 1215. Catholic children are to be educated in schools where not only nothing contrary to Catholic faith and morals is taught, but rather in schools where religious and moral training occupy the first place. . . .
> 1216. In every elementary school the children must, according to their age, be instructed in Christian doctrine.
> The young people who attend the higher schools are to receive a deeper religious knowledge, and the bishops shall appoint priests qualified for such work by their learning and piety. . . .
> 1224. The religious teaching of youth in any school is subject to the authority and inspection of the Church. . . .

It is no exaggeration to say that the whole historic conflict in temporal policy between the Catholic Church and non-Catholics comes to a focus in their respective school policies. The Roman Catholic Church, counseled by experience in many ages and many lands and with all sorts and conditions of men, takes what, from the viewpoint of its own progress and the success of its mission, is a wise estimate of the importance of education to religion. It does not leave the individual to pick up religion by chance. It relies on early and indelible indoctrination in the faith and order of the Church by the word and example of persons consecrated to the task.

Our public school, if not a product of Protestantism, at least is more consistent with it than with the Catholic culture and scheme of values. It is a relatively recent development dating from about 1840. It is organized on the premises that secular education can be isolated from all religious teachings so that the school can inculcate all needed temporal knowledge and also maintain a strict and lofty neutrality as to religion. The assumption is that after the individual has been instructed in worldly wisdom he will be better fitted to choose his religion. Whether such a disjunction is possible, and if possible whether it is wise, are questions I need not try to answer.

I should be surprised if any Catholic would deny that the parochial school is a vital, if not the most vital, part of the Roman Catholic Church.

If put to the choice, that venerable institution, I should expect, would forego its whole service for mature persons before it would give up education of the young, and it would be a wise choice. Its growth and cohesion, discipline and loyalty, spring from its schools. Catholic education is the rock on which the whole structure rests, and to render tax aid to its Church school is indistinguishable to me from rendering the same aid to the Church itself.

It is of no importance in this situation whether the beneficiary of this expenditure of tax-raised funds is primarily the parochial school and incidentally the pupil, or whether the aid is directly bestowed on the pupil with indirect benefits to the school. The state cannot maintain a Church and it can no more tax its citizens to furnish free carriage to those who attend a Church. The prohibition against establishment of religion cannot be circumvented by a subsidy, bonus or reimbursement of expense to individuals for receiving religious instruction and indoctrination.

The Court, however, compares this to other subsidies and loans to individuals and says, "Nor does it follow that a law has a private rather than a public purpose because it provides that tax-raised funds will be paid to reimburse individuals on account of money spent by them in a way which furthers a public program. . . ." Of course, the state may pay out tax-raised funds to relieve pauperism, but it may not under our constitution do so to induce or reward piety. It may spend funds to secure old age against want, but it may not spend funds to secure religion against skepticism. It may compensate individuals for loss of employment, but it cannot compensate them for adherence to a creed.

It seems to me that the basic fallacy in the Court's reasoning, which accounts for its failure to apply the principles it avows, is in ignoring the essentially religious test by which beneficiaries of this expenditure are selected. A policeman protects a Catholic, of course—but not because he is a Catholic; it is because he is a man and a member of our society. The fireman protects the Church school—but not because it is a Church school; it is because it is property, part of the assets of our society. Neither the fireman nor the policeman has to ask before he renders aid "Is this man or building identified with the Catholic Church?" But before these school authorities draw a check to reimburse for a student's fare they must ask just that question, and if the school is a Catholic one they may render aid because it is such, while if it is of any other faith or is run for profit, the help must be withheld. To consider the converse of the Court's reasoning will best disclose its fallacy. That there is no parallel between police and fire protection and this plan of reimbursement is apparent from the incongruity of the limitation of this Act if applied to police and fire service. Could we sustain an Act that said the police shall protect pupils on the way to or from public schools and Catholic schools but not while going to and coming from other schools, and firemen shall extinguish a blaze in public or Catholic school buildings but shall not put out a blaze in Protestant Church schools or private schools operated for profit? That is the true analogy to the case we have before us and I should think it pretty plain that such a scheme would not be valid. . . .

There is no answer to the proposition, more fully expounded by Mr. Justice Rutledge, that the effect of the religious freedom Amendment to our Constitution was to take every form of propaganda of religion out of the realm of things which could directly or indirectly be made public business and thereby be supported in whole or in part at taxpayers' expense. That is a difference which the Constitution sets up between religion and almost every other subject matter of legislation, a difference which goes to the very root of religious freedom and which the Court is overlooking today. This freedom was first in the Bill of Rights because it was first in the forefathers' minds; it was set forth in absolute terms, and its strength is its rigidity. It was intended not only to keep the state's hands out of religion, but to keep religion's hands off the state, and, above all, to keep bitter religious controversy out of public life by denying to every denomination any advantage from getting control of public policy or the public purse. Those great ends I cannot but think are immeasurably compromised by today's decision.

This policy of our Federal Constitution has never been wholly pleasing to most religious groups. They all are quick to invoke its protections; they all are irked when they feel its restraints. . . .

17

The Church and
Social Reform

In the second decade of this century, when Protestant churches were preoccupied with problems of personal morality, especially with temperance and sex, an obscure seminary professor achieved fame almost over night by calling upon the church to address itself to rampant social abuses. Henry Emerson Fosdick has described Walter Rauschenbusch as "the voice of his generation's Christian protest against the evils of an industrial society." It will be heard in the pages that follow.

Reinhold Niebuhr is likewise a militantly liberal social reformer. And yet, as a conservative and pessimist in theology, he has engaged in prolonged polemics against theological liberals, including—as the selection below indicates—those who have been influenced by Rauschenbusch. (Needless to say, he has been at least as severe with fundamentalists.)

The answer to this paradox is to be found in the fact that, although Niebuhr believes that man is capable of love and realizes himself most completely through love, man is also finite and sinful. Hence, like Christ, perfect love although eternally relevant to human affairs is doomed in actual history, he tells us, to frustration, i.e., to crucifixion. Niebuhr's acute awareness of man's imperfections—man's "sin"—enables him not to ask or expect too much of man, and hence to eschew sentimental optimism and escape the disappointments to which such optimism is foredoomed. "All have sinned and fall short of the glory of God." (Rom. 3:23)

A parallel position prompts Niebuhr to warn that such moral heights as the individual is capable of scaling are not for groups of men. Thus, he argues that we must distinguish sharply "between the moral and social behavior of individuals and of social groups, national, racial and economic; and that this distinction justifies and necessitates political policies which a purely individualistic ethic must always find embarrassing."[1]

None of this means that Niebuhr is a defeatist preaching the futility of effort. On the contrary his aim is to define the conditions of moral action which, he believes, can be effective only if we are aware of *both* its limitations and potentialities. That is why he takes issue, in the selections cited below, with his brother Richard's defense of an ethic of disinterestedness.

The issue is joined here by two distinguished theologians in a remarkable fraternal debate. In fairness to Richard Niebuhr it must be said that his counsel of inactivity implies no beatification of the status quo. Much quietist teaching—that is, that the spirit of God is within and that the social problem is not the church's problem, etc.—has been of this nature. Much of the church's inactivity still reflects a contentment with things as they are, if not on the part of clergymen then on the part of vocal members of their congregations, who, in the end, determine much church policy. However, few if any responsible clergymen or theologians would today take such a position, and Richard Niebuhr's creed of inactivity is clearly not intended as an apology for the existing order. Even so, many, including his brother, would contend that, like the teaching of Luther, it may serve the same purpose.

---

[1] *Moral Man and Immoral Society* (New York: Charles Scribner's Sons, 1932), p. xi.

CHRISTIANITY AND THE SOCIAL CRISIS

Walter Rauschenbusch

Walter Rauschenbusch began as a minister in Hell's Kitchen where he had a chance to observe slum life at its worst. That experience embarked him on a lifelong mission, which he pur-

---

New York: The Macmillan Company, 1907. Reprinted in *A Rauschenbusch Reader,* compiled by B. Y. Landis (New York: Harper & Row, Inc., 1957), pp. 6–22.

sued with prophetic zeal, to ally the church with the forces of social reform. More than anyone else he is responsible for a major reorientation in American Protestantism. Among his most influential writings are Christianizing the Social Order *(1912),* A Theology for the Social Gospel *(1917) and* Christianity and the Social Crisis *(1910). Many of the abuses he castigated have been corrected, an outcome to which he surely contributed by his tireless insistence that the words of the Lord's Prayer be taken seriously: "Thy Kingdom come, thy will be done,* on earth *as it is in heaven."*

The prophets . . . are the beating heart of the Old Testament. A comprehension of the essential purpose and spirit of the prophets is necessary for a comprehension of the purpose and spirit of Jesus and of genuine Christianity. The real meaning of his life and the real direction of his purposes can be understood only in that historical connection.

The fundamental conviction of the prophets which distinguished them from the ordinary religious life of their day, was the conviction that God demands righteousness and demands nothing but righteousness.

The prophets were public men and their interest was in public affairs. Some of them were statesmen of the highest type. All of them interpreted past history, shaped present history, and foretold future history on the basis of the conviction that God rules with righteousness in the affairs of nations, and that only what is just, and not what is expedient and profitable, shall endure. . . .

The prophets demanded right moral conduct as the sole test and fruit of religion, and . . . the morality which they had in mind was not the private morality of detached pious souls but the social morality of the nation. This they preached, and they backed their preaching by active participation in public action and discussion. . . .

Here then we have a succession of men perhaps unique in religious history for their moral heroism and spiritual insight. They were the moving spirits in the religious progress of their nation; the creators, directly or indirectly, of its law, its historical and poetical literature, and its piety; the men to whose personality and teaching Jesus felt most kinship; the men who still kindle modern religious enthusiasm. Most of us believe that their insight was divinely given and that the course they steered was set for them by the Captain of history.

These men were almost indifferent, if not contemptuous, about the ceremonial side of customary religion, but turned with passionate enthusiasm to moral righteousness as the true domain of religion. Where would their interest lie if they lived today?

Their religious concern was not restricted to private religion and morality, but dealt pre-eminently with the social and political life of their nation. Would they limit its range today?

Their sympathy was wholly and passionately with the poor and oppressed. If they lived today, would they place the chief blame for poverty on the poor and give their admiration to the strong? . . .

Is it likely that the same attitude of mind which enlarged and purified the religion of the Hebrew leaders would deteriorate and endanger the religion of Christian leaders? . . . If anyone holds that religion is essentially ritual and sacramental; or that it is purely personal; or that God is on the side of the rich; or that social interest is likely to lead preachers astray; he must prove his case with his eye on the Hebrew prophets, and the burden of proof is with him. . . .

There was a revolutionary consciousness in Jesus; not, of course, in the common use of the word "revolutionary," which connects it with violence and bloodshed. But Jesus knew that he had come to kindle a fire on earth. Much as he loved peace, he knew that the actual result of his work would be not peace but the sword. His mother in her song had recognized in her own experience the settled custom of God to "put down the proud and exalt them of low degree," to "fill the hungry with good things and to send the rich empty away." King Robert of Sicily recognized the revolutionary ring in those phrases, and thought it well that the Magnificat was sung only in Latin. The son of Mary expected a great reversal of values. The first would be last and the last would be first. He saw that what was exalted among man was an abomination before God, and therefore these exalted things had no glamour for his eye. This revolutionary note runs even through the Beatitudes where we should least expect it. The point of them is that henceforth those were to be blessed whom the world had not blessed, for the Kingdom of God would reverse their relative standing. Now the poor and the hungry and sad were to be satisfied and comforted; the meek who had been shouldered aside by the ruthless would get their chance to inherit the earth, and conflict and persecution would be inevitable in the process. . . .

That was the faith of Jesus. Have his followers shared it? We shall see later what changes and limitations the original purpose and spirit of Christianity suffered in the course of history. But the Church has never been able to get entirely away from the revolutionary spirit of Jesus. It is an essential doctrine of Christianity that the world is fundamentally good and practically bad, for it was made by God, but is now controlled by sin. If a man wants to be a Christian, he must stand over against things as they are and condemn them in the name of that higher conception of life which Jesus revealed. If a man is satisfied with things as they are, he belongs to the other side. For many centuries the Church felt so deeply that the Christian conception of life and the actual social life are incompatible, that anyone who wanted to live the genuine Christian life, had to leave the world and live in a monastic community. Protestantism has abandoned the monastic life and settled down to live in the world. If that implies that it accepts the present condition as good and final, it means a silencing of its Christian protest and its surrender to "the world." There is another alternative. Ascetic Christianity called the world evil and left it. Humanity is waiting for a revolutionary Christianity which will call the world evil and change it. We do not want "to blow all our existing institutions to atoms," but we do want to remold every one of them. A tank of gasoline can blow a car sky-high in a single explosion, or push it to the top of a hill in a perpetual succession of little explosions. We need a combination between the faith of Jesus in the need and the possibility of the Kingdom of God, and the modern comprehension of the organic development of human society.

Jesus was not a mere social reformer. Religion was the heart of his life, and all that he said on social relations was said from the religious point of view. He has been called the first socialist. He was more; he was the first real man, the inaugurator of a new humanity. But as such he bore within him the germs of a new social and political order. He was too great to be the Saviour of a fractional part of human life. His redemption extends to all human needs and powers and relations. Theologians have felt no hesitation in founding a system of speculative thought on the teachings of Jesus, and yet Jesus was never an inhabitant of the realm of speculative thought. He has been made the founder and organizer of a great ecclesiastical machine, which derives authority for its offices and institutions from him, and yet "hardly any problem of exegesis is more difficult than to discover in the gospels an administrative or organizing or ecclesiastical Christ." There is at least as much justification in invoking his name today as the champion of a great movement for a more righteous social life. He was neither a theologian, nor an ecclesiastic, nor a socialist. But if we were forced to classify him either with the great theologians who elaborated the fine distinctions of scholasticism; or with the mighty popes and princes of the Church who built up their power in his name; or with the men who are giving their heart and life to the propaganda of a new social system—where should we place him? . . .

The demoralization of society ought to appeal most powerfully to the Church, for the Church is to be the incarnation of the Christ-spirit on earth, the organized conscience of Christendom. It should be swiftest to awaken to every undeserved suffering, bravest to speak against every wrong, and strongest to rally the moral forces of the community against everything that threatens the better life among men.

The gospel, to have full power over an age, must be the highest expression of the moral and religious truths held by that age. If it lags behind and deals in outgrown conceptions of life and duty, it will lose power over the ablest minds and the young men first, and gradually over all. In our thought today the social problems irresistibly take the lead. If the Church has no live and bold thought on this dominant question of modern life, its teaching authority on all other questions will dwindle and be despised. It cannot afford to have young men sniff the air as in a stuffy room when they enter the sphere of religious thought. When the world is in travail with a higher ideal of justice, the Church dare not ignore it if it would retain its moral leadership. On the other hand, if the Church does incorporate the new social terms in its synthesis of truth, they are certain to throw new light on all the older elements of its teaching. The conception of race sin and race salvation become comprehensible once more to those who have made the idea of social solidarity in good and evil a part of their thought. The law of sacrifice loses its arbitrary and mechanical aspect when we understand the vital union of all humanity. Individualistic Christianity has almost lost sight of the great idea of the Kingdom of God, which was the inspiration and center of the thought of Jesus. Social Christianity would once more enable us to understand the purpose and thought of Jesus and take the veil from our eyes when we read the synoptic gospels.

The social crisis offers a great opportunity for the infusion of new life and power into the religious thought of the church. It also offers the chance for progress in its life. When the broader social outlook widens the purpose of a Christian man beyond the increase of his church, he lifts up his eyes and sees that there are others who are at work for humanity besides his denomination. Common work for social welfare is the best common ground for the various religious bodies and the best training school for practical Christian unity. The strong movement for Christian union in our country has been largely prompted by the realization of social needs, and is led by men who have felt the attraction of the Kingdom of God as something greater than any denomination and as the common object of all. Thus the divisions which were caused in the past by differences in dogma and church polity may perhaps be healed by unity of interest in social salvation.

As we have seen, the industrial and commercial life today is dominated by principles antagonistic to the fundamental principles of Christianity, and it is so difficult to live a Christian life in the midst of it that few men even try. If production could be organized on a basis of cooperative fraternity; if distribution could at least approximately be determined by justice; if all men could be conscious that their labor contributed to the welfare of all and that their personal well-being was dependent on the prosperity of the Commonwealth; if predatory business and parasitic wealth ceased and all men lived only by their labor; if the luxury of unearned wealth no longer made us all feverish with covetousness and a simpler life became the fashion; if our time and strength were not used up either in getting bare living or in amassing unusable wealth and we had more leisure for the higher pursuits of the mind and the soul—then there might be a chance to live such a life of gentleness and brotherly kindness and tranquillity of heart as Jesus desired for men. It may be that the co-operative Commonwealth would give us the first chance in history to live a really Christian life without retiring from the world, and would make the Sermon on the Mount a philosophy of life feasible for all who care to try.

This is the stake of the Church in the social crisis. If society continues to disintegrate and decay, the Church will be carried down with it. If the Church can rally such moral forces that injustice will be overcome and fresh red blood will course in a sounder social organism, it will itself rise to higher liberty and life. Doing the will of God it will have new visions of God. With a new message will come a new authority. If the salt lose its saltness, it will be trodden under foot. If the Church fulfills its prophetic functions, it may bear the prophet's reproach for a time, but it will have the prophet's vindication thereafter.

The conviction has always been embedded in the heart of the Church that "the world"—society as it is—is evil and some time is to make way for a true human society in which the spirit of Jesus Christ shall rule. For fifteen hundred years those who desired to live a truly Christian life withdrew from the evil world to live a life apart. But the principle of such an ascetic departure from the world is dead in modern life. There are only two other possibilities. The Church must either condemn the world and seek to change it, or tolerate the world and conform to it. In the latter case it surrenders its holiness and its mission. The other possibility has never yet been tried with full faith on a large scale. All the leadings of God in contemporary history and all the promptings of Christ's spirit in our hearts urge us to make the trial. On this choice is staked the future of the church.

THE ETHIC OF JESUS AND THE
SOCIAL PROBLEM

Reinhold Niebuhr

Reinhold Niebuhr is American Protestantism's most distinguished theologian. His work is as respected by professional philosophers as it is by those responsible for guiding public policy. He was awarded the Presidential Medal of Freedom in 1964.

From *Religion in Life* (Spring 1932). Copyright renewal 1960 by Abingdon Press. Reprinted in *Love and Justice,* edited by D. B. Robertson (Philadelphia: The Westminster Press, 1957), pp. 29–40. Used by permission of the author.

Dr. Niebuhr has written multitudinous articles in addition to his three best-known works: Moral Man and Immoral Society (*1932*); *the Gifford Lectures, published as* The Nature and Destiny of Man (*1943*); *and* The Children of Light and the Children of Darkness (*1944*). *His most recent book is* Man's Nature and His Communities (*1965*).

The selection below was written during a period of more militant social protest than our own and reflects the point of view of a vigorous critic of social abuses who rejects both *the opportunism of the church and the Christian Gospel Movement as represented by Rauschenbusch.*

Since Walter Rauschenbusch aroused the American church to the urgency of the social problem and its relation to the ethical ideals of the gospel, it has been rather generally assumed that it is possible to abstract an adequate social ethic for the reconstruction of society from the social teachings of Jesus. Dozens of books have been written to prove that Jesus' ideals of brotherhood represented an outline of the ideal society, that his law of service offered an alternative to the competitive impulse in modern society, that guidance for the adjustment of every political and economic problem could be found in his words, and that nothing but a little logic would serve to draw out the "social implications" of his teachings.

Most of this energy has been vainly spent and has served to create as much confusion as light. There is indeed a very rigorous ethical ideal in the gospel of Jesus, but there is no social ethic in the ordinary sense of the word in it, precisely because the ethical ideal is too rigorous and perfect to lend itself to application in the economic and political problems of our day. This does not mean that the ethic of Jesus has no light to give to a modern Christian who faces the perplexing economic and political issues of a technological civilization. It means only that confusion will be avoided if a rigorous distinction is made between a perfectionist and absolute ethic and the necessities of a social situation.

The ethic of Jesus was, to begin with, a personal ethic. It was not individual in the sense that he believed in individual perfection abstracted from a social situation. He saw that wealth tempted to covetousness and that poverty prompted the virtue of humility. He spoke of the Kingdom and not of salvation, and the Kingdom meant an ideal social relationship, even though he might emphasize that it proceeded from internal spiritual forces. His ethic was an ethic of love, and it therefore implied social relationships. But it was an individual ethic in the sense that his chief interest was in the quality of life of an individual. He regarded as a temptation the suggestion that he become a political leader or that he develop the political implications of the Messianic idea, and he resisted the effort to make him king. He was not particularly interested in the Jewish people's aspirations toward freedom from Rome, and skillfully evaded the effort to make him take sides in that political problem. He accepted monarchy on the one hand and slavery on the other, though he called attention to the difference between the ideal of his Kingdom, which measured greatness by service, and the kind of greatness which the "kings of the Gentiles" attained.

His lack of concern for social and political issues is, however, not as important from the perspective of this problem as the kind of ethical ideal which he actually developed. In terms of individual life his ethical ideal was one of complete disinterestedness, religiously motivated. No one was to seek his own. The man who asked him to persuade his brother to divide an inheritance with him was rudely rebuked. Evil was not to be resisted, the borrower was to be given more than he asked for without hope of return. A special premium was placed upon actions which could not be rewarded. In other words, the prudential motive was treated with utmost severity. There are, of course, words in the teachings of Jesus which are not as rigorous as this. He promised rewards. Some of these words belong to a humanist strain in his teachings in which he merely makes a shrewd analysis of the effect of certain actions. The severe judge will be judged severely. The proud man will be abased and the humble man exalted. Here the social rewards of social attitudes are recognized. Other offers of reward occur, but with one or two exceptions they can be placed in the category of ultimate rewards—"in the resurrection of the just," "treasures in heaven," favor with God. On the whole, they do not seriously qualify his main position that moral action must be motivated purely by obedience to God, emulation of God's attributes, and gratitude for the forgiving grace of God. An ulterior motive (desire for social approval, for instance) for a worthy action would destroy the virtue of the action and would result only in the attainment of the object of the ulterior motive—"verily, they have their reward."

Jesus did not deny that disinterested action would result in rewards; "all these things" would be added, and the man who forgot himself completely would find himself most truly. Here is the recognition of the basic ethical paradox that the highest result of an action can never be its desired result. It must be a by-product. If it is desired, the purity of the action is destroyed. If I love to be loved or to be socially approved, I will not be loved or approved in the same way as if my fellow men caught in me a glimpse of pure disinterestedness. Obviously the only way to achieve such pure disinterestedness is to have actions motivated purely by religious motives. But this very emphasis upon religious motives lifts the ethic of Jesus above the area of social ethics. We are asked to love our enemies, not because the social consequences of such love will be to make friends of the enemies, but because God loves with that kind of impartiality. We are demanded to forgive those who have wronged us, not because a forgiving spirit will prove redemptive in the lives of the fallen, but because God forgives our sins. Here we have an ethic, in other words, which we can neither disavow nor perfectly achieve. We cannot disavow it because it is a fact that the prudential motive destroys the purity of every ethical action. We have a right to view the social and personal consequences of an action in retrospect, but if we view it in prospect we have something less than the best. So powerful is the drive of self-interest in life, however, that this ideal is as difficult to achieve as it is to disavow. It remains, therefore, as an ideal which convicts every moral achievement of imperfection, but it is always a little beyond the realm of actual human history.

Though Jesus was as indifferent to the social consequences of pure disinterestedness as he was critical of concern for the personal consequences, it is not difficult to draw conclusions in regard to the social ideal implied by such disinterestedness. In practical terms it means a combination of anarchism and communism dominated by the spirit of love. Such perfect love as he demands would obviate the necessity of coercion on the one hand because men would refrain from transgressing upon their neighbor's rights, and on the other hand because such transgression would be accepted and forgiven if it did occur. This is anarchism, in other words. It would mean communism because the privileges of each would be potentially the privileges of all. Where love is perfect the distinctions between mine and thine disappear. The social ideal of Jesus is as perfect and as impossible of attainment as is his personal ideal. But again it is an ideal that cannot be renounced completely. Whatever justice men attain in the society in which they live is always an imperfect justice. The careful limitation and definition of rights which Stoicism gave to the world as a social ideal always develop into injustice in actual life because every person views rights not from an absolute but from a biased perspective. The result is a society in which the perspective of the strong dictates the conceptions of justice by which the total community operates and necessitates social conflict through the assertion of the rights of the weak before the injustice is corrected. Justice, in other words, that is only justice is less than justice. Only imaginative justice, that is, love that begins by espousing the rights of the other rather than self, can achieve a modicum of fairness.

Whether we view the ethical teachings of Jesus from the perspective of the individual or of society we discover an unattainable ideal, but a very useful one. It is an ideal never attained in history or in life, but one that gives us an absolute standard by which to judge both personal and social righteousness. It is a standard by comparison with which all human attainments fall short, and it may offer us the explanation of Jesus' words, "Why callest thou me good? no one is good save God." Perhaps it ought to be added that an attempt to follow this ideal in a world that is, particularly in its group relationships, hardly human and certainly not divine, will inevitably lead us to where it led Jesus, to the cross.

Valuable as this kind of perfectionism is, it certainly offers no basis for a social ethic that deals responsibly with a growing society. Those of us who believe in the complete reorganization of modern society are not wrong in using the ideal of Jesus as a vantage point from which to condemn the present social order, but I think we are in error when we try to draw from the teachings of Jesus any warrant for the social policies which we find necessary to attain to any modicum of justice. We may be right in believing that we are striving for a justice which approximates the Christian ideal more closely than the present social order, but we are wrong when we talk about achieving a "Christian social order." The Barthians are quite right, I think, in protesting against the easy identification of the Kingdom of God with every movement of social reform and social radicalism that has prevailed in American Christianity in particular and in liberal Protestantism in general. Those of us who dissociate ourselves from the easy optimism of modern liberalism and who believe that a just society is not going to be built by a little more education and a few more sermons on love have particular reason to reorient our thinking in this matter so that we will not come forward with a social ethic involving the use of force and coercion and political pressure of every kind and claim the authority of Jesus for it.

Our confusion is, of course, no worse than that of the conventional teachers of Christian ethics and theology who have a rather complacent attitude toward the present economic society and criticize us for violating the ethic of Jesus in our espousal of the class struggle, for instance. Our confusion is, in fact, not quite as bad as theirs. They have used every kind of exegetical device to prove that the teachings of Jesus are not incompatible with participation in nationalistic wars or, if they have been a little more clearheaded, they have found ethical justification for their actions by proving that the ethic of Jesus does not provide for the responsibilities of politics and economics, and therefore leaves them free to choose a political strategy that is most consonant with their conception of the moral good will which they believe Jesus to idealize. The critics of the former type have no ground to stand upon at all when they accuse radical Christians of violating the ethic of Jesus; for participation in a nonviolent strike action, to choose an obvious example, is certainly not more incompatible with the ethic of Jesus than participation in an international conflict. Critics of the latter type have cut the ground for criticism from under their own feet. They admit that any responsible relationship to political and economic affairs involves compromise, and they ought to have a difficult time proving that the assertion of national interest or the protection of national rights is more compatible with the perfectionist ideal of pure disinterestedness than the assertion of class interests and the protection of class rights.

But the confusion of our critics does not absolve us of the necessity of clear thought for ourselves. The struggle for social justice in the present economic order involves the assertion of rights, the rights of the disinherited, and the use of coercion. Both are incompatible with the pure love ethic found in the Gospels. How, then, do we justify the strategy of the "class struggle"? We simply cannot do so in purely Christian terms. There is in the absolute sense no such thing as "Christian socialism." We must justify ourselves by considerations of the social situation that we face and the human resources that are available for its solution. What we discover in the social situation is that human life in its group interests moves pretty much upon the basis of the economic interests of various groups. We realize that intelligence and spiritual and moral idealism may qualify economic interest, but they do not destroy it. Whatever may be possible for individuals, we see no possibility of a group voluntarily divesting itself of its special privileges in society. Nor do we see a possibility of pure disinterestedness and the spirit of forgiveness on the part of an underprivileged group shaming a dominant group into an attitude of social justice. Such a strategy might possibly work in intimate personal relationships but it does not work in the larger group relations. The Negro has been forgiving in his subordinate position in society for a long time, but he has not persuaded the white man to grant him larger privileges in society. Whatever place the industrial worker has won in society has been won by the assertion of his rights through his trade-union organizations. Even the most imaginative urban dwellers lack the imagination to envisage the needs of the farmer. The farmer has been forced to exert political pressure for the attainment of even such minimum justice as he is granted in the present economic organization of our country. No one who looks realistically at the social scene can fail to discover that economic, racial, and national groups stand on a moral level considerably lower than that of the most sensitive individuals. They are not easily persuaded to a voluntary sacrifice of privileges, and an attitude of pure nonresistance on the part of those who suffer from their exactions does not produce the spirit of repentance among them. Intelligence, which may create a spirit of justice among individuals by persuading them to grant to their fellows what they claim for themselves, is generally not acute enough to function in similar fashion in group relations. More frequently it does no more than to create rational sanctifications for special group interests. Only rarely does intellectual force rise high enough to create a perspective from which group prejudices and biases have been banished. The relations between groups are so indirect that the consequences of our actions in the life of another group are not easily discerned, and we therefore continue in unethical conduct without the restraint upon our conscience that intimate personal relations create. Very few white men have any conception of the havoc that is wrought in the souls and upon the bodies of Negroes by prevailing race prejudices; and there is not one American in a million who knows what our reparations policy means for starving workers of Germany. This unhappy group seems under the necessity of asserting its interests, not only against the rest of the world, but against the more comfortable middle classes of their own country.

The social struggle involves a violation of a pure ethic of love, not only in the assertion of rights, but in the inevitable use of coercion. Here again one need but state the obvious; but the obvious is usually not recognized by academic moralists. No society can exist without the use of coercion, though every intelligent society will try to reduce coercion to a minimum and rely upon the factor of mutual consent to give stability to its institutions. Yet it can never trust all of its citizens to accept necessary social arrangements voluntarily. It will use police force against recalcitrant and antisocial minorities, and it will use the threat of political force against a complacent and indifferent group of citizens which could never be relied upon to initiate adequate social policies upon its own accord. No government can wait upon voluntary action on the part of the privileged members of a community for an adequate inheritance or income tax. It will use political force created by the votes of the disinherited and less privileged to initiate and enforce taxation policies, designed to equalize privileges. Privileged groups may accept such legislation without violent revolt, but they will probably argue against its justice until the day of their death. An intelligent society will constantly strive toward the goal of a more equal justice by initiating a more rigorous policy just as soon as a previous and more tentative one has been accepted and absorbed into the social standards of the community. If this is not done by gradual process, with the unrealized goal of essential equality beckoning each generation to surpass the approximations of justice achieved in the past, the inequalities of the social order, always increasing through natural process, are bound to grow until an outraged sense of justice (probably spurred by actual physical want on the part of the least privileged members of a community) will produce a violent revolt. In such nations as Germany, for instance, it is really an open question whether any political measures can achieve the desired end of social justice quickly enough to prevent violent revolution.

The necessity of this kind of coercion, based upon the assertion of interest on the part of the less privileged, is such a clear lesson of history that one hesitates to belabor the point and would refrain from doing so were it not for the fact that half of the academic treatises on social ethics and Christian ethics were written as if no such necessity existed. In this respect secular moralists are frequently as naïve as religious ones. In the one case it is expected that a change in educational technique will eliminate the drive of self-interest which determines economic life and in the other case there is a naïve confidence in the possibility of changing human nature by religious conversion or religious inspiration. It is the thesis of the radical wing of Christian social theorists, whether in England, Germany, or America, that nothing accomplished by either education or religious suasion will be able to abolish the social struggle. We believe that such hopes are corrupted by the sentimentalities of the comfortable classes and are caused by their lack of understanding of the realities of an industrial civilization. In what sense, then, may we call ourselves Christian, or how do we hope to insinuate Christian and ethical values into the social struggle? The simplest answer is that we believe that the highest ethical and spiritual insight may mitigate the social struggle on the one hand and may transcend it on the other.

We believe that it makes some difference whether a privileged group makes a stubborn and uncompromising defense of its special privileges or whether it has some degree of social imagination and tries to view its privileges in the light of the total situation of a community. Education ought to create some of that social imagination, and in so far as it does, it will mitigate the class struggle or the social struggle between races. The religious contribution to the same end may consist of various elements. Real religion produces the spirit of humility and repentance. It destroys moral conceit. Moral conceit is precisely what makes privileged groups so stubborn in the defense of their privileges. The human animal is just moral enough to be unable to act immorally with vigor if he cannot find a moral justification for his actions. If the Christian church used the ethical ideal of Jesus, the ideal of pure disinterestedness, more rigorously, and if the modern pulpit made a more astute analysis of human motives in the light of this ideal, many of the rationalizations that now support the antisocial policies and attitudes of privileged and powerful people would be destroyed. At least they might be qualified. One of the most unfortunate facts about our contemporary moral situation is that the church has ceased to convict men of selfishness at the precise moment in history when human greed is more obvious and more dangerous than at any previous time. Nowhere has the liberal church played more false to its generation than in its optimistic and romantic interpretation of human nature, just when an industrial civilization revealed the drive of self-interest in all its antisocial power. The part of the Christian church that has tried to convict the generation of sin knows too little about the problems of modern life to convict men of their significant sins. Thus religion has on the whole produced moral complacency rather than the spirit of repentance. The number of men who are sufficiently sensitized by religion actually to renounce their privileges must always remain small. But it ought not to be impossible for the church to create enough contrition and consciousness of human selfishness to prompt men to a more willing acceptance of and less stubborn resistance against social policies that aim at the restriction of power and privilege. If we dealt realistically with the facts of human nature, we might be able to create an attitude of complacency toward increasing social restraint, based upon the realization that few, if any, of us are wise enough to restrain our expansive desires voluntarily in a degree sufficient for the needs of our highly interdependent society. If there were a better understanding of human nature in the church today, an understanding that we could acquire by the study of psychology and economics but which we might appropriate just as easily from the insights of great religion, there would be fewer Christian captains of industry who lived under the illusion that they were good enough and wise enough to hold irresponsible power and exercise it for the good of the community. They would know that the very possession of irresponsible power tempts to its selfish use and that the benevolent pretensions of despotism rest either on unconscious self-deception or conscious hypocrisy.

True religion could mitigate the cruelties of the social struggle by its creation of the spirit of love as well as the spirit of repentance. The love ideal which Jesus incarnates may be too pure to be realized in life, but it offers us nevertheless an ideal toward which the religious spirit may strive. All rational idealism creates a conflict between the mind and the impulses, as in Stoicism and Kantian morality. The mind conceives ideals of justice which it tries to force upon recalcitrant selfish impulses. Real religion transmutes the social impulses until they transcend the limits set them by nature (family, race, group, etc.) and include the whole human community. Real religious imagination is able, furthermore, to create an attitude of trust and faith toward human beings, in which the potentialities rather than the immediate realities are emphasized. Through such imagination the needs of the social foe are appreciated, his inadequacies are understood in the light of his situation, and his possibilities for higher and more moral action are recognized. Only the religious spirit which surveys the human scene from the perspective of its presuppositions about the character of life is thus able to disregard present facts and appeal to ultimate possibilities. The fact that in Jesus the spirit of love flowed out in emulation of God's love, without regard to social consequences, cannot blind the eye to the social consequences of a religiously inspired love. If modern religion were really producing it, it would mitigate the evils of the social struggle. It would, to emphasize the obvious once more, not abolish the social struggle, because it would not approximate perfection in sufficiently numerous instances. The fight for justice in society will always be a fight. But wherever the spirit of justice grows imaginative and is transmuted into love, a love in which the interests of the other are espoused, the struggle is transcended by just that much.

It is the fashion among many Christian idealists to criticize the political movements of the disinherited for the spirit of hatred which they generate. The church, so it is said, would espouse their cause much more readily if the spirit of love were manifest in it. What the church fails to realize is that its responsibility is chiefly for the moral and spiritual attitudes of the privileged rather than the disinherited; for it is the former who makes professions of Christian idealism. If the church wants to insinuate the spirit of love into the social struggle, it ought to begin with the privileged groups, not only because it has greater responsibility for them, but because those who hold entrenched positions in the social struggle are obviously under the greater obligation to be imaginative in gauging the needs and discounting the limitations of those who suffer from social injustice. The perfectionist ethic of Jesus allows for no such distinctions; for it demands that love be poured forth whether or not we suffer from injustice. But no one can avow such an ethic from the vantage point of privilege and security. If the portion of society that benefits from social inequality and which is endangered by a rising tide of social discontent attempts to counsel love, forgiveness, and patience to the discontented, it will convict itself of hypocrisy, except it is able first of all to reveal fruits of the Spirit, which it commends, in its own life. Even if it were to reveal some fruits, but too meager to justify a more trusting and a less vehement attitude on the part of the underprivileged, its moral ideals would be regarded as pretensions. The race situation in the South offers interesting commentary upon this point. The fine work which the interracial commission has done has failed to preserve the respect of the more eager young Negroes for it, because they feel that through its efforts of conciliation white men have yielded only inconsequential social advantages in order that they may hold to their major ones. The most perfect love may not ask for social justification, but any love within the capacity of ordinary men and groups does. The disinherited will have their spirits corrupted by hatred and their policies tinctured with violence except they are able to detect some genuinely ethical elements in the policies of the privileged and entrenched social groups. If the spirit of love is to qualify and mitigate the social struggle, the groups that profess to believe in the efficacy of love and who, at the same time, have favored positions in society are clearly under obligation to introduce this Christian element in society. They may be quite sure that any solid ethical achievement among them would result in practically immediate ethical reactions of trust and faith among those who are trying to advance socially. Only the faith and trust of the advancing group will not and ought not ever rise to the point where purely voluntary action toward equality is expected. A degree of ethical insight on the part of the whole community will not abolish the necessity of social conflict, but it may prevent violence and reduce the hatred that must inevitably arise when the disinherited are faced, not only with the stubborn greed of the powerful and comfortable social classes, but also with the protection of their privileges by the covert use of force and their hypocritical pretension of virtue.

A Christian ethical idealism that espouses the cause of proletarian groups and identifies itself with their political movements is, in short, as pure as any Christian movement that assumes a responsible attitude toward society. The compromises that it makes with the pure Christian ethic are inevitable compromises which everyone must make who deals with the social problem from the perspective of society rather than that of the individual. It might claim, in addition, to appropriate the Christian ethical ideal more closely than a type of thought that fears contamination in the social struggle. For the social struggle is a reality in society and we will be contaminated by it except we get out of society. The ascetic may possibly have a vantage point from which to criticize the ethical purity of Christian socialism or Christian radicalism. Those who stay in society have not. If our critics were less confused about the moral and social realities of modern society, they would know that neutrality in a social struggle between entrenched and advancing social classes really means alliance with the entrenched position. In the social struggle we are either on the side of privilege or need. No ethical perfectionism can save us from that choice.

THE GRACE OF DOING NOTHING

H. Richard Niebuhr

In the following selection the late Richard Niebuhr defends an ethic of disinterestedness—contending that the true Christian will, qua Christian, be inactive in the presence of social injustice. His brother responds in the article that follows. That the disagreement was provoked by events which seem in these troubled times to have occurred a thousand years ago—Japan's pre-war aggressions in China—makes no difference. Today, Red China or Russia could be substituted for the Japan of 1932. The terms in which the issue is explored are timeless. At the time this debate took place both brothers were professors of Christian ethics, H. Richard at Yale and Reinhold at Union Theological Seminary. Richard Niebuhr wrote The Social Source of Denomination *(1929),* The Kingdom of God in America *(1937), and* The Purpose of the Church and Its Ministry *(1956).*

It may be that the greatest moral problems of the individual or of a society arise when there is nothing to be done. When we have begun a certain line of action or engaged in a conflict we cannot pause too long to

From *The Christian Century* (March 23, 1932), pp. 378–380. Copyright 1932 Christian Century Foundation. Reprinted by permission from *The Christian Century*.

decide which of various possible courses we ought to choose for the sake of the worthier result. Time rushes on and we must choose as best we can, entrusting the issue to the future. It is when we stand aside from the conflict, before we know what our relations to it really are, when we seem to be condemned to doing nothing, that our moral problems become greatest. How shall we do nothing?

The issue is brought home to us by the fighting in the East. We are chafing at the bit, we are eager to do something constructive; but there is nothing constructive, it seems, that we can do. We pass resolutions, aware that we are doing nothing; we summon up righteous indignation and still do nothing; we write letters to congressmen and secretaries, asking others to act while we do nothing. Yet is it really true that we are doing nothing? There are, after all, various ways of being inactive, and some kinds of inactivity, if not all, may be highly productive. It is not really possible to stand aside, to sit by the fire in this world of moving times; even Peter was doing something in the courtyard of the high-priest's house—if it was only something he was doing to himself. When we do nothing we are also affecting the course of history. The problem we face is often that of choice between various kinds of inactivity rather than of choice between action and inaction.

Our inactivity may be that of the pessimist who watches a world go to pieces. It is a meaningful inactivity for himself and for the world. His world, at all events, will go to pieces the more rapidly because of that inactivity. Or it may be the inactivity of the conservative believer in things as they are. He does nothing in the international crisis because he believes that the way of Japan is the way of all nations, that self-interest is the first and only law of life, and that out of the clash of national, as out of that of individual, self-interests the greater good will result. His inactivity is one of watchful waiting for the opportunity when, in precisely similar manner, though with less loss of life and fortune, if possible, he may rush to the protection of his own interests or promote them by taking advantage of the situation created by the strife of his competitors. This way of doing nothing is not unproductive. It encourages the self-asserters and it fills them with fear of the moment when the new competition will begin. It may be that they have been driven into their present conflict by the knowledge or suspicion that the watchful waiter is looking for his opportunity, perhaps unconsciously, and that they must be prepared for him.

The inactivity of frustration and moral indignation is of another order. It is the way of those who have renounced all violent methods of settling conflicts and have no other means at hand by which to deal with the situation. It is an angry inactivity like that of a man who is watching a neighborhood fight and is waiting for the police to arrive—for police who never come. He has renounced for himself the method of forcible interference, which would only increase the flow of blood and the hatred, but he knows of nothing else that he can do. He is forced to remain content on the sidelines, but with mounting anger he regards the bully who is beating the neighbor, and his wrath issues in words of exasperation and condemnation. Having tied his own hands he fights with his tongue and believes that he is not fighting because he inflicts only mental wounds. The bully is for him an outlaw, a person not to be trusted, unfair, selfish, one who cannot be redeemed save by restraint. The righteous indignation mounts and mounts, and must issue at last—as the police fail to arrive—either in his own forcible entry into the conflict, despite his scruples, or in apoplexy.

The diatribes against Japan which are appearing in the secular and religious press today have a distressing similarity to the righteously indignant utterances which preceded our conflicts with Spain and with Germany. China is Cuba and Belgium over again; it is the Negro race beaten by Simon Legree. And the pacifists who have no other program than that of abstention from the unrighteousness of war are likely to be placed in the same quandary in which their fellows were placed in 1860, 1898 and 1915, and—unless human attitudes have been regenerated in the interim—they are likely to share the same fate, which was not usually incarceration. Here is a situation which they did not foresee when they made their vow; may it not be necessary to have one more war to end all war? Righteous indignation not allowed to issue in action is a dangerous thing—as dangerous as any great emotion nurtured and repressed at the same time. It is the source of sudden explosions or the ground of long, bitter and ugly hatreds.

If this way of doing nothing must be rejected, the Communists' way offers more hope. Theirs is the inactivity of those who see that there is indeed nothing constructive to be done in the present situation, but that, rightly understood, this situation is after all preliminary to a radical change which will eliminate the conditions of which the conflict is a product. It is the inactivity of a cynicism which expects no good from the present, evil world of capitalism, but also the inactivity of a boundless faith in the future. The Communists know that war and revolution are closely akin, that war breeds discontent and misery, and that out of misery and discontent new worlds may be born. This is an opportunity, then, not for direct entrance into the conflict, not for the watchful waiting of those who seek their self-interest, but for the slow laborious process of building up within the fighting groups those cells of communism which will be ready to inherit the new world and be able to build a classless international commonwealth on the ruins of capitalism and nationalism. Here is inactivity with a long vision, a steadfast hope and a realistic program of non-interfering action.

But there is yet another way of doing nothing. It appears to be highly impracticable because it rests on the well-nigh obsolete faith that there is a God—a real God. Those who follow this way share with communism the belief that the fact that men can do nothing constructive is no indication of the fact that nothing constructive is being done. Like the Communists they are assured that the actual processes of history will inevitably and really bring a different kind of world with lasting peace. They do not rely on human aspirations after ideals to accomplish this end, but on forces which often seem very impersonal—as impersonal as those which eliminated slavery in spite of abolitionists. The forces may be as impersonal and as actual as machine production, rapid transportation, the physical mixtures of races, etc., but as parts of the real world they are as much a part of the total divine process as are human thoughts and prayers.

From this point of view, naïvely affirming the meaningfulness of reality, the history of the world is the judgment of the world and also its redemption, and a conflict like the present one is—again as in communism—only the prelude both to greater judgment and to a new era. The world being what it is, these results are brought forth when the seeds of national or individual self-interest are planted; the actual structure of things is such that our wishes for a different result do not in the least affect the outcome. As a man soweth so shall he reap. This God of things as they are is inevitable and quite merciless. His mercy lies beyond, not this side of, judgment. This inactive Christianity shares with communism also the belief in the inevitably good outcome of the mundane process and the realistic insight that that good cannot be achieved by the slow accretion of better habits alone but more in consequence of a revolutionary change which will involve considerable destruction. While it does nothing it knows that something is being done, something which is divine both in its threat and in its promise.

This inactivity is like that of the early Christians whose millenarian mythology it replaces with the contemporary mythology of social forces. (Mythology is after all not fiction but a deep philosophy.) Like early Christianity and like communism today radical Christianity knows that nothing constructive can be done by interference, but that something very constructive can be done in preparation for the future. It also can build cells of those within each nation who, divorcing themselves from the program of nationalism and of capitalism, unite in a higher loyalty which transcends national and class lines of division and prepare for the future. There is no such Christian international today because radical Christianity has not arrived as yet at a program and a philosophy of history, but such little cells are forming. The First Christian international of Rome has had its day; the Second Christian international of Stockholm is likely to go the way of the Second Socialist international. There is need and opportunity for a Third Christian international.

While the similarities of a radically Christian program with the Communist program are striking, there are also great dissimilarities. There is a new element in the inactivity of radical Christianity which is lacking in communism. The Christian reflects upon the fact that his inability to do anything constructive in the crisis is the inability of one whose own faults are so apparent and so similar to those of the offender that any action on his part is not only likely to be misinterpreted but is also likely—in the nature of the case—to be really less than disinterested. He is like a father who, feeling a righteous indignation against a misbehaving child, remembers that that misbehavior is his fault as much as the child's and that indignation is the least helpful, the most dangerous of attitudes to take; it will solve nothing, though it may repress.

So the American Christian realizes that Japan is following the example of his own country and that it has little real ground for believing America to be a disinterested nation. He may see that his country, for which he bears his own responsibility as a citizen, is really not disinterested and that its righteous indignation is not wholly righteous. An inactivity then is demanded which will be profoundly active in rigid self-analysis. Such analysis is likely to reveal that there is an approach to the situation, indirect but far more effective than direct interference, for it is able to create the conditions under which a real reconstruction of habits is possible. It is the opposite approach from that of the irate father who believes that every false reaction on the part of his child may be cured by a verbal, physical or economic spanking.

This way of doing nothing the old Christians called repentance, but the word has become so reminiscent of emotional debauches in the feeling of guilt that it may be better to abandon it for a while. What is suggested is that the only effective approach to the problem of China and Japan lies in the sphere of an American self-analysis which is likely to result in some surprising discoveries as to the amount of renunciation of self-interest necessary on the part of this country and of individual Christians before anything effective can be done in the East.

The inactivity of radical Christianity is not the inactivity of those who call evil good; it is the inaction of those who do not judge their neighbors because they cannot fool themselves into a sense of superior righteousness. It is not the inactivity of a resigned patience, but of a patience that is full of hope and is based on faith. It is not the inactivity of the noncombatant, for it knows that there are no noncombatants, that everyone is involved, that China is being crucified (though the term is very inaccurate) by our sins and those of the whole world. It is not the inactivity of the merciless, for works of mercy must be performed though they are only palliatives to ease present pain while the process of healing depends on deeper, more actual and urgent forces.

But if there is no God, or if God is up in heaven and not in time itself, it is a very foolish inactivity.

MUST WE DO NOTHING?

Reinhold Niebuhr

Having expressed his misgivings about the gospel of social commitment espoused by liberal Christianity,[1] Reinhold Niebuhr here takes issue with his brother's opposite counsel of disinterestedness. His comments are followed by Richard's rejoinder.

There is much in my brother's article, "The Grace of Doing Nothing," with which I agree. Except for the invitation of the editors of The Christian Century I would have preferred to defer voicing any disagreement with some of his final conclusions to some future occasion; for a casual article on a specific problem created by the contemporary international situation hardly does justice to his general position. I believe the problem upon which he is working—the problem of dissociating a rigorous gospel ethic of disinterestedness and love from the sentimental dilutions of that ethic which are current in liberal Christianity—is a tremendously important one. I owe so much to the penetrating thought which he has been giving this subject that I may be able to do some justice to his general position even though I do not share his conviction that a pure love ethic can ever be made the basis of a civilization.

He could not have done better than to choose the Sino-Japanese conflict, and the reactions of the world to it, in order to prove the difficulty, if not the futility, of dealing redemptively with a sinful nation or individual if we cannot exorcise the same sin from our own hearts. It is true that pacifists are in danger of stirring up hatred against Japan in their effort to stem the tide of Japanese imperialism. It is true that the very impotence of an individual who deals with a social situation which goes beyond his own powers tempts him to hide his sense of futility behind a display of violent emotion. It is true that we have helped to create the Japan which expresses itself in terms of materialistic imperialism. The insult we offered her in our immigration laws was a sin of spiritual aggression. The white world has not only taught her the ways of imperialism, but has pre-empted enough of the

[1] See above, p. 451 ff.

yellow man's side of the world to justify Japan's imperialism as a vent for pent-up national energies.

It is also true that American concern over Japanese aggression is not wholly disinterested. It is national interest which inspires us to desire stronger action against Japan than France and England are willing to take. It is true, in other words, that every social sin is, at least partially, the fruit and consequence of the sins of those who judge and condemn it, and that the effort to eliminate it involves the critics and judges in new social sin, the assertion of self-interest and the expression of moral conceit and hypocrisy. If anyone would raise the objection to such an analysis that it finds every social action falling short only because it measures the action against an impossible ideal of disinterestedness, my brother could answer that while the ideal may seem to be impossible the actual social situation proves it to be necessary. It is literally true that every recalcitrant nation, like every antisocial individual, is created by the society which condemns it, and that redemptive efforts which betray strong ulterior motives are always bound to be less than fully redemptive.

My brother draws the conclusion from this logic that it is better not to act at all than to act from motives which are less than pure, and with the use of methods which are less than critical (coercion). He believes in taking literally the words of Jesus, "Let him who is without sin cast the first stone." He believes, of course, that this kind of inaction would not really be inaction; it would be, rather, the action of repentance. It would give every one involved in social sin the chance to recognize how much he is involved in it and how necessary it is to restrain his own greed, pride, hatred and lust for power before the social sin is eliminated.

This is an important emphasis particularly for modern Christianity with its lack of appreciation of the tragic character of life and with its easy assumption that the world will be saved by a little more adequate educational technique. Hypocrisy is an inevitable by-product of moral aspiration, and it is the business of true religion to destroy man's moral conceit, a task which modern religion has not been performing in any large degree. Its sentimentalities have tended to increase rather than to diminish moral conceit. A truly religious man ought to distinguish himself from the moral man by recognizing the fact that he is not moral, that he remains a sinner to the end. The sense of sin is more central to religion than is any other attitude.

All this does not prove, however, that we ought to apply the words of Jesus, "Let him who is without sin cast the first stone," literally. If we do we will never be able to act. There will never be a wholly disinterested nation. Pure disinterestedness is an ideal which even individuals cannot fully achieve, and human groups are bound always to express themselves in lower ethical forms than individuals. It follows that no nation can ever be good enough to save another nation purely by the power of love. The relation of nations and of economic groups can never be brought into terms of pure love. Justice is probably the highest ideal toward which human groups can aspire. And justice, with its goal of adjustment of right to right, inevitably involves the assertion of right against right and interest against interest until some kind of harmony is achieved. If a measure of humility and of love does not enter this conflict of interest it will of course degenerate into violence. A national society will be able to develop a measure of the kind of imagination which knows how to appreciate the virtues of an opponent's position and the weakness in one's own. But the ethical and spiritual note of love and repentance can do no more than qualify the social struggle in history. It will never abolish it.

The hope of attaining an ethical goal for society by purely ethical means, that is, without coercion, and without the assertion of the interests of the underprivileged against the interests of the privileged, is an illusion which was spread chiefly among the comfortable classes of the past century. My brother does not make the mistake of assuming that this is possible in social terms. He is acutely aware of the fact that it is not possible to get a sufficient degree of pure disinterestedness and love among privileged classes and powerful nations to resolve the conflicts of history in that way. He understands the stubborn inertia which the ethical ideal meets in history. At this point his realistic interpretation of the facts of history comes in full conflict with his insistence upon a pure gospel ethic, upon a religiously inspired moral perfectionism, and he resolves the conflict by leaving the field of social theory entirely and resorting to eschatology. The Christian will try to achieve humility and disinterestedness not because enough Christians will be able to do so to change the course of history, but because this kind of spiritual attitude is a prayer to God for the coming of his kingdom.

I will not quarrel with this apocalyptic note, as such, though I suspect many Christian Century readers will. I believe that a proper eschatology is necessary to a vigorous ethic, and that the simple idea of progress is inimical to the highest ethic. The compound of pessimism and optimism which a vigorous ethical attitude requires can be expressed only in terms of religious eschatology. What makes my brother's eschatology impossible for me is that he identifies everything that is occurring in history (the drift toward disaster, another world war and possibly a revolution) with the counsels of God, and then suddenly, by a leap of faith, comes to the conclusion that the same God who uses brutalities and forces, against which man must maintain conscientious scruples, will finally establish an ideal society in which pure love will reign.

I have more than one difficulty with such a faith. I do not see how a revolution in which the disinterested express their anger and resentment, and assert their interests, can be an instrument of God, and yet at the same time an instrument which religious scruples forbid a man to use. I should think that it would be better to come to ethical terms with the forces of nature in history, and try to use ethically directed coercion in order that violence may be avoided. The hope that a kingdom of pure love will emerge out of the catastrophes of history is even less plausible than the Communist faith that an equalitarian society will eventually emerge from them. There is some warrant in history for the latter assumption, but very little for the former.

I find it impossible to envisage a society of pure love as long as man remains man. His natural limitations of reason and imagination will prevent him, even should he achieve a purely disinterested motive, from fully envisaging the needs of his fellow men or from determining his actions upon the basis of their interests. Inevitably these limitations of individuals will achieve cumulative effect in the life and actions of national, racial and economic groups. It is possible to envisage a more ethical society than we now have. It is possible to believe that such a society will be achieved partly by evolutionary process and partly by catastrophe in which an old order, which offers a too stubborn resistance to new forces, is finally destroyed.

It is plausible also to interpret both the evolutionary and the catastrophic elements in history in religious terms and to see the counsels of God in them. But it is hardly plausible to expect divine intervention to introduce something into history which is irrelevant to anything we find in history now. We may envisage a society in which human co-operation is possible with a minimum amount of coercion, but we cannot imagine one in which there is no coercion at all—unless, of course, human beings become quite different from what they now are. We may hope for a society in which self-interest is qualified by rigorous self-analysis and a stronger social impulse, but we cannot imagine a society totally without the assertion of self-interest and therefore without the conflict of opposing interests.

I realize quite well that my brother's position both in its ethical perfectionism and in its apocalyptic note is closer to the gospel than mine. In confessing that, I am forced to admit that I am unable to construct an adequate social ethic out of a pure love ethic. I cannot abandon the pure love ideal because anything which falls short of it is less than the ideal. But I cannot use it fully if I want to assume a responsible attitude toward the problems of society. Religious perfectionism drives either to asceticism or apocalypticism. In the one case the problem of society is given up entirely; in the other individual perfection is regarded as the force which will release the redemptive powers of God for society. I think the second alternative is better than the first, and that both have elements which must be retained for any adequate social ethic, lest it become lost in the relativities of expediency. But as long as the world of man remains a place where nature and God, the real and the ideal, meet, human progress will depend upon the judicious use of the forces of nature in the service of the ideal.

In practical, specific and contemporary terms, this means that we must try to dissuade Japan from her military venture, but must use coercion to frustrate her designs if necessary, must reduce coercion to a minimum and prevent it from issuing in violence, must engage in constant self-analysis in order to reduce the moral conceit of Japan's critics and judges to a minimum, and must try in every social situation to maximize the ethical forces and yet not sacrifice the possibility of achieving an ethical goal because we are afraid to use any but purely ethical means.

To say all this is really to confess that the history of mankind is a personal tragedy; for the highest ideals which the individual may project are ideals which he can never realize in social and collective terms. If there is a law in our members which wars against the law that is in our minds as individuals, this is even more true when we think of society. Individuals set the goal for society but society itself must achieve the goal, and society is and will always remain sub-human. The goal which a sensitive individual sets for society must therefore always be something which is a little outside and beyond history. Love may qualify the social struggle of history but it will never abolish it, and those who make the attempt to bring society under the dominion of perfect love will die on the cross. And those who behold the cross are quite right in seeing it as a revelation of the divine, of what man ought to be and cannot be, at least not so long as he is enmeshed in the processes of history.

Perhaps that is why it is inevitable that religious imagination should set goals beyond history. "Man's reach is beyond his grasp, or what's a heaven for." My brother does not like these goals above and beyond history. He wants religion and social idealism to deal with history. In that case he must not state his goal in absolute terms. There can be nothing absolute in history, no matter how frequently God may intervene in it. Man cannot live without a sense of the absolute, but neither can he achieve the absolute. He may resolve the tragic character of that fact by religious faith, by the experience of grace in which the unattainable is experienced in anticipatory terms, but he can never resolve in purely ethical terms the conflict between what is and what ought to be.

THE ONLY WAY INTO THE KINGDOM OF GOD

H. Richard Niebuhr

Editor The Christian Century

Sir: Since you have given me leave to fire one more shot in the fraternal war between my brother and me over the question of pacifism, I shall attempt to place it as well as I can, not for the purpose of demolishing my opponent's position—which our thirty years have shown me to be impossible—but for the sake of pointing as accurately as I can to the exact locus of the issue between us. It does not lie in the question of activity or inactivity, to which my too journalistic approach to the problem directed attention; we are speaking after all of two kinds of activity. The fundamental question seems to me to be whether "the history of mankind is a perennial tragedy" which can derive meaning only from a goal which lies beyond history, as my brother maintains, or whether the "eschatological" faith, to which I seek to adhere, is justifiable. In that faith tragedy is only the prelude to fulfilment, and a prelude which is necessary because of human nature; the kingdom of God comes inevitably, though whether we shall see it or not depends on our recognition of its presence and our acceptance of the only kind of life which will enable us to enter it, the life of repentance and forgiveness.

For my brother God is outside the historical processes, so much so that he charges me with faith in a miracle-working deity which interferes occasionally, sometimes brutally, sometimes redemptively, in this history. But God, I believe, is always in history; he is the structure in things, the course of all meaning, the "I am that I am," that which is that it is. He is the rock against which we beat in vain, that which bruises and overwhelms us when we seek to impose our wishes, contrary to his, upon him. That structure of the universe, that creative will, can no more be said to interfere brutally in history than the violated laws of my organism can be said to interfere brutally with my life if they make me pay the cost of my violation. That structure of the universe, that will of God, does bring war and depression upon us when we bring it upon ourselves, for we live in the kind of world which visits our iniquities upon us and our children, no matter how much we pray and desire that it be otherwise.

Self-interest acts destructively in this world; it calls forth counter-assertion; nationalism breeds nationalism; class assertion summons up counter-assertion on the part of exploited classes. The result is war, economic, military, verbal; and it is judgment. But this same structure in things which is our enemy is our redeemer; "it means intensely and it means good"—not the good which we desire, but the good which we would desire if we were good and really wise. History is not a perennial tragedy but a road to fulfilment and that fulfilment requires the tragic outcome of every self-assertion, for it is fulfilment which can only be designated as "love." It has created fellowship in atoms and organisms, at bitter cost to electrons and cells; and it is creating something better than human selfhood but at bitter cost to that selfhood. This is not a faith in progress, for evil grows as well as good, and every self-assertion must be eliminated somewhere and somehow—by innocence suffering for guilt, it seems.

If, however, history is no more than tragedy, if there is no fulfilment in it, then my brother is right. Then we must rest content with the clash of self-interested individuals, personal or social. But in that case I see no reason why we should qualify the clash of competition with a homeopathic dose of Christian "love."

The only harmony which can possibly result from the clash of interests is the harmony imposed by the rule of the strong or a parallelogram of social forces, whether we think of the interclass structure or the international world. To import any pacifism into this struggle is only to weaken the weaker self-asserters (India, China or the proletariat) or to provide the strong with a façade of "service" behind which they can operate with a salved conscience. (Pacifism, on the other hand, as a method of self-assertion is not pacifism at all but a different kind of war.)

The method which my brother recommends, that of qualifying the social struggle by means of some Christian love, seems to me to be only the old method of making Christian love an ambulance driver in the wars of interested and clashing parties. If it is more than that, it is a weakening of the forces whose success we think necessary for a juster social order. For me the question is one of "either-or"; either the Christian method, which is not the method of love but of repentance and forgiveness, or the method of self-assertion; either nationalism or Christianity, either capitalism-communism or Christianity. The attempt to qualify the one method by the other is hopeless compromise.

I think that to apply the terms "Christian perfectionism" or "Christian ideal" to my approach is rather misleading. I rather think that Dewey is quite right in his war on ideals; they always seem irrelevant to our situation and betray us into a dualistic morality. The society of love is an impossible human ideal, as the fellowship of the organism is an impossible ideal for the cell. It is not an ideal toward which we can strive, but an "emergent," a potentiality in our situation which remains unrealized so long as we try to impose our pattern, our wishes upon the divine creative process.

Man's task is not that of building utopias, but that of eliminating weeds and tilling the soil so that the kingdom of God can grow. His method is not one of striving for perfection or of acting perfectly, but of clearing the road by repentance and forgiveness. That this approach is valid for societies as well as for individuals and that the opposite approach will always involve us in the same one ceaseless cycle of assertion and counter-assertion is what I am concerned to emphasize.

Part Six

Alienation in the Modern World

Although the term alienation as we now use it has a venerable history which goes back at least as far as Hegel, it has only recently acquired new prominence. We need it as we try to understand once subterranean moods and tendencies which seem suddenly to have surfaced in the 1960's. The title of one of Freud's best known works is "Civilization and Its Discontents." Were he alive today he might give us a sequel entitled "Modern Society and Its Discontents." We are, indeed, in our winter—some would say an unseasonal winter—of discontent, and alienation, for reasons now to be explored, is the condition which best explains it. The discontent is of a special kind, removed, if not entirely from war, then from storm, hunger, plague and the other immemorial disasters which have brought man grief. The object of the following pages is to examine the new alienation, especially as it prevails among young people, and then to deal with the remedy, drugs, to which many of the discontented have turned.

18

Modern Society and
Its Discontents

Industrial capitalism has always had its bitter critics as well as its ardent apologists. Usually the criticism has been economic, emphasizing the way in which the profit motive results in exploiting workers and victimizing consumers with attendant breakdowns in the economy such as occurred in the 1930's. Sometimes the criticism has been ethical, concentrating on the corrupting influence of the profit motive. Sometimes, as with romanticists, criticism has concentrated on the mechanization of production and its dehumanization of the worker. Most such criticism was inspired by the sordid beginnings of industrial capitalism when unprotected workers, including women and children, were in fact cruelly overworked and underpaid and lived under indescribably wretched conditions; or by the period of *Hochcapitalismus* when the most predatory practices of businessmen and capitalists were almost completely uncontrolled.

Today, although there are still serious defects in the social system of which industrial capitalism is the foundation, most critics would concede that vast improvements have taken place. Democracy is no longer a utopian dream. Despite great and potentially dangerous concentrations of power, democratic institutions do in fact function as they did not a century ago. An autonomous labor movement gives workers a strong voice they did not have before and Marx's prediction that they would undergo progressive degradation has not been confirmed. On the contrary, both the conditions and rewards of work have been vastly improved in the last century for the great majority of workers in Europe and America. If a sixty hour work week once made it difficult to distinguish between a free worker and a slave, the reduction of the work week, especially in the United States, is surely a spectacular achievement exceeded only by the elimination of poverty for four-fifths of our population. One-fifth of our people are still deprived of the basic necessities of life and in a society as affluent as ours this is scandalous, but it may fairly be argued that our failures should not obscure what has been accomplished for the other four-fifths. Also, education, even though it leaves much to be desired, has been made available to all. And the system provides ample opportunity for the able and talented even though ethnic prejudice mars the record. If provision for those who are not able and talented is still much too meager, it is in glaring contrast to the poorhouses and almshouses (not to mention the pesthouses) of another century.

To be sure, it is all too easy to exaggerate these accomplishments, as many do, and to use them as a pretext for ignoring the blighted condition of our cities or the desperate predicament of our ethnic minorities. Only the smug and myopic will fail to recognize that much remains to be done. Nevertheless, enough has been achieved to render strikingly paradoxical the recent appearance among many of a mood of complete disenchantment and disillusionment. Even more mysteriously, this mood afflicts a considerable number who can hardly be described as economically disadvantaged. Perhaps most bewildering is the scope of their censure which goes beyond such traditional grievances as poverty and inequality to totally fault a whole way of life. They are repelled by what they see. Recitations of past accomplishments and encouraging trends completely fail to impress them. They are supported by many of our most highly regarded writers and artists who see nothing worth recording in the world about them except the ugly and pathological. All feel trapped in a mechanized, depersonalized, regimented, over-organized society where, as they see it, hypocrisy displaces honesty, venality triumphs over generosity, ambition is mistaken for self-realization, ugliness drives out beauty. Their animadversions are directed not merely against capitalism, but against communism, at any rate communism of the variety subscribed to in the USSR. Both are seen as threatening the individual's sense of identity, as diminishing him, as manipulating him, as making him a pawn of forces external to him.

We are confronted by the protest of people, most of them young and therefore concentrated on college campuses, who feel isolated, displaced, rootless, lonely, estranged, in a word, alienated. Two major groupings are roughly distinguishable. Some have taken the way of retreat, exiling themselves from conventional society. Among these are the "hippies," who have carried their protest to the point of adopting a new style of life. They are refugees from what they choose to call the rat-race. Their advice in the curious patois which has become a trademark is, "Do your own thing."

Although they may not know it, the pedigree of the hippies goes back to Diogenes and the Greek Cynics who, like them, sought "honesty" and escape from artificial conventions by living doglike ("canine" and "cynical" have the same Latin and Greek roots), i.e., "natural" lives. It embraces Thoreau, and extends through Nietzsche, who likewise sought a transvaluation of all values, and the existentialists, with borrowings from the oriental mystics. Among the hippies a wholesale repudiation of middle-class values, whether related to propriety or property, manifests itself in sartorial eccentricity and sexual permissiveness and an attitude of complete disdain for status and wealth. It has been difficult (for those who are not their troubled parents) to regard the hippies as more than impudent teen (or tween)-agers transiently intent on savoring complete freedom—including freedom from hard work—and shocking their elders. However, the hippies are only the more visible and quixotic vanguard of a much more numerous legion which embraces large numbers of artists, writers, students, and teachers. There is therefore good reason for taking this phenomenon seriously, although the real perils and sheer boredom of living in New York's East Village or San Francisco's Haight-Ashbury may well disperse these and similar settlements. Whether the hippies and the new converts they may acquire will survive such a diaspora is not foreseeable.

If there is the way of the yogi, there is also, to recall Koestler's useful distinction, the way of the commissar. Thus, some prefer rebellion to retreat, to change the world rather than to escape it. These, exponents of the so-called "new politics," comprise the "New Left" which not only despises the profit system, but organization and discipline as well, and therefore regards Communists and liberals with the same condescension it reserves for all "Organization" men. New Leftists share with their drug-oriented cousins a complete alienation from the "Establishment." However their estrangement leads them not to beads and flowers and inner exploration but to picket lines, teach-ins, marches, demonstrations and other forms of vehement social protest. Their pedigree goes back to the youthful Karl Marx, from whose early *Economic and Philosophic Manuscripts* (which he later repudiated) they derive their notions of alienation. Many of them served their apprenticeship in the civil rights movement, bravely courting danger in Mississippi and other centers of Southern hospitality. More recently they have earned their spurs demonstrating against the war in Vietnam which they cite as confirming their severest criticism of prevailing American practices. Dedicated activists, they relish slogans such as "Black Power" and "Student Power." Since, for special reasons, universities and colleges are peculiarly vulnerable to student activists (*vide* Berkeley), their campus protests have often prospered. These campus successes have conceivably led them to exaggerate the potentialities of militancy in other areas such as the Pentagon or a Century City hotel in Los Angeles where the President is speaking. It should be added that, having repudiated what they regard as the stale left-of-center formulas of the traditional liberal, social-democratic or communist varieties, they are as vague on program as they are valiant in protest.

The emphasis in the readings which follow will be not so much on the alienating conditions—some of these are discussed in an early selection by John Dewey (see the section on "The Values of a Business Society")—as on the estranged states of the critics. How seriously should we take their protests and the value judgments on which these are based? To what extent are we dealing with the personal failure of individuals unable to cope with the problem of growing up in a complex society, or with the symptoms of a breakdown in society itself? To what extent has youthful exhibitionism been confused with authentic moral criticism? Why did the "new alienation" become acute in the 1960's instead of the 1940's and 1950's? Should we look for our answer to the family? The permissive anti-authoritarian middle-class parents of many of the new young protestants rarely invoked sanctions or imposed discipline; they preferred, especially if they were artists or intellectuals, to rely on reason and consensus. Is the total and often bitter rejection of American institutions and values by their children the result of a first, unaccustomed confrontation with irrationality—which is endemic to the human condition—and authority? These are some of the questions that concern the authors of the several selections which follow. The first reading deals with those who have chosen the way of retreat, the next two with the political activists on the left.

However, no discussion of alienation would be complete without reckoning with another area of disaffection, the New (or "Radical") Right which shares with activism on the left, albeit for quite opposite reasons, a deep discontent with prevailing practices, a disregard for principles of historical continuity, a strident scorn for compromise and the "politics of civility." Both suffer from what their critics call conspiracy fantasies inspired in the one case by "scheming" capitalists, in the other case by crypto-communists. But overshadowing these and other resemblances is, of course, a basic difference: the bitterness of radical rightists is inspired not by the triumph of middle-class values and ideals, but by what they regard as the communists' and proto-communists' betrayal of these ideals. A concluding selection will deal with their discontent. Not as visible on picket lines and not concentrated on college campuses, the radical right sometimes fails to receive the publicity accorded the new left. This is especially true during the Vietnam war when, increasingly, the need for a "stab-in-the-back" apology for lack of success in the military theater may make for disproportionate emphasis on the new left.[1] However, the radicals on the left are not even remotely comparable in power with those on the right as the discussion below will disclose.

A final caveat is in order. The selections which follow are not intended to suggest a difference in the age composition of dissidents on the left and right. The selections dealing with the former emphasize youth; the selection about the new right does not. However, the left has its aging gurus (despite a popular slogan, "you can't trust anyone over thirty"); and the right those youthful cadres abundantly in evidence at almost any convention consecrated to "God and country."

---

[1] Vice-President Humphrey recently suggested that the French lost the Vietnam war in Paris.

THE INTELLIGENT SQUARE'S GUIDE TO HIPPIELAND

June Bingham

Mrs. Bingham, wife of New York's Congressman Jonathan Bingham, is the biographer of Reinhold Niebuhr and U Thant. In addition to Courage to Change: An Introduction to the Life and Thought of Reinhold Niebuhr *(1961)* and U Thant: The Search for Peace *(1966), she is co-author with Dr. Fritz Redlich of* The Inside Story: Psychiatry in Everyday Life *(1953).*

No generation, it is said, can predict the weapons that the next one will use against it. Surely few Americans who grew up during the Depression and struggled to win middle- or upper-middle-class privileges for their family would have dreamed that, by 1967, some of their most gifted sons and daughters would purposely be hurrying from riches to rags.

Today, these visible, audible and sometimes smellable young rebels are loosely called hippies. Constituting a tiny minority, they are mostly white, carefully nurtured and educated beyond the average; some were former leaders of their class in school. Their young Negro counterpart is trying to achieve, rather than "drop out" of, higher education and professional status; or, if he is trapped in the slums, he may turn to addictive drugs, such as heroin, which are scorned by the hippies, or to violence, which is abhorred by them.

Within the hippie subculture—mostly urban—not all are intelligent and promising. Some are mentally ill or not very bright; some are merely unformed and seduced by the gross simplifications and absolute certainties that seem to result from even a rare use of LSD or a heavy use of marijuana. Mental hospitals throughout the United States report a startling drop in admissions of the two kinds of schizophrenics whose symptoms are similar to those of someone on an LSD trip: the young inappropriately laughing hebephrenics and frozenly posturing catatonics have gone to live among the hippies who tolerate them, thus discouraging their seeking psychiatric treatment.

But partly because many hippies are imaginative, articulate and artistic, their world-view has spread to the far larger number of their well-shod and well-shorn contemporaries, especially to those appalled by the American involvement in Vietnam. Hippiedom, in one sense, is part of the Vietnam fallout.

But this is not all that it is. For there are hippies in England and Canada, Denmark and France, countries not involved in Vietnam or in the credibility gap.

The hippies are in rebellion also against nuclear fission, automation, and bigness in industry, labor and government—in sum, against everything that diminishes the importance of the individual. Their slogan is, "I am a human being: Do not fold, spindle or mutilate." And their value system is the mirror-opposite of the middle-class or square system (while the hippie terms himself a "human being," he terms the square "subhuman" or "humanoid").

If one imagines the questions that a suburban father would ask of a future son-in-law, about family background and religious affiliation, academic degrees and career prospects, previous record and future plans, the hippies would say that None of These Matter (they always seem to talk in capital letters). What matters, they say, is not what a person *does* but what he is, not outer forms or "games," but "Being At One With Yourself."

The hippie phenomenon, once thought to be only a passing phase, is probably more dangerous to its conforming nonconformists than to society as a whole. For the hippie minority, though revolutionary, is neither subversive nor violent. There has been a recent divorce between the hippies and the New Left. While the hippies reject the capitalist emphasis on "mine," whether my house, my money, my gadgets, my child or my work of art, they also reject the Communist practice of job assignment and restriction of the arts and individual freedom. The love-ins, while sometimes unattractive, are an improvement over the deafening silence of the "cool" young of the McCarthy period, or the destructiveness of some beatniks, beats and hipsters, those immediate predecessors of the hippies. There is no hippie leader like Norman Mailer, who tried to link the hipster to Black Power.

The squares who wish to alert a hippie—or demihippie—to the hidden dangers to which he is exposed will find disgust less helpful than an attempt to understand the hippie "transvaluation of values." Though the hippies' positive program comprises little that is new or practical, their negative strictures may well be a judgment upon the squares' value system.

There is nothing new, for instance, in the hippies' privatism (the solipsists long ago took it to the end of the line), nor in their hedonism (ancient Greece coined the word for it), nor in their reversion to the Natural (Rousseau promoted the "Noble Savage" whether with hair on his face, like the hippie boys, or under the arms, like the hippie girls). Similarly, there is nothing new in the hippies' passivity and pipe dreaming (hashish—a stronger variety of pot—has been used for millennia).

The following hippie judgments, however, are worth square consideration:

At a time when sexual excitement by way of the media has reached laughable, if not obscene, proportions, these boys and girls in identical tight pants and shoulder-length hair are signaling that the male and female secondary sexual characteristics are not that important; their form of address for one another is "Man."

At a time when racial antagonisms erupt on the street, these boys and girls appear relaxedly integrated. The problems of poverty and the ghetto—together with those of leisure—are no problems to the hippies who embrace all three. In their own sections of cities there is little serious crime and no prostitution.

At a time when national and ideological rivalry may lead to nuclear apocalypse, the hippies preach, "Make love, not war," and refuse to offer themselves for service to their country if this means that they may have to kill or be killed.

At a time when Organization Man and his wife have been clutching material possessions not only for health and comfort but for prestige and a kind of security, the hippies share their food, their pad, their guitars, and such cash as they earn or are given. They would agree with Joseph Wood Krutch that true security depends upon how much one can do *without,* and they are proud of their own instantaneous mobility. Some move onto the land in small rural kibbutzlike settlements reminiscent of Brook Farm and other 19th-century idealistic experiments. Their guru, Allen Ginsberg, notes that the only technologically complicated item they wish to own is a stereo phonograph.

At a time when some churches have been exposed as slumlords and some church membership stems from other than religious reasons, the hippies stretch for spiritual meaning beyond the Judeo-Christian tradition. This has led some to study Hinduism and Buddhism, ancient philosophies too long spurned by the West.

At a time when planning—by government, by business, by individuals—is still highly touted, the hippies do not bother to turn the leaves of the calendar, or look at their watches (if they own any), or read or listen to the news. They wish to live by whim, by spontaneity, by the non-rules of Now. They are not interested in what someone else has said is right or has planned for them. If they feel in the mood they will neglect all appointments to marvel at the sight of an onion: intricacy and beauty enclosing the purity of the Void. In reacting against pressures of home and school that may have started in kindergarten, many are taking what Erik Erikson has called a "psychological moratorium." Said a male 26-year-old demihippie: "We don't know what we'll be when we're 40; we'll have to wait and see."

At a time of Hidden Persuaders, when politics and advertising are frankly based on image-making, on fooling as many of the people as much of the time as possible, the hippies cry, "Hypocrisy!" As for the politeness and self-restraint that grease the social, as well as business and political, wheels, the hippies prefer discussion of Birth and Death, Creation and Destruction, to small talk. Say the Diggers, a leading subgroup in San Francisco's Haight-Ashbury section, " 'Normal' citizens with store-dummy smiles stand apart from each other like cotton-packed capsules in bottles."

At a time when in any given year there is one divorce for each four weddings, the hippies point to square hypocrisy in the sphere of sex. Many adults who have preached virginity before marriage and fidelity after it have practiced neither, the hippies say, and many who have practiced these have done so out of fear rather than love—out of, if you will, a form of biological capitalism.

Says a girl hippie: "What's the big deal when a girl hoards a bit of skin just so she can exchange it for a gold ring or a ranch house in the suburbs?"

Says a boy: "In the days before the Pill, people made a virtue of necessity and praised virginity; well the necessity is gone."

while to the outsider he appears to be riding an escalator in a clump with his peer group. A hippie on a "high" will paint a picture he is certain is original; a psychiatrist can spot it at once as drug-influenced: It has no integral unity, merely repetitive motifs embellished with tiny—and often merry—detail.

All in all, the hippie, despite his high potential, often ends up with less self-knowledge than his square contemporary. Trying directly to "find oneself" seems paradoxically less effective than first becoming the kind of person upon whom others can rely and then learning existentially from this revealing experience.

The hippie honestly believes that he is practicing Love, but if you shut your eyes while he discusses suburbanites, you would think he was a bigoted white talking about Negroes.

The hippie honestly believes that he is achieving Freedom, but in fact he is slamming doors on himself, now as in the future. Because he operates on whim ("if it feels good, I'll do it"), he cannot be relied on in momentous times such as birth or death, family celebrations or crises. While dropping out he may have made himself worth dropping, by the very people who are nearest, if not dearest, to him.

The hippie honestly believes that he is honest. *He* has nothing to hide—nothing, that is, except the curved knife that he refuses to admit generically rests in the human hand. When the person the hippie cuts by way of his "honesty" cries out in pain, the hippie's first reaction is genuine surprise. His second is, "Well, that's your problem." Since, as he believes, there was, in his own purity, no wish to hurt, then the victim must surely be at fault, must have some hidden weakness that he would do well to explore.

And if the victim, in his freedom, has no wish thus to explore? Then the hippie may turn visibly hostile: "You are jealous, you wish you could live the way I do." If the older person responds that his concern is not about his own life at the moment but about the hippie's, the pat answer is that older people often use their worry as a means of subjugating the young. For the hippie, therefore, to avoid hurting his elders would be an unthinkable caving-in to pressure, a loss of his own integrity.

A clear difference between the hippies of today and their parents-when-young is that the parents handled their not so uncolorful rebellion discreetly and in the fear, if not of God, then of their parents. The hippies, on the other hand, through their ambivalent behavior—pregnancies out of wedlock, diaries left open to shocking pages—or their unambivalent appearance, trumpet their rebellion and thus challenge their parents, if not God, to smite them down.

A clear difference between the parents of today and their parents is the reluctance to smite the young down. Rarely is the cry "Never darken my doorstep" heard in the land; infrequently are the old expletives "impertinence" or "insolence" dusted off.

Instead, many concerned squares, either to keep open the paths of communication, or to help their almost-grown child, under whose truculence they think they hear a muted cry for help, or simply in the generic American willingness to admit that oneself may have goofed, are making the supreme effort to dissolve their own crystallized hierarchy of values into liquidity again. Is it possible, these parents ask themselves (or their spouse), that their dismay at their hippie is, in part, based on their own fear of loss of job, or of respect by their neighbors, or of approval by relatives?

In any event, some men and women in their 40's and 50's are putting themselves through, for a second time, the anxieties, even the agonies, of what is now called the "identity crisis"—it used to be called "growing pains." (One frantic parent in an attempt to save a hard-core hippie's marriage took LSD with the couple; the marriage did not survive, and the parent barely so.)

While the lucky parents can dissolve their value-system and reestablish one that does not make their whole past life seem futile, the unlucky ones may look back on the various crossroads of life and think, too late, that they took the wrong turn. The young person, through his unintentionally cruel questioning, may be toppling Humpty Dumpty at a time in life when all the king's horses and all the psychiatrists cannot put Humpty Dumpty together again.

Those now over 40 were often burdened by their late-Victorian and pre-Freudian parents with a harsh conscience, a tendency to over-blame themselves. They are sandwiched between a generation that questioned too little and a generation that questions too much. They themselves never had the white meat of the turkey. When they were children, the best parts were saved, as a matter of course, for the adults; by the time they grew up, the best parts were being saved, as a matter of course, for the children.

Having been children in an adult-centered world, they are now adults in a child-centered world. And how do they react to finding themselves in this historic tide rip of values? By feeling guilty.

How can parents live through the period when their hippie or demihippie is testing every parental value; when he is busily devaluing the sacrifices they have made; when, in an odd reverse of the historic wheel, his brooding presence is reminiscent of nothing so much as that of a Victorian chaperone as he counts each parental drink, each cigarette, each tranquilizer, each white lie, each hour "wasted" in front of television or in talk about nonultimate matters, each mile above the speed limit (if the parents break the law by way of a car, the hippie argues he can break it by way of drugs)?

Here are five main survival suggestions for square parents:

(1) To fight guilt and despair, since these are likely to be both inappropriate and counterproductive. The hippie-demic is in the air,

whetted by the media, and it affects young people from united as well as disrupted homes, from permissive and strict ones. Just as parents cannot predict the form of rebellion chosen by the next generation, so they are not individually responsible for it.

(2) To rely on that tough, effective teacher, the parents' ally, Experience. The young person who refuses to learn the easy way will simply have to learn the hard way. But the gnarled old teacher has tended over the generations to keep to the same lesson plan: that the work one loves can be more fun than fun, and that permanent relationships grounded in loyalty are vastly preferable to ephemeral ones.

(3) To distinguish between parental affection and approval: affection is built in, approval must be earned. Though the parents may never fully approve of their grown child—or vice versa—a family, like a nation and a world, can, with effort, make room for diversity.

(4) To try to give an object lesson in tolerance and humor, cheer-fully and admittedly borrowing those hippie attitudes that will come in handy for the time of retirement. Whereas the hippie has much to learn about work, the square may have much to learn about leisure, especially in appreciation of the arts and nature. Even before retirement the square may wish to shed some encrusted bugaboos, such as compulsive punctuality or servitude to already announced plans. Indeed, his health may benefit if he learns, as the young say, to "hang easy."

(5) To have hope that within the two years it usually takes for diminishing returns to set in, the hippie will emerge from the dangerous Children's Crusade of his time, the better prepared to cope in middle age with the gyrations of his and his children's century, the twenty-first.

WHAT'S BUGGING THE STUDENTS

Irving Kristol

Mr. Kristol is a founder of Encounter *and senior editor and vice-president of Basic Books. He is also co-editor of the quarterly* The Public Interest.

From *The Atlantic Monthly* (November 1965), pp. 108–111. Copyright © 1965 by The Atlantic Monthly Company, Boston, Mass. 02116. Reprinted by permission.

No one, except perhaps a few college administrators, mourns the passing of "the silent generation." But it must be said in its favor that at least one knew what the American university students of the 1950s were silent about, and why. They were conformists for plain, indeed, obvious and traditional, conformist reasons. We may have been distressed and vexed by this conformism; we were not mystified by it; whereas we are very much mystified by the nonconformism of the students of the sixties.

Many of the same middle-aged critics who so fervently and eloquently condemned the silent generation are now considerably upset and puzzled at the way students are "misbehaving" these days. One wanted the young to be idealistic, perhaps even somewhat radical, possibly even a bit militant—but not like this! It used to be said that the revolution devours its children. It now appears that these children have devoured this revolution.

What is it all about? One thing is fairly clear: the teach-ins, the sit-ins, the lay-downs, the mass picketing, and all the rest are not *merely* about Vietnam, or civil rights, or the size of classes at Berkeley, or the recognition of Red China. They are about these issues surely, and most sincerely. But there is, transparently, a passion behind the protests that refuses to be satisfied by the various topics which incite it. This passion reaches far beyond politics, as we ordinarily understand that term. Anyone who believes the turbulence will subside once we reach a settlement in Vietnam is in for a rude surprise. Similarly, anyone who thinks of present-day campus radicalism as a kind of over-zealous political liberalism, whose extremism derives from nothing more than youthful high spirits, is deceiving himself. What we are witnessing is an event *in* American politics, but not *of* it.

Indeed, one of the most striking features of the new radicalism on the campus is that it is, in one sense, so apolitical. It is a strange experience to see a radical mood in search of a radical program; it is usually very much the other way around. These young American radicals are in the historically unique position of not being able to demand *a single piece of legislation* from their government—their "platform" is literally without one legislative plank. Their passion for "freedom now" coexists with a remarkable indifference to everything the United States government is doing, or might do, in this direction.

If one read every campus leaflet published these past two years and attended every campus or off-campus demonstration, and knew only what one learned from these sources, one would hardly be aware that the Johnson Administration had enacted in the area of civil rights the most far-reaching reforms in a century of legislative history. There has been no campus meeting to celebrate the passage of the Civil Rights Act or the Voting Rights Act. There has not even been any meeting criticizing these laws for "not going far enough." It's as if nothing had happened—or, to put it more precisely, as if whatever happens in Washington has nothing to do with the world the students live and act in.

The same sort of thing is to be seen with regard to the war on poverty, a topic upon which students will declaim passionately and with unquestionable sincerity. But it seems that their passion is so pure, their sensibility so fine, that these would be violated by a consideration of anything so vulgar as how to get more money into poor people's pockets. The recent increase in social security and the medicare bill made their way through Congress without the benefit of so much as a benevolent nod from the campuses. Whenever I have mentioned this legislation in conversation, I have received an icy stare of incomprehension and disdain, as if I were some kind of political idiot who actually believed what he read in the New York *Times*.

Even in the single area where one would most expect specific and tangible proposals of reform, the organization of the multiversity, these have not made their appearance. For an entire year the students of the University of California at Berkeley have given dramatic evidence of dissatisfaction with their university experience—and does anyone know specifically what they would like, by way of improvement? The university officials certainly don't know, nor do the regents, nor do the faculty. Some outsiders *think* they know. Berkeley is too large, they say, too anonymous; there is no possibility of a face-to-face community of scholars, young and old. This is true enough. But the Riverside branch of this same university is a small liberal arts college, with great intimacy and comfort, and for the past decade it has had much difficulty in attracting enough students. They all want to go to Berkeley, and the reason, they will explain, is: "That is where the action is."

The denunciations of the multiversity suspiciously resemble the way New Yorkers excoriate "megalopolis"—having come there in the first place, and determinedly remaining there, for no other reason than that New York *is* a megalopolis. All Americans will always insist that they adore small towns and detest great cities, but the movement of population from towns to cities remains strangely unaffected. And Berkeley, even today, has far more student applications than it can handle; one might even say, *especially* today, for I understand that the number of applications has, in fact, slightly increased.

No, the upsurge of left-wing sentiment and left-wing opinion on the American campus today is not the sort of thing progressive parents and educators had in mind ten years ago when they benevolently urged students to become "socially committed" and "more idealistic." They naïvely wished them to have intelligent discussions of Vietnam, not to hurl insults and epithets at Averell Harriman (as happened at Cornell), or tear up their draft cards, or laud the Viet Cong. They wished them to be urbane and tolerant about sex, not to carry placards with dirty words, or demand the sale of contraceptives in the college bookstore. They wished them to be concerned for civic and social equality for the Negro, not to denounce "white America" as a pious fraud, whose "integration" did not differ essentially from South Africa's apartheid, or express sympathy with a mindless (if occasionally eloquent) black nationalism. They wished—they wished, in short, that their children be just like them, only a wee bit bolder and more enlightened. Instead, these children are making it very clear that being just like their parents, progressive or not, is the fate they wish most desperately to avoid.

And this, I think, is the crux of the matter. The new student radicalism is so fundamentally at odds with our conventional political categories because it is, above all, an *existentialist* revolt. The term is unfortunately chic, and ambiguous, too. But in this context it has a fairly definite meaning: the students are in rebellion, not so much because things are bad for them, or for others, but because things are what they are for them and for others.

Clues to the meaning of this rebellion may be found in two phrases that now appear ever more commonly in the left-wing campus vocabulary. The first is "organized America." The second is "participatory democracy."

"Organized America" is, quite simply, America, and not, as one might think, some transient bureaucratic excrescence on the body of America. As a matter of fact, today's students are immensely skillful in coping with bureaucracies and their paper work. They fill out forms and applications with a briskness and competence that startle the middle-aged observer. (I would guess that no one over the age of forty could properly fill out a college application form unless he received guidance from some kindly youngster.) What bugs the students is not these trivia but the society they emanate from—the affluent society, welfare state and all. The liberalism (and the radicalism, too) of the 1930s and 1940s has borne its fruit, and it tastes bitter to the children, setting their teeth on edge. That is why American students, amidst reasonably general prosperity and under a liberal Administration that is expanding the welfare state more aggressively and successfully than anyone had thought possible, feel more "alienated" than ever before. So many college students "go left" for the same reason that so many high school students "go delinquent." *They are bored.* They see their lives laid out neatly before them; they see themselves moving ahead sedately and more or less inexorably in their professional careers; they know that with a college degree even "failure" in their careers will represent no harsh punishment; they know "it's all laid on"—and they react against this bourgeois utopia their parents so ardently strove for.

One of the unforeseen consequences of the welfare state is that it leaves so little room for personal idealism; another is that it mutes the challenge to self-definition. All this is but another way of saying that it satisfies the anxieties of the middle-aged while stifling the creative energies of the young. Practically every college student these days understands what is meant by an "identity crisis": it is one of the clichés of the sixties. It is not, perhaps, too much to say that mass picketing on the campus is one of the last, convulsive twitches of a slowly expiring American individualism.

American youth, however, has had one grand idealistic experience: the civil rights movement. This has been the formative experience for the activists of the 1960s; it is this movement that gave them a sense of personal power and personal purpose; and it is the civil rights movement which instructed them in the tactics of civil disobedience that are now resorted to at the drop of a hat. Unfortunately, the civil rights movement has had one great drawback: so far from being a proper "dissenting" movement, it has behind it the President, Congress, the courts, the laws of the land, and a majority of public opinion. This fact helps explain why the younger militants have constantly pushed the movement toward "extremes"—for example, demanding utter, complete, and immediate *equality of condition* for the Negro, as against mere equality of opportunity.

Such equality of condition is what "freedom now" has come to mean. And since this demand cannot be fulfilled without repealing three centuries of history, and since even Lyndon Johnson hasn't figured out a way to do this, there is some satisfaction in such a maneuver. The trouble is that the students do not know how to fulfill this demand either, and are even running out of extremist slogans; which is why so many of them are receptive to the idea of switching their attention to Vietnam, where they can be more splendidly, less ambiguously, in "the opposition."

A second theme of student radicalism today, and a polar twin to the concept of "organized America," is the idea of "participatory democracy." This is a vague notion, but a dynamic one. It expresses a profound hostility toward, and proposes an alternative to, everything that is impersonal, manipulative, "organized" in the American political process. Indeed, many of these students simply dismiss American democracy as a sham, a game played by the "power structure" for its own amusement and in its own interests. *True* democracy, they insist, can only mean direct democracy, where the people's will is expressed and legislated by the people themselves rather than by elected representatives, most of whom achieve office by deceit and retain office through the substantial support offered them by the vested interests.

One is reminded by this of nothing so much as the Russian Narodniki ("populists," our textbooks call them) of the end of the nineteenth century. They, too, were largely middle-class students who selflessly turned their backs on the careers the Czarist bureaucracy offered them. They, too, "returned to the people," leaving the fleshpots of Petrograd for the villages of the interior, much as our students leave their comfortable homes in New York or Chicago for Southern ghettos and slums. And they, too, were hostile to the nascent liberal institutions of their day, seeing political salvation only in a transformed and redeemed people rather than in improvements in any kind of system of representative government. It is also interesting to recall that, though they were as individuals the gentlest and most humane of their time, they nevertheless believed in the justice and efficacy of terrorism against the status quo and assassination against its spokesmen.

The analogy is, of course, very superficial: the United States today is not Czarist Russia of yesterday. But it is nevertheless illuminating, because it helps reveal the inner logic of the idea of "participatory democracy," a logic which proceeds from the most exemplary democratic premises to the most illiberal conclusions. Though few students these days learn it in their social studies course, the Founding Fathers of the American republic were exceedingly familiar with the idea of "participatory democracy"; as a matter of fact, this was what the word "democracy" usually meant prior to 1789. They rejected "participatory democracy" (they called it "direct democracy") in favor of "representative government" for two reasons. First, they didn't see how it could work in so large and complex a nation, as against a small city-state. Second, and more important, they thought it inconsistent with the idea of free government—that is, a government that respected the liberties of the individual. For participatory democracy requires that all people be fit to govern; and this in turn requires that all people *be made* fit to govern, by rigid and uniform educational training, constant public indoctrination, close supervision of private morals and beliefs, and so forth. No legislator can be as free as a private citizen, and to make all the people legislators is willy-nilly to abolish the category of private citizen altogether.

This, of course, is exactly what the Communists do, after their own fashion. They claim to exemplify a truer, more "direct," more "participatory," more "popular" democracy than is to be found in the representative institutions of the bourgeois West. The claim has a certain plausibility, in that regimes established by mass movements and mass revolutions certainly "involve the people" more than does any merely elected government. The semblance of "involvement" is perpetuated, as we know, through the mass organizations of the Communist state, and the fact that it is done under compulsion, and becomes more of a farce with every passing Communist year, is one of the inner contradictions both of the Communist system and of the myth of direct democracy itself.

These contradictions our left-wing students are not entirely unaware of. Though many of them are, to one degree or another, either pro-Communist or belligerently "neutralist," theirs is a very qualified and unconventional version of this attitude; which is why conventional anti-Communist propaganda tends to pass them by. They are, for instance, extraordinarily uninterested in the Soviet Union, and they become ever less interested to the degree that the Soviet Union liberalizes its regime—that is to say, to the extent that the Soviet Union becomes merely another "organized" system of rule.

What they seek is a pure and self-perpetuating popular revolution, not a "planned economy" or anything like that. And this is why they are so attracted to Castro's Cuba and Mao's China, countries where the popular revolution has not yet become "bourgeoisified." As for mass terror in Cuba and China—well, this actually may be taken as a kind of testimony to the ardor and authenticity of the regime's revolutionary fervor. Our radical students, like other radical students before them, find it possible to be genuinely heartsick at the injustices and brutalities of American society, while blandly approving of injustice and brutality committed elsewhere in the name of "the revolution."

Like other radical student generations before them, they are going to discover one day that their revolution, too, has been betrayed, that "organized society" is what revolutions establish as well as destroy. One hopes they will not be made too miserable by their disillusionment. One also hopes, it must be added, that they won't make *us* too miserable before that day arrives.

THE NEW LEFT

Christopher Jencks

Christopher Jencks has served as a consultant on education to federal agencies, private corporations and local anti-poverty groups, and is co-author of a forthcoming book, The Academic Revolution. *He is a contributing editor of* The New Republic. *In the following article he attempts to explain the hatred of the New Left for authority.*

Week before last, I reported on a meeting in Czechoslovakia between 40 Americans and two delegations of Vietnamese revolutionaries. That report concentrated on the Vietnamese side of the dialogue; now I

"Limits of the New Left" from *The New Republic* (October 21, 1967), pp. 19–21. Reprinted by permission. © 1967 by Harrison-Blaine of New Jersey, Inc.

want to say something about the Americans there. The majority were young and came from what is now irrevocably christened the "New Left." Some were active in the antiwar movement, organizing teach-ins, writing, helping set up protest groups and fomenting draft resistance. Others were working with poor whites and blacks on grievances only obliquely related to the war; they knew relatively little about Vietnam when they arrived in Bratislava. But they all saw the war as an inevitable by-product of some ill-defined sickness in the American system, which could only be cured by radical political remedies. They were contemptuous of liberals who regard the war as a colossal blunder and who think that when the war is over America will get on with rehabilitating a flawed but redeemable society. For this reason almost all the young radicals at Bratislava were slightly scornful of the traditional "peace movement," which they regard as ideologically naïve and politically ineffective. They had little in common with the clergymen and pacifists from the pre-Vietnam peace movement who were also in Bratislava, except distaste for the war.

To me, the most striking fact about the young radicals was the extent to which they identified with the Viet Cong. This identification was almost entirely confined to people born after the outbreak of World War II. I myself am only a few years older, have been bitterly critical of the war and support the National Liberation Front in the limited sense that I would rather let it take power than continue either the war or the present Thieu-Ky regime. Yet I do not feel instinctively allied to the NLF, and I know hardly anyone else my age who does. Indeed, I would say that inability to identify with the Viet Cong is one of the obvious differences between the generation which came to political consciousness under Eisenhower, as I did, and the generation which worked out its political position under John Kennedy and Lyndon Johnson, as the young radicals at Bratislava had.

This New Left sympathy for the NLF is not based on any similarity of style or of temperament. The Vietnamese revolutionaries we met were not the joyless communist *aparachiks* whom the Soviet Union would send to such a meeting, but they were dignified, restrained, disciplined and apparently selfless—about as unlike the loose-tongued, anarchistic, spontaneous Americans as any group could conceivably be. It was easy to respect their courage and patience under incredibly difficult conditions, and to find them personally charming, but it would not be very easy for a young American to establish an intimate personal friendship with or psychological understanding of such strangers. Nor do I think most of the Americans at Bratislava would find life in post-revolutionary Vietnam congenial; on the contrary, I suspect most would find themselves in opposition fairly soon. The common bond between the New Left and the NLF is not, then, a common dream or a common experience but a common enemy: the US government, the system, the Establishment. The young radicals' admiration for the NLF stems from the feeling that the NLF is resisting The Enemy successfully, whereas they are not.

Speaking for the older generation at Bratislava, David Dellinger said to the Vietnamese at one point, "You are Vietnamese and you love Vietnam. You must remember that we are Americans and we love America too, even though we oppose our government's policies with all our strength." The young man next to me groaned at this expression of patriotic sentiment, and as I looked around the room at other American faces I got the impression that he was not alone in his embarrassment. Certainly he was not alone in his feeling that almost anything non-American was likely to be better than almost anything American.

The historical failures of American radicalism are, I think, linked in important ways to this distaste for American culture and American institutions. One reason why the radical revival of the early 1960's captured the American imagination and achieved modest successes was that it seemed so completely native, so true to the professed high purposes of the Republic. It appealed to the Constitution, to schoolbook stories of what America should be, to injustices which troubled millions of decent citizens.

But the New Left has never numbered patience among its virtues; it soured on America once it became clear that radical change, rather amorphously defined, would be neither quick nor easy. If America could not undo the evil consequences of racism in a few years, then America was hopeless. If America could not restrain its military, if it would not support revolutions in the underdeveloped countries, then America was a positive menace and the primary task of our time was to contain American power. Having begun a few years earlier with great residual faith in the American people, and a conviction that "the people" had strengths from which a new and better society might be built, many of the young radicals moved to the conclusion that Americans as a whole were hopelessly complacent, corrupt and self-centered. This view is not yet universal in the New Left, but it seems to be gaining ground. The result was a dramatic contrast at Bratislava between optimistic, confident Vietnamese and pessimistic, self-deprecating Americans. They sang "We Shall Overcome," but it was a nostalgic tribute to an earlier era, not an expression of confidence in the future.

The central weakness of the New Left, it seems to me, is its attitude toward authority. This came out clearly two years ago when this journal asked a number of young radicals to describe what they thought was wrong with America and what should be done about it. The essays were almost monotonous in their insistence that the people have no voice in decisions which affect their lives; that they are powerless.

That is true, but it is by no means a universal complaint. The toiling masses of Marxist memory still toil, but they do not seem to feel oppressed by the institutions within which they live. On the contrary, most defend these institutions staunchly. If, for example, you ask poor people what is wrong with America, they will usually complain about the *results* of decisions which affect their lives, not the *process* by which the decisions are made. They want good schools or good housing; relatively few of them want a voice in the operation of these facilities if the results are satisfactory. The New Left, however, cares more about how a decision gets made than about what the decision is. The Free Speech Movement at Berkeley exemplified this outlook. Very few Berkeley students had any real interest in whether the university allowed political advocacy on its property. But many came to resent the university's making such decisions arbitrarily without consulting anyone, and thousands enjoyed participating in the struggle to alter the rules.

An allergy to paternalism is not unique to the New Left, but young radicals of the kind who went to Bratislava have taken it more seriously than almost anyone in my generation and more seriously than most of their peers. It is this which has driven many into total opposition to the American way of life, which, they say, is largely shaped by big organizations and involves passive dependence on enormous numbers of remote experts, bureaucracies and commercial enterprises. Their opposition has led a growing minority to talk about the need for a revolution in America— though no one has any clear idea who would organize such a revolution, or whom it would bring to power, or how post-revolutionary America would be organized. It is this opposition, too, which has made the young radicals cynical about the anti-communism of their elders, forgetting that many liberal anti-communists were also anti-authoritarian. They are ready to support any sort of attack on the American establishment, even if it is launched by Vietnamese guerrillas with whom the New Left has only the most remote ideological or cultural kinship.

How widespread is this readiness to identify with "the enemy"? The militant, embittered sentiments described above are probably confined to one or two percent of the younger generation. But I think the basic attitudes which lead the activists to sympathy for the Viet Cong are quite general among the young, and that their impact is only beginning to be felt.

These are children of the 1940's, raised in relatively permissive middle-class homes where authority was supposed to be rational rather than arbitrary. Unlike earlier generations of Americans, their parents were reluctant to take advantage of their monopoly on physical, economic and legal power. Their youngsters were free to challenge the legitimacy of parental authority from an early age, by arguing that their parents were not using their power reasonably or wisely. Not only that, but such challenges often succeeded. Even when they failed, the children often curbed their parents' power indirectly by refusing to join in a consensus which defined certain rules as sensible and just. Without such a consensus many parents felt reluctant to impose their will, and in many cases found it impossible even when they tried.

The emphasis on consensus and rationality in these young people's upbringing was accompanied by reliance on new forms of discipline. The distinctive feature of a "permissive" home is not that "anything goes." It is that the limits are supposed to be set by the child's internalized sense of what is reasonable and unreasonable. In order to keep up this pretense, overt sanctions and punishments are frowned on. Instead, if the child behaves in what the parents regard as an unreasonable fashion, they retaliate by making the child feel he has hurt them, has let them down. Such a threat was doubtless terrifying to the very young. As they grew older, however, children discovered that they too could use such weapons. Children fear rejection, but so do parents, at least in modern America. A child who acted as if he hated his mother could frequently reduce her to tears. This leads to a system of mutual deterrence, which makes parents hesitate to use their ultimate power and produces an unprecedented equality in relations between the generations.

Such children emerged into the larger society with relatively little experience of authority structures based solely on superior force. Yet this is almost always the ultimate source of authority in large groups and organizations. Confronted with such authority these young people's first reaction was to resort to the tricks they had learned at home. First they tried reason. Racism, they argued, was a violation of the Constitution; the Saigon government was founded on a violation of the Geneva Agreements; and so forth. Such arguments had some success on the racial front, but virtually none on foreign policy. When this tactic failed the young radicals tried withholding love and approval from their elders. This was both the origin and the effect of the protest marches and of civil disobedience—a technique known to all children in all times. Like reason and legalism, emotional confrontations proved moderately effective as weapons against racism. The liberal leaders of the national establishment wanted the young to love and admire them. They did not want to play the tyrannical father and enforce order with a paddle. (Small-town Southern elites came from an older tradition, and felt no more embarrassed by using force against protesters than they did about spanking their children.) Civil disobedience has not yet been tried on a large scale to curb the Vietnam war, but the small efforts to date have not had much effect.

The failure of the techniques learned in permissive, middle-class homes has brought a crisis in America's radical movement. Ghetto Negroes have turned naturally to violence, for they have mostly been raised on it. Young middle-class whites, on the other hand, find violence almost impossible. The radicals must, therefore, either abandon the struggle and retreat into cynicism and privatism or else compete with other adults for control over the apparatus of the state—which means, ultimately, control over the apparatus of violence and coercion. One way to do this might theoretically be violent revolution, but as a practical matter this seems infeasible, undesirable, and an escape from reality. America is not Vietnam. The only real alternative seems to be creating political organizations capable of taking power, first locally and eventually nationally.

Yet it is precisely here that the young radicals' distrust of all authority becomes an apparently insuperable problem. They are allergic to leadership, hierarchy and discipline. They want a movement of small insurgent "cells," organized around mutual trust, equality and respect for every man's individuality. These are appealing values. They are, indeed, my own. But I doubt that they can lead to the creation of political organizations capable of winning and wielding power.

If the children of permissive, middle-class parents are unwilling or unable to participate in established political institutions, or if their distaste and alienation from the whole pattern of American life makes it difficult for them to communicate with a relatively complacent and chauvinistic majority, who *will* exercise power in America? The most likely answer is that power will go by default to conservatives and reactionaries from more traditional backgrounds, who are less allergic to leadership, more willing to submit to the discipline of political organization, readier to make the compromises inherent in the assumption and exercise of power. This seems especially likely if the US fails to suppress the South Vietnamese revolution and withdraws. Any such about-face in Vietnam could produce a right-wing reaction even stronger than the one produced by the collapse of Nationalist China and the stalemate in Korea. The older generation of liberals and radicals showed no great capacity for withstanding such onslaughts in the late 1940's and early 1950's. If the younger generation is also temperamentally incapable of organizing itself so as to withstand a right-wing revival, America may be headed for an era of repression which will make McCarthyism seem relatively innocuous.

THE NEW RIGHT

Daniel Bell

Daniel Bell is Professor of Sociology at Columbia University and chairman of the department in Columbia College. He was formerly managing editor of The New Leader, *labor editor of* Fortune Magazine, *and director of the international-seminar program of the Congress for Cultural Freedom (Paris). He has taught at the University of Chicago, the Salzburg Seminar in American Studies, and was a Fellow of the Center for Advanced Studies in the Behavioral Sciences. He is the author, among other works, of* The Background and Development of Marxian Socialism in the United States *(1952) and* The End of Ideology *(1959).*

I believe that the radical right is only a small minority, but it gains force from the confusions within the world of conservatism regarding the changing character of American life. What the right as a whole fears is the erosion of its own social position, the collapse of its power, the increasing incomprehensibility of a world—now overwhelmingly technical and complex—that has changed so drastically within a lifetime. . . .

The psychological stock-in-trade of the radical right rests on a threefold appeal: the breakdown of moral fiber in the United States; a conspiracy theory of a "control apparatus" in the government which is selling out the country; and a detailed forecast regarding the Communist "takeover" of the United States.

Central to the appeal of the radical right is the argument that old-fashioned patriotism has been subverted by the cosmopolitan intellectual. An editorial in the *National Review* on the space flight of astronaut John Glenn sums up this theme in striking fashion. Glenn, said the editorial, is an authentic American hero because he is unashamed to say that he gets a thrill when the American flag goes by and because he will openly acknowledge the guidance of God. "It is 'American' as in older storybooks, as in legends, and myths and dreams—brought up to technological date, of course—as, let's say it plainly, in the pre-1930 Fourth of July celebrations; and the *Saturday Evening Post* covers before they, too, not long ago, went modern; and a touch of soap opera. Yes, a bit corny—for that is the

---

From *The Radical Right,* Daniel Bell, ed. (Garden City, New York: Doubleday & Company, Inc., 1955), pp. 1–47. Reprinted by permission of the author.

traditional American style. Too corny by far for the Norman Cousinses, Arthur Schlesingers, Adlai Stevensons, Henry Steele Commagers, Max Lerners, John Kenneth Galbraiths, and those others of our enlightened age—so many of them now fluttering around the Kennedy throne—who have long left behind the old provincial corn for a headier global brew."

Here one finds the praise of the "simple virtues"—they are always simple—the evocation of small-town life, the uncluttered Arcadia, against the modern, the sophisticated, the cosmopolitan. . . . America will be back on an even keel when the simple virtues prevail.

The theme of conspiracy haunts the mind of the radical rightist. . . . The distinctive theme of the radical right is that not only is Communism a more threatening force today than at any other time in the past forty years, but that the threat is as great domestically as it is *externally*. If one points out, in astonishment, that the American Communist Party is splintered badly, its membership at the lowest point since the mid-1920s, its influence in the trade-union movement nil, and that not one intellectual figure of any consequence today is a Communist, the rightist replies do not confront these assertions at all. They range from the question that, if this is so, how did it happen that the United States "lost" China, Czechoslovakia, and Cuba to the Communists, to the outright charges, like General Walker's, that the highest officials of the Democratic Party are members of the "Communist conspiracy," or to Robert Welch's claim that former President Eisenhower was a "tool" of the Communists and that his brother Milton is an avowed one. Defeat can be possible only if sinister men were at the helm.

In fact, so great is the preoccupation with the alleged domestic threat that only rarely in the press of the radical right is there any mention of Russia's military prowess, its scientific equipment, or its ability to propel intercontinental ballistic missiles. When such facts are raised, it is often asserted either that such strength is a sham or that whatever knowledge Russia has was "stolen" from the United States (the claim made, for example, by Medford Evans, now an adviser to General Walker, in his book *The Secret War for the A-Bomb,* Chicago, Regnery Press, 1953). For a considerable period of time, in fact, the magazines of the radical right refused to acknowledge that the Russians had sent a sputnik to the moon, or that they had sent a man into space, and, like the *Daily Worker* unmasking a capitalist conspiracy, they gleefully pounced on inconsistencies in news stories to assert that we were all being hoodwinked by a hoax (as were, presumably, the American tracking stations).

One sees among the radical right, particularly among individuals in its upper-middle-class following who have never seen a Communist, the most extraordinary apprehensions about the extent of current Communist infiltration in government. If one asks them to explain these attitudes, one is constantly reminded of Alger Hiss and Harry Dexter White. Yet whatever the actuality of past Communist infiltration in the government—and its extent has been highly distorted as to the actual influence exerted—none of this offers any proof about the current status of Dean Rusk or W. W. Rostow, or any of the present foreign-policy advisers. . . . Yet the *internal* threat is the one that is primarily harped upon, along with suspicions of the "soft" attitudes of the current administration.

It is largely among the extremist fringes of the radical right that such paranoid views are peddled. But most of the radical right, uneasily aware of the difficulty of maintaining the position that the Communist Party alone constitutes the internal threat, has shifted the argument to a different and more nebulous ground—the identification of Communism with liberalism. "I equate the growth of the welfare state," says Dan Smoot, a former F.B.I. agent whose program, *The Dan Smoot Report,* is heard on thirty-two television and fifty-two radio stations, "with Socialism and Socialism with Communism." Thus it is argued that the administration is unwilling (for ideological reasons) or incapable (for intellectual reasons) of "getting tough" with Communism. (And in this fashion, the foreign-policy issue is tied in with a vast array of right-wing domestic issues, centering around the income tax and the welfare state.)

But with this shift in the argument, the nature of the debate becomes clearer. What the right wing is fighting, in the shadow of Communism, is essentially "modernity"—that complex of attitudes that might be defined most simply as the belief in rational assessment, rather than established custom, for the evaluation of social change—and what it seeks to defend is its fading dominance, exercised once through the institutions of small-town America, over the control of social change. But it is precisely these established ways that a modernist America has been forced to call into question.

Every country has a "national style," a distinctive way of meeting the problems of order and adaptation, of conflict and consensus, of individual ends and communal welfare, that confront any society. The "national style," or the characteristic way of response, is a compound of the values and the national character of a country. As anyone who has read travelers' accounts knows, there has long been agreement on the characteristics of the American style.

The American has been marked by his sense of achievement, his activism, his being on the move, his eagerness for experience. America has always been "future-oriented." Europe represented the past, with its hierarchies, its fixed statuses, its ties to antiquity. The American "makes" himself, and in so doing transforms himself, society, and nature. In Jefferson's deism, God was not a transcendental being but a "Workman" whose intricate design was being unfolded on the American continent. The achievement pattern envisaged an "endless future," a life of constant improvement. Education meant preparation for a career rather than cultivation. . . .

Hand in hand with achievement went a sense of optimism, the feeling that life was tractable, the environment manipulable, that anything was possible. The American, the once-born man, was the "sky-blue, healthy-minded moralist" to whom sin and evil were, in Emerson's phrase, merely the "soul's mumps and measles and whooping cough." . . .

American achievement and masculine optimism created a buoyant sense of progress, almost of omnipotence. America had never been defeated. America was getting bigger and better. America was always first. It had the tallest buildings, the biggest dams, the largest cities. . . .

And all of this was reflected in distinctive aspects of character. The emphasis on achievement was an emphasis on the individual. The idea of that society was a system of social arrangements that acts to limit the range of individual behavior was an abstraction essentially alien to American thought; reality was concrete and empirical, and the individual was the moral unit of action. That peculiar American inversion of Protestantism, the moralizing style, found its focus in the idea of reform, but it was the reform of the individual, not of social institutions. To reform meant to remedy the defects of character, and the American reform movement of the nineteenth century concentrated on sin, drink, gambling, prostitution, and other aspects of individual behavior. In politics, the moralistic residue led to black-and-white judgments: if anything was wrong, the individual was to blame. Since there were good men and bad men, the problem was to choose the good and eschew the bad. Any defect in policy flowed from a defect in the individual, and a change in policy could begin only by finding the culprit.

In the last fifteen years, the national self-consciousness has received a profound shock. Although the crisis in national style can be detected most forcefully in the realm of foreign policy, there have been, in the past thirty years, deep changes taking place in the social structure that are reworking the social map of the country, upsetting the established life-chances and outlooks of old, privileged groups, and creating uncertainties about the future which are deeply unsettling to those whose values were shaped by the "individualist" morality of nineteenth-century America.

The most pervasive changes are those involving the structural relations between class position and power. Clearly, today, political position rather than wealth, and technical skill rather than property, have become the bases from which power is wielded. In the modes of access to privilege, inheritance is no longer all-determining, nor does "individual initiative" in building one's own business exist as a realistic route; in general, education has become the major way to acquire the technical skills necessary for the administrative and power-wielding jobs in society.

In the older mythos, one's achievement was an individual fact—as a doctor, lawyer, professor, businessman; in the reality of today, one's achievement, status, and prestige are rooted in particular *collectivities* (the corporation, being attached to a "name" hospital, teaching at a prestigious university, membership in a good law firm), and the individual's role is necessarily submerged in the achievement of the collectivity. Within each collectivity and profession, the proliferation of tasks calls for narrower and narrower specializations, and this proliferation requires larger collectivities, and the consequent growth of hierarchies and bureaucracies.

The new nature of decision-making—the larger role of technical decision—also forces a displacement of the older elites. Within a business enterprise, the newer techniques of operations research and linear programming almost amount to the "automation" of middle management, and its displacement by mathematicians and engineers, working either within the firm or as consultants. In the economy, the businessman finds himself subject to price, wage, and investment criteria laid down by the economists in government. In the polity, the old military elites find themselves challenged in the determination of strategy by scientists, who have the technical knowledge on nuclear capability, missile development, and the like, or by the "military intellectuals" whose conceptions of weapon systems and political warfare seek to guide military allocations.

In the broadest sense, the spread of education, of research, of administration, and of government creates a new constituency, the technical and professional intelligentsia, and while these are not bound by some common ethos to constitute a new class, or even a cohesive social group, they are the products of a new system of recruitment for power (just as property and inheritance represented the old system), and those who are the products of the old system understandably feel a vague and apprehensive disquiet—the disquiet of the dispossessed. . . .

In identifying "the dispossessed," it is somewhat misleading to seek their economic location, since it is not economic interest alone that accounts for their anxieties. A small businessman may have made considerable amounts of money in the last decade (in part because he has greater freedom than a large corporation in masking costs for tax purposes), and yet strongly resent regulations in Washington, the high income tax, or, more to the point, his own lack of status. To the extent that any such economic location is possible, one can say that the social group most threatened by the structural changes in society is the "old" middle class— the independent physician, farm owner, small-town lawyer, real-estate promoter, home builder, automobile dealer, gasoline-station owner, small businessman, and the like—and that, regionally, its greatest political concentration is in the South and the Southwest, and in California. But a much more telltale indicator of the group that feels most anxious—since lifestyles and values provide the emotional fuel of beliefs and actions—is the strain of Protestant fundamentalism, of nativist nationalism, of good-and-evil moralism which is the organizing basis for the "world view" of such people. For this is the group whose values predominated in the nineteenth century, and which for the past forty years has been fighting a rear-guard action.

The present upsurge of American nativism—one aspect of the radical right—is most directly paralleled in the 1920s, in the virulent assaults on teachers' loyalty by the fundamentalist churchmen in the name of God, and by patriotic organizations like the American Legion in the name of country. . . . Intellectually, the fundamentalists were defeated and the modernists won; their views came to predominate in the country. But the fundamentalist temper of the 1920s still holds strong sway in rural-dominated states. . . . And, paradoxically, although they have become intellectually and socially dispossessed, the fundamentalist "regions" have risen to new wealth in the last fifteen years or so. The industrialization of the South and Southwest, the boom in real estate, the gushing wealth of oil in Texas and Oklahoma have transformed the fundamentalist churches and the Southern Baptist movement into a middle-class and upper-middle-class group. Small wonder that, possessing this new wealth, the fundamentalist groups have discovered the iniquity of the income tax.

The social ideas of fundamentalism are quite traditional—a return to the "simple" virtues of individual initiative and self-reliance. In political terms, this means dismantling much of the social-security program, elim-inating the income tax, reducing the role of the federal government in economic life, and giving back to the states and local government the major responsibilities for welfare, labor, and similar legislation. . . .

To list the managerial executive class as among the dispossessed may seem strange, especially in the light of the argument that a revolution which is undermining property as the basis of power is enfranchising a new class of technical personnel among whom are the business executives. And yet the managerial class has been under immense strain all through this period, a strain arising in part from the status discrepancy between their power within a particular enterprise and their power and prestige in the nation as a whole. . . .

Already in 1960 the efforts of a number of corporations, led by General Electric, to go "directly" into politics, in imitation of the unions—by taking a public stand on political issues, by sending out vast amounts of propaganda to their employees and to the public, by encouraging right-to-work referendums in the states—indicated the mood of political dispossession in many corporations. Since then, a significant number of corporations have been contributing financially to the seminars of the radical-right evangelists.[1] Despite the black eye General Electric—the most vocal

---

[1] The National Education Program, at Harding College in Arkansas, which prepares films on Communism and materials on free enterprise, has been used exten-

defender of free enterprise—received when the government disclosed that G.E. as well as a dozen other electrical manufacturing companies had been guilty of illegal price-rigging and cartelization, it is likely that the Kennedy-Blough imbroglio of 1962 will provide an even greater impetus for corporations to finance right-wing political activity in the coming years.

The irony for the American military establishment is that at a time when, in the new states, the military has emerged as the ruling force of the country (often because it is the one organized group in an amorphous society), and at a time in American history when the amount of money allocated to military purposes—roughly fifty per cent of the federal budget —is the highest in peacetime history, the military is subject to challenges in its own bailiwick. The problems of national security, like those of the national economy, have become so staggeringly complex that they can no longer be settled simply by common sense or past experience. As a writer in the *Times Literary Supplement* recently put it, "The manner in which weapons systems are likely to develop; the counters which may be found to them; the burdens which they are likely to impose on the national economy; the way in which their possession will affect international relations or their use the nature of war; the technical problems of their control or abolition; all these problems are far beyond the scope of the Joint Planning Staff study or the Civil Service brief."[2]

The fact is that the military establishment, because of its outmoded curriculum, its recruitment and promotion patterns, the vested interests of the different services, and the concentration at the top levels of officers trained in older notions of strategy, is ill equipped to grasp modern conceptions of politics, or to use the tools (computer simulation, linear programming, gaming theory) of strategic planning.

In the last decade, most of the thinking on strategic problems, political and economic, has been done in the universities or in government-financed but autonomous bodies like the Rand Corporation. A new profession, that of the "military intellectual," has emerged, and men like

---

sively by General Electric, U.S. Steel, Olin Mathieson Chemical, Monsanto Chemical, Swift & Co., and others. Boeing Aviation and the Richfield Oil Company have sponsored many of the anti-Communism seminars on the West Coast. The Jones & Laughlin Steel Company has a widespread propaganda program for its employees. One of the most active firms is the Allen Bradley Company, of Milwaukee, which makes machine tools and electrical equipment. The Allen Bradley Company advertises in the John Birch Society magazine and reprinted Dr. Fred Schwarz's testimony before the House Un-American Activities Committee, a reprint which Schwarz claims had "wider distribution than any other government document in the history of the United States, with the possible exception of the Bill of Rights, the Declaration of Independence and the Constitution." The Allen Bradley Company, which constantly extols the virtue of free enterprise, was one of the companies convicted of collusive bidding and illegal price-rigging.

2 "The Military Intellectuals," *Times Literary Supplement* (London), August 25, 1961.

Kahn, Wohlstetter, Brodie, Hitch, Kissinger, Bowie, and Schelling "move freely through the corridors of the Pentagon and the State Department," as the *T.L.S.* writer observed, "rather as the Jesuits through the courts of Madrid and Vienna three centuries ago." . . . The recent controversy over the desirability of the RS-70 bomber is a case in point. The systems analysts in the office of the Secretary of Defense, led by Charles Hitch, an economist from Rand who has become the comptroller in the Pentagon,[3] decided on the basis of computer analysis that the manned RS-70 bomber would long be outmoded by the time it could come into full production, and that it would be wiser to concentrate on missiles. Dismayed by this decision, the Strategic Air Command and its allies in the aircraft industry invoked Congressional support, and the House Military Affairs Committee voted money for the bomber.

On any single set of political or strategic issues, it is an exaggeration, of course, to speak of "the military," or "the scientists," or "the military intellectuals," as if these were monolithic entities. . . .

But the main point is that the military community is no longer the only, or even the dominant, source from which the strategists are drawn, and the older military leaders particularly, with vested interests in military doctrines and weapons systems derived from their own by now parochial experiences, find themselves in danger of being ignored or shelved. A few—Major General Walker is an example—may feel that all intellectuals are involved in a plot against the nation. No doubt most of the military men will be forced, as it is already happening, into the more complex and bureaucratic game of recruiting particular groups of scientists for their own purposes (in part through the power of the purse), or attempting to make alliances. In the long run, the military profession may itself become transformed through new modes of training, and a new social type may arise.

But one can already see, in the behavior of retired military officers, the rancor of an old guard that now finds its knowledge outdated and its authority disputed or ignored, and that is beginning to argue, bitterly, that if only "their" advice had been followed, America would not be on the defensive. A surprising number of high-ranking officers on active duty as well as high-ranking retired officers have become active in extreme-right organizations. The Institute of American Strategy, which is financed by the Richardson Foundation, has on its board, and among its members, Rear Admiral Rawson Bennett, Chief of Naval Research; Lieutenant General E. C. Itschner, Chief of Engineers; Rear Admiral H. Arnold Karo; Lieutenant General George W. Mundy, Commandant of the Industrial College of the Armed Forces; and General E. W. Rawlings (U.S.A.F., ret.), the executive vice-president of General Mills, Inc. The American Security Council, for

---

[3] Editor's note: He has since been appointed president of the University of California.

example, lists on its national strategy committee such retired officers as Admiral Arthur W. Radford, former chairman of the Joint Chiefs of Staff, who had been one of the leading exponents of "massive retaliation"; General Albert C. Wedemeyer, who served in China; Lieutenant General Edward M. Almond; Admiral Felix B. Stump; Admiral Ben Moreell (now head of the Republic Steel Corporation); and Rear Admiral Chester Ward.

More active as anti-Communist entrepreneurs are some lesser lights who have held Army posts, often in Intelligence work, and who seek political status accordingly. Thus Brigadier General Bonner Fellows (ret.), a wartime aide to General MacArthur, is the national director of a group called For America, and chairman of the Citizens Foreign Aid Committee, which, despite its name, seeks to reduce foreign aid. Lieutenant Colonel Gunther Hartel (ret.), a former Intelligence officer in Europe and the Far East, heads an organization called American Strategy, Inc. These and other retired officers are active in the various "seminars" and public meetings organized by the radical-right groups.

The stock in trade of almost all these individuals is the argument, reinforced by references to their experiences, that negotiation or co-existence with Communists is impossible, that anyone who discusses the possibility of such negotiation is a tool of the Communists, and that a "tough policy"—by which, *sotto voce,* is meant a preventive war or a first strike—is the only means of forestalling an eventual Communist victory. . . .

Within this perspective, therefore, what are the prospects of the radical right. To what extent does it constitute a threat to democratic politics in the United States? . . . It is in the very nature of an extremist movement, given its tensed posture and its need to maintain a fever pitch, to mobilize, to be on the move, to act. It constantly has to agitate. Lacking any sustained dramatic issue, it can quickly wear itself out, as McCarthyism did. But to this extent the prospects of the radical right depend considerably on the international situation. If the international situation becomes stable, it is likely that the radical right may run quickly out of steam. If it were to take a turn for the worse—if Laos and all of Vietnam were to fall to the Communists; if, within the Western Hemisphere, the moderate regimes of Bolivia and Venezuela were to topple and the Communists take over—then the radical right could begin to rally support around a drive for "immediate action," for a declaration of war in these areas, for a pre-emptive strike, or similar axioms of a "hard line." . . .

Yet, given the severe strains in American life, the radical right does present a threat to American liberties, in a very different and less immediate sense. Democracy, as the sorry history of Europe has shown, is a fragile system. . . . In America, the extreme-right groups of the late 1930s—the Coughlinites, the German-American Bund, the native fascist groups—all sought to promote violence, but they never obtained legitimate or respectable support. The McCarthyite movement of the early 1950s, despite the rampaging antics of its eponymous leader, never dared go, at least rhetorically, outside the traditional framework in trying to establish loyalty and security tests. The Birchers, and the small but insidious group of Minutemen, as the epitome of the radical right, are willing to tear apart the fabric of American society in order to instate their goals, and they did receive a temporary aura of legitimacy from the conservative right.

Barbarous acts are rarely committed out of the blue. (As Freud says, first one commits oneself in words, and then in deeds.) Step by step, a society becomes accustomed to accept, with less and less moral outrage and with greater and greater indifference to legitimacy, the successive blows. What is uniquely disturbing about the emergence of the radical right of the 1960s is the support it has been able to find among traditional community leaders who have themselves become conditioned, through an indiscriminate anti-Communism that equates any form of liberalism with Communism, to judge as respectable a movement which, if successful, can only end the liberties they profess to cherish.

19

Drugs: The Magic Carpet

The catalyst in the transvaluation of bourgeois values essayed by large numbers of the discontented is the hallucinogenic drug, mild or strong. However, the burgeoning use of such drugs involves more than hippies and their kindred spirits and suggests that alienation is a condition hardly limited to flower children and youthful rebels. Drugs are, of course, an ancient device for escaping reality. However, we now confront them in a new context calling for new decisions about their use and abuse. Such decisions, including those we make about the sanctions to invoke against the use of drugs, can hardly be intelligent unless we know something about drugs.

In the case of the so-called "hard" drugs such as cocaine and the opium derivatives (e.g., heroin, morphine) there is no disagreement about their harmfulness. The hard drugs are admittedly addictive. This means, according to the World Health Organization: "(1) An overpowering desire or need (compulsion) to continue taking the drug and to obtain it by any means; (2) a tendency to increase the dose; (3) a psychic (psychological) and generally a physical dependence on the effects of the drug; (4) an effect detrimental to the individual and society."

On the other hand, the nature of the detrimental effect is subject to much misconception. For example, competent authorities agree that the heroin addict is not aroused by the drug he takes and transformed into the "dope fiend" and rapist-killer of popular folklore; opium is a depressant tending to dull sexual appetite and reduce violent behavior. Criminal behavior generally occurs when the addict is not under the influence of the drug but desperately

needs money for a new dose. Contrary to popular opinion, there
are no known organic diseases associated with opiate addiction as
there are with heavy smoking and alcohol.

The crucial question is how to curb addiction without
encouraging the crime that occurs when drugs are bootlegged at
artificially high prices. However, this problem, important as it is,
will not be dealt with here. Limitations of space confine us to
drugs of a quite different category, the non-addictive hallucinogens
or psychedelic drugs, so-called because they alter perception and
affect the mind so as to produce hallucinations.

Notable among the mind-altering drugs are marijuana, a
mild hallucinogen derived from the hemp plant (cannabis sativa),
and LSD-25 (lysergic acid diethylamide), which is now easily
synthesized and is enormously potent. Marijuana (also variously
called grass, pot, Mary Jane, tea, etc., and closely related to
hashish, which is a stronger derivative of the same plant), while it
may cause psychological dependency, does not induce withdrawal
symptoms, nor do users develop a tolerance such that increasingly
larger doses must be taken to produce the same effect. This is also
true of LSD (although researchers report that some users do
develop a tolerance).

The use of hallucinogens has increased enormously within
the last few years and experience with marijuana, once limited to
fringe groups (beatniks, jazz musicians) and segregated ethnic
minorities, is increasingly common among otherwise conventional,
middle-class young people in quest of "kicks" and scorning as old-
fashioned their elders' reliance on alcohol. More U.S. servicemen
in Vietnam are arrested for smoking marijuana than for any other
single major offense. The use of LSD is far less common if only
because its sheer potency frightens off many would-be users, and
those who venture on an LSD "trip" are less likely to be in quest of
euphoria than are marijuana users. The power of LSD is, indeed,
quite frightening: one authority reports that a two-suiter luggage
piece could contain enough LSD to incapacitate the entire population of the United States.[1]

It is important to emphasize that, unlike most drug users,
the so-called psychedelic who has recourse to the stronger psycho-
chemicals (LSD and the weaker peyote or mescaline) is as a rule
not hedonistically motivated. To overlook this is to miss the distinctive feature of the "movement," with its missionary quality and
cult-like overtones. Most psychedelics claim not to be in search of

---

[1] Sidney Cohen, *The Beyond Within: The LSD Story* (New York: Athe-
neum, 1964), p. 231.

pleasure, but of "understanding" through self-exploration, new experience, a sense of "oneness" with the universe, etc. Their movement has its high-priest in Dr. Timothy Leary (not to mention a poet laureate, Allen Ginsberg) for whom the psychedelic drug means "ecstasy, sensual unfolding, religious experience, revelation, illumination, contact with nature." If this seems like a large order, Leary is quite undaunted either by the vagueness and magnitude of the goal or the hazards of encouraging (albeit with an experienced guide) use of an easily manufactured chemical so powerful that the slightest overdose could produce disastrous consequences. Neither is he worried about the loss of motivation and lapse of interest in their normal social ties and usual occupations which characterize the "psychedelic dropouts." ("It's nothing to worry about; it's something to cheer.") His slogan is "Turn on, tune in, drop out," the import of which is to "detach yourself from the tribal game" and escape our "air-conditioned anthill." Leary rejects as unreliable a survey cited by *Time* finding 200 victims of bad trips in Los Angeles hospitals, as he does the conclusion of Dr. Jonathan Cole of the National Institute of Mental Health that psychedelic drugs "can be dangerous . . . People get into panic states in which they are ready to jump out of their skins . . . The benefits are obscure." To be sure, not all authorities agree with Dr. Cole, as the selections that follow will indicate.

California, Nevada, and New Jersey have passed restrictive and prohibitive laws against the use, possession, distribution or manufacture of LSD. But many will question the need for such legislation, as they do laws which put marijuana in the same category with heroin and thereby encourage contact with users and sellers of the more dangerous drugs. Once again, as in the section on sex and society, we confront the phenomenon of "crimes without victims" to borrow the felicitous title of Edwin Schur's book, and once again we must ask: to what extent should society intervene?

Unfortunately, it is difficult to find in the voluminous literature on marijuana an intellectually respectable criticism that comes to grips with the really basic and overriding issue. Suppose, as may well be the case, that marijuana were as free of disadvantages and as superior to alcohol as its apologists claim it to be: no hazard to health from overuse, no hangover, no drain on a poor man's purse. Or, to avoid the legacy of controversy about marijuana, suppose that chemists were able to develop a cheap, completely harmless euphoriant. This is surely a theoretical possibility; the science of psychopharmacology is, after all, only in its infancy. In his *Brave New World* Aldous Huxley described such a drug, used by the dictatorship to keep the man in the street happy, which he called *soma*. Two questions at once suggest themselves, one psychological, the other moral: (1) Would most people avail themselves of such a drug? (2) How should we evaluate the consequences if they did? It could well be that the very virtues of a perfect euphoriant—and therefore, to a lesser degree, of marijuana —are paradoxically its real danger.

Satisfaction is usually purchased with effort, not merely in the obvious sense that most of us have to work in order to have the satisfaction of eating or living with a roof over our heads, but because in most circumstances (from which not even the rich are exempt) satisfaction is a concomitant of the successful pursuit of ends. We have enjoyment, satisfaction, gratification, whatever we choose to call it, when we have objectives and are able to encompass them, when, as Aristotle would have said, we realize ourselves. Such self-realization normally requires effort. And all such effort in its totality accounts for what we call civilization.

Suppose now that our cheap euphoriant were at hand with all its virtues. Since we have not claimed that it would also be an analgesic we would at least have to bestir ourselves to avoid the pain of hunger and exposure. Would we seek more than simple fare and shelter or, thanks to our euphoriant, live contentedly at a subsistence level? And, if we failed to seek more, what would the moral difference be? "It is better," J. S. Mill said, "to be a human being dissatisfied than a pig satisfied; better to be Socrates dissatisfied than a fool satisfied." Clearly Mill had no doubt about the moral difference. But a new breed of sybarites might respond, as the "hippies" in effect answer, that they would rather live like pigs than be caught in the "rat-race." That this attitude, if universal, would mean the decay of all culture, does not deter the committed "user." By dwelling exclusively on the defects of our culture he can find his rationalization in the charge that we have nothing worth saving.

Some light may be thrown on the question by Dr. C. J. Miras of the University of Athens who has observed chronic marijuana smokers in Greece for 20 years—much longer, according to UCLA drug experts, than American researchers. He reports that many of his subjects who were teachers and artists left their work for other jobs, but preferred most of all "to sleep and talk philosophy." One wonders if they "talked philosophy" or engaged in verbal reverie; the two are sometimes confused. As a state of vague and dreamy meditation the latter is not far from sleep. Pigs, we may suppose, do not engage in reverie, and yet one may well wonder if the state of torpor of which it is a variant is much different from the condition of porcine contentment eschewed by Mill.

As noted earlier, the effects of marijuana and LSD are widely disparate and the motives of marijuana and LSD users are often quite different. It is therefore difficult to deal with them under the same rubric. The discussion on marijuana is limited to excerpts from an official report on the assumption that in the present climate of opinion the reader will be best served by a statement that both friends and foes of the punitive laws now in effect are bound to respect—although some advocates of the laws we have seem determined to respect nothing except demands for stiffer penalties. Meanwhile the reader may marvel at our inability to decide whether marijuana is a vicious scourge, an innocuous folk euphoriant, cheaper and less harmful than alcohol and tobacco, or possibly neither. At present our law is on the side of those who believe the first.

The remaining and more extensive discussion will deal with the use of LSD. Its novelty, its great potency and potential hazard, and the claims made for it as a source of new insight and a key to new knowledge give it special interest. Certainly a new science of psychopharmacology opens up startling possibilities apart from the new moral options with which it promises to confront us. Some of these will be touched upon in the following selections which should help us decide whether most LSD users are frustrated escapists unable or unwilling to cope with the normal strains and tensions of modern life; or, as they often would prefer to think, bold spirits exploring inner frontiers even as others are exploring the frontiers of outer space.

MARIHUANA

The President's Advisory Commission on Crime and Law Enforcement

In addition to suggesting that the penalties provided for narcotics and marihuana offenses be made more flexible, the Commission would like to comment specially on marihuana, because of questions that have been

From the Commission's Report, February 1967, pp. 12–14.

raised concerning the appropriateness of the substantive law applicable to this drug.

The basic Federal control statute, the Marihuana Tax Act, was enacted in 1937 with the stated objectives of making marihuana dealings visible to public scrutiny, raising revenue, and rendering difficult the acquisition of marihuana for nonmedical purposes (the drug has no recognized medical value) and noncommercial use (the plant from which the drug comes has some commercial value in the production of seed and hemp). At the heart of the act are provisions requiring that all persons with a legitimate reason for handling marihuana register and pay an occupational tax, requiring that all marihuana transactions be recorded on official forms provided by the Treasury Department, subjecting transfers to a registered person to a tax of $1 an ounce, and subjecting transfers to an unregistered person to a prohibitive tax of $100 an ounce. Under the Uniform Narcotic Drug Act in force in most States, marihuana is defined and controlled as a narcotic drug.

The act raises an insignificant amount of revenue and exposes an insignificant number of marihuana transactions to public view, since only a handful of people are registered under the act. It has become, in effect, solely a criminal law imposing sanctions upon persons who sell, acquire, or possess marihuana.

Marihuana was placed under a prohibition scheme of control because of its harmful effects and its claimed association with violent behavior and crime. Another reason now advanced in support of the marihuana regulations is that the drug is a steppingstone or forerunner to the use of addicting drugs, particularly heroin.

The law has come under attack on all counts, and the points made against it deserve a hearing.

The Effects

Marihuana is equated in law with the opiates, but the abuse characteristics of the two have almost nothing in common. The opiates produce physical dependence. Marihuana does not. A withdrawal sickness appears when use of the opiates is discontinued. No such symptoms are associated with marihuana. The desired dose of opiates tends to increase over time, but this is not true of marihuana. Both can lead to psychic dependence, but so can almost any substance that alters the state of consciousness.

The Medical Society of the County of New York has classified marihuana as a mild hallucinogen, and this is probably as good a description as any, although hallucinations are only one of many effects the drug can produce. It can impair judgment and memory; it can cause anxiety, confusion, or disorientation; and it can induce temporary psychotic episodes in predisposed people. Any hallucinogenic drug, and many of the other dangerous drugs, can do the same. Marihuana is probably less likely to produce these effects than such moderately potent hallucinogens as peyote, mescaline, and hashish (another derivative of the plant from which marihuana comes), and much less likely to do so than the potent hallucinogen LSD.

Marihuana, Crime, and Violence

Here differences of opinion are absolute and the claims are beyond reconciliation. One view is that marihuana is a major cause of crime and violence. Another is that marihuana has no association with crime and only a marginal relation to violence.

Proponents of the first view rely in part on reports connecting marihuana users with crime. One such report by the district attorney of New Orleans was referred to in the hearings on the 1937 act. It found that 125 of 450 men convicted of major crimes in 1930 were regular marihuana users. Approximately one-half the murderers (an unstated number) and a fifth of those tried for larceny, robbery, and assault (again an unstated number) were regular users. However, the main reliance is on case files of enforcement agencies. Excerpts from these files have been used to demonstrate a marihuana-crime causal relation. The validity of such a demonstration involves three assumptions which are questioned by opponents of the present law: (1) The defendant was a marihuana user. Usually this can be determined only by the defendant's own statement or by his possession of the drug at the time of arrest. (2) He was under the influence of marihuana when he committed the criminal act. Again a statement, perhaps a self-serving one, is most often the source of the information. Chemical tests of blood, urine, and the like will not detect marihuana. (3) The influence of the marihuana caused the crime in the sense that it would not have been committed otherwise.

Those who hold the opposite view cannot prove their case, either. They can only point to the prevailing lack of evidence. Many have done so. The Medical Society of the County of New York has stated flatly that there is no evidence that marihuana use is associated with crimes of violence in this country. There are many similar statements by other responsible authorities. The 1962 report of the President's Ad Hoc Panel on Drug Abuse found the evidence inadequate to substantiate the reputation of marihuana for inciting people to antisocial acts. The famous Mayor's Committee on Marihuana, appointed by Mayor La Guardia to study the marihuana situation in New York City, did not observe any aggression in subjects to whom marihuana was given. In addition there are several studies of persons who were both confessed marihuana users and convicted criminals, and these reach the conclusion that a positive relation between use and crime cannot be established.

One likely hypothesis is that, given the accepted tendency of marihuana to release inhibitions, the effect of the drug will depend on the individual and the circumstances. It might, but certainly will not necessarily or inevitably, lead to aggressive behavior or crime. The response will depend more on the individual than the drug. This hypothesis is consistent with the evidence that marihuana does not alter the basic personality structure.

Marihuana as a Prelude to Addicting Drugs

The charge that marihuana "leads" to the use of addicting drugs needs to be critically examined. There is evidence that a majority of the heroin users who come to the attention of public authorities have, in fact, had some prior experience with marihuana. But this does not mean that one leads to the other in the sense that marihuana has an intrinsic quality that creates a heroin liability. There are too many marihuana users who do not graduate to heroin, and too many heroin addicts with no known prior marihuana use, to support such a theory. Moreover there is no scientific basis for such a theory. The basic text on pharmacology, Goodman and Gilman, *The Pharmacological Basis of Therapeutics* (Macmillan 1960) states quite explicitly that marihuana habituation does not lead to the use of heroin.

The most reasonable hypothesis here is that some people who are predisposed to marihuana are also predisposed to heroin use. It may also be the case that through the use of marihuana a person forms the personal associations that later expose him to heroin.

The amount of literature on marihuana is massive. It runs to several thousand articles in medical journals and other publications. Many of these are in foreign languages and reflect the experience of other countries with the use of the drug and with other substances derived from the hemp plant. The relevance of this material to our own problem has never been determined. Indeed, with the possible exception of the 1944 La Guardia report, no careful and detailed analysis of the American experience seems to have been attempted. Basic research has been almost nonexistent, probably because the principal active ingredient in marihuana has only recently been isolated and synthesized. Yet the Commission believes that enough information exists to warrant careful study of our present marihuana laws and the propositions on which they are based.

The Commission Recommends:

The National Institute of Mental Health should devise and execute a plan of research, to be carried on both on an intramural and extramural basis, covering all aspects of marihuana use.

The research should identify existing gaps in our knowledge of marihuana. A systematic review of the literature will be necessary. The plan should provide for an intensive examination of the important medical and social aspects of marihuana use. It should provide for surveys of the extent of marihuana use and of the nature of such use, i.e., occasional, periodic, or habitual. It should provide for studies of the pharmacology of marihuana and of its immediate and long-term effects. It might also provide for animal studies. The relation of marihuana use to aggressive behavior and crime should certainly be a subject of study. So should the relation between marihuana and the use of other drugs. The Commission of course does not wish to imply that the need for research is confined to marihuana. Much remains to be learned, for example, about the potential uses and dangers of hallucinogenic drugs.

LSD—"UTOPIATE"

Richard Blum

> Dr. Blum teaches at Stanford University and was consultant to the President's Commission on Law Enforcement and Administration of Justice. The several papers he contributed as consultant are included in its task force report Narcotics and Drug Abuse. He is project director of the Psychopharmacology Project at Stanford's Institute for the Study of Human Problems and is one of the leading authorities in this country on mind-altering drugs.

LSD-25 in the range of dosage employed by sample members (25 to 900 micrograms) has powerful effects on the minds of those taking it. There are a very few exceptions. . . . The range of effects is predictable.

The physical consequences described are incapacitation, nausea, numbness, cramps, exhaustion, and changes in facial musculature. The major mental effects are sensory changes, including alterations in intensity in attention, imagery, and hallucinations; transient feelings of anxiety, excitement, despair, power, terror, release, calm, intoxication, euphoria, or detachment; new perspectives about oneself, including insights, recollections, redefinitions, acceptance, or rejection; new views or emotions about others, including felt objectivity, closeness, withdrawal, loathing, and lovingness; changes from prior chronic states, including reduction of tension, anxiety, or anger, reduced competitiveness, or increased depression; shifts in interest, including reduced work interests and goal striving, increased artistic or philosophical concerns, greater preoccupation with internal events and self, and greater interest in drugs per se; and new integrative experiences which may be culturally acceptable, psychotically delusional, or mystically religious. . . .

On the basis of the information available it appears that LSD use is most likely to occur among psychotherapy patients whose psychiatrists have themselves had LSD, among middle-class persons living in areas where LSD institutions make the drug publicly available, among artists and professionals having informal equal-status contacts with mental-health professionals who do have access to the drug, among volunteers for drug experiments in institutions, and among active social groups of younger persons already using other drugs, whose interests or career training in the arts and professions expose them to LSD information and sources of supply among professionals. There are, however, a large number of potential or actual users who have no contact with professionals and have access to LSD only through black-market sources: homemade or imported LSD and homegrown or purchased morning glory seeds.

At the present time, LSD use would appear to be confined to a limited social strata of intellectuals in the twenty-one to fifty age group, primarily male, or the wives or girl friends of such males; they are white, often Anglo-Saxon, Protestants. It is a phenomenon concentrated among respected, conforming, successful persons with socially favored backgrounds and careers. . . .

It is clear that the use of unprescribed or illicit drugs is by no means confined to criminal, deviant, or lower-class groups. A number of otherwise law-abiding citizens experiment with, and some habitually use, drugs such as marijuana, peyote, and methedrine with little apparent risk of association with criminals or of engaging in offenses against either property or person. They also appear to run little risk of detection and arrest. There is no evidence that such illicit drug use among successful and older intellectuals is associated with sexual deviancy, overt rebelliousness, degeneracy, or untrustworthiness. Furthermore, there is no evidence of interest in or likelihood of any "steppingstone". . . .

Whether or not laws should be changed or law-enforcement effort directed more toward this group is a question that will necessarily be raised. Given the occasional occurrence of psychotic reactions and the presumptive evidence for a few persons showing reduced efficiency or effectiveness, there seems little doubt that LSD use does present hazards for those taking the drug. Whether these hazards are any greater than, or indeed as great as, those which are posed by other permissible drug activities, alcohol use, tobacco use, or use of prescribed tranquilizers, energizers, sedatives, and the like is a very important question. The evidence from this study suggests that the controlled institutional use of LSD is associated with the least extension of LSD-taking to other drugs or to the informal (unsupervised) and sometimes illicit use of LSD. Institutional safeguards do not appear, however, to exclude any of the risks of immediate psychological or physical bad results, regardless of the claims of institutional personnel to the contrary. Except to control the drug effect hazards, there would appear to be no reason to direct law enforcement toward this otherwise eminently law-abiding sector of the population. . . . [This] would be consistent with Vollmer's belief that drug use should not be a police problem. Unacceptably deviant behavior by members of groups which use these substances will no doubt emerge in other forms and can be dealt with under other laws.

Much rests on the judgment of pharmacological harmlessness and on the amount of risk that the individual is allowed to assume for himself before society intrudes to prevent or control use. In LSD, for example, the risk exists but will be balanced against the notion of the individual's rights to choose for himself or to have private experiences, even if these are publicly disapproved. Such a debate is a continuing one in our society and extends beyond the use of illicit drugs to alcohol, tobacco, and acts of sexual deviancy in private and between consenting adults. . . . Americans have a number of problems in reconciling individual rights and the public good and also in deciding whether or not laws are enacted to be enforced or merely as expressions of ideals or devices to encourage discretion. . . .

Sociologically it is clearly demonstrated that LSD use is a social phenomenon. The drug is given by one person to another along predictable lines of association and role relationship. It is usually taken in the presence of several persons—friends, relatives, and associates other than the initiator. Afterward, those who continue the use of or interest in the drug do so in association with like-minded persons and do form social groups based upon the shared experience and developing interests. . . .

Robert K. Merton's notion of "retreatism," attributed to persons in a disadvantaged social position lacking either legitimate or illegitimate means for achieving culturally sanctioned ends, is clearly irrelevant to the LSD phenomena. While one may think of the convinced LSD user as retreating, it is certainly not because he has failed to achieve at least some of the glories of this world, nor does he lack institutional means to secure more of these ends should he so desire. And whatever retreat does occur is not a withdrawal into a dismal emptiness or shadowy world of despair. As described, it is a retreat from competition and strife but also toward something felt to be positive: tranquillity and personal or religious exaltation. The retreat, then, if that is what it is, is more along the lines of "privatism," an antimaterialistic emphasis on a reliable inner world in the face of an unreliable outer one. A retreat of that order is . . . an attempt by the intellectuals, who have lost political power to bureaucracy and the state, to endow their lives with a meaning and significant order which cannot be found through empiricism and worldliness.

There are a number of variables, intrapsychic and interpersonal, rational and nonrational, which predispose some persons to take LSD and, among those taking it, predispose a minority to become regular users of it and other mind-altering drugs. The decision to accept or reject the drug is influenced by the kind of information one has about its effects and about how one feels about his life circumstances and directions at the time the drug is made available. If one's life is unpleasant, if one conceives of most of the distress to be due to some lack, need, or problem in oneself, and if one believes the drug to produce personal benefits, then the chances are that one will take LSD. If one's general motivation is curiosity and excitement-seeking or is directed toward the inner life, one is predisposed to take the drug. If, on the other hand, one is ready to blame external sources for one's distress, if one's motivation is toward known rather than unknown sources of stimulation, if one distrusts foreign substances or drugs in general, if one is holding the line against change, or if one is informed that the drug's effects are transient, superficial, or unpleasant, then the chances are that LSD will be rejected.

Those who are already more interested in the active social world maintain that interest, continue their upward climb and/or competitive striving, and do so at the cost of continued tension, perhaps resorting to sanctioned relaxers and restoratives in the form of alcohol or overeating. These persons are unlikely to take LSD and are certainly unlikely to become regular drug users. The LSD accepters, especially the continuing users, appear more willing to withdraw from striving and to abandon worldly goals; as this occurs, they become more relaxed, more preoccupied with themselves, and more euphoric. Their level of anger goes down and is replaced by more affectionate feelings. . . .

There are some subtle indications that the LSD rejectors may be better able to withstand anxiety, that they find more satisfaction in competitive striving, that they are more extroverted, and that, whatever their protestations of tolerance—which they can afford as a comfortable majority behaving in accordance with antidrug morality—they do disapprove of drug use and users on moral grounds, that disapproval sometimes lending itself to pleasant feelings of superiority. It may be that these intellectuals, schooled to accept deviancy, allow the police to be their projected conscience. Externalized, that conscience can then be criticized as well as secretly approved. Implicit is the fact of a moral conflict over the use of drugs both in those who use them and those who do not use them. That conflict is projected to beliefs about police and public reactions to drug use. This conflict is interpersonal as well as intrapsychic. Various groups are in strenuous opposition with reference to the evaluation of the dangers, menace, and benefits of drug use, and with reference to the need for control or moral suasion through punitive devices. But what is not to be overlooked is the likelihood that, the more intense positions people take and the more passionately they invoke principles, sentiments, and morality in the name of freedom or repression—mass conversion to drugs or mass imprisonment of users—the more the observer should be alert to intrapsychic conflict and defense in these expostulators. Their conflicts are likely to center on the handling of physiological and developmental needs —especially those connected with sex, defecation, exploration, and oral satisfactions; with attitudes of rebellion or overconformity toward authority, and, in general, with matters of comfort, spontaneity, and pleasure for which drug use has much symbolic significance.

The significance of drug use for some users merits special attention, especially those real groups of younger persons who use a number of mind-altering substances and for whom such use is symbolic of revolt against constraints—psychic and social—and is an affirmation of anticompulsive, anticonservative spontaneity. This same emotionality is to be found in those who react to these users with intense disgust, their reaction being a fear of overwhelming menace, and enlist noble sentiments in the cause of punitive repression. As Fritz Redl observed, a temptation which is repressed at great effort may be handled through reaction formation and the outpouring of hostility on the scapegoat caught doing the tempting deed. . . .

J. S. Slotkin has described in *The Peyote Religion* the relationships between drug values and practices and the social-historical position of the Menomini Indians vis-à-vis the whites. Becker has described the subculture of the jazz musician-marijuana user; Harold Finestone has reviewed the place of drugs in the life of the "cat," the frustrated young urban Negro interested in music and kicks, who lives solely within his own achievement-blocked social group to fashion a new kind of status which represents an indirect attack upon conventional values. For the "cat," drug use is a renunciation and rebellion, a subtle accommodation avoiding confrontation or attack, a way of finding status and self-identification, and a means to pleasure and aesthetic satisfaction. G. Morris Carstairs compares the Brahmin's acceptance of hashish and rejection of alcohol with the Western world's acceptance of alcohol and rejection of hashish and the opiates. The latter drugs are productive of a quiescence compatible with values of meditation and the turning-wheel-of-life ethos of the religous man of the East. Alcohol is incompatible with that, but is, in its effects, compatible with the Western aggressive interpersonal ethos; it is the intoxicant of the warrior, the Kshatriya.

These observations point out that the pharmacological effects of a drug will affect its selection or rejection by a culture, the requirement being that, for general sanction, employing the drug must not produce effects opposed to the predominant ethos of the culture. On the other hand, drugs rejected by the culture at large may be selected by dissident subcultural groups just because they do symbolize the rejection of that larger ethos and because the effects produced are compatible with the interests of the dissident subculture. Some drugs may not be intimately linked with the ethos because of the recency of their innovation, their unavailability, or the unimportance of the subgroups employing them. In those cases, the acceptance of a drug, ignored or disdained by the larger culture, may not symbolize rebellion or the conflict of power and values, but may reflect more moderate dissent—a desire to fashion new images, myths, or identifications or to experiment with values accepted but not encouraged in a pluralistic society. The use of hallucinogens is best seen in that light. . . .

In pursuing the matter of cultural themes and drug effects, one comes again and again to a dichotomy: inward-turning versus outward-turning. There are those who are in and of the world and those who are not; and as with any simple typology, there are those who fall somewhere in between. In psychology, the words are introversion and extroversion; in sociology, inner-directed and other-directed. In anthropology, the words are more diverse: cultures of contemplation and cultures of action or Dionysian cultures of ecstasy and Apollonian cultures of moderation. And in religion, there is a division between the mystics and the ascetics—and, unfortunately for the typology, the majority who are neither, or those who become one to achieve being the other. . . .

Max Weber expanded the history, circumstance, correlates, and consequences of mysticism as opposed to asceticism. His was the delineation of the Protestant ethic and the evaluation of the ascetic Protestant quest for salvation through worldly work alone. Taking this organized asceticism, together with the history of Christianity, capitalism, and the evolution of the modern state, what are the predominant "givens" in the Western world which Weber describes? We list them as follows: inner worldly asceticism; rationalism; a sober and dominant bureaucracy; the ideal of order and security; the ideal of alertness and self-control; the exaltation of commerce and vocations with a power distribution to maintain them and military force to protect and facilitate them; the proliferation of the apparatus of the state; indifference to religious feeling and the emphasis on institutional religious forms accompanied by suspicion of the independent religious seeker; the rejection of personal ethics and personal loyalties or feelings as dictating modes of economic and bureaucratic intercourse; and success in business as the proof of favor with God, as proof of salvation, and as the finest fruit of a rational way of living. The dominant modes, as Weber saw them, are anti-intellectual, antiromantic, antimagical, anti-irrational, antierotic, and antiaesthetic. Politics devotes itself to the dominant interests of the state and to realism; it is opposed to every residue of the religious ethic of brotherhood, just as are the economic institutions.

What is the outcome? The world as we know it in all its progress, efficiency, and rational smoothness. But for individuals who accept the heritage of mystical religions, or who regenerate that heritage in their own experience, there can be a sense of loss. Humility and brotherly love are gone. There can be a sense of guilt, a "secret anguish" Weber calls it, as men are compelled to act in spite of their spiritual propensities and to experience "godless sin" as they participate in an eminently impartial, intrinsically honest, and overwhelmingly well-organized system. There can be, among intellectuals especially, but also among the middle class or aristocracy who have lost their power to bureaucrats and the military, a reaction against the entire system. The reaction is "apolitical emotionalism," a revulsion against the perfection of rationality and impersonal manipulations—in essence, a revolt against a system which works but which does not gratify. The direction of the revolt? As long as it is apolitical, then it must turn inward, and that flight is into mysticism.

Parsons, in discussing Weber, rightly notes that one modern term for the disaffection of men for the impersonal social system in which they find themselves is "alienation." The nature and effects of that social system have been the subject of continuing sociological discourse the last decades. Whyte's *The Organization Man,* for example, shows the business system molding its participants; *Crestwood Heights* has described how the system prepares the young for the rational control of their own personalities as saleable commodities; Stein has documented *The Eclipse of Community* in the anonymous urban monolith, and others have discerned how difficult it is to identify oneself as something special when so much of one is controlled, constrained, and molded for the market place.

Sociological theory, beginning with the brilliant symbolic interactionism of Mead and expanded by current writers has taken role theory quite beyond the business of attributes and "as if" behavior and has moved from attending to the forces shaping social behavior to social forces shaping personality. As this has occurred, role has slowly been converted into "self" and social status into "identity." The play is reality, and persons are only actors, players, masks, or other outward-oriented, feelingless entities. There are no more persons, merely personae. . . .

The drug movement provides a framework for the intellectual apolitical rebel. It is his revolution, a quiet revolution with no thundering rage. Its participants are too well acculturated and have benefited too much from the good things of our society to have the audacity or the ingratitude to overrun the ethic itself. Like the violence-eschewing "cat" of the Negro ghetto, the LSD-using white professional is too committed to the values of the larger society and, in his case, too well rewarded for his good conduct to think of overturning a social order which is exactly what a properly reared citizen must think it should be: efficient, fair, honest, healthy, secure, charitable, and rational. The bind is on. He is what the society would have him be, eminently hard-working, successful, honest, and all the rest. The controls are built into his personality—indeed over controls, as the evaluation of ego control and distrust showed. Such a man cannot actively rebel. But the constraints which negate an active protest do not prevent him from experiencing emotions of reaction against that kind of a life and world. These are the feelings expressed by the words "unfulfilled," "tense," and "anxious," which most LSD users, and most of the controls as well, use to describe themselves.

The response to these symptoms is biologically determined by a desire to escape from pain and, culturally, by that optimism and activism which permeate the myth of progress: the belief that one need not accept things as they are and that one can change things, oneself included, for the better. So it is that LSD use remains consonant with the Western articles of faith; cure is possible, there are better worlds beyond, and science does provide a means for control—in this instance, one more pharmaceutical miracle.

The notion of control is an important one. This is a control-oriented society; technology and the whole apparatus of rational endeavor work to control nature and to control men. But that effort, one which is usually considered beneficial to man's comfort and security, has generated instruments so ponderous that the individual can lose all hope of controlling the instruments themselves. The state, organizations, and the various forms of collectivity are Frankenstein monsters, for they have moved from being instruments in the hands of men to being instruments which hold men in their hands. This is the nature of bureaucracy and the culmination of an efficient technological revolution.

For some, especially those who refuse to take LSD, the challenge of life in the machine age is met with some optimism. There is enough gratification found in remaining with the mainstream, seeing just how far one can swim against the current, seeing what eddies and backwaters one may turn to advantage, or, for many, the heady pleasure of plunging ahead, swimming with the current in full confidence that where it is taking one is exactly where one wants to go. For others, especially those who use LSD regularly, there is disinterest in remaining in those turbulent waters. Some are not optimistic about any benefits to be accrued, for the cost in malaise is great enough to annul the worth of any ends. For some, the awareness of the hopelessness of trying to control any part of oneself, once it is committed to the real world's torrent, looms uppermost. Others are discouraged because they fear they will not reach the goals they wish, a failure which will cost them dearly in self-esteem. Rather than seek and fail, they renounce those ends and seek new and easier glories. Their ambition is converted but not lost. For them, there is success achievable in the approval of friends or, for those who have become gurus, in the admiration of their disciples.

Individuals who have lost interest in or hope of controlling themselves and events in the real social world may try to control that area that can be controlled, the inner life. Appropriately enough, the devices employed still reflect their commitment to the world outside, for self-control is not achieved by oneself alone; it is achieved with a technological boost from the world of pharmacy.

Individuals sold on the system itself, sold on the self that is part of the system and yet still miserable, do not question the fundamental values, but seek only to alter that reality which can be changed without encountering direct and massive disapproval. Real revolutionaries are shot; illicit drug users are jailed, but LSD users are law-abiding people who behave in proper ways. They choose a pill in a society which advocates pills. They are initiated by one of the elite of that society—a doctor or sometimes an executive or engineer. And they use a drug which was or was believed to be perfectly legal to use at the time and under the circumstances when most of the professionals who were seeking the approved ends of personal benefit and improvement took LSD. The perfect regard for propriety characterized not only the use, but the reaction to the drug of the entire sample of legitimate users.

That regard for propriety was much less evident among the younger people [surveyed by the author] who used LSD in the black-market setting. They had already taken other drugs illegally, they took LSD without benefit of medical supervision, and their response to the drug was erotic and orgiastic. No legitimate user of LSD engaged in orgiastic eroticism after taking the drug. But regardless of his greater immediate unconventionality, the black-market user's revolution is also a quiet one. He is willing to enjoy himself, but he is by no means attacking the world, nor is he reacting against the broad ascetic ethic. He has no intention of renouncing his career goals nor that wonderful, active, beckoning, big wide world. Obviously the life situation and propelling motives of the black-market user cannot be interpreted as symptoms of suffering which are to be relieved by a flight into contemplative mysticism. The use of LSD by the black-market group is associated with unconventional response, but not with mysticism and not with any withdrawal from commitment to the external world. Their short-term active unconventionality does not forebode any long-term unconventionality. The professional and legitimate

LSD user, on the other hand, initially proper in use and response, may nevertheless be suffering, and that suffering may move him to mysticism and a long term of quiet unconventionality.

For the older, more successful people who are in need of lasting change, LSD does provide relief. It does not change basic personality structure nor the external world itself; it does change relations to that world by altering feelings, beliefs, and actions. The "anesthetic revelation" establishes contact with a lost inner psychic world—and William James would say with real and grander worlds of religion and God as well. For the user who does move in the direction of contemplative mysticism, there is a fleeing from the world and the re-establishment of the ethic of brother-hood, symbolized in becoming more loving. But as with most brother-hoods, and certainly as with many fellowships of the mystery religions, brotherhood and the personal ethic is limited to the elect, to spiritual kinfolk. And so, demonstrating the pattern of personal ties and clan loyalties which have characterized the "little communities" of tribesmen and peasants, the LSD user's brotherhood is confined, ethnocentrically, to those in the drug movement and, indeed, because of the factionalism therein, only to some in that movement.

Having become "loving" is one of the most important changes which the regular LSD user reports in himself. It is real because it is felt to be real. But it is also inferred in the warm reactions of others to some of these people. That lovingness arises not just because of the regeneration of the ethic of brotherhood, but also because of the biological, psychological, and social fact that human beings have the capacity to love, a capacity which does grow as one makes peace with oneself and as one has intense emotional experiences with others during critical periods. Certainly the LSD initiation, fraught as it is with anxiety, uncertainty, danger, symbolic affirmations, great hopes, and group support, is one of those critical periods. Indeed, under some LSD institutions' procedures, that initiation is planned so as to maximize anxiety and dependency ties which are then molded to a special form of "lovingness."

The balance of lovingness also rises as the heavy weight of tensions and hatreds fall. As the individual does move even a bit away from the exhausting competition with others and the never-ending striving for goals that are always one step ahead, his aggressiveness and socialized anxiety, which have been in the service of vocational gain, and his hostility in response to the competitive threats posed by others recede. Thus what is felt as a new lovingness is partly the result of the diminishing of strife and hatred.

This lovingness need not be manifest to others. For one thing, the mystically oriented person may not be actively benevolent. He may be disinterested in those overt forms of charity and aggressively helpful inter-vention of those who subscribe to the conventions of philanthropy and humanitarianism. These acts are themselves part of the other-directed motifs of an ethical and rational society. Thus, what the LSD user feels to be loving and what the observer requires as "proofs of love" are quite different. Second, it is to be recalled that Morimoto, in observing normal persons under LSD influence, found them to seek support from others, but not to be brotherly. Since the drug incapacitates the user, he does, in fact, rely on others for assistance and for reassurance. He becomes physically and psychologically dependent upon the initiator. Most initiators accept that and encourage dependency with warmth and understanding. The background of most of the LSD users is one which has discouraged dependency. "Self-reliance," "stand on your own two feet," "bear your pain in manly silence"; those are the watchwords. But the LSD experience alters that, encouraging intense interrelationships, dependency, and, psychoanalytically speaking, regression. What a luxury and relief it must be! To indulge in that relaxation and to be allowed it. One feels loved and is allowed to love in return. That accepted dependency and resultant interpersonal tie may be the root of the LSD lovingness and would account for the absence of reciprocal, brotherly conduct, as observed by Morimoto. That dependency might also account for the feelings of protectiveness sometimes reported by observers; it and the earlier lack of active benevolence can account for the discrepancy between the observer's impression of a few users as simply passive, unconcerned, or selfish and the users' description of their own lovingness. . . .

  An important consideration is the extent to which LSD produces a full commitment to the inner life, that is, produces full-time mysticism. . . . Most LSD users stayed on the job and compromised their inner visions with the demands of the outer world. That they have done so augurs well for their adjustment to that world, for there is no headlong flight from reality. The ascetic observer will approve and think well of the common sense of the LSD user. On the other hand, if one, longing for passionate commitments, hopes that it alone can make Dionysians out of molded Apollonians, he will be disappointed. The intellectuals who use LSD, with the possible exclusion of the younger black-market orgiasts, are incapable of altering themselves to such an extent that they go to any extreme. Should they try to achieve extremism through the continued use of drugs, they are more likely to suffer chronic drug effects rather than be transported to any state of ultimate and continuing enlightenment. It does not appear that LSD is a short cut to personality reconstruction or to nirvana.

  . . . Those who compromise . . . must adjust inner desires and outer demands. What these persons propose is to "play the game." One is to go through the motions of a vocation but to do so without conviction, enthusiasm, or the investment of personal feelings. It is in this that regular LSD users may differ most dramatically from most, but not all, rejectors.

  The LSD user who proposes to play the game is in fact carrying the rational impersonal system to its logical next step. By proposing further to divest himself of feelings in his relations with other men, by proposing to analyze the system and play it exactly according to its rules, without feelings, without a personal ethic, but with a willingness to abide by external moralities, that man completes his alienations from society. He becomes the very model of modernity. Nothing could be more rational. That modern man, wrote Weber,

> performs his duty best when he acts without regard to the person in question . . . without hate and without love, without personal predilection . . . but sheerly in accordance with the factual material responsibility imposed by his calling, and not as a result of any discrete personal relationship.

It is ironic that the sensitive intellectual who seeks spontaneity and richness denied him by the cold and ungratifying outer world by turning to inner experiences which are drug-induced, that sensitive man who renounces "the slave goals" of success and status which are part of an "inhuman bureaucracy," can in fact become the epitome of that dehumanization in his worldly interactions. Not all who use LSD repeatedly would so evolve, of course. That some will is the inevitable consequence of the massive effects of having lived in that world too long, of taking a drug which reduces "with" behavior and which leads to the association with social groups which, as they espouse "playing the game," not only reflect the awareness of a need to compromise and a desire to turn inward, but which represent the triumph of alienation in their own motifs. The existentialists are concerned about commitment, about "being." So too are many LSD users—and their peers. LSD helps the user to feel more intense and alive, but whether or not it allows him "being" in the existential sense remains an open question. If commitment to private experience is sufficient, it does. If commitment must be as a human being with other human beings, that is, if the axis of reality also runs through shared experiences, if *being* alone is not sufficient and requires also *being together,* then one must wonder if LSD will provide lasting fulfillment.

The alienated man will be divorced from it all, a perfectly rational man acting impersonally in an automatic system. In that sense the euphoria produced by LSD and maintained, in regular users, by frequent use of mind-altering substances, is completely compatible with the evolution of an alienated society. The LSD user responds to alienation initially with despair, but then he makes an adjustment which is reportedly very satisfying, but which serves further to alienate him from that society and his own feelings about that society. The LSD rejector, on the other hand, suffering too, but in all fairness perhaps not so sensitively as the LSD user, is willing to continue to suffer rather than to abandon his emotional investment in the world. Lest the drug rejector's position be overly glorified, let it be made clear that he needs some escapes, palliatives, and restoratives too, and may very well guzzle alcohol, overeat, take sleeping pills, chew aspirin, use tranquilizers, or find his brand of ecstasy in a modified form of the "imperial madness" by becoming—as some most certainly do—drunk on power. . . .

That there is a need for the drug movement is demonstrated by its emergence, granting the premises of functionalism. For the intellectuals from whose ranks the movement draws its recruits, perhaps the world does require a new mythology. Murray describes the current state of affairs in which there is

> the senescence of the traditional religions and their present in-capacity . . . to bring forth a new vision of a better world, to generate widespread passionate belief in their own doctrines, or in all sincerity, to guide individual self-development and conduct in the light of an acceptable ideal.

In the world of today, writes Murray, there is "the spread of existential anxiety, affectlessness, meaninglessness, spiritual loneliness, hollowness, alienation and regressive emotional drift." Given these curses of our time, no wonder Murray concludes that the world needs some new mythology, "radical and revolutionary."

The drug movement is an expression of that need. It is a dream, an idea; its converts, like all those aflame with their own convictions, have charisma. That is why the observer is so often drawn to convinced LSD users, for they *are* alive, and the observer must sense the strength of their convictions. It *is* contagious. For those who subsist on the jejune diet of social accommodation, Protestant rigor, and reason, the charisma emanating from ones who have conviction evokes a psychic tropism. The movement promises much—a return to paradise, a Utopia of the inner life—and so LSD-25 becomes, if one may be allowed a neologism, a "Utopiate."

Whether the movement fulfills its promise or whether it falters because of some insufficiency in its mythology, some undesirable side effects in its means, or the intensity of its worldly opposition, the need for *something* will be no less strong. It is this need which must be kept in mind. Whatever happens to the drug movement as such, drugs will continue to be used to alter states of consciousness. To the extent that ordinary consciousness remains in a state of reactive despair to the world of reality—or is empty of that experience which mind senses as its own potential—people will join together to seek new meanings in some mythology.

CELEBRATING WITH DR. LEARY

Diana Trilling

> *Reverberations of the psychedelic movement are felt not*
> *only, as one might have thought, in psychology laboratories,*
> *but also in seminaries, symposia occupied with the problems*
> *of epistemology and ethics, art galleries, discotheques, and*
> *even lower Manhattan's Village Barn where, for a time, one*
> *might have attended "The Death of the Mind" presented by*
> *the League for Spiritual Democracy and starring Timothy*
> *Leary. If unwelcome at Harvard, Dr. Leary is cordially re-*
> *ceived in Greenwich Village. Impressions of his performance*
> *are recorded in the following selection by an able essayist,*
> *Diana Trilling. They afford at least as good an insight into*
> *the psychedelic movement as a scientific treatise.*
>
> *Mrs. Trilling is an editor, a literary critic, and an author*
> *who frequently writes on sociological and political topics. She*
> *has been fiction critic for* The Nation, *a columnist for the*
> New Leader, *and has contributed to leading magazines and*
> *newspapers. A collection of her writings has appeared under*
> *the title* Claremont Essays *(1964).*

Although we had been told on what was presumably sound authority that the previous Tuesday evening, the opening night of Dr. Leary's scheduled series of Psychedelic Celebrations, the audience had been "tough" and that therefore on our evening too we must expect some element of danger, or at least unpleasantness, actually it would be hard to imagine a milder scene than awaited us at the Village Barn, the small theatre in Greenwich Village to which Dr. Leary's show had suddenly moved from the Village Theatre where it had originally been booked. . . . There had been confusion about the arrangements because of the change of theatre, so that we arrived almost an hour before the announced curtain time. But the entrance to the Barn was already jammed—no fewer than two hundred people, probably closer to three hundred, were waiting for admission and as time went on the crowd became so dense that it blocked traffic through the street. But the conduct of Dr. Leary's audience was exemplary. There was no sign of impatience about the possibility of not getting seats; no one pushed or showed any of the usual impulse to assert

---

From *Encounter* (June 1967), pp. 36–46. Reprinted by permission of the author.

territorial claims. On the other hand I should scarcely describe it as a friendly gathering, and this despite the fact that most of Dr. Leary's audience was of much the same age—under thirty—and of roughly the same situation in life: middle-class dissident, above the average in education.

It was not a crowd that talked or laughed; I saw no exchange of greetings, it was even difficult to particularise couples. The group seemed to be made up of strangely isolate young people who, if they were acquainted with each other, were not concerned to further the connection. The general atmosphere was nevertheless one of virtually palpable benevolence. If one can speak of the face of a gathering, this was the face of an entire, an almost programmatic, good-will and peaceableness—it reminded me of the mandatory calm of recent converts to Christian Science. At first I was surprised by this prevalence of benignity in young people many of whom might be assumed to be in some degree involved in the subversive world of drug-taking and who, at any rate, were all of them dressed in the rather violent contemporary uniforms of dissent, either harshly black or, at the other extreme, colourful in refusal of middle-class conformities of dress—until I reminded myself that, after all, there lies at the heart of the LSD movement as of most contemporary movements of youthful protest the conviction that it is those who accept, or at least accommodate themselves to, the values of Western society who have lost the knowledge of peace and kindliness. Then, too, LSD would seem to have a gentling effect on the personality. I have observed this curious transformation in all the young people I know who have taken the drug; even after only one or two trips they attain a sort of supra-humanity, as if they had been purged of mortal error; and as far as I can make out, this change persists. But one must be cautious with conclusions drawn only from personal observation. In our present highly-deficient state of scientific understanding of LSD, we know with certainty only that its power to work alterations on the brain is enormous: it is 5,000 times more powerful than mescaline. But the precise nature of the changes it makes and how far they extend or how long they last we do not know—which is of course why those who use it or who for whatever reason do not wish to oppose its use can persuade themselves that all warning of its danger is without scientific foundation. . . .

Is it perhaps straining for consistency that I found in Dr. Leary's prose, written or spoken, a character not unlike that of his audience—the same imperviousness achieved at an equal cost in substantive actuality? For instance, a placard was posted in the lobby to explain the last-minute switch of Dr. Leary's show from the Village Theatre to the Village Barn. Later I copied it out:

> With regard to Dr. Leary's Psychedelic Celebration at the Village Theatre: It is with regret that Dr. Leary has discovered inequities and is experiencing financial problems with the theatre. Therefore

he is forced to announce that he will no longer appear at the
Village Theatre. Instead, Dr. Leary will conduct a psychedelic
religious celebration tonight at the Village Barn at 9:00. There
will be no admission charge.

Prose like this, at once so plain and "elegant," colloquial and fine,
commonplace and yet formal, almost legalistic, is compounded of entirely
familiar elements of communication. Certainly it has no shock value. But
when we examine it we see that although it is offered in explanation, it
explains nothing; it merely seduces one into the belief that one has been
addressed with a familiar cogency. And so with Dr. Leary's spoken
language. It creates the illusion of coherence, it seems to proceed reasonably enough; it is only when one applies oneself to it that it eludes the
grasp. Dr. Leary's impossible plausibility would not seem, however, to be
consciously contrived, and in this his verbal style differs from that of more
orthodox evangelists. Dr. Leary is nothing if not sincere; his language
could not be less ornate or theatrical. In fact, it is precisely from its
naturalness and sincerity that its hallucinatory quality derives. . . .

    But, more, what particularly struck me when I came back to Dr.
Leary's notice in the lobby after I had become better acquainted with his
mode of discourse was its premise of innocence. It is of course its innocence that constitutes a chief appeal of Dr. Leary's doctrine to the
privileged young who, perhaps because they are the offspring of a parent-
generation intent on keeping no knowledge from them, now regard their
elders as uniquely impure in motive and behaviour. If the audience at the
Village Barn was a fair sampling, and I think it was, Dr. Leary's followers
are certainly not to be associated with any ordinary image we may have of
juvenile delinquency. The class difference, involving as it does not only
differences in education but in social assumption, significantly separates the
users of LSD from the young world of street gangs and violence. The LSD
phenomenon therefore represents a quite separate social problem located, I
think, at that special place in society where cultural influences tend to
supplant the better-understood social pressures.

    Still, nothing I learned in my evening with Dr. Leary proposed the
idea that because his young followers make so urgent an option for virtue
and purity of motive, they have any special endowment of native goodness,
or even any notable sensitivity to ugliness, or inability to sustain it. As to
the first, there is no ground for the belief that behind their benevolence
there do not lie the usual human angers and aggressions. As to the second,
in the course of my evening at the Barn I came to suspect that if we are
going to stay with the "frightened generation" explanation of the LSD
phenomenon we need to be precise about what we mean. Far from suggesting any extreme vulnerability to the terrors of life, these young people
seemed to me to be unduly armoured—and if this is because LSD has
reduced their moral alertness, then we must regard the drug as perhaps

more dehumanising than we have yet recognised. My point could not be simpler: at the most alarming moments of the evening, when Dr. Leary announced that he knew no child over the age of seven who was not on drugs, or when his coadjutor, Dr. Alpert, in response to a question about 16-, 17-, or 18-year-olds on LSD, said, "Even if they end up in a hospital or prison for a few months, it doesn't bother me," there was no slightest sign of dismay in their audience. Fearful these young people may be, like the rest of us; they have a fearsome world in which to be young. But fear can show itself in a number of ways, and defines character only by the form it takes and the ends it is made to serve. To express concern for the children of Viet Nam and yet remain unmoved by the idea of submitting 7-year-olds to hallucinogenic drugs is surely to obey the dictates of culture rather than of reliable feeling.

Dr. Leary and Dr. Alpert have both been university teachers, teaching psychologists. I daresay my own response to statements as cruelly irresponsible as these—they were casual remarks, really, spoken with an entire ease—is underscored by the importance I assign, the special importance, to their former profession. In a society as mobile as that of America, the school is more than an institution for teaching the intellectual disciplines, it is the matrix of our ongoing culture, the chief source and guardian of our personal and social morality. What the school establishes today, the home will have absorbed by tomorrow—most of the precepts of our post-Freudian family culture were first formulated in our teacher-training programmes. But the problem is that it is exactly because America is so open-ended that youth is valued as it is, beyond its possible emotional and social capacities. And this means that the teacher whose task it is to instruct the young in the complexity of the conditions on which the continuing life of society depends and in the limitations imposed upon the individual by emotional and social reality must himself be able to resist the seductions of rebelliousness for its own youthful sake—which seems to be a difficult demand to make today of anyone of radical spirit and imagination. No one in American public life, certainly no one in government, has the ear of the young like their university instructors, unless it is the advanced social and literary critics, and these are often the same persons, so that if—as now is increasingly happening—the teacher is reluctant to surrender the glamour of youthful rebelliousness and to discover its own grave satisfaction in the exercise of the parental role, he leaves his students in the position of children who have been robbed of the definition they can only achieve when those who train them, and whom they naturally rebel against, have a firm authority of their own; they face emptiness, a world without boundaries. I am not suggesting that the tide of nihilism in which the young appear to be more and more caught up takes its sole or primary force from the school, but only that if anything is to be done to stem it, the salvage will have to be undertaken by the same class of people who did such a successful job of bringing the failure of modern culture to our educated consciousness. Dr. Leary was dismissed, as Dr. Alpert was too, from his Harvard post for engaging his students in his experiments with drugs, but I doubt he would have reached the young as he has were it not for his earlier professional certification.

But, at our evening in the Barn, Dr. Leary was not resting with his pedagogic function. He also made it a religious occasion, and thus drew on the shared fund of recollected church-going his audience, even his young audience, might be supposed to have brought to his celebration. (We keep it in mind, however, that Dr. Leary is under indictment for illegal possession of drugs and if he is to plead freedom of religion under the First Amendment, he does well to put public emphasis on his religious convictions.) His show our night was called "The Incarnation of Christ"; he also does an "Illumination of the Buddha." The ceremonies had been advertised on the theatre rather than the religious pages of the papers, with Dr. Leary "IN PERSON" as the leading attraction. His religious purpose was nevertheless kept dominant. In addition to the film-and-dance portion of the programme, itself ritualistic, there was a sermon, there were prayers by Dr. Leary, and even a moment of silent prayer on the part of the "congregation." Early in the performance Dr. Leary reminded us that while we were gathered here in New York for our religious ceremonies our opposite numbers in India were enjoying the religious ecstasy on the shores of the Ganges, and our opposite numbers in Mexico attaining their exaltation with peyote. Of ecstasy and exaltation there might actually be none, either in Dr. Leary's programme or his audience, but unmistakably a spirit of devoutness permeated the auditorium. The religious emotions of Dr. Leary seemed, however, to be considerably interfered with by the strains and temptations of showmanship. And he was very tired, one saw his fatigue from the start, as soon as he took his place on the platform in the darkened hall; he might have been managing a hangover. This was a weary impresario and performer, a weary pedagogue, a weary Messiah—the multiplication and confusion of roles that Dr. Leary now assumes are his burden as the leader of a movement which even he could not have guessed would grow so fast.

We had been shown to our seats at a Press table; amusingly, not unexpectedly, a disproportionate space in this small auditorium had been set aside for those Dr. Leary might hope would give his movement still more of the publicity it has already had in such abundance. Although it was legitimate enough that we should present ourselves as members of the Press, at least for me even this means we had used to procure seats added to the self-consciousness I had felt ever since I had arrived at the hall. It is always uncomfortable to sightsee in other people's emotional universe; and after all it had come only as an afterthought, when we were already seated, that I might some time want to write about the occasion and should therefore take notes. Some days later I was to read a review of our evening in the *New York Times,* by a reporter who apparently spotted us for the tourists we were. She got us by name and described us as "initiates of the older cults of politics and psychoanalysis." We were likened—and this is uncommonly vivid reporting for the *Times*—to "atheists attending a religious ritual out of sociological interest . . . our expressions faintly tinged with boredom and distaste." Well, the sociological posture was unquestionably readiest to hand, but I am afraid I was unprotected by scientific distance from the objects of my study. I looked around the theatre at this strangely subdued and isolate audience, and I was painfully aware of the chasm that stretched between the world of these young people and my own at the same age, of the difference between this dedication of theirs and the political dedication of the Marxist '30s in which I had come to maturity. We too, at their age, had pointed to the violence of those in power. My contemporaries, too, had set themselves to make a revolution in consciousness, which would make us "free." But our means had been social and political, and now the very concept of society was inoperative. But if ours had been an ideology of social involvement, not of withdrawal, this could now be no boast—it had led to a blockage of hope which could perhaps never be, certainly had not been, surmounted by a succeeding generation. And for us there had been no atomic bomb. And there had been no such limitlessness in our world, no such vacuum as now passes for the social and personal structure of life. It was not necessary to find any particular emotional vulnerability or even feelingness in Dr. Leary's followers to recognise that they had sufficient ground for confusion and despair, a good bit more even than we had had when we rejected our society as given.

The unease of my situation was much relieved as soon as Allen Ginsberg came to sit at my side, and this is surely not the least interesting aspect of the evening, that by some marvellous transmutation of things as we think them to be, the fact that Ginsberg sat next to me throughout most of the performance was more than a comfort, it provided my chief link with sanity. We had seen him entering the hall and had waved. He had come over to say hello and just then the performance began. To avoid disturbance, Ginsberg sat down at my side. His beard was by far the most lavish in this well-bearded audience; were it still not a blackest black, he should be called the good grey poet of the psychedelic movement, such is his air of venerableness and wisdom, such the authority with which he now seems vested. . . . It was very little later that Dr. Leary mentioned, in all mildness, the presence in the hall of agents from the Narcotics Squad; for a bad instant, as I looked around me and saw no one who met the description, I supposed it might be the four of us Dr. Leary was referring to—except, of course, we had Allen Ginsberg to vouch for us, he was our security in this alien territory. Throughout the ceremonies, speaking in a low steady voice, precise, in firm pedagogic control of knowledge it pleased

him to share, this former student of my husband's gave me the assurance I
needed of my own identity, unchallenged, in no subtlest degree suborned.
The adroitness with which Ginsberg made his aesthetic and critical removal
from what was going on onstage while keeping intact his old ties of
theoretical and even practical approval of the drug-taking enterprise was
something of a triumph. Everything about him indeed, his weight of
purpose no less than his canniness, freshly pressed upon me the importance, in the psychedelic universe as elsewhere, of the wish for fame and
immortality, that most traditional impulse of the gifted. For what is it,
finally, other than the force of this desire, that has sustained Ginsberg,
regulated the degree of his involvement in dangerous personal experiment,
urged him beyond the anonymousness implicit in the pursuit of selfhood
through drugs.

Is Dr. Leary, as well, an exception to the harsh rule of self-eradica-
tion in drugs? I doubt it. Certainly drug-promotion is now giving Dr. Leary
a rare celebrity. And by the evidence of these religious ceremonies he
courts immortality in the largest possible way by identification with
immortal principles and personages. . . . as the evening wore on,
with Dr. Leary up there on the platform and Allen Ginsberg at my side, I
had the sense of a certain entertaining ambiguity in the relation of these
two psychedelic figures. At least before friends like ourselves from an
earlier period in his career Ginsberg seemed to me to make a point of his
poetic pride, of his superiority to the leader, even of his superior scholarship, but I may have misread him. At any rate, in the course of the
ceremonies, he several times alluded to the need for humour in dealing with
the LSD subject. For the poverty of Dr. Leary's show as art he was carefully and courteously apologetic.

There was, first, the darkening of the hall and Dr. Leary's entrance
into the spotlight, behind him a white and still-empty screen. From the
wings of this makeshift theatre came the soft strumming of a guitar, and
immediately the audience was churchy-still—except that the comparison is
absurd: church is where people cough and rustle and squirm and there was
no coughing or rustling or squirming in the Barn, unless on the part of four
unlicensed sociologists. Through the next two hours (I guess the show
lasted) Dr. Leary had his audience in entire control; he could be envied by
the professionals.

With his opening remarks Dr. Leary effectively formulated, if one
can put it so, the incoherence through which I would try to grope for the
remainder of the evening. I have a friend who shares his apartment with a
painter; one day my friend's mother (this is a Jewish story) came to see
him, examined the paintings on his walls and turned to her son with the
question, "Who authorised these pictures?" It was the question I would
have put to Dr. Leary: Who, or what, had authorised this particular
conglomerate of pageant, preachment, classroom, revival meeting, dance,

movie, and off-Broadway amateur night? Where had this performance come from, what was the source of its inspiration? How much was it the psychedelic experience itself that was being reproduced for us, how much an "artistic" derivation? How much was Dr. Leary improvising a gospel, and how much was he bearing witness to the accepted doctrine? Where did the play end and pedagogy begin, where did pedagogy end and the play begin? Had Dr. Leary and his co-performers recently taken LSD and was the drug thus so-to-speak present in the talk that accompanied the film, or had there been at least the intention of artistic detachment from the actual drugged state? It was reported of the movie, *Flaming Creatures,* whether accurately or not I have no way of knowing, that its actors were all of them under drugs when it was made; this one could credit from the loose automatism of their movements and their dispersed sexuality. Dr. Leary's film and the sporadic miming that took place in front of the screen and the words Dr. Leary himself spoke and those that were intoned antiphonally by the male pantomimist and a woman at the side of the stage were certainly all of them sufficiently lifeless to suggest some similar interference with normal process. Still, I realise that an actor has to be highly skilled to simulate nature unimpeded by human awkwardness. What looked like blocked transmission in Dr. Leary's show may simply have been amateurishness. "You have to go out of your mind to come to your senses." "We don't pray to anyone up there but to what is inside ourselves." Even announcing his best-shaped slogans, Dr. Leary himself, and despite his naturalness and sincerity, failed to take significant shape except in a form already made iconographic by nightclub and television "personalities." The essential quality he conveyed was that of a schoolmaster acting the master of ceremonies in a school show—a good-looking, tired, essentially vulgar, still-boyish teacher, histrionic, equally pleased with his popularity with his students and with the privileges of office which he could exercise as occasion demanded.

He stayed in the spotlight, quite alone, for rather a while. I had no sense it was too long for his audience. His lecture-preachment-patter covered a general territory already well known from repeated accounts of the doctrine. What one had not been sufficiently prepared for was the vagrancy of Dr. Leary's thought, its bold (however tired), bald carelessness of the ordinary rules of reasonableness, of intelligible discourse. For the occasion of ceremony everything was spoken with the cadence of ceremony, something between a croon and a subdued exhortation. *We pray we are not hung up and that you will have a good trip* (did he mean in our next LSD session, or only metaphorically, here in the theatre?). . . . *The voyage is always the same* (did he mean reliable, or was he remarking the singleness of the indicated path?). . . . *We re-new and re-enact the ancient myths* (this could refer to the play, but it could also refer to the sacred journey to which we were being urged). . . . *We pass on what we* (an editorialized Dr. Leary, psychologist?) *have learned in ten years of hard work. . . . We* (Dr. Leary and his audience? Dr. Leary and others under the influence of LSD?) *meet in our retinas, we meet on the screen in the vibrating beams of light, also we meet in the liquid canals of the ear; then we move within to resurrect the body, rediscover the timepiece of the universe: the heartbeat. . . . Then we breathe together. . . . You should not take a trip without a road map. . . . Myths are cellular. . . . The myth is a blueprint. . . . Tonight we invite you to re-live the myth of Jesus Christ. . . . The resurrection of Jesus Christ has been a rough trip for all of us* (Dr. Leary and his co-authors? All of us in the 20th century who are the inheritors of the Christian tradition?). . . .

First we ran into Christian backlash, second the backlash from Jews and atheists. . . . The Christian myth means, once there was a man who took all the guilts, the shoulds and shouldn'ts, on his own shoulders and wiped them out. If you experience this myth* (before you take the drug? afterwards) *you are free. . . . Go back and free the world from good and evil. . . . The tolling of the bell at Millbrook* (here the clanging of a loud bell presumably took us to Dr. Leary's "institute") *takes us on a voyage of discovery. You have to have a guide in the person who has been there before you: an old witch or a frog or a hunchback. Today, your teen-age child. . . . They have the key to the voyage and it always involves a chemical tick.* (Trick?) *This is the Chalice, the Holy Communion, and always the Last Supper: good-bye to all back there. . . . I welcome you in the name of the Father, the Son and the Holy Ghost. . . . Give thanks as we take the Chalice and let our thanks ascend. Drink. This is my flesh, bone and blood. . . . As often as you do this, do this in memory of me.*

Lights had now begun to flash on the screen and Dr. Leary moved to the side of the stage. His voice rose in intensity. *Open the naked eye, find the centre!* Great circles of light appear on the screen, and the show complicates itself:

GIRL'S VOICE: *Can you float through the universe of your body and not lose your way?*

No one directly answers the question. Mushroom-like patterns form on the screen. In front of the screen a man in black trousers, bare above the waist, sways slowly, it would seem painfully, his arms weaving and reaching in the familiar dance-idiom of tortured quest.

GIRL'S VOICE: *What is happening?*

DR. LEARY: *Float to the centre.*

MAN'S VOICE: *I am drowning in blood. . . . Help. . . . Please make it stop. . . . No, no, don't make it stop.*

GIRL'S VOICE: *Blood to death. . . . Out. . . . Out. . . . Blood to death. . . . Life. . . . Life. . . . Life. . . . Scarlet. . . .*

MAN'S VOICE: *So warm. . . . Drifting down. . . . Melting. . . . Breathing. . . . Breath of life. . . .*

Here my notes indicate a certain amount of groaning on the stage but not who is the sufferer. Unfortunately, I have no shorthand. But if at first I am troubled by my inability to catch every word being spoken on the stage, soon enough as I catch the drift I realise that the drift is all. It is said of LSD that it taps the unconscious in order to add to the store of the conscious; this is indeed its principal and much-vaunted value, that it is supposed to augment consciousness. But surely to call the LSD experience consciousness-enhancing is to merge two meanings of the word "consciousness"—that which we oppose to *un*consciousness and by which we mean those activities of the mind which we can take note of as they proceed, and, second, the honorific meaning, that of active and useful awareness. If one is to judge the LSD state by Dr. Leary's representation or adumbration of it in his ceremonies or by anything one has so far read of it, what happens under LSD may very well be a flooding of the mind with images or emotions from which it is otherwise closed off. But what the mind does with this new material speaks not at all of a significantly enhanced mental activity such as we usually adduce in our appreciation of awareness. The problem is, of course, an old one in aesthetics. It is not without interest that the new Coleridge scholarship demonstrates with some persuasiveness that "Kubla Khan" was not actually an opium dream and that Coleridge offered it as such only in polemic, as a defence of the role of nonreason in the writing of poetry. But it is not solely an aesthetic problem, it is also a scientific problem and a vexing one: how define what we mean by consciousness, especially in the creative process?

The dialogue between male and female voice now peters out and Dr. Leary relinquishes the spotlight so that the full attention of the audience can be focused on the screen. The pictures that appear look to me like magnified blood cells or other organic matter. Then gradually they become more complex, "social," sometimes fleetingly identifiable. Also, the background music now rises in volume, becomes more assertive—Ginsberg whispers to me, "The *Missa Luba,* a Congo version of the Catholic Mass," and obediently I hear what could perhaps be the *Kyrie Eleison;* he whispers "Verdi's *Requiem"* and, more reluctantly, I hear that as well. Without my having quite noted, the guitar has eliminated itself, been replaced by a sound-track to accompany what is apparently intended as a representation, or evocation, of the evolutionary process, a kind of psychedelic March of Time. Ginsberg mentions a word that sounds like *Straboscopia,* which I take to derive from the same root as *Strabismus: "Med.* A disorder of the eye in which the optic axes cannot be directed to the same object because of incoordination of the muscles of the eyeballs. . . ." In later dictionary consultation I realise he said *Stroboscopic,* pertaining to "an instrument for observing the successive phases of a periodic motion by means of light periodically interrupted." But the difference is only objective. The camera's wish to catch the speed of psychedelic imagery affects me like a sickness of the eye. From my Press table I no longer see Dr. Leary. I assume he is seated stage right. His voice resumes the incantation:

Let's return to the 20th century and reincarnate Jesus Christ. Let's do it everyone of us right now. . . . You have to take on all the guilt, sin and wretchedness of the world. . . . You have to do this for everyone so that there won't be any more. . . . Then we're all through with the good-evil thing and you will be reborn. . . . All-embracing, Dr. Leary invites the police and the narcotics agents to join in the rebirth, and for the first and only time in the evening his audience is vocally responsive. "You're right," come several voices from the audience, soft, devout.

My notes do not say if Dr. Leary is now once more stage centre, in full spotlight, but I recollect him to be. The film has now run its spotty course, from our unicellular origins to our modern metropolitan medi-ocrity, and we can have the sermon. Certainly it is in fullest stage centre that Dr. Leary makes his biggest pitch of the evening, inviting someone to come up from the audience on to the platform, take off his clothes and be nailed to the cross. *Let's look in the bag. There are some nails here and a crown of thorns.* The audience remains unmoving. Dr. Leary is apparently not surprised, he had expected no volunteers; one wonders, in fact, what he would do if a too-eager listener profferred his services. He repeats: *Will anyone volunteer to be nailed to the cross if we guarantee you there will be no more evil in the world?* He dissipates the reverential hush, or at least lifts it a fraction, with a prepared comment: Dr. Leary confides to us that he had been warned that if he made such a proposal in this setting, "four hundred and ninety-seven exhibitionists, sado-masochists and faggots would storm the platform." There is no laughter. *No, we must not do it that way, we must do it with our clothes on, or even our uniforms. . . . But let's do it.*

There follows the more formal sermon, wholly Dr. Leary's own show and, like all sermons, lengthy. Its text, Dr. Leary announces, is from William Blake *who had been in our profession a couple of hundred years ago* (sic). *. . . He who is a fool persists in his folly* (sic). *. . .* We must start a new religion, says Dr. Leary, and start a new country. *We have been working six years*—it had been ten, I recall, a few minutes back—*to work out a plan to turn on this country and this planet. . . . Starting a new religion is like starting a new business. Or a garden. There are inevitable sequences. . . . A series of ordeals or tests. . . . We have no paranoia or hostility about our opposition, it's a rough business starting a new religion. It's a rough business but highly-stylised, more classic than baseball or football. . . . We must turn on, tune in, and drop out. . . . Turn off your mind and go within. . . . You need a sacrament and today it is a chemical. The chemicals we use are ancient. . . . Treat these sacraments with the respect they deserve. Before you turn on you must be in a state of grace. You must look into yourself and see where you have sinned. On*

*your own chessboard. You are the only one who can forgive yourself. You
look in your mirror, in your retina is the history. You confess to yourself.
If you don't go to confession before you take a sacrament you may writhe,
suffer, call for a doctor. . . . Once you turn on, then you tune in, show
others what has been shown to you.* Dr. Leary calls on Rudi and Jackie,
assistants, to come forward and testify. They have apparently helped to put
the show together, now they will help us tune in.

DR. LEARY: *Rudi, where are we now and where are we going?*

RUDI (thinking): *We are working from a core which is a circle of
love. A very beautiful and pure thing.*

DR. LEARY: *Jackie, where are we?*

JACKIE (who is a girl): *We are here and happy to be here. And we
are going from here out, to turn on the world.*

DR. LEARY: *We have to work with the young, the artists, the
underground groups for a new breakthrough. Artists change consciousness
and the change lasts. . . . We work to change family life. . . . Encourage
husbands and wives to take LSD together. . . . I can't imagine a husband
being turned on without wanting to turn on his wife. I can't imagine parents
being turned on without wanting to turn on their children. I know no child
over the age of seven who hasn't been given drugs and I know many of
them. The parents turn on the children.*

Dr. Leary has a practised device of irony. He echoes his outrages
of decency in the voice of outraged respectability:

Imagine turning on children!

There is a pregnant pause, and Dr. Leary recapitulates:

*The psychedelic experience is one you want to share with those
you care most about. . . . Inconceivable that parents would take LSD and
not want their children to share the experience.*

The audience continues to be dead still: no one stamps, hisses,
rises to object. No one leaves the theatre. (And no reporter, to my knowledge, undertakes to report what we all of us at Dr. Leary's Press tables so
clearly heard.) From this point forward, the rest of Dr. Leary's sermon is
bound to be anti-climax:

*We are now in a legal and political phase. . . . Several million
Americans are taking LSD, more taking marijuana, for serious purposes.
. . . They need an institution. . . . We are working with the courts to
license small groups to take LSD. . . . After you tune in you drop out. It
happens so gracefully. . . . A detachment from old ambitions and drives.
. . . What we meet and work for is what you want and know is possible.
. . . We need and invite your comments and questions.*

The comments and questions that comprise the remainder of the programme may be what Dr. Leary invites, they cannot be what he needs. But then, what speaker ever gets the questions he needs, and these were at least intended neither to provoke nor challenge. Dr. Leary fares better than most public speakers when they finish a talk and discover to whom they have been speaking and what they are thought to have said. A man rises from the audience to say that he has confronted the beast: Is this what Dr. Leary meant by confrontation with the wolf? Myself, I had heard no mention of wolves, singular or plural. I wonder if the questioner has in mind the beast one confronts in the mirror when one confesses to oneself, or merely an encounter on the psychedelic journey. Dr. Leary is perhaps himself confused. At any rate, he chooses this moment to call to the stage "his well-known colleague" Dr. Richard Alpert, recently returned from California. Together, Dr. Leary and Dr. Alpert respond to the question that has been asked by explaining the uterine recapitulation of man's long slow evolution. *Memory cards flash through your brain when you take LSD, so it doesn't fit your tidy 20th-century mind.* I conclude from this that when you take LSD you return to the womb and re-live the pre-natal development.

The second questioner is a priest; he is recognised by Dr. Leary and Dr. Alpert as a friend. The priest wants to know whether after many trips you could not have the same experience without taking the drug. It is Dr. Alpert who undertakes to reply: *After a trip you get depressed by your new sense of your daily life. After enough of this, you stay high all the time because you have revised your life. . . . LSD is not a substitute for the conscious effort of digging here and now. . . . LSD is a constant reminder of our divinity. We mustn't stop because we are too busy. . . . Find someone not on LSD and find out how he and I are us.* This is the point at which I recall, with a certain syntactical confusion, the priest in Ilf and Petrov's wonderful *The Little Golden Calf* of whom the verb "befuddle" is used as an active verb of expression: "Yes," befuddled the priest—"No," befuddled the priest. But of course this was in another country. . . . The priest sits down; he is apparently satisfied with the answer that has been given him.

And now the master of ceremonies introduces Allen Ginsberg from the audience, calls him to the stage. Ginsberg rises modestly but readily—had he been forewarned?—to join the circle on the platform. While he is threading his way through the audience, Dr. Leary intersperses some remarks on electrons, heightens the scientific authority of the occasion. He also addresses himself to the subject of people killing themselves under the effects of LSD: the percentage is negligible, he assures us, and anyway these are the people who failed to go to confession and expunge their guilts. Dr. Leary gives the nod to the next questioner.

This time the question, although manifestly not intended to give offence, does suggest criticism; it is carefully larded with apology. It seems that although the questioner himself understands the moral nature of the LSD enterprise, there are people of his acquaintance who take the drug just for kicks. Would Dr. Leary comment on this? From the other side of the theatre, I have no trouble hearing the question. But Dr. Leary seems to have difficulty; he turns to his coadjutors in appeal but meeting no help he invites his interrogator to the stage. But on his way, this young man is checked by another member of the audience who rises to protest that such a question can only come from someone caught "in the game"—which is to say, someone under the influence of this-worldly, non-psychedelic, values. A moment of tension develops between the two men at the foot of the platform—it represents something of a relief amidst all this benignity—and then Allen Ginsberg intervenes: *You're taking it too seriously, keep some humour.* The questioner addresses the stage in self-defence: *But I want a successful revolution.* To which Leary responds soothingly: *Tell us why, how are we sliding back from the centre?* The questioner identifies himself as an instructor in a college in South Jersey. Grievingly he explains that some of his students fail to understand the moral purpose of LSD, they take it for the sensation, they are not *serious*. (He hits the word as I have not heard a word hit since the days when the comrades would accuse each other of being *subjective*.) *And I want you to win, I want a revolution like you do.* The troubled comrade from South Jersey is at last disposed of by Dr. Alpert, judiciously: *It doesn't matter from what motive these kids of 16, 17, or 18 take LSD, if they turn on for 30 seconds the experience is so profound. Even if they end up in a hospital or prison for a few months, it doesn't bother me. . . . The confusion is the greatest kind of confusion for these kids, at any age. It opens the door and makes a mensch of them.* The audience is relieved and ready for the catharsis of humour after such unblessed controversy.

The necessary humorous relief is supplied by a Negro, a solid and comely man who rises at the rear of the hall and announces in a big resonant voice that he has only a single question to ask: *What is LSD?* Although he has produced through the hall the only titter of the evening, he meets a wall of impenetrable silence on the stage. The questioner repeats his question, once, twice, a third time. He becomes insistent: *I'm just asking a single question. I hear you all talking about LSD. What I want to know is, what is LSD?* After what seems forever—the audience is becoming restive—someone onstage has the presence of mind to answer firmly: *It is a chemical.* And the subject is closed; the questioner sits down. Dr. Leary makes a few remarks about his LEAGUE FOR SPIRITUAL DIS-COVERY, much in the spirit of a preacher before the plate is passed; no plate is passed, the evening has been an expense to no one. *We in the League are working, at risk, to legalise marijuana and LSD. . . . It is an intimate family thing we're doin.* Allen Ginsberg steps forward and announces an anti-war rally on the following Saturday—no, not an anti-war rally, a "peaceable march, a transcendence over anger." The meeting is at an end.

There is again no elbowing or pressing as the crowd begins to leave the hall. Now, as not before the performance started, I begin to see couples, pairs of boys and girls holding hands, much as married couples leave funerals or weddings with clasped hands, bound in the intimacy of shared deep emotion. (Dr. Leary, incidentally, could not be more pious than he is about coupling: approaching the sexual subject, he speaks only of "making love to your wife.") It also becomes possible, here and there, to particularise other sightseers among the dedicated: the sloweddown man in his late thirties who wears the mark of yearning, of loneliness, of the failed artist; the dykish, tight-lipped girl who belongs at the side of the swimming-pool of a women's *"Y"*; the bookkeeper, as I am certain, who stands out in the crowd for her excruciating neatness and spinsterishness no less than for her advanced years—it is she whom I overhear greeting an acquaintance: "What did you think of it? Weren't you *impressed?"* These are the wanderers between worlds.

But for the most part the audience is as one had first perceived it: young, Village but middle-class, good contemporary faces of the kind one wants to trust, the faces of people to whom intellectual leadership might be thought appropriate, except that they had made another choice and the signal of it is in their eyes. The four of us appeal to each other: Is it only the gifted who go in for this sort of thing? Are these the best, the brightest, of their generation? We of course haven't the answer, any more than we have the answer to a corollary question, How can any enlightened person of whatever age take this psychedelic leader with intellectual seriousness, assent in an ideology so barren of ideas? As we move out on to the street, away from the theatre—unregenerate, we are looking for a beer—this becomes, in fact, the nub of our anxiety. For us, Dr. Leary's religious ceremony had been ridiculous when it had not been despicable, but we had been surrounded by young people of good education who not only could take Dr. Leary's drug and this celebration of it but had also somehow managed to issue to the whole subject of LSD a safe-conduct which exempted it from rational inspection, creating—or perhaps only responding to?—an atmosphere in which whoever would put it to adverse question is automatically taken to be repressive, retrograde, lacking in imagination, deficient indeed in scientific open-mindedness.

But Dr. Leary's epiphany gave rise to perhaps even bleaker thoughts than these. In the past month I had heard of four more young people, four adolescent children of friends, who had broken down as a result of LSD—two college boys and a college girl who had had to be hospitalised, a high school boy who, on the edge of psychosis, had had to be withdrawn from school. This made, so far, seven LSD casualties within my own small circle of acquaintance. Of course, some or all of them may have been predisposed to mental breakdown. And we had no figures to tell us whether they were in any way representative of what could happen to Dr. Leary's followers. This being so, how long were we to wait for the statistics to accumulate and be got in order?

For Dr. Alpert there were surely no such anxieties. "These kids" were simply casualties of the new dispensation, eggs that had to be broken to make Dr. Leary's omelette. But I could no more shrug off this concern, retreat into "scientific" or ironic detachment, than I could muster "objectivity" to meet the destruction of the young for the sake of some new Jerusalem of the political imagination. The destruction of a person's mental powers is *actual,* like hunger, poverty, death. It happens in actual life; it entails actual anguish. No, the nub of my anxiety as I left Dr. Leary's show was not that his audience could give credence to the nonsense he spoke—clever as so many of his young followers are, they have no doubt already learned to trust the LSD tale rather than its teller—but the recognition that the direction we take from our present-day assumption that the new and dissident are good in themselves, no matter what their form, may very well lose for us the basic and ordinary knowledge of human decency, including the knowledge that the human mind, even in all its weakness and error, is valuable.

20

Escape from Alienation

Are we succumbing to a progressive malaise, or is it possible to revive a sense of belonging and, beyond this, a sense of commitment and a new spirit among those who need more than economic security and more than an endless succession of technological miracles to make them feel at home in their world? Does the latter require a redefinition of purpose in modern society and, if so, can this be accomplished within the framework of our existing values? Do the deep differences expressed throughout this volume suggest that such a redefinition of purpose is chimerical, or can we find a kind of value consensus within which difference thrives without degenerating into discord and distemper? The concluding essay in this volume is addressed to such basic questions.

TOWARD A MORE HUMAN SOCIETY

Kenneth Keniston

Dr. Keniston, a former Rhodes scholar, is professor of psychology and psychiatry at Yale. Much of his attention has been concentrated on chronicling and describing new tenden-

From *The Uncommitted* (New York: Harcourt, Brace & World, 1960), pp. 3–4, 429–447. Copyright © 1960, 1962, 1965, by Kenneth Keniston. Reprinted by permission of Harcourt, Brace & World, Inc.

cies in student life, especially the emergence of a new breed of "professionalists" whom he describes as "academically committed young men and women, who value technological, intellectual and professional competence above popularity, ambition or grace" and whom he contrasts to the "professionalists manqués" who are described in the preceding selections.

Our age inspires scant enthusiasm. In the industrial West, and increasingly now in the uncommitted nations, ardor is lacking; instead men talk of their growing distance from each other, from their social order, from their work and play, and from the values and heroes which in a perhaps romanticized past seem to have given order, meaning, and coherence to their lives. Horatio Alger is replaced by Timon, Napoleon by Ishmael, and even Lincoln now seems pallid before the defiant images of hoods and beats. Increasingly, the vocabulary of social commentary is dominated by terms that characterize the sense of growing distance between men and their former objects of affection. Alienation, estrangement, disaffection, anomie, withdrawal, disengagement, separation, noninvolvement, apathy, indifference, and neutralism—all of these terms point to a sense of loss, a growing gap between men and their social world. The drift of our time is away from connection, relation, communion, and dialogue, and our intellectual concerns reflect this conviction. Alienation, once seen as imposed *on* men by an unjust economic system, is increasingly chosen *by* men as their basic stance toward society.

These tendencies can of course be exaggerated in individual cases. As many or more men and women now lead individually decent and humane lives as ever did. There are pockets of enthusiasm in every nation. Old values are clung to the more tenaciously by some as they are disregarded by others. And the growing sense of alienation brings reactions in the form of new efforts to reconstruct commitment. But other facts are equally incontrovertible, at least in America: that there has seldom been so great a confusion about what is valid and good; that more and more men and women question what their society offers them and asks in return; that hopeful visions of the future are increasingly rare. The prevailing images of our culture are images of disintegration, decay, and despair; our highest art involves the fragmentation and distortion of traditional realities; our best drama depicts suffering, misunderstanding, and breakdown; our worthiest novels are narratives of loneliness, searching, and unfulfillment; even our best music is, by earlier standards, dissonant, discordant, and inhuman. Judged by the values of past generations, our culture seems obsessed with breakdown, splintering, disintegration, and destruction. Ours is an age not of synthesis but of analysis, not of constructive hopes but of awful destructive potentials, not of commitment but of alienation.

Thus it happens that terms like alienation gain ever wider currency, for despite all their vagueness they seem to point to something characteristic of our time. We feel this "something" in the growing belief in the inherent alienation of man from man and from the universe, in our preoccupation with the rifts, traumas, and discontinuities of psychological development, in the increasingly problematical relationship between men and their society, in our concern over national purposes and the breakdown of established values, even in our wavering faith in the progressive drift of history. And we see alienation especially clearly in American youth, poised hesitantly on the threshold of an adult world which elicits little deep commitment. Despite the achievement of many of the traditional aspirations of our society, we commonly feel a vague disappointment that goals that promised so much have somehow meant so little real improvement in the quality of human life. Whatever the gains of our technological age, whatever the decrease in objective suffering and want, whatever the increase in our "opportunities" and "freedoms," many Americans are left with an inarticulate sense of loss, of unrelatedness and lack of connection.

Thus, paradoxically, at the very moment when affluence is within our reach, we have grown discontented, confused, and aimless. The "new alienation" is a symptom and an expression of our current crisis. The individual and social roots of our modern alienation . . . are complex and interrelated; yet if there is any one crucial factor at the center of this alienation, it is the growing bankruptcy of technological values and visions. If we are to move toward a society that is less alienating, that releases rather than imprisons the energies of the dissident, that is truly worthy of dedication, devotion, idealism, and commitment, we must transcend our outworn visions of technological abundance, seeking new values beyond technology.

In the next decades of this century, Americans will be called upon to choose between three fundamentally different options concerning the future course of our society: whether to attempt to turn the clock back so as to "re-create" a bygone society in which our modern alienations did not yet exist, whether to "continue" the present triumphant march of a technological process which has created these same alienations, or whether to begin to define a new vision of a society whose values transcend technology. The first two choices would lead, I believe, to regression or stagnation; only by beginning now to articulate a vision of a society in which technology is used for truly human purposes can we create a nation of individuals, a society, that *merits* the commitment of its citizens. Yet such a redefinition of purpose has not been forthcoming, and social and political thought in America continues to be dominated by those who would have us regress to the past or those who would merely have us continue our present drift. What is it that prevents our imagining a society radically better than and different from our own?

. . . I have emphasized the inherent hostility of technology to

Utopian and visionary thinking. The fundamental assumptions of technology and science are metrical, comparative, analytic, and reductive. Technology concerns itself with instrumental questions and dismisses Utopian visions as impractical or irrelevant. Moreover, the growing pressure for ego dictatorship increasingly subordinates and suppresses the passions and idealisms from which cogent criticisms of our society and radical propositions for its reform might spring. Convinced that all Utopian thinking is impractical and self-defeating, we therefore cling to a technological empiricism that merely perpetuates the status quo. No doubt all established orders and all great ideologies resist fundamental change; but the technological society we live in is unusually well armored against attack, especially well equipped to subvert its critics, peculiarly able to discourage thinking that does not start from technological assumptions.

But beyond this, the very speed with which technology has accomplished its original goals has caught us off guard. The triumph of technology has occurred in an extraordinarily brief span of time: only one century separates our own era from the Civil War, technology triumphant from the beginning of the industrial era. Like a victorious and powerful army whose enemy unexpectedly surrenders, we now find ourselves without clear goals, mobilized for action that is no longer needed, and scarcely aware of the extent of our victory. We have been overtaken by success, surprised by triumph, caught off guard by victory. We have only begun to realize how far we have come, let alone to think of what might lie beyond.

Paradoxically, then, we live in a society in which unprecedented rates of technological change are accompanied by a fundamental unwillingness to look beyond the technological process which spurs this change. Even those who are most concerned over the future course of our society continue to conceive that course in primarily technological terms, emphasizing quantity, comparisons, economic output, and dollars and cents. And the imagination and commitment needed to define a future qualitatively different from the technological present are deflected—even for those most concerned with our social future—by a series of specific fallacies about the social process.

The fallacy of the psychosocial vise—A characteristic conviction of many modern men and women is the sense of being trapped in a social, cultural, and historical process they have no power to control. This sense of being inescapably locked in a psychosocial vise is often most paralyzing to precisely those men and women who have the greatest understanding of the complexity of their society, and who therefore might be best able to plan intelligently for its future. And although the sense of being trapped in history is widespread, it often appears to receive particularly cogent justification by social scientists. Recent years have seen a growing understanding of the connections between individual character, social process, cultural configuration, and historical change. Just as psychoanalysis has shown that even the most aberrant behavior "makes psychological sense" and serves definable psychic ends, so sociologists argue that social patterns that seem senseless also make a kind of sociological sense, serving "latent functions" corresponding to the unstated needs of individuals. We now know that the link between how men are raised as children and how they lead their lives as adults is a close one; that small changes in one sector of society can have enormous repercussions in other areas; and that apparently small historical transformations may spread and generalize to transform an entire community.

This awareness that individual, social, cultural, and historical processes are intimately connected is often taken as the basis for social pessimism. Because social institutions have a function, it is assumed this function can never be changed; because individual behavior, even the most irrational, has adaptive value, it is thought that no other behavior could be more adaptive. The fit between individual character and social structure is seen as a perfect fit, and the "gears" which convert historical pressures to psychological responses are seen as having a fixed and invariant ratio. The result is a deterministic sense of being caught in a psychosocial vise, locked so tightly it cannot be loosened without destroying it altogether. As a consequence, we dare change nothing at all.

In practice, the fallacy of the psychosocial vise can lead either to despair or complacency. Those who despair are usually all too aware of the enormous problems of our age: they despair because they can see no way of changing anything short of changing everything. Those who are complacent take comfort from the fact that (in retrospect) everything that happens in American society in some way "makes sense," can be explained and understood in terms of individual motives and social processes. The most dangerous trends in American society can be explained away as mere "reactions to social strain" which an omniscient sociologist could well have anticipated.

The facts, however, justify neither despair nor complacency. The "fit" between individuals and society, culture and history is never a perfect fit and is not always even a good fit. . . . the closeness of fit between, for example, family structure and social structure does not entail a comparable closeness of fit between family demands and the psychological needs of family members. There is, then, a kind of "slippage in the gears" of psychosocial transmission. Social institutions that now serve one function can later serve another or be replaced altogether; two men with essentially the same potential can end very differently; cultural needs and values that are salient today may become subordinate tomorrow. A "functional view" of social institutions does not require the assumption that comparable functions cannot be assumed by still other and better institutions.

To be sure, all social planning must be undertaken with the greatest possible understanding of its likely consequences. And we are probably in a better position than any previous generation to assess and gauge what these consequences will be. But the obvious fact that changes in one area of society have repercussions in others need not prevent social action. On the contrary, an understanding of the complexity of society can be an aid to social planning, helping us identify those points and moments of maximum leverage where small actions can have large consequences. There is often a kind of social "multiplier effect"; there are virtuous as well as vicious circles. Far from discouraging social planning and action, an understanding of psychosocial process can help us guide and direct it more intelligently.

The fallacy of romantic regression—One of the most common reactions against technological society is to deplore it by invoking images of a romanticized past as a guidepost for regressive social change. In future years, as at present, Americans will be increasingly called upon to accept or reject the ideology of romantic regression. This ideology starts from the valid observation that our post-industrial society has lost intact community, socially given identity, stable and accepted morality, certainty and a clear collective sense of direction. From this valid observation, the regressive position attempts to re-establish a simple "organic" community, longs for Jeffersonian agrarianism, seeks a "new conservatism" which will "preserve" the values of the nineteenth century, turns to Fascism with its appeal to blood feeling and the "corporate state," or is tempted by the syndicalist vision of re-attaining "genuine" self-governing communities of workers. All of these outlooks see the solution to the problems of post-industrial society as some form of restoration, re-creation, or reconstruction of the simpler, more intact world that technology has destroyed.

Given a romantic idealization of the past, programs for social action invariably have regressive aims: to *reduce* the complexity of the world, be it material or moral; to *limit* the choices and opportunities which now bewilder men; to *inhibit* freedoms to which men owe their modern anxieties; to *narrow* the alternatives which give rise to current indecision; to *constrain* those who complicate moral, social, political, and international life; to *simplify* moral dilemmas into clear-cut decisions between good and evil. In short, the romantic seeks to solve the problems of the modern world by regressing to his image of an earlier world where these problems did not exist—be it the New England village, the grit-and-gumption ethic of the nineteenth-century entrepreneur, or even the Polynesian island.

Among social scientists, this ideology often takes the form of an idealization of primitive communities or peasant life. In such static communities, the problems of social change cannot arise; in an undifferentiated society, the problems of a divided life, "not belonging," and being forced to choose do not exist; the family cannot be specialized because it has too much work to do to survive; and ideological crises rarely occur because men and women unthinkingly accept the ideology they were born to.

The image of such a primitive community is, I believe, useful in highlighting the contrasting qualities of our social order. But it is a grave mistake to take primitive society, peasant life, the New England village, medieval life, or the entrepreneurial ethos of the nineteenth century as an adequate model for the future of our own society. On the contrary, few of us would freely choose to inhabit such a world. However romantically appealing the technicolor image of the Polynesian village, the idealized portrait of the "intact" peasant community, or the zest and simplicity of the frontier, harsher realities lie behind these romanticized images: endemic disease, grinding poverty, high infant mortality, lawlessness, and often the absence of the most elementary requirements for subsistence. Nor is the low standard of living in such communities accidental: it results from attitudes to change, to social organization, and to child-rearing that make a prosperous society impossible. And even if we could put up with such material deprivations, few of us could tolerate the oppressive social demands of such communities. Americans today may "conform," but we usually do so from choice; in most primitive societies the issue of conformity cannot arise as such because there *is* no choice. Our society may demand the arduous achievement of individual identity, but peasant communities "solve" this problem simply by allowing the young no options. We may suffer from the pressures of chronic social change, but we would suffer more in a society that persisted in its traditional ways despite evidence that they were destructive. And we may lament the loss of mythic vitality in the twentieth century, but we would lament even more an age where those who challenged the collective myth were outlawed or destroyed.

Moreover, in appealing to the image of the primitive or "intact" community as a guide for social action, we forget the eagerness with which those who dwell in such communities seek to abandon them. The destruction of tribalism, of feudalism, and of "intact community" continues to correspond with the wishes of the vast majority of those who have a choice: in the emerging nations of the world men lust after affluence and technology, not after tribal embeddedness. And even in our own history, the development of political liberalism and representative government, like the growth of technological society, was a response to the felt wishes of those who sought to escape the rigors of previous societies. Those who hark back to the values of their grandparents forget the eagerness with which these same men and women sought to create a "better world" for their grandchildren. We would find even the rigidity, complacency, and intolerance of the recent Victorian era hard to live with; the total absorption of the individual in most "primitive" societies would be even more intolerable.

However instructive the comparison of our own society with "intact" communities may be, today's problems cannot be solved by regressing to that kind of society. The new problems, the new alienations of technological society, require not regression to a romanticized past but new definitions of purpose, new forms of social organization, new goals for personal development. We must not return to the past, but transcend the present.

The fallacy of unfinished business—Perhaps the most potent deterrent of all to any fresh thinking about the purposes of our lives and our society is the fallacy of unfinished business—exclusive concentration on the remaining problems of productivity, poverty, education, and inequality as defined by technological values. This fallacy is most dangerous because it affects most those who are genuinely concerned with the problems of our society, critical of its achievements, impatient with the slowness of its "progress." Politically and socially, the only articulate alternative to those who would have us regress to the past is found among those who emphasize the unfinished business of technology, the "incomplete revolutions" which must be completed. From Lyndon Baines Johnson to Paul Goodman, the main thread of "progressive" thinking about American society assumes that our task is to complete our unfinished technological business.

I do not mean to deprecate this position. It is not wrong but inadequate; the evils pointed to are real and urgent. Gross prejudice and inequality are daily realities in much of America; poverty is a grinding and destructive fact to a fifth of the nation; millions do not and cannot get the minimal education necessary for an honored place in American life; it is genuinely alarming that we have not solved the problems of chronic unemployment. Nor will it be politically easy to solve these problems; the programs so far proposed only scratch the surface.

But the adequacy of this view to the problems of our society can be questioned. The "unfinished business" of technological society is, on a historical scale, increasingly vestigial, a "mopping-up operation." Revolutionary causes lose their impact when they have been largely accomplished; men are seldom stirred to arms in a cause already victorious. What is historically most salient is that *only* a fifth of the nation remains, by today's high American standards, poor. What should astound us is that *only* 30 per cent fail today to complete twelve years of education. And even in very recent American history, an unemployment rate of *only* four to six per cent would have been an unprecedented breakthrough to prosperity. Our efforts to relieve these problems should not abate; on the contrary, these efforts are still inadequate. But our technological accomplishments mean that if real "new frontiers" are to be found, they must lie beyond technology; and that if we do not now live in a "Great Society," then expanded Medicare, poverty programs, job-retraining, and anti-dropout campaigns will not suffice to create it.

Moreover, the values and instruments of technology will no longer suffice even to finish a technological society's own unfinished business. Our pursuit of quantity leads us to focus on such numerical indices of national and social success as the gross national product, the growth rate, the percentages of Americans employed, the proportion in high school, the divorce rate, the number of cars, telephones, and washing machines. We rejoice when these indices of success show us "ahead" of the Russians, and worry when our growth rate falls below theirs. But in each area of "unfinished business" in American life, our traditional techniques are inadequate. That traditional panacea, an increase in national output, no longer affects the poor, insulated from the main streams of the economy. More money poured into existing schools does not solve the problem of dropouts, whose prior problems are human and psychological, not merely educational. New technological innovations in industry are producing more, not less, chronic unemployment among the unskilled. And no matter how much we speed up the slow movement toward greater equality for Negro Americans, full citizenship cannot be achieved by traditional legal means alone. It also requires a deeper (and non-technological) effort to overcome the bitter legacies of slavery and oppression; and it may even require that we learn to recognize, accept, and enjoy the differences between white and Negro Americans that this legacy has created. In almost every area where our "technological revolutions" are incomplete, the instruments and values of technology will not alone suffice to carry us farther. Our urban sprawl, the chaos, disorganization, blight, and congestion of our society, our new alienations—all were *created* by our exploding, unplanned technological society; the technological process alone will not solve their problems.

But most important, the fallacy of unfinished business overlooks the crucial questions for most Americans today: What lies beyond the triumph of technology? After racial equality has been achieved, what then? Abundance for all for what? Full employment for today's empty jobs? More education that instills an ever more cognitive outlook?

It is all too easy to imagine a society in which the triumph of technology is complete. It would be an overwhelmingly rich society, dominated by a rampant technology and all of its corollaries—science, research and development, advertising, "conformity," secret invidiousness, overwhelming nostalgia for childhood, the dictatorship of the ego, a continuing deflection of the Utopian spirit. It would be a prosperous, ugly, sprawling society which men had learned not to see. It would have many entertainers but few artists, many superhighways but few open spaces to go to on them. It would be a science-fiction dream of automation, preprocessing, and home-care conveniences. Skyscrapers would rise ever taller and more sheer, and "developments" would burgeon outside the blighted urban cores.

Yet the central problems of today would merely be magnified. The pace of social change would increase and, without an over-all sense of direction, Americans would huddle ever more defensively in the present.

For some, the romanticized stability of the past would grow more and more attractive, and this attraction would express itself more and more forcibly in political and social reaction. Life, already divided today, would be further divided tomorrow; and the vast majority of Americans, who could create no community within their own hearts, would be altogether without a home. As the pressures toward cognition grew, private escapes into irrationality, cults, and fads would flourish. The atmosphere would become ever more hostile to speculation, to idealism, and to Utopianism; the cult of efficiency, spread into human relations and industrial management, would relegate idealism and the noble dreams of youth to the hours after work or to "entertainment." In such a society the most talented would be alienated, yet they would be unable to find a positive voice; and their alienations would be, as now, self-destructive, carping, and self-defeating. To complete our incomplete revolutions, to finish our unfinished business, is therefore not enough, nor can it be accomplished by technological means alone. For their solution, the vestigial tasks of technology require values beyond technology.

If we are to seek values beyond technology, purposes beyond affluence, visions of the good life beyond material prosperity, where are these values, purposes, and visions to be found? Must we, as many secretly fear, await the coming of some new prophet who will create, out of nothing, a new Utopian vision for Americans? Are we condemned to a continuation of technological society until some Messiah arrives to save us?

I believe the answer is closer to home. When, a century ago, Americans began to take seriously the goals of prosperity and freedom from want, these values were not created out of nothing: they had long been part of the Western tradition. What changed was that a dream of the good life previously considered beyond the reach of the ordinary man passed into his hands and was accepted as a concrete goal that could be achieved by ordinary men and women. The turning point at which we stand today requires a similar translation of already existing dreams of human fulfillment and social diversity into the concrete goals of individuals and of our society. The values we need are deeply rooted in our own tradition: we must merely begin to take them seriously.

The ideal of full human wholeness is as old as Periclean Athens. But in the course of Western history, this goal could be taken seriously by few men and women: as in Athens, only a small number of the leisured and wealthy, supported by the vast majority of their fellow citizens, attained the freedom from want which is a prerequisite for the implementation of this ancient goal. Even in the Renaissance, when the Greek ideal of full humanity was rediscovered, the vast majority of men and women were far too preoccupied by their incessant struggle against poverty, oppression, and sickness to have time for such lofty ideals. And even today, for most citizens of most nations of the world, the vision of a more harmonious integration of self, a more complete development of talent and ability, must await the attainment of more urgent goals of attaining freedom from want and oppression. Only those who have been able to conquer poverty and tyranny have energy to cultivate their full humanity.

But for those who do not want materially and are not oppressed politically, the quest for fulfillment beyond material goods becomes possible and urgent. There is in human life a hierarchy of needs, such that the higher needs are fully felt when, and only when, the lower needs have been satisfied. Just as thirsty men do not seek food, and the starved have no strength for sex, so freedom from political oppression and material want are prerequisites for any attempt to achieve a more harmonious integration of self, a fuller development of human potentials. Today, in America, and increasingly in other technological nations, these preconditions are rapidly being met: we can now begin to imagine realistically that a whole society might commit itself to the attainment of the greatest possible fulfillment for its members.

To be sure, by the quantitative and reductionistic standards of our technological era, goals like "human wholeness," "personal integration," "the full development of human potentials" are inevitably vague and imprecise. They point to the quality of individual life, rather than to quantitatively measurable entities. Partly for this reason, our knowledge of the sources of human wholeness and fulfillment is woefully inadequate, despite a half-century's systematic study of man. But we do know more than previous generations about the causes of human malformation, distortion, and blighting. Our systematic and scientific knowledge is, no doubt, no more than a confirmation of what a few wise men have intuitively known in the past. But what was heretofore the special wisdom of the sagacious few (which they often carried to their graves) is on the way to becoming communicable public knowledge. Gradually, we are learning to pinpoint the obstacles to full human growth, specifying those especially "lethal" psychological combinations of parentage and social circumstance for children, defining more adequately the antecedents of human pathology, and even at times learning how to intervene positively to foster full human development.

Yet even today, it is far simpler to list the obstacles to full human development, to personal integration, to self-actualization, than to prescribe the precise path to these ancient goals. For just as there are from birth many distinct individuals, each with his own unique genetic and environmental potential, there must remain many paths to fulfillment. Our modern search for a single definition for "maturity" and "positive mental health" that will apply to everyone is probably doomed to failure from the start. Responsiveness, activity, excitability, and even the capacity to learn are not only shaped by the environment, but partly determined by birth.

"Fulfillment" depends on individual potential and on social opportunity; human "wholeness" depends on what there is to be made whole.

But though no single definition of human fulfillment is possible, some of its results can be defined. A whole man or woman has the capacity for zest, exuberance, and passion, though this capacity may often be in abeyance. An integrated man does not cease to experience tension, anxiety, and psychic pain, but he is rarely overwhelmed by it. Though all men must at times "close" themselves to that which would be subversive of their commitments, a whole man nonetheless retains the *capacity* for openness, sensitivity, and responsiveness to the world around him: he can always be surprised because he remains open to that which is alien to himself.

Above all, human wholeness means a capacity for commitment, dedication, passionate concern, and care—a capacity for wholeheartedness and single-mindedness, for abandon without fear of self-annihilation and loss of identity. In psychological terms, this means that a whole man retains contact with his deepest passions at the same time that he remains responsive to his ethical sense. No one psychic potential destroys or subverts the others: his cognitive abilities remain in the service of his commitment, not vice versa; his ethical sense guides rather than tyrannizing over his basic passions; his deepest drives are the sources of his strength but not the dictators of his action. We recognize whole men and women because their wholeness is manifest in their lives: what they do is "of a piece."

If no unitary definition of fulfillment and integration is possible, then a society that is to support these goals must necessarily be a diverse, heterogeneous, pluralistic, and open society. And like the ideal of individual fulfillment, the goal of social diversity is one we have never seriously considered implementing. Although the ideal of political pluralism is entrenched in our liberal tradition, this ideal has most often meant the toleration of political factions, not the encouragement of the full diversity of human talents. Politically, we may tolerate lobbies and believe in political parties; but socially our goals are given by slogans like "Americanization," "the melting pot," and increasingly today "the search for excellence" defined in cognitive terms. Though we think of ourselves as a "tolerant" society, in ordinary speech we most often couple the term "tolerate" with the modifier "barely." All too often, the "tolerance" of Americans is a thin veneer over the discomfort created by all that is different, strange, and alien to them. Once, to be sure, the image of this nation as a vast melting pot suggested the noble vision that the millions of diverse immigrants who came to this shore could be welded into a single coherent nation. But today there is no menace of an America excessively fractured along ethnic, regional or class lines. The current danger is excessive homogeneity, sameness, uniformity. Already, ethnic distinctions, regional differences, even class lines have been blurred beyond recognition in a land where almost everyone lives in the same city apartments and suburban dwellings, eats the same frozen foods and watches the same television programs at the same time on the same networks. Even the current effort of some Americans who are fearful of conformity to be "different," to develop distinctive styles of consumption and life, paralleled by the attempts of advertisers and industry to promote "personalized" and "individualized" products, tends to become only another sign of the homogenization of American society.

Romantic regionalism or the idealization of ethnicity are of course not virtuous in themselves: and even if we chose, distinctions of region and ethnic background could not be naturally preserved. But there *is* an inherent virtue in the appreciation of genuine human differences and the encouragement of a new social diversity based not on region, ancestral origin, class, or race, but on the special accomplishments, potentials, talents, and vital commitments of each individual. Pluralism must be extended from politics to the individual, implemented as a concrete social goal. Human diversity and variety must not only be tolerated, but rejoiced in, applauded, and encouraged.

A society of whole men and women must, then, be a society which encourages diversity, enjoying the differences between men as well as the similarities among them. Social diversity has a double connection to individual fulfillment: not only is a diverse society a precondition for human wholeness, it is its consequence—the kind of society whole men and women choose to live in. Those who are inwardly torn, unsure of their psychic coherence and fearful of inner fragmentation, are naturally distrustful of all that is alien and strange. Those whose sense of inner unity is tenuous are easily threatened by others who remind them of that part of themselves they seek to suppress. Our "one-hundred-per-cent Americans" are those whose own Americanism is felt to be most tenuous; the bigoted and the prejudiced cannot live with the full gamut of their own feelings. And conversely, those who can still sense their shared humanity with others of different or opposite talents and commitments are those who are sure of their own intactness. The goals of human fulfillment and social diversity require each other.

Both of these ideals, I have argued, are ancient ones. They are rooted deep in our Western tradition, and they arise almost spontaneously in those whose material and physical wants have been satisfied. But it remains for us to implement these visions. These are values beyond technology, credal ideals of our civilization which we can now begin to take seriously. Probably for the first time in human history, we can move toward a fullness of life beyond a full larder, human fulfillment beyond material satiation, social diversity beyond consensus.

History is always made by men, even in an era like ours when men feel they are but the pawns of history. The inability to envision a future different from the present is not a historical imposition but a failure of imagination. It is individuals, not historical trends, that are possessed by a self-confirming sense of social powerlessness. The decision to continue along our present course rather than to take a new turning is still a decision made by men. One way men sometimes have of shaping the future is to be passive and acquiescent before it. Our collective and individual future, then, will inevitably be shaped by us, whether we choose inaction and passivity, regression and romanticism, or action, imagination, and resolve. Men cannot escape their historical role by merely denying its existence. The question is therefore not *whether* Americans will shape their future, but *how* they will shape it.

What is lacking today in America is certainly not the know-how, the imagination, or the intelligence to shape a future better than our present. Nor do we lack the values that might guide the transformation of our society to a more fully human and diverse one. Rather, we lack the conviction that these values might be implemented by ordinary men and women acting in concert for their common good. The Utopian impulse, I have argued, runs deep in all human life, and especially deep in American life. What is needed is to free that impulse once again, to redirect it toward the creation of a better society. We too often attempt to patch up our threadbare values and outworn purposes; we too rarely dare imagine a society radically different from our own.

Proposals for specific reforms are bound to be inadequate by themselves. However desirable, any specific reform will remain an empty intellectual exercise in the absence of a new collective myth, ideology, or Utopian vision. Politically, no potent or lasting change will be possible except as men can be roused from their current alienations by the vision of an attainable society more inviting than that in which they now listlessly live. Behind the need for any specific reform lies the greater need to create an intellectual, ideological, and cultural atmosphere in which it is possible for men to attempt affirmation without undue fear that their Utopian visions will collapse through neglect, ridicule or their own inherent errors. Such an ethos can only be built slowly and piecemeal, yet is it clear what some of its prerequisites must be.

For one, we need a more generous tolerance for synthetic and constructive ideas. Instead of concentrating on the possible bad motives from which they might arise (the genetic fallacy) or on the possible bad consequences which might follow from their misinterpretation (the progenitive fallacy), we must learn to assess them in terms of their present relevance and appropriateness. To accomplish this task will be a double work. Destructively, it will require subverting the methodologies of reduction that now dominate our intellectual life. Constructively, it will require replacing these with more just measures of relevance, subtlety and wisdom, learning to cherish and value the enriching complexity of motives, passions, ethical interests, and facts which will necessarily underlie and support any future vision of the good life.

Secondly, we must reappraise our current concepts and interpretations of man and society. It is characteristic of the intellectual stagnation of our era, an era so obviously different from former times, that we continue to operate with language more appropriate to past generations than to our own. Many of our critiques and interpretations of technological society, including most discussions of alienation, apply more accurately to the America of the 1880's than to the America of the 1960's. We require a radical reanalysis of the human and social present—a re-evaluation which, starting from uncritical openness to the experience, joys, and dissatisfactions of men today, can gradually develop concepts and theories that can more completely comprehend today's world. American society does not lack men and women with the fine discrimination, keen intelligence, and imagination to understand the modern world; but we have yet to focus these talents on our contemporary problems.

But above and beyond a more generous atmosphere and a more adequate understanding of our time, ordinary human courage is needed. To criticize one's society openly requires a strong heart, especially when criticism is interpreted as pathology; only a man of high mettle will propose a new interpretation of the facts now arranged in entrenched categories. And no matter how eagerly the audience awaits or how well prepared the set, only courage can take a performer to the stage. There are many kinds of courage: needed here is the courage to risk being wrong, to risk doing unintentional harm, and, above all, the courage to overcome one's own humility and sense of finite inadequacy. This is not merely a diffuse "courage to be," without protest, in a world of uncertainty, alienation, and anxiety, but the courage to be *for* something despite the perishability and transience of all human endeavors.

Commitment, I have said, is worthy only as its object is worthy. To try to "reconstruct" commitment to American society as it exists today is less than worthy, for our society is shot through with failings, failures, and flaws. It is, as the alienated truly perceive, "trashy, cheap, and commercial"; it is also, as the alienated seldom see, unjust, distorting of human growth and dignity, destructive of diversity. It has allowed itself to be dominated by the instruments of its own triumph over poverty and want, worshiping the values, virtues, and institutions of technology even when these now dominate those they should serve. Only if we can transform the technological process from a master to a servant, harnessing our scientific inventiveness and industrial productivity to the promotion of human fulfillment, will our society be worthy of commitment. And only the vision of a world beyond technology can now inspire the commitment of whole men and women.

America today possesses a vast reservoir of thwarted and displaced idealism; there are millions of men and women who sense vaguely that something is amiss in their lives, who search for something more, and yet who cannot find it. Their idealism will not be easily redirected to the creation of better lives in a better society; it will require imagination, vigor, conviction, and strong voices willing to call for many years, before we dare raise our aspirations beyond vistas of total technology to visions of fuller humanity. But for the first time in American history, and probably in the history of the world, it is conceivable that a whole nation might come to take seriously these ancient and honored visions.

In defining this new vision of life and society, we must remember the quests of the alienated. Though their goals are often confused and inarticulate, they converge on a passionate yearning for openness and immediacy of experience, on an intense desire to create, on a longing to express their perception of the world, and, above all, on a quest for values and commitments that will give their lives coherence. The [alienated] of modern American life are often self-defeating; they cannot be taken as exemplars of human integration or fulfillment. But the implicit goals they unsuccessfully seek to attain *are* those of integrated and whole men—openness, creativity, and dedication. Today we need men and women with the wisdom, passion, and courage to transform their private alienations into such public aspirations. We might then begin to move toward a society where such aspirations were more fully realized than in any the world has known.

We can hope for such new commitments in the future only if men now begin to resolve their alienations by committing themselves—through the analysis, synthesis, and reform of their own lives and worlds—to the preparation of such a new society, a society in which whole men and women can play with zest and spontaneity, can work with skill and dedication, can love with passion and care—a society that enjoys diversity and supports human fulfillment.